Copyright, Congress and Technology: The Public Record

opyright, ongress and echnology: he Public ecord

olume I:
he Formative Years, 1958-1966

olume II:
he Political Years, 1967-1973

olume III:
he Future of Copyright, 1973-1977

olume IV: CONTU:
he Future of Information Technology

olume V: CONTU'S Final
eport and Recommendations

dited with an introduction by
cholas Henry.

Operation Oryx, started more than 15 years ago at the Phoenix Zoo to save the rare white antelope—believed to have inspired the unicorn of mythology—has apparently succeeded. The operation was launched in 1962 when it became evident that the animals were facing extinction in their native habitat of the Arabian peninsula.

An original herd of nine, put together through *Operation Oryx* by five world organizations, now numbers 47 in Phoenix with another 38 at the San Diego Wild Game Farm, and four others which have recently been sent to live in their natural habitat in Jordan.

Also, in what has come to be known as "The Second Law of Return," rare biblical animals are being collected from many countries to roam freely at the Hai Bar Biblical Wildlife Nature Reserve in the Negev, in Israel, the most recent addition being a breeding herd of eight Arabian Oryx. With the addition of these Oryx, their collection of rare biblical animals is complete.

Published by The Oryx Press
2214 North Central at Encanto
Phoenix, AZ 85004

Published simultaneously in Canada

Printed and Bound in the United States of America

Library of Congress Cataloging in Publication Data

Main entry under title:

CONTU: the future of information technology.

(Copyright, Congress, and technology : the public record ; v. 4)
1. Photocopying processes--Fair use (Copyright)--United States. 2. Copyright--Computer programs--United States. 3. Fair use (Copyright)--United States.
4. Photocopying services in libraries--United States.
5. United States. National Commission on New Technological Uses of Copyrighted Works. I. Henry, Nicholas, 1943- II. United States. National Commission on New Technological Uses of Copyrighted Works. III. Series.
KF2994.A1C57 vol. 4 [KF3030.1] 346'.73'0482 79-23160
ISBN 0-912700-32-7

TO MY PARENTS

Contents

Acknowledgements

I am indebted to a great many people in compiling these books, especially to Ms. Valari Elardo, my graduate assistant, who spent untold hours over a smoldering photocopying machine copying the necessary documents. Ms. Gwen Weaver has been both efficient and cheerful in putting out the necessary typing, and officials at the National Commission on New Technological Uses of Copyrighted Works have been cooperative and forthcoming in permitting me to reprint some of their important research in Volumes IV and V.

Ms. Phyllis Steckler, President of the Oryx Press, deserves recognition for her perceptiveness in seeing the need for this set, as well as her personal encouragement.

Of course, and as always, I am indebted to my understanding wife, Muriel, and my children, Miles and Adrienne, for their support in the completion of this project. This set is dedicated to them.

NH
Tempe, Arizona

Introduction to the Set

Copyright, Congress, and Technology: The Public Record is a compendium of selected public documents that were published during the remarkable effort to revise American copyright law which occurred during the twenty-one years between 1955 and 1976. Simply as an example of the policy-making process, the campaign waged to change U.S. copyright law is fascinating in and of itself; few pieces of legislation have taken as long to be enacted as a revised copyright law. This five-volume set, however, is designed not only to trace the development of the Copyright Act of 1976, but also is meant to set the record straight in the areas of how the new copyright law affects the use of new information technologies, notably photocopiers and computers, for the benefit of librarians, educators, authors, publishers, and public officials. The impact of copyright on these technologies is both profound and complex, and perhaps the most simple way of conveying the thinking of policy-makers and interest groups in their effort to resolve copyright and technology is to provide a format that allows them to speak for themselves.

These volumes also describe the actual policy-making process as it related to the attempt to revise the United States Copyright Act of 1909 in a manner that would accommodate the new information technologies, notably photocopying and computer-based information storage and retrieval systems. These are the primary "neo-publishing" technologies (in the sense that they permit the massive republishing of copyrighted works by the populace), and the "politics of neo-publishing" was the effort to reconcile these technologies with copyright law.

While there are other neo-publishing technologies, those that have engendered the greatest concern among copyright owners and copyright users are photocopiers and computers. Of these two, the photocopier is preeminent. There are approximately 600,000 photocopiers in this country alone, churning out an estimated 30 billion copies every year. Most of these copies are made in public and research libraries, and empirical studies of photocopying use patterns in libraries indicate that as much as 60 percent of all the photocopies made each year may be of copyrighted publications. Increasingly, publishers are convinced that their sales of periodical subscriptions and books are being undermined by popular and massive photocopying practices, and that this is particularly the case for publications in science and technolgy.

The other major neo-publishing technology is the computer. There are more than 100,000 computer-based information storage and retrieval systems in the United States. While we know that these systems are reformatting and disseminating vast quantities of the information on demand and at an incredibly rapid rate, we do not know what proportion of that information may be protected by copyright. Some material, certainly, that is processed by computers is protected by copyright, and it is highly unlikely that information system operators and programmers are soliciting the permission of the copyright owners to use their material to any significant degree, if at all.

Both copyright owners and copyright users perceive copyright law to be virtually the only public policy that is concerned with the relationships among the new neo-publishing technologies, intellectual creativity, intellectual property, and, to quote the Constitution (Article I, Section 8), the paramount social value of promoting "the Progress of Science and useful Arts . . .". Revising copyright law to accommodate the new information technologies thus is a public policy of some consequence.

Two conclusions may be drawn from the public record about copyright law revision. One is that the process represented, and no doubt will continue to do so, a politics of technological elites. Copyright is one of the least recognized but most important public policies of our time, affecting an industry of vast magnitude. In fact, the "knowledge industry" comprises the largest single segment of the American economy, and it has been estimated by economists that the knowledge industry accounts for a third of the Gross National Product. More than 40 percent of the nation's economic growth is attributable to advances in education, and the "copyright industries" alone are the equivalent size of mining, banking, and utilities. Copyright is not merely big business, it is the biggest.

In light of the implications of the new information technologies and copyright law, it is both discomfiting and surprising to learn how small the group is that has been debating how to reconcile technology and copyright during the past three decades. The elitism of this debate is brought out in these volumes. The same names appear and reappear with frequency, but the overwhelming reality remains that public policy for new information technologies has affected and will affect far more people than those who have been talking about it. We have here a case of very small elites "representing" very limited elements of society that nonetheless are forming public policy for the new information technologies.

Why is this elitism the case? A major reason appears to be that the sheer complexity of the subject inhibits participation. Yet, complexity is a growing fact of political life in techno-bureaucratic societies, such as ours. Political decision-making in twentieth century America deals with technology, and technology is complicated. Those who understand the complex technological issues of modern political life (or who say they do) become the policymakers. Nowhere is this better illustrated than in the instance of what some have called "the politics of neo-publishing." As the reader will quickly discern, very small elites have made a public policy that affects us all.

The second conclusion that one may draw from reading these public documents, is that the politics of neo-publishing is frankly Marxist. Revising copyright law was a political brawl involving the redistribution of political and economic power between haves and have-nots. While it was not a class war in the traditional sense, the politics of neo-publishing clearly is, to use Marxian language, a fight between the owners of a means of production and the users of their products. Indeed, the formal terminology of copyright law reflects the language of Marxism: copyright "owners" and copyright "users." The neo-publishing technologies have provided an opportunity to the "exploited masses" of copyright users. By dint of these technologies, proletarian copyright users may become bourgeois copyright owners. Publishers, the historic owners of the means of intellectual production, are witnessing the undermining of their ownership through the popular use of new information technologies. As Marshall McLuhan has noted "in an age of Xerox, every man is a publisher."

Copyright is the single public policy concerned with the economics of commercial publishing. It is predicated on the idea that a would-be publisher must put up a considerable amount of capital in order to begin publishing—that is, in order to control a means of production. It follows, therefore that publishers ought to be granted certain monopolistic rights or "exclusive license" to their products. This is what copyright does, or at least did, until the neo-publishing instruments made their debuts. These technologies are redistributing a means of production and, in so doing, are undermining copyright as a standing public policy. For these reasons, the documents included in this set can be understood most satisfactorily as a Marxian class conflict—owners against users.

While such conclusions may be interesting, and perhaps even important, the major reason why this set will be useful to most readers is that an enormous amount of confusion surrounds the impact of the new copyright law on librarians, authors, educators, and publishers. Thus, these volumes are organized in such a way that they will be of optimal use to these professionals in tracing how the thinking of their colleagues has evolved just as information technologies have developed.

Volume I of *Copyright, Congress, and Technology: The Public Record* focuses on those early public documents that emerged between 1958 and 1966. The discerning reader will note that the tone of the copyright proceedings in these years is substantially different from the tone found in public documents emerging in 1967 and beyond. I have referred to this phenomenon elsewhere as "noetic politics," or the peculiar style of politics that derives from knowledge, logic, and the scientific method.[1] We see in these documents a conscious effort by the participants in copyright politics to devise legislation that will work for the benefit of all society. The normal, grubbing interest-group politics that we associate with the legislative process is relatively absent, although there are many moments of passion and greed.

It was during this period that the Register of Copyrights commissioned thirty-four scholarly studies on copyright, and issued a major report in 1961 that was hailed as a seminal work in the area. Experts, lawyers, and policy-makers of various stripes were consulted on a continuing basis during these years, and the Commission on New Technological Uses of Copyrighted Works (CONTU) was first proposed. All these instances and others represent an effort to form policy on the basis of knowledge rather than on the basis of the political power of particular interest groups.

As noted, however, this tone changes—and I think rather precipitously—in the years following. In the 1967 Congressional hearings, for example, we see spokespersons for various groups calling each other names during their testimony. The balance of power in the dispute appears to shift away from copyright owners (largely publishers and authors) and toward copyright users (largely librarians and educators), but not necessarily for reasons of wise public policy (although it may well turn out that way). Rather, the gains made by

---

1. See: Nicholas Henry, *Copyright/Information Technology/Public Policy. Part I: Copyright/Public Policies* and *Part II: Public Policies/Information Technology.* New York: Marcel Dekker, Inc., 1975 and 1976.

copyright users over the interests of copyright owners are made because the users have the votes and the owners do not. Thus, Volume II covers the years 1967 through 1973, and the tone throughout is overtly political, although there is some hard and creative analysis available in these years, which is included.

The third volume in the retrospect reprints documents emerging between 1973 and 1977, including pertinent selections from the several Congressional hearings on copyright law revision. An effort has been made to include those public documents that point the way toward the future of copyright. The entire Copyright Act of 1976 also is reproduced.

Volume IV, *CONTV: The Future of Information Technology,* reproduces the ground-breaking studies sponsored by the National Commission on New Technological Uses of Copyrighted Works, which dealt with computer software, photocopying and copyrights, public photocopying practices, library photocopying and the economics of periodical publications. The Commissions final report, the result of years of testimony by experts from across the nation, comprises Volume V.

Taken together, the five volumes are a collection that should be both convenient and authoritative in guiding copyright users and owners through the maze of copyright, technology, and public policy.

NH
Tempe, Arizona

Introduction to Volume IV

As the title of Volume IV indicates, this book is dedicated to the early work accomplished by the National Commission on New Technological Uses of Copyrighted Works, or CONTU. Unique in the annals of copyright law, CONTU represented an unusual blend of political acumen and a wholly scholarly approach to the problems of copyright and information technology.

The Commission was created as a part of the Library of Congress "to study and compile data on: (1) the reproduction and use of copyrighted works of authorship—(a) in conjunction with automatic systems capable of storing, processing, retrieving, and transferring information, and (b) by various forms of machine reproduction, including reproduction by, or at least at the request of, instructors for use in face-to-face teaching activities; and (2) the creation of new works by the application or intervention of such automatic systems or machine reproduction." The Commission was also authorized to "make recommendations as to such changes in copyright law or procedures that may be necessary to assure for such purposes access to copyright owners." These recommendations were to be made to the President and to Congress within a three-year period, at which time the Commission would be disbanded. To assist in compiling its report, the Commission was authorized to hold hearings, administer oaths, and subpoena witnesses.

The concept of creating a National Commission on New Technological Uses of Copyrighted Works can be traced back to the mid-1960s. In 1968, a bill authorizing such a Commission (S.2216) was passed by the Senate but subsequently died in the House. The 1968 bill called for a 23 member Commission comprised of the Librarian of Congress, 2 Senators, 2 Representative, 7 copyright users, 7 copyright owners, and 4 members from the general public. In 1971, the proposed Commission was included as Title II of the Copyright Law Revision bill (S.644), and in 1973, it was included as Title II of the Revision bill (S.1361). Beginning with its inclusion in the 1971 Copyright Law Revision bill, the composition of the Commission was changed from 23 members to 13 members comprised of 4 copyright users, 4 copyright owners, 4 members of the general public (all to be appointed by the President), and the Librarian of Congress. The Register of Copyrights was to serve *ex officio* as a non-voting member.

CONTU does not seem, at first glance, to be a body fraught with politics but, given the intensity of the politics of neo-publishing, it should not be too surprising that even the proposed Commission was exceptionally controversial. Organized education interests took the most umbrage at the proposal for CONTU which, when all is said and done, amounted to little more than a study group on the subject of technology and copyright law.

Educators were particularly outraged by Senate *Report No. 640* (reproduced in Volume II of this set) released in 1967 by the Committee on the Judiciary to accompany S.2216. This *Report* was a brief statement recommending the establishment of a National Commission on New Technological Uses of Copyrighted

Works. The Report stated that although it "is not the intent of the Committee that the Commission should undertake to re-open the examination of those copyright issues which have received detailed consideration during the current revision effort, and concerning which satisfactory solutions appear to have been achieved," the Commission, nevertheless, was expected to consider the copyright ramifications of photocopying. As the report noted: "photocopying in all its forms presents significant questions of public policy, extending well beyond that of copyright law. No satisfactory solutions appear to have emerged in the limited considerations devoted to this problem during the current revision effort." This passage, along with other factors present in 1967, upset members of the Ad Hoc Committee of Educational Organizations and Institutions on Copyright Law Revision, which was the umbrella organization for education interests in the copyright law revision process. Harold Wigren, chief spokesman for the Ad Hoc Committee, noted "with dismay the failure to exclude from the Commission's scope of duty the matter of 'fair use' by photoduplication and recording" when he spoke during the congressional hearings held on copyright revision that year. Indeed, the very fact that the Commission did include the problem of photocopying in its purview was a major motivation behind the Ad Hoc Committee's decision to terminate its agreements with copyright owners, and the irony of professional educators arguing vehemently against the creation of a research group dedicated to discovering new knowledge in the areas of information technology and use cannot be overlooked.

In 1971 and 1972, a movement to push the creation of CONTU was begun at the grassroots. Central in this movement was Gerald Sophar, past President of the Committee to Investigate Copyright Problems and an official of the National Agricultural Library. In 1971, the American Society for Information Sciences (in which Sophar was quite active), the Information Industry Association (a group that spoke largely for copyright owners), and the National Federation of Science Abstracting and Indexing Services called for a "Parliament on New Technological Uses of Copyrighted Works," which had as its theme, "Planning for a National Commission."

The Parliament was successful, and in 1972 a second Parliament on New Technological Uses of Copyrighted Works was held in Washington which was far more inclusive in its representation of the major participants in the politics of neo-publishing. Attending the second Parliament were representatives from the Ad Hoc Committee of Educational Organizations and Institutions on Copyright Law Revision, the American Association of Law Libraries, the American Bar Association, the American Business Press, Inc., the American Chemical Society, the American Institute of Biological Sciences, the American Institute of Physics, the American Society for Information Science, the American Society for Testing and Materials, the Association of American Publishers, the Association of American University Presses, the Association of Research Libraries, the Association of Scientific Information Dissemination Centers, the Authors League of America, the Copyright Society of the United States, the Council of Biology Editors, the Information Industry Association, the Institute of Electrical and Electronics Engineers, the Inter-University Communications Council, the Joint Council on Educational Telecommunications, the McGraw-Hill Information Systems Company, the National Bureau of Standards,the National Federation of Science Abstracting and Indexing Services, the National Microfilm Association, the National Technical Information Service, the Williams and Wilkins Compamy, Xerox Corporation, and the Special Libraries Association. Clearly, there was a great deal of grassroots interest in the formation of a National Commission.

Congress appeared to hear the message, and on September 9, 1973, Senator John McClellan of Arkansas, Senator Howard Baker, Jr., of Tennessee, and Senator Hugh Scott of Pennsylvania, introduced S.3976, which extended copyright duration another two years pending eventual passage of a revised copyright law, increased criminal penalties for the piracy and counterfeiting of sound recordings and, of special note to this Volume, established the National Commission on New Technological Uses of Copyrighted Works. The objective of the Bill was not only to establish the long-pending National Commission, but was also an effort to protect copyright owners until a revised copyright bill could be enacted. The senators saw no problems in any portion of the Bill, and S.3976 sailed smoothly out of the Senate by a voice vote and into the House, where it immediately ran into choppy water.

Representative Robert W. Kastenmeier, who would be chairing the House hearings on the 1973 Revision Bill, introduced S.3976 to the congressmen on December 19. The major provisos of S.3976 concerned the extension of copyright protection and the setting up of the National Commission, and Kastenmeier was sensitive to the potential controversy involved in these clauses. He observed that the extension proviso would constitute the ninth such extension of the copyright law since the extensions had first been enacted in 1962; about 150,000 copyrighted works would be affected by the proviso—some of which would be under copyright protection for a total of 66 years as a result—and roughly two-thirds of these works were musical compositions. Kastenmeier noted on the floor of the House that, while he was obligated to duly report the opinions of his subcommittee, it was nonetheless his considered view that, "I cannot concur in the action of my colleagues in ordering a further extension of expiring renewal terms of copyright. I continue to be of the opinion that in too many instances the measure will operate to provide an unjustifiable windfall at the expense of the public domain."

Kastenmeier also notified the congressmen that his subcommittee, as well as himself, thought that the National Commission should be established forthwith, although some close legislative oversight of the Commission's budget would be exercised. The Commission's estimated three-year budget of $2,461,400 was felt to be high, and the House Judiciary Committee had amended Section 205 of S.3976 in order to "limit the authorization to appropriate funds . . . the authorization applies only to funds for the period preceding June 30, 1976," or within a year and a half. In this vein, S.3976 also was amended so that the Commission would submit an interim report to the House in 18 months.

Representative John Dingell was among those few congressmen who were not only against passing S.3976 but also retained a modicum of interest in copyright. Dingell, while noting that the proposal undoubtedly would pass, nonetheless characterized S.3976 as "an incredibly bad piece of legislation . . . a Christmas tree."

Dingell observed acidly that the bill would not extend copyright for the benefit of "a bunch of poor old ladies who hold copyrights," but rather for "the big publishing houses who are going to have their copyrights extended for the ninth time" and the American Society of Composers, Authors, and Publishers (ASCAP), "one of the curious institutions which hold copyrights, and which holds them not for the benefit really of the authors, but which holds them for the benefit of its own interests." Dingell concluded that "these copyrights have passed to the big publishing houses. They have passed to the recording companies. . . . That is who the beneficiaries of this legislation are. They are not the widows and they are not the children and they are not the heirs and they are not the authors, but they are often a bunch of possible antitrust violators. . . ." Other members of the Judiciary Committee rose to echo Dingell's sentiments, noting that they "had crossed that [extension] wire for the last time."

Congressman Dingell also lowered his sights at CONTU. He saw in the composition of the proposed Commission (*i.e.*, 4 copyright users, 4 copyright owners, 4 nongovernmental members from the general public, and the Register of Copyrights) a plot by big copyright proprietors to "extort further from the reading public, the listening public, and the consuming public." Dingell stated that such a body represented "nothing more than a rip-off of the American consumer. . . . I say 'Shame.' "

Other members of the House Judiciary Committee also objected to aspects of the Commission. It was observed that the Bill did not require that the Senate give its advice and consent in appointing members of the Commission, but that the President could make these appointments with the utmost autonomy. It was also suggested that financing independent researchers to study the topic would be considerably cheaper and would be less likely to achieve biased results. Complaints were aired that the Commission would be too closely involved administratively with the pro-owner Library of Congress. Finally, it was contended that no less than 8 of the Commission's members "must be chosen from among those who have a vested interest in preserving and extending copyrights," and thus enhancing "entrenched economic power."

Although Congressman Dingell made an effort to delay passage of S.3976 by arguing that a quorum was not present, the House voted to suspend the rules by a two-thirds vote (292:101), and passed the Bill by voice vote.

The Bill establishing CONTU, enacted virtually in the final hours of the 93rd Congress, was quickly sent to President Gerald R. Ford for his signature. Ford signed the Bill into law and duly appointed the 13 commissioners.

By most accounts, the President made wise choices in his appointments. Representing copyright oweners were the distinguished John Hersey, President of the Authors League; Herschel B. Sarbin, President of the Ziff-Davis Publishing Company; E. Gabriel Perle, Vice-President of Law for Time, Inc.; and Dan Lacy, Senior Vice-President of McGraw-Hill Publishing Company. Representing copyright users on the Commission were Elizabeth Hamer Kegan, Acting Deputy Librarian of Congress; William S. Dix, Librarian Emeritus of Princeton University; Alice E. Wilcox, Director of Minitex, an information technology firm located in Minneapolis; and Robert Wedgeworth, Executive Director of the American Library Association. Representing the public on the Commission were George Cary, former Acting Register of Copyrights; Rhoda H. Karpatkin, Executive Director of the Consumers Union; Arthur R. Miller, Professor of Law at Harvard University; and Melville B. Nimmer, Professor of Law at the University of California, Los Angeles who also served as vice-chairman of the Commission. Appointed as Chairman of the Commission was the Honorable Stanley H. Fuld, a former federal judge and special counsel for Kay, Scholer, Fierman, Hays, and Handler, a law firm in New York City.

At CONTU's inaugural meeting, held on October 8, 1975, Judge Fuld, as Chairman of the Commission, stated, "It is my view that the reprography problem is the most urgent of those on our list. The computer problem certainly will become increasingly important as the techniques of using copyrighted works in storage and retrieval systems develop with further advances in the art. Further, too, our directive is to devise a system that will allow access to copyrighted works for the purpose of their reproduction and use on computer systems, again with the recognition of the rights of the copyright proprietors. Whether or not the system which we work out for dealing with the conflicting economic interests under the heading of reprography will also fit the computer problem is a matter for future consideration.'' To outline the photoduplication problem for the Commission, Chairman Fuld appointed an ad hoc committee comprised of two representatives of copyright owners (Lacy and Hersey) and one representative of copyright users (Dix).

CONTU held a total of 21 formal meetings between 1975 and 1978. The verbatim transcripts of these meetings are not included in this set for reasons of space and appropriateness; nevertheless, a CONTU bibliography is reproduced in Volume V (Appendix G of the Commission's final report) which synopsizes the remarks of the witnesses called by CONTU and the topics they addressed. These transcripts are available from the National Technological Information Service for a moderate fee.

CONTU was involved with the politics of neo-publishing during the final years of the copyright revision debate, both peripherally and, on occasion, centrally. As we have noted, copyright users, especially education interests, had deep reservations about the very existence of the Commission, and copyright owners, particularly publishers, had been especially active during the years of the Commission's existence in reorganizing themselves politically.

In early 1975, Curtis Benjamin, who was retired from McGraw-Hill and who was a publisher long active in copyright law revision, formed the Coalition for Fair Copyright Protection, a group of only 11 members, but 11 members who represented a broadly-based amalgam of owner-oriented interests. The Coalition's members included the Association of American Publishers, the Information Industry Association, the National Music Publishers Associaiton, the Magazine Publishers Association, the Educational Media Producers Council, the American Medical Publishers Association, the Music Publishers Association of the United States, the National Association of College Stores, the National Audio-Visual Association, the National Newspaper Association, and the P.E.N. American Center. Benjamin stated in forming the group that, ''What we are concerned about is piracy, and piracy on a national scale. The plain hard fact is that we need a strong, modern copyright law to cope with the new technological age.'' Benjamin went on to note that the Coalition wished to ''combat the growing practice throughout the country of using duplicating equipment to make repeated copies of original material from books, magazines, television, tape recordings, and computer programs.'' In short, the Coalition for Fair Copyright Protection was almost a countergroup to CONTU, and one with a far firmer vision of where it was going. Specifically, in 1975 and 1976, the Coalition wanted to preserve Sections 107 and 108 of the Copyright Law Revision Bill, which were under attack by copyright users.

On a broader scale, publishers created in 1974 the American Book Publishers' Political Action Committee (PAC) which is registered with the Federal Election Commission under the Federal Election Act as a lobbyists' group. PAC had, and has, as its mission the influencing of the congressional Committees on Education, the Postal Service, Ways and Means, and, of course, the Judiciary, which was chiefly concerned with copyright law revision. To quote *Publishers Weekly,* the industry's major trade magazine, publishers were ''now looking down the road to a time when publishers themselves can build a grassroots organization concentrating on five publishing centers—New York, Boston, Philadelphia,

Chicago, and San Francisco.'' Publishers would, of course, have a long way to go compared with the grassroots organizations of educators and librarians, but they were, and are, moving in the same direction.

In this political milieu, CONTU functioned both effectively and in the public interest. Not only did it sponsor important empirical studies on copyright and on the new technological uses of copyrighted works (all of which are contained in this Volume), but it was instrumental in reconciling key areas between copyright owners and users in enacting the Copyright Act of 1976.

As noted in Volume III of this set, a major sticking point in reconciling copyright owners and users was the guidelines surrounding ''systematic copying'' in libraries and educational institutions for non-profit uses. In early 1976, the principal representatives of publishers, authors, educators, and librarians agreed to a rephrasing of Section 107 on fair use of the revision bill and, according to a number of reports, memebers of CONTU were instrumental in facilitating that agreement. The Register of Copyrights was quoted in *Publishers Weekly* as stating that, ''the Commission's contribution may come more usefully in the form of guidelines for library photocopying to be included in the House-Senate Conference Report,'' and an article in *Science* Magazine stated that, ''observers say that CONTU, itself a microcosm of the vested interests involved, helped to bring the discussion along. On 3 March, the subcommittee adopted an amendment to the fair use section of the bill which seemed to open the way for reasonable use for multiple copies for classroom use. . . . CONTU stepped into a potential breach on 2 April by offering to assist the interested parties in preparing guidelines on library photocopying. Kastenmeier [chairman of the subcommittee considering copyright revision] accepted the order and it is now understood that if guidelines acceptable to both sides can be worked out, they will be included in the Committee's final report.'' As it turned out, these guidelines were acceptable to all parties involved in the dispute and provided a key to the speedy enactment of a revised copyright law. CONTU was instrumental in this reconciliation; indeed, the Commission had done what previous groups had been unable to do—notably, the National Commission on Library and Information Science (NCLIS)—which, with the Copyright Officed, had convened in 1974 a Conference on Resolution of Copyright Issues and had as its specific objective accommodating the library photocopying problem. While the resultant NCLIS study (reproduced in this Volume) was of use to CONTU, it appeared that CONTU itself was the group that was truly able to accommodate the conflicting interests over the photocopying issue. As *Publishers Weekly* observed, ''the new Commission's work may very well supersede that of the conference.'' And this appears to be what happened.

Despite the good works of CONTU, it would be an error to conclude that the politics of neo-publishing generally, and the dispute over library and educational photocopying specifically, are over. Far from it. In late 1977, with no guidance from CONTU (not that any was required), publishers formed a Copyright Clearance Center. The objective was to centralize the process of receiving copyright permissions by copyright users and free them from the time-consuming problem of dealing with individual publishers. Libraries were expected to report their photocopying activities to the Center, which would sort things out by computer and distribute the money accrued from fees paid by librarians to publishers and other copyright owners who were members of the Center. Libraries were to report their photocopying use in one of three ways: by bundling up copies of the first page of each article photocopied and sending them to the Center; submitting periodic log sheets of photocopies made to the Center; or submitting computer-based records of photocopying. Within its first year of operation, more than 900 publications had registered in the Copyright Clearance Center, and the Center's formation and popularity with publishers were an indication of tensions between copyright owners and users continuing far beyond the enactment of a new Copyright Act and the termination of CONTU.

Partly because the Center was formed principally under the aegis of the Association of American Publishers, the publishers' major trade association, librarians in particular were concerned that the device was yet another rip-off of the copyright user. Indeed, in early 1978, the American Library Association (the major organization of librarians) took the "extraordinary step" (to use its own words) of addressing the members of the Association of American Publishers directly, "primarily in an attempt to avoid a major confrontation which we see developing between the publisher/author and the library communities." In a letter written to all members of the Association of American Publishers, the Executive Director of the American Library Association (who also served as a CONTU commissioner) stated, "We will not be intimidated by tactics illustrated by the recent public attacks questioning the integrity of the several national library associations. We sincerely hope that these tactics do not represent the dominant attitude toward libraries of the members of the Association of American Publishers."

In summary, it seems that not only will the politics of neo-publishing be roiling into the foreseeable future despite the conclusion of the revision process, but that CONTU, in even its brief duration, was as closely involved with those politics as a nonpartisan Commission could be. Nevertheless, this involvement by CONTU does not appear to have been of a biased nature and, indeed, was quite constructive.

Volume IV begins with a report by Yale Brownstein and others on the economics of property rights as applied to computer software and databases. Brownstein and his colleagues conclude, importantly, that copyright encourages the provision of scientific and artistic works even as they are formulated in the context of modern computer systems. In this light, however, Brownstein is concerned to some degree with the problem of "transaction costs," or the expenses associated with collecting permissions fees from copyright users by owners, and states that when these costs become too high the viability of copyright can be called into question.

Brownstein's analysis is followed by that of Marc Breslow, Allen R. Ferguson, and Larry Haverkamp, which approaches both the computer and photocopying questions from the viewpoints of the general public. This is a fairly general report designed to explain the issues to the citizenry.

The report by Breslow, Ferguson, and Haverkamp is followed by a fascinating survey of publishers' practices and present attitudes on authorized copying and licensing of journal articles by Bernard M. Fry, Herbert S. White, and Elizabeth L. Johnson. The survey uncovered a number of findings of interest to those involved in the economics of publishing. The journal editors were "overwhelmingly unwilling to grant blanket permission for copying, or blanket permission for interlibrary loans," and this was the case despite the fact that more than half the respondents were nonprofit journal publishers.

The survey of publishers is followed by a report by Harbridge House, Inc., on the legal protection of computer software. The report finds that the typical software company is less than a decade old, has less than 100 employees, and expends about $100,000 a year on research and development. Computer software companies are not particularly interested in taking advantage of legal protection, if available, but, if they were to do so, the protection would have to be simple, accessible, and inexpensive. The absence of legal protection of computer software programs, however, does not appear to deter the typical software company from developing or marketing new programs.

We move away from the problems of computer software developers to the problems that librarians face in grappling with copyright and photocopying. In an impressive investigation of library photocopying practices in the United States by King Research, Inc., it was found that the amount of photocopying occurring in libraries is substantial. The study's authors estimated that there were almost 40,000 paper-to-paper photocopying machines in the 21,280 libraries from which they chose their statistical sample, which was representative of academic, public, federal, and special libraries, with public libraries accounting for the largest share of photocopying of all library materials. Significantly, the study was confined to photocopying performed only by library staffs of library materials, and even with this limitation an estimated 114 million photocopies were made in 1976; however less than half of this number was made of copyrighted materials.

The sixth and final study commissioned by CONTU was performed by the Public Research Institute, a division of the Center for Naval analyses, and examined the costs to a library of owning, borrowing, and disposing of periodical publications. The Institute developed a formula for determining the most economic means of acquiring publications based on the levels of use by the library, and created useful "crossover points" that indicate the economic wisdom of borrowing or owning periodical publications.

The Institute study concludes Volume IV. The Commission's important *Final Report and Recommendations* are contained in Volume V of this set.

CONTU was a remarkable experiment for a number of reasons. One was that it was a blue-ribbon panel which accomplished not only what the normal blue-ribbon panel is supposed to accomplish but was instrumental in expediting the copyright law revision process itself. The studies commissioned by CONTU will prove useful to library managers and information specialists in virtually every nation. CONTU has made an important contribution to the world of information science.

NH
Tempe, Arizona

Economics of Property Rights as Applied to Computer Software and Data Bases

SUMMARY

The Major Issues

This report addresses two issues, one general and one specific. The general issue is whether economic analysis can provide insights into the proper scope of copyright coverage for works stored in or used with the assistance of computers or other automated data processing systems. The more specific issue is whether computer software should be copyrightable and, if so, what the terms of that copyright should be.

Advantages of Copyright

We show that, if one wishes to encourage the private provision and us of scientific and artistic works, the net value of output of goods and services to the public as a whole can be increased by the broadest possib specification of property rights by means of copyright. This conclusion remains valid even when one considers the economics of modern computer syst

Our analysis proceeds by showing how the economics of investment in the product of intellect influences the structure of the market for th works. Economic theory is then used to show that in such a market there is an optimal structure of prices. Here "optimal" means that economic welfare of society is maximized given the requirement that the producers break even or make some minimum level of profits. We then show that this implies that fees for the usage of copyrighted material be charged for as many of the uses as possible. This then leads to the conclusion that if any groups of users are exempted from paying, those users who are charged will have to pay more than they otherwise would (or the profits of the copyright owners and the incentives for the production of new works will be reduced).

There is one possible exception to the general rule that charges should be levied in every market. This exception arises when the costs of collection of user fees are likely to be so high relative to the sums involved as to render that collection uneconomical. These administrative costs are commonly referred to as "transactions costs". In computer information systems, costs of storing, transforming or manipulating data are generally much lower per datum supplied than are those of non-computer systems. Moreover, costs of monitoring the usage of those data also turn out to be correspondingly low. We conclude that the transactions costs are, in general, sufficiently insignificant, so as not to invalidate the argument for user fees and broad copyright protection.

Copyright vs. Trade Secrecy

The two prime methods available for the protection of computer software -- copyright and trade secrecy -- have opposite effects on usage. Whereas copyright promotes disclosure, reliance on the trade secrecy statutes requires suppression of information on advances in software design. We analyze these effects and infer that the use of copyright for protection will have beneficial effects on the quality and variety of software.

If producers have to rely on trade secret laws, they will have an incentive to keep their programs and data bases secret to prevent unauthorized use. Programs will tend to be written in obscure form, which makes it difficult to modify them or transfer them to a different computer. Potential buyers of computer software will lack information on what is available. Competition will lead to a duplication of efforts. Too many resources will be devoted to the development of software which is similar to existing products, so that a firm can capture a portion of a lucrative market, at the expense of others. Too few resources will be devoted to highly innovative and more risky software developments, which are beneficial to society, but less profitable to an individual firm.

Copyright protection has the advantage of giving better market infor-mation to software users; it encourages the development of software which can be used for many purposes and on many different computers since that gives a producer a wider market without fear of unauthorized use of his products; it reduces duplication of efforts; and it will tend to lead to the availability of a wider variety of products.

Choice of Copyright Period

For how long a period should a copyright of computer software or data bases be granted? On the one hand, the longer the period of protection the more profitable is the development of new software and the more will be produced. But the temporary monopoly during which a producer can charge a price for the use of his products also discourages some potential users, and in this way reduces the social usefulness of whatever amount of software is produced. The optimal time span for the period of protection yields the best compromise between these two effects. This optimal period depends on a number of economic and technological factors. In this report formulas are given which permit computation of an optimal protection period from empirical data. The following four factors all tend to favor a short protection period: a short useful life-span of software packages; rapidly increasing costs with an increase in the production of software; demand which is very responsive to price changes; and a high discount rate. Of course, the opposite factors all favor a longer protection period.

The actual choice of optimal protection period will require further research in gathering the pertinent data. It is research that is surely worth undertaking because the copyright period selected can make a substantial difference in the general welfare.

Other Conclusions

It should be noted that there is empirical evidence which implies that for the encouragement of the development of truly innovative software and fundamental breakthroughs in software design public support of research institutions will continue to be needed even if copyright protection is provided.

In any event, it is clear that encouragement of software design, whether through copyright protection or by other means, is important as an element in the stimulation of economic growth. Declining costs of computer hardware and expanding opportunities for automation imply that computer hardware and software together will play an increasingly crucial role in our economic future.

TABLE OF CONTENTS

I

OVERVIEW OF THE ISSUES

A. Historical Perspective

Since the passage of the 1909 copyright act (and in some ways, since the enactment of the first U.S. copyright law in 1790) it has been necessary for the courts and the Copyright Office to interpret that act in the light of technological and business advances. Two trends have emerged: First, utilitarian (non-artistic) creations and compilations of data such as interest tables and telephone books have been found to be copyrightable.[1,2] Second, the relationship of the copyright act to the products of and information transmitted by new technologies has frequently created difficult cases and often bad, or at least unclear, law. Among these technological advances have been sound recordings, radio and television broadcasts, photocopying, and cable television.[3]

Although the Supreme Court has expressed "the conviction that encouragement of individual effort by personal gain is the best way to advance public welfare through the talents of authors and inventors..,"[4] the decision concerning new techniques have sometimes appeared to ignore that conviction. (Fortnightly and Williams and Wilkins are perfect examples.) As a result several copyright revision bills have in recent years been considered by Congress; these addressed various parts of the issue of the

---

[1] Edwards and Deutch Lithographing Co. v. Boorman, 15F. 2d 35(7th Cir. 1926).

[2] Leon v. Pacific Tel. & Tel. Co., 91 F. 2d 484 (9th Cir. 1937).

[3] Among the more distinctive cases are: White-Smith Music Publishing Co. v. Apollo Co., 209 U.S. 1 (1908) (Piano roll not a copy of copyrighted music); Capitol Records, Inc., v. Mercury Records Corp., 221 F. 2d 657 (2d Cir. 1955) (phonograph record not copyrightable); Williams & Wilkins Co. v. United States, 420 U.S. 376 (1975) (Wholesale governmental photocopying no infringement); and Fortnightly Corp. v. United Artists Television, Inc., 392 U.S. 390 (1968) (CATV system does not "perform" works it makes available to its customers.)

[4] Mazer v. Stein (347 U.S. 201, 1954).

proper scope of copyright protection in light of new technology.[1] The 1969 revision bill (S.543) and the version finally enacted in 1976 (P.L. 94-553) each contained a section (§ 117) that stipulated that the case law on the use of copyrighted works in computer systems would be unaffected by the new law. In an action which may have permitted the passage of the new copyright act, the National Commission on New Technological Uses of Copyrighted Works (CONTU) was established to recommend legislation in the area of the reproduction and use of copyrighted works by computer and photocopying systems.[2]

In general terms the conflict to be resolved is that between the desire for a free flow of ideas, on one hand, with the establishment of incentives for the creation of ideas on the other. This balance is addressed by the copyright and patent laws, both of which grant, under certain circumstances, limited monopolies to the creators of inventions, books, and other forms of products of intellectual creativity.

B. Specific Issues in the Area of Computer-based Information

There are three basic questions that underlie this discussion of the proper scope of copyright protection:

(1) What is the product, i.e., what exactly is copyrightable in the context of items used with the aid of a computer system?

(2) How do we define usage in this context?

(3) How do we detect and monitor such usage?

These questions obviously do not pertain only to information used in a computer or automatic data processing system. There are natural parallels, say, to the use of copyrighted phonographic recordings by radio stations or the transmission of copyrighted still or motion pictures by means of television. But in the computer field these questions can not simply be

[1]For example, see H.R.2512 and S.597 (1967), S.543 (1969).

[2]P.L.93-573, enacted on Dec. 31, 1974. The Commissioners were appointed on July 25, 1975.

answered by analogy with other forms of communication.

Although the Commission has received considerable testimony and advice on whether input to, storage in, or output from a computer whould constitute usage,[1] we shall take a step back to the basic underlying principle which has given rise to these questions:

Principle 1.1 The more complete and certain the specification of property rights, the greater the level of economic efficiency that is possible.

It is because of this principle that one seeks to define what is meant by property in reference to information used by a computer system. As the Data Base Subcommittee has indicated, it seems clear that the intention of Congress was that computer data bases be considered a proper subject for copyright.[2] However in the discussions of proprietary rights in computer programs and software, arguments have been made for protection by means of copyright, patent, or the trade secret laws.[3] It is in the comparison between protection by means of copyright and reliance on trade secrecy and restrictive licensing that the contrasts are most apparent. Copyright promotes disclosure while trade secrecy results in minimal disclosure and dissemination (if it works).

We shall examine the economic issues such as the trade-off between the incentives to create and the incentives to use new information or products. Although we shall not be able to disregard completely many of the legal issues, they shall not be in the forefront of our discussion.

---

[1] See, e.g., Data Base Subcommittee report, Feb. 18, 1977.

[2] Ibid., p.1.

[3] For example, see D. Bender, "Trade Secret Protection of Software," G. Washington Law Review 38:909 (1970); C.N. Mooers, "Computer Software and Copyright," Computing Surveys 7 (March 1975), 45-72; and O.R. Smoot, "Development of an International System for Legal Protection of Computer Programs," Communications of the ACM 19 (April 1976), 171-174.

C. Introduction to the Economic Analysis

The subject of copyright gives rise to a number of complex economic issues. After pointing out some fundamental relationships that will underlie our discussion, it is well to begin with a survey of these issues. From there we turn to a brief indication of the evaluation of these issues to which one is led by economic analysis. Our report then turns to a rather more probing discussion of a number of these matters, and ends up with a careful description of a novel and powerful method by which one can evaluate one of the key issues in the area -- the optimal length of copyright.

The need for copyright or some substitute arises from what economists call difficulty of exclusion from the use of printed material, software, and various other such products whose initial cost of production is quite high but for which the cost of replication is very small. Ability to exclude means that the producer of such an item can prevent a potential user from employing it unless that person is willing to provide payment for the item. Difficulty of exclusion means that people can help themselves to the item without payment and with little or no fear of untoward consequences. Such goods, particularly when they are expensive to produce, normally will find no private suppliers. Firms will surely be discouraged from investing in new software if the products will be immediately available to anyone for the taking. To prevent this is, of course, the purpose of copyright. It is intended to protect the investment of firms that put resources into valuable new products, not only as a means to protect the interests of those firms, but perhaps even more important from the social viewpoint, to encourage the production of valuable items from whose use it would be difficult to exclude anyone without such protection.

However, there is another side to the matter which will play an important role later in the analysis. These same products which seem to require statutory protection are also, generally, items which, in the view of economists, should be offered with maximal encouragement of widespread use. That is, these items generally involve a heavy (sunk) cost of development to which little or nothing is added when there is an increase in number of users. This is in sharp contrast with other products such as food or clothing in which additional usage requires substantial additional use of resources -- additional users are not free. Thus, economists argue, while goods like shirts or potatoes should have a high price reflecting the high costs imposed by additional users, there is something undesirable about a commensurately high price for the use of a software package since that high price will discourage widespread use even though such added use costs society little or nothing over and above the sunk cost of development of the package.

D. Issues in Copyright Policy

Having discussed the logic of the underlying problem we can turn next to a listing of the issues which must be faced by copyright policy. In the following section we will see how the analysis which has just been summarized helps us to provide a fruitful evaluation of these issues.

The most obvious issue that arises in this area is whether copyright is the only way to go about dealing with the problem that copyright protection is designed to solve. As a matter of fact there are several alternatives to copyright, and the issue is to determine whether anyone of them as generally better than the others, or, what may be more likely, whether some work well in some circumstances while others are better suited under different conditions.

Since copyright is intended to protect the interests of those who invest in the design of certain types of new products and to encourage that sort of investment, an obvious alternative to copyright is the provision of added protection to industrial secrets. If a potential investor in a software package can be made to feel reasonably confident that others will be unable to discover the secrets underlying his product so that he will be able to retain a monopoly over its use, then that may perhaps be as effective a stimulus to this sort of investment as copyright protection.

There is also a third possibility where neither secrecy nor copyright protection is applicable or effective, then private investment will obviously be discouraged. In that case the substitute possibility is investment by the public sector. This helps to explain the heavy investment of government agencies in a wide variety of types of research, most notably in basic research which is preponderantly carried out under government sponsorship.

Thus there are alternatives to copyright, and we will see in the nex section that for each of them there are areas in which it promises to be more appropriate than the others.

The second set of issues that arises in the area of copyright policy is the nature of the terms that should be permitted. Here several issue arise immediately:

(1) Over how long a period should the copyright extend?

(2) Should the length of copyright be uniform for all items protecte

(3) Should there be any restrictions upon the monopoly power conferr upon the holder of a copyright?

(4) In particular, should there be compulsory licensing of the copyrighted product?

(5) If there is compulsory licensing, how should the price be set?

(6) Should there be classes of uses or classes of users of copyright products who are exempted from the copyright provisions?

Finally, there are a variety of issues that arise in carrying out copyright policy in light of the complications inevitably injected by reality. These force policy-makers to accept compromises which can be avoided altogether only in theoretical discussions. Only two examples will be offered, both of them arising because of problems of enforcement.

First, are there types of use which should be exempted from copyright protection, not because their exemption is inherently desirable but because the cost of entering copyright protection in these areas exceeds the potential benefits of enforcement? If so what can one say about the nature of such exemptions? (This is one of the issues addressed by the "fair-use" section (§107) of the 1976 Copyright revision.)

Our second example relates to charges for the use of copyrighted material. Here the question is whether the imposition of charges based directly on use is always practical, and if not, what alternatives constitute a second-best solution.

This brief discussion has been intended to provide a short list of the main economic issues involved in copyright policy. It certainly does not pretend to be exhaustive nor does it even begin to suggest the noneconomic (e.g., legal, political and social) issues. This list should, however, serve as an adequate working framework for our discussion.

We proceed now to a brief commentary upon each of these issues, indicating how economic analysis suggests they should be viewed. After that, we will turn to a somewhat more extensive examination of several of the more crucial topics.

E. Copyright and Its Alternatives

We have indicated that copyright is only one of three avenues to encourage investment in the development of the pertinent new products, trade secrecy and direct government investments being the two prime alternatives. What is the appropriate role of each of these instruments?

Later we will discuss in some detail the differences in the consequences of secrecy and copyrighting. But, in brief summary, secrecy necessarily restricts the range of direct users of the product involved, whereas copyright does not necessarily do so and certainly does not do it where there is compulsory licensing at reasonable prices. Second, resort to secrecy does encourage expenditure on product features which inhibit discovery of the secrets. There are other costs, extending even to outlays on espionage which this process encourages. On the other hand, if the copyright remains valuable as its expiration data approaches this can encourage research expenditures whose only purpose is to discove product variations just sufficient to justify a new copyright, an exercis which obviously has little payoff to society.

Secrecy is likely to work most effectively where the uncopyrighted product is an intermediate good which is itself used in the production of other goods, e.g., if it is a computer program used to process other people's data. When this is the case it is easier for the investor to earn the cost of his investment without revealing his secret because his product need never leave his hands. On the other hand, if the investor must rely for his earnings on the sale of the uncopyrighted product itself (e.g., by selling the program itself to users) then it is very difficult to retain secrecy. This distinction naturally suggests the sort of item in which innovation can be expected in the absence of copyright protection, and the sort of product which requires copyright if private investment in development is to be obtained.

But there are reasons why the third way of obtaining this sort of investment -- direct government financing -- should at least sometimes be utilized. We saw earlier that for at least some potentially copyrightable products the cost of serving additional users is negligible, so that a high price which discourages use is undesirable socially. However a very low price is likely to be incompatible with recovery of initial investment outlays for its development. Where this is a significant consideration (and precise conditions for this case can be enunciated --

see Baumol and Ordover [1977] appended to this report),[1] then neither copyright nor secrecy will be in the social interest, for both operate via the extraction of prices sufficiently high to bring a return that will be attractive to private investment. It is clear that in such a case, if the investment in the product is worthwhile to society but compensatory pricing is not, then the only alternative is government financing. Even if one were to think of another method of making such investment attractive financially to private enterprise, it would, by definition, be no more satisfactory than the use of copyright or reliance on secrecy.

F. Terms of Copyright

We come next to the issue of which conditions should be applied to the granting of a copyright where that is the procedure adopted.

The first issue to be considered is the period of time over which the copyright should remain valid. It is shown in detail in this report that this is an issue which need not be settled ad hoc, on the basis of tradition or compromise. There are strong economic considerations which can serve as an underpinning for an analysis of optimal copyright life. The point is that a very short copyright period will fail in its purpose by being insufficient to attract any significant amount of investment into the development process. On the other hand a very long copyright period can extract an excessive price from society by granting monopoly powers to investors for an excessive period. The optimality calculation consists of a balancing of these two considerations to determine that duration of copyright which maximizes its net contribution to social welfare.

This immediately indicates that, at least in principle, the optimal

---

[1] Baumol, W.J. and Ordover, J.A., "On the Optimality of Public-Goods Pricing with Exclusion Devices," Kyklos 30 (1977) Fasc. 1, pp. 5-21 (copy attached).

period of protection will vary from case to case. It will depend on the annual profitability of the investment, the magnitude of the monopoly price extracted from the public, the "natural" rate of obsolescence of the product of the investment[1] and a variety of other such considerations which are indicated specifically in detail later in our analysis. That means that one industry or one type of product may call for a copyright life different from another. A computer program may be encouraged most effectively by a copyright lasting x years while a novel may call for a y year copyright. Obviously, a case-by-case approach to copyright period is totally impractical, but it is certainly worth considering whether the establishment of, say, two or three different categories of materials eligible for copyright protection, each with its own copyright period, may not be desirable and feasible administratively. Often it has proven to be true that where administrative simplicity calls for uniformity while other efficiency considerations call for variability, a very small number of categories add very little to administrative costs and yet contribute enormously to efficiency -- sometimes capturing the bulk of the gains that are potentially available. It is because of this possibility that this report devotes so much space to a model for the evaluation of optimal copyright duration. Should it be determined that the possibility of several copyright periods is worth further exploration, our model indicates just how this issue should be investigated.

Other potential provisions of the copyright that require comment are the idea of compulsory licensing, the possibility of restrictions upon pricing and the notion of exemptions from the terms of the copyright

---

[1] In general, for example, the optimal period of protection will be less than the useful economic life of the item covered. This is necessary in order to make sure that the net gains from the project are shared by the investor and by the general public. Obviously, the latter's gains are limited until after the expiration of the copyright since before that time the copyright holder may be able to use the monopoly power it confers to extract the bulk of the gains flowing from the copyrighted product.

of certain categories of use or certain categories of users.

All of these possibilities share one common feature. Each of them constitutes some restriction upon the avenues which the holder of the copyright can use to pursue profits. This means that, if statutory protection is to serve as an incentive for investment in the production of material subject to that protection, any provision of the sort now under discussion must weaken this incentive.[1] To achieve any given degree of stimulation of such investment, a price ceiling, a requirement of licensing or other such restrictions must be offset by a commensurate improvement in some other inducement, e.g., it may call for a countervailing increase in length of the period of copyright protection. But we have seen that a lengthening of this period is not without its social cost, so that the decision becomes a trade-off in which the advantages expected to flow from the restrictions in the copyright holder's monopoly power are balanced against the social cost of the lengthened protection period.

Compulsory licensing and restrictions upon the price charged for a license obviously must constitute a gain to those who decide to acquire a license as well as to the customers for their products. This will necessarily be so since those who obtain a license do so voluntarily, and hence to them it must be worth its price. Without compulsory licensing they would be deprived of this gain.

But one must be careful not to jump to the conclusion that this is a net gain to the community. It is equally certain that compulsory licensing must constitute a net loss to the holder of the copyright, at least in his own view of the matter, for otherwise there would be no together rather than separately.) The interrelation between scale economies and production complementarities can be seen in the operations

---

[1] This argument only considers the economie incentives for investment in the production of intellectual works. There are, of course, other incentives.

of the abstracting and indexing services. For example, the American Society of Civil Engineers produce printed and machine readable abstracts and indices as part of the same operations. The development costs for this computer-assisted abstracting and indexing system were approximately $25,000. It now costs less than $2,000 per month for the input of 100 items.[1]

The econometric studies reported in this section lead us to the following tentative conclusion: Most STI systems -- scientific journals, CS, CDB -- are characterized by scale economies and in many cases by production complementarities.

C. Setting Prices to Cover the Costs

We have seen already that marginal cost pricing has desirable properties from the standpoint of the society. Thus, if price is equal to marginal cost, all those who are willing to pay the price are per force willing to pay for the resource which is used to provide them with the commodity in question. Ideally, then, we would like to have all the commodities priced in this manner. For a single-product firm, or for a multi-product firm in which all fixed costs can be rationally allocated among various products, i.e., when fixed costs are product specific, the simplistic prescription is to switch from marginal cost pricing to the average cost pricing. By definition, a firm that charges a price equal to or exceeding the average cost can recover all its costs. Setting aside the difficulties associated with the definition of the say, to certain classes of nonprofit users, but there seems to be no reason to require the burdens to be borne by other users of the same copyright. Economists are not opposed to all subsidies, but where they support them they prefer general subsidies that are provided openly and explicitly and financed by the community as a whole through the tax

---

[1]See P.A. Parisi, "Composition Innovations at the American Society of Civil Engineers," presented at the 1975 IEEE Conference on Scientific Journals, p. 33.

system, rather than subsidies which are concealed and extracted from some fortuitously chosen group from whom it happens to be convenient to obtain the funds.

There is a second reason why economists generally do not favor broad exemptions of particular classes of users. As we have noted earlier, a price for the use of some copyrighted material always tends to discourage its use -- the higher the price, the less use will generally be made of the product. Now a zero price to one group of users compensated by a higher price to other users will cause a lopsided change in demand patterns which generally cause a larger overall social loss than a balanced spread of the price increases. There are carefully worked out principles in economic analysis which indicate how the social losses from such distortions can be minimized, and these principles are generally inconsistent with broad exemptions.[1]

G. Compromises Required in Practice

As has already been noted, even if an ideal copyright system can be designed in theory one can be sure that it will require considerable compromise to make it workable in practice. Thus, we noted that while ideally the length of the copyright should vary from product to product, in reality such lattitude could only result in an administrative nightmare.

At least two other compromises also suggest themselves immediately, though others will undoubtedly arise in practice.

First, the economic principles of optimal charging which were discussed in the preceding section call not only for payments to be borne by all classes of producer, but also for payments to be required for every use. For example, if a charge is imposed upon photocopying of materials pro-

[1] See for example, Y. Braunstein, "An Economic Rationale for Page and Submission Charges by Academic Journals," Center for Applied Economics Discussion Paper, New York University (1976).

tected by copyright, such a charge should, ideally, be required for every such act. Yet (aside from the issue of fair use) with current technology it is literally impossible to monitor every instance of photocopying done in a library or elsewhere. Consequently, user charges for the photocopying of copyrighted material can only be approximated at best. One may be able to impose a flat fee on a photocopying machine or upon a library, or one can base a payment upon the number of recorded uses of a photocopier. However, these all involve three serious compromises: First, there is no way of knowing whether it is the individual who uses the copyrighted material who actually bears the cost. Such a crude payment process must bear as heavily upon the person who copies his own handwritten page as upon the person who copies a journal article to avoid buying that journal. Second, payment will generally not correspond closely to the amount of use of material under copyright. Finally, there is no way of allocating the payments among the producers of the copyrighted materials in proportion to their use. One is driven instead to resort to some sort of pooling arrangement such as the one used to compensate composers of music. Fixed annual payments for performances of recorded music are, for example, made by the television networks to the composers' organization which then divides these proceeds among the composers on the basis of some rule of thumb. This is all a very crude approximation to the theoretical ideal of payment proportioned to use, but enforcement and administrative problems leave no choice except some such compromise arrangement. This type of accomodation may frequently have to characterize payment under copyright in the future.

A second compromise which seems unavoidable is the exemption of very limited usage, for example the photocopying of a single reproduction of a short passage from a journal. The main argument for such an exemption from the viewpoint of the economist is not that such a limited use is "fair", but rather that potential gains from payment for such limited use are likely to be swamped by the administrative and policing costs.

The main issue raised by the necessity of compromises such as have been discussed is whether they should be written into the rules of copyright with an attempt to fix the boundaries of permitted compromise, or whether one prefers to permit time and usage to soften the working rules formulated without exceptions. But this is a choice which lies outside the economist's area of special competence. It is therefore appropriate to turn from this outline of the general issues, to a more careful examination of those directly amenable to economic analysis.

II

IMPLICATIONS OF ECONOMICS OF PRICING FOR STRUCTURING PROTECTION OF COMPUTER SOFTWARE AND COMPUTERIZED DATA BASES

The main purpose of this Chapter is to apply some recent advances in the economic literature on pricing decisions to the question of the scope and nature of property right protection that the society should grant to those who develop and disseminate computer software (CS, hereafter), and to computerized data bases (CDB, hereafter). The major premise that underlies the discussion in this section of the report is that the applicability long-cherished principles of incremental cost pricing to the pricing of CS and CDB is severely hampered for two basic reasons.

(1) The structure of the costs in the STI industry is, in general, such that with prices set at the incremental cost of providing an additional user with the CS package or with the use of a CDB the production costs will not be covered.

(2) Once we grant a property right to the producer we vest him with a certain degree of monopoly power. It is well-known that a monopolist has no incentive to set prices at incremental cost. The question then arises as to the kind of pricing policies that the monopolist should be allowed to engage in.

It should be noted that in this section we abstract from the difficult problem of the duration of the property right. This is the subject of Chapter IV of our report. We begin by stating some fundamentals of pricing and then show how those fundamentals bear on the question of copyright.

A. Economics of Pricing: Some Basic Principles

In the introduction we have already noted some difficulties in applying the long-cherished principles of incremental cost pricing to the pricing of computer software and to computerized data bases. The difficulty that we isolated stemmed from the fact that with price set at marginal cost the total costs of CS and CDS can in general, not be recovered.

This problem is best illustrated with an example. Let us assume that the development, maintenance and updating costs of a particular piece of software, i.e., the fixed costs, are $10,000. The cost of providing the package to an additional customer, i.e., the marginal (or incremental) cost is 10 man hours at $50 per man-hour, or $500. If the firm charges $500, then the initial costs will be uncovered. If the firm charges anywhere above $500, there is a resource misallocation. To see this, note that the cost of serving an additional customer is $500. Consequently, all customers who are willing to pay this amount should be allowed to purchase the commodity. If the price is pushed above $500 because the firm must be able to recoup its total costs, then some prospective customers who are willing to pay the cost of providing them with this commodity will be priced out of the market. Thus

Principle 2.1 If the price of a commodity is set above its incremental cost, some prospective consumers who are willing to pay that incremental cost will be deprived of this commodity.

We should note that *Principle 2.1* applies not only to commodities but also the services that various commodities provide. To illustrate, if the (incremental) cost of accessing one additional entry in the bibliographic data base is five cents, and the price of an access is 5 1/2 cents then all those users who are willing to pay less than 5 1/2 cents will not make the additional search of the bibliographic data base. Unfortunately *Principle 2.1* clashes with the following

Principle 2.2 If the firm is operating at the point at which there are economies of scale in production then it cannot cover its total costs by charging prices equal to the incremental cost.

To a non-economist this principle is not as simple as the previous one. It is imperative therefore that we explain carefully the concept of economies of scale. This is best done with an example. Consider, therefore, a firm that is producing one output, a particular software package. The total cost of providing this CS package to 100 users is $5000. If output (sales) double then total costs of production increase to $9000. Thus doubling of output causes the total costs to increase less than two fold.

The presence of economies of scale can easily be inferred once it is ascertained that in the relevant range of outputs the average cost is decreasing with output. This situation is depicted in Figure 1.

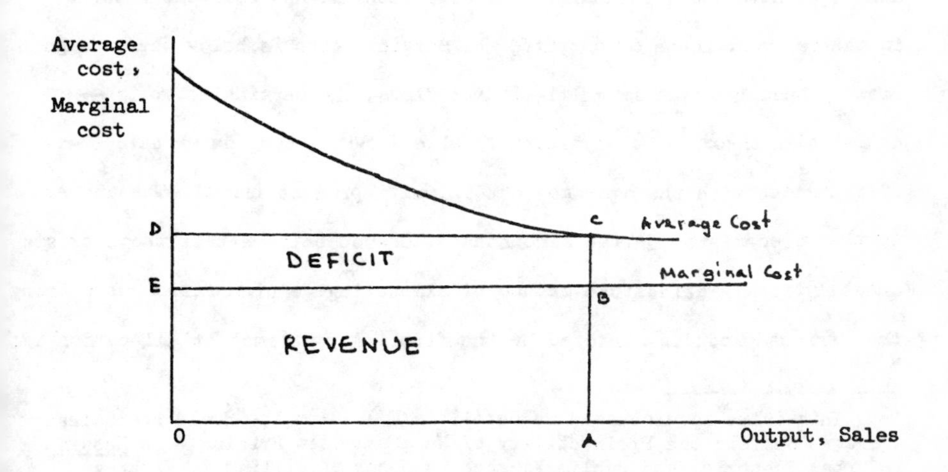

Figure 1

On the vertical axis, we measure in dollars per unit of output the two types of costs: the average cost and the marginal cost. On the horizontal axis we measure output. To fix ideas, the reader may think of output as being the number of sales of a particular CS package. If the firm charges the price equal to OE, its sales are OA. The revenue is given by the area of a rectangle OABE. The total cost is, however, equal to the area of OACD. Hence, the deficit is equal to BCDE.

We have been less than careful in specifying the notion of output. In some cases it may be perhaps relatively easy to specify and measure what the output is. It may be, as in the example above, the number of CS packages sold. Or, in the case of CDB, it may be the number of bibliographic entries extracted from the data base. We shall, however, not attempt to deal with the questions of the appropriate measures of output but rather assume that output is well-defined and measurable.

If we leave the unrealistic world of a single-product firm for the more likely multi-product firms, it becomes more difficult to ascertain those situations in which the marginal cost pricing is not feasible.[1] Here, it suffices to point out that a conceptual difficulty arises because in such firms the notion of the average cost is not well-defined. And as we have seen, the marginal cost pricing is not feasible when, in the relevant range of outputs, the marginal cost is below the average cost. (Luckily, even in multi-product firms, the marginal cost is -- at least in theory -- always identifiable.) Why, then, do we have these difficulties with the average cost in multi-product firms? The answer is that economists, unlike accountants, do not believe that there exists an analytically defensible method of allocating genuine fixed costs among the various products marketed by the firm. Any attempt at allocation is

[1]This issue is discussed in detail in W.J. Baumol, "Scale Economies, Average Cost and the Profitability of Marginal Cost Pricing," in Essays in Urban Economics and Public Finance in Honor of William S. Vickrey (Lexington, MA: Lexington-Heath, 1975).

inherently arbitrary. Consequently, depending on the allocation method, some of the products may be priced at the marginal cost while others are not. But a change in accounting practice may lead to the revision of the cost allocations and, therefore in the list of those commodities which can be priced at incremental cost. Fortunately, as we shall see, the economic theory of pricing does not hinge on the notion of the average cost but focuses instead on the marginal costs.

Principle 2.3 In a multi-product firm average cost pricing is arbitrary because the relevant average costs cannot be rationally computed.

In order to motivate our discussion later in the chapter on non-marginal cost pricing, we digress for a moment in order to consider the cost structures in various segments of the scientific and technical information industry (STI).

B. Costs in the STI Industries: Empirical Analysis

1. Examples from the scientific journal publishing sector.

Our econometric studies of the cost relationships in the journal publishing sector of the STI industry revealed that both single and multi-product firms generally meet the Baumol tests for the infeasibility of marginal cost pricing. We undertook three separate studies -- one was a cross-section analysis of the publishers of 56 journals; the other two were in-depth studies of large journal publishing organizations. We present a summary of our findings.[1]

Our cross-sectional study of journals indicated that, within the sample range, the annual costs of publishing a journal declined as the number of different journal (titles) published by the same publisher increased. This inverse relationship was estimated by a statistical regression analysis of cost and output data of 56 journals from three

[1] Our detailed findings are presented in W.J. Baumol and Y.M. Braunstein, "Empirical Study of Scale Economies and Production Complementarity: The Case of Journal Publication," Journal of Political Economy, October 1977.

years. (These data were collected by B Fry.)[1] The regression technique allows us to isolate the effect of the number of journals has on cost from the effects of changes in the circulation and in the number of pages published per year. In particular, a publisher with 36 journals would have average costs of approximately 80% of a single journal publisher after correcting for circulation and number of pages.

The exact equation estimated was

$$\log TC = -.735 + .171 D_s + .588 \log C + .793 \log P - .0621 \log J .$$

In this equation, the journal's total annual cost (TC, in $10,000's) is a linear function of its circulation (C, in 1,000's), the number of pages published per year (P, in 100's), and the total number of journals published by this publisher (J). There is also a "dummy variable" (Ds) which indicates that the costs are higher for journals in the scientific and technical fields. Each coefficient was statistically significant (diffe from zero) and the R^2 was .8524.

This cross-section procedure has associated with it several difficulties. The major one is that the per-journal costs from a multi-journal publisher necessarily involve an arbitrary accountant's allocation of fixed costs (generally overhead, administration, etc.). The presence of this problem in our data was confirmed by our finding that statistically there appeared to be no fixed costs; all reported costs could be divided into those varying with changes in circulation and those varying with number of pages.

For example we estimated the following cost function for six journals from one publisher for nine years using standard econometric methods:

$$TC_{it} = -.168 + .184 C_{it} + .647 P_{it} ,$$

[1] Fry, B.& H.J. White, "Economics and Interaction of the Publisher-Lib Relationship in the Production and Use of Scholarly and Research Journals", final report, National Science Foundation Grant GN-4398 (November, 1975). Also published by Lexington-Heath.

where

TC_{it} = cost of each journal i (i = 1,...,6) for year t (t = 1,...,9) (in $10,000)

C_{it} = circulation for journal i in year t (in 1000's)

P_{it} = pages published by journal i for year t (in 1000's).

The R^2 was .978. This again shows that costs are linearly related to the circulation and the number of pages. Here the constant term (-.168) was not statistically significant. More formally we could not reject the hypothesis that the true value was zero (at the 95% level).

But we know there are fixed costs in publishing journals. Among the possible explanations one that has a great deal of logic and appeal is that most publishers (or their accountants) allocate these fixed costs among the various titles on the basis of pages, circulation, or some other factor correlated with one or both of them. If true this indicates that we cannot capture all of the economic phenomena in which we are interested unless we find some way to obtain unallocated cost data.

In addition to describing statistically the production process in general, our other interest was in confirming (or denying) the presence of production complementarities in the publication of journals. Here the issue, in non-formal terms, is whether the consolidation of publishing activities or the combining of publishing and other activities results in savings over doing these things individually. The econometric problem was an interesting one: could we develop a specification (a relationship between costs and outputs) that enabled us to measure complementarities and scale economies without, *a priori*, prejudging whether or not they existed?

One family of specifications that has just these properties is

$$C = a_0 + a_1x_1 + a_2x_2 + a_3(x_1x_2)^{\gamma}$$

where

C = total costs

x_1 and x_2 = outputs, and

$1 \geq \gamma \geq 0$.

Here the a_i and γ are numbers whose magnitudes are to be estimated econometrically.

It can be proved that if a_0, a_1 and a_2 are positive (and $a_3 = 0$), we have scale economies but no complementarities in production. If, in addition, a_3 is negative, these complementarities do exist.[1]

We employed this analysis using two alternative sets of data. The data in the first case study came from a publisher with two distinct types of journals -- those reporting original research and those containing translations of articles first published in another language. The cost data were annual costs for each of nine years. The output data were indices that indicated both the magnitude of circulation and the number of pages in the two types of journals. Our estimated cost function was

$$TC = 582.8 + 2.38S_1 + 8.00S_2 - 345.7(S_1S_2)^{0.13}$$

where

TC = Annual costs (in $1,000,000's).

The R^2 was .8012 (but the F was 6.72 because of the low number of observations).

This first analysis confirmed the existence of scale economies and production complementarities. Therefore we can conclude that the consolidation of publication of the original and translation journals resulted in cost savings.

---

[1]See Baumol and Braunstein, op. cit.

The second case study involved an organization which has affiliated with it a large number of learned societies, each of which publishes a journal as well as providing other services and activities for its members. The data covered fourteen years of operation for twenty-five of the affiliated societies. Using these data we found and measured the economies that arose from the combining of membership and publishing activities.

The estimated function was

$$TC = 153.4 + 1.86M + .680P - 13.17(MP)^{0.1}$$

where

TC = annual society costs (in $10,000's)

P = pages (in 100's)

M = membership (in 1000's)

The R^2 was .794. This confirmed the presence of economies from the combining of activities. This time the range of the observations was much greater than in our previous calculation. The number of pages varied from 20 to 3000 per year and membership ranged from 6000 to 18,000, giving us observations that can be considered to fall very close to the axes and the origin. However, we are less certain of the implications of this cost function because there is necessarily a high correlation between membership and circulation and because we were forced to use number of pages alone to measure the publishing activity of the societies.

2. Scale Economies in Computer Software and Computer Data Bases.

a. Computer Software (CS)

There is an increasing tendency for computer systems managers to utilize standard instead of custom-made computer software. This change has partly been caused by the unbundling of computer software and hardware and has partly resulted from the underlying economics.

> In the first place, standard software generally contains far fewer logical errors; secondly, it is more flexible in that it has been created for generalized criteria, making it easily classifiable and, therefore, readily adaptable to the ever-increasing requirements of the users of data processing; it is easily programmable and thus lends itself to shortening substantially the critical phase, rapidly achieving results and, in sufficiently reliable conditions, attaining ultimate objectives.[1]

However, the production of computer software closely parallels the process of publishing in that there are substantial "first-copy" costs that must be incurred irrespective of the number of units produced and sold. If the computer software is a complex operating system, for example, there may also be substantial costs associated with the production and installation of the second and later "copies." However, if these costs decline with each additional unit produced (possibly because of "learning-by-doing") or if some of the pre-production investment is generalizable to all of the copies, there will be economies of scale in the production of computer software.

We were able to obtain some estimates of the development costs of one large on-line retrieval system. This system cost approximately $1,000,000 to develop (including hardware acquisition) over a three year period. This development cost has been divided into five categories. (The approximate percentages of the total follow each category.)

Software Design/Implementation	5-10%
Hardware Acquisition	60-70%
Maintenance	5-10%
Testing & Experimentation	10%
Marketing & Education	10%

The organization that created it is now marketing this system. The development costs amounting approximately to $250,000 - $300,000 (the

[1]A. Leggio, "Economic Results of Technical Decisions in Large Data Centers," in A.B. Frielink, ed., Economics of Informatics, (New York: American Elsevier, 1975).

sum of the design, testing,and marketing costs) are, at least partially, fixed costs that do not have to be repeated for each "copy". This certainly indicates that there are substantial economies of scale in the production of additional copies or versions of this operating system.

b. Computer Data Bases (CDB)

Here again an analogy with publishing can be shown to be reasonable. The development of a CDB also has large initial costs relative to both the cost of making additional copies and to the cost of periodic up-dating of the data base. The time profile of the costs of one CDB are shown in Figure 2.

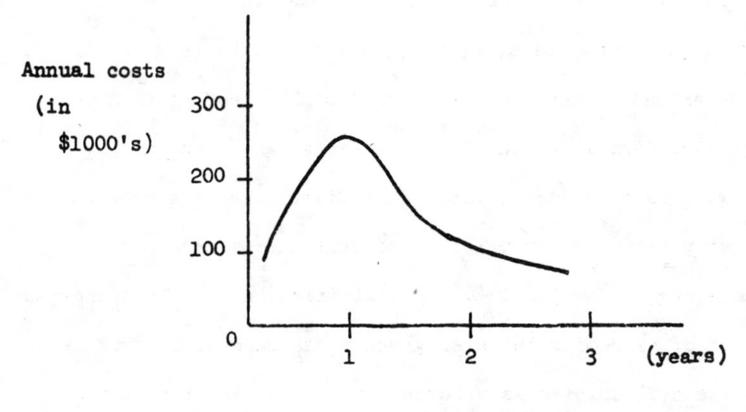

Figure 2

In addition to the scale economies in the production of CDB, there may also be substantial complementarities in production. (Production complementarities occur when it is less expensive to produce two products together rather than separately.) The interrelation between scale economies and production complementarities can be seen in the operations of the abstracting and indexing services. For example, the American Society of Civil Engineers produce printed and machine readable abstracts and indices as part of the same operations. The development costs for this computer-assisted abstracting and indexing system were approximately

$25,000. It now costs less than $2,000 per month for the input of 100 items.[1]

The econometric studies reported in this section lead us to the following tentative conclusion: Most STI systems -- scientific journals, CS, CDB -- are characterized by scale economies and in many cases by production complementarities.

C. Setting Prices to Cover the Costs

We have seen already that marginal cost pricing has desirable properties from the standpoint of the society. Thus, if price is equal to marginal cost, all those who are willing to pay the price are per force willing to pay for the resource which is used to provide them with the commodity in question. Ideally, then, we would like to have all the commodities priced in this manner. For a single-product firm, or for a multi-product firm in which all fixed costs can be rationally allocated among various products, i.e., when fixed costs are product specific, the simplistic prescription is to switch from marginal cost pricing to the average cost pricing. By definition, a firm that charges a price equal to or exceeding the average cost can recover all its costs. Setting aside the difficulties associated with the definition of the average cost, we shall demonstrate that average cost pricing has little to recommend it except in a rather unlikely situation which we shall soon describe. Consequently in this section we shall provide some general principles which should guide those responsible for setting prices. The rules to be developed apply to firms that sell an identical product to various categories of users as well as to the firms which sell a variety of products. More importantly the same sets of rules apply

(a) to a firm which attempts to maximize the welfare of its consumers

---

[1] See P.A. Parisi, "Composition Innovations at the American Society of Civil Engineers," presented at the 1975 IEEE Conference on Scientific Journals, p. 33.

subject to the proviso that the firm earns an adequate rate of return;

(b) to a firm which strives to maximize its profits.

In order to simplify our exposition of the basic rules, we begin with the very simple case of a firm which sells one commodity. That commodity, however, is bought by two distinct classes of users. For example, a CS package is sold both to profit-making firms as well as to nonprofit research institutes. What distinguishes those two groups is, however, not their goal but the responsiveness of their demands to changes in the price for a CS package. In economics the measure of responsiveness of demand to price changes is known as the <u>elasticity of demand</u>. More formally, the elasticity of demand is given by the percentage change in demand as a result of a (small) percentage change in product price. Mathematically, if Q is the quantity sold and P is a product's price, then its elasticity, e, is given by $e = - (\frac{\Delta Q}{Q})/(\frac{\Delta P}{P})$
where the symbol Δ stands for change. For example if some price increases from \$3 to \$5 than ΔP is equal to \$2. Similarly, if that price increase causes sales to drop from 10,000 units to 8,000 units then ΔQ is simply 2,000. If e is greater than one it is said that demand is elastic. Similarly, if e is less than one, the demand is said to be inelastic. In Figure 3, we depict two demand relationships which reflect the quantity sold as a function of price.

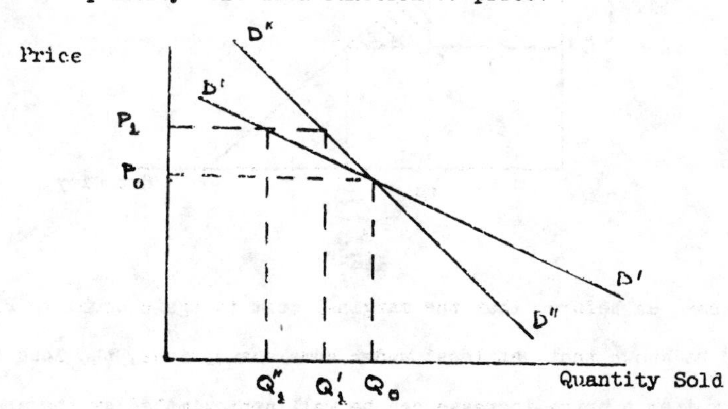

Figure 3

At the price equal to P^0 the same quantity, Q^0, is sold in both markets. However, the demand relationship D"D" is less elastic at the current price than is the demand relationship D'D'. Note that a price increase from P^0 to P^1 reduces the demand in the former market to Q_1 and to Q_1" in the latter. Clearly Q_1' exceeds Q_1''.

We have argued before that, if feasible, the price should be set at marginal cost. In many markets the forces of competition for consumer's purchases accomplish just that: competition drives down the price to the level of marginal cost. In our example that price is equal to P^0, say. If the firm does not break even at that price, the price must be raised. There will be an undesirable decrease in the quantity sold; this reduction will be most substantial in the markets in which the demand is most elastic.

It turns out that we can give a rather precise measure of the loss to the society caused by a deviation of the price from the commodity's marginal cost. In Figure 4, we plot only one demand relationship.

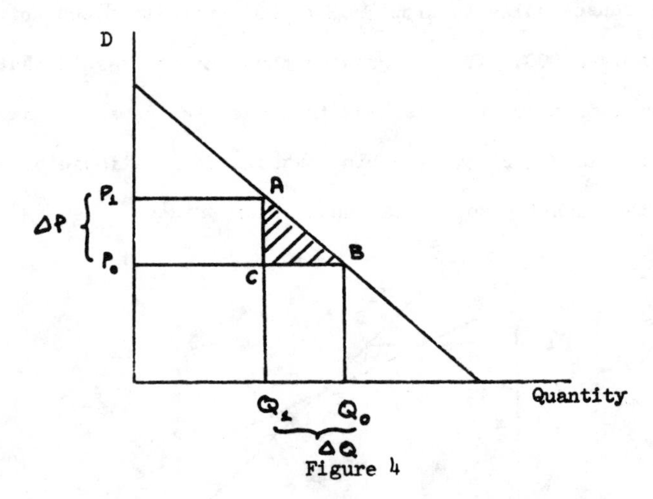

Figure 4

We assume, as before, that the marginal cost is again equal to P_0. It can be shown that, at least under some assumptions, the loss to the society from a price increase can be well approximated by the area of the shaded triangle ABC. In our example this area is obviously given by $(1/2)\cdot\Delta Q\cdot\Delta P$. It measures the loss in consumer's surplus as a result of the price increase.[1]

Principle 2.4 Consumer's surplus measures the difference between the maximum amount that a consumer would be willing to pay for a given quantity of any commodity or service rather than to go without it and the actual amount that he pays for that quantity.

To illustrate, with price at P_0 the consumer's surplus is given by the area of the triangle P_0BD. If the price goes up to P_1, consumer's surplus decreases to the amount given by the area of the triangle P_1BD.

It should be already clear that if marginal cost pricing is not feasible then prices should deviate from the marginal cost in such a way that the total loss in consumer's surplus is minimized and at the same time the total cost of the operation is covered. As it is apparent from our Figures 3 and 4 for any given price increase the area of the welfare loss triangle will be the smaller the more inelastic the demand curve. Hence, we have this general rule:

Principle 2.5 If prices cannot be set equal to marginal cost(s), then percentage deviation of price from the relevant marginal cost should vary inversely with the elasticity of demand.

In otherwords, in those markets in which consumers react strongly to price changes, the price should be set close to the incremental cost.[2] However, in those markets in which sales do not respond significantly

---

[1] The interested reader is referred to R.D. Willig's "Consumer's Surplus Without Apology," American Economic Review, 66 (September 1976), pp.589-97, for a full review of the concept of consumer's surplus and its uses.

[2] The validity of this Principle is, however, limited to those instances in which the change in price in one of the firm's markets does not affect the sales in other markets served by the firm. In other words, the rule stated above is valid when there are no cross-elasticities of demand. When these cross-market effects are present some modifications have to be introduced. We shall not discuss those complications here, but rather refer the reader to W.J. Baumol and D.F. Bradford, "Optimal Departures from Marginal Cost Prices," American Economic Review, 60 (June 1970), and J.A. Ordover and R.D. Willig, "On the Optimal Provision of Journals Qua Excludable Public Goods," forthcoming in the American Economic Review. In particular, in the second of the two papers, the authors derive workable pricing rules for the case of interconnected markets.

to price increase, the price should be marked-up substantially above incremental cost. It should be apparent why in the economic literature our *Principle 2.5* is refered to as a Inverse Elasticity Rule of optimal pricing.

It is important to realize that a firm which is allowed to price-discriminate, i.e., to charge diverse prices for the same commodity if it strives to maximize its profits it will follow a rule similar to the one just stated: it will change a high price in the inelastic market. The difference between the prices set by the profit-oriented firm and by the firm which has also the interests of the consumers in mind is that the former firm will set prices that will be uniformly higher than those set by the latter.[1] What is important about *Principle 2* is that it can serve as a valuable guide to firms since its use will enable them to earn a higher rate of return on their investments.

Charging diverse prices for an identical product is referredto as price discrimination. Some forms of price discrimination are often considered illegal. However, what is not often realized is that

Principle 2.6 Price discrimination may often benefit not only a producer but also consumers. Furthermore, in some situations it is the only way by which a producer can realize enough revenue to induce him to provide a socially desirable product.

We should close this section by pointing out that the general economic theory of pricing as just described, applies to a firm which serves more than two distinct markets as well as to the firm which sells more than one distinct product. In the latter case the marginal costs may, of course, differ from a commodity to a commodity. Still we would find that in a multi-product firm prices should be set in such a way that

[1] See W.J. Baumol and J.A. Ordover, "On the Optimality of Public-Goods Pricing with Exclusion Devices," Kyklos, 30 Fasc. 1 (1977), pp. 36-4 [Copy attached].

for each commodity percentage deviation of this commodity's price from the respective incremental cost should vary inversely with the elasticity of demand for this commodity. The percentage deviation can be readily calculated as (price minus incremental cost) ÷ (price). In the "Manual of Pricing and Cost Determination for Organizations Engaged in Dissemination of Knowledge,"[1] the authors provided a survey of various pricing methods that could be effectively utilized by producers of computer programs and data bases to improve their financial position. Without going into the details of the argument here, we may suggest nevertheless that the length of the patent or copyright protection could be shortened if the holder of a patent or of a copyright can reap high returns in the initial period of patent or copyright protection for his CS package or CDB.

We shall now turn to ascertaining what are the implications of this general theory of pricing for the proper structure of copyright protection of software packages and data bases. We shall refer to the theory just elucidated as the theory of optimal pricing.

D. The Implications of Optimal Pricing for the Statutory Protection of CS and CDB.

There are important lessons to be learned from the theory of optimal pricing for the proper structuring of copyright laws. We begin by reminding the reader of our basic assumption -- supported by some empirical evidence -- that in the software and data base segments of the STI industry, marginal cost pricing is not feasible because of a significant fixed cost component in the total cost. This fixed cost will have to be recovered from the users/buyers of the commodity.

Let us note that one of the purposes of statutory protection is to secure a return to the developers of CS and CDB sufficient to induce them

[1] See this Report for more detailed information concerning this argument. W.J. Baumol, Y.M. Braunstein, D.M. Fischer, J.A. Ordover, New York University, April 1977, prepared under the grant SIS74-12785 from the Division of Science Information of the National Science Foundation.

to provide those products to the market. Consequently, the content and scope of that protection should be such as to secure the necessary return at the minimum dislocation to the efficient allocation of resources. From the standpoint of society that misallocation will be minimized if the prices to all users follow the inverse elasticity rule. This implies, in particular, that the scope of the protection should be quite wide because without such protection it will not be possible to charge the prices that are desirable under the inverse elasticity rule. Specifically it should enable the owner of the legal "rights" to collect payment for the use of his product. To summarize,

Principle 2.7 Unless there are strong reasons to the contrary, the recovery of the fixed cost component of the total costs should be spread over as wide a set of customers and users as feasible. (The contrary reasons include the costs of collection, presence of externalities, and income distribution considerations, and will be discussed in the subsequent sections of this Report.)

The prescription contained in *Principle 2.7* is consistent with the theory of optimal pricing. To see why, let us consider a firm, say a developer of a computer software package, who can sell a CS package outright to the users -- firms or nonprofit research institutions -- who then have free and unlimited access to the package that is stored in the computer's memory. Let us assume, for simplicity, that once the program is stored in the memory it costs nothing to make it available to the user. In other words, the incremental cost of providing the service of the program is zero; the stored computer program is a public good in the sense used in Chapter I. But should the price per use be zero? The answer is no. Note that the fixed cost has to be recovered. This can be accomplished by charging prices, perhaps different, above the marginal cost to the two classes of buyers. (These two prices will be different if the two demand elasticities are different.) The marginal cost that is relevant is the cost of installing and maintaining the package. Now, if a user charge is levied then there will be an inflow of revenue from this source. True, some users will, in general, be discouraged, causing a resource misallocation. However, because of the user charge the two sale prices can be reduced to stimulate the purchases of the package thereby also bringing the price closer to the marginal costs of installation and maintenance. This downward variation in prices will, by definition, improve resource allocation. In otherwords

Principle 2.8 Spreading of revenue collection over a wide spectrum of users reduces the welfare loss which arises from the inability to price the commodity or service at the relevant marginal cost.

The ability to charge user fees is desirable because it spreads the burden of paying for the fixed costs of the package over a wider group of customers. There is, however, little reason to expect that a firm which is granted the privileges of charging user fees will necessarily lower its basic sale prices. Instead, it is likely simply to keep the larger profits that can be obtained from this source. However this result is not unnecessarily undesirable, because it may enable the society to reduce the period of statutory protection. Hence, by allowing the firm to earn greater profits initially the society can reduce the time it waits for the full benefit that will accrue to it from the new computer software package or a data base.

Principle 2.8 The more sophisticated the pricing policy of a firm the higher are the net revenues that it can expect to earn during the period that its product is protected by a property right be it in the form of a trade secret, patent or a form of a copyright.

Incidentally, the annual loss to the community from the monopoly power conferred by copyright can be measured in the same way as the misallocation loss from quasi-optimal pricing. In Figure 5, we plot a demand curve for a service of some product whose marginal cost of production is given by MC^0.

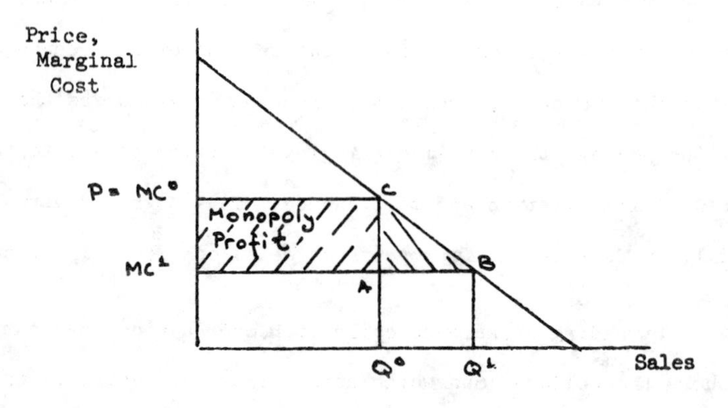

Figure 5

If perfect competition obtains in the production of this commodity, then the price will be set at P^0 and the quantity sold will be Q^0. Let us assume next that by employing some specialized computer program, the firm is able to reduce the marginal cost to MC^1. If it does not have to license its new program to competitors, then for the duration of the copyright it will be able to charge the initial price P^0, keeping all of the savings for itself and passing none of them on to consumers.

The firm's monopoly profits will be given by the area of the rectangle (MC^1) AC (MC^0). Some of these profits will be charged against the costs of developing the cost reducing innovation over which the firm has a copyright. The loss in social welfare per year of duration of the copyright is measured by the area of the triangle ABC. This triangle measures the consumer's surplus that is lost because the firm has monopoly power over the copyrighted cost-saving innovation.

In theory it is rather simple to calculate the social loss due to monopoly power. In practice such calculations are very difficult to carry out. It suffices to point out that estimates of annual welfare losses due to monopolistic pricing practices in the American economy vary from one tenth of one percent of national income to around six percent of national income.[1] There is unfortunately, no easy way to determine the percentage of that loss that can be attributed to monopolistic pricing in the STI sector of the economy. If we assume that total knowledge producing industries in the United States comprise anywhere from 16% to 28% of the Gross National Product, then the welfare loss originating in the STI industries must constitute a rather small percentage of the GNP.[2]

Clearly, the more ingenious the pricing methods employed by the copyright holder, the larger is the consumer's surplus that the firm will be able to extract from the buyers of its products. In deciding, therefore, on the appropriate duration of the copyright, the policy-maker must weigh the benefits of speeding the moment at which the society can capture the full benefits flowing from the cost-saving invention against the costs of extracting substantial monopoly profits during the period throughout which the copyright is valid. As we have seen, the scope for realization of monopoly profits depends on the range of prices that the firm can legally charge.

The urgency of capturing the full benefits of the innovation can be measured by the social rate of discount or time preference. For example, if the social rate of time preference is 10% then a dollar's worth of benefits a year from now has a present value of approximately 90 cents. Consequently, if the discount rate is high, early capture of invention's benefits is particularly beneficial. It is not obvious how such an early release can be accomplished through an interplay of the allowable

---

[1] See A. Bergson, "On Monopoly Welfare Losses," American Economic Review 63, (December 1973), pp. 853-871; and J. Hirshleifer, Price Theory, Prentice-Hall, 1976, pp. 287-8.

[2] The lower figure is from M.U. Porat, The Information Economy, vol. 1 Center for Interdisciplinary Research, Stanford University; the higher from F. Machlup, The Production and Distribution of Knowledge in the United States, Princeton U. P., Princeton, NJ, 1962. Both numbers are reported in Porat, op. cit., Table 4.1, p. 85.

pricing practices and the duration of protection. Surely, the scope and the duration of protection should be so chosen as to generate a requisite rate of return to the firm. If the duration of protection is short, the firm must be allowed to earn significant monopoly profits early in the period. But the society weighs heavily those initial losses in consumer's surplus relative to the full benefits that will accrue in the future. To reduce those early losses, monopoly profits must be diminished, conceivably by restricting the scope of discriminatory pricing and other special pricing practices. On the other hand if early profits are low the duration of protection must be extended in order to secure the requisite rate of return on investment.

Principle 2.9 The minimization of social welfare loss due to monopoly power can be accomplished by an interplay of the length of protection and allowable pricing practices. For example, if it is necessary that a particular innovation be fully exploited as soon as possible the society may opt for a very low compulsory license fee coupled with the assurance that the developer will have a long period of protection from new products.[1]

It should be noted that our case for user fees does not rest on legal considerations, for example on whether or not the use of a software package constitutes a violation of the copyright.[2] Our preference for user fees stems from the application of optimal pricing analysis. To repeat, the theory calls for positive percentage deviations of prices from marginal costs for all goods and services provided by the firm.

---

[1]For a similar discussion in the area of regulation see V. Goldberg, "Regulation and Administered Contracts," Bell Journal of Economics 7 (Autumn 1976), pp. 426-448. Goldberg discusses the issue in terms of protecting the producer's right to serve.

[2]See "Legal Protection of Computer Software," Computer/Communication Secretariat Report of Working Group No. 12 (September 1976), Canada.

E. Some Extensions of the Theory of Quasi-Optimal Pricing and Their Relevance for the Structure of Copyright Laws

The standard inverse elasticity formula discussed in Section II-C has built into it several simplifying assumptions. The one simplifying assumption that was already discussed earlier stated that there are no cross-market effects of price changes. Unfortunately, the complications that have to be introduced into the formula to take account of the effects of a change in the price of one product upon the demand for another are not easy to describe. Fortunately, the implications for the proper structure of the copyright law in no way depend on those complications.

There are other considerations, however, which may have significant implications for the nature of copyright protection. The first involves the problems of income distribution. We observed earlier that the welfare loss from monopoly pricing can be fairly well approximated by the triangle ABC of Figure 5 which measures the dimunition in consumer's surplus resulting from "incorrect" prices. Now, the decision-maker may well consider the loss in consumer's surplus in one market to be more serious than an equal loss in some other market in which the commodity -- a CS package or a CDB -- is sold. This differentiated evaluation should lead the policy-maker to reduce the price in the market in which losses of consumer's surplus are considered highly detrimental <u>and</u> to raise the price in the remaining market or markets. For example a new computer routine can be used to improve the manufacture of various commodities bought mostly by low-income people as well as to lower the costs of some luxury commodities. If the demand for luxury commodities is more elastic than that for the necessities the profit maximizing firm which follows the inverse elasticity rule (see *Principle 2.5*) will set a high price in the latter market and a lower price in the former market. However, for reasons of equity the society in general will value more the loss of a dollar in benefits to the low income groups than a loss of a dollar's worth of benefits to the high income groups. Consequently, from society's standpoint welfare loss figures have to be modified by correction factors designed to reflect the policy-maker's concern about income distribution.[1]

The profit-maximizing firm, however, is not concerned with the niceties of differential evaluation of welfare losses. It focuses on elasticities of demand and sets prices in accord with what the traffic will bear. But the policy-maker can introduce incentives which will cause the profit-oriented firm to respond, at least partly, to those differentiated evaluations. The simplest route, perhaps, is to reduce the period of copyright protection for commodities sold in the preferred markets. Such a move would have to be accompanied it would seem, by a compensated increase in protection elsewhere in order to guarantee the rate of return judged necessary to stimulate the developed process. A reduction in the period of protection in the socially favored segment of the market, holding the flow of new products constant, would increase the pool of substitutes which would be available at low (or zero) prices. This increased competition would tend to increase demand elasticity for the CS package or CDB that has just come on the market. We have seen already (cf. *Principle* 2.5) that an increase in the elasticity in demand reduces the profit maximizing percentage mark-up of a price over the relevant incremental cost. Consequently such policy may have the desired effect of lowering the price in that sector of the market in which it is important from a social standpoint that the loss in consumer's surplus be held down to the minimum.

Unfortunately the policy prescription just stated may suffer from

---

[1] See R.D. Willig and E.E. Bailey, "Ramsey-Optimal Pricing of Long Distance Telephone Services," Bell Laboratories Economic Discussion Paper #77, January 1977.

two perhaps fatal difficulties:

(1) It is not obvious that the flow of new products will not be adversly affected by the reduction in the length of protection.

(2) The compensatory extension of the length of protection in the socially less-favored segments of the market for CS and CDB may prove to be of little economic value.

Let us take up each of those points starting with the second one. The value of an extended life of the property right depends on the additional profits that can be earned because of this extension. If the economic value of the property right expires before the end of the period of legal protection then the extension is valueless. There is some evidence that the economic life of a new product is much shorter than the period of legal protection, particularly in the rapidly developing segments of the STI industry such as computer software. The average economic life of computer software has been estimated to be around three years, which is substantially less than the proposed period of legal protection.[1] However, there are two additional considerations: First the variance may be high; some CS packages (e.g., BiMed, SPSS, etc.) may have relatively long economic lives. In testimony to CONTU, Lockheed estimated the economic life of the DIALOG operating system to be on the order of ten years. Second, the documentation can have an independent copyright thus enabling the creators to obtain payments from the users. It is likely that these two considerations go hand-in-hand; i.e., CS with longer economic lives may be the CS for which the documentation can be independently sold. Nonetheless, it may be that the "long-lived" CS's are just those we seek to protect because of their usefulness to society. Therefore a short <u>average</u> economic life is not, <u>per se</u>, an argument for a shortened period of protection.

---

[1]Canada Department of Consumer and Corporate Affairs, <u>Working Paper on Patent Law Revision</u>, Ottawa, Canada, June 1976.

It is also arguable that a manipulation of protection length in the various sectors of the market for CS and CDB may affect the flow of new products. In addition, there may be substitution in the products' design so that the products would be more suitable for use in those markets where competition is less strenuous. This long-run effect -- the alteration in the flow of new products -- can reverse the short-run, transitory benefits which may accrue to some users because in the short-run the flow and composition of the new products will not be significantly affected.

This, incidentally, provides a guarded argument against various exemptions that have been contemplated in the copyright law. Those exemptions simply exclude various groups from contributing their share of the total cost of producing and disseminating the product. The proponents of such exemptions must implicitly assume that there are unexplored profit margins in the other segments of the market for STI in which the producers can make-up their lost revenue, and that there is a clear case for this sort of cross-subsidy by the one type of consumer by another. Thus we have this loose economic rule:

Principle 2.10 Exempting some users from payment or arbitrarily restricting the charges that can be assessed against them leads to increased costs and charges to the less-favored users.

Similar remarks apply to the proposals for compulsory licensing. Under compulsory licensing, the prices charged in all markets may well turn out to be uniform. Such pricing is not necessarily desirable either from the standpoint of profits or social welfare measured by the size of consumer's surplus generated in the industry. This follows from our previous analysis which revealed that some form of price discrimination is preferable in general to uniform prices. The effect of compulsory licensing serves to reduce monopoly profits but the undesirabl long-run effect of such licensing may be a reduction in the flow of new products to the market place.

Principle 2.11 Compulsory licensing and other artificial restrictions on prices reduce the welfare loss from those products that reach the market. However, the total effect of such restraints may be undesirable if it impairs the flow of innovations.

We close this chapter of our report with a conclusion, albeit tentative one, that the protection afforded to the producers and disseminators of CS and CDB should not include unreasonable restrictions on the admissible pricing schemes. If the pricing practices employed by the producers are found undesirable they should be attacked directly, using the existing antitrust laws. In addition, if it is found that legal prices charged by the producers are undesirable for reasons of income distribution or externalities that are generated by some buyers of CS and CDB, then those problems should be also attacked directly, through subsidies, for example, of some classes of users or producers.[1]

F. Transactions Costs in Computer Information Systems

We have noted previously that the likelihood that transactions costs will be high can lead either to a decision against user fees, in general, or to the exemption of certain classes of users from payment because the volume of usage by them is so small that it is not practical to levy a charge. The economic issue is the comparative efficiency of user charges versus free provision and the relative magnitude the transactions costs. For this comparison to be valid it is necessary that all the accounting, billing, collection, and enforcement costs be included as transaction costs.

[1] See J.A. Ordover and R.D. Willig, "On the Role of Information in the Design of Social Policy Towards Externalities," Center for Applied Economics Discussion Paper #76-03, New York University, for a guide to various methods of coping with external effects.

The level of these costs will depend on the coverage required and on the form of the license. For example, if infrequent use in personally owned mini-computers is exempted, the transactions costs for the collection of royalties for the use of some computer programs may be substantially reduced. Similarly, blanket licenses generally result in lower accounting costs for one or both parties because detailed information on the level of usage is not required.

Operators of two different types of computer systems provided us with estimates of the costs of monitoring of use, accounting, billing, etc. One was a large "service bureau" organization with a large number of customers. They estimated that their transactions costs were generally 15 to 18 percent of total costs. The other organization operated only an on-line information retrieval system. Their costs of monitoring and recording usage were approximately 10 to 15 percent of their total system costs. However, it is important to note that in neither case do these costs include the expense of determining how to disburse any royalties or fees due to copyright owners.

The obvious archetypes of a clearinghouse that collects royalties and then makes payments to the copyright owners are the performing rights societies. ASCAP usually has been able to hold the level of its operating costs below 20 percent of its revenues. The disbursement costs are a function of the payment scheme used. The more detailed the information required (by monitoring or some reporting plan) the more expensive it will be for the parties involved. In general, usage of a variety of goods or services such as copyrighted works does not follow a uniform distribution. In fact, usage is usually highly skewed. To use an example from the photocopy field, the British Lending Library reported that of the 14,967 serial titles in their collection, the most requested 210 titles accounted for 20 percent of the demand for photocopies while the 6000 least requested titles amounted to only 10 percent of the demand.[1] This sort of skewness can lead to a substantial reduction in monitoring and other transactions costs if there is some minimum level of usage for which no royalty payments are distributed. On the other hand, the absense of such a "threshold" may require quite accurate and complete monitoring to insure the detection of the smallest levels of usage.

III

THE CONSEQUENCES OF TRADE SECRECY AND COPYRIGHT PROTECTION FOR THE QUALITY, VARIETY AND QUANTITY OF NEW PRODUCTS

In the last chapter we discussed some implications of economic theory of pricing for the structure of property rights that are to be granted to producers of software and data bases. In particular we found that there exists a trade-off between the length of protection afforded the producers and the breadth of this protection in terms of allowable pricing practices. We also argued that there are strong reasons for not interfering with the price mechanism through the copyright laws but rather for leaving the stamping out of the undesirable pricing practices to the authorities responsible for the enforcement of the antitrust statutes. Specifically we tentatively concluded that if copyright protection is in the end extended to the producers of CS and CDB they should be entitled to sophisticated user charges and that no classes of users should be exempt from payment. We also noted that compulsory licensing may have undesirable consequences for the long-run flow of new software and data bases.

The discussion in the last chapter implicitly assumed that some form of statutory protection will be in place. In this chapter we examine the differential impacts of trade secrecy and copyright protection on the quality, variety and the quantity of new commodities that will be available in the marketplace for the computerized scientific and technical information.

[1] M.B. Line and D.N. Wood, "The Effect of a Large Scale Photocopying Service on Journal Sales," Journal of Documentation 31:241 (1975).

Specifically we shall find that trade secret protection biases the quality of new output in the direction of unnecessary complexity. It also channels the innovative efforts into those forms of software which are not particularly well-suited to general use. In other words trade secret protection is particularly detrimental to private provision of non-specialized, general interest types of software. Copyright protection diminishes that type of distortion. Certainly under compulsory licensing the producers would strive to provide the product with as wide a applicability as possible.[1]

There are no general conclusions to be drawn as to the quantity of the new products that would be forthcoming under various regimes of property rights as compared to the socially optimal quantity. Copyright protection may be expected to intensify competition in the software and data base industry, vis á vis a situation that would be obtained under trade secret protection. It has been shown by various authors that competitive structure of the industry is not necessarily most conducive to innovative effort. In fact the purpose of copyright protection is to transfer a competitive situation into a (temporary) noncompetitive one.[2]

Protection based on trade secrets may lead to larger concentration in the software and data base industry which may be more conducive to the optimal flow of new products. It is well known, however, that the presence of trade secrets does often lead to significant duplication of effort because of informational imperfections.

---

[1] It is often argued that if compulsory licensing is instituted the unusual tastes may go unsatisfied. For example some say that if General Mi[illegible] were to have to license the production of Cheerios it would optimally adjust the receipe to conform to more standard tastes.

[2] For a recent mathematical study of the problem of the interrelationship between market structure and the flow of new products see G. Lowry, "Market Structure and Innovation," The Center for Mathematical Studies in Economics and Management Science, Discussion Paper #256, Northwestern University.

It is obvious, nevertheless, that the flow of products will be directly related to the expected monopoly profits that the innovator hopes to realize from the product. We have noted in the previous sections that the welfare loss during the duration of the monopoly is the price that the society must pay in using copyright as its inducement for investment in the development of new products. The longer this period the more such investment it should stimulate, but the greater the interim loss in social welfare. Weighing these two factors against one another one must use them to determine how long this monopoly should last. In part, the question may be somewhat academic in that the economic value of the copyright may evaporate much sooner than the copyright itself. For example, the economic life of a software package has averaged some three years -- much less than the prospective length of the copyright protection. (See our discusison of the relevance of "average" economic life in Chapter II-B above.)

The question of the optimal length of protection can also be rendered academic if the society opts for trade secret protection as opposed to the statutory protection. Under a trade secret approach the duration of effective protection is in fact a random variable whose realization depends on the success of the possessor of the secret in preventing it from falling into the public domain. We do not, of course, have any data on how successful the possessors of trade secrets have been in securing their monopoly power. However, it is an interesting fact that the holders of patents have had a difficult time in defending their property rights. As Professor David Bender notes, "statistics indicate that in about 70 percent of infringement suits litigated to conclusion, the defendant emerges the victor."[1] Although Bender realizes that patent protection is inherently uncertain he seems not to note that the same applies to

---

[1] D. Bender, "Trade Secret Protection of Software," The George Washington Law Review, 38 (July 1970), pp. 909-57, 915.

trade secrets. Unfortunately, we do not have comparative data on the riskiness of the two forms of protection. The substantial investments that firms make to protect their secrets do indicate, however, that the probability of losing trade secret protection is rather substantial.[1]

The expected probabilities of losing protection under the two distinct regimes -- trade secrets vs. statutory protection through patents or copyrights -- figure quite significantly in an evaluation of the virtues of the two systems. The main criticism of trade secrecy is that, because it depends on the prevention of disclosure, it inevitably leads to a wasteful duplication of effort. There is no need to recount here the horror stories that are being told about the duplication of the programming work in many corporations. The costs of duplication and the attendant waste must be weighed against the benefits of the probability of quick disclosure at a zero price to the general public. Thus, before the idea of increased reliance on protection based on trade secrets is discarded those costs and benefits must be ascertained. The general presumption is, nevertheless, that the trade secrecy method of creating incentives for innovation is inefficient.

In the next two sections of this chapter we examine the structure of incentives for innovation under various regimes of property rights. We postpone until Chapter IV the discussion of the optimal duration of protection.

A. Qualitative Effects of Trade Secrecy and Copyright Protection

The producers of products have not only the choice of how much to invest in the research, development, marketing, etc., of new products but also a choice of characteristics of the products that will be developed. The effects on the choice of the product or products are classified here as qualitative effects of protection. In other words,

[1] See Bender, ibid., pp. 912-13.

the nature of the protection that is allowed for intellectual property will affect the quality and the variety of the commodities produced in the economy.

Trade secrecy protection favors developments of those products which cannot easily be duplicated or engineered backward. Consequently, under such a regime, one is likely to find that producers will build into their products various special features that may complicate appropriation of the secret by unauthorized users. For example, there may be an unnecessary tendency for complication of the structure of the product, so as to obscure its essential properties and increase the costs of unauthorized use. In computer programs there may be a need for introducing special safety devices.

A typical list of features of computer programs which are designed so as not to be usable by outsiders is the following:

(1) Frequent use is made of special features of the machine on which the program is currently running (such as machine language instructions, features which depend on the word length, on the representation of characters by bit-strings, etc.)

(2) All comments, which may make the logical flow of the program clear to a reader are omitted.

(3) The loop structure of the program is unnecessarily complicated, with transfers of control back and forth within the code.

(4) Mnemonic variable names, which could reveal the meaning of a variable are avoided.

(5) Unnecessary portions of code are added to confuse a potential user.

It should be clear that all these features reduce the social value of a program or software package, and do not only make it more difficult, or nearly impossible, for an outsider to use the program or appropriate its logic, but also make it harder for the original programmer to maintain and modify the program. But many programs are, in fact, written in the manner just described to protect them against non-paying users.

Principle 3.1 Trade secrecy protection leads to the waste of social resources through overly complex product design. Another distortion that may occur is that programs and data bases will be tailored to the needs of specialized groups of users. By making the program more specialized the developer minimizes its usefulness to others and diminishes the probabilities of disclosure. To borrow language used in the economic theory of investments in human skills, trade secret protection makes specific investment more valuable than general investment.[1] General investment is to be understood as the investment in the development of programs and data bases which can be employed by a wide variety of users. However, the more widespread the use the more difficult it is to prevent the leakage of the technical desscription of the products into the public domain which, in turn, undermines the protection afforded under the law of trade secrets. This qualitative variety bias of trade secrets has not been discussed in the literature. It seems, however, that it may be a cause of even worse misallocation of resources than the effort duplication commonly viewed as the most serious consequence of trade secrecy protection. To minimize this bias, direct support on contractual basis may have to be provided to those institutions which may be expected to develop the general purpose programs or data bases.[2]

Principle 3.2 Trade secrecy protection may lead to overprovision of specialized CS and CDB and to underprovision of general-use CS and CDB. Another form of the quality-variety distortion occurs when, for

---

[1]See G.S. Becker, Human Capital (NBER and Columbia University Press, New York, 1964).

[2]The economic analysis of this type of governmental support is provided in J.A. Ordover and R.D. Willig, "On the Role of Information in the Design of Social Policy Towards Externalities," Center for Applied Economics Discussion Paper #76-03, New York University.

maintainance of secrecy, the maintenance, revisions, and so on, of programs and data bases is undertaken by the developer of the CS package or CDB even though efficiency would dictate that this task be carried on to some extent by the user himself. For example, we find that computations in the structural analysis of buildings or airplanes are carried out by the owner of the program rather than by the firm which needs the calculations. It is not clear whether such an arrangement is optimal, for it necessitates a significant flow of information between the user and the owner. This type of use of a program, in which the user supplies the data and receives the final results, but is not allowed to put his hands on the program itself, is particularly inconvenient when the program in question ought to be part of a larger model. For example, it is impossible to apply an optimization routine, which the user may have available on his own computer installation, to a structural analysis program which he cannot transfer to his computer, but for which he has to supply the input data for each run in prespecified form to the firm who owns the program.

Lastly, we must allude to the fact that various forms of protection may cause greater or smaller reliance on bundling and tie-in sales. Bundling and tie-ins are widely used as a method of indirect collection of payment for a commodity for which exclusion of nonpayers may prove to be difficult. Thus, in the brokerage industry, research was routinely provided "for free" as part of services generally performed by stockbrokers.

With computer software, bundling may take the form in which a producer of a software package makes its use available "for free", provided the user runs the program on the producer's computer and purchases computer time simultaneously, at an inflated rate. One would expect that unbundling -- perhaps partial -- would be a consequence of greater reliance on copyright or patent protection of CS packages and CDBs. The possibility of unbundling arises in the regime of copyright protection because the sellers are not forced to collect payment through roundabout routes. Previously bundling and roundaboutness were introduced to reduce the fear that the product will fall into the public domain and lose any protection from the nonpayers.

Principle 3.3 Copyright protection may reduce the efforts of the sellers of software and data bases to bundle their products with other products or services for which the costs of collecting the sale price or user fee are low. However, there would probably be a continued reliance on tie-ins for the purposes of extracting more profits from buyers of these products. We have discussed the advantages and disadvangages of tie-ins elsewhere and there is no reason to review our findings at this point.[1] Here we simply want to point out that bundling and tie-ins can be used as devices to increase the transaction costs of unauthorized use. Whatever the reason for the use of bundling, there will be a gain in profits and, in the short-run at least, losses in that component of social welfare that is measured by consumers' surplus.[2]

Statutory protection through copyright or patents has as its cornerstone the disclosure of the fundamental properties of the product. With

[1] See W.J. Baumol, Y.M. Braunstein, D.M. Fischer, and J.A. Ordover, "Manual of Pricing and Cost Determination for Organizations Engaged in Dissemination of Knowledge," New York University, April 1977.

[2] Bundling adds flexibility to the pricing schemes to be used, and in this way offers a potential to increase welfare in a way similar to price discrimination, which was discussed earlier. If bundling is used by an unregulated monopoly, it will always increase profits. It may increase or decrease consumers' surplus. An example where price bundling increases consumers' surplus (and therefore social welfare, since it also increases the producers' surplus) is a case in which a software package will be developed only if the producer can recover costs through price bundling, but not otherwise. The users' willingness to pay for the package must exceed their actual payments, by definition, since they are not forced to buy. If the package could not be produced at all, because of a prohibition of price bundling, then the consumers' surplus would be zero in this particular example. But there are also many cases where the use of price bundling reduces social welfare, as shown for example by W.J. Ada and J.L Yellen, "Commodity Bundling and the Burden of Monopoly," Quarterly Journal of Economics, XC (August 1976), 475-98.

(more or less) full disclosure there will be no special need to design new programs to have features which increase the transaction costs of unauthorized appropriation. This leads to the hypothesis that statutory protection may spur the development of general use programs. Under statutory protection, disclosure of the characteristics of the product to the general public need not have significant effects on the profitability of any given product. As a matter of fact, the demand for the product -- a software package, for example -- is generally stimulated by knowledge of the product's availability. But such knowledge can be detrimental to profits. Improvement in the information about products increases competition for prospective buyers who now can make better choices. Competition, of course, drives down the rate of return on new commodities. Consequently, our hypothesis will be valid if the reduction in profits due to better consumer information is small relative to an increase in expected profits due to a reduction in the probability that the CS package will be appropriated without payment.

It is implausible that statutory protection will have an adverse effect on the flow of specialized programs. Disclosure should not be harmful to those products. They are intended, to begin with, for a small group of users and in the limit for only one user. In those situations, the value of the product to others may be quite low and not worth the price of "cracking" its structure.

Principle 3.4 We tentatively conclude that a shift from trade secrecy protection to statutory protection should have stimulating effects on the variety of the products developed and marketed by the software industry. We expect that under the latter form of protection, private firms will have stronger incentives to produce general use software packages without substantial funding commitments from the government.

Funds for the development of general purpose software packages have occasionally been provided by the government and by private foundations.

For example, the Time Series Processor (TSP), an econometric package, was developed at the Harvard Institute of Economic Research with the support of the Energy Policy Project of the Ford Foundation, the Office of Emergency Preparedness, and additional funds provided by the participating academic institutions. NASTRAN, a program for use in structural analysis, was developed by NASA and then made available without charge to any potential user. Many general purpose algorithms have also been written and published by academic researchers who performed sponsored or non-sponsored research. A representative collection of these is contained in "Collected Algorithms of the Communications of the Association for Computing Machinery," which is updated regularly and is available to potential users for a small subscription fee that merely covers printing costs. One hopes that with a clearer form of protection for software, private industry may begin to develop the general use programs the development of which, until now, relied heavily on government subvention.

B. Quantitative Effects of Trade Secrecy and Copyright Protection

In the previous section we noted that the mode of protection will affect the variety of products in the marketplace. It is equally clear that the choice of protection systems should affect the quantity of the products. Thus, it is generally known that a monopolist will choose not only inappropriate product characteristics but given the chosen product then will underprovide it to the public. In the last section we have seen that the reliance on trade secrecy may cause the (prospective) developer to shy away from products that are intended for wide circulation because the costs of enforcing the trade secret are high for those types of products.

Abstracting from a product's characteristics, we may inquire about the supply of products under various forms of protection. The general result which emerges from theoretical discussions is that irrespective of the kind of protection, competition will tend to overprovide inventions and innovations with high private value, and simultaneously underprovide those with high social value. These are two opposing forces, one of which tends to increase the supply of inventions over the socially optimal level, and another tendency which decreases the amount. Which effect will outweigh the other depends on the specific situation. There will be an increased supply of inventions and innovations which bring a private advantage to the supplier, possibly at the expense of the rest of society. On the other hand, inventions which are useful to society as a whole, but difficult to sell and therefore of relatively small value to the producer, will be supplied in a less than socially optimal amount. For example, programs which imitate or duplicate existing programs and therefore add very little to social welfare, but which enable the producing firm to capture a portion of the corresponding market and enter a lucrative business, will tend to be overproduced. But programs of a highly innovative nature, which could be beneficial for a wide variety of users for a long time period, but which it may be more difficult to market, will tend to be underproduced. The net effect can be an increase or decrease in innovative activity from the socially optimal level, but it is clear that with competition the <u>wrong kind of innovation</u> will be forthcoming.[1] It is also clear that with competition a larger amount of resources will be devoted to the production of any given amount of innovation than is socially necessary.

Under trade secret protection, the dangers of overprovision are magnified because there is lack of information as to the existing products. Overprovision in the regime will take the form of too many identical products being developed by independent producers. As we have

---

[1]For a discussion of these ideas, see J. Hirshleifer, "The Private and Social Value of Information and the Reward to Inventive Activity," <u>American Economic Review</u> 61 (September 1971), pp. 561-574.

seen, however, the variety may also be affected adversely.

Although trade secrecy may lead to an overprovision of new computer software and data bases, because of a lack of communication, it also may lead to excessive concentration in the industry, which in turn brings with it the monopolistic tendency to restrict output in order to maintain higher prices.

The proposition that there will be overprovision under competitive market structure depends on the assumption that the number of firms which engage in the development of new computer software and data bases is fixed. However, as we noted above, the use of trade secrets can lead to excessive concentration in the industry. The argument can be summarized as follows: Lack of information about existing CS packages places a premium on the control of a large portfolio of those packages whenever there are some complementarities between various items of software. In the literature, those gains are referred to as economies of scope. Economies of scope exist whenever the total costs of producing two or more items of software in separation exceed the total costs of producing them in one firm.[1]

The complementarities between various items of software may be attributable, for example, the interchangeability between subsets of computer programs. If a firm cannot obtain the information about other programs which can be useful in the development of the new one then it will have to waste resources on reinventing the existing complementary software. A firm with a large portfolio of programs is at a comparti- tive advantage over a small firm with the proprietary programs. If copyright protection is substituted for trade secrecy then the flow of information is facilitated and firms can fully utilize the existing stock of knowledge. Hence

[1]See John C. Panzar and R.D. Willig, "Economies of Scale and Economies of Scope in Multi-Output Production," Quarterly Journal of Economics, (forthcoming), for a complete discussion of the concept.

Principle 3.5 Barriers to entry, and hence competition, will be diminished by a move from trade secrecy to copyright protection.

Disclosure also facilitates competition because the downstream firms -- the purchasers of software -- have better knowledge of the available products. An improvement in consumer information should drive down the price. More important, it may also ease entry into the upstream -- software -- industry. Then the argument is that with better information the downstream firms can more easily search out alternative sources of supply. Hence, the well-established firms need not have a special advantage over the newcomers because the newcomers can advertise widely and specifically their products without the fear of losing trade secrecy protection. This discussion brings out a point which curiously seems to have been missed in the current literature, namely that disclosure not only reduces wasteful duplication of the research effort, but also reduces search costs for the ultimate buyers. This reduction in search costs facilitates improved matching between buyers and sellers and improves social welfare.

Principle 3.6 Copyright protection reduces the transaction costs of matching buyers and sellers relative to those costs that would be incurred under policy of trade secrecy.

There is no agreement in the literature on innovations on the sign of the correlation between the market structure and the flow of innovations. The Schumpeterian view is that monopoly leads to improved flow of research over time. It adds credance, therefore, to those policies which lead to market concentration in the upstream industry. That is, monopolization yields an improvement in intertemporal allocation of resources. On the other hand, monopoly has detrimental consequences for static or temporal efficiency: As we showed earlier, it leads to a loss in consumer's surplus. (There may be also a loss in producer's surplus if the marginal costs are not constant over some range of output.)[1] Consequently, if our argument that trade secrets lead to market concentration is correct, then the gains in intertemporal welfare which arise from increased concentration and the reduction in the duplication of research effort should be measured against the known static (temporal) costs of monopoly.

We found in this chapter that there are strong arguments in favor of copyright protection in terms of the quality and variety of output of software and data bases. Trade secrecy protection leads to overprovision of specialized types of software and CDB's relative to the socially optimal level and to the concommitant underprovision of general, widely applicable software and data bases. Those tendencies are attenuated by disclosure policy which is an essential component of copyright protection.

We may also conclude that trade secret protection leads to the concentration in the STI industry because it creates artificial barriers to entry into the industry and impinges on the efficient matching of buyers and sellers.

To the extent that competition is baneful to the provision of new products as suggested by the Schumpeterian hypothesis then the monopolistic tendencies encouraged by trade secrets should be welcomed. However, the benefits of improved flow of innovations have to be measured against the quality distortions and transaction costs caused by trade secrets protection.

In the next chapter we shall study the appropriate length of protection on the assumption that such protection does not exceed the expected economic life of the property.

---

[1] See M.I. Kamien and N.L. Schwartz, "Market Structure and Innovation: A Survey," Journal of Economic Literature, 13 (March 1975), pp. 1-27.

IV

THE OPTIMAL DURATION OF COPYRIGHT

A. Factors Which Influence the Optimal Duration of the Monopoly

It has been mentioned before that in order to induce firms to produce computer software,[1] some form of protection has to be granted to them. For if every computer program or data base were to become public property as soon as it was developed, the firm which invested resources in its development would hardly be able to recover its costs, and would consequently have very little inventive to undertake such research activities. A temporary monopoly on the rights to use or sell a piece of computer software will give a financial reward to the successful innovator, which encourages him to undertake such activities. The longer the period for which such a monopoly is granted to an innovator, the greater will be his incentive to devote resources to the development of computer software, and the more abundant will be the stream of new programs and data bases being developed.

But a long period of protection also has an adverse effect on public welfare. The longer a monopoly is granted to an innovator, the longer the period will last during which there is a misallocation of resources. The sooner restrictions on the use of a computer program or data base are lifted, the more useful will that particular item be to society, because, as discussed earlier, the cost of additional uses is likely to be negligible.

The problem is, then, to find an optimal compromise between the two extremes of too short or too long a lag period during which protection in the form of a copyright is granted to the producer.

---

[1]The same analysis applies to innovations in general. For a more thorough discussion of these issues, see "Optimal Lags in a Schumpeterian Innovation Process," by W.J. Baumol and D.M. Fischer, mimeo, New York University, 1976.

In the next section we construct a model that shows how a firm reacts to various periods of protection. In that model we will assume that there are diminishing returns to scale in the production of computer software for two reasons. First, we assume that there is an unlimited number of potential projects which can be undertaken by a computer software firm. Some of them promise very high benefit to cost ratios, while this ratio will be lower and lower for the less attractive projects. The firm will undertake all those projects for which its expected benefits exceed its expected costs. Here the benefits to the firm consist of both the gains it derives from its own use of the computer software it has developed, and of the revenues from sale of the program or from the licensing of its use. Costs will include a normal rate of return on invested capital. They will also include some premium for risk taking, because of the risky nature of any innovative activity, such as the development of a new computer program, where it is difficult to estimate in advance the difficulties and obstacles to be encountered and consequently the number of manhours to be expended. In many cases, it may even prove impossible to complete successfully a project that has been started, so that the investment will turn out to be a complete failure. Riskiness of this sort is typical of any kind of innovative activity, for example the development of new drugs or new products in general. Incidentally, in dealing with this problem larger firms, which can pool risks, have an advantage over smaller firms. Small for-profit firms will tend to engage in the development of computer software that follows more or less established lines and has direct applications, whereas the more risky basic research in new computer languages and algorithms will be left to research units within large firms, or to publicly supported academic institutions.

A second element which causes returns to diminish with increased activity is the considerable variation in the skills of computer programmers. One brilliant programmer may well be able to accomplish more than twenty mediocre ones.[1] As a firm expands its operations, it will first tend to hire the most skilled personnel, and gradually have to resort to less and less talented employees. These two factors, the declining benefit to cost ratio of software projects considered for implementation, and the declining abilities of incremental personnel, tend clearly to lead to diminishing returns to scale in the production of computer software, at least at the level of the industry as a whole. Although these will be some cost advantages in concentrating the development of computer software in a few large firms, which can benefit from internally shared information and reduced risk, every firm will operate at a level where it encounters increasing costs per unit of output with expanding activity.

Obviously, the longer the period of property right protection that is granted to a firm, the higher will be its revenue from any particular project it may undertake, and the more profitable, on the average, that innovative activity will therefore turn out to be. On the other hand, a langer period of protection will reduce the availability, and with this the usefulness to society, of any given amount of computer software produced. The model in the next section will permit us to calculate the optimal length of the period of protection under given assumptions about the shape of the cost curve and the structure of demand for computer software.

On the demand side, we assume that the amount users are willing to pay for any given computer software package declines over time, because new and better products become available, which render the old

---

[1] Although programmers with greater skills usually command higher salaries, the differences in pay will usually hardly be commensurate with the much greater differences in productivity. But even if programmer salaries were to capture all of the benefits of superior productivity it would still be true tautologically that the best programmers can yield the largest product. All that changes in this case is the identity of the recipient of the benefit.

ones obsolete. In exceptional cases, the demand for the use of a program which embodies some ingenious idea may also increase over time, because the use of computers is expanding, and because the existence of the program may become more widely known. But we will confine our analysis to cases in which the social value of a program diminishes over time. It seems intuitive that the more rapidly the value of a program declines, the shorter should the period of protection be that is granted to its producer. In the next section, we will establish the relationship between the optimal period of protection and the useful lifetime of a computer program.

B. A Model to Simulate the Behavior of a Typical Software Firm[1]

The computer software industry is composed of a very large number of firms, some of them controlling a substantial share of the total market, others being very small, sometimes consisting of a single self-employed individual. All of these firms produce products which are similar, but not identical. They are substitutes to some degree, but not perfect substitutes. We can therefore assume that the firms are engaged in monopolistic competition, where each one of them faces a downward sloping demand curve of some sort for its products. Instead of looking at the industry as a whole, with its rather complex structure, it should suffice to analyze the behavior of a single, typical and representative firm to gain insight into how the software industry will tend to react to any proposed policy measure.

We assume that every firm maximizes the discounted stream of future net revenue. Its behavior (that is, the amount of computer software it produces in each year) is then completely determined by the demand curve it faces as a function of time, its internal cost curve over time, and the nature of protection granted to it. We will specify in turn the

[1] This section is of a more technical nature and may be skipped without loss by readers who are more interested in policy issues.

assumptions we have made about each of these functions.

In this model we do not distinguish between the sale of a program for unlimited use, and the leasing for a fee to be paid for each use. We simply assume that for any given software package a firm has developed there is some number of users who are willing to purchase it, and that this number is larger, the lower the price is which the firm charges for the package.[1] We also assume that there is a single price for each software package; that is, the firm does not practice price discrimination among users.[2]

We first look at the demand curve for one particular software package, during a given relatively short time interval. The simplest shape for the demand curve will be a linear function, and in one version of our model we assume a linear demand curve (Figure 1a). But this may introduce some bias. It seems more natural to us to assume that with a very low or even zero price, the number of users will tend to increase by considerably more than a linear demand curve indicates. We have also experimented with a demand curve which approaches the horizontal axis asymptotically, as shown in Figure 1b.

---

[1]It has been observed that there have been cases in which a firm was unable to sell a software package at a low price, but found interested buyers when it increased the price, apparently because they believed in the quality of something expensive, but were suspicious about something cheap. But we do not concern ourselves here with such psychological anomalies of decision-makers in a firm.

[2]If a firm is allowed to charge discriminatory prices, it can extract a larger amount of surplus from the consumers, and therefore needs a shorter period of protection to be induced to produce a given amount of computer software.

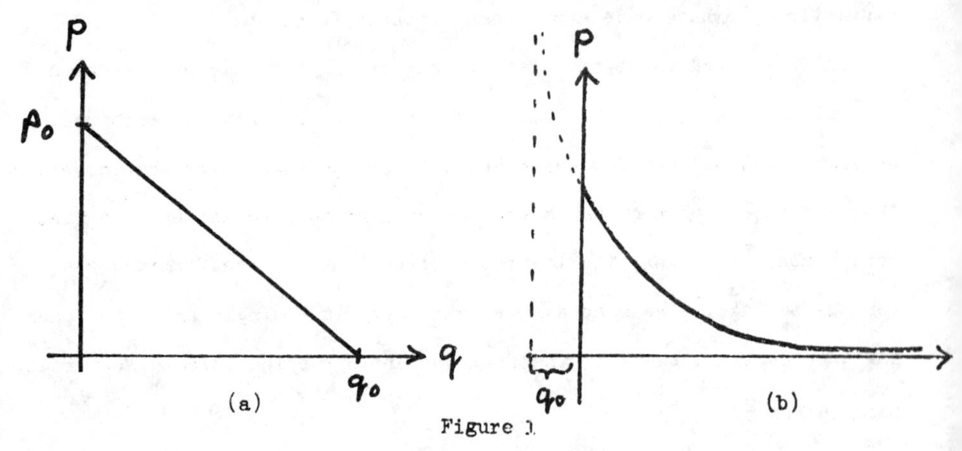

Figure 1

(a) A linear demand curve $p = \begin{cases} p_0(1 - q/q_0) & \text{if } q \leq q_0 \\ 0 & \text{if } q > q_0 \end{cases}$

(where p is the price and q the corresponding quantity sold

(b) A nonlinear demand curve of the functional form

$p = k(q + q_0)^{-u}$, where $u > 1$.[1]

Both of the demand curves shown in Figures 1a and 1b apply to one particular software package, at a given point in time (or, more realistically, for a relatively short time interval, which may, for example, be an entire year). We next define how the demand function declines over time. We assume that the price which any given consumer is willing to pay declines exponentially over time at a constant rate (Figure 2).

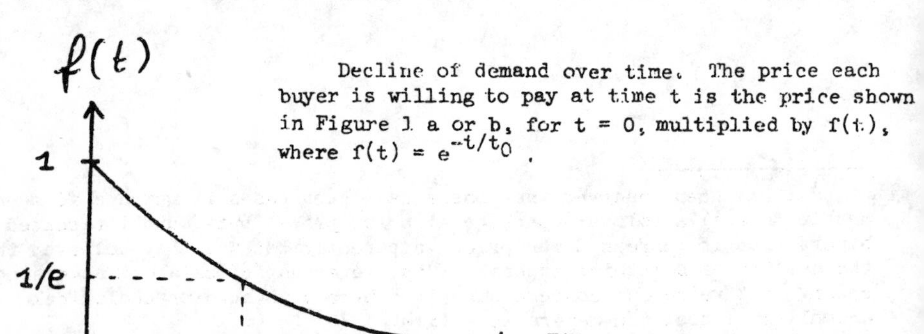

Decline of demand over time. The price each buyer is willing to pay at time t is the price shown in Figure 1 a or b, for t = 0, multiplied by f(t), where $f(t) = e^{-t/t_0}$.

Figure 2

[1] The condition $u > 1$ is necessary because otherwise the consumers' surplus would be unbounded when the price p is equal to zero.

Up to now we have looked at the demand for only one particular software package. (Of course, the same package may be sold over and over again to different users once it is produced, unlike a private good.) We now ask how the various demand curves faced by a firm look for different software packages. It is clear that some of them can be sold at a much higher price than others, but these will also tend to be the ones which are most expensive to produce. We now make the somewhat heroic assumption that there is some measurable unit of output of software, which is defined in such a way that each unit of output can yield to the firm the same amount of revenue (say, e.g., $1000), if the firm is granted a permanent monopoly on the sale of the software it has produced.[1] We also assume that the decline of demand over time progresses at the same rate for each unit of software so defined, so that the demand curve as function of time is identical for each unit of software.[2]

We are now in a position to define a cost function. We assume that each additional unit of software output has an increasing cost, for the two reasons stated. (The firm will have to choose from less and less attractive projects and hire progressively less efficient personnel.) An example of an increasing marginal cost function is shown in Figure 3.

If the firm is granted a permanent monopoly, it will produce the amount X_1 (see Figure 3). If its protection period is limited so that it can earn only the amount MC_0 on each unit of output, then it will produce only the smaller amount X_0 of software, at which marginal cost is equal to marginal revenue per unit.

---

[1] Of course, the shorter the period of protection, the smaller is the revenue the firm can obtain from each unit of output.

[2] Without these simplifying assumptions, the amount of information required to specify the model would simply grow beyond any reasonable bounds.

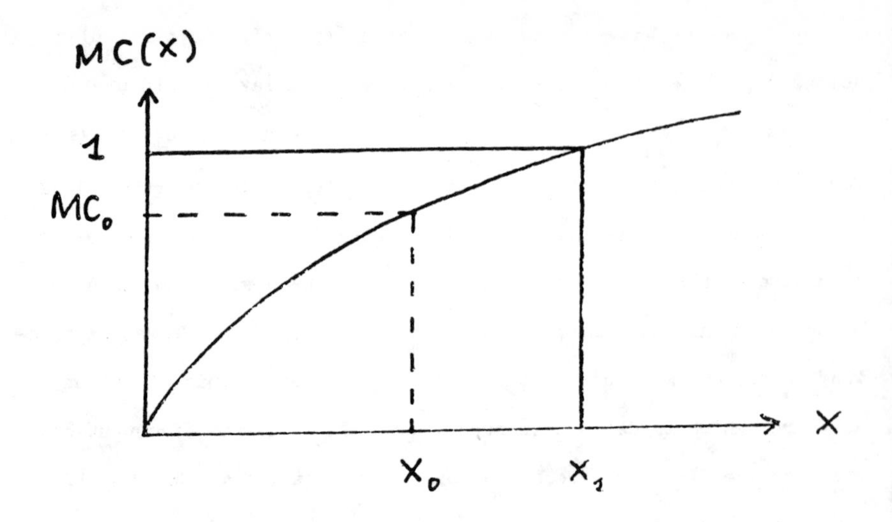

Figure 3

Marginal cost MC(X) as a function of the number of "units" X of software produced: $MC(X) = X^v$ with $v > 0$.

We assume that all costs are incurred over a short time period when the program is developed, and that later maintenance costs are negligible. Maintenance costs could easily be built into the model, if information about them were available. But they could simply be discounted back to the point of creation of a new program and would therefore not modify the results obtained here in any essential way.

For the nature of the protection offered we make the simple assumption that the firm is granted a monopoly for a time period of length T after it has produced a new program, and that the program becomes public property thereafter.[1]

---

[1] One might also consider an institutional arrangement in which firms enjoy a total monopoly at first, with complete freedom of setting prices for their products and then are required gradually to lower the fees at which they make their software packages available to other firms. But it is probably too complicated to administer such a scheme equitably in reality.

To summarize, our model is characterized by the following set of equations:

(1)	$p^{(0)} = p^{(0)}(q)$	price at which a unit of software can be sold q times, per time unit, at time $t = 0$.
(2)	$p^{(t)}(q) = f^{(t)}p^{(0)}(q)$	where $p^{(t)}$ is the price at which a unit can be sold q times per time unit at time t, and f(t) characterizes the decline over time of prices consumers are willing to pay.
(3)	MC(X)	marginal cost of producing the Xth unit of output.
(4)	$p^{(t)}(q) = 0$ for $t > T$,	expiration of the monopoly after T time units.

We now want to determine what period T of protection is optimal from society's viewpoint given the profit-maximizing behavior of the firm. The optimal period T will be the one which maximizes the net present value of the discounted stream of social welfare W, which we shall define soon.

Our procedure will be the following. First we will calculate the price the firm will charge for a unit of software during the period of protection, depending on the demand curve. From the duration of the protection period we can then calculate the discounted net present value of the revenue a firm can derive from each unit of computer software. By comparing this revenue with the marginal cost curve MC(X) for production of the Xth unit of computer software, we can derive what amount of software the firm will produce during each time period. Next we can compute, for a given period T of protection, the discounted net present value of the future stream of social welfare derived from one unit of computer software. As we have noted earlier, the amount X of computer software produced during one time interval will be an increasing function of the protection period T, whereas the social welfare arising from any particular unit produced will be a declining function of T. By multiplying the amount of software produced by the welfare arising from each unit, we obtain total welfare generated as a function of the period of protection T. This function will increase at first, reach a maximum, and then decline again. The point at which this welfare function reaches its maximum corresponds to the optimal lag period T.

We will now execute that program, step by step. First, we will derive the solution in general algebraic terms. Then we will specialize to the particular demand and cost functions shown in Figures 1, 2, and 3.

We will measure social welfare as the sum of consumers' and producers' surplus, as it is customary in economic literature.[1] The producer's surplus or, equivalently, the firm's net profit is the difference between revenue and costs. The consumers' surplus is the difference between what they would be willing to pay at most for a piece of computer software, and what they actually pay. In Figure 4, the consumers' surplus is represented by the area PRP_0. The lower the price, the larger will be the consumers' surplus. Since the producer's costs are independent of the number of times he can sell a given unit of computer software, we look here only at the variable portion of producer's surplus, which alone depends on the quantity sold (or, indirectly, on the price the firm charges for a unit of computer software). This variable portion of the producer's surplus is represented by the rectangle OQRP in Figure 4.

---

[1] This definition of social welfare ignores considerations of distributional equity, and simply adds up the monetary gains to each participant in the economy. For a discussion of other types of welfare functions and their implications for equity, see for example, "The Output Distribution Frontier. Alternatives to Income Taxes and Transfers for Strong Equality Goals," by W.J. Baumol, mimeo, New York University, January 1977.

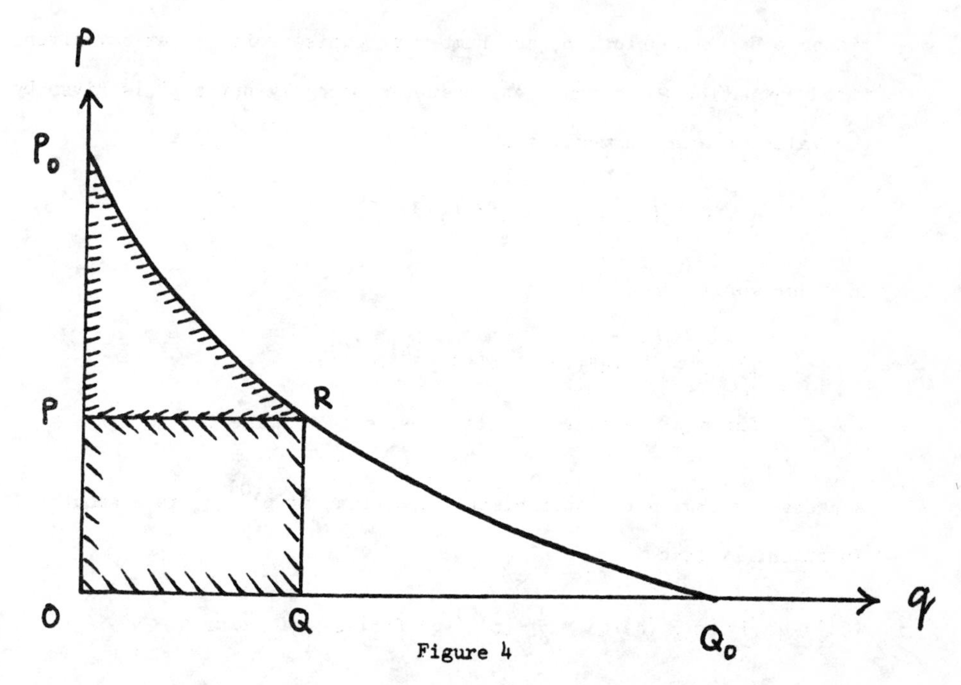

Figure 4

Consumer's surplus PRP_0 and variable portion of producer's surplus OQRP as function of the price OP the firm charges. This figure applies to one particular unit of computer software, during one time interval.

We can see that as the firm increases the price OP it charges, starting from zero, its revenue OQRP increases at first, but later declines again, as the number of sales it can make gradually drops to zero with increasing price. Somewhere in between, say when OP = p*, the firm's revenue reaches a maximum. p* is then the monopoly price the firm will charge as long as it is protected. The corresponding number q of copies sold will be denoted by q*. After a period of length T, when the firm's copyright expires, the price it can charge drops to zero, and the consumers' surplus then comprises the entire area OQ_0P_0 in Figure 4.

Let us now compute the monopoly price p*, which the firm will charge per unit of computer software, as a function of the time interval t elaspsed since the production of that unit. Formally using the relationship between price, p, and number of copies sold, q, at any given time t (equation 2) we can state that the monopoly price p* is given by the value of p which maximizes

$$q \cdot p^{(t)}(q) = qf(t)\, p^{(0)}(q).$$

In other words,

$$(5) \qquad q^*(t) \cdot p^{(t)}\,(q^*(t)) \geq q(t) \cdot p^{(t)}(q^{(t)})$$

for any quantity $0 \leq q(t) < \infty$ sold at time t.

A necessary (but not a sufficient) condition, if $p^{(0)}(q)$ is a smooth function, is that

$$(5') \qquad \frac{d}{dq}\,[p^{(t)}(q) \cdot q] = \frac{d}{dq}\,[p^{(0)}(q) \cdot f(t) \cdot q] = 0 \quad \text{for } q = q^*.$$

We will assume that both the firm and society use a discount rate r. Then the net present value of the revenue a firm can obtain from one unit of software during the period T of protection is equal to

$$(6) \qquad R(T) = \int_0^T p^*(t) q^*(t) e^{-rt}\, dt,$$

where the monopoly price p*(t) and the corresponding quantity q*(t) are given by formula (5).

The number of units of software produced, X(T), as a function of the protection period T, can now be obtained from the marginal cost function MC(X) by setting

$$(7) \qquad MC[X(T)] = R(T),$$

and finding the amount X(T) which satisfies (7).

Our next step is to calculate the net present value of the discounted stream of welfare, W(T), generated by one unit of software if the protection period is T.

The contribution to social welfare, $w(t)$, generated by one unit of software, per time unit, at time t <u>during the period of protection</u> is equal to

$$(8) \qquad w(t) = \int_0^{q^*(t)} p^{(t)}(q)dg \qquad \text{for } 0 \leq t \leq T$$

This corresponds to the sum of the two shaded areas $OQRP^0PO$ in Figure 4.

After the protection has elapsed, the social welfare is equal to the consumers' surplus, which now includes the entire area under the demand curve (area $0\ Q_0\ P_0$ in Figure 4):

$$(8') \qquad w'(t) = \int_0^{\infty} p^{(t)}(q)dq \qquad \text{for } t > T.$$

The present value of the discounted stream of the sum of consumers' surplus and the producer's revenue, generated by one unit of software, is then equal to

$$(9) \qquad S(T) = \int_0^T w(t)e^{-rt}dt + \int_T^{\infty} w'(t)e^{-rt}dt.$$

Since $w'(t) > w(t)$, (the welfare contribution of a unit of software is larger without protection than with protection), we see that $S(T)$ reaches its maximum at $T = 0$ and declines with increasing T.

To obtain the contribution of a unit of software to social welfare, we would have to subtract its production costs. But average production costs will depend on the amount X of software produced, and we will therefore have to take each into account separately. The cost of producing $X(T)$ units of software, $C(T)$, is equal to

$$(10) \qquad C(T) = \int_0^{X(T)} MC(x)dx$$

No discounting is necessary here, since we assumed that all costs are incurred at the point of production when $t = 0$.

The contribution to social welfare of all units of software produced during one time unit at $t = 0$, discounted to infinity, as a function of the protection period T, is now equal to the amount $X(T)$ of computer software produced, multiplied by the consumers' and producer's surplus, $S(T)$, generated by each unit of software, minus the production costs $C(T)$:

$$(11) \qquad W(T) = X(T) \cdot S(T) - C(T).$$

Figure 5 shows some typical shapes for $X(T)$, $S(T)$, $C(T)$ and $W(T)$. The value of T which maximizes $W(T)$, T^*, is the optimal period of protection:

$$(12) \qquad W(T^*) \geq W(T) \quad \text{for } 0 \leq T < \infty \quad .$$

Results obtained for the optimal period of protection as a function of various parameters, such as the discount rate, the average useful life of a software package, and the structure of costs and demand will be presented in the next subsection. We will also compare the maximum amount of welfare that can be obtained through a copyright system, when the optimal protection period is granted, with the social welfare that could be achieved in principle through some form of central planning. In the latter case, we will assume that a firm produces the socially optimal amount[1] of computer software, financed through gevernment support, and makes the software it has produced available for free (that is, at marginal costs) to anyone who wants to use it.

[1]For the socially optimal amount to be produced, the marginal cost of the last unit of software produced must be equal to marginal social benefit.

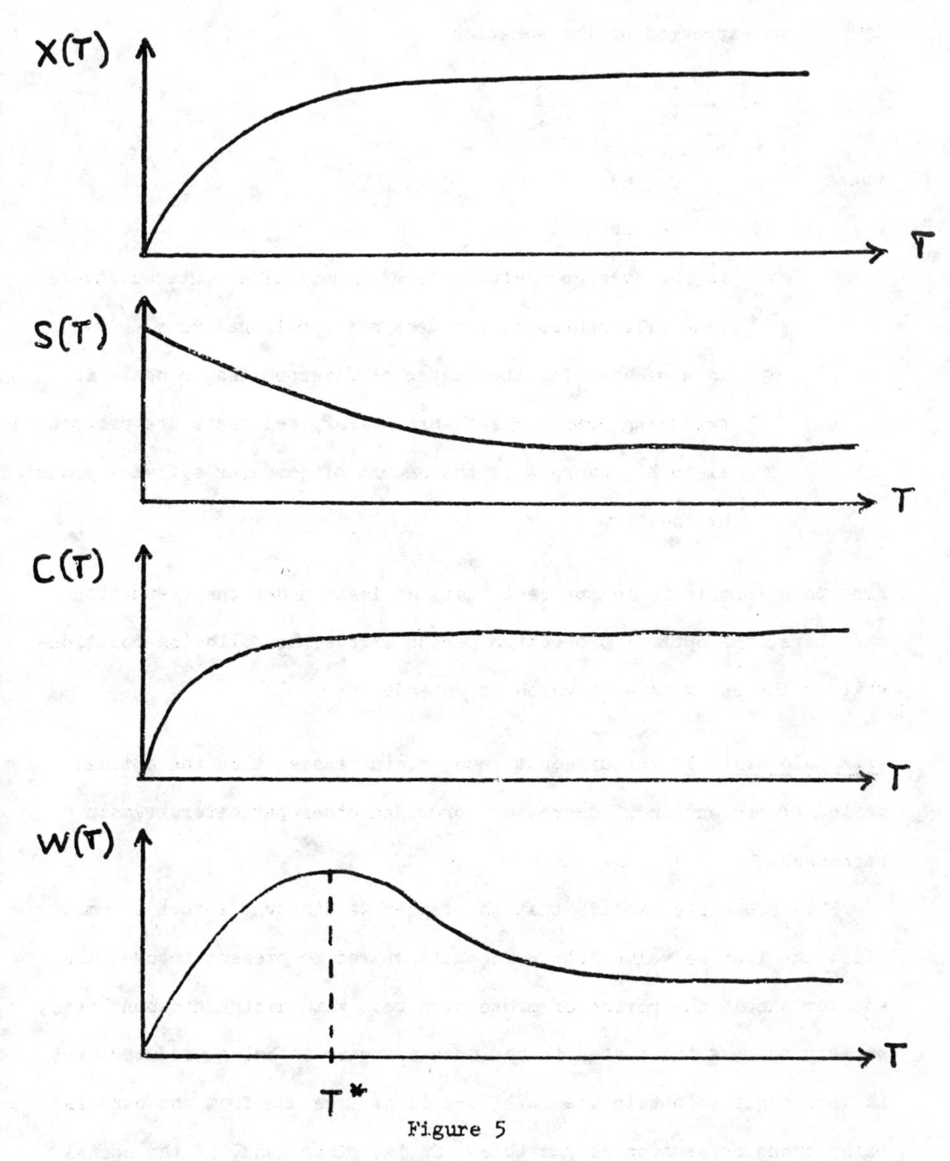

Figure 5

Amount of software produced, X(T), consumers surplus and producer's revenue generated per unit of software, S(T), total cost of all units of software produced, C(T), and present value of discounted stream of welfare, W(T), as functions of the protection period T. T* is the optimal period of protection.

C. Results Obtained from the Model and Their Policy Implications

Let us first consider a linear demand curve (as shown in Figure 1a). As is shown in Appendix IV-1, the optimal period of protection,

T^*, can be expressed by the equation

$$(13) \qquad T^* = \frac{1}{r+1/t_0} \ln \frac{v+3}{v-1} \quad ,$$

where

r is the discount rate

t_0 is the average useful life of a unit of computer software (the willingness to pay decays proportional to e^{-t/t_0})

v is a measure for the degree of diseconomies to scale in producing computer software. (Marginal costs are proportional to X^v, where X is the amount of computer software produced by the firm.)

From this formula it is apparent that, at least under the assumptions made here, the optimal protection period T^* has the following relationship to the parameters on which it depends:

Principle 4.1 If the discount rate, r, increases, then the optimal period of protection T^* decreases, provided other parameters remain unchanged.

This principle implies that the faster we discount future income, i.e., the less we value future income compared to present income, the shorter should the period of protection be. With a high discount rate, society is less interested in how much software is being produced, but is more eager to obtain the full benefit of free use from whatever is being produced as soon as possible. On the other hand, if the social discount rate is low, society is willing to grant a longer protection period and make some sacrifices in the near future in order to promote the production of software to a fuller extent and have more to live on in the more distant future. This relationship corresponds to what one would naturally expect.

Principle 4.2 If the average useful lifetime, t_0, of a unit of computer software increases, the optimal period of protection should be increased.

This principle, again, corresponds to our intuition that the longer it will take until a piece of computer software is superseded by a better one, the longer it is worth to protect it, in order to have a greater amount of computer software produced.

Principle 4.3 The stronger the diseconomies of scale are in the production of computer software (as measured by the exponent v), the shorter ought to be the optimal period of protection T*.

This principle is somewhat less obvious than the first two principles. But it too has a natural interpretation in hindsight. If there are very strong diseconomies of scale, this means that there is some limited number of software projects which it is worthwhile to undertake, but anything beyond that selection will be very expensive to produce, as costs increase rapidly. In this situation, a longer protection period, which is designed to give more revenue per unit of software to the producer and in this way to encourage him to produce more, will have very little effect. Only a few projects, if any at all, will be made cost-effective if they were unprofitable under a shorter protection period. That means, by increasing the protection period, society would forego a large amount in potential welfare from the free use of existing computer software, in order to stimulate the production of only a small additional amount of computer software. A short period of protection is therefore indicated in the presence of strong diseconomies of scale. Just the opposite is true if there are only weak diseconomies of scale or almost constant returns to scale. In that case, a slight increase in revenue per unit of software produced will now make a wide range of new projects financially feasible - projects which were unprofitable under a shorter protection period. Therefore, by giving up only a limited amount benefit from existing computer software through a prolongation of the producer's monopoly, society will induce producers to create a considerably larger amount of software. Therefore, if diseconomies of scale are weak, a long protection period is indicated.[1]

We turn next to the nonlinear demand curve shown in Figure 1b. Here, monopoly pricing excludes a much larger number of potential users who are willing to pay only a low price for the use of a software package than was the case when the demand curve is linear. We will therefore e the differences in social welfare between monopoly pricing during the protection period and free use after the lapse of the protection period to be larger than in the case of a linear demand curve. In other words, the penalty paid by society during the protection period is higher than in the previously considered case.

As is shown in Appendix IV-2, the optimal period of protection, T*, in the case of the nonlinear demand function assumed is

$$T^* = \frac{1}{r+1/t_0} \ \ln \frac{1}{1-z^*} \quad \text{with } z^* = \left(\frac{u}{u-1}\right)^u \cdot \frac{u-1}{uv+2u-1} \tag{14}$$

where
- r is the discount rate
- t_0 the average useful life at a unit of software
- v is a measure for the degree of diseconomies of scale, and
- u indicates how rapidly the willingness to-pay declines with incraasing numbers of consumers ($p = k(q_0+q)^{-u}$, where q is the number of copies of a unit of software sold at price p, and k and q_0 are parameters defined earlier.) The higher u the less demand responds to a change in price, i.e., the les price elastic is demand.

[1]Mathematically oriented readers will have noticed that the optimal protection period under the model assumptions made here is finite only if $v > 1$, that is, marginal costs of production increase at a faster rate than the amount produced. This implies that total costs increase more rapidly than the square of output. If the diseconomies of scale are any weaker, then the optimal protection period is infinite.

As before, (in equation 13) we find that the optimal period of protection decreases with increasing discount rate r, increases with increasing average life time t_0, and decreases with increasing diseconomies of scale in production, represented by v. In addition, we have the new relationship

Principle 4.4 The less demand responds to a change in price, the longer should the period of protection be.[1]

This principle agrees with the intuitive relationship between the shape of the demand curve and the penalty paid by society for having a monopoly, which we just discussed. If the willingness to pay declines rapidly for additional potential users, i.e., if demand is inelastic, then little is sacrificed by having a non-zero monopoly price charged for the use of software, and society can afford to grant a longer period of protection. On the other hand, if monopoly pricing excludes many potential users from taking advantage of existing software - that is, if demand is more price-elastic - then the loss resulting from a monopoly is more serious and a shorter period of protection is appropriate.

D. Data Requirements and Estimates of Optimal Protection Periods

In order to estimate the shape of the demand curve for computer software, it would be necessary to collect information on the number of sales of a given software package that a firm has been able to make at various prices. If demand can be represented sufficiently well by a linear demand curve, then this information alone is sufficient to permit the calculation of an optimal period of protection from the discount rate, the average life-time of software, and the cost curve. It is not necessary to have any more detailed estimates of demand.[2] How

[1] It is a little tricky to see that T* increases with u (by the definition of u, the higher the value of u, the more rapidly the demand curve declines). But we will soon see graphs which show the dependency of T* on u and other parameters.

[2] That is, it is not necessary to know the slope of the demand curve, and the intercepts p_0 and q_0 in Figure 1a.

the discount rate r is to be estimated should pose no problem. The average life-time of a piece of software, t_0, can be obtained from information on how rapidly the sales-price, or the number of sales of a software package at a constant price, decline. To estimate the degree of diseconomies of scale in the production of software (as represented by the parameter v), it would be necessary to ask software firms by how many percent their costs would increase if they were to increase their output by, say, 10 percent (where output is measured by the dollar volume of sales). Given these three parameters, r, t_0 and v, the optimal period of protection T* can be calculated from equation (13). For example, if we take a 10 percent annual discount rate (r = .10), a 5-year average life-time of a software package, and a parameter v = 2 (indicating that marginal costs are proportional to the square of the quantity of software produced), then we obtain

$$T^* = \frac{1}{r+1/t_0} \ln \frac{v+3}{v-1} = \frac{1}{.10+.20} \ln \frac{5}{1} = 3.33(1.61) = 5.36,$$

i.e., a copyright protection for a period of about 5 years is optimal.

Figures 6 to 8 indicate how the optimal protection period T* depends on r, t_0 and v.

How serious is it if the length of the protection period departs from the optimum? To gain insight into this problem, we can calculate the relative efficiency of various protection periods T, where the relative efficiency indicates what fraction of the maximum feasible amount of welfare[1] is reached by a copyright of a duration of T years. As is shown in Appendix IV-1, for a linear demand curve the relative efficiency E(T), is given by

$$(15) \qquad E(T) = (1/v)\ (z/2)^{1/v}\ (v+1 - (v+3)z/4),$$

[1]This maximum could be reached through some ideal form of central planning.

where $z = 1-e^{-sT}$ and $s = r + 1/t_0$.

Figure 9 shows the relative efficiency E(T) as a function of the protection period T, for the set of parameters used in the example just given.[1] Table 1 lists efficiencies for some selected values of T.

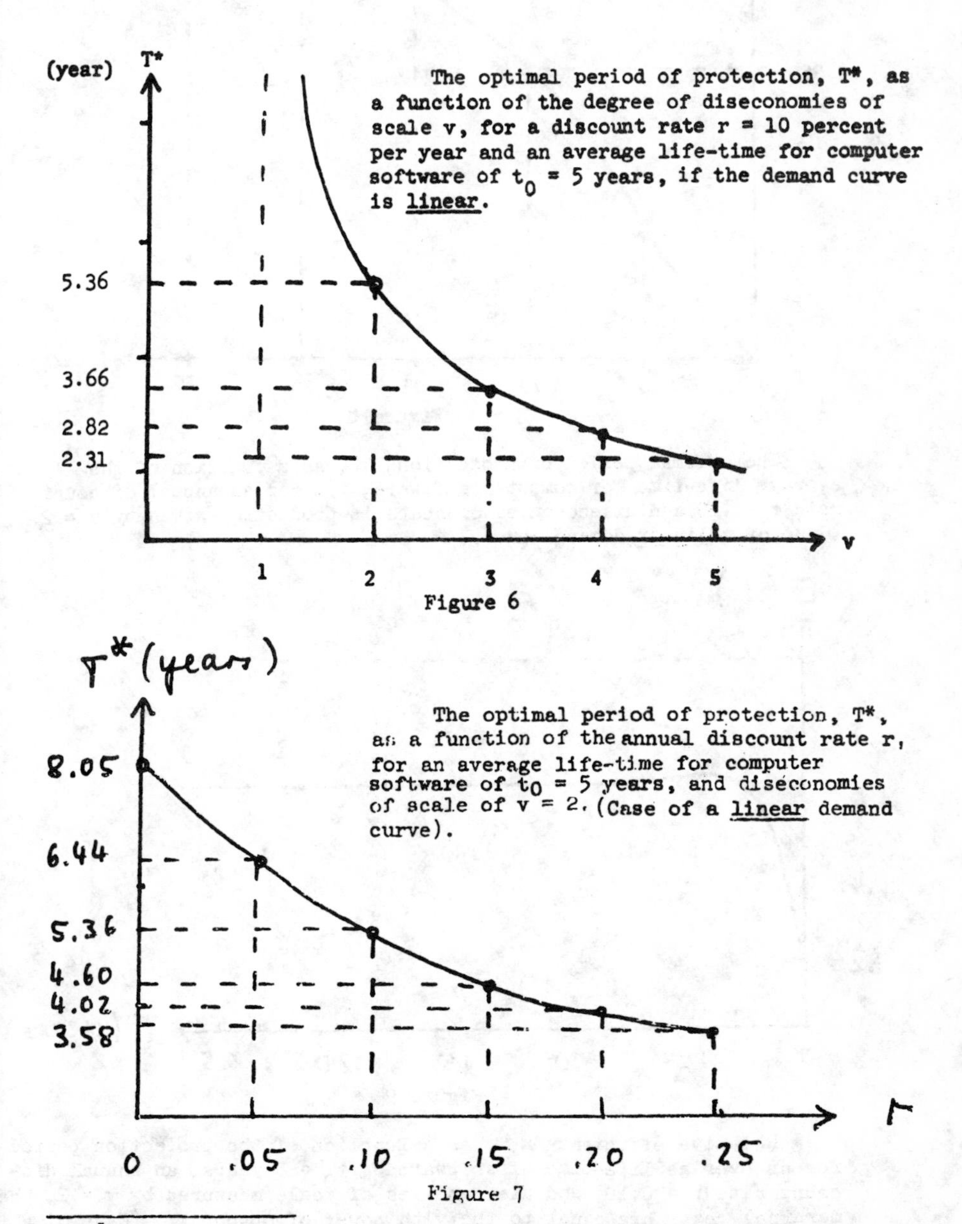

Figure 6

Figure 7

[1]This diagram corresponds to the social welfare W(T) shown in Figure 5.

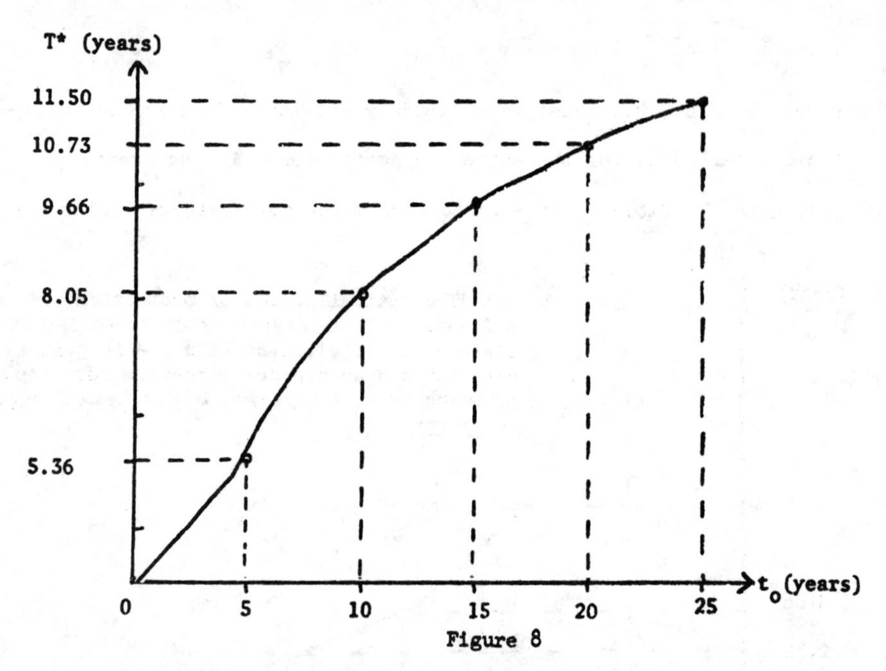

Figure 8

The optimal period of protection, T*, as a function of the average life-time for computer software, t_0, for an annual discount rate r = .10 and diseconomies of scale in production given by v = 2. (Case of a linear demand curve.)

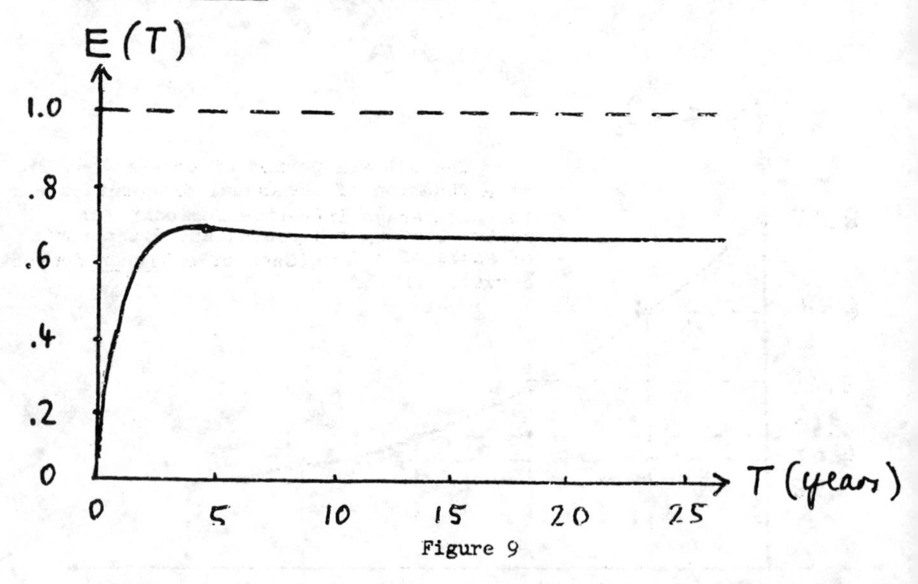

Figure 9

Relative efficiency E(T) as a function of the protection period T for an average life-time of software of t_0 = 5 years, an annual discount rate r = 0.10, and diseconomies of scale measured by v = 2, when marginal costs are equal to the v'th power of output x. (Case of a linear demand curve.)

T	0	0.1	.25	.5	1	2	5.36	10	1000
E(T)	0	.180	.277	.373	.482	.579	.632	.625	.619

Table 1

Relative efficiency E(T) as a function of the protection period T (in years), for the same parameters as in Figure 9 (for a linear demand curve).

As Figure 9 and Table 1 indicate, the maximum of the efficiency is very flat. There may be some loss in efficiency if the protection period T is much too short, but even if T is only 2 years (less than half of the optimum of 5.36 years), the loss in relative efficiency is less than 10 percent. And if the protection is granted for as long as 1000 years, the loss in efficiency is only about 2 percent.

The fact that the relative efficiency curve is almost flat to the right of the optimum was also pointed out by Nordhaus, in a slightly different context.[1] This is typical for linear demand curves. As we shall see soon, however, for some non-linear demand curves, too long a protection period can bring a considerable loss in welfare.

Table 2 lists the optimal protection period T for various parameter combinations. It also shows that relative efficiency that can be obtained with the optimal protection period, and the relative efficiency that would result from permanent protection (when T approaches infinity).

[1]See Invention, Growth and Welfare by W.D. Nordhaus (MIT Press, Cambridge, MA, 1969) esp. pp. 83-84. In his model, Nordhaus considers patent protection on cost-saving inventions.

L		V= 0.1	V= 0.2	V= 0.5	V= 1.0	V= 2.0	V= 5.0	V=10.0
L= 1	T◆	◆◆◆◆◆◆	◆◆◆◆◆◆	◆◆◆◆◆◆	◆◆◆◆◆◆	1.463	0.630	0.334
	E◆	0.003	0.062	0.312	0.500	0.632	0.758	0.829
	E	0.003	0.063	0.313	0.500	0.619	0.696	0.723
L= 2	T◆	◆◆◆◆◆◆	◆◆◆◆◆◆	◆◆◆◆◆◆	◆◆◆◆◆◆	2.682	1.155	0.613
	E◆	0.003	0.062	0.312	0.500	0.632	0.758	0.829
	E	0.003	0.063	0.313	0.500	0.619	0.696	0.723
L= 5	T◆	◆◆◆◆◆◆	◆◆◆◆◆◆	◆◆◆◆◆◆	◆◆◆◆◆◆	5.365	2.310	1.226
	E◆	0.003	0.062	0.312	0.500	0.632	0.758	0.829
	E	0.003	0.063	0.313	0.500	0.619	0.696	0.723
L= 10	T◆	◆◆◆◆◆◆	◆◆◆◆◆◆	◆◆◆◆◆◆	◆◆◆◆◆◆	8.047	3.466	1.839
	E◆	0.003	0.062	0.312	0.500	0.632	0.758	0.829
	E	0.003	0.063	0.313	0.500	0.619	0.696	0.723
L= 20	T◆	◆◆◆◆◆◆	◆◆◆◆◆◆	◆◆◆◆◆◆	◆◆◆◆◆◆	10.730	4.621	2.451
	E◆	0.003	0.062	0.312	0.500	0.632	0.758	0.829
	E	0.003	0.063	0.313	0.500	0.619	0.696	0.723
L= 50	T◆	◆◆◆◆◆◆	◆◆◆◆◆◆	◆◆◆◆◆◆	◆◆◆◆◆◆	13.412	5.776	3.064
	E◆	0.003	0.062	0.312	0.500	0.632	0.758	0.829
	E	0.003	0.063	0.313	0.500	0.619	0.696	0.723
L=100	T◆	◆◆◆◆◆◆	◆◆◆◆◆◆	◆◆◆◆◆◆	◆◆◆◆◆◆	14.631	6.301	3.343
	E◆	0.003	0.062	0.312	0.500	0.632	0.758	0.829
	E	0.003	0.063	0.313	0.500	0.619	0.696	0.723

◆◆◆◆◆◆ INDICATES THAT THE OPTIMAL PROTECTION PERIOD IS INFINI

Table 2

Optimal protection period (T*), optimal relative efficiency (E* and relative efficiency obtained with permanent protection (E), for a <u>linear demand curve</u>, for various values of v, the degree of diseconomies of scale in software production, and various average life times L (in years). The annual discount rate r is assumed to be 10 percent.

As Table 2 shows, the highest relative efficiencies which can be obtained through a copyright system are achievable when there are very strong diseconomies of scale in the production of software, i.e., when the parameter v is high. A high value of v means that the protection period should be kept relatively low, and that additional protection, which increases a firm's revenue, will induce it to increase its production only by very little. If v = 10, that is, if a 10 percent increase in output raises marginal costs by a factor of $(1.1)^{10} = 2.6$, then a copyright of optimal duration will yield about 83 percent of the maximum amount of welfare that is achievable in principle. But if diseconomies of scale are not as strong, then the efficiency of a copyright system, even one of optimal duration, is considerably lower. If marginal costs are proportional to output (i.e., $v = 1$), then the efficiency is 50 percent. If v is as low as 0.1, meaning that a 10 percent increase in output raises marginal costs only by 1 percent, then the efficiency of a copyright system is less than 1 percent of what is feasible in principle, with the right amount of public funding of software development.

Let us now look at some results for a non-linear demand curve for software, of the type shown in Figure 1b:

$$p(q) = k(q+q_0)^{-u}$$

As is shown in Appendix IV-2, the optimal period of protection in that case is given by

$$(14) \quad q\ T^* = -\frac{1}{s}\ \ell n\ (1-z^*)$$

where $z^* = (\frac{u}{u-1})^u \ \frac{u-1}{uv+2u-1}$ and $s = r+1/t_0$.

Here the parameter u indicates how rapidly the price drops with an increase in supply. For example, if $u = 2$ and $v = 2$, and $t_0 = 5$ and $r = .10$ as before, we find $s = 0.3$, $z^* = 4/7$, and $T^* = 2.82$. The behavior of the optimal protection period with respect to the parameters v (diseconomies of scale), r (discount rate) and t_0 (average life-time of a software package) is similar as before in the linear case. What is new is the way T^* depends on u, where a low value of u indicates more elastic demand, and a high value of u indicates inelastic demand for software. Figure 10 shows how T^* increases with increasing values of u, given that all the other parameters are held fixed.

Again, we ask how serious it is to depart from the optimum duration for the protection period. In Appendix IV-2 it is shown that the relative efficiency, E(T), of a protection period of length T is given by

$$(16) \qquad E(T) = \frac{v+1}{v} (yz)^{1/v} \left(1 - \frac{u}{u-1} yz\right) - \frac{1}{v} (yz)^{(v+1)/v}$$

with $z = 1-e^{-sT}$, $s = r+1/t_0$, and $y = (u/(u-1))^{-u}$

In Figure 11, a graph of the function E(T) is shown for a specific combination of parameter values. Table 3 lists selected values of E(T).

As Figure 11 and Table 3 clearly show, there may be a substantial penalty for granting too long a protection period, if demand for software is not linear and rather elastic in the lower right tail of the

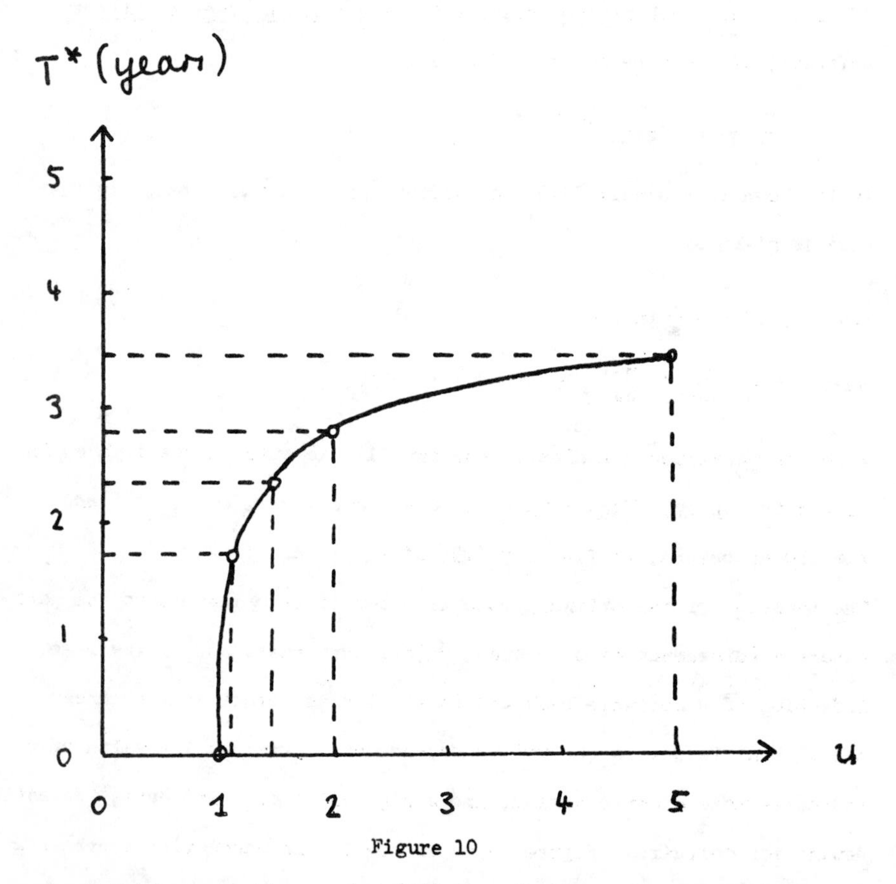

Figure 10

Optimal protection period (T*) as a function of u, where high u means inelastic demand. Parameter values are v = 2 (diseconomies of scale), t_0 = 5 (average life-time of software in years) and r = .10 (annual discount rate). The demand curve is <u>nonlinear</u>, as shown in Figure 1b.

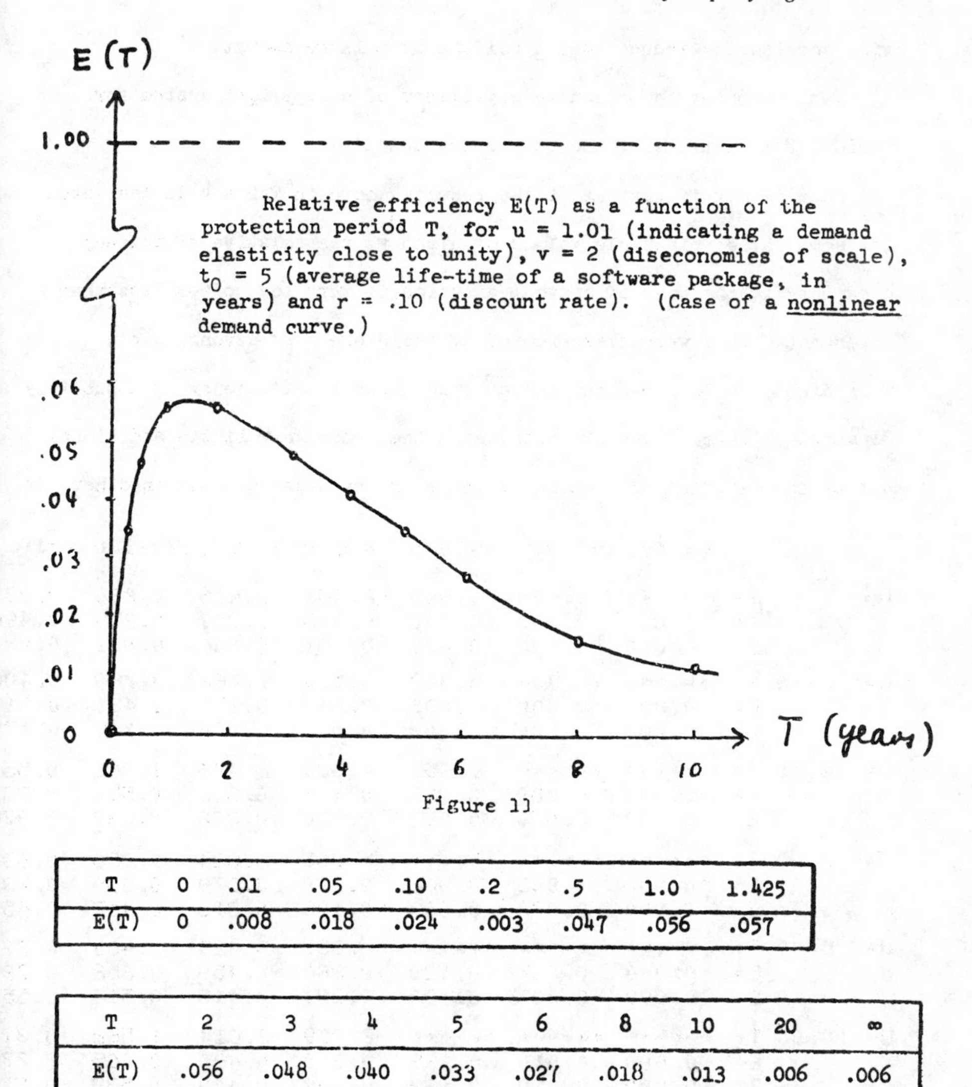

Relative efficiency E(T) as a function of the protection period T, for u = 1.01 (indicating a demand elasticity close to unity), v = 2 (diseconomies of scale), t_0 = 5 (average life-time of a software package, in years) and r = .10 (discount rate). (Case of a <u>nonlinear</u> demand curve.)

Figure 11

T	0	.01	.05	.10	.2	.5	1.0	1.425
E(T)	0	.008	.018	.024	.003	.047	.056	.057

T	2	3	4	5	6	8	10	20	∞
E(T)	.056	.048	.040	.033	.027	.018	.013	.006	.006

Table 3

Relative efficiency E(T) for selected values of T, for the same parameters as in Figure 11 (for a <u>nonlinear</u> demand curve).

demand curve. The reason is that during the protection period a very large number of potential users are excluded from enjoying the benefits of already existing software, because of the monopoly price being charged for it. Thus, any extension of protection, beyond the mininum period needed to encourage the production of at least some software, will necessarily reduce public welfare by a large amount.

Table 4 shows the relative efficiency of a copyright system for various combinations of the parameters u and v.

What is significant about the results shown in Table 4 is that even for some rather plausible values of u and v, the relative efficiency of a copyright system of optimal duration is very low, often less than 1 percent. Only when diseconomies of scale are very strong (i.e., v is high) does a copyright system come close in efficiency to a publicly financed software industry, because in that case very little additional output can be obtained from an increase in investments. But in other

		V= 0.1	V= 0.2	V= 0.5	V= 1.0	V= 2.0	V= 5.0	V=10.
U= 1.01	T◆	9.581	6.689	3.943	2.454	1.425	0.638	0.33
	E◆	0.000	0.000	0.000	0.005	0.057	0.278	0.49
	E	0.000	0.000	0.000	0.001	0.006	0.021	0.03
U= 1.10	T◆	◆◆◆◆◆◆	13.904	5.347	3.120	1.766	0.780	0.40
	E◆	0.000	0.000	0.003	0.043	0.171	0.431	0.61
	E	0.000	0.000	0.003	0.025	0.076	0.143	0.17
U= 1.50	T◆	◆◆◆◆◆◆	◆◆◆◆◆◆	9.653	4.520	2.444	1.065	0.55
	E◆	0.000	0.000	0.033	0.143	0.316	0.555	0.70
	E	0.000	0.000	0.033	0.126	0.236	0.337	0.37
U= 2.00	T◆	◆◆◆◆◆◆	◆◆◆◆◆◆	◆◆◆◆◆◆	5.365	2.824	1.226	0.63
	E◆	0.000	0.002	0.062	0.200	0.378	0.599	0.73
	E	0.000	0.002	0.063	0.188	0.313	0.417	0.45
U= 5.00	T◆	◆◆◆◆◆◆	◆◆◆◆◆◆	◆◆◆◆◆◆	6.851	3.429	1.483	0.77
	E◆	0.000	0.007	0.120	0.286	0.459	0.652	0.76
	E	0.000	0.007	0.120	0.280	0.413	0.514	0.55
U= 10.00	T◆	◆◆◆◆◆◆	◆◆◆◆◆◆	◆◆◆◆◆◆	7.359	3.614	1.562	0.81
	E◆	0.000	0.010	0.139	0.310	0.480	0.665	0.77
	E	0.000	0.010	0.139	0.306	0.440	0.539	0.57
U=100.00	T◆	◆◆◆◆◆◆	◆◆◆◆◆◆	◆◆◆◆◆◆	7.829	3.775	1.631	0.85
	E◆	0.000	0.013	0.155	0.331	0.498	0.676	0.77
	E	0.000	0.013	0.155	0.327	0.461	0.559	0.59

◆◆◆◆◆◆ INDICATES THAT THE OPTIMAL PROTECTION PERIOD IS INFINI

Table 4

Optimal protection period (T*), optimal relative efficiency and relative efficiency obtained with permanent protection (E), various values of u (when a high u indicates inelastic demand) a v (high v indicates strong diseconomies of scale in production). average life-time of a copyright, t_0, is assumed to be 5 years, the discount rate r = .10. (Case of a <u>nonlinear</u> demand curve.)

cases, where costs do not increase prohibitively with an expansion of output, it turns out that a reliance on profit motive of private firms does not help to generate an amount of computer software close to the social optimum. Even when these firms are given just the proper amount of property right protection, not too little and not too much, it will still be observed that many potential investments in the development of computer software, which are worthwhile to be undertaken from the point of view of society as a whole, will be unprofitable for any one firm. The deeper reason for this state of affairs is, of course, the public goods aspect of information, which can be shared without being used up.

These findings do not imply that a copyright system for computer software is a bad idea, and should be abandoned in favor of the current reliance on trade secret laws. For reasons expounded elsewhere in this report, trade secrets are even worse from the point of view of public welfare. What these results mean is that if the software industry has a certain cost and demand structure (moderate diseconomies of scale and elastic demand), then a reliance on private enterprise to produce a desirable amount of computer software will exact a high price from society. Whether such demand and cost conditions prevail in the computer software industry has to be determined from empirical observation. We hope that this study has indicated how important it is to undertake such an empirical investigation.

E. Protection vs. Public Subsidies for the Production of Software

As we have seen at the end of the previous section, in some cases the granting of a monopoly to producers of computer software for a period of optimal length can yield a contribution to public welfare which comes close to what would be possible in principle through government planning. But in some other cases, especially when demand for computer software is quite elastic, the welfare loss caused by protection of 1000 years reduces welfare only very slightly over a patent of optimal duration, which we found to lie between 6 and 20 years, depending on the parameter assumptions. But as we have seen, these findings critically depend on the model assumptions made.

If it should turn out from empirical observations that private firms do not produce the optimal amount of computer software, because many projects that would be worthwhile to undertake from the viewpoint of society as a whole are not profitable to an individual firm, even if it is granted a monopoly of limited duration, then it is worth it to consider whether alternatives to statutory protection should be explored. Among other possibilities we think primarily of increased public support for the production of computer software, at universities and other non-profit research organizations.

If the development of new computer software is supported with public funds, there is no need to grant a monopoly of a certain duration to the producer, and new computer programs and data bases can be made available immediately to all potential users and benefit the entire economy. Of course, public funds must come from somewhere, and they will have to be financed through taxes imposed by the government. But taxes can be spread among a large group of firms and other users, scaled according to each one's ability to pay, and they do not discourage potential users of software to the same extent as a price charged under a monopoly.

In a related study, two of the coauthors of this report[1] have shown that in a simple economic model with innovation the economy grows faster if innovation is sponsored by the government and the results are made available to everybody, than if the government grants

---

[1]See "Optimal Lags in a Schumpeterian Innovation Process" by W.J. Baumol and D.M. Fischer, mimio, New York University, 1976.

a patent of optimal duration to innovators and leaves innovation to private firms. In the system with a patent, less will be invested in innovation than is socially optimal. It was also found that the loss in welfare resulting from the misallocation of resources under a temporary monopoly is considerably larger than the monopoly profits earned by the innovating firm.

In the model studied in Baumol and Fischer, innovation played a central role in the entire economy, and a short-fall in the amount of innovation forthcoming led to a retardation of the growth of the whole economy. Even a slight reduction in the annual growth rate will ultimately make a great difference in the output level of the economy, if the growth rate is compounded year after year over an extended period.

If we look specifically at computer software, and not innovations in general, then the effect on the U.S. economy of underproduction in that sector will be less serious, at least for the present time, since the software industry amounts to less than one percent of all economic activities. We would therefore not expect a noticeable slowdown in economic growth to result, even if there is some measurable loss of welfare because less software is being produced than would be socially desireable. But this situation could change if our economy were to rely more and more on computers and automation. And trends indicate that this will indeed soon be the case. We shall return to this point in the final paragraphs of this section.

Of course, a system of publicly financed production of computer software is not without problems of its own. Having the government pay for the production of computer software and make it available for free to everybody on request eliminates the test of the market, whether a newly produced software package meets a real demand. Once this test for profitability is eliminated, it is necessary to replace it by equivalent, or if possible better criteria to evaluate which activities in the software field deserve to be supported. Without any screening, researchers will have a tendency to do what is interesting rather than what is needed for economic progress.

What type of activities in the software field should be supported with public funds? As was discussed in Chapter III-B, firms who develop software which is very similar to what already exists, simply to capture a share of a lucrative market for themselves without contributing to an increase in public welfare, will not be able to justify such activities for public support. But other institutions do deserve to receive government support in the public interest. Among them will be especially those who are engaged in highly innovative activities which hold potentially great promises for uncovering new opportunities. These activities are more risky, and their benefits may be realized only in the more distant future, making them commercially less attractive. Among the type of projects primarily deserving public support are the development of new computer algorithms; the mathematical specification of algorithms in unambiguous form; the development of translating systems which allow programs to be written in machine independent form, without reference to the specific hardware used; the development of more flexible programming languages, which are free of artificial restrictions stemming from historical developments; the automation of the programming process itself, allowing a user to specify only what would be needed to explain to an intelligent person what a program is designed to do, and leaving all the details of memory allocation, efficient coding, etc. to a powerful compiler; and, finally, research in artificial intelligence, which may one day make feasible new types of thought processes which we would never have imagined.

In the absence of a commercial test of what is demanded, there ought to be a constant dialogue between users and developers of new software. to assure that the needs of users are met.

An alternative to either statutory protection or government support is the reliance on trade secrecy to give producers of software sufficient financial incentives, which is the current situation. Trade secret laws, which allow firms to conclude binding agreements among each other about conditions for the sale and lease of computer software, imply that there is some period of protection of a random duration and of decreasing efficiency, as the number of imitations increases. The secret may be lost through unauthorized users, for example an employee who changes his job and keeps a copy of a computer program developed by his previous company. The resulting random period of protection will hardly happen to be of optimal length. But what is even more serious, the lack of public disclosure of computer programs, out of fear of unauthorized use, reduces the revenue a producer might win from sales. Also, software producers tend to undertake efforts to make programs obscure and difficult to transfer from one machine to another, in an effort to discourage unauthorized users.[1] Programs which are poorly written in order to prevent others from using them also make it much more difficult for the firm who developed the programs to maintain and modify them.

All of these effects (the lack of public disclosure and the obscure programming style) will tend to reduce social welfare. For these reasons we do not believe that reliance on trade secrecy in the field of computer software is a desirable state of affairs. However, the advantages of a copyright system, or of public support for the development of computer software, must be weighed against the administrative costs of these systems, which may be higher than for a system of trade secrets.

Let us add here a few remarks on the relative merits of a patent vs. a copyright system. One may argue that what is essential about a computer program is the idea behind it, not the specific form it assumes, as is the case with literary works, and that therefore patenting of

---

[1]Some ways in which this is done were discussed in Chapter III-A.

computer algorithms is more appropriate than a copyright. But this could endanger creativity. A law that grants property rights to producers of computer software should be formulated so as to prohibit any deliberate copying, which is an unambiguous violation. But it should not prohibit anyone from developing new programs, based only on ideas generally available in the scientific literature, and on a programmer's own original ideas. Such a policy would unduly hamper progress. For example, methods for the solution of linear programs are described in many standard textbooks. It should not be against the law to translate any such algorithm into a program, only because someone else has done this before. Only if it is obvious that the program has been copied from a copyrighted code should this be prohibited. People may well be expected to be honest, and it is perfectly reasonable to request that before anyone copies someone else's code, he assure himself whether he is entitled to do so, or may have to pay a fee to the copyright holder. But it would be unreasonable to expect from a creative person that before he develops a new computer program he should check whether anybody in the entire nation has ever written a similar program, and that he might therefore be liable of (unwitting) imitation. Such a provision of the law would be a paralyzing fetter on creative minds. For this reason, and because of the difficulty to prove the novelty for a patentable item, we consider a copyright law to be preferable to a patent law for computer software.

Is there any empirical information on how the amount of consumers' and producers' surplus from computer software obtained in reality compares with what is theoretically feasible? We have seen that in order to achieve the theoretical maximum of social welfare, all those software projects which yield benefits to society higher than the costs of production ought to be undertaken. Our analysis showed that since the revenue to a producer is only some fraction of the benefits to society, he will produce less software than is optimal for society. Some of the projects near the borderline of profitability will have a benefit to cost ratio greater than unity for society, but a revenue to cost ratio of less than one for the firm, and will therefore not be undertaken.[1] But from our theoretical analysis we would expect that, at least in the case of protection, the producer's revenue is a reasonably large fraction of the social benefits,[2] and that therefore all those projects whose social benefits substantially exceed their costs will be undertaken, even by private firms. But an empirical sutdy recently performed by Mathematica, Inc. shows evidence that this is not true.[3]

NASA developed a computer program, called NASTRAN, for the stability of flying rockets and their resistance to stress and vibrations of various frequencies. The same program can also be used to study the structural stability of airplanes and large buildings, for example a building's ability to withstand shocks from earthquakes of various amplitudes and frequencies. NASA made this program available for free to any individual or firm who wanted to use it. The costs to NASA for developing this program (in constant 1976 dollars, at an annual discount rate of 5 percent) were equal to 12 million dollars. The estimated economic benefits to all the firms who used it were estimated at $684 million. This corresponds to a benefit to cost ratio of 58:1. Doubtless, sooner or later someone would have undertaken to develop a similar project, given its great economic advantages. For the calculation of the above benefit to cost ratio, it was assumed that NASA's contribution only accelerated this development by 4 years. If it is assumed that it would have taken 10 years until an equivalent program had become

---

[1] On the order of about 50 percent, depending on the assumptions about the shape of the demand curve made.

[2] This is true, to various extents, both for the case of trade secrecy and of copyright protection.

[3] See "Quantifying the Benefits to the National Economy from Secondary Applications of NASA Technology," prepared for NASA by Mathematica, Inc., June 30, 1975.

available, then the benefit to cost ratio increases to a staggering 145:1. A few large firms, such as Ford Motor Company and Computer Sciences Corporation estimated their annual benefits from using the program to be comparable to its production costs of $12 million.

The question arises why did no private firm spend the resources to develop such a program, given its high benefits? There are a number of possible reasons. First of all, it is impossible for a producer of software to realize all the benefits himself, through sales, because of the public goods nature of computer software. In addition, it is difficult to market a software package and sell it to all potential users, even to those who could derive benefits exceeding the sales price, because it is difficult to convince the management of a firm of the benefits of something new and unfamiliar. NASA had an advantage in this respect insofar as its prestigious name will be taken as a güarantee for quality by many users. Furthermore, if something is free, many potential users will be willing to take the risk of spending some time to try it out, and as they get to know it, they begin to appreciate it. This still leaves unexplained the fact that some large companies, who by themselves derived higher benefits from the program than its production costs, still did not invest the resources to develop something equivalent. A possible explanation is that top management in those companies is overly conservative and only willing to invest in something which has immediate tangible benefits, but they invest too little in more fundamental research and development.

Another area, where most of the fundamental research and innovation is performed at universities or other government supported research institutions, is agriculture. Most of the new seed strains, insecticides, or fertilizers have been developed at public non-profit institutions, not by farmers.[1] Not even large agribusiness enterprises invest an appreciable amount in innovation. Observations of this sort would indicate that governments do have to assume an important role in supporting basic research and innovation, including probably certain types of computer software.

One form, among others, in which the government could support the development of new software is through open competitions, with rewards for the most elegant and practical solutions. An institution similar to Research Applied to National Needs (RANN) could solicit proposals for important problems that are waiting for a solution. It could then send out and publish these lists, with a deadline for submitting porposed solutions in the form of computer programs, written in a standard language, which do the required job. The authors of the best solutions could be rewarded, and the results published and made available to the general public without payment. Many programmers have great talent in finding an ingenious solution to a problem they are given, but lack the ability to market the products of their work. They normally end up doing repetitive types of work with very narrow, specialized applications, for some company. But if they were given an opportunity to solve problems of a more general nature with wider applications, and could make their programs available to anyone who can use them, they would be able to make a much greater contribution to public welfare.

How important is it to have effective institutions to encourage the production of new computer software? The costs of computer hardware, per arithmetic operation, have declined steadily at a rate of 55

---

[1] According to a report in the New York Times of April 14, 1977, a research team at Michigan State University has isolated a substance called triacontanol from alfalfa, which in the tiny amounts of 4 milligrams per acre can increase the yield of many food crops by 10 to 40 percent. The enormous cost savings that this discovery can bring to people all over the world are hard to imagine.

percent per year over the last 20 years,[1] and there are good indications that this trend will continue for some time to come.[2] With this trend, computers will begin to play an increasing role in our daily lives. Perhaps the most important role they can play lies in the automation of many production processes, which can free people to devote their time to more creative activities than monotonous, repetitive tasks. Computers will play an increasingly important role in the area of storage and transmission of information, potentially replacing libraries and the publishing industry as we know it today. Other areas where automation has wideranging applications are banking operations, transportation (with automatically guided public transportation there is no need for drivers), in communication (human telephone operators will no longer be needed), even in agriculture where plans exist for robots to take over the decreasing number of tasks still left to people.

Automation is seen by many people today as a threat to their jobs and income, and is resisted on those grounds. This is understandable, because the potential benefits from automation have not always been shared equally in the past, benefitting employers at the expense of employees who were replaced by machines. But potentially automation could be used to increase the income and reduce the workload of everybody, not just a priviledged few. We anticipate that in time workable solutions to these problems of equity will be found.

With an increase in automation, the computer and software industry will not be limited to a few percent of GNP, but will become a major,

---

[1]This figure is taken from Economics of Academic Libraries by W.J. Baumol and M. Marcus (American Council on Education, Washington, DC: 1973). Data used covered the years 1951-1967, but a similar trend has persisted since then.

[2]Many advances in the miniaturization of large scale integrated circuits have already been made, but not yet fully exploited in large computers available today. A price collapse, such as the one that took place for pocket calculators over the last few years, is likely to follow for more powerful computers as well.

perhaps even the major industry. Then it will be extremely important that the economy can develop, with a sufficient amount of easily usable software available, rather than still being plagued by incompatibilities between different types of hardware and different conventions on computer software[1] and by a sprawling proliferation of programming languages.[2] A failure to solve these problems satisfactorily today may be a major retarding factor for economic development in the future.

APPENDIX IV-1

Derivation of the Optimal Protection Period for a Linear Demand Curve

We shall calculate here what period of copyright protection maximizes social welfare, given demand for software can be represented by a linear demand curve (as shown in Figure 1a). To do this, we will compute the relative efficiency of any given period of protection, where the relative efficiency is defined as the ratio between the amount of social welfare forthcoming under a given duration of protection, and the maximum amount of welfare that is possible in principle with ideal central planning. Then we will determine the optimal protection period T^* which maximizes the relative efficiency.

In order to calculate the amount of welfare generated by any given protection period, T, we will first derive the maximum revenue $R(T)$ that the producer of a unit of software can generate through monopoly pricing during the period T. Then, by setting the incremental cost of the last unit of software produced equal to revenue per unit, we can calculate what amount $X(T)$ of software the firm will produce. Next we will compute the discounted stream of consumers' and producer's

---

[1]Such incompatibilities make the life of programmers unnecessarily difficult and frustrating, and cause an enormous waste in human talent.

[2]A survey conducted by the Office of Naval Research revealed that the Pentagon is using more than 1000 different programming languages!

surplus, S(T), forthcoming before and after the expiration of the protection period from one unit of software. By multiplying the amount of software produced, X(T), by the surplus generated per unit, S(T), and subtracting total production costs, C(T), we obtain the amount of welfare, W(T), resulting from a protection period of length T.

In order to calculate the maximum amount of social welfare feasible under the given cost and demand structure, W*, we assume that the amount of software produced, X*, is determined in such a way that the incremental cost of the last unit is equal to the social benefit generated per unit. It is assumed that software will be made available for free to all potential users, so that the consumers' surplus is equal to the entire area under the demand curve (e.g., area OQ_0P_0 in Figure 4). Again, the maximum possible amount of social welfare to be generated, W*, is equal to

$$W^* = X^*S^* - C^*,$$

where X* is the amount of software produced, S* is the surplus generated per unit, and C* is the total cost of producing X* units of software.

For guide reference, we list here all the essential equations of the model, using the same numbering as in section B of this chapter:

(1a) $$p^{(o)} = \begin{cases} p_0 \ (1-q/q_o & \text{if } q \leq q_o \\ 0 & \text{if } q > q_o \end{cases}$$

linear demand curve

(2) $$p^{(t)}(q) = p^{(o)}(q)e^{-t/t_o}$$

exponential decay of the value of a unit of software

(3) $$MC(x) = c \cdot x^v$$

incremental cost of the xth unit of software produced. The exponent v indicates how rapidly marginal costs increase with increasing output.

(4) $p^{(t)}(q) = 0 \quad \text{for } t > T$

expiration of the monopoly after T time units.

(5) $\frac{d}{dp}(p \cdot q) = 0$

for the monopoly price $p = p^*$

(6) $R(T) = \int_0^T q^* p^* e^{-t/t_o} e^{-rt} dt$

monopoly revenue during protection period T, given the discount rate is r and the average useful lifetime of a unit of computer software it t_o.

(7) $c \cdot X(T)^v = R(T)$

marginal revenue equals marginal cost

(8) $W(t) = \int_0^{q^*} p^{(t)} dq \quad \text{for } t \leq T$

consumers' and producer's surplus generated per time unit, per unit of software, during the protection period.

(8') $W'(t) = \int_0^{\infty} p^{(t)} dq \quad \text{for } t > T$

consumers' and producer's surplus generated per time unit, per unit of software after expiration of the protection period.

(9) $S(T) = \int_0^T W(t) e^{-rt} dt + W'(t) e^{-rt} dt$

discounted stream of consumers' and producer's surplus generated per unit of software, during and after the period of protection

(10) $C(T) = \int_0^{X(T)} MC(x) dx$

total cost of producing X(T) units of software

(11) $W(T) = X(T) S(T) - C(T)$

amount of social welfare generated through a protection period of length T (by a single firm).

We begin by calculating the amount of software a producer will supply, and the price he will charge per unit, as long as he is granted a monopoly. If the demand curve is given by

$$q = q_o(1-p/p_o),$$

the linear shape shown in Figure 1a, then the revenue per time unit that the monopolist can earn, if he charges price p, is

$$r(p) = p \cdot q = pq_o(1-p/p_o).$$

By taking the derivative of r(p) with respect to p and setting it equal to zero, it is easy to see that the price which maximizes the monopolist's revenue in this case is equal to $p^* = p_o/2$. This applies at time $t = 0$. After a time span t has elapsed, all the prices consumers are willing to pay decline by a factor $f(t) = e^{-t/t_o}$. The monopoly price also declines to

$$p^{*(t)} = p^*e^{-t/t_o} = \frac{p_o}{2} e^{-t/t_o} \quad ,$$

but the quantity q^* sold by the monopolist remains unchanged.

The discounted stream of revenue a monopolist can earn during the life-time of copyright protection is equal to

$$R(T) = \int_o^T q^*p^*e^{-t/t_o} e^{-rt}dt$$

$$= \frac{q_o p_o}{4} \int_o^T e^{-(r+1/t_o)t}dt$$

Using the notation

$$s = r + 1/t_o \ ,$$

we obtain

$$R(T) = \frac{q_o p_o}{4} \int_o^T e^{-st}dt$$

The total cost of producing $X(T)$ units of software is

$$C(T) = \int_0^{X(T)} c \cdot x^v dx = c \cdot X(T)^{v+1}/(v+1) .$$

Finally, the amount of welfare generated through a protection period of length T is equal to

$$W(T) = X(T)S(T) - C(T).$$

Using the notation

$$z = 1 - e^{-st} ,$$

and substituting all the expressions we obtain

$$W(T) = \left(\frac{p_o q_o}{4sc} z \right)^{1/v} \cdot \frac{p_o q_o}{2s} (1-z/4) - \frac{c}{v+1} \left(\frac{p_o q_o}{4sc} z \right)^{(v+1)/v} .$$

We now go on to calculate the maximum amount of social welfare that can be achieved if the government purchases the socially optimal amount of software from the firm under consideration,[1] and makes it available without payment to the entire society. In that case, we have the set of equations

$$(17) \qquad S^* = \int_0^\infty W'(t)e^{-rt}dt,$$

$$(18) \qquad X^* = \left(\frac{1}{c} S^* \right)^{1/v}$$

$$(19) \qquad C^* = \frac{c}{v+1} (X^*)^{v+1} , \quad \text{and}$$

$$(20) \qquad W^* = X^*S^* - C^* .$$

We find

$$S^* = \int_0^\infty (1/2)p_o q_o e^{-(r+1/t_o)t} dt = \frac{p_o q_o}{2} \cdot \frac{1}{s} .$$

[1]The way this would happen in practice is that the government sets a price for software it purchases, which is equal to the estimated marginal social benefit, and then lets the firm produce as much as it wants at the given price.

$$= \frac{q_o p_o}{4} \cdot \frac{1}{s} (1-e^{-sT}).$$

To find the amount being produced by the monopolist, $X(T)$, we set marginal revenue equal to marginal cost:

$$c \cdot X(T)^v = R(T) \quad \text{or} \quad X(T) = (\frac{1}{c} R(T))^{1/v}$$

At time $t = 0$, the producer's surplus (corresponding to area OQRP in Figure 4) will be equal to $p^*q^* = p_o q_o/4$. The consumers' surplus (the small triangle corresponding to area PRP_0 in Figure 4) will be equal to $p_o q_o/8$. Thus, at time $t = 0$, the consumers' and producer's surplus generated by one unit of software is equal to $(3/8)p_o q_o$. At time t during the protection period, the contribution to the surplus is

$$W(t) = (3/8)p_o q_o \, e^{-t/t_o} .$$

After protection has elapsed, the contribution to the consumers' surplus (area OQ_0P_0 in Figure 8) is equal to

$$W'(t) = (1/2)p_o q_o \, e^{-t/t_o} .$$

The discounted stream of consumers' and producer's surplus generated by one unit of software is equal to

$$S(T) = \int_o^T W(t)e^{-rt}dt + \int_T^\infty W'(t)e^{-rt}dt$$

$$= \int_o^T (3/8)p_o q_o e^{-(r+1/t_o)t}dt + \int_T^\infty (1/2)p_o q_o e^{-(r+1/t_o)t}dt$$

$$= (3/8)p_o q_o \cdot \frac{1}{s}(1-e^{-st}) + (1/2)p_o q_o \cdot \frac{1}{s} e^{-st}$$

$$= (1/2)p_o q_o \cdot \frac{1}{s} - (1/8)p_o q_o \frac{1}{s}(1-e^{-st}) ,$$

where $s = r + 1/t_o$.

The optimal amount of software to be produced is

$$X^* = \left(\frac{1}{c} S^* \right)^{1/v} = \left(\frac{p_o q_o}{2sc} \right)^{1/v} .$$

The cost of production is equal to

$$C^* = \frac{c}{v+1} \left(\frac{p_o q_o}{2sc} \right)^{(v+1)/v} .$$

The maximum feasible amount of welfare is therefore

$$W^* = X^* S^* - C^* = \left(\frac{p_o q_o}{2sc} \right)^{1/v} \cdot \frac{p_o q_o}{2s} - \frac{c}{v+1} \left(\frac{p_o q_o}{2sc} \right)^{(v+1)/v}$$
$$= \left(\frac{1}{c} \right)^{1/v} \left(\frac{p_o q_o}{2s} \right)^{(v+1)/v} \left(1 - \frac{1}{v+1} \right) .$$

We are now able to compute a coefficient of relative efficiency, $E(T)$, for a protection period of length T:

$$E(T) = W(T)/W^* .$$

After some algebraic manipulations, one will find

$$(15) \qquad E(T) = \frac{1}{v} \left(\frac{z}{2}\right)^{1/v} \left(v+1 - \frac{v+3}{4} z\right),$$

where $z = 1 - e^{-sT}$.

The optimal protection period T^* is the one which maximizes the relative efficiency $E(T)$. It corresponds to the optimal value z^* for z. Taking the derivative of $E(T)$ with respect to z, and setting it equal to zero, we obtain

$$\frac{d}{dz} E(T) = \frac{1}{v} \left(\frac{z}{2}\right)^{1/v-1} \left(\frac{1}{2}\right) \cdot \frac{1}{v} \left(v+1 - \frac{v+3}{4} z\right) + \left(\frac{z}{2}\right)^{1/v} \cdot \frac{1}{v}\left(- \frac{v+3}{4}\right) = 0.$$

By simplifying and solving for $z = z^*$ we find

$$z^* = \frac{4}{v+3}$$

Substituting back

$$z^* = 1 - e^{-sT^*},$$

we finally get the formula

$$(13) \qquad T^* = \frac{1}{s} \ln \frac{v+3}{v-1} = \frac{1}{r+1/t_o} \ln \frac{v+3}{v-1} .$$

APPENDIX IV-2

Derivation of the Optimal Protection Period for an Example of a Nonlinear Demand Curve.

In this Appendix we will calculate the relative efficiency of a period of copyright protection T and the optimal duration T* for the case of the nonlinear demand curve shown in Figure 1b. All the steps are essentially the same as in Appendix IV-1, except that the demand equation (1a) is replaced by the equation

$$\text{(1b)} \qquad p^{(o)}(q) = k(q+q_o)^{-u}, \qquad \text{where } u > 1.$$

We will therefore limit ourselves to indicating the major steps in the calculation, and refer for their motivation to Appendix IV-1.

To maximize his revenue from each unit of software produced, the monopolist, at time $t = 0$, will sell q^* copies of each unit of software he has produced, where for $q = q^*$ we have

$$\text{(5)} \qquad \frac{d}{dq}(p^{(o)}(q) \cdot q) = 0 = \frac{d}{dq}(k(q+q_o)^{-u}q)$$

$$= kq(-u)(q+q_o)^{-u-1} + k(q+q_o)^{-u}$$

This yields the monopoly quantity and price

$$q^* = \frac{q_o}{u-1} \quad \text{and} \quad p^* = k\left(\frac{u}{u-1}q_o\right)^{-u} .$$

The revenue earned by the monopolist is equal to

$$\text{(6)} \qquad R(T) = \int_0^T p^*q^*e^{-(r+1/t_o)t} = p^*q^* \int_o^T e^{-sT}dt = \frac{kq_o}{u-1}\left(\frac{uq_o}{u-1}\right)^{-u} \cdot \frac{1}{s}(1-e^{-sT}).$$

We will again use the abbreviation

$$z = 1-e^{-sT} .$$

By setting revenue per unit equal to marginal cost, we obtain for the quantity produced

(7) $$X(T) = (\frac{1}{c} R(T))^{1/v} .$$

During the protection period, consumers' and producer's surplus generated by one unit of software is equal to

(8) $$W(t) = e^{-t/t_o} \int_o^{q^*} p dq = e^{-t/t_o} k \int_o^{q^*} (q+q_o)^{-u} dq.$$

Solving the integral and inserting $q^* = q_o/(u-1)$ we obtain

$$W(t) = e^{-t/t_o} \cdot \frac{k}{u-1} (q_o^{1-u} - (\frac{uq_o}{u-1})^{1-u}) .$$

Similarly we find for the surplus after the expiration of the protection period

(8') $$W'(t) = e^{-t/t_o} \cdot \frac{k}{u-1} q_o^{1-u} .$$

The discounted stream of consumers' and producer's surplus generated by a unit of software is

(9) $$S(T) = \int_o^T W(t)e^{-rt}dt + \int_T^{\infty} W'(t)e^{-rt}dt = \frac{k}{u-1} \cdot \frac{1}{s} (q_o^{1-u} - (\frac{uq_o}{u-1})^{1-u} \cdot z)$$

with $z = 1 - {}^{e-st}$.

Total cost is given by

(10) $$C(T) = \frac{c}{v+1} X(T)^{v+1} .$$

Combining the expressions (6), (7), (9) and (10) yields

(11) $$W(T) = X(T)S(T) - C(T),$$

$$= [\frac{kq_o}{sc(u-1)} (\frac{uq_o}{u-1})^{-u} z]^{1/v} [\frac{k}{s(u-1)} (q_o^{1-u} - (\frac{uq_o}{u-1})^{1-u} z)]$$

$$- \frac{c}{v+1} [\frac{kq_o}{sc(u-1)} (\frac{uq_o}{u-1})^{-u} z]^{(v+1)/v} .$$

For the maximum social welfare feasible under public financing we evaluate formulas (17) to (20) and obtain

$$(17) \qquad S^* = \int_0^\infty W'(t)e^{-rt}dt = \frac{k}{s(u-1)} q_o^{1-u}$$

$$(18) \qquad X^* = \left(\frac{1}{c} S^*\right)^{1/v} = \left(\frac{k}{sc(u-1)} q_o^{1-u}\right)^{1/v}$$

$$(19) \qquad C^* = \frac{c}{v+1} (X^*)^{v+1}$$

$$(20) \qquad W^* = X^*S^* - C^* = \frac{v}{v+1} c\left(\frac{k}{sc(u-1)} q_o^{1-u}\right)^{(v+1)/v} .$$

We can now compute the relative efficiency E(T) of a given protection period T as

$$(16) \qquad E(T) = W(T)/W^* = \frac{v+1}{v} (yz)^{1/v} \left(1 - \frac{u}{u-1} yz\right) - \frac{1}{v} (yz)^{(v+1)/v}$$

where z stands for $1 - e^{-sT}$ and y for $(u/(u-1))^{-u}$.

In order to find the optimal protection period T*, we take the derivative of the coefficient of relative efficiency, E(T), with respect to z and set it equal to zero. This yields

$$z^* = \left(\frac{u}{u-1}\right)^u \cdot \frac{u-1}{uv+2u-1} \quad \text{and} \quad T^* = -\frac{1}{s} \ln (1 - z^*).$$

By replacing s by $r + 1/t_o$ we obtain equation (14) in Section IV-B.

An Analysis of Computer and Photocopying Copyright Issues from the Point of View of the General Public and the Ultimate Consumer

EXECUTIVE SUMMARY:

THE CONSUMER INTEREST IN APPLYING COPYRIGHT PROTECTION TO COMPUTER-BASED INFORMATION AND PHOTOCOPYING

THE EXPERIMENT

Public Interest Economics Center (PIE-C) and Public Interest Satellite As (PISA) are participating in a unique experiment in providing a federal agency informed consumer input. The issue is how would consumer interests be affect by changes in the copyright laws governing photocopying and computer based in mation.

In 1974, Congress, recognizing that new forms of communication or informa transfer, rapidly gaining in importance, might not fit neatly into the existi system of exclusive rights, created the National Commission of New Technologi Uses of Copyrighted Works (CONTU). The Commission is charged with investigat what changes in copyright law may be necessary to "assure...access to copyric works and to provide recognition of the rights of copyright owners" in regard the reproduction and use of copyrighted works, and the possible creation of r copyrightable items, by means of:

- automatic data processing systems, and
- machine reproduction.

For present purposes, this means:

- photocopying of copyrighted periodicals and books,
- use of computer programs or, more generally, computer "software",
- use and dissemination of copyrighted materials in computer data bases, and
- possible protection for new works of authorship created with the aid of computers.

By December 31, 1977, CONTU is required to submit to Congress a report, inclu recommendations for legislative and administrative action.

PIE-C is preparing, under contract, an analysis of the impacts of changes copyright laws in these areas of new technology. The project has two purpose to provide the basis for PIE-C testimony to the Commission in support of the public (or consumer) interest and perhaps, more far reaching, to provide othe public interest groups with information that will help them formulate and pre their positions on the issue. To reinforce the effort to provide opportunity informed public interest participation, CONTU has also contracted with PISA t do three major things: to reach out to and inform public interest organizatio about CONTU's issues, to organize conferences among such groups to discuss th issues and to criticize drafts of the PIE-C report, and third, to present tes mony of its own on the public interest aspects of CONTU's policy choices.

A. INTRODUCTION

Article I, Section 8 of the United States Constitution states:

"The Congress shall have the Power...to promote the Progress of Science and useful Arts, by securing for limited Times to Authors and Inventors the exclusive Right to their respective Writings and Discoveries."

Under this authority Congress, early in United States history, established the copyright and patent systems, giving forms of exclusive rights to authors and inventors.

The copyright laws now in effect date from 1909. Over the years subsequent to 1909, the copyright system was expanded to incorporate several new forms, or uses, of creative works which were deemed to be eligible for protection as equivalent to more traditional "Writings" of authors. For example, copyright royalty fees are paid for the use of musical broadcasts to the general public over the radio. Not until 1976 did Congress enact a major revision of the 1909 statute. Public Law 94-553, a "General Revision of Copyright Law," will go into effect on January 1, 1978. One product of that statute is The National Commission on New Technological Uses of Copyrighted Works (CONTU).

A copyright gives its holder exclusive rights to use or sell the item in question. The scope of a copyright may, in general, be said to extend only to the way in which ideas are expressed, or their form, not to the ideas themselves. That is, an infringement occurs where a second "writing" is done that uses the same or similar written expressions, but not where only the same general idea is used. For example, it has been said that the basic plots used in novels are relatively few in number; plots cannot be protected, and innumerable copyrighted books can be produced by varying the way in which plots are expressed. The term of copyright protection granted an individual is the life of the author plus fifty years; a copyright issued to a corporation is valid for seventy-five years.

Patents, on the other hand, give exclusive rights to use of ideas contained in inventions. To be patented ideas must be original, have commercial value, and be non-obvious advances over existing knowledge. Hence, patents are more difficult to obtain but confer much stronger protection than do copyrights.

Copyrights (like patents) are grants of limited monopoly. They permit their owners to impose conditions on reproducing a work or to prevent copies from being made at all. Generally this means exacting a royalty(fee), but even if payments are not required by the holders, protection can still be used to prevent unauthorized changes from being made in the material, using it without attribution, or using it for specific purposes, such as advertising.

It is our belief, based on the information available to us, that copyrights would be used very little to prevent dissemination of information altogether. The major commercial use would be to impose royalties to maximize the income of copyright holders. This same use would be important to some other holders. In addition, many holders, especially non-commercial holders, would prefer that works be widely and freely distributed. To them, the major advantage of copyright protection would lie in controlling abuse of their work, obtaining rec through attribution or similar benefit.

The basic question to which this report is addressed is whether the inte of consumers would be advanced by increasing or decreasing the stringency of present copyright law as it applies either to photoreproduction of copyright materials or to computer based materials.

A number of associated questions emerged in the discussions with public advocates:

- Should any royalty charge be permitted?
- Should any royalty charge be permitted only for particular uses or users?
- Closely related, several participants asked whether and some urged that not-for-profit organizations, individuals or public interest groups should be exempt from payment of royalties, under some sort of fair use doctrine?
- Should research or development paid for by the government be subject to copyright assignable to private parties?
- Should copyrights be available only to individuals, as distinct from corporations or government entities?
- Since an individual or small firm can not be expected realistically to be able to prevent infringement by large corporations what, if any, adjustments in copyright law should be made?
- Will technology overtake us?

B. PIE-C'S GENERAL CONCLUSIONS

The key questions relate to the power to charge royalties. The PIE-C an strongly suggests that the answer to those questions differs between the pho copying and the computer areas:

- No royalty charge should be allowed on photocopying other than for resale,
- Copyrights with authority to charge royalties, and non-disclosure contracts should both be available to independent software firms,
- Neither should be available to large hardware manufacturers
- Copyrights should be available both on information incorporated in data bases and on material disseminated from them, including "computer created" works,

- To make copyright protection effective for individuals, non-profit organizations and small business, the federal government should explore means of assisting small copyright holders in protecting their copyrights.

More detailed conclusions follow the discussions of the major areas of concern. But it is important to note that the main conclusions in the two areas are substantially different.

C. <u>GENERAL ANALYSIS</u>

To focus on the question of how the interest of consumers would be affected by increasing or decreasing the power of providers of information to charge royalties for use of photocopying copyrighted works or for use of computer-based information, it is necessary to define consumer, the consumers' role and interest and the analytic issues presented. PIE-C defines "consumer" to mean the ultimate consumer, i.e., the individual or households, not for example, commercial customers of computer software companies. Although all people are consumers, most people play other economic roles as well, for example, as workers, investors, savers. We are concerned with people not in those roles but only in their function as consumers of goods and services for their own use.

The only legitimate function of economic activity is to increase (relative to what it would otherwise be) the well-being of the members of society. This means basically the well-being of consumers and workers. Because all costs of producing goods and services must be borne, in the end, predominantly by consumers or workers, their well-being tends to increase as the efficiency of the economy increases. Efficiency in this statement must be broadly defined to include all costs. In addition, it is consumers who ultimately benefit from the availability of any new product that is, in fact, of value.

The economy is becoming progressively more dependent on information; the production of information and its use in productive processes are expanding dramatically. This appears to be particularly true of computer-based information and of photocopied information, as well as of information for final consumption, such as entertainment and cultural "information." The consumers' interest lies in assuring that adequate amounts of information are produced and are made available for use, both in the present and in the future.

The institution of copyrights empowers providers of information to constrain its use. The justification for this governmentally-enforced system can be thought of as the holders' property "right" to his/her work, or as a necessary inducement to produce and disseminate intellectual creations which are of value to society. It is the latter which constitutes the economic rationale for providing copyright protection or other compensation for creativity.

In turn, the basis for granting monopoly in this area of the economy rests on a recognition that the products of intellectual work, which may be classi as "information", (where we are subsuming "entertainment" under information) constitute a special type of commodity. For most products (carrots, automob etc.) the producers are able to exact a price from every user by maintaining physical control of the objects until payment is assured. However, once a p of information exists in tangible form, it is physically possible to copy it without let or hindrance. Only if the producer of the information is provid with an enforceable property right, can it demand payment from all the benef aries who might copy it. This characteristic of intellectual work is referr as "non-exclusivity" (the producer cannot exclude all users from obtaining t benefit it may provide) or "non-appropriability" (the producer cannot approp a share of the benefits obtained by every user). In the case of information, there is a second problem: a large portion of the price that is paid for the material is not due to the costs of producing that copy of the work, but to the original efforts of creating the information in the first place. As a r once a copy of a piece of writing or programming, etc. has been made availab to the public, it can be reproduced at far less cost than that required to create it in the first place.

The social significance of such a situation would be that to the extent that creativity and the dissemination of creative work is stimulated by the prospect of monetary reward, publishing and other information-production wou tend to be curtailed below the optimal level--consumers would be provided wi less information than they would be willing to pay for.

For example, the price of a mass market mystery novel includes a per-volume royalty paid by the publisher to the author, as well as the costs of editing and the risks of market failure. Without the existence of copy-right protection, a second publisher could reprint the same novel at a pric lower than the first, reducing the author's return for his/her writing, and making it impossible for the publisher to recoup its total costs.

Within this general rationale for a copyright system, three basic issues appear to be relevant:

- To what degree (if any) does the supply of intellectual products respond to the monetary incentive of royalties?
- To the extent that the supply of information is dependent on royalties, there is a clear tradeoff--the greater the costs imposed on users of copyrighted material, the higher will be the returns to producers and the greater the supply of information. What return to creators will, over the long run, assure that the optimal amount of information will be made available? Higher prices to consumers will

raise the cost of using existing information and, hence, reduce its effective availability, but lower prices will tend to reduce production of future information. To the extent that new research or other creative work is dependent on using existing information, the problem is made complex: higher royalties exert some pressures on the production of new information.

- Given that producers of information respond to monetary incentives, is a system of exclusive rights to reproduction the best means of providing these incentives?

Stated alternatively, the question is: would each potential extension of copyright power contribute more to consumer welfare by stimulating the production and dissemination of new information than it costs in terms of availability of the presently existing stock and in increasing the cost of creating more information for the future?

One unifying theme does seem to apply in examining the entire range of issues identified above: the basic concept of monopoly. In economic policy--certainly within any form of market system--there is always a presumption against the granting or extension of monopoly power: the burden of proof is on him who would see monopoly expanded. While all copyrights confer a monopoly on reproduction of the specific item involved, the cost that such limited monopoly can impose on users of the material is restricted by the degree to which other, similar, sources of information can be substituted for any particular one. To use the example of mass-market novels again, for most of them the copyright confers little ability to charge a high price because there is substantial competition among them. There appear, in contrast, to be two primary categories in which substitution is low, permitting a high degree of marketpower.

- Individual ability allows the author to create an outstanding work, for which there is great demand even at prices well above cost. The desirability of copyright protection in such cases depends on the degree to which such talented individuals respond to the prospect of large monetary gains.
- A large corporation, or a few firms acting in collusion, have effective control over one of the information industries, or a specific market within an industry, allowing them to restrict output, thus raising prices and generating monopoly profits.

In such cases action of some form should be taken to break up the corporations or to control their monopoly.

We can say that increased copyright powers would serve the public (consumer) interest if:

- the supply of information is less than is socially optimal and if more stringent copyright authority would increase the supply toward that optimum,
- it were the most efficient way to do so,
- royalty payments reflect the value of the product to its users, and
- there are no significant barriers to entry into each information market in question.

The peculiar characteristic of non-appropriability strongly suggests that without copyright or other protection the supply of information would tend to be less than is socially optimal. Public subsidization of the production of information would tend, in the opposite direction, to make the amount of information produced exceed the optimum level as determined by the market. However, for purposes of analyzing the desirability of copyright protection, it seems appropriate to assume that public subsidization reflects an effort to raise the production of information above the market level to some politically determined, more general concept of a socially optimal level.

Having greater freedom to impose royalties, producers of any kind of information could be expected to use it only if doing so would increase their revenue. In the absence of severe constraints on market entry, any increase in revenues above the current levels would increase the supply of information--unless producers were totally insensitive to monetary returns.

In light of the fact that the payers of royalties would, in all practical cases, appear to be those who intended to benefit from having a copy of the material, there is little chance (with an important exception in the case of photocopying) that the royalty could exceed the value (at the margin) to the customer on whom the burden fell.

For all these reasons it appears that there may be some justification for expanding the role of copyright. Several questions remain, however:

- To what extent are producers of the relevant form of information responsive to the prospects of monetary reward?
- Are there more efficient ways of achieving the same ends?
- Are there significant barriers to entry in the relevant markets?

The remainder of this summary discusses the specific conditions applicable to the areas of computer software, computer data bases, computer-created works and photocopying, and will present PIE-C's policy recommendations, while identifying some major unresolved questions.

D. COMPUTER SOFTWARE

Computer programming, or production of computer software, is a recent, but rapidly growing, form of information. While clearly possessing aspects of human expression, software constitutes a significant break with previous modes of communication that have heretofore come under copyright law. The instructions are primarily directed towards the mechanical operations of a machine, rather than directly to human users. As a result, programs can be considered "processes which might well be eligible for patent protection.

While software may represent as much as one-half to three-quarters of total computer costs for computer users in the United States, the vast majority of software development is currently done in-house, by firms and other institutions for their own use, by their own employees. Copyright (or other) protection is largely irrelevant for such software used only internally.

Separately-purchased software "packages" are taking a rapidly growing share of the market. While the giant corporations which dominate the "hardware" (the actual computer) market--IBM, Burroughs, etc.--sell a substantial portion of total program packages, their positions are steadily being eroded by the "independent" software firms, and among the latter there is very little concentration, the largest firms having very small market shares. The overall structur of the software industry is, then, unclear, as the hardware firms have historical possessed monopolistic advantages but, due to substantial freedom of entry, are gradually losing their dominant share.

Unlike the production of written works, the production of computer software is not undertaken primarily by authors working independently but is done by employees of user or producer corporations. It appears certain, then, that the supply of separately purchased software is responsive to the prospects of monetary reward. However, copyright or patent protection is not the only method of providing such incentives.

The industry currently relies heavily on trade secrecy. One survey of independent software firms showed that the vast majority use some form of contractual licensing arrangements with their customers, by which the purchasers agree not to disclose the contents of software packages to other firms--"trade secrecy" contracts. About three-quarters of responding firms felt that such arrangements are "somewhat", or "completely" effective in protecting their software against unauthorized copying and use.

Copyrights on software have been available, by decision of the Register of Copyrights, since 1964. While a number of firms do file copyright notices on their program packages, it appears that this is done mostly as a precautionary measure without any real confidence that the copyright alone provides effective protection.

Very few instances were cited in which firms viewed the fear of inadequa protection as being a barrier to the development of programs representing a "significant level of innovation."

Available evidence on proprietary protection, along with the rapid grow of the industry, suggests, then, that methods for retaining control of softw products are in most cases adequate to give firms the necessary incentive to produce. Major reasons for this appear to be that currently most packaged software is either custom-designed or appropriate only for a limited number customers, and that separately-purchased softwear constitutes only a very small percentage of total automatic data-processing (ADP) costs for computer using firms (due to the predominance of in-house development and other intern personnel costs). Program purchasers simply do not find the potential savin worth the effort and risk of trying to obtain unauthorized copies rather tha buying from the software provider;

The major questions in software protection are:

- Does the predominant system of licensing (trade secrecy) have inefficiencies which would be reduced or avoided by a statute making copyrights clearly available for software?
- If the above is done, should trade secrecy agreements be banned?
- Should patents, rather than or in addition to copyrights, be available for software?
- Is software a unique enough form of information to justify a new form of statutory protection designed specifically for it?

A number of arguments suggest that trade secrecy is less satisfactory--socially less efficient--than are copyrights. These include:

- arranging and enforcing contracts involves substantial "transaction costs", raising prices to purchasers and reducing the supply of software,
- maintenance of such contracts has "economies of scale," so that large producers can use them more effectively than can small ones, tending to create concentration within the industry,
- the need for maintenance of trade secrecy tends to steer producers away from general-purpose and mass-marketed software, towards specialized programs which face less risk of disclosure, and
- the term of protection is unregulated; thus, if contracts are effective, the term is unlimited.

While conclusive data are not available, there is no evidence to show that transaction costs are a significant fraction of industry costs, or that large firms have important advantages in enforcement. In fact, industry trends suggest just the opposite. Moreover, there is little reason for believing that copyrights, with the bringing of infringement suits still being the responsibility of their holders, would change matters noticeably.

Contractual licenses do indeed confer an unlimited term of protection. However, under copyright law, with a 75-year protection period for corporate products, the term is effectively unlimited anyway, since no piece of software is likely to be commercially valuable for anything approaching that many years.

Thus, for the kinds of software largely produced to date, consumers appear to have little interest in either the constriction or expansion of copyright protection. However, copyrights do seem to have a substantial advantage over trade secrecy for mass-marketed programs, which are beginning to emerge with major potential. Clearly firms selling large volumes of software over-the-counter could not enforce non-disclosure contracts. Copyrights, however, automatically provide important protection against unauthorized copying. An analogy with records and tapes sold at retail is appropriate. While a copyright does not prevent single copies from being made using home tape-recorders, it does greatly inhibit competing firms from reproducing and selling copyrighted works on a mass scale. The same would presumably be true for software. Hence, making copyrights clearly available for programs appears to be desirable.

Even with the availability of unambiguous copyright protection we do not find it desirable to ban all secrecy contracts. Independent software firms are likely to continue to find secrecy more effective than copyrights in a large proportion of cases. Again, given close competition among firms, it is in the interests of software buyers and ultimately of consumers that sellers have the option of using one or the other (or both) means of protection.

Software innovations do have characteristics which are essentially indistinguishable from those for which patents are traditionally granted, and the standard justification for patents--to stimulate the creation of new processes and inventions--would appear to apply here. However, without more extended analysis of the patent system as a whole, this alternative is best put to the side.

Software's dual traits as both a "writing" and a "process" for use by a machine have led to an argument that it should not come under the same law as forms of expression designed for direct human communication. An example of a possible new form of protection would be a middle ground between copyrights and patents, in which "ideas" would receive protection but there would be no ban on independent development of software containing a given idea. In practice it is questionable if determinations could be made wether an innovation had been developed independently or "stolen." Also trade secrecy does, in effect, protect ideas while not preventing other firms from developing the same ones on their own.

Our arguments supporting the availablity of both copyrights and contractua licensing are applicable only where monopoly power is absent. Only is that cas could the increased revenues obtainable through such protection be expected to bring about the expansion in the supply of information that is the social objec of any form of protection of information. The major hardware manufacturers appear to have very substantial monopoly positions, and measures which would accelerate their displacement by independent producers should increase overall economic efficiency to the ultimate benefit of consumers.

Our recommendations for software are:

1. For independent software firms not in control of a substantial portion of the market, continued use of non-disclosure contracts should be allowed.
2. For these same firms, copyright availability should be formally enacted, probably under a separate title of the copyright law, but with the term of protection still equal to or longer than the expected commercial life of most software.
3. Research should be done to find methods of making copyright protection more effective (enforceable for small copyright holders.
4. Research should be undertaken immediately to ascertain the extent to which hardware manufactureres have monopoly power in the software industry or are likely to develop it.
5. Measures should be taken to eliminate the existence and danger of monopoly power in the software field. In decreasing order of desirability measures are:

a. denial of trade secrecy and copyrights to large hardware manufacturers.

b. statutorily forcing hardware manufacturers to spin off their software operations.

c. antitrust litigation to force hardware manufacturers to divest themselves of their software activities and to split up any (future?) software firms with market power.

d. compulsory licensing with regulation of prices, holding profits down to competitive levels.

E. COMPUTER DATA BASES AND COMPUTER-CREATED WORKS

Computer data bases are, in general, compilations of information ("data") taken from one or more written or observational sources and stored in (or prepared for storage in) a computer memory in a systematized way. The organization of the data within the computer is designed so that retrieval of particular categories of information desired by users is rapid and efficient. Data bases may be regarded as analogous to various well-known material sources such as bibliographic indexes, social science abstracts, and encyclopedias. The major advantages of computerized systems are that (1) through use of programmed instructions, the computer itself can search the files, at a great savings in time and manpower, and (2) the files can be rapidly and relatively cheaply updated or expanded.

Access to, or output from the computer take any of several different forms, including paper copies, microform, or on-line electronic access, the last of which is probably most common. Data bases may be roughly categorized into three classes: bibliographic, statistical, and specialized. Bibliographic bases contain citations or abstracts of professional or other technical literature in one or in a variety of fields. Statistical bases consist of masses of data, such as financial statistics, and usually have facilities for high speed access and sophisticated analysis and graphical display. Specialized bases exist for a wide variety of applications. Examples include real estate listings, airline schedules, books in print, technical tables, and information on business and consumer credit ratings.

On-line, general-purpose bases appear to be the most important and have the greatest potential for growth. The firms which operate on-line services are generally known as "wholesalers." The wholesalers provide computer facilities and a distribution network, but for the most part do not compile information banks themselves. Rather, these are bought from data base "manufacturers" and from publishers of standard written reference works. Each computer data base may contain information from as many as 40 or 50 hard-copy data sources.

At present the general-purpose on-line market is highly concentrated, with two firms (Lockheed and SDC) controlling most of the market. However, entry into the market has occurred recently, and with that entry some prices reportedly fell markedly. That suggests that there were substantial monopoly rents going to the original "wholesalers" and indicates that there is at least some price competition now. However, there is no clear indication of whether it will persist or how effective it will be. Several data bases are only available from one company, leaving little room for competition.

Regarding the information sources, preliminary indications are that the degree of competition varies greatly depending on the field of information. In some cases, there are a number of firms vying to market data bases which have comparable content, while in others there is only one supplier. As has been discussed earlier, however, concentration in itself does not imply monop oly power if barriers to entry are low. Also, non-profit corporations such as professional societies may strive for maximum dissemination even if market power is present.

Publishers of journals, reference works and written data bases have available to them standard copyright protection against use of their material by computer data base "wholesalers." Because computerized information vendin is a highly visible, public business, and since the materials used are re-sol to the public, there is not at present much opportunity for computer firms to evade paying royalties to their sources or meeting any other conditions for u Hence, at the stage of transfer from data base/written index to computer-info mation vendor there is apparently a well-functioning system for protecting th property interest of data suppliers. Typically the copyright holder receives a percentage royalty on the sales of the wholesaler.

On the output side there does not seem to be at present a major protecti issue, largely because users of computerized data bases receive individually-tailored output, unsuitable for use by other potential customers. Any unauth ized transferral of output copies that might occur is also limited by the dif ficulty of locating other users who would want the same listings and arrangin a transaction with them.

There may be some problem due to another computer operator paying for an obtaining virtually all of a data base, then reselling its contents without incurring the "wholesaler's" setup cost. This practice is again hampered by the necessarily public nature of marketing computer data bases, and so it is probably not possible to avoid paying fees for any large-scale resale.

In this area, then, present law appears to provide adequate protection for the holders of copyrights. However, to the extent that firms possess market power, and thus the ability to control prices, at any stage of the process the ultimate customers of data-base services will suffer in the end, due to higher prices, reduced supply, and hindered responsiveness to consumer needs. For lack of more imaginative solutions, we return to the standard remedies for monopolistic practices.

Computer-created works may be regarded as output which has been transformed to such an extent within the computer that it constitutes an original piece of work, eligible for copyright. Its value may be dependent in part on one or more copyrighted information sources, the software used to manipulate the data, the hardware and data transmission facilities, and the skill of the retrieval operators. We see no policy difficulties here. The rights to any revenues resulting from the newly created work should be allocated by private contractual agreements. In the absence of any rights of the input owners, the owner of the computer operation would retain ownership of the output. If an individual programmer renting computer time, with no strings attached, created such a work, that person would be entitled to the copyright. Other arrangements would again be of concern only to the parties involved. There does not seem to be any reason why works created with the aid of a computer should not be provided with the same proprietary copyright protection as any other intellectual work. In no case does a computer alone "create"--there are always human authors.

Again, because production is largely a corporate activity, there is reason to believe that the supply of computer data bases and computer created works is responsive to pecuniary incentives. In this case there is no established alternative to copyrights. Further, there is little reason to expect that payers of royalties would pay more than the marginal value of the input or output. Consequently, our recommendations are:

1. Copyrights should be available for both the information inputs into and the outputs from computerized information systems and other uses of computers to aid creative work.
2. Empirical studies of the structure and functioning of the industry should be initiated, and continuous monitoring of changes should be performed.
3. Federal policies to reduce or prevent monopolistic tendencies--policies analogous to those suggested for computer hardware firms operating in the software market--should be undertaken.

F. PHOTOCOPYING

The CONTU mandate includes recommending legislative change with regard to copyright protection against machine reproduction. The PIE-C study was restricted to photocopying. The quantity of the use of photocopying and the extent to which it has permeated the society have increased tremendously in recent years as the per page costs of copying have fallen dramatically. While hard evidence on what is being reproduced is limited, the existing data suggest that most photocopying is done in public, university and commercial libraries, in research establishments and in business operations. CONTU's policy concern related only to reproduction of copyrighted materials. It appears that a very small fraction of copying is copying of copyrighted materials, most reproduction being either internal documents used by firms and other organizations, or letters, reports and publications which are not copyrighted.

The publishing industry has argued that photocopying should in general be subject to copyright restrictions and has begun to establish clearinghouse mechanisms to enforce and administer the charging of royalties on photocopying.

The basic question is whether making virtually all photocopying (exclusive of face-to-face educational use) subject to copyright restriction would efficiently assure that the supply of copyrighted works would be moved to or toward the socially optimal level. The imposition of additional royalties would (in the absence of monopoly power) tend to increase the supply of published works, by making that activity more remunerative. But is there any reason to think that in the absence of such policy the supply of published works (that are subject to a significant amount of photocopying) is or would be too small?

Because of the non-appropriability of information, the low and declining cost of photoreproduction could mean that the supply is less than optimal. To the extent that photocopying is done for resale or is a substitute for the purchase of a book or journal, the publishers' product is appropriated without compensation. Further, it could be argued that free benefits from the existing publications are garnered by users of free library services including photocopying. This is the essential argument for restrictions on photocopying of copyrighted materials. The question is what does the evidence show. Unfortunately there is not nearly as much evidence as one would wish.

There is general agreement--but little hard evidence--that within libraries a high proportion of photocopying, by patrons and for interlibrary loans, is of scientific and professional technical--primarily academic--journals, and that a large part of the remainder is of small sections of academic or technical books. Other heavily-copied items would be expected to include high-priced financial publications. Under current circumstances there appears to be little reason for concern over the royalty revenues of authors. Most scientific and technical literature is written by individuals on academic or other salaries, for whom royalties constitute an insignificant portion of their incomes. Most academic journals pay little or no royalty to authors, and some even charge publication fees. Besides, many authors publish for other than pecuniary motives.

To the degree that photocopying is a substitute not for individual subscriptions, but for manual note-taking, as seems likely in a large proportion of cases, duplication can be said to reduce publishers' revenues below what they would have been without photocopying. To the extent that persons are demanding a photocopying service rather than a publishing service when they make a photocopy, a royalty would tend to contribute to misallocating resources, tending to encourage more than the optimal amount of publication of the journals in question. Funds are transferred from the photocopying users to publishers despite the fact that the photocopying service requires many inputs in addition to the copyrighted materials themselves and despite the fact that if the photocopying is not a substitute for purchase, it is performed at no cost to the publishers. The output of photocopying services would tend to be decreased, that of publication increased, resulting in a misallocation of resources.

Moreover, there is a mechanism by which publishers can, and do, appropriate part of the benefits of multiple library usage, in any form. That is the practice of price discrimination, by which libraries and other institutions are charged a higher subscription price than are individuals. Publishers realize that libraries, in the recognition that many periodicals are heavily used, are less likely to cancel a subscription due to a price increase than is an individual subscriber. How satisfactory a mechanism this is complicated by the nature of public libraries, as 1) their budgets, and ability to afford subscriptions, depend on governmental budget situations and the political process, and 2) paying a high subscription fee for, as an example, a weekly financial publication implies an income transfer from all taxpayers to one particular group of users.

General evidence on the state of the publishing industry as a whole does not support a claim that photocopying has caused the industry any substantial harm. In recent years sales have grown at a steady pace, and the stock market values of individual firms indicate that publishing remains a profitable field. Further, only a small fraction (about ten percent) of total sales of commercial publishers is through channels that would permit substantial non-educational photocopying--libraries in particular. Consequently there is no basis for any concern about the effect of unrestricted photocopying on the economic health of the publishing industry in general. It would be desirable to have evidence on the economic and financial position of professional journal publications but little is systematically available. However, the existence of many small journals which have a very small number of subscribers suggests that the possible loss of a few subscriptions due to photocopying is not likely to discourage publication of many journals or substantial curtailment of their scope or content.

As photocopying costs continue to decline it is likely that the incidence of copying will grow substantially and extend beyond scientific and technical journals to various other types of written materials. However publishers can be expected to maintain a technological advantage over consumers in photocopying in that their costs of <u>printing</u> an additional unit of a publication should always be lower than the costs to the consumer of photoreproducing it. But as this differential narrows, it may be outweighed by 1) the absence of a royalty fee paid to the author due to making a photocopy, and 2) the low cost of copying only portions of printed works.

elements have enormous potential to increase general public access to information sources greatly. Yet for this to occur completely different methods of providing compensation to information producers may be necessary, and attempts to retain the current forms of proprietary rights could severely retard progress in increasing information creation and dissemination.

At present the costs of searching out and obtaining desired information are very high, and growing. Given the tremendous volume of new information produced each year, for most people it is quite difficult to find those specific books, journals, and other information they want. Moreover, the high costs of distributing knowledge means that a high proportion of authors and researchers cannot get their work published, or published in a sufficiently accessible form that it receives appropriate attention.

Prices of mass-circulation magazines, technical journals, and books, particularly reference and scholarly works, are increasing rapidly. Expenses for public education, at all levels, which can in large part be regarded as costs of information transfer, are on the order of $100 billion a year. Large and growing governmental subsidies exist for public libraries, mailing privileges for books and magazines, and federally-funded research activities.

Copyright royalties appear to amount to no more than a few billion dollars a year, small in comparison to the total cost of the information system, yet they may play a disproportionately important role, partly because copyright stabilizes property rights and encourages specific modes of exchange and transmission of information.

Telecommunications and other technologies have the potential to revolutionize access to information by separating the intellectual content of information from the medium on which it has traditionally been carried. The dissemination of information can be greatly aided by reducing to a small fraction of current costs the expense of efficient and appropriate distribution, which tends to dominate the costs of production.

For example, the collection of books in the Library of Congress could be converted into electronic form using existing optical technology and transmitted for home consumption at very low cost via television, using either current towers and transmission stations or satellites.

Utilization of such possibilities may require compensation systems based on entirely different methods from the present collection per-unit at point of final purchase. The one major alternative currently in use,

Should photocopying become as inexpensive as to be a widespread substitute for purchases of information materials, it could cause returns to some authors and publishers to fall to such an extent that the supply of information would be reduced below what is optimal from the standpoint of consumers. This problem does not appear to be significant now or in the immediate future. Should it become so one can count on the publisher interests to make the fact known through the political process and would, presumably, become evident in the quintenniel review of photocopying called for in the 1976 Act. It is important to note that copying of copyrighted materials in libraries constitutes only one portion of total library usage, all of which can be regarded as reducing publisher revenues by allowing multiple usage of publications. The arguments used for charging royalties on photocoping in libraries are in large part applicable to all use of free libraries.

Conclusion: Under current conditions

- the narrow range of materials that are photocopied
- the lack of evidence of impact on authors
- the availability of the price discrimination mechanism
- the general health of the publishing industry and lack of evidence of serious financial problems in the most directly parts of publishing
- the danger of misallocation of resources

We conclude that the imposition of royalties on most photocopying is unjustified. In those cases where reproduction is done for resale, and can be presumed to have an impact on sales or subscriptions, royalties are more likely to have the socially desirable effect of enabling producers to cover their costs and, hence, to enter or continue in operation. Consequently it is appropriate that the fair use doctrine be extended to cover all photocopying other than for resale.

G. NEW TECHNOLOGIES

The bulk of the PIE-C analysis and the work of CONTU has been concerned with "new technological uses of copyrighted works," but has looked almost exclusively at the impacts of information transmission methods which have already come into major use. We have left aside consideration of the impacts of technological changes which can be expected to occur during the next few years, let alone over longer periods in the future.

It is reasonably clear that technological advances are currently causing and will continue to cause drastic reductions in the real cost of using machine reproduction, computers, and, possibly most important, telecommunications. Systems incorporating these three and possibly other financing of television, radio and to some extent other media indirectly via advertising, is highly deficient in obvious ways. What is needed is systematic development of experimentation for organizing and financing the dissemination of information in ways which are as restrictive and as conducive to general access as possible.

H. SPECIFIC QUESTIONS

A number of the questions posed at the beginning of this summary have not been addressed directly.

We have concluded that copyright protection for photocopying should be available in the event of reproduction for resale and should be available for all computer-based information. Should the fair use doctrine be extended to exempt public interest groups from paying royalties on materials they copy (by photoprocesses or by some computer recovery mechanism)? In terms of economic efficiency, there is no general basis for making such exemption. However, social policy is based on more than efficiency considerations. It is social policy to grant some categories of not-for-profit organizations special advantages.

Further, there are, in economics, several bases for such treatment. First, the product of such organizations is believed to be of broad public value, greater than the value placed on it by the market.

Second, many such organizations are involved in redistribution of wealth in one manner or another, and market efficiency is not socially optimal unless the distribution of wealth is itself socially optimal--which is believed by many, including the authors--to be far from the case. Third, there is a more modern justification for subsidizing the generation of information from sources other than the established producer-oriented sources of much policy information. Theoretically there could be more efficient means of providing the assistance that is deemed socially desirable for such organizations. Practically, the only way to support them appears to be through instrumentalities such as providing special small advantages such as reduced postage rates. Consequently, there are good practical and theoretical arguments for such exemption, but there is no unbiased way that we know of determining whether the social gains would exceed the social cost of such exemption. Our judgement is that such exemption would be socially desirable and for administrative convenience should be extended to all 501(c)(3) corporations.

It would appear to be undesirable to restrict copyright ownership only to individuals. First, many creative activities are now carried on in corporations, with mutually reinforcing research and development teams: the contribution of individuals is indeterminate. Second, to deny individual copyright holders the opportunity to sell their rights to corporations would greatly reduce the value of copyrights to the individual owners.

The question of whether research and development funded by the federal government should be subject to copyrights assignable to private parties would require more analysis than was possible in our study.

To make copyright holders effectively equal under the law, some form of assistance to small business, individual and non-profit copyritht holders appears to be highly desirable. However, to determine the appropriate form and the practicality of any form lies beyond the scope of the study reported here.

Finally, will technology overtake us? Our recommendations pertain only to the present and clearly visible applications of existing technology. This is based first on our lack of clairvoyance but also on the observations that private interests are amply capable of seeking protection when a demonstrable need for protection arises. On the other hand to remove protection for almost any vested interest has historically proven to be politically most difficult. Hence, it seems entirely appropriate to recommend no protection to cover future contingencies. Further, the 1976 Act provides for review of the technology of photocopying at five year intervals. We recommend not only that the review be extended to cover computer-based information but that there be a sunset provision: unless existing protection in both photocopying and computer-based information is justified every five years it should be discontinued.

INTRODUCTION

A. PURPOSE

This report has been prepared by the Public Interest Economics Center (PIE-C) in partial fulfillment of its contract with the Commission on New Technological Uses of Copyrighted Works (CONTU) to study the impact on consumers of increasing or decreasing the stringency with which owners' interest in computer-related and photo-reproducible information is protected by copyrights.

The basic purpose of earlier versions of this report was to provide background for discussion with and among consumer group leaders and other public interest advocates at conferences held in Washington on May 2 and June 13, 1977, under the direction of the Public Interest Satellite Association (PISA). Those versions and this final report were and are intended to provide public interest leaders with background information which would be valuable to them in preparing any testimony they elect to present to CONTU, to provide information specifi-cally for PISA for such purposes, to provide information to the CONTU staff to be the basis for testimony by PIE-C.

B. <u>NATURE OF COPYRIGHT PROTECTION</u>

The special characteristics of the markets for information and creativity (discussed in Chapter II) led (or at least contributed) to the patent and copyright systems. The two systems have historically served diffe purposes.

The patent system is designed to encourage invention by offering a grant of monopoly to the originator of an "idea"--a process, design, or othe form of useful physical invention. To obtain a patent, one must show (in actua pay a fee for the U.S. Patent Office to determine) that the idea is orig-inal (never before patented), has commercial value, and is a non-obvious improvement to existing knowledge to an expert in the field. Once granted, a patent gives exclusive rights to the holder to produce or use (or to with-hold or transfer the rights to produce or use) the innocation. Should the same or a similar item be developed independently by someone else, no matter how soon afterwards, the later developer is prohibited from making any commercial use of the item. Whichever individual or firm first puts in the patent application will, assuming it is accepted, obtain exclusive rights to the invention. Thus, patents not only solve the problem of non-exclusivity, but they go much farther. They prevent anyone else from benefiting from rese on exactly the same item, even if it had been proceeding simultaneously, and they allow the patent holder not only to obtain returns from his/her (or the firm's) own work but to have a monopoly on the <u>entire market</u> for the inventio It is clear that patents create great incentives for first development of an innovation, but that they also impose high costs on society.

Copyrights offer a much more restricted degree of protection than do patents. Applied to communications via print, audio, and television media (among others) copyrights give exclusive rights to the specific <u>expression</u> communicated, but give no rights to the ideas <u>contained</u> therein; and there is no prohibition against independent development of the same idea or substantia similar expressions. Thus, since most ideas, such as themes or plots for stories, can be expressed in innumerable ways, copyrights afford the holders a monopoly much less extensive than do patents.

The distinction between patent and copyright protection can also be de-scribed as the former protecting <u>meaning</u> while the latter protects form.[1] We have these associations:

patents: physical--invention--idea--meaning

copyrights: communication--expression--form

To the degree that the above are separable phenomena the patent and copyright systems can be analyzed separately. But in reality the two are intertwined. Copyrightable items may contain not only commercially saleable forms but also ideas which are original and valuable in themselves. While we are not able to deal extensively with this subject in the present paper, it does appear that as the advanced nations move towards becoming "information economies," in which communications of all forms compose an increasing share of national income, it will be of vital importance to clarify such distinctions. In Chapter IV on computer software, we make evident one area in which advancing technology may be making the copyright vs. patent dichotomy unsatisfactory.

Specifically, copyright protection of anything creates a limited but long-lived monopoly, given typically to the producer of the material. It can be thought of as a confirmation of his/her property "right" in his/her creation or it can be thought of as an inducement to producers (of all sorts) to create and provide more new works. It is the latter that constitutes the economic justification for copyright protection or other compensation for creativity.

Copyrights permit the holder to impose conditions on copying or permit the holder to keep a work from being copied at all. The most obvious condition for reproduction is the payment of a royalty. But other conditions may be important as well. For example, a copyright provides some protection against making unauthorized changes in the material, or using it without attribution, using it for unauthorized purposes, such as advertising. The existence of a copyright does not imply or require that royalties be charged or that any other restriction on use be imposed; it merely permits such imposition. Obviously, all these kinds of protection have potential value to any copyright holder. For some the non-monetary aspects may be the most important, for those individuals and corporations whose income depends on receipts from producing copyrightable material, the royalty is likely to be the most important.

There is clearly a possibility of drawing a copyright statute that would provide some but not all these forms of protection. For example, the power to preclude copying of a product could be replaced by a requirement to license its use. One could also imagine a law which provided all forms of protection other than the collection of royalties. For reasons discussed below none of these options appear to be very significant in reality.

It is our belief, based on the information available to us, that copyrights would be used very little to prevent dissemination of information altogether. The major commercial use would be to impose royalties to maximize the income of copyright holders. This same use would be important to some other holders. In addition, many holders, especially noncommercial holders, would prefer that their works be widely and freely distributed. To them, the major advantage of copyright protection would lie in controlling abuse of their work, obtaining recognition through attribution or similar benefit.

It is possible that copyrights serve other ends. Because a copyright holder can prevent any (legal) dissemination of the copyrighted information, the copyright could be used to suppress information. It is a not uncommon practice to buy patents not to exploit them but to prevent their being exploi We know of no way of systematically exploring whether such use of copyrights substantial or is likely to become so with future technology.

C. QUESTIONS

The basic question to which this report is addressed is whether the interests of consumers would be advanced by increasing or decreasing the string of present copyright law as it applies either to photoreproduction of copyrig materials or to computer based materials.

There are a number of associated questions that emerged in discussion w public interest representatives:

- Should any royalty charge be permitted?
- Should any royalty charge be permitted only for particular uses or u
- Closely related, should not-for-profit organizations, individuals or public interest groups be exempt from royalties, under some form of fair use doctrine?
- Should research or development paid for by the government be subject to copyright assignable to private parties?
- Should copyrights be abailable only to individuals, as distinct from corporations or government entities?
- Since an individual or small firm can not be expected realistically to be able to prevent infringement by large corporations what, if an adjustments in copyright law should be made?
- Will technology overtake us?

It is not within the purview of the study reported here to examine the question of whether copyrights are, *per se*, socially desirable, Although, if had evidence that that they were not, we would have examined the cases studie in light of such evidence. Not only do we know of no such evidence, but we f some circumstances in which copyrights are clearly desirable.

D. THE NATURE OF CONSUMER INTEREST

1. Definition of Consumer

In order to address the question of how consumer interest would be affe ted by changes in copyright law, it is necessary to define consumer and to sp the nature of the interest of consumers as a group in copyrights.

To understand the relevance to consumer interests of the protection of novation and production, whether in information or in physical products, it i essential to appreciate the key role of consumers in the economy. In welfare economics, the only legitimate function of economic activity is to increase (relative to what it would otherwise be) the well-being of the members of society. This means basically the welfare of consumers and workers. In light of the fact that all costs of producing the goods and services created in the economy must ultimately be borne predominantly, and perhaps exclusively, by consumers and workers, their well-being tends to increase as the efficiency of the economy increases. (Efficiency in this statement must be broadly defined to include all costs and the concept of output must be correspondingly broad.) In addition, it is consumers who ultimately benefit from the availability of any new product that is, in fact, of value.

Throughout this report we define consumers as the ultimate consumers (or households); not, for example, commercial customers using copyrighted information. Thus, we are defining consumers as people, natural persons. A problem of communication may arise from the fact that whereas all people are consumers, most people also play other economic roles, for example, as workers, investors, savers. We are concerned with people, not in those roles, but only in their role or function as consumers of goods and services for their own use.

Several alternative definitions might have been used (some of which were suggested by public interest advocates), including:

- consumer representatives,
- public interest groups,
- non-profit organizations,
- small business, and
- customers.

The last of these is in common use in some simplified forms of economic analysis where it is necessary only to distinguish between the suppliers and demanders in a market. However, many customers, particularly in commercial ADP (automatic data processing), are producers--businesses or government--using information just as they use any other input in their productive processes. As is well established in the public choice literature (and by casual observation), businesses and governmental entities typically are well represented in legislative and regulatory proceedings. It is our understanding that it is CONTU's interest to be presented with ideas as to the typically under-represented interests of the mass of people in their role as <u>consumers</u>. Hence, we do not consider all customers consumers.

With regard to the other possible definitions of consumer, two questions arise: are the various groups really "consumers" in some sense that is useful here? Is it socially desirable that they be granted preferential treatment under the fair use doctrine?

Consumer representatives could, of course, be thought of as surrogate consumers. Small businesses are clearly not performing the function of consumers, nor are non-profits in general or all public interest groups. Further small business includes some amply represented producer groups such as physici attorneys, independent oil producers, and non-profits include many business-related organizations.

The question of whether any of these groups are entitled to some preferential treatment has to do with the question of exemption from royalty payment ("fair use" exemption) not with copyrights per se. In terms of economic efficiency, there is no general basis for making such exemption. However, social policy is based on more than efficiency considerations. It is social policy to grant some categories of not-for-profit organizations special advantages.

Further, there are, in economics, several bases for such treatment. First, the product of such organizations is believed to be of broad public value, greater than the value placed on it by the market. Second, many such organizations are involved in redistribution of wealth in one manner or anothe and market efficiency is not socially optimal unless the distribution of wealt is itself socially optimal--which is believed by many, including the authors--to be far from the case. Third, there is a more modern justification for subsidizing the generation of information from sources other than the established producer-oriented sources of much policy information. The argument can be mad on the basis of the public choice literature, that genuine public interest representatives should be subsidized in the general interest. In brief, frequently, the actions that benefit the majority are disadvantageous to the interested small groups, but because of the concentration of impact the special interest groups have greater motive for making their voice heard in policy decisions. It can be shown that the provision of objective or countervailing information will tend to increase the quality of policy decisions under such circumstances.

Theoretically, there could be more efficient ways of providing the socially desirable level of assistance to public interest advocates, through direct subsidy. Practically, however, doing so is frequently, if not always, impossible. Consequently, there are good practical and theoretical arguments for special treatment. However, we know of no unbiased way of determining whether the social gains would exceed the social cost. Our judgment is that such exemption would be socially desirable. However, the problem of defining a genuine public interest organization is rather baffling. To avoid some kind of new identification of "deserving" groups and for administrative simplicity, it seems appropriate to exempt from royalties, through explicit extension of fair use, all 501(c)(3) corporations.

2. The Consumer Interest

The consumers' interest in an increase or decrease in the level of copyright protection in these rather special areas of economic activity is typically remote. With present technology, there is virtually no direct use of computer products by consumers. Consumers' interest lies almost entirely in increasing the availability or reducing the price of other goods and services in whose production computer materials are employed. Eventually some consumers may make more direct use of computer materials; at that time their interests will be served by increasing the availability and reducing the price of particular types of computer products.

Some small fraction of consumers make direct use of photocopying of copyrighted materials. However, again the main use is made by intermediaries producing some good or service that may eventually redound to the interest of consumers. Such intermediaries, as in the case of commercial users of computer based information may be thought of as surrogates for consumer interests, but the linkage is remote. In particular most of the relevant use of photocopying appears to be, as shown in Chapter III, by professionals using specialized literature in research and academic pursuits. Except for some educational use, the consumers' interest is diffuse and lies in the overall efficiency of the production of technical and cultural information and in the eventual efficiency with which future consumer goods and services are produced.

People in their other major economic role--as workers--similarly have indirect interests for the most part. Improved availability of computer materials or photocopyable materials may indirectly affect conditions in the workplace. Finally, it is important to note that consumers have an interest in the efficiency with which government services are provided. This extends to services they consume directly, such as education or policy protection, and to those from which they benefit indirectly such as defense or environmental protection.

The consumer interest in other aspects of copyrights may be more direct, for example, the applicability of copyrights to musical reproductions, but in the area of our concern, their interest is in the overall efficiency of the economy and the contribution of information to that.

3. The Basic Trade-off

Because information is a vital ingredient in virtually all productive processes, the consumer's interest lies in a maximum flow of new information becoming available over time and in maximum availability of the presently existing stock of information.

It is obvious that the consumer interest includes maximum accessibility to the stock of existing information. Any increase in the cost of using information would tend to increase the costs of producing other goods and servic retard the development of new ideas, and reduce direct consumption of infor Hence, any system that increases the cost of access to existing information or in any other way restricts access to it, imposes some costs on consumers and society as a whole. However, because information is so vital in both p duction and consumption, it is also of importance to consumers that the cre of new information be maximized.

The concept of copyrighting and patenting new ideas derives from the belief that, first, the amount of new information will be greater the great the expected rewards to those who might create it and, second, that one eff tive way--perhaps the best way--to provide adequate compensation for new id of commercial value is to make available to those who develop them, a degre of monopoly power over exploitation of their ideas. Because the income der from a patent or copyright depends entirely on how much the society is will to pay for access to the protected information, there is a strong presumpti that, however much the copyright holder receives, it is no more than what h her ideas are worth to society.

Thus, we are left with a conflict: to the extent that greater string in copyrights decreases the availability of existing materials, it is disad tageous to consumers; to the extent that it increases the production of new materials it is advantageous to consumers. In simplest terms, the purpose this report is to explicate this conflict in the areas of photocopying and computer-based information. It appears, at first, as if there is a simple trade-off: the greater the stringency the greater the opportunity, on aver for innovators of ideas to reap economic gains from innovating; the higher price for access to existing materials (presumably high prices, i.e., royal yield higher returns to innovators) the greater the present costs to consum In such a situation the optimal degree of restriction, from the consumers' point of view is that which creates the ideal balance of access to existing information versus stimulation to production of new information.

The nature of the gains and the losses from such trade-offs are relati easy to specify in theoretical terms. However, in this case there is a maj complication. The amount of new information that will be produced is, like any other commodity, dependent upon not only the expected revenues to be derived from the new ideas but also on the costs of producing them. Since an essential ingredient in the creation of new knowledge is access to existing knowledge, the trade-off is obscured. To the extent that greater stringency in protecting existing knowledge increases the cost of developing new information, such stringency tends to counter its intended contribution to new knowledge. It is impossible to quantify the impact of greater stringency o either the inducement to create new information or on the cost of doing so. Indeed, if copyright law were made more stringent that would, as already indicated, not necessarily dictate that greater royalty payments (or other restrictions) would be imposed--such change would only permit such action.

In coping with this three-way trade-off, the government has available three major kinds of policy variables: the scope of copyright (or patent) protection, the duration of protection, possible exemption of some uses or users from copyright restrictions. Scope of protection includes such considerations as what materials should be subject to copyright? Should all of the historical forms of protections be continued (or added to), for example, should the power to hold material off the market altogether be precluded? The question of duration is obvious, the longer the duration of protection (up to the full economic life of the material) the greater the potential return to the holder and the greater the cost to consumers. This report is concerned with two broad questions of exemption, whether particular materials and uses--computer-related information and photocopying of printed material, respectively--should be exempted from copyright protection and whether there should be exemptions for particular users.

We can say that increased copyright powers would serve the public (consumer) interest if:

- the supply of information is less than is socially optimal and if more stringent copyright authority would increase the supply toward that optimum,
- it were the most efficient way to do so,
- royalty payments reflect the value of the product to its users, and
- there are no significant barriers to entry into each information market in question.

THE PROBLEM AND THE PIE-C APPROACH

A. WHY CONSIDER COPYRIGHTS?

As long as the American economy is predominantly a market economy with consumers' material wants being met--to the extent that they are met--largely through the response of profit-oriented producers to monetary demand for goods and services, there is a strong presumption against any form of monopoly. Yet there is a long history of granting specific monopolies through patents and copyrights. The basic rationale for doing so and the conflicts inherent in doing so have been alluded to in the first chapter. Here we shall discuss some of the factors that have led policy makers to support granting to producers of new information monopoly rights to the exploitation of that information. It is important to understand that we are dealing with the intellectual considerations in determining whether greater or less stringency in such protection of innovations is in the public interest, not with the power politics of copyright (and patent) policy.

In a market that functions in accordance with the precepts of a free enterprise economy there would be no economic justification for copyrights. In this section we review the characteristics of such a market. Then, in the next, we discuss the nature of the markets for information and indicate their very special characteristics, in particular, how they differ from the competitive ideal.

In a market economy the unregulated forces of supply and demand in a particular industry, and in all industries together, can be shown to maximize--for any given distribution of wealth-- the economic well-being of consumers as a group, if a number of assumptions regarding "perfect competition" are effectively fulfilled. The assumptions relevant to the present study include:

- Absence of externalities: the impacts of the industry fall entirely on the sellers and buyers of the goods involved, with no effects, either positive or negative, on third parties; such effects include pollution (on the negative side).
- Exclusivity or appropriability: only those consumers who purchase the product at the price set by the producer can obtain its full benefits.
- Competition: producers are in close enough competition with each other that no individual firm can raise the price it receives by reducing the amount it produces and, hence, no producer can obtain (over the long run) profits above a "normal" rate of return.
- Comparability: the products of different firms in each market are identical (undifferentiated), so that consumers purchase solely on the basis of price.
- Marginal-Cost Pricing: the price at which a good is sold is equal to the cost (including the "normal" profit) incurred by the firm in producing and selling the marginal unit of the good.

The proposition that a competitive market maximizes consumer well-being not only abstracts from the distribution of wealth, but also leaves aside the questions of <u>which</u> consumers benefit and to what degree. Thus, if one believes that the current distribution of wealth is unjust, one would expect a "perfectly functioning" competitive market to produce unjust results. However, the ideal way--and the only promising way--to reduce such injustice substantially is to change the distribution of wealth directly. Efforts to rig markets to offset inequities in the distribution of wealth typically risk doing more harm than good, although there are important exceptions concerning information, as indicated in Chapter I.

B. THE MARKET FOR INFORMATION

The markets for information and for literary or artistic creativity contrast sharply with this ideal. For each of the information markets considered in this paper the industry has its own characteristics, but they have, as well, some important attributes in common.

1. The Nature of Information

First, information itself has special characteristics;

- Information is complex. It is used at virtually every stage of the production process and in consumption. In many cases, the complexity of information may make it accessible only to a select group of "experts" and require large costs to process the information to make it more universally intelligible.
- Information is costly. This is often forgotten since the explicit cost of obtaining an additional piece of information is often zero, but there are costs involved in the production, storage, retrieval, processing and transmittal of information.
- Information is valuable. This may seem readily apparent. It is important to remember, however, that information is never so valuable that its cost should not be counted. Anyone who continues to search for the very last bit of information to become perfectly informed before making a decision is rarely using good economics in his search process. The very last bit of information is typically inordinately expensive compared to the benefits deriving from it.
- Knowledge can be destroyed and storing knowledge is costly. The death of "wisemen" typically destroys much valuable information. Retrieval of knowledge from human memory is not costless and must be kept effective by constant mental exercise. Storage in computer memories or in written records requires substantial initial cost and at least some maintenance cost.
- Ordinary use does not deplete the stock of knowledge. In this respect, information differs importantly from material goods such as mineral resources or an auto dealer's inventory. One person can use a stock of knowledge yet there is no diminution in the amount available for others. This means that there is little or no cost to society from use of available information, once it has been created. For example in the case of widely demanded items such as news stories, their sometimes high initial

production costs need be incurred only once, while the case of reproduction brings the cost per reader down to a tiny figure.

- The production of knowledge. In some instances, such as some computer applications, a "creator" may come up with part of an idea, a "user" suggests ways in which his use of the idea could be increased, thereby triggering a new idea or alteration of the old idea by the "creator." Such a process reduces the private nature of knowledge or the extent to which knowledge should be considered an exclusive property of a single creator.
- Information may be substituted for other commodities and other commodities for information. Consulting services provide a very apparent example of this information characteristic. More profoundly, the rise of the modern multi-national corporation may to a large extent be explained in terms of this characteristic of information. This is valid to the extent that the multinational exports technology (e.g., technological competence) or managerial skill as well as the commonly recognized export of physical capital.
- In some instances information may actually be over-abundant and this is a major and costly problem in itself. The term "information pollution" has been coined to describe the situation of people assailed by an excess of trivial messages. Simply adding more information is not necessarily helpful unless it is information relevant to the user. Television ads or real estate want ads, for example, may give one more information than is helpful and may actually overwhelm or mislead the buyer.
- Much information, especially that which has been processed into relatively accessible form, is often easily used at no price to the user beyond the cost of helping himself. Many knowledge producers (and a lesser number of knowledge distributors) not only do not obstruct but often actively encourage the unpaid appropriation of their work.

2. Cost and Price Characteristics of the Industry

The "industry" producing information has some characteristics that fai in important ways to match the competitive model. Some of these derive fro the characteristics of information just discussed.

We have found no adequate economic description in the secondary literature of either the publication industry or the computer software data-base industries. However, the following general outlines appear to be broadly applicable.

Each publishing house typically produces many products and several product lines: a company may publish mass market paperbacks, trade and text books, magazines and journals, for example. Within each product line there are many titles--many text books and several professional journals, for example. Each edition of a book may go through one or more printings and the size of run in each printing may vary, from a few hundred to tens of thousands. Each magazine or professional journal is published, typically, on some schedule, and each issue could be printed in a varying number of copies.

The industry is characterized by a complex of "fixed" costs (or "joint" costs). It would carry the discussion far afield to discuss the subtleties of joint versus fixed costs, so we refer to them all as fixed costs. A publisher may have--typically does have--a management and marketing complex that handles many or all of its products. Similarly a publisher may own or have long-term contractual access to printing and other facilities. Whereas the size and nature of these assets are presumably determined by the expected volume and kind of publication to be performed, they and their costs do not change with short-term, say monthly, changes in the actual number of pages printed.

It may be that there are substantial economies of scale in the organization and procurement of such assets. That is one possible explanation of the high concentration ratios observed in the industry (Chapter III). It is not these corporate-wide fixed costs that are central to our discussion, but they have to be identified and set aside in order to avoid confusion with some fixed costs that do lie near the heart of the argument.

Two sets of costs are critical, a fixed component of the costs of each individual product--its setup costs--and the short-run variable costs, i.e., the costs of making copies of each product. In publication, the setup costs of the publishing house consist of such activities as working with the author, editing, and, in some areas, gathering and compiling data. The authors' setup cost is essentially the cost of writing the manuscript and performing the research or other creative tasks underlying that process.

Information available on the relevent portions of the computer industry is even less complete. It appears, however, that there are analogous setup costs associated with production of software, data bases and computer-created works. These costs, again, appear to be independent of the extent of use of the computer materials--the number of times they are copied. The setup costs in production of software, data bases and computer-created works include the accumulation and categorization of data, analysis, and programming.

In both industries setup costs are one-time costs--for each book, journal article, data bank, program. The fact that in many instances they have to be updated does not change the basic fact that once the task is performed a potentially valuable asset has been created, and created at a cost to the producer and the society.

Unless producers of computer works and printed materials can foresee with a high level of confidence that they will at least recoup the total costs--including the fixed costs--they incur in bringing new information into existence and making it available, they will have no economic incentive for doing so and, in most instances, can be expected to discontinue or (perhaps more important) not begin developing and disseminating new information. Consequently, it is necessary for them to price copies of their output at more than the cost of reproduction. In the ideal perfectly competitive market, short-run marginal cost should equal price--just as should long-run marginal cost. That condition of perfect competition apparently can not be met in the information industries, without protection or price discrimination, which are, themselves, inconsistant with perfect competition.

Further, once its setup cost has been incurred, copying a work is relatively very cheap. Other publishers could, in the absence of copyright protection, reprint books, journals or articles at only the cost of printing (and binding, etc.). Individuals can photocopy parts or all of publications at low and rapidly declining absolute cost per page (although higher than the cost of mass producing most printed materials). Given access, existing data banks, new computer works or computer software can also be readily copied for individual use or, potentially at least, for resale. In practical terms, this means that if a producer charges a price adequate to recoup total cost--including fixed cost--others can reproduce the work at less than its price. Whereever doing so constitutes a substitute for buying the work from the original producer at its full unit cost or, a fortiori, reproducing the work makes copies available for resale to others who would be potential customers of the original producer, the difficulties of covering full cost are potentially large.

3. Non-exclusivity

This is one of the central aspects of the traditional rationale for copyrights and patents. However, many industries have high fixed costs, including costs exactly analogous to the setup costs alluded to here. Most of them are able to attract the resources needed to meet the market demand for their goods without privileges analogous to copyrights and, in many cases where industries enjoy analogous protection, consumers would be demonstrably better off were those protections removed.

In the information industry there is, however a major and nearly unique problem, non-exclusivity (or non-appropriability) unlike the case of physical goods (at least those whose design is not highly original), the producers or creators of useful information are often unable to assure that its benefits are restricted to those customers who purchase the information. This applies to both physical inventions and to knowledge and creativity embodied in written and other forms of communication. Once the original producer has sold--or other wise provided unrestricted access to--the work, without governmental intervention, it has no sure way of appropriating all the value that might be realized through using or copying the work.

The nature of costs prevents providers of information from equating short run marginal cost and price; at the same time, the non-appropriability of information makes it impossible to assure that all beneficiaries of proprietary information pay for using it. Thus, the conditions of perfect competition are not met, so the prospect that governmental intervention could improve on market results is well founded in theory.

The practical consequences of these characteristics of the industry are equally important. The combination of the fact that works can be copied at costs far below the total unit cost of producing new information coupled with the non-appropriability of information means that in the absence of some protection of proprietary rights in information or some form of compensation for innovation, the market would produce less than the socially optimal amount of new information, to the ultimate detriment of consumers.

Copyright (or patent) for protection, however, permits (to the extent that it is enforceable) the originator of information to charge a royalty for the use of reproduction of the material, thus appropriating more of the benefits of use than would otherwise be possible. If the expectation of the returns from such royalty (plus any other income associated with producing the work in question) is adequate to cover the total costs and provide an adequate return, the potential producer will have economic motivation for producing new information. If revenues from doing so are large relative to costs, others will be encouraged to enter the field, expanding the supply of such information.

4. Competition, Monopoly and Product Differentiation

There is a wide range of variation in the degree of competition among sellers in various markets for information. In some cases effective competition appears to be keeping profits and prices down, while in other cases an important element of monopoly control (or market power) is exercised by one or a few producers. One must be careful to define the relevant market correctly. For example, it is inadequate to say that since a large number of popular, or general circulation, magazines exist that there is effective competition from the standpoint of consumers. The magazines cater to a wide variety of needs and tastes, and for any particular type of periodical (photography, gardening, financial, etc.) there may be only a limited number of firms in t market, resulting in costs and prices above competitive levels and in excess profits. Such uniqueness of each product (magazine)--known as product diff entiation--is inconsistent with competition.

5. Externalities

For some categories of information and creativity, society has historically decided (via the political and other processes) that there are signifi cant benefits deriving from their production and dissemination that are exte to both the actual producers and consumers involved. (The possibility of negative externalities, as suggested, for example, by those who favor censor is not considered here). That is, it is widely believed that the whole soci gains from having more knowledge produced and from having more people become knowledgeable, to a greater degree than would be indicated by market transac alone. Much basic research, even with effective systems of exclusive reproduction rights, while of significant social value is too remotely related (if at all) to marketable products to be commercially valuable. In such cas private markets do not adequately serve the public welfare, and subsidies--n sarily paid for by consumers (often through taxes)--are used. The subsidies given to academic research, libraries, and students by the government and various philantl ic organizations are indications of the widespread benefi which information is considered to promote.

A second reason for public subsidies is the fixed-to-marginal-cost relationship. Subsidizing producers to the extent of their fixed costs, and then having prices to customers equal the (low) short-run marginal cost of distributing the intellectual product is one alternative. The government could also hire its own researchers (as it does in some areas) instead of paying subsidies to private individuals and groups.

It does not follow, nor is it obviously true, that all the research undertaken is justified by the expected benefits. In addition there may be some negative externalities in adding to the stock of available knowledge associated with difficulty in obtaining the small fraction of it that may be useful and relevant in any particular case.

In conclusion, because of the fact that any effectively competitive market does use resources efficiently in meeting the demands ("needs") of consumers, there is a presumption against any policy that introduces monopoly power. Further, the fact that markets have "imperfections"--such as those just indicated for the markets for information--by no means sugges that the way to offset them is to introduce any element of monopoly, such as copyrights or patents. Market imperfections are only a necessary not a

sufficient condition for introducing such instruments. Whether introducing or strengthening the limited monopoly power provided by copyrights is in the interest of consumers is, then, an empirical question.

C. STAGES OF PRODUCTION

We have discussed the creation and dissemination of knowledge as if there were a single entity which brings knowledge into existence, reproduces copies of the work (in whatever form) and makes it available to the public. For written materials, both books and periodicals, the authors are, in the vast majority of instances, separate from the publishers (which also applies, for example, to musical recordings). The authors operate as independent economic entities, not employees of the publishing house; there are, of course, exceptions--in journalism and the financial press, for example. For present purposes, the major significance of this dichotomy between the two stages of production is that the response to economic incentives may be much different at the different stages. The distinction between the two stages appears to be of far greater significance in the publishing industry than in the computer business, although there has not been enough empirical analysis of these relationships to permit making such an assertion with confidence.

Any policy based on ensuring that providers of a good or service obtain adequate returns on their investment obviously is based on the assumption that production is responsive to the level of returns. In the case of authors, we are considering the response of intellectual creation to the availability of royalties from copyrights or patents (or some other source of compensation). There are two reasons why this assumption must be re-examined.

First, a substantial proportion of informational and (to a lesser degree) artistic production is done by individuals or research groups receiving university salaries, government or philanthropic grants, or other sources of income independent of royalties on their work. To the degree that royalties constitute a small portion of their incomes, and/or their salaries are enough that their effort responds only slightly to the opportunity for earning more income, royalties will have little effect on their supply of intellectual work.

Secondly, it can be argued that the quality and quantity of work done, particularly in academic and creative fields, is dependent more on non-monetary incentives than on a desire for greater income. To the degree that production responds to the intrinsic satisfaction gained from doing the work, to altruistic motivation, to a desire for recognition, and to other factors, royalties will, again, have little effect on the supply of intellectual work.

Thus, to the extent that these conditions prevail in particular fields of creativity, the result of royalties in those fields might appear not to make more information available but simply to transfer income from the consumers of those products to their producers.

The situation is, however, more complex. First, even though many authors may not be responsive to monetary rewards directly associated with their producing publishable works, undoubtedly some are. Although some creative people are willing to undergo very substantial material deprivation for the sake of pursuing their creative endeavors, casual observation suggests that far more of them will publish if to do so they do not also have to perish.

There are alternative ways of compensating producers of information. As stated above, a large amount of research is publicly supported. To simplify, if there were no monetary reward for writing for publication only those authors who had no monetary incentive would write. As the amount of the expected monetary reward rose, more and more of those authors motivated by the prospect of pecuniary gain would undertake to produce. Further, even those whose primary motives were non-monetary might find that with adequate monetary compensation they would (perhaps could "afford to") devote more effort to writing.

Further, the second portion of the producer sector is made up of institutions, for-profit corporations and not-for-profit institutions. Both must cover their total costs of production if they are to survive in publishing or data processing, and potential new entrants must foresee the ability to do so if they are to be able to enter. Some publications can be cross-subsidized to cover their costs by for-profit organizations, as loss leaders, for example, or by not-for-profit institutions as part of achieving their broader purposes, but the greater the prospects of recovering costs, the greater the incentive for both groups to expand their publication activities.

Where there is effective competition among publishers, any pure monopoly profits for the firm as a whole will, in the long run, be competed away. However, this will occur only on the average for all the publications of a given publisher, or for all the publications of a particular category: trade, mass market. etc. Marketing a piece of literature involves great uncertainty in that the sales of a book, or, to a lesser degree, magazine, cannot be predicted with accuracy, and, as discussed above, some substantial fixed costs are incurred once the publication is undertaken. One of the functions of publishers is to absorb part of the risk by selling a large number of items, some of which will do better and some worse than expected. Unusually successful works will mean high profits for the publisher (and, typically, large royalties to the author), while disappointing ones may mean losses. Wherever a publisher has considerable monopoly power, for example, through effectively differentiating its product, it may be possible to realize monopoly profits.

The availability of copyright protection prevents publishers from only copying those works of other publishers that have been proven successes (thus avoiding the risks of publishing works of unknown commercial appeal). If applied more extensively to photocopying, copyrights would also permit supplementing revenues from sales by the imposition of royalties for photocopies. Thus, copyrights tend to increase the prospects that enough works will be profitable to offset the risks that some other publications will generate losses. The greater the profits on individual successful works, the larger will be the number of works published, unless there are barriers to entry. Copyright protection, as already stated, may serve to offset the tendency for non-appropriability in face of the relatively low cost of copying existing works to cause the market to produce less than the socially optimal amount of new information.

Thus, we have the basic case for copyright protection. Before proceeding to the more specific analysis, it is desirable, however, to point out that even given a need for revenues that will cover the entire cost of production (including normal return on investment for the for-profit sector, at least), it does not necessarily follow that stringent copyright laws are the most efficient and equitable way of providing expected returns adequate to induce the optimal amount of creativity.

One alternative is government subsidization of authors, with their works then put in the public domain. Such policy has the advantage that, although consumers must still pay, through taxes, the absence of royalties would encourage maximum dissemination of the material. However, there are various serious difficulties with governmental subsidies, not the least of which is accurately making the amount of support proportional to the social value of the research or creative endeavor. Under a copyright system, where demand determines the returns to the author, this allocation function is performed by the market.

Possibly more important is the danger in further centralized, institutional control, of the creation and provision of information. Subsidies must necessarily be given out by a commission of some sort, which is certain to have biases which will restrict the free flow of research and dissemination of knowledge. Under copyrights an author is responsible to the general public for the quality and relevance of his/her work. While this is certainly not a perfect mechanism, it is likely to involve less danger of censorship and governmental use of public funds to serve its own ends than would a more extended system of subsidies. Even under the present system, it can be argued that research is undesirably constrained by, for instance, the parochial attitudes which may exist in academic departments pressuring faculty to follow certain lines in their work. Increasing governmental power (or centralized control of any form) has well-recognized drawbacks, that appear to be particularly severe in the field of information. On the other hand, it is not always clear that information that is demanded by the market constitutes the socially optimal quantity and quality of information, witness TV programming which for the most part reflects only "what will sell."

1. Conflict-of-Rights

One approach to the issues raised in this report is to assume a basic conflict between the rights of two groups--the producers of intellectual works, on the one hand, and the using and consuming public, on the other. The "rights" of the producers involve having proprietary rights in their work firmly established and protected. The "right" of the public is to have unrestricted access fo and use of (including the right to copy) existing intellectual material. The approach assumes the existence of rights on both sides, and weighs the awards in favor of the side with the greatest rights. Viewing the issue as a conflict of rights has drawbacks. The major drawback is the normative nature of the approach, and the inherent, subjective nature of any resolution of the conflict.

2. Maximizing Benefits to the Public

An alternative approach which, among other things, needs fewer philosophical assumptions to arrive at a conclusion is to seek to maximize benefits to the public. This approach considers benefits to producers only to the extent that they are members of the public. The size of the costs and benefits to individual members of each group from various policies is considered as is the relative size of each group. The "public" is defined as all those persons who gain from the provision or use of copyrighted material. The ratio of "producers" to the relevant public is typically very small.

Under this approach, therefore, the optimal amount of protection of copyrighted work is that which necessary in order to maximize benefits for the public (as defined above).

The differences in the two approaches is summarized in the table below:

TABLE 1

Characteristics of Two Approaches

	Conflict of Rights	Maximization of Public Bene
Basis of policy analysis	"Right" of opposing parties	Aggregate net benefits to all parties
Emphasis	Normative	Positive
Is relative size of group considered?	No	Yes
Is net benefit to each group considered?	Yes	Yes

The advantage of the approach which maximizes public benefits as opposed to one which tries to resolve conflicting rights is that benefits may be more easily defined than "rights". Factors which increase welfare are said to increase consumer benefits. Examples include decreasing costs to consumers, increasing availability (quantity) of services to consumers, and increasing the quality of benefits to consumers. A rigid application of this approach would involve concluding that the policy that created the maximum net benefit to society as a whole is the best policy--without regard to how those benefits are distributed. As mentioned above, distributional impacts should be considered in analyzing the application of copyright powers. The necessary adjustments are made without losing the advantages of the benefits approach.

"Rights" of parties involve judgments which are difficult to define on any objective criterion, let along to quantify. A still more difficult question than "What rights exist?", is "What rights should exist for each of the parties?" Furthermore, the kind of information one might desire in order to answer the question, "What rights should exist for the various parties?" would be likely to be contained in the analysis of benefits to the public. This is especially true if benefits to the public is the basis of allocation of property rights among competing interests. Therefore, the benefit to the public approach is more general and also based more on readily defined, objective criteria than is the property "rights" approach.

In light of these considerations, PIE-C has elected to use the approach based on maximizing net benefits to the public. Whereas, as was discussed in Chapter I, all of the public, whatever its other roles, plays the part of consumers this approach is likely to yield results identical with or close to maximizing consumer interests, as we have defined consumers.

3. Basic Tradeoff, Again

The stated objective of copyrights and patents under the U.S. Constitution is to "promote the useful arts and sciences"--to provide an opportunity for the creators of information to obtain a return on their work, and, thus, to be encouraged to innovate. Our explication of this has been in terms of avoiding the consequences of non-exclusivity--of permitting producers to obtain payment whenever their work is used. Yet it is clear that such payments imply costs to the rest of society. As discussed in Chapter I, consumers have an interest both in maximizing the generation and production of new information and in seeing that these products, once created, are available at the lowest possible price. It was pointed out that these two objectives conflict to some degree, as do the buyers' desires for maximum production and minimum price in the market for any good. In the cases we are considering, there is one basic tradeoff between more innovation and production on the one hand and, on the other, higher costs of accessibility to existing works.

Looking only at the copyright case (patents will be discussed in the chapter on software), there appear to be two prime variables that affect the extent of this tradeoff: the term, or duration, of protection and the scope of protection. The latter involves not only determination of such issues as the classes of information and the uses and users to be subject to copyright protection, but also it involves making some complex qualitative distinction on how similar work must be to constitute infringement. We do not get into that issue here. It is the term of protection which is relevant as the major policy tool, within any class of protection. Presumably, for any given scope of protection, the longer the term of copyright protection, the greater the potential returns will be, thus, both increasing the expected production and raising costs to consumers.

In Economics of Property Rights as Applied to Computer Software and Data Bases[1] a mathematical model is developed for "The Optimal Duration of Copyright" as applied to computer software. The study essentially assumes that duration of copyright is highly correlated with, if not identical to degree of protection. A second study, by two of the same authors, deals in parrallel fashion with the question of scope of coverage as reflected in expansion or curtailment of fair use.[2] It reaches analogous conclusions. Further, the findings of both studies comport with a widely accepted theory that shows what pricing structure will, for any given level of revenues, minimize consumer losses from monopolistic power. The theory is applicable to situations in which (as is generally the case in information industries) the high fixed costs of production neccessitate that for a firm to cover total costs (again including a "normal" profit) the price of at least some units of the product must be above short-run marginal cost. Consumers are divided into as many distinguishable groups as is administratively feasible, according to the degree to which the demand for the product responds to a change in price (the elasticity of their demand). Then:

> "the theory prescribes that for each product and for each class of buyers, percentage deviation of price from marginal cost ought to vary inversely with the elasticity of demand."

That is, prices should be raised most for those classes of consumers whose purchases are least affected by the change, and raised the least (or lowered) for those consumers whose demand would be most altered by the change. Empirical evidence suggests this course is pursued by producers whenever they are able to discriminate in pricing, which one would expect to be the case since such a pricing scheme maximizes their revenues. Some of the features and conclusions of "The Optimal Duration of Copyright" are applicable to copyright policy in general.

An interpretation for general policy of the conclusions of that study, is:

- The extent to which society prefers benefits in the present to those in the future (as measured by the discount rate) is an important factor in giving protection to any form of intellectual work. The more society is concerned with the present, and the less it is concerned with the future, the less protection should be given to creators, i.e., the greater should be the dissemination of (the lower the price of) existing work.
- The desired degree of protection, as reflected in the duration of copyrights depends, in most cases, on the sensitivity of demand to changes in prices. The more the amount demanded tends to increase as price falls and to decrease as price rises, i.e., the more "elastic" demand is said to be, the less the amount demanded changes with price changes.

  "...if demand is inelastic then little is sacrificed by having a...monopoly price charged for the use of software, and society can afford to grant a longer period of protection. On the other hand, if monopoly pricing excludes many potential users from taking advantage of existing software--that is, if demand is more ... elastic--then the loss resulting from a monopoly is more serious and a shorter period of protection is appropriate."[3]
- The longer a form of intellectual work remains commercially valuable, the longer it should be protected. In balancing the desire for increased future stocks with that for maximum dissemination of existing stocks, lengthening the period of restriction is more worthwhile the longer will be the later period of low-cost availability.

The model (and the other theorizing alluded to above) is designed to show what policies would maximize total social welfare, defined as "the sum of consumers' and producers' surplus, as it is customary in economic literature." However, as the authors point out, "This definition of social welfare ignores considerations of distributional equity, and simply adds up the monetary gains to each participant in the economy.[4] In other words, the conclusions are reached without regard to who is getting most of the benefits from the maximizing policy--the producers or consumers of intellectual work. Clearly the question of distribution of welfare should be taken into account in any choice of policy.

The factor which determines the split of benefits between producers and consumers in these theories is the shape of the demand curve facing the individual firm. This shape can be taken to mean simply the degree to which consumers respond to price changes, so that the less they respond, the fewer consumers stop buying the product due to an increase in price. Hence, their conclusion that the less change in level of output the better, as consumption of the information remains relatively unaffected. Meanwhile, more expensive (in real resources) goods will be produced, that would not otherwise have been because the higher prices paid by customers mean greater profits for producers. This increase in supply (here meaning not more units of one particular sales item, but a greater variety of items) causes total welfare to increase in most cases. The analysis appears to be couched in terms of the demand for all the output in a particular market. However, the shape of the demand curve facing an individual firm can also be taken to indicate the degree of monopoly power in a market--the degree to which producers are able to control the market so as to maximize their profits, at the expense of consumers. In an industry with effective competition, the firm can sell all it wishes to at the market price, but initially nothing at any significantly higher price. In such a situation, an increase in the term of protection will have no effect on the distribution of benefits between producers and consumers, because the producer can not raise its price significantly anyway. Competition implies that, in the long run, producers tend to obtain about the "competitive" rate of return. An increase in the length of protection, allowing producers to profit from sales farther into the future, would permit reducing the price on current sales, as entry into the market with close substitutes occurs. Thus, an implication of our reasoning is that under competition there is no identifiable limit to the period of protection.

The more a market deviates from perfect competition (due to product differentiation, a limited number of sellers, and/or collusion among sellers) the more each firm can raise prices by restricting output. The more monopolistic an industry is, the more a lengthening of the term of copyright, or otherwise increasing protection, will transfer income from consumers to producers.

In analyzing the appropriate policies for each of the various fields of intellectual production, this point is crucial. While an evaluation of total economic welfare may imply the desirability of protection, regardless of the structure of the industry, the impact on consumers is critically determined by the degree of competition in the industry.

4. Extent of Monopoly

In any industry, monopoly power is a function of substitutability of other goods for the monopolized one and of the barriers to entry. To the extent that each firm's product takes on substantially unique characteristics, it no longer has close substitutes, and significant market power comes into existence. For example, in choosing between two different makes of subcompact cars, the consumer faces some degree of monopoly in part because the cars are not exactly alike--they are not perfectly interchangeable--and so each producer has a measure of leeway in setting prices. A case where there is less substitutability is in the choice between taking a bus or a taxi to a particular destination--the options are not highly interchangeable and, if there is only one bus company or one taxi company, each firm can exercise substantial monopoly power (which is the rationale for regulating taxis and buses).

A major barrier to entry--and the only one we address--is large initial expenses, in production, distribution or marketing, that must be made in order to gain entry into a market. In the classic case of the auto industry, again, a new firm would face tremendous barriers in the capital needed.

Our questions are to what degree is there substitutability among copyrightable items, and to what degree are there barriers to entry into the relevant market? For simplicity consider for the moment only authorship of written work. It is clear that in most categories of creative, scientific, and technical writing there is a large number of competitors. Entry barriers appear not to be so high that one or a few authors have tremendous advantages.

Substitutability is a function of the quality of the work. There is a high degree of interchangeability between, for example, various mediocre journal articles or mediocre novels. In both cases there are many people with abilities and training in the field, each of whom can write according to consumer preferences (or commercial and academic needs for research). Thus, based on the N.Y.U. analysis, neither the entry barriers nor substitutability appear to create the conditions under which copyright protection would afford significant market power to authors for <u>most</u> written work.

It is only when we come to very original research or excellent writing that there appears to be a significant possibility of monopoly profits to authors, due to the small number of people (possibly only one) capable of doing the particular work in some area of creativity or scientific investigation. Such works may indeed be virtually unique--little substitutability is possible. If there is a substantial market for them they can command a very high price, with the attendant costs to consumers and society as a whole. On the other hand, it is clear that the social costs in reduced dissemination (relative to the zero-price case) can only increase monotonically as the benefits to society increase as a consequence of the work's having been done at all. It may be, as already indicated, that the possibility of large monetary returns is not necessary to bring about some, or all, highly innovative and creative work. In those cases the efficiency justification for copyright protection is eliminated. But obviously there are substantial risks that valuable research and writing would be discouraged if protection were removed. Also there are some equity questions in depriving those who would produce without monetary reward of the chance of receiving it. There is the countervailing consideration that, making existing work more readily available (at no royalty) reduces the cost of new information. However, this last seems likely to have a small effect in the relevant cases.

The great number of people who have creative skills adequate to meet much of the commercial demand for writing, suggests that concentration of monopoly power in the hands of authors is not likely to prove to be a major problem. This does not mean that some authors will not make occasional large rents, but that averaging out the gains and the losses, the income of authors as a group will not be expected to exceed their potential earnings in other fields.

Similarly there appears to be relatively close substitutability among the products of various publishing houses with the exception, perhaps, of a few specialized journals. So relatively little monopoly power can be expected to derive from that quarter. Monopoly power in the publishing industry would appear to derive from economies of scale in marketing. As described elsewhere there are relatively high fixed costs or setup costs associated with the publication of a particular book or journal--costs, that once incurred, need not be incurred again as more and more copies are made. However, since any one publication is typically a small fraction of the output of the large publishers, this is not apparently a significant entry barrier.

In the chapters on software and computer data bases, it is shown that there appears to be substantial monopoly in the data-base "wholesaling" industry but substantial competition among independent software producers.

5. Regulation and Antitrust Action

In subsection 3 above, we discussed the distributional implications of exclusive rights to intellectual products, as opposed to the efficiency analysis done in the model "The Optimal Duration of Copyright," showing a major inadequacy of examining only the latter criterion. However, in theory at least, it is possible to reconcle distributional equity with maximizing efficiency. The model (if its other analytics are correct) does tell us what term or degree of protection will maximize total welfare. If protection results in excess profits for producers, an alternative to reducing it is to regulate the prices (royalties) charged. In principle, ignoring the costs of regulation, the latter policy would produce more favorable results for consumers than would reducing the extent or instituting a term of copyrights. In another paper, directed at scientific and technical information systems (STI), two of the authors of the model for software state:

> "If the policymakers are fearful that the abandoning of the fair use doctrine may generate unconscionably high profits for the producers and disseminators of STI by increasing the extent of monopoly power, then they should turn their attention to the problems of regulation of the industry. Regulatory restrictions,

if desirable, should be placed on the price level and not on the pricing structures that the industry may present to the market."[5]

Whether complete freedom of producers to discriminate in pricing maximizes the welfare of information consumers depends on the degree of monopoly power which producers are able to exercise. From the consumer standpoint, discrimination which increases revenues to information sellers is desirable to the extent that more sellers are able to cover their total costs of production and distribution (including a competitive rate of profit), thus making more information available to consumers. In such cases, the market approaches the optimal solution without governmental intervention. However, for some information producers that have relatively large degrees of market power, price discrimination above a certain level will result in excess profits. If this is the case, it is still socially desirable to discriminate among different groups of customers so as to minimize effects on consumption; but excess profits should be eliminated either by 1) antitrust action, or 2) regulation which reduces prices to all classes of customers so as to leave the producing firm with a competitive rate of profit.

There are, of course, costs involved in a regulatory system, the most obvious of which are the expenditures needed for running the agency. The indirect costs, though, are probably more significant. The agency may not perform its function according to the announced intentions. There are, for example, great problems in determining costs and the competitive rate of return. It might restrict prices greatly, harming both producers and consumers as supply is forced down due to inadequate returns. More likely, experience suggests that the agency will tend to become a "client" agency, serving the interests of the regulated industry rather than the general public. Producers may also be able to restrict the effectiveness of the agency through expensive, time-consuming litigation about the agency's rulings. Finally, there is always a danger in legislating more power for another government bureaucracy, particularly discretionary authority, because any agency can be expected to serve its own interests.

Regulation has been deemed to be economically justified when the regulated industry constitutes a "natural monopoly." That is, the minimum size of an efficient firm is so large relative to the market that it would be highly inefficient to have a number of firms competing; in such cases, all but the largest firms tend to be driven out. Examples are local public utilities (water, electric, etc.). There appears to be no significant natural monopoly characteristic of the information industries. It is also possible to have situations of market power where there is no apparent "natural" monopoly present. An example of this seems to be IBM in the software field. In these cases anti-monopoly action (antitrust litigation or statutory change) is the preferred policy, so as to restore competition and eliminate the need for regulation.

FOOTNOTES

[1] Braunstein, Yale M., Fischer, Dietrich,M., Ordover, Janusz A., and Baumol, William J., Economics of Property Rights as Applied to Computer Software and Data Bases, New York University, May 1977.

[2] Braunstein, Yale M. and Ordover, J. A., "Economic Views of Copyright in Scientific and Technical Information Systems," New York University, February 1977.

[3] Braunstein, et al, op cit, pp. 21-22.

[4] Ibid, p. 11 (text and footnote).

[5] Braunstein and Ordover, op cit, p. 19.

PHOTOCOPYING

The issue addressed in this chapter is whether it is desirable--serves the interests of consumers--to refrain from imposing further restrictions or photocopying of copyrighted works.

Under the 1976 Act, the only photocopying to be permitted which is not specifically authorized by the copyright holder is that provided under secti 107 and 108. Section 108 allows certain uses of library photocopying and section 107 allows photocopying under "fair use". In addition photocopying for direct face-to-face teaching is authorized without constraint.

It is currently unclear what constitutes "fair use" under section 107. Williams and Wilkins vs. the National Library of Medicine is the only majo test case of photocopying of copyrighted works and that case resulted in a standoff, setting no general precedent. A major policy recommendation of th study relates to breadth of the definition of "fair use" that would maximiz consumer well-being.

CONTU"S mandate includes "machine reproduction", an area considerably broader than photocopying. However, it has been possible to study only photocopying and consequently our report is restricted to that area.

A. NATURE OF THE PROBLEM

From the consumers' point of view, unrestricted (royalty-free) photoco seems, at first, to be clearly preferable, because it gives the consumer a costless (or reduced cost) choice between copying and not copying. Photocop restriction, on the other hand, reduces (raises the cost of) present consum and, by increasing the cost of research and other creative activity, increas the cost of relatively near-term future consumption. However, as pointed ou in Chapter II, protection of photo-reproducible material will, it is hypothe stimulate relatively remote future consumption by influencing the quantity of future copyrighted works.

In addition to the more obvious advantages of increasing the output of intellectual products, it is sometimes suggested that by increasing the numer of journals published the number of pools of referees would also be increased. Given that referees make errors and have biases, the probability that worthwhile articles would be rejected would be correspondingly reduced.

The basic question is whether making virtually all photocopying (exclusive of face-to-face educational use) subject to copyright restriction would efficiently assure that the supply of copyrighted works would be moved to or toward the socially optimal level. The imposition of royalties from new sources would (in the absence of great monopoly power) tend to increase the supply of published works, by making that activity more remunerative.

As discussed in the following section, photocopying of non-technical publications appears not to be important. The available evidence suggests that for the commercial publishers any such effect has not been critical; publisher profits have remained very healthy throughout the current period of rapidly rising photocopy machines sales.

The problem arises because of the non-appropriability characteristic of information. The case of printed material is something of a hybrid. Copies of journals (or books) are sold, largely to subscribers. In this way publishers do appropriate the benefits gained by the subscribers. Similarly by selling to institutions--typically at a higher subscription rate or price--they appropriate some of the benefits of other users (e.g., library users). Once either of those sets of copies are in circulation, cheap photocopying means that other users can, in the absence of protection, readily obtain benefits whose value cannot be appropriated by the publisher.

As just mentioned, some of the photocopying revenues are appropriated by publishers through price discrimination. Some photocopying revenues are not appropriated by publishers. It is not totally clear, however, that publishers should appropriate photocopying revenues since much of those revenues are the result of demand for photocopying service, not publishing services.

A substantial amount of photocopying takes place in public libraries, however, non-appropriated use results from use of library materials at no charge, not from the photocopying of these materials. Photocopying articles may be considered a particular use, but in terms of non-appropriability it is not distinct from borrowing the materials for any use. The single fact that libraries lend materials at no charge makes the services from those materails non-appropriable. Photocopying, reading, notetaking, or any other use of the materials does not affect their appropriability. The non-appropriability problem derives not from photocopying, but from the institution of free (lendin libraries themselves.

The institution of the library itself is the source of the non-appropriabili It is the library that lends to persons who do not pay the publisher for the journal or the book. The institution of the library itself is designed to encourage free use. Within libraries, photocopying makes use of the material more convenient for each non-payer (free-rider). But library photocopying does nothing to make (say) journal costs more or less appropriable to journal users. Library existence and library usage is the sole source of non-appropriability of journal costs and publishers outputs in general. If publisher are sincerely worried about appropriability of their output, charging individual library users rather than photocpiers would seem to be a more logical target.

It is a matter of some historical curiosity that publishers have not taken issue with the institution of lending libraries. This source of non-appropriability of costs from publishers output is clear-cut and long standing. In Europe, organized authors have, in contrast, frequently urged payment of royalties for use of books circulated by public libraries.[1] (Of course, none of this is intended to suggest that the institution of free libraries is not socially desirable. A strong case for them can be made on both equity and externality grounds.)

The fact that there are a large number of technical journals now, apparently in stable operation, clearly indicates, however, that some large portion of the benefits are appropriable without the imposition of royalties on photocopying The fact that the commercial publishing industry appears to be thriving, strongly indicates the same conclusion for that part of the industry. The question is, would a more nearly optimal amount of technical (and other) publication take place if such royalties were permitted. To the extent that photocopying is a substitute for purchase of journals (or books) restricting photocopying--through charging a royalty or more restrictive methods--would tend to increase subscriptions (sales) and, all else equal, publisher revenues, thus increasing publishers' appropriation of the public benefit they create. If photocopying were predominantly a substitute for subscription or purchasing books, the impact on revenues could be very large indeed. This affect is independent of whether the copies made are resold by the copier. However, if they were to be resold to other individuals who, absent the availability of the photocopied materials, would subscribe to the journal the impact of photocopying, or of restricting, it would be greater.

If photocopying is not a substitute for subscribing, restricting it would have no effect on subscriptions. Royalties from photocopying could, however, contribute to publishers' revenues, and, hence, encourage additional publication. Royalties would also decrease disposable income of consumers spent in other sectors and decrease consumption and future production in those sectors. Whether royalty charges which have these effects are a good idea is a very difficult empirical question. The theoretical framework within which this question may be analyzed and answered is shown in Appendix C.

Any policy decision should take account of the equity considerations. Would alternative policies on copyright application to machine reproduction be fair? How, if at all, would they affect the distribution of income, wealth and power? Are there particular portions of the population who would benefit or suffer? These questions, as well as the efficiency questions are addressed in the analysis that follows. The existing data are extremely limited and do not permit a complete factual analysis. However, they appear to be an adequate base for defensible conclusions.

B. THE NATURE OF PHOTOCOPYING

1. What is Copied?

In order to examine the question posed above it is necessary to begin by specifying the nature of photocopying of copyrighted materials.

Casual observation suggests that most photocopying is reproduction of non-copyrighted material. According to Robert Frase[2] here are no good U.S. figures on this, but a University of Amsterdam study in 1972 showed the following ratio of copying copyrighted materials to non-copyrighted materials in the Netherlands.

TABLE 2

Category	Photocopies		Offset and Stencil	
	Total	Under Copyright	Total	Under Copyright
	1000x	1000x	1000x	1000x
Government	201,220	1,020	184,220	60
Education	53,540	13,570	715,430	62,170
Business	956,160	49,610	958,810	5,660
Libraries	8,350	5,450		
Total	1,219,270	69,650	2,858,460	67,890

Consequently it seems reasonable to assume that most photo reproduction is of other than copyrighted works.

Further, it appears that technical journals (we use "technical" publication throughout to encompass all academic and professional writing) are the most commonly photocopied publications. This is to be expected because photocopying cost relative to the purchase price is lowest for this type of publication. Where the photo-copying cost is high relative to price, the benefit from photocopying and, hence, the probability of extensive photocopying is low.

This is shown in Figure 1 below.

Photocopying Incidence and Copy-Cost/Purchase-Cost Ratio

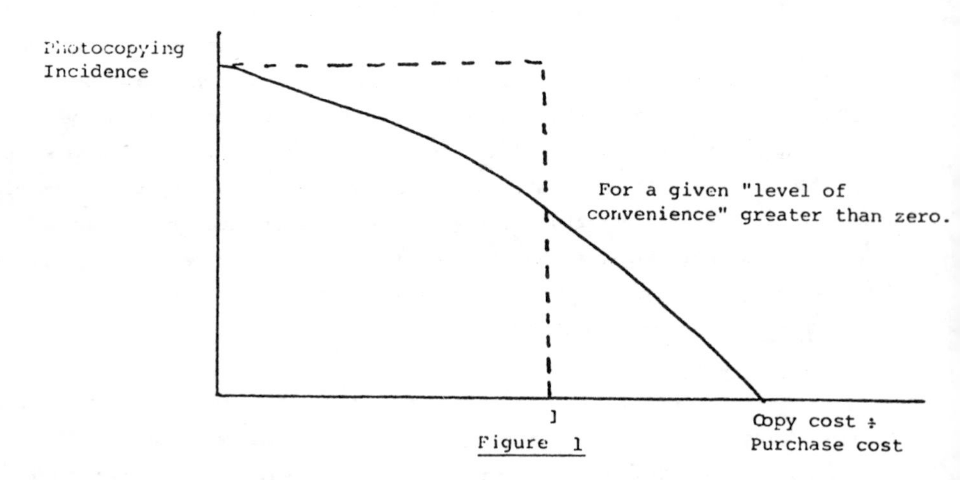

Figure 1

One might argue that the relation shown in Figure 1 should be discrete rather than continuous: That is, photocopying costs would always be either above or below purchase costs. At a copy/purchase cost ratio less than 1, one would always choose to copy. At a copy/purchase cost ratio above 1, one would always choose to purchase. The dotted lines and horizontal axis would then show this relation in Figure 1.

The reason this is not the case shown in the figure is that variables other than copy cost and purchase cost affect photocopying incidence and these have been held constant at a positive level in Figure 1.

Convenience of photocopying relative to purchase is probably the most important of these variables and this may vary among individuals. For exampl at a low copy to purchase cost ratio everyone would find the convenience factor overwhelming and choose to copy. As the copy/purchase cost ratio increased, a few persons would choose not to copy for every (small) increase in the ratio until only very wealthy persons would choose to copy at high copy/purchase cost ratios. This explains the continuous nature of the graph in Figure 1.

Thus photocopying incidence is seen to depend primarily on three factors copy cost, purchase (of book or journal) cost, and relative convenience of copying as opposed to purchase. Figure 1 shows two relations with one held constant. To give a concrete example, novels are rated less economical to photocopy than to purchase. Evidence on this suggests that, for books at least, purchasing prices average 1 1/2 to 2¢ per page.[3] The reason for this is fairly clear. It rests on a technological asymmetry in favor of publishers. This technological asymmetry in favor of the publisher also holds for offset printing and mimeographing or any other technology available to consumers. Hence, publishers' costs would be expected to equal or be less than consumers' cost of reproduction of entire works.

Unfortunately the analysis is not so straight-forward. Cost advantages do not lie entirely on the side of the publisher. There is a somewhat offsetting asymmetry in favor of consumers--namely consumers may presently photocopy without incurring royalty costs while this is not true for publishers. Further, users need copy only those parts of a publication in which they are particularly interested. Consequently although their costs of copying, per page copied, are higher than those of publishers their costs of copying what they want may be less than the cost of printing an entire journal or book.

With regard to technical journals, there is no possible cost advantage of purchase over copying when only one or two articles (or parts of articles) are to be copied. To some extent, the same is true of technical books in which it is likely that only small portions will be photocopied. It may well be true as well for a number of other kinds of printed matter, such as sheet music, pictorial or graphic material, costly newsletters. However, we found no relevant data on photo reproduction of such items.

Because of the cost differential just referred to, it appears that to the extent that photocopying affects the quantity of publication, its impact falls primarily on technical books and journals and possibly a few other categories. Photocopying all of a novel or non-technical book or magazine is simply too uneconomical to merit much concern.[4]

Restricting free photocopying would presumably increase the number of technical journals that could be published at or above cost and in this way could increase the number or size of such journals, increasing the number of published articles. This should increase the number of worthwhile ideas in circulation.

2. Purpose of Photocopying

A key question is whether photocopying is a substitute for journal purchase or whether it is a substitute for notetaking. If it is a substitute for journal purchase then at least some of the hypothetical advantages from photocopy restriction may be realized. Put differently, that photocopying be a substitute for journal purchase is a necessary but not a sufficient condition for directly increasing journal sales (and future creativity and consumption?) via photocopy restriction. On the other hand, to the extent that photocopying is merely a substitute for notetaking, photocopy royalties would have no effect on subscriptions.

This question readily boils down to an empirical issue: Is photocopying primarily a substitute for journal purchase or for notetaking? The empirical evidence is, however, very meagre at present, at least while some current rese activities are completed. However, Line and Wood (1975) provide evidence on the question of whether photocopying serves as a substitute for journal purcha or notetaking. Their evidence indicates that in almost no case does photocopy serve as a substitute for journal purchase.

The answer to this question is so central to any policy remedy, however, that PIE-C strongly recommends that policymakers should not ignore it. Lacking hard evidence, CONTU members might ask themselves questions such as: "If I suddenly found that the option of photocopying (say) journal articles became less attractive (because of increased photocopying costs or for some other reason), would I resort to more notetaking or to journal purchase?" Conversely, "What would be my reaction if photocopying became more attractive for some reason? Would this decrease my notetaking of journal articles or would it cause me to cancel current journal subscriptions and substitute photocopying?" "What would be the reaction of other persons faced with the same decisions?"

These are not trivial questions. To a very large extent, the facts on the use of copying in lieu of notetaking will determine the effectiveness of any policy remedies.

It is worthwhile to quote at length an authority on the subject. Dr. Gordon Williams, Director of the Center for Research Libraries in Chicago, cites his observation on coin-operated photocopy machines in libraries.

> "In my own observation, use of these machines, and indeed my own use, in lieu of any possible purchase is so rare as to be absolutely insignificant! They are primarily used in lieu of more time consuming, and inefficient notetaking by hand. I would suppose that most of you would agree that, indeed, this is most of your own personal use in the use of photocopying machines for copyrighted materials--notetaking
>
> "This kind of use--in lieu of notetaking--I take to be fair use. But if the operation of these machines is to be stopped or hindered, I am confident that virtually no <u>more</u> book or journal sales would result. Or, if taxed for what is fair use (and without a monitor there to oversee each operation and forgive each fair use, this would be the result of a blanket charge) either this is unfair to the user, or it will inhibit his use, and waste his time and effort in the legitimate development and use of new technology."

Similarly, the available evidence indicates the number of people who faced with photocopying restrictions would subscribe to journals may be small. For example, many journals have few readers, hence, a person might occasionally photocopy an article from a journal but not subscribe to it, even if he could not photocopy.

Dr. Williams notes;

"Several publishers, and I think specifically of the American Chemical Society and the American Psychological Association, have done surveys to discover the number of readers of the articles in their publications. The American Psychological Association found that the average number of readers was only 7 per article in their publications, and the American Chemical Society found the average to be only 10 persons for articles in their publications."

Speculating on a general explanation for this phenomenon, Dr. Williams notes:

"Not many people use journals except, perhaps, for a few current general ones such as Science or Nature. What they use are articles in journals. But the peculiar thing about periodicals is that you cannot subscribe to articles, but only to the whole miscellaneous collection of articles that constitute the periodical. In addition, you must subscribe and pay in advance without knowing what the articles will be about or who their authors will be. In effect, subscribers are being required to buy ten or twenty articles they are not interested in to get one that they are."[5]

C. EVALUATION OF PHOTOCOPYING RESTRICTIONS

1. Impacts on Producers

Three parties are directly affected by the degree of stringency in the application of copyrights to photocopying: authors, publishers and the "photocopying public" (those who do photocopying). In Chapter II, we indicated that the two stages of production consist of authors and publishers, for the most part separate and very different kinds of entities. In this section, we show that photocopying and charges for or restrictions on it are more likely to affect publishers and their output than authors and theirs. That either is substantially affected by photocopying is shown to be unlikely so long as photocopying is restricted to personal use.

In light of the fact that the existing evidence suggests that technical journals are the form of copyrighted publication most commonly photocopied the first question is the effect of photocopying on subscriptions. For the most part the same comments could be made about its effect on sales of books, although the magnitudes would presumably be smaller.

As was indicated in the preceeding sub-section, use of photocopying as a substitute for subscriptions (or purchase and a fortiori for resale could have an adverse impact on publishers revenues. Extensive use of photocopying for such purposes would deny publishers the opportunity to appropriate a portion of the benefits generated through their publications.

It was also shown that under present and at least near future technology, publishers have and will retain a cost advantage per page in producing copies of existing works. Further the existing evidence indicates that photocopying is not a substitute for subscription (or purchase) in the vast majority of cases. Consequently, although there might be some slight reduction in the production and circulation of journals it is likely to be small and there is no empirical evidence available so far as we know that such reduction has occured.

The fear has been expressed that photocopying might impair the financial strength of the publishing industry. There is no evidence to support any general argument along these lines. First, most of the kinds of materials produced by commercial publishing houses are not widely photocopied (Appendix B). Second, the commercial publishing industry has prospered during the period of expansion of the photocopying industry. The industry has grown: its profits have risen.* The evidence seems to indicate that the industry is not suffering as a consequence of photocopying. The evidence would be more relevant and conclusive if the industry relaxed its secrecy and reported on a line-of-business basis. Third, a large portion of the types of journals most commonly photo-reproduced are published by not-for-profit organizations. In unpublished research done for CONTU, Dean Bernard Fry collected data showing that 31.6% of technical journals are published by commercial publishers. The remaining 68.4% are published by societies, university presses, and other non-profit publishers.[6]

Actual earnings of journals operating various levels of subscription sales are not known. However, there are a number of journals operating with very small subscription levels, less than 2,000, some with substantially less. For example, the Journal of Economic Theory and the Journal of Mathematical Economics are reported to have roughly 1,500 and 900 subscribers respectively. From this easily observable data it may be inferred that these journals are presently receiving revenues adequate to keep them operating and, for those that are not subsidized, it indicates that the minimum efficient size of a technical journal is small. If they were not receiving enough to cover costs these journals would not be published.

The fact that many journals are published by not-for-profit organizations, often as a benefit of membership in a professional association, means that for some the effective break-even point may be very low indeed.

---

* Cf. Standard and Poor's Industry Surveys: Communication. New York, 1976, pp. C90-C93.

Consequently, it appears that most journals are operating considerably above the minimum efficient level for survival. To the extent that that is true, small reductions in their volume of subscriptions would not threaten their continuation.

More refined tests should be made to measure the effects of photocopying on technical publications. Such studies should control for variables, in addition to photocopying incidence, which affect publishing revenues and profits over time. Changes associated with changes in competition might be one such variable. As already stated photocopying for resale could impinge significantly on publishers revenues. Further the existing publishers' cost advantage in reproduction of existing works could be eroded in the relatively near future, at least for copying progressively larger parts of whole books or issues of journals. Consequently, it is desirable to examine also the question of whether technological developments are apt to effect the producers' cost advantage. However, all the available evidence supports the conclusion that no large adverse effects of free photocopying appear to impinge on the publishers, even on publishers of technical books and journals which constitute the only vulnerable portion of the industry. Finally, free photocopying may add something to revenues of publishers by increasing library demand by users who photocopy parts of journals. Many of these users would not buy the journal were free photocopying not available to them.[7]

Conceivably adverse effects could accrue to authors of such works. The actual prospect of such result is patently small because there is no evidence that even increased photocopying would reduce sales substantially.

As discussed in Chapter II, authors of professional and related works appear not to be motivated substantially by the prospects of reward through royalties. First, their incomes frequently comes from other sources, university, industrial or governmental salaries or grants. Second, authors are often motivated by non-monetary incentives, interest in the subject-matter, personal recognition, increased opportunity for professional advancement, for example. Evidence that indirect monetary and non-monetary rewards from technical research often outweigh the direct monetary rewards from copyrighted publication is found in the preferences of academicians. Many of them, for example, typically prefer to publish in academic journals which pay no royalty and may charge a page fee, over publishing in books of readings which offer a small royalty or stipend. Most importantly, non-royalty related rewards from technical publishing are not reduced by unrestricted photocopying; if anything, they are increased, since photocopying increases dissemination of their works.

2. Impacts on Users and Consumers

It appears that may restriction on photocopying for personal use would have little impact on the total number of subscriptions (or book sales). Consequently, given the power to restrict such photocopying, the economically rational action for publishers would appear to be to establish royalties rather than to restrict such photocopying altogether.

Obviously, users of photocopies of copyrighted works would suffer a loss of income, income would be transferred from them to publishers. It is conceivable that receipts from new royalties would exert downward pressure on subscription prices. Under conditions of effectice competition there would be a tendency for this to occur as a consequence of some expansion of the number and size of journals. The question of how any new balance among level and structure of royalties, individual prices and institutional prices for subscriptions and books would evolve is complicated and is not central to the issues at hand. What is clear is that direct users of photocopying of copyrighted works would lose income to publishers. Substantial royalty income would, of course, permit the expansion of existing journals and the introduction of new ones. One of the potential benefits of increased production of technical journals, referred to above, is expanding the pool of referees. As stated in Chapter I, the consumer interest is often remote but real, in the issues at hand. This is a good example, increasing the number and kinds of worthwhile ideas in circulation should redound eventually to the benefit of consumers. However, the number of journals is so large now in most of the major technical fields that it seems unlikely that the benefits to consumers of increasing the number of referee pools would be significant.

There is another aspect of the efficiency of royalty payments. Introducing royalty payments would involve some very substantial administrative costs. The administration of a royalty system would require charging for each copy of copyrighted material but not, presumably for other copies: allocating the royalty receipts to producers; accounting and reporting. This appears to be a very complex set of tasks. The costs of carrying them out would appear to be very substantial.

The photocopy question has equity as well as efficiency implications. To the extent that the income and wealth of the users of photocopies of copyrighted materials is less than those of publishers, photocopy restriction will result in a more concentrated (and less egalitarian) distribution of income and wealth. For profit-making publishing firms, all photocopy restriction alternatives tend to have this effect, at least in the current period.

There are no data on the income or wealth position of users of photocopying, so there is no way of making a simple statement about the distributional effects of introducing payment for photocopying. However, it is clear that the costs of increased copying will be borne in the relatively near future by consumers as a group, and their income and wealth levels are less than those of stockholders on the average, and hence, presumably less than those of stockholders of commercial publishing houses. Hence, royalty payments tend to have undesirable equity consequences. Income and wealth distribution effects are unclear for the case of not-for-profit publishers and for any case of for-profit publishers who, for some reason, consistently subsidize particular journals.

The expected consequences of any increase in publisher revenues brought about by new royalties appear to be several. Publishers who were operating prior to the imposition of royalties would make windfall gains. For previously successful for-profit publishers these would be windfall profits; for some, such gains might permit continuing an erstwhile unprofitable operation. For non-profit publishers, they might permit expansion in otherwise economically infeasible areas or they might permit higher salaries for managers. For both there would be some incentives to expand output. To the extent that the relevant publishing market is competitive, the availability of royalties on photocopying would exert some downward pressure on future subscription rates. This would partially offset the stimulus to expansion, and reduce future windfall gains, but would leave the royalties on old issues of journals as pure windfall gains.

In examining another equity aspect an analogy may be instructive. Most library users use a desk when reading the material of publishers. To a large extent, use of the desk makes reading of the publishers' materials easier. If forced to use (say) journals only in libraries and if forced to stand (or sit on the floor) while reading them, patrons would be far more likely to give up on library journals and purchase their own journals. As a result, one might question whether libraries should rent out desk space to journal users and return this rent to publishers.

If this were done, competitively priced journals published after the "desk charge returnable to publishers" were imposed, might be priced lower. The sum of desk charges plus the lower journal price would then return the competitive profit to publishers. To publishers who earned the competitive return (profit) prior to the desk charge, however, the desk charge would represent a pure windfall to publishers.

Since any refunds on the purchase price of journals purchased prior to the royalty arrangement is unlikely, royalties on these (old) journals would represent a pure windfall to publishers (one which expects no downward pres ure on prices).

The point of the above analogy is that redirecting revenues from photocopiers to publishers is a somewhat arbitrary choice. Users of any item indirectly connected to publisher output (e.g. journals) could be redirecte to publisher profits with the same logic.

The possibility that net benefits will occur from restricting (charging for) photocopying is much less clear than is the timing of these benefits. Benefits to users from photocopying access occur in the period in which the copying takes place. However, benefits to most consumers--technological or other intellectual advances--occur only in the future, possibly the distant future. This is important because there is strong evidence that people pre consumption in the present to consumption in the future. This increases th net benefits of unrestricted photocopying. How much present consumption is preferred over future consumption can be determined by use of a rate of time preference which may be taken as being equal to the discount rate. Th higher the discount rate--i.e., the greater the society's preference for satisfaction now rather than in the future--the less the value today (prese value) for any given future benefit.

Finally, it is conceivable that the nature of research will vary depend ing on the degree to which photocopying is restricted. If the cost of phot copying were to rise substantially research might be of a different type from that performed if photocopying remains fairly accessible. With restrictions, returns to publishers and some authors of intellectual works, such as books of readings, can be expected to be greater. However, returns to authors--especially non-monetary returns--of technical articles would be slightly less. The amount of their expected loss would depend on the amount of their returns from non-royalty sources -- e.g., from recognition, from grants and from the tenure/non/tenure decision in academic institution To the extent that through unrestricted photocopying authors are made more dependent on grants, government, industry or foundations may gain more cont over the research activities and over the orientation of authors who derive a greater portion of their incomes from royalties on copyrighted works. Th is not thought to be a very important point and is mentioned here more or less in passing for the sake of completeness.

Finally, even in the unlikely event that photocopy restriction could make some marginal difference in the type of research conducted, it is not clear whether more non-governmental research would result in a greater social benefit than other research that might benefit from low priced photo copy accessibility. Nor is it clear whether an increase in subsidies would lead to greater or less academic freedom. Thus, it may be possible to say something about the slight effects on types of research from photocopy accessibility. It is very difficult, however, to say what are the effects of increases and decreases in these types of research on the general good or the social welfare.

3. Overall Impacts

There is a basic problem of economic efficiency relating to the extension of royalty charges for photocopying copyrighted works. It is more fully developed in Appendix A. One can think of two separate sets of activities or "sectors", publication and photocopying.

Permitting publishers to impose a royalty on the photocopying of their copyrighted works would increase the cost of photocopying. That would deprive users of photocopiers (for this purpose) of some of the value (consumers' surplus, in technical terms) to them of photocopying that material. Similarly, it would tend to appropriate revenues of providers of photocopying services. Providers of photocopying are not solely manufacturers of hardware; the service installations where machine reproduction is provided for sale or for"in-house" or library use are the actual providers of the service. Although the percentage impact on photocopying (as well as offset and stencil copying) would apparently be small (Section B above) in absolute terms they might be substantial; especially in the future. The royalty would constitute an increase in the cost of photocopying, tending to increase its price and to reduce the amount of photocopying service produced and consumed, as well as reducing the producers and consumers surplus (net benefit) in that sector.

These sums would be transferred to publishers. The transfer would occur despite the fact that the photocopying service requires many inputs in addition to the copyrighted materials themselves and despite the fact that if the photocopying is not a substitute for purchase, it is performed at no cost to the publishers.

The increase in publishers' revenues can best be thought of as equivalent to a reduction in the (net) cost of producing the type of publication involved. A decrease in the price would, under conditions of effective competition, tend to increase output in the publishing sector, benefiting both customers and producers in that sector.

The output of photocopying services would tend to be decreased, that of publication increased, resulting in a misallocation of resources. Only in the event that in the status quo ante publication levels were below the socially optimal amount could the conclusion be reversed. It is impossible to determine whether the level of publication is at, above, or below the socially optimum level. However, if publishers are failing to appropriate a large portion of the benefits they create, there is a tendency for publication to be too little in social terms. A key question, then, is whether publishers have and use adequate alternatives to royalties as a means of appropriatin the value of their product.

D. ALTERNATIVES TO ROYALTIES

There is an alternative way of compensating publishers for their full cost of production and facilitating the appropriation of a large portion of the benefits created through publication of copyrighted works, namely price discrimination.

The basic rationale for price discrimination was sketched out in Chapter II-D. Here it is appropriate to point out that price discriminatio may, to a large extent, overcome the difficulties of non-appropriability in photocopying of publishers' output: by charging higher prices to e.g., lib for non-appropriable multiple use than to individual subscribers for fully appropriable use. Similarly higher prices can be charged to other institu (e.g., business and government) which distribute publishers' output to mult users and create non-appropriability difficulties.

As already indicated, a large portion of photocopying is copying of technical journals in libraries and other institutions. Obviously more people typically want to use a library's copy of any particular journal tha want to use any individually subscribed journal (usually one person presumably). An institution's demand for a journal subscription can be thought of as a monetary expression of the cumulated wants of all the libra clients who want (use) the journal. A price change of any given (absolute) amount tends therefore to be smaller relative to the total income of the demanders of institutional than of individual subscriptions. This tends to make the institutional demand less elastic than individual consumer demand. As a result the publisher can charge a higher price to the institution than individual subscribers.

If prices were set on the basis of long run marginal cost adjusted in accordance with the inverse elasticity rule, if libraries (and other instit dealt with publishers on an arms-length basis, and if there were effective competition in the relevant portions of the publishing industry, revenues of publishers of photocopied materials would move toward the optimal level.

A quick empirical check shows that price discrimination is widely used The subscription price of many technical journals (and of some books) is higher to libraries than to individual subscribers. This would not be rational were library demand for journals not less elastic than individual demands. Library demand would not be as inelastic (and possibly not as hig as it is now were the photocopying option not available to library journal users.

It is possible to formalize the publishers' calculation of revenue-maximizing price discrimination. This is done in Appendix C.

However, it is important to note that commercial publishers are not entirely free to discriminate between institutional and individual subscribers: postal rules prohibit their use of class-two permits if price discrimination exceeds two to one. Non-profit publishers are free to discriminate without such constraint. As mentioned above a recent study showed 68.4 percent of technical journal publishers to be non-commercial publishers.

Although there is no way, at least without extensive empirical study, to determine whether virtually all the benefits would be appropriated by a combination of price discrimination and charging royalties on reproduction for sale, it is clear that a large proportion of them would be. The fact that there are a large number of the type of journals most vulnerable to competition from photo reproduction as well as the fact that publishing in general is flourishing, indicate that enough of the benefits currently being produced are captured to provide a virile source of printed information.

E. IMPLICATIONS FOR POLICY

The general conclusions of the analysis presented in this chapter indicate that CONTU should not recommend any further restrictions on photocopying beyond those that are included in the 1976 Act and that fair use should be formally defined to include photocopying and similar reproduction for personal use. The basis of this recommendation and a summary of the major and minor arguments for both sides of the issue are summarized below:

Major arguments against expanding restrictions on photocopying of copyrighted works

1) Photocopying royalties shift revenues from the photocopy "sector" to the publishing "sector" and in this way misallocate resources. That is, persons seeking convenience (a substitute for notetaking) wind up paying for publishing output under royalty schemes, which was not their intention.

2) Substantial administrative costs are involved in any royalty scheme.

3) A method currently exists for allowing publishers to recover most if not all non-appropriable costs from non-paying users of published works (principally library users) and not exclusively photocopy users. The method is price discrimination, by which publishers charge institutions more than the individual subscription rate.

4) The size of the minimum efficient scale for journal subscriptions is small. Therefore, large publisher outputs are unnecessary to sustain existence of a large number of technical journals. The fact that most technical journals are subsidized strengthens this argument (and allows for a small minimum efficient journal scale size).

5) Publisher profits are healthy and not currently in need of being revived.

6) A royalty system would be likely to generate windfall gains to publishers from three sources:

a) Even if publishing is highly competitive some windfall gains will accrue to existing publishers during the period before the competitive market adjustment is being accomplished. Some of the publishers who were operating before the change would retain windfall gains permanently.

b) To the extent that the publishing industry is not effectively competitive increased revenues from price discrimination via a royalty syste would not be entirely offset by corresponding decreased revenues from price discrimination via different institutional and individual subscription charg

c) Royalties to publishers from photocopying of pre-royalty publications would involve pure windfalls to publishers unless a system is set up to make refunds on the subscription price to previous purchasers of journals--which is unlikely.

7) Increased future creativity from royalties or other photocopy restrictions are questionable, at best. This is largely because authors of technical works--which have the greatest photocopy incidence--would not get significant royalties from such publications nor are they motivated to any large extent by the pecuniary rewards flowing directly from their technical publications.

8) In many cases, the economics of photocopying are outweighed by the economies of publishing. In these cases, it is more economical (cheaper) fo a user to purchase a publisher's output rather than to copy it.

9) Any royalty system is likely to have very large administrative costs associated with it. These are deadweight losses borne ultimately by consumers.

Minor arguments against additional restriction

1) Easier photocopy access may increase the ease of future creation because of the increased accessibility of source materials for authors.

2) Any potential benefits to consumers from photocopy royalties and their restrictions occur in the future, mostly in the distant future. A posi social discount rate is desirable to promote egalitarian inter-generational income transfers. This makes present consumption more desirable than future consumption and argues for less photocopy restriction, thereby favoring present over future consumption.

3) Any royalty scheme results in a redistribution of resources from consumers to publishers. To the extent that the income of consumers of photocopiers of copyrighted works is less than the income of stockholders of publishing houses (which is likely) photocopy royalties result in a less egalitarian (more concentrated) income distribution.

Major arguments for restricted photocopy access (through a royalty scheme or some other mechanism)

1) Future creativity and output may be increased as a result of more technical journals being published and possibly larger remuneration and incentives to authors. This is to be contrasted with minor argument #1 for unrestricted photocopy access.

2) To the extent that photocopying is a substitute for purchase of publishers' output, a photocopy restriction (and/or royalty) will result in better resource allocation among sectors in the economy.

Minor arguments for restricted photocopy access (through a royalty scheme or some other mechanism

1) A royalty scheme would increase non-government-subsidized output which might reduce governmental influence on creativity.

2) If future creativity and publishers' outputs are increased, this may increase the future supply of photocopiable materials and increase demand for future photocopying. This effect may somewhat offset the decline in quantity demanded of photocopiable materials as a result of photocopying royalties.

Finally, there is a question of whether it is desirable to try to legislate now to handle future technological developments. Photocopying technology is advancing rapidly, changing the availability and cost of reproduction outside publishing houses.

The intent of Congress seems to reflect a "cross-one-bridge-at-a-time" attitude by requiring periodic review of the provisions of Section 22 every five years.

CONTU testimony, however, is not without queries concerning future technology. In most cases, the emphasis is on the subject of the need for more and more stringent photocopying restrictions now.

The dangers of presently legislating against the vaguely perceived threats of future technological change are seldom discussed.

Two considerations mitigate against imposing restrictions in the present to forestall future contingencies. First, once a governmental function is established that grants monopoly status to any set of suppliers, a vested interest in the perpetuation of that status builds up. That economic interest provides resources for perpetuation of the position, even after any social justification for its initiation has long past. Second, commercial interests can be counted on to press vigorously, and with ample resources, for any protectionist action that would benefit them as soon as the situation changes so that they are threatened by new developments. Consequently, it would appear appropriate not to recommend any restrictions greater than the minimum required to meet current conditions.

FOOTNOTES

[1] Letter dated June 22, 1977 to Public Interest Economics Center from Robert W. Frase, Assistant Executive Director and Economist CONTU.

[2] Letter of June 22, 1977, cited above.

[3] Economic Council of Canada, Report on Intellectual and Industrial Property, (Ottawa: Information Canada), 1971.

[4] Ibid

[5] Gordon Williams, CONTU Testimony, October 1976, pp. 128-129.

[6] Letter from Frase, op. cit. above.

[7] CONTU Testimony, October 1976, pp. 128-129, op. cit. above.

APPENDIX A

OPTIMAL PRICE DISCRIMINATION

A large proportion of photocopying of technical publications is done in libraries. Technical publishers are aware of this and are able to price discriminate by charging higher subscription rates to libraries than to the general public. In fact, if publishers have knowledge as to the incidence of photocopying of their journal, they may (and possibly do) estimate revenues lost from library photocopying. This is estimated by the publisher from considerations such as frequency of journal photocopying times the probability that photocopy restriction would result in an additional journal sale. This equals the number of lost journal sales as a result of library photocopying. Multiplying this number by price per journal yields gross revenues lost as a result of free library photocopying = GR. Publishers are free to raise prices to libraries somewhat. Doing so would tend to recover revenues lost through library photocopying.

What would be the revenue maximizing price differential? The answer depends upon the new demand curve which is generated by libraries.

The price of individual subscriptions depends upon the demand for subscriptions by individuals. Here $q_i = f(p_i)$ represents individual demands where i refers to the ith subscriber, q = number of journals sold and p = the journal price.

In the case of libraries, $q_e = g(p_e)$; $p_e = h(\sum_{i=1}^{n} q_i)$, where e refers to the eth library. Hence, in the case of libraries, demand for a subscription at each library depends upon demand by the n individuals who demand the publication from the library.

The important point here is that more persons want a library journal than the number of persons who demand any individually subscribed journal. Therefore, the quantity demanded of a library journal is much less subject to price fluctuation (less elastic) than is demand for an individually subscribed journal. As a result, the publisher can charge the library a higher price for the journal than he can charge an individual user.

Some library users are, presumably, persons who would buy the journal had it not been available to be photocopied. The switch of these persons from individual subscribers to library users does not result in a loss to the publisher equal to the revenues they would have paid the publisher from subscribing defined as "GR" above. Rather, it is equal to "GR" minus additional revenues the library is able to earn as a result of marginal individual subscribers (persons who would not subscribe were the photocopy and library option available) entering the library photocopy market and increasing library demand for the journal. Call this additional revenue "AR". The difference is equal to net revenues resulting from a switch from individual subscription demand to library demand called "NR" = GR - AR. The sign of NR may be positive, negative or zero, depending on all the factors mentioned above.

It is important to recognize that it is unlikely that NR = GR. If AR is greater than zero, publishers would not lose from photocopying an amount equal to the loss of subscriptions from persons who choose to photocopy rather than to subscribe.

For readers so inclined, this model of "reduced adverse effects to publishers as a result of photocopying by library users contributing to price discrimination opportunities for publishers" is shown in the graphs in Figure 2.

Explanation of Figure 2.

First, it should be pointed out that individuals switching from market i to market L did not necessarily increase demand but likely made it more inelastic. Compare graphs showing "library" and "individual subscription" markets in Figure 2. This is because increased library demand for a journal's use will not necessarily result in more journals ordered by the library but will result in more use of (photocopying of) the existing journal(s) owned by the library. This is especially true if journals are for library use only.

Profits of the publisher are maximized where the last journal sold in the individual market adds as much to total revenues as the last journal sold to libraries; that is, where the marginal revenues in the individual and library markets are equal.

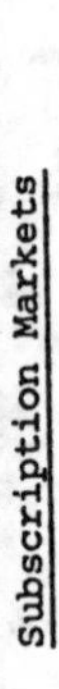

Publisher Price Discrimination Between Library and Individual Subscription Markets

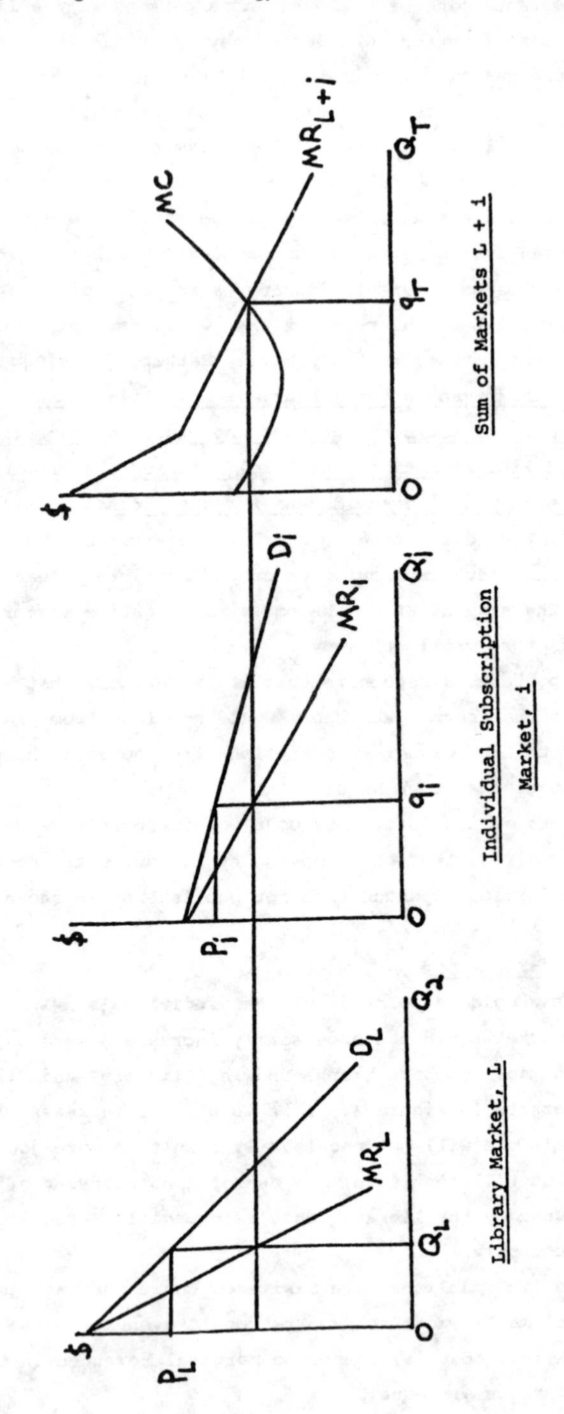

Library Market, L

Individual Subscription Market, i

Sum of Markets L + i

Figure 2

To accomplish this, the marginal revenue curves of the two markets are summed horizontally, giving combined marginal revenue function MR_{L+i} in the far right panel of Figure 2. MR_{L+i} is equated to marginal cost MC, indicating the optimal output q_T. To equalize marginal revenue in each market at the profit maximizing value, we construct a horizontal line from the point where $MC = MR_{L+i}$. The optimal output in each market is found where this horizontal line intersects the markets' MR function, and the profit maximizing price is found by reading off the relevant demand function the price at which the optimal quantity is demanded. This gives the pictoral explanation of the theory behind the observation that the higher priced O P_L is optimal in the less elastic library market and the lower priced O P_i is optimal in the more elastic individual subscription market.

Once again, the moral of this story is that publishers reap new gains as well as suffer new losses when increased photocopying (even with no royalty charge) results in decreased individual journal subscriptions and increased library photocopying. The loss results from a decline in (individual) subscriptions ($\downarrow q_i$). The gain results from less elastic and possibly higher library journal demand resulting in price and possibly quantity increases in the library journal market. ($\uparrow P_{L'}$, possible $\uparrow Q_{L'}$). (See Figure 2.) Net effects are uncertain, but are probably less than the gross loss effect ($\Delta p_i q_i$) and may even result in a net increase in publisher profits.

An Impediment to Market Self-Regulation

A problem with the price discrimination solution is that institutional factors prevent it from working to the degree it might work if unencumbered. Currently, U.S. law prevents more than a 2:1 ratio of prices charged institutions vs. individuals for journal subscriptions. The penalty for violating this law is loss of the second class mailing privilege. This is no small loss and nearly all technical journals keep within the 2 to 1 pricing rule in order to keep their second-class mailing privilege.

It may be desirable to re-examine the rationale for the 2 to 1 pricing rule in light of the social advantages of price discrimination. Allowing price discrimination to work in a less encumbered fashion would increase the viability of the market vs. government as a regulator of photocopying of copyrighted works. Suggesting re-examination of this pricing rule may lie on the periphery of the area of authority and responsibility of CONTU.

APPENDIX B

THE PUBLISHING INDUSTRY:

EMPIRICAL DESCRIPTION

A. <u>SIZE AND COMPOSITION</u>

As shown in table 3, publisher's receipts have grown steadily througho the first half of this decade and preliminary figures indicate a continuatio of this trend.

TABLE 3

Publishing Industry Sales 1971-76

Year	Sales ($ Billions)	Percent Change from 1971
1971	2.9	–––––
1972	3.0	3.4
1973	3.1	6.8
1974	3.5	20.6
1975	3.8	31.0
1976p	4.6	58.6

Source: extracted from <u>American Association of Publishers Report</u> and <u>Publish Weekly</u> 6/76

In 1975 12 billion copies of books were distributed: this is roughly 5.5 books per capita. These billion-plus copies were composed of 39,372 new and revised book titles. (This means that there was an average of about 30,500 copies of each title). 16% of all titles were in economics and sociology, wh 10% of all titles were fiction. 1976 figures are not yet available.

These statisties together with the data on stock market value and profit of the publishing industry indicate that it is a profitable and growing in- dustry and has remained so during the period when photocoping became a major activity.

B. ROYALTY PAYMENTS & MARKETING EXPENSES

Publishing industry analysts typically divide the industry into six major divisions: Mass market paperback, College textbooks, Elementary and High School textbooks [EL-HI], Trade books (fiction & non-fiction; juvenile and adult; hard and soft), Professional and Book Club. Consolidated accoun- ting statements are available for each of the above divisions. Of particula interest to CONTU were the data presented on royalty payments in each divisi as a per cent of net sales. New sales are gross sales minus returns and allowances. Royalty payments are those monies paid to authors for the prima rights to their work. Sometimes publishers also purchase subsidiary rights which allows reprinting, translations, syndication and the like. Subsidiary rights are important in only one division--trade books.

Table 4 shows royalty payments for primary rights as a percent of net sales for each division.

TABLE 4

Division	Royalty as % of Net Sales
Mass Market	29
College	15.2
Trade	13.7
Professional	10.1
El-hi	6.0
Book Club	6.0

More detailed statistics do not reveal any systematic variations in royalty payments either by firm size or profitability.

Within trade publications, 20% of the sampled firms recieved 91% of the income from subsidiary rights. Normally the publishing house and the author split the subsidary revenues (after expenses) on a 50-50 basis. There are exceptions. The publishers' share from juvenile books is typically 66%, while the authors' share from adult paperbacks averages 60%.

Marketing expenses fall into two catagories, selling expenses and promotion. In general they are expenditures made by the publisher to attract or capture the attention of a prospective buyer. There is a relationship between marketing expenses and royalty payments. This is portrayed in Table 5.

TABLE 5

Relationship between Royalties & Market Expense

Royalties as % of Net Sales	Market Expense as % of Net Sales
Book Club (6.0)	Mass Market (7.8)
El-hi (6.0)	College (14.4)
Professional (10.1)	Trade (15.6)
Trade (13.7)	Professional (16.9)
College (15.2)	El-hi (20.8)
Mass Market (29.0)	Book Club (35.0)

In general high royalties are paid to those authors who can penetrate markets with a minimum of marketing support. Conversely, high marketing expenses--such as book clubs where the publisher creates and organizes a market--mean low royalty payments. Simple linear regression techniques indicate that for every $10 increase in marketing expense, royalty payments decline $7.36.

What this means is, publishers pay writers not for the quality of the id nor for the potential impact on the human condition but for the writers' abil to attract the attention of prospe :ctive buyers.

C. DISTRIBUTION CHANNELS

The most important book distribution channels are shown in Table 6.

TABLE 6

1975 Distribution Channels

	Gross Revenues ($ billions)
General Retailer	1.1
Direct mail	1.0
El-hi stores	.7
College stores	.7
Libraries & others	.4

Very little photocopying is to be expected along the two major distribution channels, general retailers and direct mail. There is, simply, no opportunity. El-hi stores and college stores similiarly offer little if any opportunity to photocopy or tend to be excluded by the face-to-face teaching clause.

Libraries and other institutions are expected to be the major places whe copying will occur. These channels account for only about 10% of all sales.

The above expectation about the location of photo copying is based on two considerations:

there is more ability to copy at the library because of the presence of self-service, coin-operated machines and

there is more interest in doing so because books distributed thru libraries tend to be more expensive than those offered thru other sources. Evidence on this second point is contained in the following table.

TABLE 7

Revenues per unit by Channel

Channel	$/unit
Direct Mail	5.84
Library	4.97
College store	4.30
El-hi store	2.55
General Retail	2.53

D. MARKET POWER

There are two places where market power may arise, between author and publisher and between publisher and consumer. PIE-C focused on market power because with increasing concentration of economic power, prices tend to rise, output to be reduced and resources tend to be used inefficiently.

Theoretically market power exists whenever the elasticity of demand is less than infinity. As a practical matter, economists inspect the cross-elasticity of demand and concentration ratios to test for the presence of significant monopoly power.

Concentration ratios are computed by dividing industry sales into the sales of the some of the largest firms in the industry. The shares of the 4 largest or 8 largest firms are often used.

Below, table 8 portrays concentration ratios for five categories of books. These catagories unfortunately differ from those used earlier. Textbooks include both El-Hi and college; technical compares rather well with professional; and religious, general and reference make up the Trade, Mass Market and Book Club categories.

TABLE 8

Concentration Ratios in Book Publication

Product	Percent of sales by 4 largest	Percent of sales by 8 largest
Textbook	33	54
Technical	39	57
Religious	36	51
General	29	47
References	71	82

Source - Census of Manufactures 1972

It is clear that the greatest concentrations occur in the reference-work area. Furthermore the 8 largest firms control over half the market in all but one of the product categories.

It is useful also to recall that revenues from subsidiary rights are concentrated in the hands of a few publishers.

The relationship between author and publisher is more problematic. authors are free to seek any publisher from among those who publish in their field. Once an author selects and is selected by a publisher no further competition takes place. The terms of the author-publisher relationship vary but patterns do emerge. As noted above in general author-publisher terms are strongly related to marketing considerations. If an author can attract attention he/she will receive higher royalties.

- The publishing industry is financially healthy and growing with no-fee photocopying.
- Consumers spend 4.6 billion dollars a year on books
- Royalty payments are strongly related to marketing strategy
- Subsidiary rights are not important in 5 or 6 categories
- 10% of all books are distributed thru libraries
- Photocopying is likely to occur in libraries
- some monopoly power may exist in the publishing industry, especially in the reference category.

APPENDIX C

Determining Optimal Photocopy Restriction

The theoretical framework for determining the optimal amount of photocopy restrictiveness is set forth below. This framework determines optimal price and quantity of photocopying, price and quantity of journals and the optimal photocopy charge (royalty). The theoretical framework shows how these price, output, and royalty levels would be determined. That is, it shows the data requirements necessary for their determination. Data requirements are supply and demand elasticities for publishers' outputs in general and photocopied materials in particular as well as total dollars spent for publishers' outputs and for all photocopying.

The theoretical framework itself does not (without the above data) tell the optimal photocopy charge. Very importantly, it does not tell whether the optimal charge (royalty) is positive or negative. A negative royalty would imply publishers' subsidization of consumers' photocopying. It is an important result of this theoretical framework that in absence of any particular empirical restrictions, the case for consumer subsidization of publisher profits (via royalty or some other arrangement) is not more compelling than publisher subsidization of consumer photocopying--an option not considered in the public debate.

Consumer and Producer Surplus

Analysis of consumer and producer surplus is another approach which may be taken to analyze the photocopy issue. By this approach, policy makers seek to maximize the sum of consumer and producer surpluses. Consumer surplus is defined as the additional amount consumers would be willing to pay for the product. Producer surplus is defined as producer profits. These concepts are shown graphically below in the supply and demand diagram:

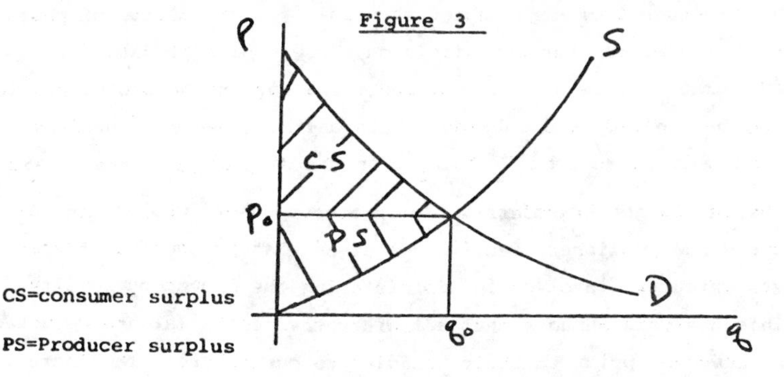

Supply and Demand for Photocopy Service

The demand curve above represents demand for photocopying of journals. It is in equilibrium at P_o Q_o. If a per unit royalty on each use of photocopy service is imposed, it will shift the supply curve from S_o to S_1 as shown in figure 4.

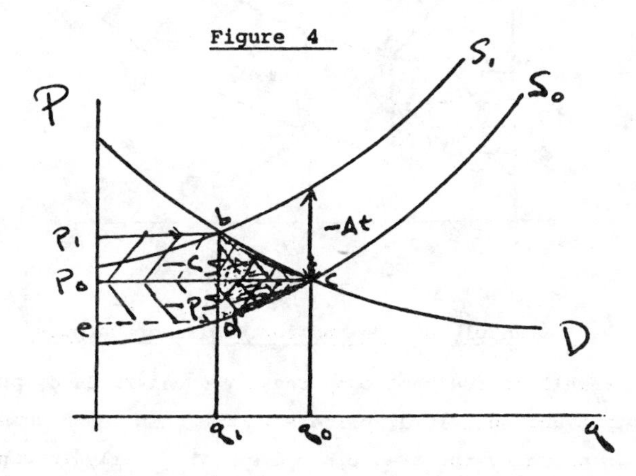

The area marked -cs shows the loss of consumer surplus. The area marked -ps shows the loss of producer surplus. The rectantles, -cs and -ps show revenues flowing from persons who phtocopy (consumers) and photocopy manufacturers (producers) to publishers. The darkened triangle is known as a "dead weight loss" or "excess burden". It is equal to the net loss of consumer and producer surplus. That is, it is equal to the loss of consumer and producer surplus which is not offset in some other sector (e.g. offset by increased revenues of publishers). This is the net loss which results from the photocopy charge. (If the supply curve were perfectly elastic, all the loss would be borne by consumers.) The size of the loss depends only and entirely on supply and demand elasticities as well as the size of photocopy revenues from copyrighted materials. Desirability of photocopy charges therefore, turns entirely on these empirical data.

From the point of view of the publisher, the royalty on photocopiable materials may be treated as a subsidy. This may be shown as a positive shift in the supply curve from S_0 to S_1. In the diagram 5 , the entire amount of the tax is not transferred from photocopy users who pay (-) ΔT to publishers since publishers receive (+) Δt-a. "a" is equal to transactions costs which are involved in administering the photocopy royalty program. This analysis assumes that administrative costs (a) are deducted from royalty revenues prior to their transfer to publishers. The increase in producer surplus of publishers and consumer surplus (excluding consumers who photocopy) for users of publishers' outputs is shown below in figure 5.

Figure 5

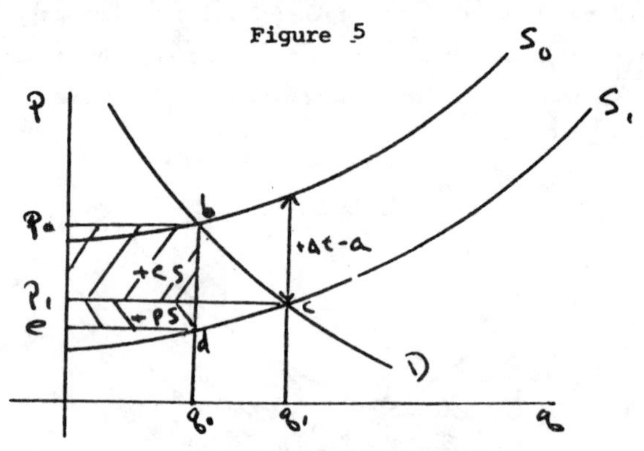

Supply and Demand for Publisher Outputs

As a result of the photocopy royalty equal to Δt-a, publishers produce q, of output and sell it at price P_1. The gain in consumer and producer surplus is shown by the area p_0b c d e. This analysis considers long run supplies, when all inputs are variable. It also considers in the supply curves discounted future effects on creativity and output -- which might be positive or negative as shown in the photocopy discussion section.

To determine net effects one would subtract from p_0b c d e in figure 5 , the area p_1 b c d e in figure 4 . If the difference is positive, one would conclude that photocopy royalty charges increase consumer and product surplus and are worthwhile. If the difference is negative, one would conclude that these charges are not worthwhile.

It seems desirable to set forth this framework since the results of this analysis indicate the information which is necessary to answer the desirability of photocopy charges.

Although the data are not easy to come by (supply and demand elasticities for photocopies in particular) they may not be impossible to come by. Industrial organization literature has attempted a number of estimates of the dollar size of the dead-weight loss which results from the presence of monopoly power in the U.S. economy. A parallel study of useable accuracy net dead weight loss which would result from a photocopy surcharge may also be feasible.

SOFTWARE

A. THE PRODUCT AND THE INDUSTRY

1. Description of the Product

Computer software may be defined to be a set of instructions designed for use by a computer to perform specific functions. Software, or computer programs, may be divided into a number of different categories, depending primarily on the closeness of the "language" employed to ordinary human language-source, compiler, object program, etc. The closer a language comes, in the several stages required, to stating the instructions in a form that actually can be used by the computer to carry out tasks, the less it is recognizable or comprehensible to a human reader.

Software can be represented in a number of different forms, including written listings, tapes, discs, silicon chips, and temporary storage within computer memory. "Hardware" is generally taken to mean permanent circuitry which is purchased as a physical machine unit rather than in a form that is easily reproducible by users and transferable between machines. However, the distinction between software and hardware may be becoming increasingly difficult to make, as intermediate forms of storage take hold in the field. The relevant distinction for this study seems to be made by considering as software anything that can be conveniently reproduced [or examined for content], by a user without the necessity of going back to the provider.

Software is the major area at present where the separation between protecting expressions and ideas is a matter of concern. While all communications contain ideas as well as expression, it has (possibly incorrectly) been considered that the value of non-physical intellectual work could be adequately protected by means of protection of the expression alone.

The nature of software, with its primary intent being communication with a computer (or through a computer to humans) which cares nothing about style or expression, tends to bring out more clearly the fact that the work may contain both detailed, tedious successions of steps <u>and</u>

innovative programming ideas. (It has been pointed out that in, for example, programming for education use, the intent is not only communication with the computer but also with a student.) For present purposes the significance of the distinction is that, as discussed in Chapter II, materials that communicate ideas but are heavily dependent for their value on expression have been subject to copyrights while physical entities and the design of new material products, where the uniqueness lies in the idea rather than in its mode of expression, have been subject to patents.

The fact that these ideas, when translated into simplest program form, actually perform the operation of a computer leads to the possibility that new software falls into the realm not only of communications (copyrights), but also to that of physical product innovations, which if novel could be subject to patent. CONTU Commissioner John Hersey has argued that programs, as amalgams of writings and processes, are appropriate for neither copyright nor patent protection and should therefore be protected by a mechanism specifically designed for them.

It is unclear what the division in commercial value is between the detailed expression contained in a program and the novel ideas or processes, if any, (also known as algorithms) developed for that specific piece of software. Any such division probably varies from one program to another to a degree which can not be known in advance. Most observers seem to believe that a high proportion of the value is, in general, due to the former--the expression--[1a] component.

For public policy towards protection, the significance of understanding this distinction is that specific innovative algorithms can possibly be copied or initiated for commercial use by examining a program or by passing on the ideas from one programmer to another. On the other hand, for the typical lengthy program, making use of the details is probably only worthwhile if an actual copy can be obtained and run or reproduced. This has implications both for what protection (if any) is theoretically adequate, and for the practicalities of enforcement.

2. Present Industry Structure

Data on the software industry are difficult to evaluate unambiguously, because of overlap in statistical categories, lack of product-line reporting by firms selling both hardware and software, and the large amount of programming which is done for in-house use, and hence, is never sold.

Looking, first at purchases: In 1976 U.S. computer users spent $38.4 billion in total computer usage, of which $20 billion (52%) was computer goods and services $10 billion (26%) was user salaries, and $8.4 billion (23%) was user overhead.[2] Another source gives data by user industry and by cost component of total data processing expenditures. Hardware ranges from 33 to 46 percent of total costs, depending on the industry. Internal personnel costs, a large proportion of which is presumably in-house software development, ranges from 35 to 54 percent of total expenses. "Packaged software," meaning programs purchased externally and separate from hardware, constituted only 1.3 to 3.5 percent of total data processing costs. The portions of such programs bought from the "mainframe" (hardware) manufacturer versus independent software firms varies tremendously by industry, with more than 2 to 1 ratios in either direction.[3] A different estimate concluded that of $30.99 billion spent on electronic data processing (EDP) in 1976, only $1.72 billion was for "software packages/facilities management."

If in-house developed and separately purchased programs are lumped together, one calculation shows that the proportion of total computer costs accounted for by software has risen dramatically in recent years, to an estimated 75 percent currently.[4,5] But of an estimated $12 billion in software expenditures, an overwhelming proportion was done in-house, rather than through package buying.[6]

Turning to producers: Total worldwide revenues of U.S. computer manufacturing and service firms were $31.9 billion in 1976, of which $26.6 billion was for computer equipment and supplies, and $5.3 billion was computer services.[7] Worldwide hardware sales constituted about $12.8 billion of the total.[8] Software sales were approximately $840 million--less than 3% of total revenues-- in 1976, up substantially from $500 million in 1974.[9]

Revenues in the data processing industry are highly concentrated, with the top 6 firms accounting for about 75 percent and IBM alone controlling 50 percent of the market.[10] Another source shows that of 1976 total revenues for U.S. EDP systems manufacturers of $18.4 billion, IBM has 60.2 percent, with the other seven significant producers ranging from 7.9 percent down to 2.9 percent of the market.[11]

Independent software producers are clearly highly competitive among themselves, with 1972 figures showing (although they are difficult to interpret) more than 1500 firms in the industry, and the top 46 firms (those with sales over $50 million) probably receiving less than one-fifth of the total revenues of independents.[12]

Unfortunately, we have not been able to obtain data showing the share of the software market held by hardware manufacturers (IBM et al), who are, of course, typically orders of magnitude larger than the independent software firms. Without requirements for product-line reporting by corporations, this important information for determining competition in the industry is difficult to arrive at. One indication is the large fraction (mentioned earlier) of software purchases made in many industries from "mainframe" manufacturers. Another, possibly misleading, bit of evidence is the dominance of IBM and Burroughs in copyright registrations of software, of which they have about 75 percent between them.[12a]

Thus, the picture of industrial market structure is obscure. The hardware industry is highly concentrated. The software industry is characterized by a very large number of relatively and (absolutely) very small firms, but the huge hardware companies are also in this market to an unknown degree with, one suspects, major monopolistic advantages.

There is remarkably little data on the process of soft-ware innovation, who does how much of it, in what institutional setting, for what motives. It is obvious that some is done in many settings ranging from secondary school pupils through industrial and governmental research, developmental and operational activities to the most advanced centers of scientific exploration. Further, there are some individuals who believe that future technological developments will permit individuals to do some programming useful to themselves and potentially valuable to others in their own homes. It is also obvious that much of the commercially available programming is created by private corporations, software houses and manufacturing firms. The supply of innovative programs from software firms appears to be directly dependent upon the expected software innovation. Hence, the aggregate supply of new software is obviously responsive to prospective monetary gain. Consequently our analysis, based on the assumption that protection is at least one major instrument for encouraging production of new programs, appears to be well founded.

3. Projections of Technological and Market Structure Changes

One forecast of total expenditure by computer users has it rising from 3.2 percent of US GNP in 1975 to 5.2 percent in 1980 and to 8.3 percent in 1985.[13] CONTU gives a projected growth rate of 20 percent per year for the independent software industry. A projection by a market research firm has software sales rising to $3.5 billion by 1984, a four-fold increase from their estimate of $840 million in 1976.[14]

Software is expected to constitute a continually increasing share of total ADP costs, as high as 90 percent by 1985.[15] While most programming is currently done in-house, this is expected to change greatly, as independent software companies increase their share of total employment of computer specialists from the present 15 percent to about 50 percent.[16]

CONTU's data project a continuing trend towards more rapid growth by independent software producers than by hardware manufacturers, possibly implying increasing competition in the industry. Other observers, noting the many small firms and rapid entry into the market, believe that software development will buck the trend of most industries, remaining an unconcentrated "cottage" industry. However, there is by no means total agreement on this forecast:

> "Today, there are more than 400 independent suppliers of software in the U.S. . . . Which of the 400 will survive the next 10 years is the big question. Even a casual observer would agree that a big shakeout is coming. Just as in other aspects of our industry, software has attracted hundreds of small entry companies which will eventually dwindle down to 10 or 20 key firms."[17]

Technological progress is occurring at a rapid rate in the hardware field, as costs continually fall and miniaturization, including the development of "mini"- or "micro"-computers, remains a major trend. According to CONTU testimony, progress in the efficiency with which software is written, however, appears to be slow. Techniques remain relatively primitive, based largely on individual skill, and observers do not project much change in the foreseeable future.

The trend towards falling costs and miniaturization, plus other qualitative evidence, suggests that computers will not only constitute an increasingly large share of national income, but will also begin to enter substantially into direct consumer-goods purchases in such areas as entertainment, education, and home appliances. Changes in computer and programming technology may also make possible a degree of do-it-yourself programming by consumers.

B. PROTECTION OF SOFTWARE

1. Present Means of Protection

Protection of proprietary rights or privileges in software is sought and attained in a multiplicity of ways. Copyrighting of software was first allowed in 1964 but, even since that date, has not appeared to be the dominant form of protection. The major means appear to be various forms of contractual provisions.

Data on the utilization and effectiveness of presently available protection for computer software are limited. A survey of practices for protecting software property was undertaken in 1972 by Harbridge House The data obtained in that study show that the vast majority (77 percent) of firms responding to the survey use contractual licenses or leases, with a "confidential disclosure" provision. Fifty-one percent of firms believe these arrangements are either "very" or "completely" effective, with another 23 percent saying they are "somewhat" effective. The other modes of protection all overlap greatly with this dominant category; trade-secret licenses, copyrights, and "physically limiting access to technology" all being employed by a majority of respondents. These three categories were all viewed as having similar effectiveness, with 49 percent or more saying each was a least "somewhat effective." Other modes were used relatively little, with patents in particular employed by only 3 percent of the firms.[18]

Of the respondents, only 13 percent (four companies) could think of any instance in which inadequate protection was a barrier to the development of programs representing a "significant level of innovation."[19]

A study done in Sweden (probably in 1974) found that of 77 firms surveyed 45 percent reported having experienced infringements of proprietary rights in software.[20]

The figures on use of copyrights for protection must be regarded with caution. From 1964 to 1977 only about 1200 programs had been registered, with varying forms of deposit, with the Register of Copyrights. While the vast majority of registrations were from only two companies, IBM and Burroughts, the reported "use of copyrights" reflects simply the placing of a copyright notice on all marketed copies of the software. Under present law such notices entitle a firm to protection; registration need be made only prior to bringing an infringement suit. As it is virtually costless to file notices, and since no copyright infringement suit for software has yet been brought, its effectiveness must be regarded as largely speculative, depending on the belief that notices have some deterrent effect.

2. Problems in the Existing System

As noted, the limited survey evidence available gives only slight support to arguments that lack of effective protection hinders software development. Interpretations of the data must be ambiguous. While only 13 percent of firms could cite specific instances of hindrance, if the "contractual licensing" category of protection is regarded as encompassing all the others, then a few firms (3 percent) felt protection was "not at all effective" with 23 percent regarding it as only somewhat effective. Judging from the rapid growth of the software industry in recent years it is clear that there is plenty of profit to be made despite any difficulties in maintaining proprietary rights, although it cannot be proven that growth might not have been even faster under different circumstances.

One major reason why current protection appears to be adequate in most cases is that a large portion of "packaged programs" are either custom-developed or are designed for limited, specialized markets. In turn part of this specialization is due to non-standardization of hardware, with each different type requiring software designed specifically for it. Second, "physically limiting access to technology," may, where used, make it impossible to violate non-disclosure provisions. Third, the data discussed earlier show that packaged software is currently used almost exclusively as an input into production processes (defined broadly) not as a final consumption good, and that it constitutes a very small percentage of total ADP costs. For a firm which has purchased use of software, and another wishing to obtain use without going to the manufacturer, to seek each other out and come to an agreement involves breaking a valid contract and putting a great deal of effort into arranging the transaction. It seems that in most cases the possible reduction in costs is simply not worth the trouble and the risks of a suit for contract violation.

A number of reasons have been alleged as to why the prevailing system of confidential-disclosure/trade-secrecy contracts is not entirely satisfactory, despite the apparent health of the industry:

- arranging and enforcing contracts involves substantial "transaction costs," raising the prices to buyers, reducing supply of software;
- contracts currently fall under different state laws, which are not uniform and make it more difficult to write and enforce agreements;
- because non-disclosure provisions can fail, the risk to sellers of incurring losses is substantial, tending to reduce innovation;
- the need for maintenance of secrecy tends to steer producers away from general-purpose and mass-marketed software, towards specialized programs which face less risk of disclosure;
- as opposed to a copyright system where the item would be deposited and could be examined, buyers have difficulty in comparison shopping and, hence, necessarily have inadequate information on which to base purchasing decisions;
- the "ideas," "processes," or "algorithms," contained in innovative programs are not protected, on the other hand;
- secrecy means that not only are the expressions involved kept under proprietary control but disclosure of general programming ideas is inhibited, impairing innovation through building one program on another.
- the term of protection is unregulated and, thus, if contracts are effective the term is unlimited;

- maintenance and enforcement of secrecy agreements appear to have "economies of scale," so that large producers can use them more effectively than small ones, tending to create concentration within the industry.

3. Alternative Policies

The principal alternatives for federal policy towards software appear to be:

- status quo: continued protection via state common-law regarding trade secrecy contracts, provisional availability of copyrights according to the 1964 decision of the Register of Copyrights;
- trade secrecy under state law continued, copyrights not allowed;
- trade secrecy under state law continued, availability of federal copyrights formally enacted by Congress;
- federal trade secrecy law replaces state law, copyright availability enacted;
- federal trade secrecy law replaces state laws, copyrights not allowed;
- copyright availability enacted, trade secrecy banned;
- no protection-state laws allowing trade secrecy banned, copyrights not allowed;
- any of the above options, with patents made available for those programs meeting the criteria of utility, novelty, and non-obviousness--(all options except this one assume no patents);
- new form of protection for software--difficult to characterize, as there may be numerous possibilities--one example would be a modified patent, in which there would be protection for "ideas" or "algorithms," but no ban on independent development;
- any of above options, with expanded federal subsidies for some types of software development, which would then be in the public domain.

Besides the long list of alternatives, there are several variable characteristics of the forms of protection which may greatly affect their impacts: First, there is the term of protection granted under any form of protection for software; second, the type of deposit/degree of disclosure required under copyrights; third, the practical effectiveness of the mechanisms available for enforcing copyrights, particularly for small producers; fourth, any of the alternatives could be implemented along with other measures designed to limit the costs of monopoly power that occurs in the industry. Protection could be denied to firms which have substantial monopoly control of the relevant market; compulsory licensing could be instituted; or antitrust action could be taken to split up dominant firms. There is an obvious problem in making recommendations in this area, in that it might be very difficult to tie together a federal system of protection with provisions for anti-monopoly action.

C. COSTS AND BENEFITS

1. Trade Secrecy and Copyrights

Evaluation of alternatives revolves largely around an evaluation of the degree to which the present system is operating non-optimally, a subject on which there is much controversy. Above we listed, without comment, the reasons why the predominant mode of protection, non-disclosure contracts, has been argued to be undesirable. Examining these arguments adequately requires data which for the most part are unavailable, so our conclusions are in all cases tentative.

It has been argued that the costs involved in maintaining proprietary rights through non-disclosure contracts under common law are a fairly small component of the costs of developing and marketing software. While we have no hard evidence on this subject, current conditions in the industry suggest that, at least at present, this statement is correct. To the degree that it is, the hypothesis, that large firms have an advantage in using secrecy agreements, is of less importance.

The same memo states that non-uniformity among state laws is an insignificant barrier to marketing by software firms, one reason being that for practical purposes the laws are, in fact, fairly similar.[21] We have found no contrary evidence, but this remains a subject for investigation.

The survey data previously cited, while ambiguous, appear to indicate that the present system, in part due to the types of software being produced, performs reasonably well although the risks involved to producers, of disclosure and loss of investment, may be significant enough to warrant concern.

All of the above applies to current conditions, and may not hold as rapid changes occur in the industry, particularly if mass-market programs become a reality on a large scale. It has been argued that the customized or restricted-market nature of most software means that protection is relatively easy to maintain.[22] What will happen for more general-purpose programs is unclear. The likelihood of copying would seem to be much greater. On the other hand, to reach a large market, such programs will have to sell at relatively low prices, which may make the inconvenience and stigma of illegal copying outweigh the savings to the user. An analogy with phonographs and audio tape recordings may be appropriate here, as the market for records and tapes appears to flourish despite the ease of making unauthorized recordings. More difficult to evaluate at all is the degree to which software firms may be dissuaded from entering the mass-market field because of its (possibly) higher risks of disclosure.[22a]

To continue the analogy, it does appear that copyrights could perform a valuable function for mass-market software. As we understand them, non-disclosure contracts can only apply to the original purchasers of a software package, and it seems infeasible to require such contracts for software packages sold at retail. Without copyrights, there would be no legal prohibition against a firm's mass-producing "stolen" programs, purchased at retail. In contrast, in the case of contraband records and tapes the threat of copyright infringement suits presumably provides some deterrent.

Returning to current conditions, it is not clear that copyrights would alleviate any of the other hypothesized drawbacks of trade secrecy listed above. Copyrights are presently available, yet are not relied upon, one must assume because they are viewed as ineffective, or no more effective than private contracts. Under present circumstances, copyrights and non-disclosure agreements essentially duplicate each other, with no evidence that availability of clarified copyright protection would significantly reduce transaction costs or the risks of unauthorized reproduction. Unless some change occurs which would make copyrights easier to enforce than contracts, they do not offer any important advantage to producers. CONTU has pointed out that with copyrights there is "availability of (a) statutory damages, (b) attorney's fees from infringers," which between them might make infringement suits a marginally (or substantially?) more viable option than contract violation suits.[23]

Another suggestion is to provide publicly-supported legal assistance for small producers who bring infringement suits.[24] While potentially valuable, this last possibility involves difficult questions of implementation and governmental bureaucracy, which we do not go into here.

On the other side, we do not see that availability of more stringent copyrights would have any important costs. As an alternative to private contracts, they cannot provide any more restrictive protection than do the latter, and would not appear to provide any greater opportunity for monopoly power than does trade secrecy. The option of using either or both forms of protection should simply mean that a firm would use copyright if it believed that would reduce its transaction and/or enforcement costs.

It might also be possible to make copyrights clearly available while banning trade secrecy for any software covered by copyrights. If the two forms of protection are essentially equivalent this would lead to little change from the status quo. To the degree that private contracts can be written which are more effective than copyright law (greater penalties, technological constraints, etc.) the elimination of non-disclosure agreements would increase the risk to producers (assuming no monopoly power in the industry--see below). There are also constitutional questions in banning private parties from entering into contracts freely agreed upon.

We can identify only two possible substantial advantages of copyrights over trade secrecy:

First, if banning non-disclosure contracts can be legally implemented, use of copyrights could greatly limit the term of protection (see below) if that is desirable.

Second, a copyright statute could require disclosure/deposit of enough identifying material that while the entire programs could not be copied, the ideas--algorithms--could be examined and passed on, possibly directly encouraging innovation through greater sharing of knowledge. It appears that programs which are currently registered have various forms of deposit, enough for identification purposes, but we are unclear as to whether algorithms can be deduced. Whether the disclosure of innovative algorithms is desirable is another question (again, see below).

The "no protection" alternative is one in which we can see no net advantages, as per this paper's introductory discussion of the non-exclusivity characteristics of information. We doubt that prohibiting all protection is legally possible, and if done it could only have harmful consequences on the supply of software.

2. Competition and Monopoly

Clearly our arguments have been based on the assumption that protection is desirable from the standpoint of consumers. In Chapter II, we showed that consumer interests are best served by the maintenance of proprietary rights, as long as there is effective competition in the industry. Available evidence indicates that this is indeed the case among independent software producers, although we lack evidence on the role and power of the hardware manufacturers in software markets. While more empirical work needs to be done, on balance it appears that, whatever their historical dominance, the hardware corporations lack the ability to control entry into the software market, and that their market shares are being steadily eroded by the independents. Thus, we can tentatively conclude that protection of software, at least for the independent producers, serves to benefit consumers by enhancing competition and increasing long-run supply. For the hardware manufacturers, or any independent software firms which have a substantial share of the market, it is doubtful whether protection is in the interests of consumers.

However, should conditions change in the future (see C. Projections of Technological and Market Structure Changes), with the software industry becoming subject to control by a few firms, other actions (in our view preferably -- anti-monopoly legislation and enforcement) would become necessary. If such action is feasible, effective protection would still be desirable (see II.G, Regulation and Antitrust Action). Should effective anti-monopoly action or regulation of some form prove infeasible, it would be necessary to reconsider the nature and extent of protection.

3. Term of Protection

The term or duration of copyright protection is, as discussed in Chapter II, an important component in the value of a copyright to its holder. The longer the term, all else equal, the larger the amount of income potentially transferred from customer to producer on the particular item in question. To recapitulate, the social justification, if any, for such a transfer is that only the expectation of such transfer (profit) will induce some potential producers of innovative software to produce it. In light of the fact that there is substantial risk that any innovation will fail, i.e., return to its innovator less than the costs incurred, a steady flow of innovation is impossible without either subsidization or protection.

Regarding the optimal term of protection there are difficulties in arriving at any satisfactory conclusion. Economics of Property Rights As Applied To Computer Software And Data Bases (see II. E. Basic Tradeoff and Term of Protection) concludes that, under most conditions, the term of protection should be shorter than the expected commercial life (average useful lifetime) of a unit of software. Given the usually (at present) short period before which programs become obsolete, this suggests a period of protection for software much shorter than that traditionally given to written works, possibly only one or a very few years.

On the other hand, on the basis of our analysis, one would find that in effectively competitive markets for software, the term should be as long as the period of commercial usefulness. With effective competition, denying payments to the original producers on software sold a few years in the future does not reduce monopoly profits under competition (there are none). (See Chapter II.) Thus, a short period of copyright protection would mean reducing innovation in software below the level that is optimal in terms of consumer interest.

If optimal policy requires that the copyright be effective throughout the commercial life of a software item, that implies that, under conditions of competition, there is no simple justification for any terminal date at all on the copyright: once an idea is of no commercial value there is no substantial cost to society of not having it freely available. There may be non-substantive costs in permitting anyone to have the power to restrict access to anything that is not of commercial value. Hence, a position that copyrights should be valid in perpetuity would be false.

The picture changes dramatically if there is substantial monopoly in the software market. If there is monopoly, the availability of copyrights, especially in the absence of trade secrecy, would serve to strengthen monopoly positions. The longer the duration of the copyright the greater that effect and the greater the transfer of income from customers (ultimately consumers) to the monopolists. The economically preferred remedy would be not a reduction in the term, but rather removing should be used to evaluate it, we will attempt no complete examination of their validity and importance.

The House Subcommittee on Patents, Trademarks, and Copyrights reported:

> "From the social point of view patents are not an ideal means of encouraging inventive effort. They may come into the hands of firms which, technically, are less advantageously equipped than their competitors to use the invention. The patentee may have investments in competing technology or in competing lines of manufacture which make it temporarily unprofitable for him to employ an invention which his competitors would exploit immediately. More fundamentally, patentees, since they enjoy a degree of monopoly power, are unlikely to exploit inventions to the extent warranted by their usefulness to society, and may be overcompensated in terms of their costs. Production by any monopolist is likely to be at a lower level, and his prices higher, than would prevail if the industry were competitive. Moreover, the production policies of a monopolist are likely to leave some opportunities unexploited, thus forcing other productive resources into socially less useful lines of manufacture, or to work with inferior technology."[25]

The critical factor which distinguishes patent from copyright protection is the ability to gain monopolistic control over an idea--a physical design, process, or other innovation. Unlike a copyright, a patent prevents anyone else in the entire community which is bound by the law from utilizing the same ideas, no matter how important, and no matter whether developed totally independently of the patent holder. To take one example close to the subject at hand, it has been estimated that in 1967 Xerox Corporation, holder of a patent on their dry-copy process which was (and is) far superior to any others available, was making more than

1,000 percent profit on its machines, selling copiers for $29,500 that cost $2,400 to manufacture.[26]

While we do not explore the historical roots of patents, and although it is true that public policy is in many cases in part due to inertia, the continued widespread acceptance of the patent system gives some indication that it is socially valuable. There is an apparent trade-off between the economic benefits from innovation and the economic costs of granting monopoly power to exploit individual inventions."

Two considerations relate more directly to our specific interest in the possibility of patents for software. First, there is a prohibition under patent law that "laws of nature and mathematics" shall not be subject to patent rights. This is obviously one means by which it is intended monopoly power or, possibly, regulating the prices charged so as to provide only a competitive rate of return. If such action were impractical, a reduction in the term would be of some benefit.

Another difficulty with the conception of a short term is the need for using an <u>average</u> of commercial viabilities. Since there is likely to be substantial variation in the commercial life of programs and particularly valuable innovations may have unusually long economic lives, an average will give unsatisfactory results for many if not most programs. Of course, if our reasoning in regard to the desirable policy under effective competition is correct, this difficulty is irrelevant.

In light of the fact that there appears to be substantial competition among the independent software producers but a very substantial degree of monopoly in computer manufacturing, it would appear to be appropriate for hardware manufacturers or any of their affiliates to be ineligible to obtain copyrights on software. A more complex rule would be that no hardware producer with more than some small share (say 5 percent) of the market would be eligible for normally available copyright and trade secrecy protection.

4. <u>Patents</u>

Our discussion so far has centered on the desirability of protecting the <u>expressions</u> contained in computer software, and in fact we have suggested that a desirable feature of copyrights over trade secrecy might be the disclosure of the <u>ideas</u> or underlying logic of programs, which would aid programmers in building on each others work. However, the reverse argument can be made, that the promotion of software innovation requires that proprietary rights be given to their producers. To some unclear extent trade secrecy presently does protect basic programming ideas, performing much of the private function (as contrasted to social function) of a patent. Objections to patent protection can be divided into two categories--those applicable to patents in general, as a very restrictive form of protection, and those which depend on the characteristics of software as a specific form of innovation.

To object to patents in general means, obviously, to make a more general criticism than is the subject of this paper. While quite valid, it is beyond the scope of our work to do a complete cost-benefit analysis of the patent system. While we will state some of the criteria which to restrict patents from creating great social costs. Depending on the exact interpretation, it may be that this provision would eliminate a large portion of innovative programming sequences from patent consideration. This would appear to be socially desirable.

Secondly, it has been pointed out that the greatest social costs from the patent system occur when there is a concentration of patents in the hands of one firm or a few firms. In such cases the firm may gain substantial control over the direction of research and technical change in the field, and may seek to maximize its own welfare at large cost to society.[27] Here we return, not to monopoly control over one piece of creativity, but to the problem of dominance of an industry by one or a few firms. In the software industry, despite the apparently large degree of competition, the position of IBM and other hardware firms is certainly such as to warrant concern over concentration of patent control if patents were made available for software.

In sum, while there does appear to be a socially valuable function to be performed by the awarding of patents for innovative algorithms or other programs, the evidence suggests that there are great risks in doing so. With the evidence now available to us, we can reach no conclusions on this subject.

5. Other Alternatives

It has been argued that computer software represents a form of intellectual product which is not analogous to writing and other forms of communication and to artistic expression, and thus should not be given standard copyright protection. We do not agree that there is any "cultural" danger involved in the availability of such protection, as we can see no reason why the fact of software and cultural works coming under the same form of protection should either (1) degrade cultural work in the eyes of society, or (2) harm the traditional protection for cultural works.

On the other hand, we agree that software does appear to be different from other "new technologies" (broadcast music, etc.) which have been historically given copyrights, due to its dual nature as both a writing and a mechanical process.[28] Our consideration of both copyrights and patents for software confirms its unusual characteristics. We see no objections to putting software in a separate title of the copyright law, particularly as this might simplify giving it a non-standard term of protection (if desirable) and setting up special deposit requirements for copyright registration. Whether an entirely new form of protection is desirable depends on what that new form is, and we have not yet seen a promising alternative. Our example stated earlier, of a modified patent which would protect ideas but not ban independent development has important theoretical advantages: it would allow innovators to reap some rewards from their own work, but not from precluding rewards to others through simultaneous development. Unfortunately, it does not appear to be feasible, because proving whether a second developer had done the work independently would probably be a next-to-impossible job.

6. Public Subsidization

Development of computer software, analogously to other forms of research or development, may in some cases have benefits which are not closely enough related to commercial usage, or are too large in scope for individual firms to undertake, to be done by the private sector [29] (see II. L. Public Subsidization). If the potential benefits to society are substantial, it may be worthwhile in many cases to give public support to needed research, despite the drawbacks of allocating funds through the governmental process. It is also important to ensure that a program of public support is not simply a disguised subsidy for an industry or particular firms which would have done the work anyway for their own purposes.

D. POLICY RECOMMENDATIONS

Our limited data both on present conditions in the industry, and more so, on likely future technology and market structure, necessitate that our conclusions be regarded as tentative and subject to modification as further evidence emerges.

The present system of contractual licensing is operating with reasonable success, although not optimally due to variations between state laws, transaction costs, some degree of risk of theft and the possibility of excessive constraint on new software development because no disclosure of any sort is required. To the extent that the software industry is competitive, the more important features of secrecy--(1) unlimited term of protection, and (2) some degree of exclusive control of programming ideas, would seem to be desirable. Non-uniformity of relevant state laws does not appear to be a serious enough problem to warrant federal action, especially if copyright protection is strengthened.

Under present conditions copyright protection is only marginally valuable to producers. However, it may generate some social benefits in that it would probably be used largely in cases where it would involve lower transactions costs than would trade secrecy. Further, it has negligible costs to society so long as trade secrecy is available. It may become an important stimulus for the development of mass-marketed software, which may be of relatively large benefit directly to consumers. The appropriate term of protection, we have argued, should, under effective competition, cover the full period of commercial usefulness.

All of the serious disadvantages of copyright protection arise with or are greatly exacerbated by the existence of monopoly power. Consequently, the major concern of public policy is with the degree of actual and potential monopoly power in the software market.

Patent protection, or some new form of protection, may be desirable alternatives (or patents could be available along with copyrights/trade secrecy), but much further research is needed before any such action should be taken.

Our recommendations are:

1) For independent software firms not in control of a substantial portion of the market, continued use of non-disclosure contracts should be allowed.

2) For these same firms, copyright availability should be formally enacted, probably under a separate title of the copyright law, but with the term of protection still equal to or longer than the expected commercial life of most software.

3) Research should be done to find methods of making copyright protection more effective (enforceable) for small copyright holders.

4) Research should be undertaken immediately to ascertain the extent to which hardware manufacturers have monopoly power in the software industry or are likely to develop it.

5) Measures should be taken to eliminate the existence and danger of monopoly power in the software field. In decreasing order of desirability these measures are:

a. denial of trade secrecy and copyrights to large hardware manufacturers,

b. statutorily forcing hardware manufacturers to spin off their software operations,

c. antitrust litigation to force hardware manufacturers to divest themselves of their software activities and to split up any (future?) software firms with major market power,

d. compulsory licensing with regulation of prices, holding profits down to competitive levels.

6) Research should be undertaken to ascertain whether there are general operationally useful criteria for the federal subsidization of software innovation.

FOOTNOTES

1. Manfred Kindermann, "A Comparative Study of Special Protection Systems for Computer Programs," 1976, p. 321.

2. Information Processing in the United States, American Federation of Information Processing Societies (AFIPS), April, 1977, p.5.

3. "1976 DP Budgets," Richard A. McLaughlin Sr., Datamation, Feb. 1976.

4. "Software and Its Impact: A Quantitative Assessment," Boehm, Datamation, May, 1973, p. 48.

5. "Burgeoning Computer Software Industry Foresees Fivefold Increase in Jobs by 1985," N.R. Kleinfield, The Wall Street Journal, May 2, 1977.

6. Boehm, op. cit., p. 49

7. AFIPS, op. cit., p. 4.

8. EDP Industry Report, April 22, 1977.

9. Kleinfield, op. cit.

10. AFIPS, op. cit., p. 5

11. Computer Manufacturers-1976, International Data Corporation (IDC), August

12. "Aspects of Software Policy," CONTU staff memo, p. A-1 (rough estimation f their data).

12a. Ibid, p. 26.

13. AFIPS, op. cit., p.6.

14. Kleinfield, op. cit.

15. Boehm, op. cit., p. 49.

16. Kleinfield, op. cit.

17. "The Developing Software Industry," F.L. Harvey, Info systems, June 1976.

18. Legal Aspects of Technology Utilization, Richard I. Miller, of Harbridge House, Inc., Lexington, MA: D.C. Heath and Co., 1973, p. 58.

Footnotes 19 through 25 were not referenced
in the original CONTU report.

COMPUTER DATA BASES AND COMPUTER-CREATED WORKS

A. DESCRIPTION OF THE PRODUCT

Computer data bases are, in general, compilations of information "data" taken from one or more written or observational sources and stored in (or prepared for storage in) a computer memory in a systematized way. The organization of the data within the computer is designed so that retrieval of particular categories of information desired by users is rapid and efficient. Data bases may be regarded as analogous to various well-known material sources such as bibliographic indexes, social science abstracts, and encyclopedias. The major advantages of computerized systems are that (1) through use of programming instructions, the computer itself can perform, at a great savings in time, an information search that would otherwise be done by hand, and (2) the data files can be rapidly updated or expanded by inputting new material and deleting old material in the computer memory.

Access to, or output from the computer may be in several different forms, including standard paper copies, microform, or on-line electronic access, the last of which is probably the most common. Data bases may be roughly categorized into three classes: bibliographic, statistical, and specialized. Bibliographic bases contain citations or abstracts of professional or other technical literature in one or in a variety of fields. Statistical bases consist of masses of data, such as financial statistics, and usually have facilities for high speed access and sophisticated analysis and graphical display. Specialized bases exist for a wide variety of applications. Examples include real estate listings, airline schedules, books in print, technical tables, and information on business and consumer credit ratings.

In this chapter we consider the proprietary rights involved both in input into the computer and in output. Inputs into data bases may be characterized as having one or both of two valuable properties--(1) the content of the material is useful, such as would be the case for an entire journal article or other manuscript put into computer memory, or (2) the organization of the material gives it its primary value, such as for a bibliographic index, in which the individual entries are public-domain information.

For the former case, output from the data base would normally be in the same form as the input, with the source clear. For the latter case, however, the information is likely to be rearranged within the computer, items from several or many different sources may be combined in one output listing, and the sources of the output may be unrecognizable.

In relation to proprietary protection, it is clear that both the sources of the information and the firm operating the data base have an interest in the output, regardless of whether the material is put out in a form totally different from the original. Only the sources of information have any proprietary "right" at risk on the input side.

Output whose value lies largely in the reorganization of the data done in the computer can legitimately be considered a new product or creative expression, potentially subject to protection. We will evaluate the likely effects on consumers of such protection, but will not evaluate non-economic arguments over whether such output constitutes "derivative" or "original" work in some legal sense. Such distinctions are not relevant to the impacts on consumer welfare of alternative policies.

Similarly, in this chapter we consider the purer case of "computer-created works," by which we mean those not derived at all from other copyrighted material.

B. PRESENT INDUSTRY STRUCTURE AND PROJECTIONS

Very little quantitative information is readily available on the computer data-base industry. Relevant to our analysis are both the providers of data bases themselves and the sources from which they draw their data. Computer data base vendors use a broad range of sources, including individual journals, hard-copy data bases, indexes, newspapers, and public-domain material put out by the government. Qualitative evidence indicates that for many of the journals and, in particular, for a large proportion of the comprehensive indexes, the publishers of the hard-copy possess a large degree of monopoly power in selling to computer data-base operators. In many cases there are only one or two sources of information which have been arranged in the needed manner, (for example, Social Science Citation Index and Moody's or Dun and Bradstreet). Also, it appears that one or a few firms control a major portion of the entire indexing market.[1] For a number of the journals and some reference works the publisher is a non-profit professional society, which may not be attempting to maximize profits. However, for-profit firms are probably the major force in the industry (see data in Chapter III. Photocopying). Further, a not-for-profit organization living within a limited budget or trying to minimize its deficit, may operate very much like a profit maximizer.

At present the on-line bibliographic computer data base industry is highly concentrated, with two firms controlling most of the market (Lockheed and Systems Development Corp. [SDC]), with only one other significant firm in existence (Bibliographic Retrieval Services, or BRS). Specialty data bases are operated by a number of other firms, including the New York Times and several legal reference services. There are also a few data bases put out by non-profit firms, and major reference bases provided by the government, including MEDLINE. Observers report that, despite the high levels of concentration, there appears to be at present effective price competition among the few firms involved, in at least a large portion of the categories of data base usage. In some cases, however, certain data bases are available from only one company.

It should be noted that Lockheed, SDC, etc. are generally known as "wholesalers," while their sources are actually referred to as data base proprietors. These sources are often not originally in machine-readable form. Often they are not derived from copyrighted works, but are developed directly by the data base firm. While each base, in general, has unique features, there appears to be a substantial degree of competition among them.

The continuing rapid decline in hardware and other computer costs, and the increase in demand for easily-accessible information, indicate that the on-line computer data base industry should enjoy rapid growth. It may be that more specialized data bases will be developed with the possibility of competition from firms with expertise in specific areas. However, for the near future it is unlikely that there will be any new large-scale entrants into the on-line market which would challenge the dominance of Lockheed and SDC.

In such a new and volatile field it is risky to make projections, but the nature of data-base services suggests that the industry is likely to remain one with high initial, or fixed costs, and consequent substantial barriers to entry. We may surmise that monopolistic tendencies will be a continuing problem. However, the degree of monopoly power that will be exercised is unknown, particularly in light of the potential for market control that currently exists but apparently is not being fully used. There are a number of prospects in this connection. The existing large participants may not be charging full monopoly prices for any of several reasons. They may want to discourage new entrants, seeking to maximize long-run rather than immediate profits. SDC with its origins as a not-for-profit corporation may still have some technocratic, rather than profit maximizing, motivation in its management. Lockheed with its history of being repeatedly buoyed up by government contracts and support in largely non-competitive markets may, similarly, be less vigorously profit seeking (and more security-seeking) than a firm whose history is characterized by participation in free enterprise markets. The degree of future concentration in the market will depend on the growth of the market and the growth of the present suppliers. As the market grows, it is possible that they will have difficulty in retaining their dominant market shares.

C. PRESENT MEANS OF PROTECTION

Publishers of journals, reference works and written data bases have available to them standard copyright protection against use of their materials by computer data base "wholesalers." Because computerized information vending is a highly visible, public business, and since the materials used are re-sold to the public, there is not at present much opportunity for computer firms to evade paying royalties to their sources or meeting any other conditions for use. Hence, at the stage of transfer from data base/written index to computer-information vendor there is apparently a well-functioning system for protecting the property interest of data suppliers. Typically the copyright holder receives a percentage royalty on the sales of the wholesaler. In some cases where the publishers of data bases are abstracting journal articles or other materials there is a question as to whether royalties should be paid to the journal publisher or other copyright holder.

On the output side there does not seem to be at present a major protection issue, largely because users of computerized data bases receive individually-tailored output, unsuitable for use by other potential customers. Any unauthorized transferral of output copies that might occur is also limited by the difficulty of locating other users who would want the same listings and arranging a transaction with them.

There may be some problem due to another computer operator paying for and obtaining virtually all of a data base, then reselling its contents without incurring the "wholesaler's" set-up cost. This practice is again hampered by the necessarily public nature of marketing computer data bases, and so it is probably not possible to avoid paying fees on a large-scale.

D. <u>PRESENT AND PROJECTED PROBLEMS</u>

In this area present law appears to provide adequate protection for the holders of copyrighted materials. There has been a large amount of discussion within CONTU as to whether computer vendors should be subject to suits against copyright infringement at the point of <u>input</u> of material into a computer or at the point of <u>output</u> to the user. We do not see this as an important point of contention. Regardless of the stage at which protection is formally defined to occur, it is clear that the copyright holders have legal rights in connection to any use that is made of their work, whatever the final form of presentation. Thus, computer vendors would be, as they are now, required to negotiate agreements with the source of copyrighted inputs prior to inputting it for resale to users of the computer service. The terms of such an agreement are a private market matter with no apparent policy implications.

For computer-created works, where the output may be considered a new creative work, and whose value may be dependent in part on one or more copyrighted information sources, the software used to manipulate the data, the hardware and data transmission facilities, and the skill of the retrieval operator, we see no policy difficulties. The rights to any revenues resulting from the newly created work should be allocated by private contractual agreements. In the absence of any rights of the input owners, the owner of the computer operation would retain ownership of the output. If an individual programmer renting computer time, with no strings attached, created such a work, that person would be entitled to the copyright. Other arrangements would again be of concern only to the parties involved. There does not seem to be any reason why works created with the aid of a computer should not be provided with the same proprietary copyright protection as any other intellectual work. In no case does a computer alone "create"--there are always human authors.

Our major policy concern is with the existence of monopoly (or monopsony--on the buyer's side) power at any of the stages of bringing computerized information to the ultimate user. Copyright protection is desirable from the standpoint of consumers, assuming effective competition in an industry. It is apparent, however, that there are various degrees of market power among publishers of the input materials, and the data base wholesalers. We do not have the information needed to make an adequate assessment of the current impacts of that power, nor can we project the future of the industry. A detailed empirical analysis should be done of the data base market.

To the extent that firms possess the ability to control prices at any stage of the process, consumers will suffer in the end. This need not require the existence of only one reference source or only one computer service. Because each bibliographic source/data base or computer vendor may offer largely unique materials or services, there may be little effective competition (or substitutability) among them. In such a case each could set a price that would yield some monopoly profit, but not enough to induce a rival to make the initial outlays necessary in effect to duplicate the product of the first. Monopoly power among information sources, for example, would enable them to raise prices to computer data base vendors, ultimately causing increased prices to consumers. Simultaneous market power on the buying side by the computer data base firms would yield an indeterminate arrangement between them, as both sides bargain for the best deal. Consumers would in no way be helped by such rivalry. The conflict would determine only how the monopoly profits were to be divided between the monopolist and monopsonist. A situation, as at present, of strong monopoly on the part of the wholesalers may enable them to force data base publishers out of business, with the latter selling out to the former, causing vertical integration in the industry, thus consolidating the monopoly profits into a single entity. In any case, the consumers of computer data base services are likely to be faced with the standard losses due to monopoly (or oligopoly)--higher prices, reduced supply, lack of responsiveness to consumer needs.

E. POLICY ALTERNATIVES

The relevant alternatives for federal policy towards protection are:

1) Modified status quo--copyright protection for copyrighted inputs and for computer-created works.

2) No protection--neither information sources nor computer operators would have protection available to them.

3) Continued copyright availability for data publishers (sources), but no protection for computer data base vendors.

4) Continued copyright protection for both stages of production. Antitrust action or regulation of prices to be used where appropriate against firms with market power.

5) Public provision of or subsidies for creating some data base systems.

The status quo is adequate if competition remains reasonably effective, but granting the possibility that that will not be the case, it reduces for our purposes to option (4). Both alternatives (2) and (3) are unlikely to have any desirable results for consumers. (2) would require a restructuring of the entire copyright law, as there is no distinction between materials which can be used on computers and other works of authorship, and so no basis for denying copyright protection to that segment of the information industry. (3) might be legally plausible, on the theory that once information is put on the computer its owner no longer is eligible for the standard privileges. It could be argued that denying protection at this stage might enable new entrants to make unauthorized use of the data bases of the dominant firms, enhancing competition in the industry. The probable results of (2) or (3) would not however, be any increase in competition or in the overall availability of data bases. As has been emphasized a number of times, unless the producer can expect to recover at least the set-up costs, there will be no economic incentive for continued production of data bases. In light of the ease of copying (reproducing) a data base, absence of copyright protection would be likely to result in a move towards strict reliance on trade secrecy, no-disclosure contracts, physical protection, and careful limitations on access to large portions of data bases, leaving us with no more competition and possibly greatly increased costs of transacting business.

Instead, for lack of more imaginative solutions, the appropriate response to monopoly is alternative (4) with the possibility of some usage of (5), public support for information services: For a full discussion of these matters, including the optimal pricing scheme under regulation, see Chapter II. G. Regulation and Antitrust Action. There are significant costs involved in any government intervention into markets, and issues of public management and political control involved in choosing the best (or least undesirable) form of involvement; so that pragmatic trade-offs must be made which we cannot evaluate here. As a general rule, however, large degrees of market power do require, in the interests of consumers, public action to break them up or, at least to limit the undesirable consequences of that power.

Our recommendations are:

1) Copyrights should be available for both the information inputs into and the outputs from computerized information systems and other uses of computers to aid creative work.

2) Empirical studies of the structure and functioning of the industry should be initiated, and continuous monitoring of changes should be performed.

3) Federal policies to reduce or prevent monopolistic tendencies--policies analogous to those identified at the end of the preceeding chapter--should be undertaken.

FOOTNOTES

1. Conversation with Kathy Ray, Brookings Institution Acquisitions Librarian, April, 1977.

ADDENDUM

DESIGNING POLICY FOR THE FUTURE OF THE INFORMATION SYSTEM

Most of this report has dealt with the attributes and problems of the information protection system under current conditions. However, it is clear that technological changes in various areas, including photocopying, computer and possibly most important, telecommunications, are likely to have an enormo impact on the workability and desirability of present laws and institutional arrangements. While advancing technology holds out great promise, there appears to be a significant danger that it will be hindered or have its potential uses distorted by the actions of groups with interests in the status quo. In other words, the technological feasibility of new informatic systems should not be taken to imply their rapid acceptance--there are severe institutional constraints which must be dealt with first, among which the proprietary rights for information producers (copyrights) play an important part. Below we attempt a preliminary exposition of the issues which should be considered in designing a system for the production and dissemination of information that is compatible with the maximum possible benefits that can be realized by the public at large. It is hoped that, although these rough ideas are not central to the basic analysis of this report, they will be usef in stimulating discussion leading to more direct policy implications.

I. COPYRIGHTS MUST BE CONSIDERED IN A LARGER CONTEXT

Copyrights, patents, and trade secrets have grown up over many centuries as part of public policy to encourage the production and use of intellectual products. Their scope, terms, administration, and encouragement has been refined and changed as elements, not entities by themselves, of a larger public system of encouraging appropriate flow of information.

As early as the Magna Carta, preservation of copyright was an essential aspect of public life. Guilds were granted royal charters and were supported in their preservation of the secrets of their trade. These grants, patents, and charters were subsidized further by access to the courts for their enforcement.

Early in the life of the American republic there was established an office within the Library of Congress for the registration of copyrights, in a way parallel to the registrar of patents. These offices are subsidized out of public funds. Their purpose is to facilitate the enforcement by private parties of their grants of partial monopoly from the public.

Perhaps the largest expense of the public institutions is involved in facilitating the usage of copyrighted materials--education for general literacy. When extended through general education at the college level it accounts for about $100 billion dollars a year. This expenditure comes out of the conviction that the private market is likely to underinvest in instruction which facilitates, among other things, the usage of intellectual products. The above figure includes $1 billion a year for school texts.

The distribution of intellectual products is also heavily subsidized. A major part of the cost of the postal system is caused by the partial subsidy of rates for books, magazines, newspapers and the like. This is likely to be on the order of several billion dollars a year. Further, usage of the public airwaves for radio and TV is granted without sizable fee to private usage, rights which on a commercial auction basis would probably bring rents of several billion dollars a year.

Production of scientific and technical information, as provided by the general market, has been considered to be insufficient, and public support of these activities through government expenditures and tax write-offs is on the order of $50 billion per year. To this figure should be added the costs of research done at colleges and universities. Much of this support is either direct public subsidy or tax write-offs for donations.

Most companies and government agencies are involved in continuing an adult education and training of their employees. Approximately 9 million Americans are involved in such activities, with an annual cost of approximately $15 billion per year. In addition, the purchase of books and magazines for professional purposes is a tax write-off worth perhaps a billion dollars a year for personal use and $2 billion for private libraries in businesses.

Public libraries, beyond the many found in schools and universities, also obtain their funds from the public, with combined budgets of several billion dollars a year.

Thus, all in all, the annual public expenditure, either in terms of direct public subsidy and support, in terms of rights to the air waves, or in terms of tax write-offs, in the support of the production and distribution of intellectual goods is on the order of about $200 billion. At the same time, the annual payments within the USA for copyright royalties is only a few billions (with a similar amount coming from abroad).

It should be clear from the above discussion that the part played by copyrights in the distribution of royalties for usage is small in comparison with the public expenditure. But copyrights are probably a crucial part of the system in two ways: first, the few percent of the system involved in royalties is discretionary money on top of stable and assured money, and thus attracts unusual attention. Thus, this small amount becomes a steering current for the whole. Second, copyright stabilizes property rights and encourages specific modes of exchange and transmission of the information. For example, even though the same information could be distributed in a Sunday newspaper format for 50¢ (and, if sold for $1.50, earn much more income as an annual piggyback on the usual newspaper) it is easier to control the copyright and to manage arrangements if it is sold as a $500 encyclopedia.

However, there are now emerging new technologies which can revolutionize the structure of the system. Basically, they separate the intellectual content from the carrier medium (the book is a physical item, though it is the content which is copyrighted). By so doing, property rights and dissemination processes can be arranged in ways which are quite different, and perhaps very difficult to manage under old ways which grew up with different technologies.

II. POTENTIALS FOR NEW TECHNOLOGY OF INFORMATION TRANSFER

Let us, for a moment, imagine what could be done with technology which is already available, but configured in a slightly different form to take care of some current needs and usages.

The bulk of this country's population is covered by TV channels, much of which could be piggybacked by a few additional channels at very low costs (using the current towers and transmission stations). If there were only a way to convert written information into electronic form, and then to reconvert it to ordinary page copy, the costs of transmission would be almost zero. One TV channel could transmit the content of the Library of Congress in a week, with the most popular million books being run every day. All the correspondence carried by the Post Office could be transmitted on another channel daily, with enough room to broadcast all the letters, regulations, and other documents in the public domain by the government. The total cost for such piggybacking would be less than 50¢ per citizen per year. Another way of performing the same feat would be via a highpowered TV satellite in synchronous orbit, with similar costs, but probably poorer reception for the moment (this can be fixed soon).

The costs of translating written material into electronic form, or capturing as such in the first place, are rapidly declining. An office-size OCR (optical character reader) which can process electric typewriter fonts is now about $5,000. An experimental library instrument which not only reads books placed on them by the blind, but simulates speech, costs about $50,000 each in prototype; the prices are expected to plummet soon, expecially in versions which do not require special mechanical elements for the blind. Office electronic typewriters are now only a few thousand dollars, and record information electronically in a form which could be transmitted by phone or other electronic media. Thus, these prices are coming down to the level where a system could be begun almost immediately.

The receivers are a little more trouble for the moment. A device which can be attached to a TV set for reading electronic material now costs a few hundred dollars, including keyboard for writing. Like TV games, these costs can be expected to drop precipitously in the next few years. A serviceable paper printer is also a few hundred dollars now, and dropping rapidly in cost.

These devices can be attached to a $20 cassette recorder as a storage medium capable of holding about a book's length of information, or to an $800 TV recorder which can hold about 100,000 books worth of information.

Thus, for homes and offices equipped with devices as costly as a color TV set, the possibilities exist now for inexpensive information transmission. These devices can be hooked up to the telephone system immediately without waiting for any large scale conversion. The costs for coast-to-coast correspondence is now about the cost of first class postage. In a few years is should be much less.

By using an OCR at the office and then in the home systems, a group of friends could use a chain letter method in a way very similar to samizdat of Soviet dissidents to distribute a copy of a new book across the country to 1000 others for a communications cost of about 5¢ per person, given that non-mass market book readers tend to be concentrated in metropolitan areas with toll-free telephone rates. With such systems around, copyright as we know it will be unenforceable.

Thus, for a cost of only a few billion dollars a year to all parties concerned, the present library system, Post-Office correspondence system, and government information systems could be replaced. If there is not such a shift in usage, there will be strong incentives to evade current institutions using private systems.

Before getting into the institutional problems more deeply, it may be worthwhile to point out some other technologies which might have some impact.

While the TVR (such as the BetaMax) has the capacity for large scale evasion of current institutional arrangements, the Videodisk could be used for large scale decentralization of archives. The marginal cost--that is, the cost of making an additional copy once the material has been put into electronic form--of storing the contents of all of the libraries in the world in a stack of videodisks is now about a thousand dollars; in a decade it could be about the current cost of an encyclopedia. If it were offered, many graduating high school or college students would want one.

A satellite in synchronous orbit could beam the content of all the world's printed information to all the world's peoples. This would not only speed up the intellectual development of developing countries, but would make censorship and intellectual repression very difficult. The long-range consequences for world peace might be enormous.

TV and other broadband communications present a much greater problem. The bandwidth required by TV for the same time-usage by humans is millions of times greater than for writing. But this problem can be handled by placing a larger satellite in orbit. An array of antennas about a mile square could pinpoint a message to any place on the earth's surface electronically (by using phase differences in transmission from different parts of the array, a place a hundred yards away would receive many millions of times weaker signal). Thus it could beam many billions of channels of information down to the earth, but with some requirement for switching instructions from the user--one can order several channels with a few seconds' delay before delivery. Thus any small area could have its own unique channel. The practical and cost-effective implementation of this idea is perhaps a decade away, but it is worth moving towards.

Privacy can be maintained in such systems by use of inexpensive microprocessors and sophisticated coding systems. Thus private post can be distributed to someone's code number. While a very large computer could probably decipher the message it would be costly, and would take special effort just as information can be intercepted now by special effort and expense. Such codes and ciphers could be used to protect private postage or copyrights in such a system, but in ways and with a logic quite different from protection based on possession of a physical carrier. It may well be possible to arrange actual usage to better reflect needs for information and intellectual products.

In a purely electronic information system, the essential requirements for use of a product is knowing where to find it (its "address"), and knowing the code cipher required to decode the information ("access"). These correspond to possession of the physical carrier, and knowing the language in which it is written, respectively. Restrictions of use to those who would pay is based on different principles: In the physical, material form of distribution, control is based on being able to spatially lock up the carrier, the effort and costs required in carrying it off and in reproduction. In the electronic form, it is based on the intelligence, time, and attention required to find and decode the content.

A reference to an article, an enjoyable book or picture can be passed on to a friend or colleague very easily when the address and access are pure information themselves. This kind of diffusion can be realistically controlled in four ways:

(1) Tie the information to a physical location either of use or access. Thus the information or enjoyment is tied directly to some physical trans-

formation which is itself controlled by other factors. This is a point of implementation, and may well be tied into some societal economic or cultural system. Information of this kind may be likened to the category of trade secrets, and the controls which would evolve would be a generalization of the experience there.

(2) Protect the distributors from other public and overt purveyers, and allow them to try to regain their investment before private diffusion has depleted their market advantage. Expressive literature which builds on fad and fashion and so has a limited lifetime would fall under this category. The protection and experience is most similar to traditional copyrights. What would not easily be protected in a new electronic environment would be those rare classics which have universal appeal and applicability and yet long drawing power over the years. However, there is little evidence that such are any more predictable or encouraged by long-term commercial benefits than short-term expressive products. Indeed, in the scientific and technical experience, such ideas are often held not to be patentable or copyrightable.

(3) Target the information so that it is especially valuable only to a small or limited audience which is predictable ahead of time. This type of product is most similar to that protected by the patent system. There is a sense of specific value added in terms of building on previous factors of production, and having a predicted audience or clientele in mind, with some relatively specific sense of value added for that clientele by use of the information provided. Usage of the information can be protected if the who and what of the usage is predicted in advance, just as in the case of patents. This mode of operation is also similar to the practice in the scientific literature: it is expected that users of ideas exercise due diligence in searching for antecedents, and that they give due credit and citation to those which they find; failure to do so may result in partial exclusion from that community, or in job sanctions. Positions, promotions, and prestige are allocated in large measure based on who cites and uses one's ideas, and with what further benefits.

(4) The information is individualized in the sense that there is interaction between the purveyer--who has in stock many ideas, processes, or tools, and the client--who has a problem or need, but is not sure of exactly what is needed or available. The heart of this process is a series of interactions out of which the two develop a better model (diagnosis) of the situation, and a sense (prescription) of what will work. In the personal sphere, this is the action of a professional or practitioner such as a physician, lawyer, or teacher. In the new technological areas, it is the function of a data-base purveyor, or modern librarians. The value

added in the client's situation is the administration of a specific recipe (Rx), and the improvement experienced. But there can be purveyors to the professional or practitioner, too. This would be in the form of better diagnostic tools, and better information stocks (recipes) for application; these products are in the form discussed under (3) above. To complete the model, the products listed under (1) above are those supervised by pharmicists or therapists; those discussed under (2) above are "patent medicines" sold over-the-counter, with a strong expressive or psychosomatic aspect. The area of (4) is generally controlled by licensure.

Thus, the potential effect of the new information technologies is to facilitate the on-going shift from mass-media intellectual products which tend to aim at the median audience very efficiently, but are much more costly, or less well adaptive, for smaller groups.

The overall direction which seems to come out of the considerations sketched above is better and more timely adaptation of information and services to individual need and situation. But this process is dependent upon the retrieval of appropriate information, or upon the prediction of where the intellectual product is likely to find use. This then focuses attention upon the modelling and switching capacities of the system, or upon the computer use patterns. Since the principle value added comes from the timely individual adaptive or accurate model, there will be a tendency for the basic content of the system to be not the final display product to an individual, but rather the program which generates the display. Since this is a rather different concept from current perception, let us discuss possible examples or viewpoints of this idea, and then discuss the technological potentials and principles behind it.

As an immediate example, we can take the individualized book. Already, one can buy for very little additional cost, a children's book which has been computer-printed with the child's name in it, together with names of local towns, streets, dogs and cats. In the practice of programmed instruction, it has been found that about 15 to 20 students will provide about 95-98% of all the questions and difficulties in mastering a particular article, and that it is possible to provide answers and assistances which will allow almost all to master the material; unfortunately, it takes about 5 times as much space to provide all the extra materials, and a lot of students are bored if they have to slog all the way through. Thus computer assisted instruction, in effect, attempts to individualize the material so that each student only sees that part of the material needed, and yet get a much higher fraction of the students through-- at sizable economic savings in terms of cost-effectiveness. It is reasonable to expect that similar principles could be applied in expressive literature, with the turns and pacing of the plot adaptable to individual temperaments of the readers, with much greater psychological satisfaction. Thus, in this case, we can see a possible trend: books initially were in category (1), with the Gutenberg Bible highly illustrated so that the book was a sumptuous physical instrument itself. Then came the invention of the novel as an instrument of mass expressive appeal, and with almost all quickly passing out of fashion into oblivion, per category (2). With better information on clienteles, fiction and literature has been focused, for example, for specific set of Zip Code residential areas, or even individualized to specific households based on a list of 50 common names used in the area (the local dogs and cats of the example above). It is now becoming possible to develop interactive computer programs which present in effect an individualized book depending upon the instantaneous mental state of a particular person.

The availability of technology, or the size of the market, while classical economic prerequisites to the potential improvements sketched in the evolution above, are not sufficient. Also important has been the development of better information on current situations, and better models for predicting likely outcomes. Thus, in the case of programmed books, as above, or in the corresponding medical case of models of clinical judgement which can in some instances out-perform on a more reliable basis ordinary physician diagnosis from a slate of test results, the situation requires good information about the very large range of potential customers or users, and well-developed computer models which predict with some reliability the benefits the clients are likely to gain. These informations and programs become factors of production behind the final application, and themselves become economic commodities.

As a second example, consider the evolution of computer programming. At first, and still to an uncomfortable degree, programs have been somewhat specifically tied to particular machine configurations (category (1)). But rapidly changing technology with the manufacturer's needs to update the machines without recurring software expenses, the demands by customers to have new machines without further software costs, and the ability of machines to simulate each other's operations all tend to make software ever more machine independent.

Quite a few specialty programs have been developed as part of the marketing strategy of computer companies to establish visibility, to break into a new market such as accounting systems, or general purpose graphics packages (category (2)). Major houses have also developed detailed packages to entice specific clienteles, with large and especially developed software under trade-secret or patent protection. But there has been continued competitive pressure to make the programs modular in format so that many companies can participate in suggesting new improvements without the need to develop a whole new system. This is similar to the forces which act to keep major industrial labs publishing their general research, while keeping their applications to individual internal company problems secret. Thus, the market has tended to bifurcate into two major categories: very large and complex programs affordable only by the largest of companies in specialized international competition; and, a generally open market of sub-programs which is hovering between the ethical product mode of (pharmaceutical) distribution, and the scientific model of open dissemination for visibility and prestige. Given the preceding analysis and experience from similar areas (together with the ability of machines to mimic each other) it seems likely that the second model will emerge for the factors, with the pharmaceutical mode merging into the practitioner mode (category (4)). There are some preliminary indications that procedures and models for operating the practitioner mode are beginning to diffuse.

In these several examples we have seen at work a classical pattern in the shift in the texture of a market area. It starts out with individual craftsmen or artists employed by a wealthy patron to use some expensive material or technology to achieve some effect (frequently spectacular or monumental) on the particularities of the patron. There is a long-range shift of the system to involve the participation of many diverse specialists handling portions of the problem using smaller, cheaper, and more easily distributed materials in ways which can be combined in predictable ways to meed differentiated categorical needs by individual consumers. Since the practitioner portion of the system is crucial for information implementation, the system could be organized in a highly decentralized manner; since the carrier for the information is a prerequisite, it could also be organized around several large providers of that service; the choice is partly a matter of public policy.

Which would be the likely final mode of economic organization is not easy to predict because of the possibility that models of practitioner judgements may not themselves become a market, but may be highly centralized. The bases for such centralization would be derived from advantages of central collection of data from a very wide range of users (and thus, greater reliability of models), the likely continuing economies of scale of super-large central computers, and from the scarcity of highest creative talent in the generation of new insights. But as a matter of public policy it may be possible to provide some of these services in a disaggregate or common carrier mode, or to encourage the most creative people to take academic or government lab positions as contributors to the externalities of smaller-scale situations.

It should be possible to develop an experimental set of different arrangements, with analysis of the data using both psychological and economic models. The above discussion brings out that the central factors permitting enforcement of ownership or attribution of creations depend on factors of learning psychology, and of the value added through better prediction; both of these areas have theoretical models which would facilitate the analysis. Let us for a moment highlight some of the principles involved.

One of the central results of learning psychology is that learning and utility of information is only secondarily based on the availability of the information: people are surrounded by far more data than they can ever hope to absorb or use. The critical factors are:

a. Motivation--which is based on a reasonable experience or expectation that the data will be useful in obtaining some satisfaction or speeding up some previously learned operations.

b. Timely appropriateness--the information fits into some motivated scheme of operation in current effect. The information must be formulated to be absorbed easily into that scheme, and must arrive or be easily retrieved when needed; if either condition fails, the information will be almost useless.

c. Frustration--if the costs or efforts involved, or the timing is off, the futilities may outweigh the utilities and the whole scheme be abandoned or put off. Thus the pattern of interaction is critical, and a major aspect of the purveyence of information is the scheme of presentation, and how well it matches the needs of the client.

This psychological model (derived from Pribram's research on brain functioning, as well as the work of Piaget and Bruner) emphasizes the matching of schemas of client operation and supplier presentation in time as well as effect. From the perspective of economics, the problem of the supplier is that of formulating a scheme from past factors which he can reasonably predict will be recognized as useful by a predictable client and at a predictable time. Thus, his production function contains the following components:

a. prediction of a distinguishable or cheaply recognizable schema in operation at a particular time, place (at least in the space used by the retrieval system);

b. reliable availability of schemas which can be compounded together to provide the client's needed schema.

The situation is complicated or enriched by a number of other aspects. The schema "for sale" can become more valuable (better adapted to an individual user, or resulting in less futility) or of wider appeal (adaptable to a wider range of users) if it is constructed in ways which make it changeable during usage; thus, if it is not a static presentation, but one controlled by an intelligent program (another schema!) it becomes more valuable. Information on the behavior of clients, when organized in ways which match the schema of adaptation of the supplier also can become a factor of production. But these kinds of functional distinctions between different kinds of factors are familiar to economists, and are susceptible to analysis.

In summary, let us highlight the following points:

1. Beyond the arrival of cheap reprography (one in every home) there is another technological revolution now available which can change the economic and enforcement configurations radically, and essentially eliminate most distribution and printing costs.

2. There are still enforcement and economic considerations which revolve around classical problems of utility (psychological satisfaction) and predictability (economic value-added). It should be possible to arrange a system which can resolve the fine details of individual utility, and provide far greater general predictability, or more rapid evolution of appropriate services. There are pregnant models to extrapolate from.

3. As examples, a new system could focus on: reliable improvement in the operation of particular physical situations, with known measures; timely provision of services in a mode conducive to expressive expectations; predictable suggestion of information for specific situations which would be monitored not on the basis of examining the information (royalty for purchase of access to content) but on actual use (when the result comes out as predicted, as with patents); and individualized services based on maps of needs and abilities.

III. DRAWBACKS TO THE EXISTING INFORMATION SYSTEM

Below we point out a number of what are (from our viewpoint) undesirable aspects of the existing information production and distribution system. While there are a number of factors interacting to determine the structure of this system, the copyright law is an important feature in the overall result, and will become of increasingly greater importance as the availability of new technologies puts strains on the system.

The total costs of operating the system are high and growing at a rapid rate, making it difficult for the various modes of information dissemination to function effectively. For example, libraries are facing skyrocketing costs, (10 to 15 percent per unit of service per year), due both to increases in purchase prices of books and journals and to the hidden, but high, costs of operating a circulation system, meaning primarily personnel costs.

Textbooks, particularly in the upper levels of the educational system, are steadily being priced out of usage, with increases of 7 to 10 percent per page per year. The postal system is another example where the expense of handling information transfer via obsolete methods is showing up in unmanageable cost increases of 10 to 15 percent per year. With library and postal service budgets not receiving corresponding increases, services to consumers are being cut back.

The high setup costs of initially putting together an information package and setting up a distribution system greatly limit the range of information which can achieve wide dissemination. For books, journals, television, etc., despite the relatively low costs of serving the marginal consumer, it is very difficult for information producers (authors, prospective writers of TV shows, etc.) to obtain space in the media. The middlemen between information and entertainment creators and the consuming public--publishers and broadcasting networks--in attempting, due to the pressures of the system, to serve the widest possible audience and thereby minimize their risks and maximize expected revenues, strongly influence the communications channels towards serving only what are perceived as the predominant tastes and needs. Consequently, the incentives for authors are to innovate only in certain narrow directions, for otherwise the odds are overwhelmingly in favor of their being shunted aside in favor of the "mainstream" trends of expression. There are strong tendencies towards development of a "monoculture" as the diversity of local and regional cultural traits are absorbed and eliminated by pressure towards a uniform center. In general, the highly centralized form which modern communications mechanisms have taken is a great barrier to variety of expression and informational content.

- Consumers of information have very poor product data on which to base their purchasing choices. The channels for evaluating information sources prior to purchase are limited and ineffective, but payment must be made at the point of access to the material, not according to the utility gained as the result of usage. Purchasing decisions are made according to such uncomprehensive, unreliable means as friends' recommendations. Choices are highly susceptible to product promotion--seller type--and often tend to be faddish, responding to recent influences.
- The centralizing tendencies of the information content also encourage increasing concentration in the control of information flows, as the "middlemen" industry tends toward greater degrees of monopoly. For example, the evident trend towards reduction

of competition between newspapers in any local area, and the growth of large newspaper chains across the country.

- The commercial, monetary reward structure of the copyright system tends to drive out production of information--based on other incentives. In academia, research and publication of scholarly papers is based on securing one's tenured position in the academic world, and on rewards in the forms of renown and recognition. But for the publishing of textbooks, of the materials needed for the crucial function of educating students, there is very little in the way of status in the scholarly community involved, but rather the hope of substantial monetary gain. As a result only a very small portion of the eminent people involved in the various academic fields put time and effort into textbook writing, despite its obviously determining impact on the quality of education. Moreover, the previously discussed high setup costs of production and distribution cause a centralizing trend in the content of texts. It is clear that much greater variety, detailed explanation, and separation of texts into modular units is needed to serve the needs of individual students but under the present distribution system this appears to be economically unfeasible.

  Similar difficulties due to the effects of monetary incentives exist in other fields of creativity, such as for artists and mass-market writers. The necessity for publishers to advertise and promote in other ways the most popular "mainstream" works tends to drive others out of the market, or away from public attention.

- The system by which "free" television and radio, and other media, are paid for indirectly by advertising has well-known but nonetheless drastic effects on the quality of information and entertainment presented, on the product choices made by consumers outside of the information market, and on the general cultural and other basic features of society. Due to the indirect means by which, in effect, the publishers of mass media programming are paid for their work, consumers are induced to absorb highly persuasive advertising along with their entertainment, and the programming itself is designed to be compatible with and enhance the desired effects of the advertising.

IV. SHORING UP THE OLD SYSTEM VERSUS NEW DIRECTIONS

As new technologies begin to impact on the preexisting system of protection for copyrighted works there are basically two approaches which can be taken by public policy. Attempts to "patch up" the current methods, principles, and procedures so as to accommodate new developments within the general framework of existing institutions and laws are possible; or systematic exploration and experimentation with substantially new concepts for regulating the dissemination and usage of information can be made. Marginally amending the present system will only hinder the advent of new technologies which hold great promise. Instead experimentation with common carriers for the transmission of information, with alternative payment mechanisms, and with reliance upon non-monetary incentives should be instituted.

Insistence on using a patchwork is likely to lead to one of two possible results. First, a constituency may arise with a strong vested interest in the institutional arrangements which are solidified by marginal changes in the laws. Through politicized governmental regulatory activities, the constituencies will maintain their economic interests at the expense of society's interest in implementing technologies with vastly greater efficiency in information transfer. Also, the possibilities for creative construction of new institutional arrangements will be greatly restricted. Second, if and when powerful new technologies force their way upon the system despite the efforts of groups with commitments to present structures, it is likely that costly disruptions and sub-optimal changes will occur during the transition period, which could conceivably drag on for some time due to political maneuvering.

In either case, it is important to (for once) recognize the implications of technological change, and to anticipate the needed rearrangements of economic and social structures. While there may be uncertainty and dangers in regulating for the future, a systematic exploration of the various options which may be open to society to make most effective use of its opportunities is certainly preferable to stagnation with the status quo.

BIBLIOGRAPHY

Breyer, Stephen, "The Uneasy Case for Copyright: A Study of Copyright in Books, Photocopies, and Computer Programs. "Harvard Law Review 84:281-361, December 1970.

Bush, George P., ed., Technology and Copyright: Annotated Bibliography and Source Materials. Mt. Airy, Maryland: LoMond Systems, Inc., 1972.

Cambridge Research Institute, Omnibus Copyright Revision: Comparative Analysis of the Issues. Washington, D.C.: American Society for Information Science (ASIS), 1973.

Economic Council of Canada, Report on Intellectual and Industrial Property (Ottawa: Information Canada), 1971.

G. Gipe, Nearer to the Dust (Baltimore: Williams & Wilkins Co.), 1967.

Hanson, D.E., "Copiers: the Indispensable Machines", Administrative Manageme December, 1976, pp. 35-55.

Hattery, Lowell H. and Bush, George P., eds., Reprography and Copyright Law. Washington, D.C.: American Institute of Biological Sciences, 1964.

L. Heilprin, "Technology and the Future of the Copyright Principle", Phi Delta Kappan, Jan. 1967, pp. 220-225.

Joint Economic Committee, Invention and the Patent System (Washington, D.C.: U.S. Government Printing Office), 1964.

Line, M., and Wood, D., "The Effect of a Large-Scale Photocopying Service on Journal Sales", Journal of Documentation, Vol. 31, No. 4, December 1975, pp. 234-245.

National Commission on New Technological Uses of Copyrighted Works (CONTU), Transcript CONTU Meeting #9 (Springfield, Va.: U.S. Department of Commerce), October, 1976.

National Commission on New Technological Uses of Copyrighted Works (CONTU), Transcript CONTU Meeting #11 (Springfield, Va.: U.S. Department of Commerce), January, 1977.

W. Nordhouse, Invention, Growth, and Welfare: A Theoretical Treatment of Technological Charge. (Cambridge: MIT Press), 1969.

J. Schmookler, Patents, Invention, and Economic Charge (Cambridge: Harvard Press), 1972.

Hearings Before the Subcommittee on Courts, Civil Liberties, and the Administ tion of Justice of the Committee on the Judiciary, House of Representati First Session on H.R. 2223, Copyright Law Revision) Part I (Washington, D.C.: U.S. Government Printing Office), 1976.

Subcommittee on Patents, Trademarks, and Copyrights of the Committee on the Judiciary, General Revision of the Copyright Law, October 19, 1976.

Subcommittee on Patents, Trademarks, and Copyrights of the Committee on the Judiciary, An Economic Review of the Patent System, Study No. 15 by Fritz Matchlup (Washington, D.C.: U.S. Government Printing Office), 1958.

Survey of Publisher Practices and Present Attitudes on Authorized Journal Article Copying and Licensing

PROJECT BACKGROUND AND SUMMARY OF FINDINGS

History

In the late summer of 1976 the Research Center for Library and Informatic Science at the Indiana University Graduate Library School was approached by th National Commission on New Technological Uses of Copyrighted Works (CONTU) abc the feasibility of distributing, tabulating and analyzing a questionnaire to be provided by CONTU to the publishers of United States scholarly and research journals. The IU Graduate Library School was selected for this task because, in an earlier study for the National Science Foundation*, it had developed a core list of 2,459 U.S. scholarly and research journals. Inclusion criteria for this list are explained later in this report. It was believed that this list, initially developed in 1974, could be updated to serve as the basis for this survey. Moreover, since the IU GLS Research Center had already establish contacts with these journal publishers in the completion of the NSF questionna it was felt that this familiarity would improve cooperation and response rates

The agreement for Indiana University to distribute and analyze the questi naire was completed on September 27, 1976. The development and pre-testing of the proposed questionnaire by CONTU (one for publishers of scholarly and research journals, one for each journal included) after the new copyright act was signed on October 19, 1976, did not permit these questionnaires to be distributed until February 15, 1977, with a requested response date of March 25, 1977. At the request of CONTU, a follow-up mailing was made on April 15, 1977, and all responses received by May 10, 1977 are included in these tabulatio

The list of 2,459 journals published by 1,634 publishers used in the NSF survey was updated through a review of Ulrich's International Periodicals Directory, 16th edition (1975-76), which lists both cessations and new journal starts. The list was modified in the light of the responses of publishers themselves, some of which indicated that journals still listed had actually

---

*Fry, Bernard M. and White, Herbert S. "Economics and Interaction of the Publisher-Library Relationship in the Production and Use of Scholarly and Research Journals". Final Report on NSF Grant GN-41398, PB 249108, 1975. Also available as: Fry and White--"A Study of Scholarly and Research Journal D.C. Heath & Co., Lexington, Mass., 1976.

ceased publication, while others called our attention to journals not in our survey for a variety of reasons, including the fact that they were too new to be listed in Ulrich's. The result of these changes was a revised survey population of 2,552 U.S. scholarly and research journals, distributed by 1,672 publishers.

Project Personnel

Bernard M. Fry, Dean of the Indiana University Graduate Library School, has served as Principal Investigator for this project. Herbert S. White, Professor in the Graduate Library School and Director of its Research Center for Library and Information Science, has served as Co-Principal Investigator. Elizabeth L. Johnson has served as Research Associate.

Purpose of Investigation

The questionnaires, which were distributed with explanatory and background material also developed by CONTU, were designed to elicit information concerning attitudes toward photocopying and various methods for dealing with licensing or the supply of authorized photocopies for such article copying not exempt under the provisions of the 1976 Copyright Revision Act, and which would require authorization of the copyright owner. It was felt that these would help the National Commission to fulfill its statutory responsibility to make recommendations to the Congress and the President "as to such changes in copyright law or procedures that may be necessary to assure...access to copyrighted works and to provide recognition of the rights of copyright owners". (Public Law 94-553)

Response Rates

The response rate for publishers was 31.8% (531 of 1,672); for journals they published it was 38.2% (974 of 2,552). Some additional responses have also been received since the May 10, 1977 cut-off date, and the data taken from these have been retained in case further analysis is desired.

There is clear evidence, moreover, that a large portion of the non-response comes from journals which are not copyrighted, and which may therefore have felt relatively unaffected by the questions being posed. A total of 872, or 89.5% of responding journals indicated that they were copyrighted. By contrast, analysis of the records of the Copyright Office indicates that only about 60% of the non-responding journals are copyrighted. The response levels therefore represent, in all probability, a greater proportion of those journals whose views and decisions concerning copyright policies are of significance in the measurement of attitudes. Confidentiality of all responses has been strictly maintained, and the completed questionnaires are being returned to the respondents.

Techniques of Analysis

Responses to the questions provided by CONTU were analyzed in total for the publisher or journal group responding. As appropriate, responses were also analyzed to determine differences between the for-profit and non-profit publications sectors; between the subject disciplines of pure science, applied science and technology, social science, and humanities; and by size of circulation for each journal. At the request of King Research, Inc., an organization involved in a related study for the National Science Foundation, National Commission on Libraries and Information Science, and CONTU, publisher responses were also broken down as between those who published only one journal, and those who published more than one.

SUMMARY OF FINDINGS

General

Although the tabular and descriptive data which follow present a wealth of information, it is somewhat difficult to draw clearcut generalized conclusions. There are several reasons for this. At the time of the distribution and completion of these questionnaires, the new copyright law had been enacted only a few months earlier and will not come into effect until January 1, 1978. In addition, no specific proposals for the establishment of clearinghouses or royalty payment centers had as yet been promulgated, let alone publicized.

Of the responses, 449 come from publishers who publish only one journal in the survey. This represents 84.6% of the responding publisher population, and 46.5% of the responding journal population. Of responding publishers in the survey, 95.5% distribute five or fewer journals, and these in turn include 61.3% of the responding journals. Scholarly and research publishing consists predominantly of relatively small non-profit journals, whose publishers probably have little knowledge of or have paid little attention to the complex and lengthy provisions of the new copyright act. Clearly, a number of major publishers, both in the for-profit and non-profit sectors, have done so, but this number represents only a small minority. The inexperience and lack of prior thought by the larger proportion of the response group shows up clearly in responses which are somewhat difficult to track. Appended comments, which provide valuable insight, indicate that many of these respondents are reluctant to be involved at all. Many of them have little if any expectation of receiving payment through any copyright mechanism. They have no particular interest in involvement in any system which they might consider complex, and they expect no remuneration of any sizeable proportions. At the same time, many of these same respondents are apparently suspicious of considering agreements the implications of which they do not fully understand. This leads to a contrasting posture in many cases of unwillingness to give permission, while at the same time having no expectation of return. They supply reprint copies to authors, or assign back issue rights to agents, and they would just as soon be left out of what they fear might become a substantial entrapment in bureaucratic routine. It is, of course, interesting, and perhaps ironic, that many libraries have expressed this as their greatest fear as well, rather than the potential payment cost.

At the other extreme there are few publishers who give voice to payment expectations which are undoubtedly unrealistically high. The most significant finding, in general terms, is the need for further information and education, which must reach in particular the small journal and fringe publisher who is such an important part of this field. Proposals made by the Association of American Publishers and others must be widely publicized, and there is a major educational and dissemination role which must be undertaken, perhaps by or with the cooperation of CONTU. Such assistance could include the development and explanation of alternative specimen statements as part of copyright notices, as well as the calculation of assessment of the impact of implementation of the new copyright law, in particular for small journals and individual publishers. For publishers wishing to copyright but who are willing to adopt a liberal policy on copying, specimen terminology to be distributed as potential notices in journals could deal with concepts such as "for private study and research", "willing to let non-profit users copy", "restrictions limited to the first year following publication", but in much more specific form. To a substantial degree respondents are willing to grant tights to non-profit users that they are not willing to grant to commercial users, whether out of principle of expectation of return. They do not appear to know, however, how to go about implementing this preference, or others which they may feel.

Journal Survey

1. Publication Frequency: The survey indicates differences in publication frequency not only as between the commercial and non-profit sectors, but also as among subject disciplines. Better than half of non-profit journals publish quarterly or even less frequently, while the same holds true for commercial journals in only 36% of the cases. Humanities journals appear quarterly or less frequently in 73% of responding cases, which is more than twice the reported rate for pure and applied science journals, which appear with considerably greater frequency. (See page 241)

2. Size of Journals: Scholarly and research publishing is heavily populated by small journals. Better than half of the journals in the survey had a circulation of under 3,000 copies, and this figure is even higher for commercial than for non-profit journals. However, large (between 10,000 and 100,000 circulation) journals, while representing only 19.5% of the journals, include 74.2% of the issues distributed. (See page 243)

3. Foreign Circulation: Less than half of responding journals report a

foreign circulation which exceeds 20% of the total, and only 27% have foreign circulation of above 30%. However, smaller circulation journals are more heavily dependent on foreign subscribers. (See page 246)

4. Copyrighting: The great majority of journals which responded to this survey, in particular commercial journals, copyright each issue published. They do not, however, include individually copyrighted articles in many cases, and commercial journals tend to avoid this in particular. (See page 250)

5. Page Charges: About three fourths of the journals responding do not employ page charges at all, and only 3.5% have mandatory page charges. Commercial journals make less use of page charges, and large commercial journals responding don't use them at all. (See page 252)

6. Selling Reprints of Articles: Better than half of responding journals currently sell reprints directly (although it is not known if minimum quantity limitations are applied), but only about one third sell reprints through an agent. The use of such agents is fairly concentrated among commercial journals to two agents (Xerox University Microfilm and Information Unlimited), and dominated by Xerox University Microfilm for non-profit journals. (See page 254)

7. Current Prices of Reprints: Rates charged by journals which presently sell reprints vary widely, although most non-profit journals are willing to accept $3 or less for a ten page article, and better than half of commercial journals are willing to accept orders for $5. However, a sizeable minority, particularly in the commercial sector, charges $7 or even more for a ten page article, supplied on pre-payment to domestic customers. (See page 261)

8. Comparative Prices of Reprints: Perhaps surprisingly, and indicative of lack of informed judgement mentioned earlier, journals which do not sell reprints express themselves as satisfied with lower payments, in response to a hypothetical question, than journals which do sell them. (See page 280)

9. Volume of Reprint Sales: Two thirds of the responding journals indicate no reprint sales at all or sales which average under 6 reprints a week. Only 13% of responding journals sell more than thirty reprints per average working day, and can be considered to be "in the business of selling reprints".

Responses indicate that more than half of the journals fill orders within five days of receipt, although over 17% take a month or longer to comply. (See pages 275 and 277)

10. Expected Prices for Authorized Copies: More than 50% of responding copyrighted journals expect no payment to them from the operation of a clearinghouse, or from an agent, and this lack of expectation was particularly pronounced among commercial journals. Where compensation was expected, 50 cents was acceptable in about half of the cases. However, a small but insistent minority indicates considerably greater expectations, in some cases well above $5. (See page 291)

11. Expected Prices for Licensed Photocopying: At the same time, perhaps because of lack of information, responding journals hesitate to commit themselves to licensing directly or through an agent or clearinghouse. Where there was willingness, 50 cents is an acceptable payment in more than half the respondents, but a small minority (See no. 10 above) hold out for as much as $7 or more. (See page 294)

12. Microform Editions: By a substantial margin, journals prefer to sell microform editions through an agent rather than directly. At the same time, they are not willing to authorize copying from microform during the current year of publication, and only slightly more willing to permit unrestricted copying from past year microforms. (See page 291)

13. Policies on Liberal Provisions to Copy: Although many journals do not presently exact payment charges from libraries, they are overwhelmingly unwilling to grant blanket permission for copying, or blanket permission for interlibrary loan. This negative reaction to "carte blanche" subsides only to some extent for back year permission, and is particularly strong with relation to libraries in for-profit organizations. Where there is willingness for back year unlimited copying, the cut-off is most frequently set at one year (See page 301)

Publisher Survey

14. International Standard Serial Numbers (ISSN): Only a small percentage of

in only 36% of cases. Humanities journals appear quarterly or less the

provision of reprints or photocopies at a lower price. This may be true in part because only slightly more than one third of responding journals presently identify their journals with ISSN numbers, and some responding publishers may not even have been aware of what ISSN numbers were. (See page 316 and also Appendix)

15. Licensing Preferences: Under licensing preferences, all types of publishers indicate a strong preference for direct licensing, as against the use of either agents or clearinghouses. It should be stressed that this question was answered as something of an abstraction, since no specific clearinghouse mechanism proposal had as yet been promulgated and distributed, either by the AAP, or by any other organization. (See page 317)

16. Use of Agents: For what are probably some of the same reasons, responding publishers expressed a strong preference for supplying authorized copies directly, rather than through clearinghouses or agents. As stressed in the general comments, the use of clearinghouses and agents is a concept which is probably little understood by some of the publishers of small and scattered journals, and it would require explanation and publicity to gain wider acceptance. (See page 320)

17. Teletype Equipment for Ordering Reprints: Responding publishers saw little practical utility in teletype equipment for receiving orders, in large part because very few publishers have such equipment at present. Additionally, few publishers foresaw the usefulness of another form of electronic communication. (See pages 326 and 329)

18. Telephone Orders: Better than two thirds of responding publishers, and in particular commercial publishers, indicated a willingness to accept telephonic orders, with a majority also willing to do this at a standard charge. (See page 328)

19. Preferred Methods of Payment: The receipt of individual one-time payment for the filling of a one-time order is the most preferred method of handling copy requests, since it avoids either billing or record keeping. Only about one fifth of the responding publishers found open accounts or deposit accounts

acceptable, and this positive response is largely limited to large commercial publishers, who might have reason to expect a larger volume of business, and the same response patterns held for the use of stamps or coupons. Slightly less than half of the responding publishers were agreeable to billing with shipment of the order, although it is not certain that all of these would be willing to do this for single copy orders as well as multiple copies. Large non-profit publishers were particularly reluctant to endorse this approach. (See page 329)

20. Future Policies: Of the 43.5% of publishers who responded to a question which implied that they did not presently sell reprints or photocopies directly or through an agent, about three fourths continued to express their unwillingness to do so in the future. (See page 331)

AVAILABILITY OF ADDITIONAL INFORMATION

The data base from which these reported data were extracted will continue to be maintained at the Research Center of the Indiana University Graduate Library School. Additional tabulations and analyses can be undertaken by Indiana University on a cost recoverable basis. Requests for such work should be directed during the life of CONTU to the National Commission on New Technological Uses of Copyrighted Works, Washington, D.C. 20558. After the statutory life of CONTU has expired requests should be directed to the Register of Copyrights, Washington, D.C. 20557.

Journal Questionnaire

Definition of Survey Population

(Also described in Publisher questionnaire)

The population for this survey was drawn from the list of U.S. scholarly and research journals identified by the Indiana University Graduate Library School Research Center in its study on "Economics and Interaction of the Publisher-Library Relationship in the Production and Use of Scholarly and Research Journals", prepared for the National Science Foundation under Grant GN-41398*.

---

*A book describing the methodology and conclusions of this study is available as "Publishers and Libraries: A Study of Scholarly and Research Journals", by Bernard M. Fry and Herbert S. White. D.C. Heath & Co., Lexington, Mass. 1976.

This study, which identified 2459 journals, published by 1634 publishers, defined scholarly and research journals through the exclusion of certain categories of periodicals believed to be inappropriate because the category would not ordinarily contain communications useful for scholarly purposes or would have little economic impact. Journals were therefore excluded if they fell into any of the following categories: 1) newsletters; 2) house organs; 3) general mass audience magazines; 4) popular culture magazines; 5) periodicals intended for a juvenile audience; 6) "little" magazines; 7) reprints; 8) patents; 9) secondary periodicals or services; 10) periodicals intended for a local audience; 11) trade journals; 12) periodicals not indexed by an indexing or abstracting service except in subject areas in which such services are inadequate, or where the journal began publication after 1970 and might therefore not reasonably be expected to be indexed; 13) processed periodicals; 14) tabloids; 15) free periodicals; 16) government publications; and 17) controlled circulation periodicals. On the advice of statistical consultants, any journal with a circulation above 100,000 was excluded under category 3), because it was felt that data from these journals would hopelessly skew reported information and conclusions.

The initial list, compiled in 1974 through reviews of Current Contents and Ulrich's International Periodicals Directory, was then updated through a review of Ulrich's 16th Edition 1975-76, since Ulrich's lists both cessations and new journal starts. Finally, the list was impacted by the responses of publishers themselves, some of which indicated that journals still listed had actually ceased publication, and some of which called our attention to journals not in our survey for a variety of reasons, including the fact that they were new. These publisher-induced changes to the list of scholarly and research journals were relatively minor. Our survey is ultimately based on potential responses from 1672 publishers, who distribute 2552 scholarly and research journals.

Rate of Response

In asking the 1672 publishers of the 2552 journals in the survey universe to respond, they were asked to complete one questionnaire as publisher, and an additional questionnaire for each journal. The journal survey response was 974, or 38.2% of the universe. This was considerably better than the 31.8% response to the publisher questionnaire reported in the other section of this study, and indicates that publishers of more than one journal were more likely to respond than publishers of only single journals.

The assumption that this may be because larger publishers could be expected to have a greater interest in questions of copyright is borne out in an examination of the copyright status of responding and non-responding journals. A total of 872, or 89.5% of the responding journals indicated that they were copyrighted. By contrast, an analysis at the Library of Congress of the copyright status of 1550 of the 1578 journals (the other 28 could not be located in LC files) which either did not respond or responded too late to be included indicates that only 59.0% of these journals are copyrighted. For these reasons it can be postulated that, while the survey elicited usable response from only 38.2% of the eligible journal population, it represents a far greater percentage of those journals whose views and decisions concerning copyright policies are of significance in the measurement of attitudes. This assumption is also borne out by an examination of responses by publisher groups. For-profit journals, at 46.0%, showed a considerably higher rate of response than non-profit journals, at 35.4%. The small other-not-for-profit journals showed the lowest level of response, at 27.7%. University presses, at 60.5%, while a small group, were the most responsive, an observation which repeats the experience of the NSF questionnaire mailed out in 1974, in which university presses were also the publisher group most likely to respond. It is probable that this is a small homogeneous group, which maintains close contact, and which is used to collecting and reporting data. The for-profit journals, because of their higher response rate, represented 31.6% of the response population, although they constituted only 26.3% of the sample. Society journals, the largest sampling group at 43.1%, was also the largest response group, at a slightly diminished 41.8%.

In analysis of subject disciplines. social science journals were the largest group in the sample, at 38.6%, and are an approximately equal percentage of the response population, at 38.1%. Applied science and technology journals, the second largest sample group at 30.8%, showed the smallest percentage response, and therefore represent only 27.1% of the response population. By contrast, almost half of the 437 pure science journals in the sample responded, and this caused an increase of from 17.1% of the sample to 22.2% of the response population. Humanities journals were the smallest percentage sample group, and declined further because of a relatively poor response rate. It is known that many of these humanities journals are published in the small other-not-for-profit sector, which, as indicated above, also had a small response rate.

The for-profit sector, which represented 38.2%, of the responding journals is most heavily concentrated in the applied science and technology discipline, in which it accounts for 43.2% of the responses. By contrast, only 8.9% of the responding humanities journals are published by commercial institutions. Societies are the largest responding publishing groups in all disciplines except for the humanities. They distribute 44.0% of the pure science, 42.9% of the social science, and 42.4% of the applied science journals. By contrast, the responding humanities journals are only 33.3% published by professional societies, and in this discipline the small other-not-for-profit journals account for 42.4% of the responses, more than twice their impact in any other discipline, and four times their share of the applied science and technology discipline as recorded in survey responses.

These data confirm conclusions about publishers in the NSF questionnaire, in that commercial publishers are most active in the applied and then pure sciences, and in that humanities publishing is dominated by small individual publishers. This last observation is also borne out statistically. For-profit publishers in our survey published an average of 3.90 journals each, not-for-profit publishers 1.47. Of these, societies averaged 1.55, university presses 3.71, and the "other" non-profit publishers only 1.07

JOURNAL RESPONSE TO SURVEY

Total Query N=2552

	Number	Percentage	No. Copyrighted	% Copyrighted
Responding Journals	974	38.2%	872	89.5%
Non-responding Journals	1578	61.8%	914	59.0%

By Type of Publisher

	Total in Survey Population	Percent of Survey Population	No. Re-sponding	Percent Response	Percent of Response Population	Response No. Copy-righted	Popul % Cop right
For-profit Journals	670	26.3%	308	46.0%	31.6%	296	96.1
Not-for-profit Journals	1882	73.7%	666	35.4%	68.4%	576	86.5
a) Societies	1099	43.1%	407	37.0%	41.8%	356	87.5
b) University Press	129	5.0%	78	60.5%	8.0%	75	96.2
c) Other NFP Journals	654	25.6%	181	27.7%	18.6%	145	79.6

By Subject Discipline

	Total in Survey Population	Percent of Survey Population	No. Re-sponding	Percent Response	Percent of Response Population	Response No. Copy-righted	Popul % Cop right
Pure Science	437	17.1%	216	49.4%	22.2%	200	92.6
Applied Science and Technology	785	30.8%	264	33.6%	27.1%	238	90.2
Social Science	986	38.6%	371	37.6%	38.1%	329	88.7
Humanities	344	13.5%	123	35.8%	12.6%	105	85.4

By Publisher and Discipline

Showing % of Response Population

	Pure Science	Applied Science	Social Science	Humanities
For Profit	38%	43.2%	27.2%	8.9%
Non-profit	62%	56.8%	72.8%	91.1%
Society	44.0%	42.4%	42.9%	33.3%
University	5.6%	3.8%	10.0%	15.4%
Other NFP	12.4%	10.6%	19.9%	42.4%

Question 1a. What is the publication frequency? ____________ times per year

Publication Frequency of Responding Journals

More than half of the responding journals, 51.2%, publish between 2 and 4 issues per year, and can be assumed to be largely semi-annual or quarterly. An additional 42.9% publish between 5 and 12 issues annually, and are usually either bi-monthly or monthly, although some monthly journals skip summer months and only publish 9, 10, or 11 issues per year. The vast majority, 94.8%, publish no more frequently than monthly, a pattern which is not surprising for scholarly and research publications which do not concentrate on information with short-term news value.

There was some differentiation between the for-profit and non-profit sectors, with commercial journals publishing monthly or less frequently in 90.9% of the cases, while non-profit journals reported 96.8% in this category. There was also a markedly greater tendency for non-profit journals to publish only between 2 and 4 issues per year, with 59.4% reporting this or an even lower frequency, compared for 36.0% for the commercial sector. This greater frequency of publication, when added to the larger number of published pages for commercial journals already reported from the NSF study, may account at least in part for the greater prices being charged by commercial journals.

Substantial differentiations also emerge among subject disciplines. For humanities journals, 73.1% publish no more than 4 times a year, and for social science journals the figure is 69.0%. By contrast, for pure and applied science journals, for which currency of reporting may be postulated to be more significant, the figures are 35.2% and 32.0%, respectively.

With the exclusion of journals with circulations above 100,000 already explained earlier, significant trends by circulation size emerge. Over 75% of the large (10,000 or more) circulation commercial journals are published between 5 and 12 times annually, and 18.4% are published more frequently than monthly. By contrast, 39.0% of the smallest circulation (under 3000) commercial journals are published no more frequently than quarterly, and only 8.5% are distributed more frequently than monthly.

In the non-profit sector, similar trends, although not as pronounced, emerge. Almost the same percentage of large non-profit as commercial journals are published between 5 and 12 times annually, but only 8.2% are published more frequently than monthly. Small circulation non-profit journals have very infrequent distribution patterns, with 83.5% published quarterly or even less frequently, and virtually no distribution more frequent than monthly.

Question 1a: What is the publication frequency? ____________ times per year

	Total Journal Response (N=974)	Type of Publisher: For Profit (N=308)	Type of Publisher: Non-profit (N=666)	Journals by Subject: Pure Science (N=216)	Journals by Subject: Applied Science (N=264)	Journals by Subject: Social Science (N=371)	Journals by Subject: Humanities (N=123)
Less than 2	.7%	0	1.1%	0	.8%	.8%	1.6%
2-4	51.2%	36.0%	58.3%	35.2%	31.1%	68.2%	71.5%
5-12	42.9%	54.9%	37.4%	51.9%	62.1%	29.9%	25.2%
13-26	4.3%	7.5%	2.7%	12.0%	4.5%	.8%	.9%
27-52	.9%	1.6%	.5%	.9%	1.5%	.3%	.8%
mean	7.078	8.416	6.459	8.838	8.871	5.437	5.089
median	4.457	6.080	4.317	6.144	6.418	4.189	4.099
mode	4.000	4.000	4.000	4.000	12.000	4.000	4.000

Question 1a: What is the publication frequency? ____________ times per year

	For Profit 0-2999 (N=177)	For Profit 3000-9999 (N=47)	For Profit 10000-max (N=49)	Non-profit 0-2999 (N=297)	Non-profit 3000-9999 (N=234)	Non-profit 10000-max (N=134)
Less than 2	0	0	0	.7%	2.1%	0
2-4	39.0%	27.7%	6.1%	82.8%	50.9%	16.4%
5-12	52.5%	66.0%	75.5%	16.2%	42.7%	75.4%
13-26	8.5%	4.3%	10.2%	.3%	3.8%	6.7%
27-52	0	2.1%	8.2%	0	.5%	1.5%
mean	7.119	8.894	14.694	4.519	6.906	10.000
median	5.855	6.333	11.966	4.005	4.439	10.375
mode	4.000	12.000	12.000	4.000	4.000	12.000

Question 1b. Circulation as of January, 1977

(1) Total ___________ copies per issue

Circulation Statistics for Surveyed Journals

Reported circulation was collected into three categories; 1) journals with circulation per issue up to 2999 copies; 2) journals with issue circulation between 3000 and 9999 copies; and 3) journals with issue circulation of 10,000 and more. As reported earlier, journals with circulations above 100,000 had been excluded from the initial NSF survey because of the recommendation from consulting statisticians who felt that their inclusion would distort the data, and these journals were left out of this survey as well. The three categorizations used were selected at the request of King Research, Inc., which is carrying out parallel studies for the National Commission on Libraries and Information Science (NCLIS), NSF, and CONTU, and which felt that calculation in this manner would provide useful information for its own studies.

Better than half, or 50.5% of the responding journals, had circulation below 3000 copies per issue. Perhaps surprisingly, a larger percentage of commercial than non-profit journals fell into this category, with 64.8% of for-profit journals in this range, compared to only 44.7% of non-profit journals. At the other end of the spectrum, 19.5% of all journals which responded to this question distributed over 10,000 copies per issue, including 17.9% of commercial and 20.1% of non-profit publishers. Of the large circulation non-profit group, 83.6% are society journals. In fact, these society journals account for 61.2% of all journals in the survey with circulation over 10,000 copies. It is obvious that much if not most of the high level of circulation comes from distribution to society members.

Among subject disciplines, only applied science journals showed a deviation from the "small" journal phenomenon, and was the only discipline in which less than half the journals had a circulation of under 3000. Over 30% of these journals reported circulation of 10,000 copies and more, and the mean of 12,935 was more than twice the mean for pure science and humanities journals, with social science journals falling about halfway between the two groups.

Although the journals with distribution above 10,000 copies represented only 19.5% of the journals reporting, they represented 74.2% of the 8,354,266 issues distributed by the total of all responding journals, with more than two thirds of this total coming from the non-profit sector. Journals with circulation between 3000 and 9999 copies were 18.1% of the total, with non-profit circulation more than 4 1/2 times commercial circulation. The smallest (under 3000) category of journal, while including more than 50% of the re sponding journals, represented only 7.7% of the circulation distribution, with non-profit journals two thirds of this total.

For-profit journals represented 27.3% of the circulation, a somewhat smaller percentage than their share of the journal survey itself, and an indication of the large circulation enjoyed by societal journals, which represented more than half of the entire total. Applied science journals, with 40.9%, had the greatest distribution share, followed by social science at 35.4%. Pure science and humanities trailed substantially, at 15.0% and 8.7%, respectively.

Question 1b: Circulation as of January, 1977

	Total Copies per Issue						
	Total	Type of Publisher		Journals by Subject			
	Journal Response (N=938)	For Profit (N=273)	Non-profit (N=665)	Pure Science (N=216)	Applied Science (N=264)	Social Science (N=335)	Humanities (N=123)
0-2999	50.5%	64.8%	44.7%	57.9%	39.0%	51.6%	59.3%
3000-9999	30.0%	17.3%	35.2%	30.6%	30.3%	30.1%	27.6%
10000-max	19.5%	17.9%	20.1%	11.6%	30.7%	18.3%	13.1%
mean	8906	8349	9135	5818	12935	8839	5866

Question 1b: Circulation as of January 1977

	Total Copies per Issue by Type of Publisher		
	0-2999	3000-9999	10000-max
For Profit (N=273)	64.8%	17.3%	17.9%
Non-profit (N=665)	44.7%	35.2%	20.1%
Society	19.5%	24.2%	16.8%
University	7.3%	3.7%	.3%
Other NFP	17.9%	7.3%	3.0%

JOURNAL RESPONSE BASED ON TOTAL 1977 DISTRIBUTION

Journals by Type of Publisher

	No. Distributed	% of Total Distributed
For Profit	2279314.000	27.3%
Non-profit	6074952.000	72.7%
Society	4520849.000	54.1%
University	259448.000	3.1%
Other NFP	1294655.000	15.5%
Total	8345266.000	100%

Journals by Size of Circulation

	No. Distributed	% of Total Distribution
0-2999	639882.000	7.7%
For Profit	206291.000	2.5%
Non-profit	433591.000	5.2%
3000-9999	1507060.000	18.1%
For Profit	264940.000	3.2%
Non-profit	1242120.000	14.9%
10000-max	6207324.000	74.2%
For Profit	1808083.000	21.6%
Non-profit	4399241.000	52.6%
Total	8345266.000	100%

Journals by Subject

	No. Distributed	% of Total Distribution
Pure Science	1256740.000	15.0%
Applied Science	3414831.000	40.9%
Social Science	2961184.000	35.4%
Humanities	721511.000	8.7%
Total	8345266.000	100%

Question 1b. (2) Outside U.S. ____________ copies per issue

Circulation Outside the United States (As Shown as a Percentage of the Total)

Only 27.1% of responding journals indicated a circulation outside the United States of 30% or more of the total, and less than half report over 20%. Commercial journals are far more likely to be distributed outside the United States, with 48.4% of the journals in the for-profit sector reporting that 30% or more of their distribution went to foreign countries, and 64.7% reporting a foreign circulation of 20% or more. By contrast, only 18.6% of non-profit journals report a foreign circulation above 30%, and the group reporting 15% is still less than half of the non-profit total. It is surmised that this is partly true because commercial publishers tend to have better developed international marketing organizations or contacts, and also because much of the non-profit circulation is from American society journals to its own American society members.

Pure science journals show a far greater tendency for foreign circulation than any other subject discipline. The 56.7% of pure science journals who indicate that 30% or more of their distribution is foreign are more than twice the percentage of any other subject discipline. Social science journals, in particular, report a foreign circulation of 10% or less for half of the journals reporting.

Perhaps surprisingly, smaller circulation journals are frequently more apt to have foreign subscribers. This may be because small disciplines are truly international in scope, with a relatively small number of researchers in close contact regardless of geographic boundaries. Over 62% of the smallest commercial journals have a foreign circulation of 30% or more. By contrast, only 8.5% of the largest commercial and 2.3% of the largest non-profit journals report foreign circulation in excess of 30% large non-profit journals, in fact, report foreign circulation above 10% in only 46.1% of the journals in this category, presumably in large part because of heavy societal member distributions.

Question 1b. (2) Outside U.S. ____________ copies per issue

Shown as Percentage of Total Circulation

	Total Journal Response (N=907)	Type of Publisher: For Profit (N=258)	Non-profit (N=649)	Journals by Subject: Pure Science (N=210)	Applied Science (N=249)	Social Science (N=326)	Humanities (N=122)
0	5.8%	4.3%	6.5%	.5%	4.0%	12.0%	2.5%
0.01-0.99%	4.9%	2.3%	5.9%	1.0%	3.2%	9.2%	3.3%
1.00-4.99%	10.7%	7.4%	12.0%	4.3%	10.0%	14.4%	13.1%
5.00-9.99%	12.9%	9.7%	14.2%	8.6%	13.3%	14.4%	15.6%
10.00-14.99%	10.7%	6.2%	12.5%	5.2%	9.6%	12.3%	18.0%
15.00-19.99%	8.0%	5.4%	9.1%	6.2%	8.4%	8.3%	9.8%
20.00-24.99%	10.3%	7.8%	11.2%	8.1%	14.5%	8.6%	9.8%
25.00-29.99%	9.6%	8.5%	10.0%	9.5%	11.7%	6.7%	13.1%
30.00-max%	27.1%	48.4%	18.6%	56.7%	25.3%	14.1%	14.8%
mean %	20.783%	29.220%	17.429%	33.075%	21.330%	13.857%	17.013%
median %	18.182%	28.477%	14.396%	35.943%	20.000%	9.941%	13.171%
mean no. of copies	1137.015	1320.729	1063.983	1257.090	1706.108	742.831	822.131
median no. of copies	468.000	459.500	488.000	740.500	700.000	290.000	268.500

Question 1b (2) Outside U.S. ____________ copies per issue

Shown as Percentage of Total Circulation

Journals by Size of Circulation

	For Profit: 0-2999 (N=172)	3000-9999 (N=39)	10000-max (N=47)	Non-profit: 0-2999 (N=290)	3000-9999 (N=229)	10000-max (N=130)
0	5.8%	2.6%	0	8.3%	4.4%	6.2%
0.01-0.99%	1.2%	5.1%	4.3%	3.8%	6.6%	9.2%
1.00-4.99%	2.3%	5.1%	27.7%	10.7%	11.4%	16.2%
5.00-9.99%	5.8%	17.9%	17.0%	13.8%	10.0%	22.3%
10.00-14.99%	3.5%	15.4%	8.5%	12.1%	12.2%	13.8%
15.00-19.99%	4.1%	5.1%	10.6%	8.3%	8.3%	12.3%
20.00-24.99%	4.1%	7.7%	21.3%	11.0%	12.2%	10.0%
25.00-29.99%	10.5%	7.8%	2.1%	11.4%	9.6%	7.7%
30.00-max%	62.8%	33.3%	8.5%	20.7%	25.3%	2.3%
mean %	35.000%	23.093%	13.150%	18.447%	19.733%	11.098%
median %	37.952%	18.990%	13.333%	15.910%	19.068%	9.598%
mean no. of copies	417.029%	1141.410	4776.681	276.762	1030.131	2879.723
median no. of copies	327.500	910.000	2428.000	199.611	858.000	2000.278

Question 1b. (3) 'Special' subscription(s) __________ copies per issue (Please report here only subscriptions, either in hard copy or microform, which include some authorization to copy greater than that for regular subscriptions).

Special Subscription Copies Per Issue

This question, not surprisingly, drew very poor level of response. Over 75% responded that they had no such subscriptions, and an additional 13.6% left the question blank, leading to at least the possible conclusion that these fall into the same response category. Only 10.5% of the journals indicated that they had such subscriptions, and for 97.1% this was a figure less than 10% of their total circulation. For 93.2% it was less than 5%. Because of this sparseness of response, no tabulation of data was attempted.

Question 1c. Total circulation as of January, 1972: __________ copies per issue

Circulation Statistics for Journals in the Survey

Better than half of the 907 journals which responded have circulation of under 3000 copies. Perhaps surprisingly, commercial journals are even more heavily concentrated in this grouping than non-profit journals, with 74.1% of the journals in the profit sector compared to 51.0% of non-profit journals. Non-profit journals are more heavily concentrated in the largest (over 10,000) category, with 18.1% of the non-profit journals, compared to only 13.7% of commercial journals.

Applied science and technology journals have the greatest distribution, with 28.0% in the largest category of journals, compared to only 9.6% of humanities journals, the most sparsely distributed of the subject disciplines.

Circulation growth for the period 1972-77 averaged 21.5% for all journals, for an annual average growth of about 4%. This, of course, includes foreign as well as domestic subscribers, and individual as well as institutional (library) customers. For-profit journals grew at a far more rapid rate than non-profit journals, with the commercial sector reporting 40.0% over the 1972-77 span, compared to 15.8% for the non-profit. Within subject disciplines applied science and technology showed the most rapid growth, at 28.4%, pure science the slowest at 9.5%.

Question 1c. Total circulation as of January, 1972: ______ copies per issue

	Total Journal Response (N=907)	Type of Publisher: For Profit (N=278)	Type of Publisher: Non-profit (N=629)	Journals by Subject: Pure Science (N=200)	Journals by Subject: Applied Science (N=243)	Journals by Subject: Social Science (N=350)	Journals by Subject: Humanities (N=114)
0-2999	58.1%	74.1%	51.0%	59.5%	44.4%	64.3%	65.8%
3000-9999	25.1%	12.2%	30.8%	29.0%	27.6%	21.4%	24.6%
10000-max	16.8%	13.7%	18.2%	11.5%	28.0%	14.3%	9.6%

Percentage Increase over 5 years 1972-1977

Total Circula-tions 1977	8,354,266	2,279,314	6,074,952	1,256,740	3,414,831	2,961,184	721,511
Total Circula tions 1972	6,874,979	1,628,657	5,246,322	1,147,237	2,660,238	2,448,451	619,053
% Increase 1972-1977	21.5%	40.0%	15.8%	9.5%	28.4%	20.9%	16.6%

Question 1d. International Standard Serial Number (ISSN) ______________
(Enter the ISSN only if the ISSN is printed in each issue of the journal itself).

Use of ISSN Number

Only 36.0% of the responding 974 journals include the ISSN number in each issue of the journals. This percentage, however, is still considerably higher than that of journals which did not respond to the survey or whose responses were received too late to be included. Analysis at the Library of Congress indicates that only 14.3% of these journals have been assigned ISSN numbers. Since it has already been reported earlier that these non-responding journals are also far less apt to be copyrighted, it can be assumed that the response population includes a greater proportion of more substantial journals, more interested in and concerned about issues of library copying and copyright in general.

Journals in the for-profit sector which responded are more likely to include ISSN numbers, with 40.9% reporting their inclusion in each issue, compared to 33.8% in the non-profit sector. Almost half of the responding pure science journals carry ISSN numbers, applied science journals are at the other end of the spectrum, at 29.9%.

It might be expected that journals with larger circulations would be more likely to include ISSN numbers. However, the very reverse pattern occurs. Over 55% of the smallest commercial journals include ISSN numbers, compared to only 20.4% with circulations above 10,000 copies. For non-profit journals 33.3% of the smallest and 26.9% of the largest circulation groupings include ISSN numbers.

Question 1d. International Standard Serial Number (ISSN) _______________

	Total Journal Response (N=974)	Type of Publication		Journals by Subject Breakdown			
		For Profit (N=308)	Non-profit (N=666)	Pure Science (N=216)	Applied Science (N=264)	Social Science (N=371)	Humanities (N=123)
Print ISSN	36.0%	40.9%	33.8%	47.2%	29.9%	33.2%	38.2%
Do Not Print	64.0%	59.1%	66.2%	52.8%	70.1%	66.8%	61.8%

Journals by Size of Circulation

	For Profit			Non-profit		
	0-2999 (N=177)	3000-9999 (N=47)	10000-max (N=49)	0-2999 (N=297)	3000-9999 (N=234)	10000-max (N=134)
Print ISSN	55.4%	23.4%	20.4%	33.3%	38.0%	26.9%
Do Not Print	44.6%	76.6%	79.6%	66.7%	62.0%	73.1%

Question 2a. Do you copyright each issue of this jouranal? Yes _____ No _____

b. Are individual articles in this journal copyrighted by the authors or others?

None ________; Few _________; Some __________; Many ___________

Policy Toward Copyrighting of Issues and of Specific Articles

A great majority, 89.5%, of journals, all but 1.5% of which responded to this question, copyright each issue. As reported earlier, Library of Congress analysis indicates that the tendency toward copyrighting for non-responding journals is much smaller. Commercial journals in particular, with a rate of 96.1%, responded affirmatively to this question, but even non-profit journals report a rate of 86.5%. There is relatively little difference between subject disciplines, with pure science at the greatest rate of 92.6%, and humanities at the lowest, 85.4%. Surprisingly, the tendency by commercial journals to copyright each issue decreases as the circulation of the journal increases, with large for-profit journals copyrighting in 89.8% of the cases. By contrast, the tendency to copyright non-profit journals increases with increasing size, with the rate of 93.3% for the group with the largest circulation.

The great majority of journals do not include articles individually copyrighted by the author or by others. In particular, commercial journals completely avoid this practice in 83.4% of the cases, and report no instances in which many articles are individually copyrighted. Non-profit journals report a greater rate of individual copyrighting, although even here for 73.7% of the journals there are no copyrighted articles, and the combination of none and few exceeds 90%. In particular, pure science journals avoid individually copyrighted articles. The practice tends to occur more readily in social science and humanities journals, but even here 2/3 of the journals do not have individually copyrighted articles. Circulation size of the journal seems to have little impact on the practice, except that small commercial journals are least likely to include individually copyrighted articles.

Question 2a. Do you copyright each issue of this journal? Yes______ No______

b. Are individual articles in this journal copyrighted by the authors or others?

None________; Few___________; Some_________; Many__________.

		Total Journal Response (N=974)	Type of Publisher: For Profit (N=308)	Non-profit (N=666)	Journals by Subject Breakdown: Pure Science (N=216)	Applied Science (N=264)	Social Science (N=371)	Humanities (N=123)
a.	Yes	89.5%	96.1%	86.5%	92.6%	90.2%	88.7%	85.4%
	No	9.0%	3.6%	11.5%	6.0%	8.7%	10.0%	12.2%
	No answer	1.5%	.3%	2.0%	1.4%	1.1%	1.3%	2.4%
b.	None	73.7%	83.4%	69.2%	85.6%	76.5%	67.1%	66.7%
	Few	16.9%	8.1%	21.0%	8.8%	11.0%	24.0%	22.8%
	Some	4.4%	4.6%	4.4%	2.8%	3.7%	5.1%	6.5%
	Many	.7%	0	1.0%	.5%	.4%	.9%	1.6%
	No Answer	4.3%	3.9%	4.4%	2.3%	8.4%	2.9%	2.4%

Question 2a. Do you copyright each issue of this journal? Yes_______ No_______

b. Are individual articles in this journal copyrighted by the authors or others?

None_________; Few________; Some___________; Many_________.

Journals by Size of Circulation

	For Profit 0-2999 (N=177)	3000-9999 (N=47)	10000-max (N=49)	Non-profit 0-2999 (N=297)	3000-9999 (N=234)	10000-max (N=134)
a. Yes	97.7%	93.6%	89.8%	79.8%	91.0%	93.3%
No	2.3%	6.4%	8.2%	17.8%	7.3%	5.2%
No answer	0	0	2.0%	2.4%	1.7%	1.5%
b. None	88.1%	68.1%	69.4%	70.7%	67.9%	67.9%
Few	4.5%	10.6%	24.5%	20.5%	20.5%	23.2%
Some	5.1%	6.4%	4.1%	4.7%	4.3%	3.7%
Many	0	0	0	.7%	1.3%	1.5%
No answer	2.3%	14.9%	2.0%	3.4%	6.0%	3.7%

Question 3. Page charges

a. Not employed _________ b. Required ___________

c. Employed but not mandatory __________

Use of Page Charges

Approximately 3/4 of the journals in the survey do not employ page charges at all, and only 3.5% of the responding journals have mandatory page charges. For profit journals are least likely to utilize page charges, with only 7.5% reporting their use at all, and only 3.6% making them mandatory. Non-profit journals are more likely to use page charges, but not on a mandatory basis, with 17.6% having such non-mandatory charges. Pure science journals are most active in the use of page charges on a non-mandatory basis, (29.6%) but conversely few have mandatory charges (4.2%).

Circulation size of journal has little discernable impact on the practice. Commercial journals, as reported earlier, shun page charges, and large commercial journals use them least of all. In fact, none of the large commercial journals responding to the questionnaire indicated the use of page charges, even on a non-mandatory basis. The use of optional page charges is greatest in medium circulation non-profit journals, and falls off toward both extremes.

Question 3: Page charges

a. Not employed_____________ b. Required_____________

c. Employed but not mandatory_____________

	Total Journal Response (N=974)	Type of Publisher: For Profit (N=308)	Type of Publisher: Non-profit (N=666)	Journals by Subject: Pure Science (N=216)	Journals by Subject: Applied Science (N=264)	Journals by Subject: Social Science (N=371)	Journals by Subject: Human-ities (N=123)
a. Not employed	74.3%	87.7%	68.2%	63.0%	76.1%	79.5%	74.8%
b. Required	3.5%	3.6%	3.5%	4.2%	1.5%	5.1%	1.6%
c. Employed but not mandatory	12.8%	3.9%	17.6%	29.6%	10.3%	5.9%	9.8%
d. No answer	9.4%	4.8%	10.7%	3.2%	12.1%	9.5%	13.8%

Question 3: Page Charges

Journals by Size of Circulation

	For Profit 0-2999 (N=177)	For Profit 3000-9999 (N=47)	For Profit 10000-max (N=49)	Non-profit 0-2999 (N=297)	Non-profit 3000-9999 (N=234)	Non-profit 10000-max (N=134)
a. Not employed	85.3%	78.7%	95.9%	71.4%	59.8%	76.1%
b. Required	4.5%	6.4%	0	3.4%	3.8%	3.1%
c. Employed but not mandatory	5.6%	4.3%	0	13.8%	24.4%	10.4%
d. No answer	4.6%	10.6%	4.1%	11.4%	12.0%	10.4%

Question 4. Do you now sell directly or through an authorized agent reprints or authorized photocopies of articles from this journal? If you do not sell copies directly or through an agent skip to question 10 after answering this question.

a. Directly Yes __________ No __________

b. Through an authorized agent Yes __________ No __________

c. Name of authorized agent(s) ______________________________

Present Sale Directly or Through an Agent of Reprints or Photocopies

In requesting responses to this question, no distinction was made between sale of reprints of copies in bulk or in minimum quantities, and individual one-copy sale which would most directly affect libraries. In responding, some journals did in fact append the comment that they did not honor single copy requests, that they sold only copies of entire issues, that they sold only to authors, that they sold only in bulk, that they sold only in-print issues, or that they sold only current article reprints. The impact of these restrictions must be borne in mind before any attempt is made to generalize from these responses any policy or willingness to honor single copy requests by libraries.

With these constraints, 56.8% of the journals in the survey indicated that they did sell reprints directly on request. The proportion of commercial journals willing to do this was somewhat higher (64.3%) than of non-profit journals (53.3%). The practice was most prevalent for applied science and pure science journals, and least common for humanities journals. Large circulation journals indicated a far greater willingness to engage in this practice than small circulation journals, with large for profit journals reporting 87.8%, and large circulation non-profit journals at 72.4%. The percentages drop fairly sharply for smaller circulation journals, but remain near 50% in all cases.

A considerably smaller percentage of journals reported a present practice of selling reprints or copies through an agent. This practice was affirmed by 32.8% of all journals, 38.3% of commercial, and 30.2% of non-profit journals. The number of non-respondents also rose sharply, indicating perhaps some uncertainty concerning what sale through an agent was or implied, and as to whether or not the journal was in fact engaging in the practice. Applied science journals, which indicated the heaviest probability of direct sale, fell to third place in sale through agents, with pure science journals the most likely to be available through this channel, and humanities journal articles or reprints the least likely to be available through agents, as through direct supply. The practice of selling through agents appears most attractive to small circulation journals, but even small non-profit journals saw some advantage to this approach, in 31.6% of the responses. Both large circulation commercial and non-profit journals reported the practice to the same extent, 30.6%.

Commercial journals show some concentration in their selection of agents, with Xerox University Microfilm and Information Unlimited, between them accounting for 85.7% of the responses. Non-profit journals listed 23 agents in their responses, but Xerox University Microfilms dominate the field, with a frequency of 67.2%.

It should be noted that the Institute for Scientific Information has standing arrangements with a large number of publishers, under which ISI pays royalties to these publishers for photocopies made and sold as part of its OATS service. The fact that relatively few respondents indicated ISI as an agent indicates that they think of this organization as a customer rather than as an agent. However, as has been pointed out by ISI, the present relationship is easily convertable into an agent status, if journals wished to refer requests for copies made to them to the Institute for Scientific Information.

Question 4. **Do you now sell directly or through an authorized agent reprints or authorized photocopies of articles from this journal? If you do not sell copies directly or through an agent skip to question 10 after answering this question.**

a. Directly Yes__________ No____________
b. Through an authorized agent Yes____________ No________
c. Name of authorized agent(s)__________________________

	Total Journal Response (N=974)	Type of Publisher: For Profit (N=308)	Non-profit (N=666)	Journals by Subject: Pure Science (N=216)	Applied Science (N=264)	Social Science (N=371)	Humanities (N=123)
a. Directly							
Yes	56.8%	64.3%	53.3%	63.0%	65.5%	50.7%	45.5%
No	40.0%	35.1%	42.3%	34.7%	31.8%	45.6%	50.4%
No answer	3.2%	.6%	4.4%	2.3%	2.7%	3.8%	4.1%
b. Through an authorized agent							
Yes	32.8%	38.3%	30.2%	39.4%	29.5%	32.6%	28.5%
No	43.5%	45.1%	42.8%	37.0%	46.2%	45.8%	42.3%
No answer	23.7%	16.6%	27.1%	23.6%	24.3%	21.6%	29.2%

Question 4:

	Journals by Size of Circulation					
	For Profit			Non-profit		
	0-2999 (N=177)	3000-9999 (N=47)	10000-max (N=49)	0-2999 (N=297)	3000-9999 (N=234)	10000-max (N=134)
a. Directly						
Yes	56.5%	57.4%	87.8%	47.5%	49.6%	72.4%
No	43.5%	40.4%	10.2%	47.1%	46.5%	24.6%
No answer	0	2.2%	2.0%	5.4%	3.9%	3.0%
b. Through an authorized agent						
Yes	50.8%	27.7%	30.6%	31.6%	27.8%	3 0.6%
No	36.2%	55.3%	42.9%	42.1%	44.4%	41.8%
No answer	13.0%	17.0%	26.5%	26.3%	27.8%	27.6%

Question 4c: Name of Authorized Agent

For Profit

Agent's Name:	
Diversified Services	2
Fred B. Rothman	1
Information Unlimited	22
Kraus Reprints	2
McGraw-Hill Circulation Market Division	1
Petersen Press, Inc.	3
Wm. S. Hein & Co., Inc. Micro-Film Division	1
Xerox University Microfilms	38

Non-profit

Agent's Name	
Allen Press	3
Bell& Howell Micro Photo Division	1
Bismarck S. Williams	1
Dennis & Co.	1
ERIC/RCS	3
E.O. Pointer	4
Engineering Societies Libraries	1
Inst. of Scientific Information	1
Interstate Printers	1
J.S. Canner	1
Kraus Reprints	11
Microfilming Corp. of America	1
NTIS	8
Rothman Reprints, Inc.	4
Swets & Zeitlinger	2
Sociological Abstracts	1
Thomson Ltd.	3
Walter J. Johnson, Inc.	4
Warner Modular Publications, Inc.	2
Waverly Press	1
William R. Brown Printing	1
Wm. S. Hein & Co., Inc., Micro-Film Division	1
Williams & Field	1
Xerox University Microfilms	117

Question 5. If so, for how many years back do you or your agent sell reprints authorized copies for this journal? Back to ______ year

Question 6. What was the starting date of publication of this journal? ______ year

Ability to Supply Back Issues, As Related to Age of the Journal

The expressed ability to supply back issues was plotted against the age of the journal, for the entire group of journals, for commercial and non-profit journals, and by subject discipline. In general, correlation between the two lines was fairly consistent, with reporting journals in all categories expressing an ability to supply copies for at least three or four years back. They can supply copies in 92% of all cases back two years, and this gradually drops to 85% for 10 year old issues. Thereafter it begins to improve again. The relatively few older journals report a greater ability to supply back copies, and only one fifth of the 20% of journals in existence more than 50 years ago indicate an inability to supply issues that far back.

The gap is somewhat more substantial for commercial journals, which are more likely to limit print quantities and therefore exhaust their stocks. Of the 58% of the commercial journals which were in existence 10 years ago, 31% indicate an inability to supply copies that far back, but better than half of the 10% still in existence after 50 years can make those copies available. In the non-profit sector both journal longevity and supply access are improved, with 77.7% of the journals in existence 10 years ago and 85% of these able to supply copies from 10 years ago. Of the 25.5% of non-profit journals in existence over 50 years ago, a remarkable 86.3% indicate an ability to furnish copies from 50 years back. Little in the way of deviation is indicated in an analysis by subject discipline. Humanities journals could be expected to have a greater longevity than, for example, applied science journals, but this appears, from these data, to be only fractionally the case. In fact, it is social science journals which have been in existence the shortest period of time, although not to a significant extent.

Since the question permitted positive response for availability of back issues through an agent, it may be that, in many cases, such availability is through reproduction from microfilm which may be difficult for individual articles. It should also be noted that publishers normally supply back issues from stock until these are exhausted, and that they don't run out at constant rates. It may be possible, therefore, for a journal to indicate availability of copies back to 1965, but mean by that only that some 1965 issues and not all 1965 issues are available.

Question 5. If so, for how many years back do you or your agent sell reprints or authorized copies for this journal? Back to ______________
year

Question 6. What was the starting date of publication of this journal?__________
year

COPYRIGHTED JOURNALS

	Total Journal Response (N=737)	Type of Publisher: For Profit (N=256)	Non-profit (N=481)	Journals by Subject Breakdown: Pure Sciences (N=184)	Applied Sciences (N=198)	Social Sciences (N=272)	Humanities (N=83)
mean	1954	1962	1950	1953	1956	1954	1951
median	1966	1969	1959	1967	1966	1965	1961

	Total Journal Response (N=823)	Type of Publisher: For Profit (N=289)	Non-profit (N=534)	Journals by Subject Breakdown: Pure Sciences (N=197)	Applied Sciences (N=229)	Social Sciences (N=296)	Humanities (N=101)
mean	1949	1957	1945	1950	1947	1951	1947
median	1958	1966	1951	1961	1956	1959	1956

Questions 5 and 6 Total Journal Response

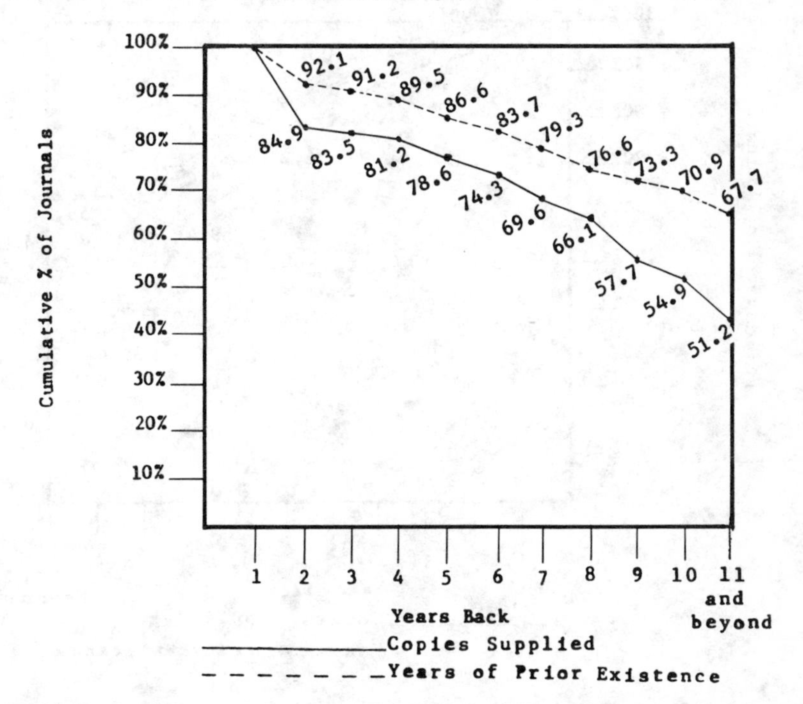

Questions 5 and 6 Total Journal Response

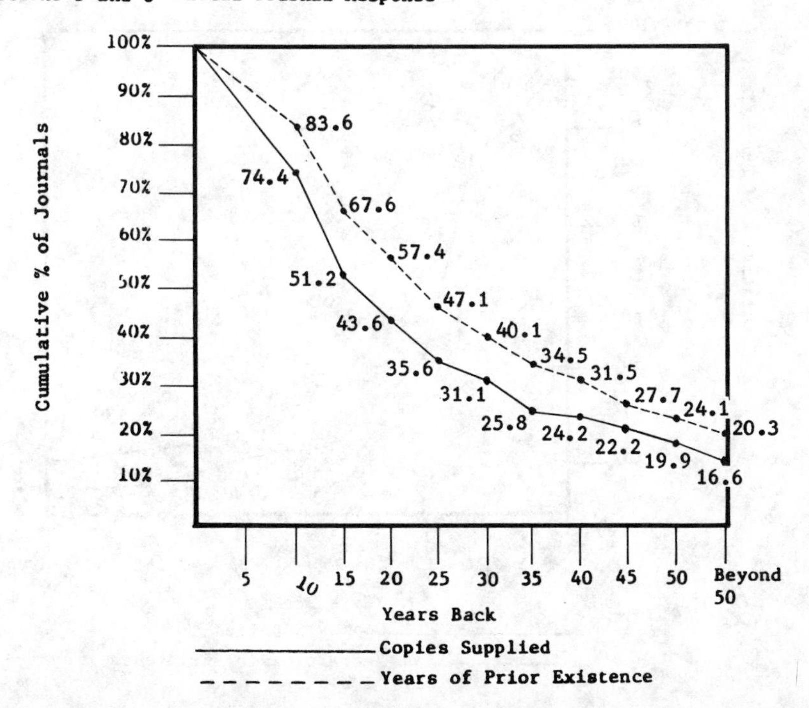

Questions 5 and 6 Journals by Type of Publisher For Profit

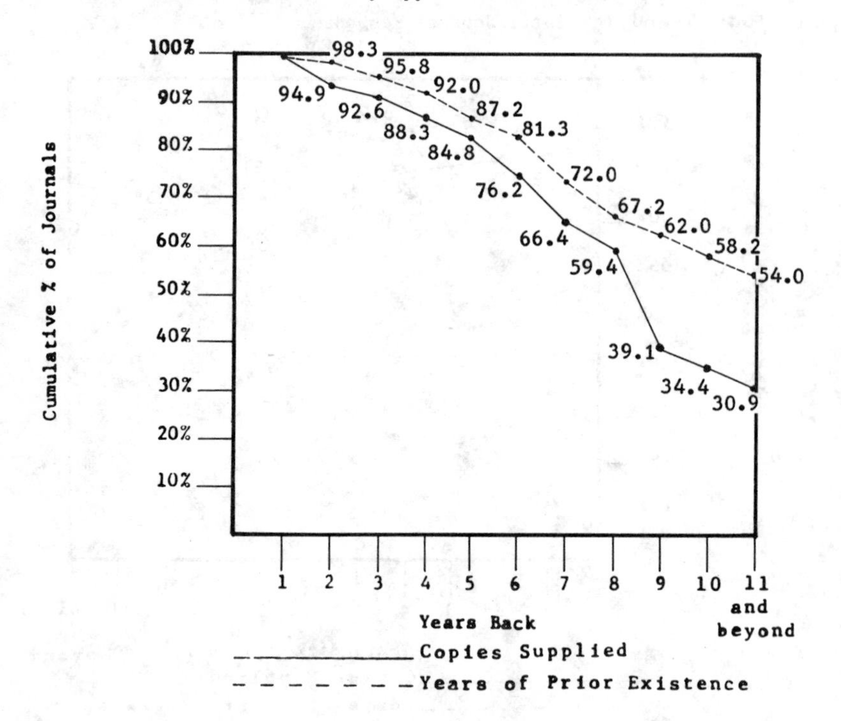

Questions 5 and 6 Journals by Type of Publisher For Profit

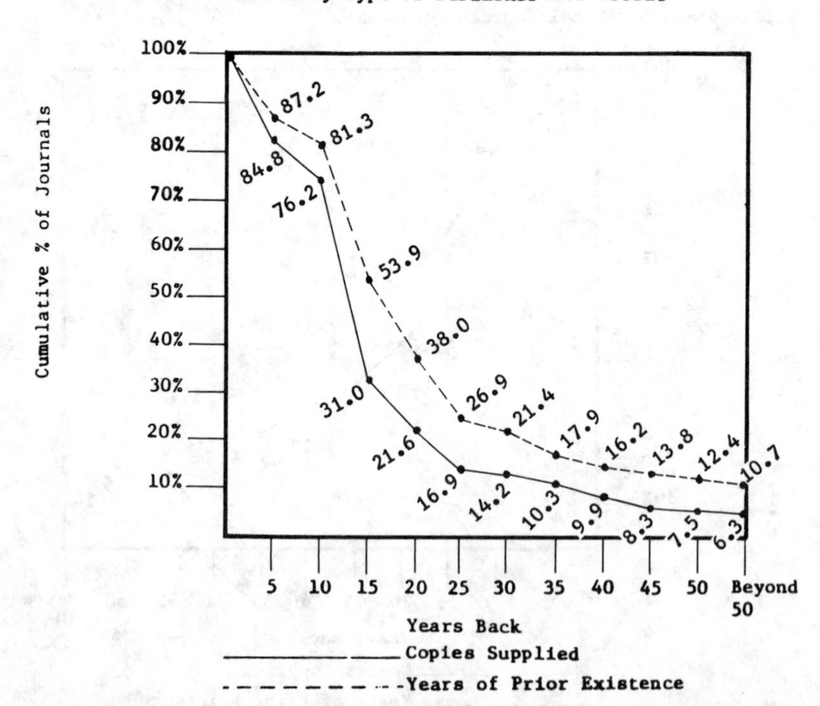

Questions 5 and 6 Journals by Type of Publisher Non-Profit

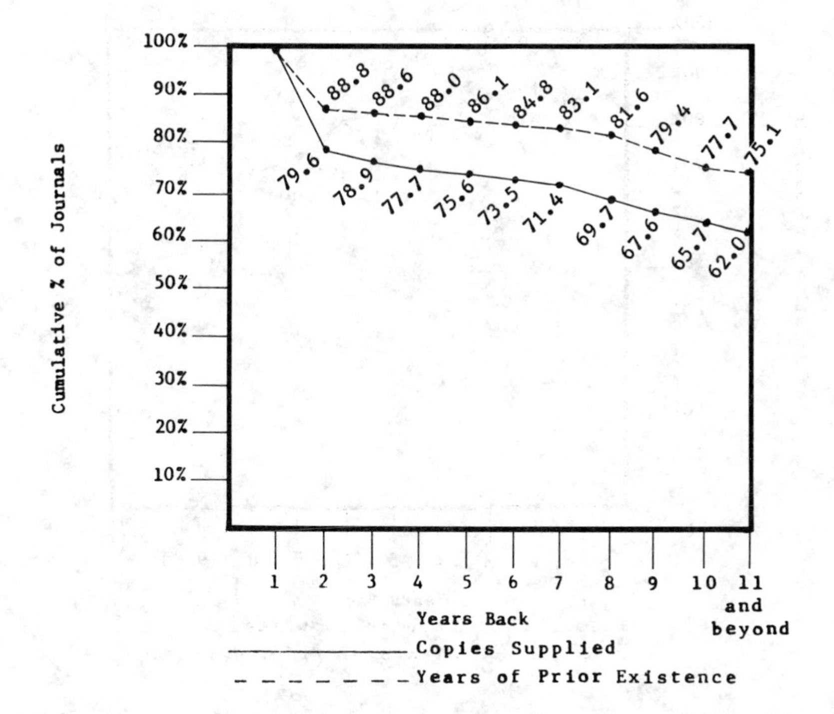

Questions 5 and 6 Journals by Type of Publisher Non-Profit

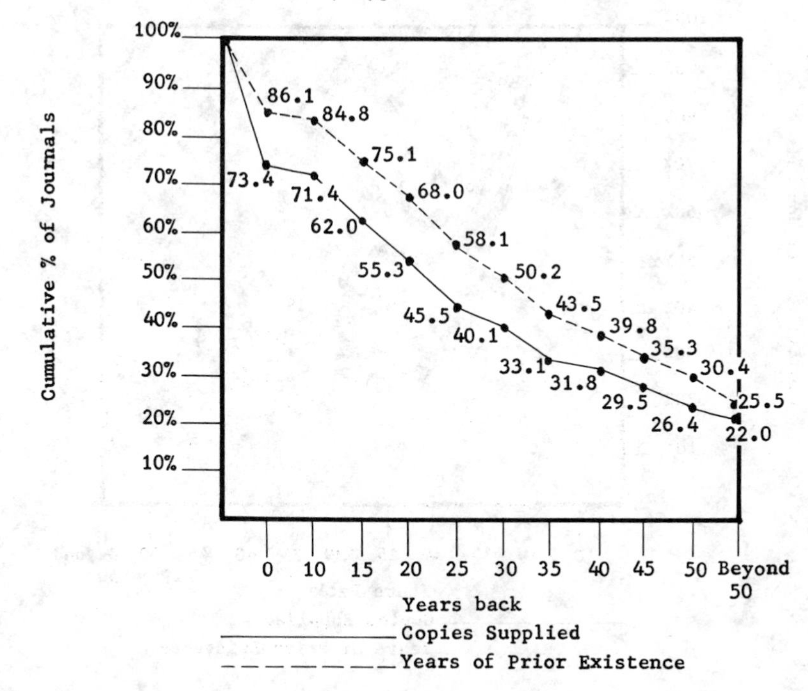

Questions 5 and 6 Journals by Subject Pure Science

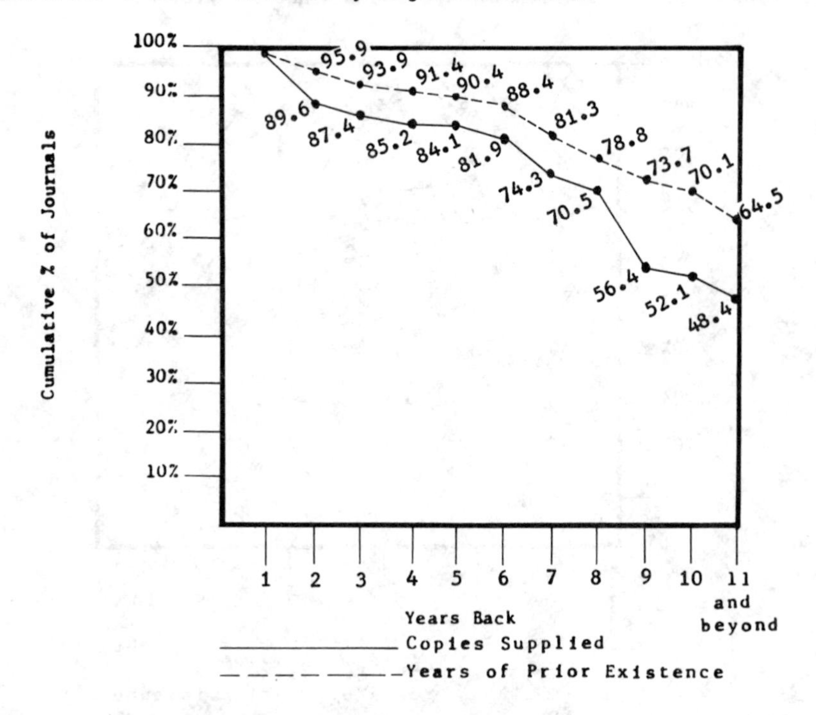

Questions 5 and 6 Journals by Subject Pure Science

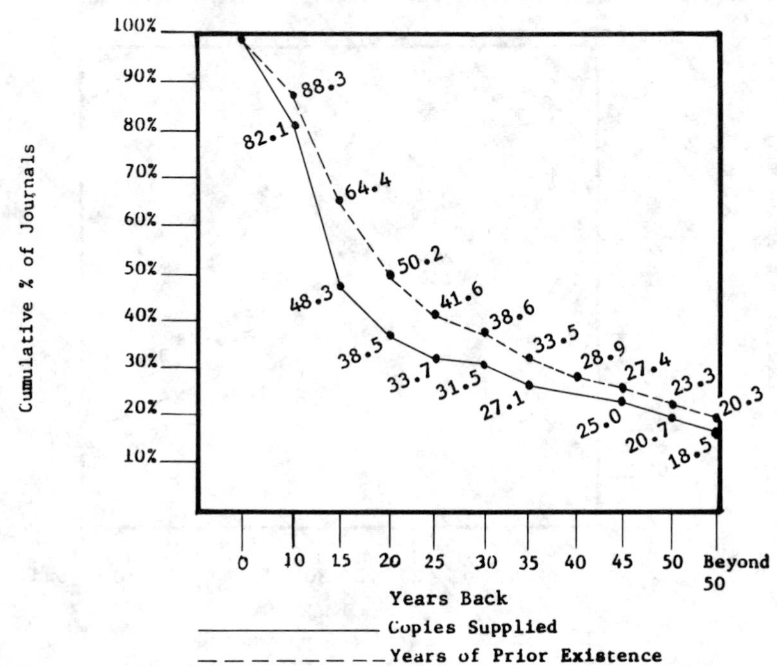

Questions 5 and 6 Journals by Subject Applied Science

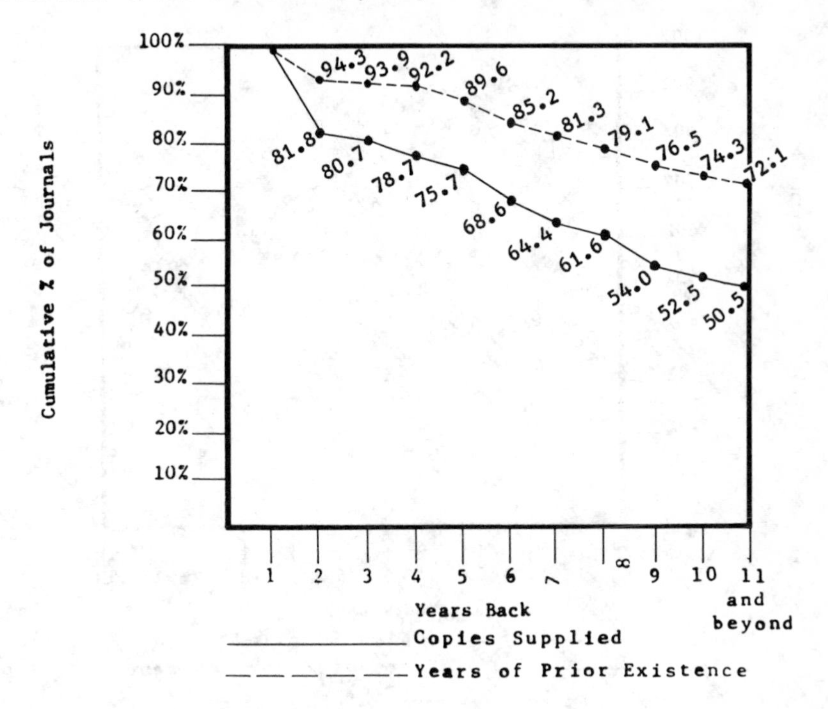

Questions 5 and 6 Journals by Subject Applied Science

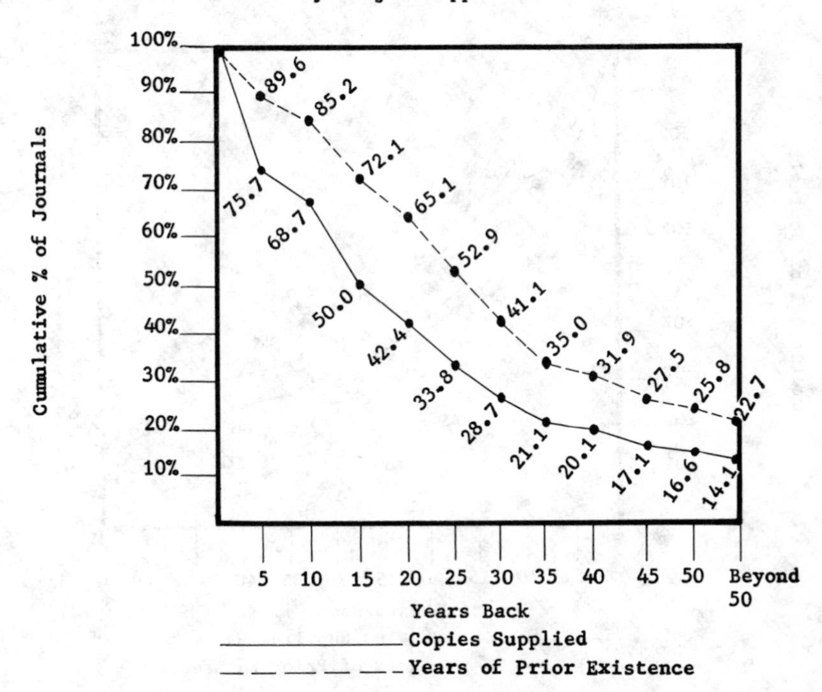

Questions 5 and 6 Journals by Subject Social Science

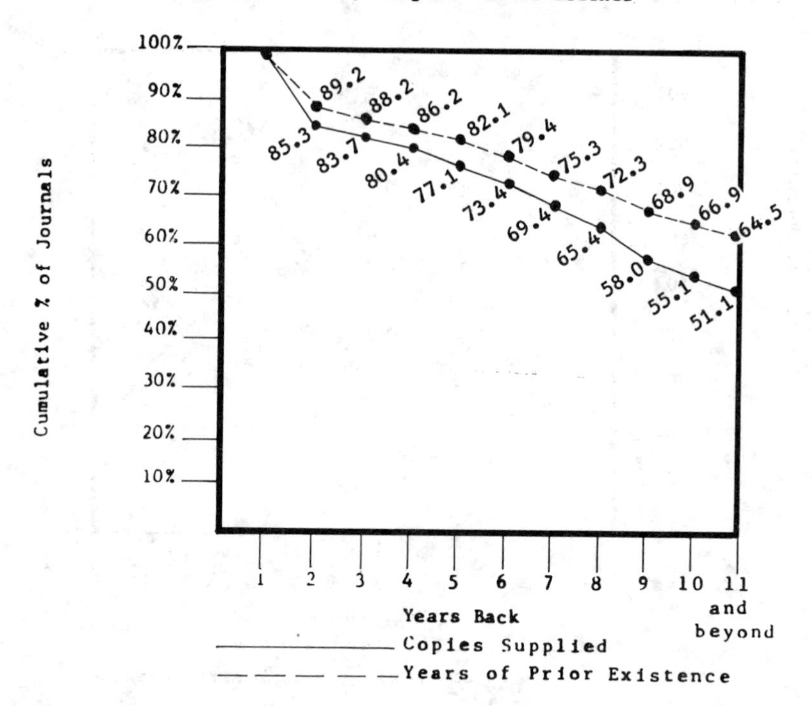

Questions 5 and 6 Journals by Subject Social Science

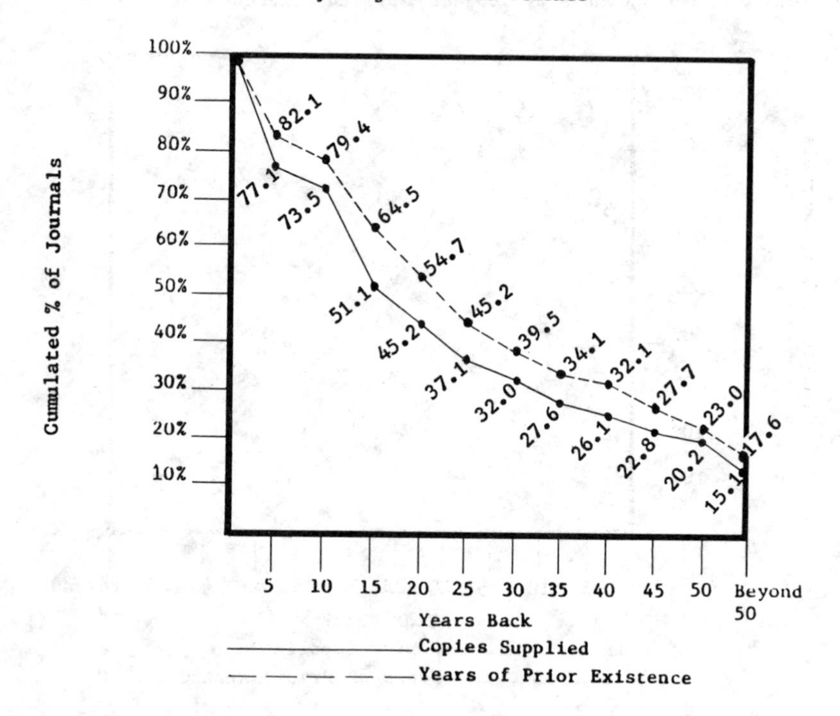

Questions 5 and 6 Journals by Subject Humanities

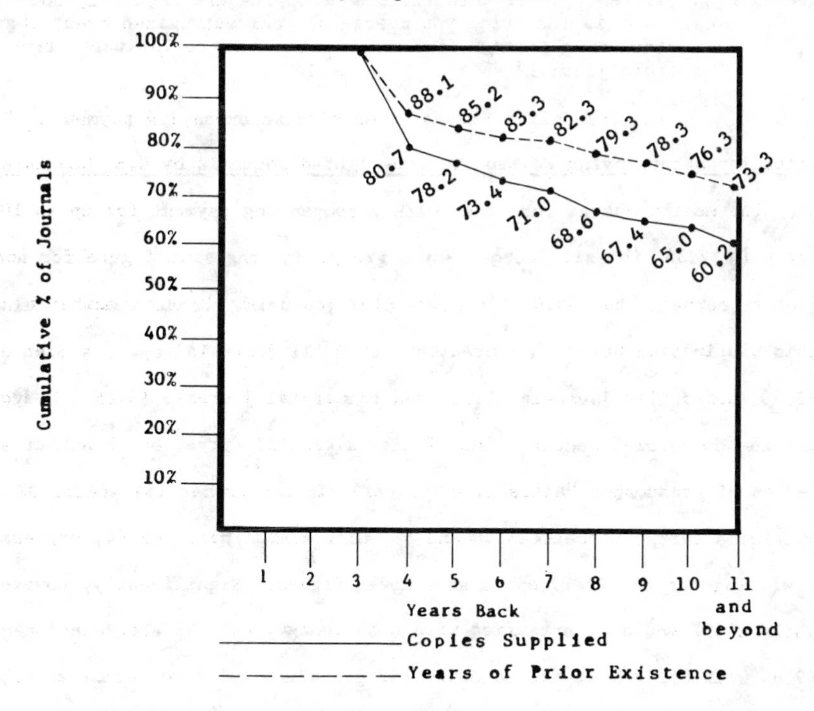

Questions 5 and 6 Journals by Subject Humanities

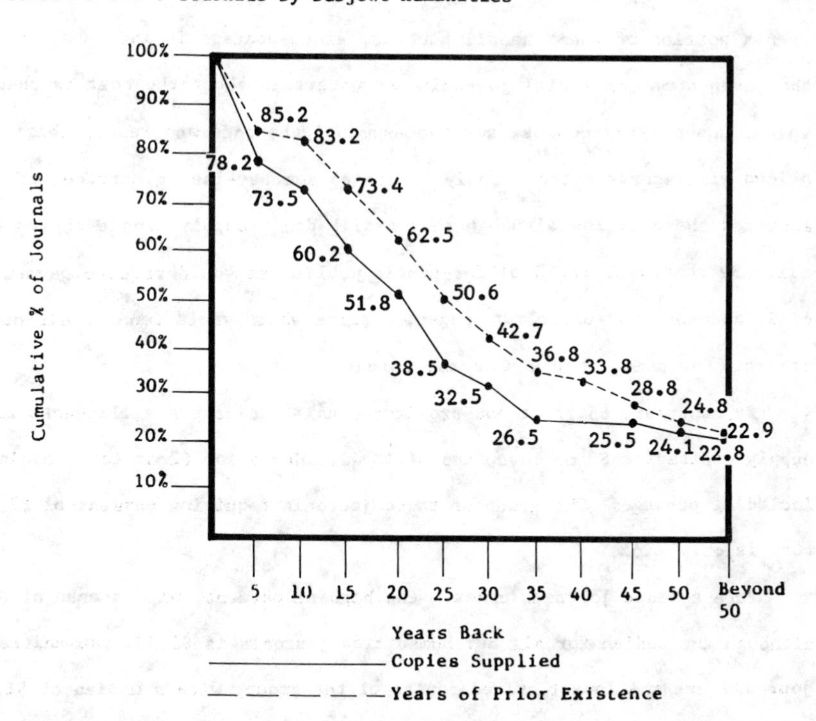

Question 7. If reprints or authorized photocopies are regularly sold, what is the price you charge or your authorized agent charges, including postage, for an article of up to ten pages from this journal?

a. For United States order with accompanying payment $________

Rates for Accompanying Payment to Copyrighted Journals by U.S. Requestors

The median charge for order with accompanying payment for up to 10 pages is $2.50 for all journals as a group, and the same figure for non-profit journals, but $5.00 for commercial journals. Means somewhat blur this distinction but do not eradicate it. All journals report a mean of $3.38, non-profit journals $2.98, and commercial journals $3.85. Responses for the commercial sector do not follow a general curve, but bunch at a series of presumably "attractive" prices. In the commercial sector 32.3% opt for a charge of between $5 and $6, with almost half, 49.6%, expressing a willingness to offer copies at a lower figure. Significantly, however, while 81.9% would be satisfied with a $6 charge, and the aforementioned 49.6% with $5, almost the same percentage, 47.1% would be satisfied with $3, and 26.6% with payments of less than $1, an amount not likely to recover even a portion of their handling costs, since postage is included. It appears that even some commercial journals are uncertain about the cost to them involved in supplying copies, and that some of the ones who report this low-priced willingness either supply copies as a money-losing service, or answered the question although they really don't supply single copies at all. By contrast, 17.4% of for-profit publishers would require payment of $7 and more for up to ten pages, a price which would tend to discourage orders. For some, that may be the intent.

By contrast, 65.1% of non-profit journals indicate a willingness to supply copies for $3 or less, and 41.1% will do so for $2 or less, again including postage. The group of these journals requiring payment of $7 and more is only 6.5%.

Pure science journals exact the highest payment, with a mean of $3.66, although the median for all but humanities journals is $2.50. Humanities journals are the lowest priced copies of the group, with a median of $1.78, and a mean of $2.56. A total of 68.4% of humanities journals indicate a willingness to supply copies at $3 or less, while the similar figure for pure science journals is only about half, and for both applied and social science journals less than half. No humanities journals report an insistence on payment of $7 or more, while for the pure sciences this group of journals totaled 16.2%.

Size of circulation had a sharp impact in the for-profit sector, with large (10,000 or more circulation) journals willing to distribute copies at a mean of $2.63 and a median of $2.48, while the smallest (under 3000) journals reported means of $4.19 and medians of $5.00. Almost 70% of these small journals would charge $5 or more, and 19.9% would charge $7 or more. By sharp contrast, 83.3% of the large commercial journals charge under $3. The pattern is not as clear in the non-profit sector, with both large and small journals tending to charge less than medium circulation ones.

It should be noted that responses to this question introduce the possibility for at least some potential error through the fact that no opportunity was provided in the questionnaire to indicate whether or not reprints or authorized photocopies were sold. It was apparent from appended comments that at least some of the journals which did not engage in the practice (even if the journals were copyrighted) did not know how to answer the question. It would appear that some did ignore the question as intended, while others may have responded as to a hypothetical question. It cannot be determined from non-responses that such journals do not in fact offer reprints or photocopies for sale, because some journals which do may not have answered the question. It might be assumed that responding journals are in fact willing to accept and fill requests for single copies, but some journals which responded made it clear in their comments that they would not.

Responses which reported a zero charge were eliminated from calculations, since such journals obviously do not sell. In addition, some responses had to be eliminated because they would not or could not provide dollar figures. These answers included replies of "at actual cost" or "at actual cost plus 15%", and could not therefore be tabulated.

Question 7a: For United States Order with Accompanying Payment

If reprints or authorized photocopies are regularly sold, what is the price you charge or your authorized agent charges, including postage, for an article of up to ten pages from this journal?

a. For United States order with accompanying payment

Copyrighted Journals

	Total Journal Response (N=424)			For Profit Publishers (N=195)			Non-profit Publishers (N=229)		
	Absolute Frequency	Adjusted Frequency	Cumulative Frequency	Abs. Fr.	Adj. Fr.	Cum. Fr.	Abs. Fr.	Adj. Fr.	Cum. Fr.
0.01-0.25	15	3.5%	3.5%	7	3.6%	3.6%	8	3.5%	3.5%
0.26-0.50	10	2.4%	5.9%	3	1.5%	5.1%	7	3.1%	6.6%
0.51-0.99	58	13.7%	19.6%	42	21.5%	26.7%	16	7.0%	13.5%
1.00-1.99	71	16.7%	36.3%	8	4.1%	30.8%	63	27.5%	41.0%
2.00-2.99	87	20.5%	56.8%	32	16.4%	47.2%	55	24.0%	65.1%
3.00-3.99	17	4.0%	60.8%	3	1.5%	48.7%	14	6.1%	71.2%
4.00-4.99	12	2.8%	63.7%	2	1.0%	49.7%	10	4.4%	75.5%
5.00-5.99	72	17.0%	80.7%	63	32.3%	82.1%	9	3.9%	79.5%
6.00-6.99	33	7.8%	88.4%	1	0.5%	82.6%	32	14.0%	93.4%
7.00-7.99	29	6.8%	95.3%	23	11.8%	94.4%	6	2.6%	96.1%
8.00-8.99	0	0	95.3%	0	0	94.4%	0	0	96.1%
9.00-9.99	20	4.7%	00.0%	11	5.6%	100.0%	9	3.9%	100.0%
mean		$3.38			$3.85			$2.98	
median		$2.50			$5.00			$2.50	
mode		$5.00			$5.00			$2.50	
min/max		$0.15/$9.99			$0.15/$9.99			$0.15/$9.99	

Question 7a. For United States or with Accompanying Payment.

Copyrighted Journals

Journals by Subject

	Pure Sciences (N=128)		Applied Sciences (N=134)		Social Sciences (N=124)		Humanities (N=38)	
	Absolute Frequency	Adjusted Frequency	Abs. Fr.	Adj. Fr.	Abs. Fr.	Adj. Fr.	Abs Fr	Adj Fr
0.01-0.25	5	3.9%	4	3.0%	5	4.0%	1	2.6%
0.26-0.50	1	.8%	2	1.5%	4	3.2%	3	7.9%
0.51-0.99	26	20.3%	21	15.7%	8	6.5%	3	7.9%
1.00-1.99	7	5.5%	22	16.4%	30	24.2%	12	31.6%
2.00-2.99	28	21.9%	35	26.1%	17	13.7%	7	18.4%
3.00-3.99	2	1.6%	5	3.7%	9	7.3%	1	2.6%
4.00-4.99	1	.8%	3	2.2%	7	5.6%	1	2.6%
5.00-5.99	30	23.4%	23	17.2%	17	13.7%	2	5.3%
6.00-6.99	8	6.3%	3	2.2%	14	11.3%	8	21.1%
7.00-7.99	17	13.3%	8	6.0%	4	3.2%	0	0
8.00-8.99	0	0	0	0	0	0	0	0
9.00-9.99	3	2.3%	8	6.0%	9	7.3%	0	0
mean		$3.66		$3.26		$3.50		$2.56
median		$2.50		$2.50		$2.50		$1.78
mode		$5.00		$2.50		$5.00		$1.00
min/max		$0.15/$9.99		$0.15/$9.99		$0.15/$9.99		$0.20/ $6.00

Question 7a: For United States order with accompanying payment

Copyrighted Journals by Size of Circulation

	For Profit			Non-profit		
	(N=141) 0-2999	(N=24) 3000-9999	(N=30) 10000-max	(N=90) 0-2999	(N=87) 3000-9999	(N=51) 10000-max
0.01-0.25	2.1%	0	13.3%	5.6%	2.3%	2.0%
0.26-0.50	.7%	0	6.7%	2.2%	3.5%	3.9%
0.51-0.99	24.1%	29.2%	3.3%	11.1%	3.5%	5.9%
1.00-1.99	2.1%	8.3%	10.0%	27.8%	24.1%	33.3%
2.00-2.99	7.8%	25.0%	50.0%	18.9%	27.6%	27.5%
3.00-3.99	.7%	8.3%	0	6.7%	8.0%	2.0%
4.00-4.99	.7%	4.2%	0	3.3%	3.4%	7.8%
5.00-5.99	41.1%	8.3%	10.0%	4.4%	2.3%	3.9%
6.00-6.99	.7%	0	0	14.4%	18.4%	5.9%
7.00-7.99	15.6%	4.2%	0	2.2%	3.5%	2.0%
8.00-8.99	0	0	0	0	0	0
9.00-9.99	4.3%	12.5%	6.7%	3.3%	3.4%	5.9%
mean	$4.19	$3.39	$2.63	$2.78	$3.24	$2.85
median	$5.00	$2.50	$2.48	$2.00	$2.50	$2.00
mode	$5.00	$2.50	$2.50	$1.00	$2.50	$1.50
min/max	$0.15/ $9.99	$0.70/ $9.99	$0.15/ $9.99	$0.15/ $9.99	$0.20/ $9.99	$0.15/ $9.99

Question 7b. For foreign order with accompanying payment

Rates for Accompanying Payment for Copyrighted Journals for Foreign Requestors

There is slight increase in the mean, and in general the same median, as reported for domestic customers. Since the question postulates that the journal will include postage costs in the payment fee, answers to this question are very much predicated on assumed method of mailing. There is suspicion, based on comments, that some responding journals ignored the impact of postage variances, although of course they were asked to include these in their calculations. This would explain why so many journals used the same rates for domestic and foreign customers. Similar patterns also emerge by circulation of journals.

Question 7b. For foreign order with accompanying payment.

COPYRIGHTED JOURNALS

Journals by Subject

	Pure Sciences (N=123)		Applied Sciences (N=121)		Social Sciences (N=105)		Humanities (N=35)	
	Absolute Frequency	Adjusted Frequency	Abs. Freq.	Adj. Freq.	Abs. Freq.	Adj. Freq.	Abs. Freq.	Adj. Freq.
0.01-0.25	5	4.1%	4	3.3%	4	3.8%	1	2.9%
0.26-0.50	2	1.6%	2	1.7%	4	3.8%	3	8.6%
0.51-0.99	25	20.3%	11	9.1%	6	5.7%	2	5.7%
1.00-1.99	5	4.1%	21	17.4%	25	23.8%	10	28.6%
2.00-2.99	25	20.3%	15	12.4%	11	10.5%	6	17.1%
3.00-3.99	4	3.3%	22	18.2%	10	9.5%	2	5.7%
4.00-4.99	0	0	3	2.5%	6	5.7%	1	2.9%
5.00-5.99	29	23.6%	24	19.8%	14	13.3%	2	5.7%
6.00-6.99	8	6.5%	3	2.5%	13	12.4%	8	22.9%
7.00-7.99	17	13.8%	7	5.8%	4	3.8%	0	0
8.00-8.99	0	0	1	.8%	0	0	0	0
9.00-9.99	3	2.4%	8	6.6%	8	7.6%	0	0
mean		$3.70		$3.60		$3.61		$2.75
median		$2.51		$3.00		$3.00		$1.98
mode		$5.00		$3.00		$5.00		$6.00
min/max		$0.15/ $9.99		$0.15/ $9.99		$0.15/ $9.99		$0.20/ $6.00

Question 7b. For foreign order with accompanying payment

Copyrighted Journals

	Total Journal Response (N=384)			For Profit Publishers (N=183)			Non-profit Publishers (N=201)		
	Abs. Freq.	Adj. Freq.	Cum. Freq.	Abs. Freq.	Adj. Freq.	Cum. Freq.	Abs. Freq.	Adj. Freq.	Cum. Freq.
0.01-0.25	14	3.6%	3.6%	7	3.8%	3.8%	7	3.5%	3.5%
0.26-0.50	11	2.9%	6.5%	3	1.6%	5.5%	8	4.0%	7.5%
0.51-0.99	44	11.5%	18.0%	31	16.9%	22.4%	13	6.5%	13.9%
1.00-1.99	61	15.9%	33.9%	7	3.8%	26.2%	54	26.9%	40.8%
2.00-2.99	57	14.8%	48.7%	11	6.0%	32.2%	46	22.9%	63.7%
3.00-3.99	38	9.9%	58.6%	24	13.1%	45.4%	14	7.0%	70.6%
4.00-4.99	10	2.6%	61.2%	1	.5%	45.9%	9	4.5%	75.1%
5.00-5.99	69	18.0%	79.2%	62	33.9%	79.8%	7	3.5%	78.6%
6.00-6.99	32	8.3%	87.5%	3	1.6%	81.4%	29	14.4%	93.0%
7.00-7.99	28	7.3%	94.8%	23	12.6%	94.0%	5	2.5%	95.5%
8.00-8.99	1	.3%	95.1%	0	0	94.0%	1	.5%	96.0%
9.00-9.99	19	4.9%	100%	11	6.0%	100%	8	4.0%	100.0%
mean		$3.56			$4.13			$3.04	
median		$3.00			$4.99			$2.50	
mode		$5.00			$5.00			$2.50	
min/max		$0.15/$9.99			$0.15/$9.99			$0.15/$9.99	

Question 7b: For foreign order with accompanying payment

Copyrighted Journals by Size of Circulation

	For Profit (N=137) 0-2999	(N=18) 3000-9999	(N=28) 10000-max	Non-profit (N=76) 0-2999	(N=81) 3000-9999	(N=43) 10000-max
0.01-0.25	2.2%	0	14.3%	6.6%	1.2%	2.3%
0.26-0.50	.7%	5.6%	3.6%	2.6%	4.9%	4.7%
0.51-0.99	21.9%	5.6%	0	9.2%	3.7%	7.0%
1.00-1.99	2.2%	11.0%	7.1%	30.3%	18.5%	37.2%
2.00-2.99	4.4%	5.6%	14.3%	17.1%	30.9%	18.6%
3.00-3.99	4.4%	38.9%	39.3%	6.6%	8.6%	4.7%
4.00-4.99	.7%	0	0	2.6%	3.7%	9.3%
5.00-5.99	42.3%	11.0%	7.1%	3.9%	2.5%	2.3%
6.00-6.99	.7%	0	7.1%	15.8%	18.5%	4.7%
7.00-7.99	16.1%	5.6%	0	1.3%	3.7%	2.3%
8.00-8.99	0	0	0	1.3%	0	0
9.00-9.99	4.4%	16.7%	7.1%	2.6%	3.7%	7.0%
mean	$4.32	$4.15	$3.19	$2.79	$3.35	$2.85
median	$5.00	$3.02	$2.92	$1.99	$2.50	$1.84
mode	$5.00	$3.00	$3.00	$6.00	$2.50	$1.50
min/max	$0.17/ $9.99	$0.40/ $9.99	$0.15/ $9.99	$0.15/ $9.99	$0.20/ $9.99	$0.15/ $9.99

Question 7c. For United States order with bill required

Bill Required, for Copyrighted Journals, United States Customers

While commercial publishers charged slightly more when a bill had to be rendered than when payment accompanied order (a mean of $3.94 versus a mean of $3.85, with the same $5.00 median in both cases), non-profit publishers reported a lower mean ($2.62 versus $2.98) and a lower median ($2.00 versus $2.50) where billing is required. The number of responders to the accompanying payment alternative was 424, for this question only 339. It is only conjectured, but perhaps reasonable to assume, that many of those who would fill pre-paid orders but not bill with order feel that they would have to charge so much as to make the whole process untenable. This would help to explain why the statistics could report a lower non-profit charge for bill-with-shipment orders than prepaid orders. The potential impact of those would not sell at all under such conditions, or who would not sell single copies under such conditions, becomes particularly speculative.

Question 7c. For United States order with bill required

Copyrighted Journals

	Total Journal Response (N=339)			For Profit Publishers (N=168)			Non-profit Publishers (N=171)		
	Absolute Frequency	Adjusted Frequency	Cumulative Frequency	Abs. Freq.	Adj. Freq.	Cum. Freq.	Abs. Fr.	Adj. Fr.	Cum. Fr.
0.01-0.25	11	3.2%	3.2%	3	1.8%	1.8%	8	4.7%	4.7%
0.26-0.50	9	2.7%	5.9%	3	1.8%	3.6%	6	3.5%	8.2%
0.51-0.99	48	14.2%	20.1%	32	19.0%	22.6%	16	9.4%	17.5%
1.00-1.99	61	18.0%	38.1%	6	3.6%	26.2%	55	32.2%	49.7%
2.00-2.99	69	20.4%	58.4%	29	17.3%	43.5%	40	23.4%	73.1%
3.00-3.99	16	4.7%	63.1%	3	1.8%	45.2%	13	7.6%	80.7%
4.00-4.99	9	2.7%	65.8%	2	1.2%	46.4%	7	4.1%	84.8%
5.00 5.99	68	20.1%	85.8%	61	36.3%	82.7%	7	4.1%	88.9%
6.00-6.99	8	2.4%	88.2%	1	0.6%	83.3%	7	4.1%	93.0%
7.00-7.99	24	7.1%	95.3%	23	13.7%	97.0%	1	0.6%	93.6%
8.00-8 99	0	0.0%	95.3%	0	0.0%	97.0%	0	0.0%	93.6%
9.00-9.99	16	4.7%	100.0%	5	3.0%	100.0%	11	6.4%	100.0%
Mean		$3.27			$3.94			$2.62	
Median		$2.50			$5.00			$2.00	
Mode		$5.00			$5.00			$2.50	
min/max		$0.15/ $9.99			$0.15/ $9.99			$0.15/ $9.99	

Question 7c. For United States order with bill required

COPYRIGHTED JOURNALS

Journals by Subject

	Pure Sciences (N=111)		Applied Sciences (N=111)		Social Sciences (N=88)		Humanities (N=29)	
	Absolute Frequency	Adjusted Frequency	Abs Freq	Adj Freq	Abs Freq	Adj Freq	Abs Freq	Adj Freq
0.01-0.25	5	4.5%	0	0	5	5.7%	1	3.4%
0.26-0.50	1	.9%	2	1.8%	4	4.5%	2	6.9%
0.51-0.99	25	22.5%	14	12.6%	5	5.7%	4	13.8%
1.00-1.99	6	5.4%	21	18.9%	23	26.1%	11	37.9%
2.00-2.99	24	21.6%	29	26.1%	12	13.6%	4	13.8%
3.00-3.99	3	2.7%	5	4.5%	6	6.8%	2	6.9%
4.00-4.99	0	0	3	2.7%	6	6.8%	0	0
5.00-5.99	29	26.1%	21	18.9%	16	18.2%	2	6.9%
6.00-6.99	2	1.8%	1	.9%	2	2.3%	3	10.3%
7.00-7.99	13	11.7%	7	6.3%	4	4.5%	0	0
8.00-8.99	0	0	0	0	0	0	0	0
9.00-9.99	3	2.7%	8	7.2%	5	5.7%	0	0
mean		$3.47		$3.45		$3.20		$2.06
median		$2.50		$2.50		$2.50		$1.10
mode		$5.00		$2.50		$5.00		$1.00
min/max		$0.15/$9.99		$0.32/$9.99		$0.15/$9.99		$0.20/$6.00

Question 7c: For United States order with bill required

Copyrighted Journal by Size of Circulation

	For Profit (N=132) 0-2999	(N=17) 3000-9999	(N=19) 10000-max	Non-profit (N=68) 0-2999	(N=62) 3000-9999	(N=40) 10000-max
0.01-0.25	2.3%	0	0	7.4%	3.2%	2.5%
0.26-0.50	.8%	5.9%	5.3%	2.9%	3.2%	5.0%
0.51-0.99	22.7%	5.9%	5.2%	13.2%	6.5%	7.5%
1.00-1.99	2.3%	5.9%	10.5%	35.3%	27.4%	35.0%
2.00-2.99	8.3%	35.3%	63.2%	17.6%	33.9%	17.5%
3.00-3.99	0	11.8%	5.3%	8.8%	8.1%	5.0%
4.00-4.99	1.5%	0	0	2.9%	3.2%	7.5%
5.00-5.99	43.9%	11.8%	5.2%	1.5%	3.2%	7.5%
6.00-6.99	.8%	0	0	7.4%	3.2%	0
7.00-7.99	16.7%	5.9%	0	0	1.6%	0
8.00-8.99	0	0	0	0	0	0
9.00-9.99	.8%	17.6%	5.3%	2.9%	6.5%	12.5%
mean	$4.08	$4.22	$2.71	$2.15	$2.79	$3.10
median	$5.00	$2.63	$2.50	$1.22	$2.50	$1.85
mode	$5.00	$2.50	$2.50	$1.00	$2.50	$1.50
min/max	$0.15/ $9.99	$0.40/ $9.99	$0.50/ $9.99	$0.15/ $9.99	$0.20/ $9.99	$0.15/ $9.99

Question 7d. For foreign order with bill required

Bill Required, for Copyrighted Journals, Foreign Customers

The same phenomenon reported earlier occurs here as well. In this case, even commercial, in addition to non-profit journals, purport to charge less for bill with orders than for pre-payments. As previously, it is assumed that the explanation comes from the sharp drop-off in journals answering the question, from 384 to 324, and it is postulated that, to a large extent, the 60 journals involved would consider a foreign bill-with-order account so speculative and problem-filled that realistic costing becomes impossible, or that they would refuse such an order under any circumstances.

Question 7d. For foreign order with bill required

Copyrighted Journals

	Total Journal Response (N=324)			For Profit Publishers (N=164)			Non-profit Publishers (N=160)		
	Absolute Frequency	Adjusted Frequency	Cumulative Frequency	Abs. Fr.	Adj. Fr.	Cum. Fr.	Abs. Fr.	Adj. Fr.	Cum. Fr.
0.01-0.25	7	2.2%	2.2%	0	0.0%	0.0%	7	4.4%	4.4%
0.26-0.50	8	2.5%	4.6%	2	1.2%	1.2%	6	3.7%	8.1%
0.51-0.99	46	14.2%	18.8%	32	19.5%	20.7%	14	8.8%	16.9%
1.00-1.99	57	17.6%	36.4%	6	3.7%	24.4%	51	31.9%	48.7%
2.00-2.99	45	13.9%	50.3%	9	5.5%	29.9%	36	22.5%	71.2%
3.00-3.99	36	11.1%	61.4%	23	14.0%	43.9%	13	8.1%	79.4%
4.00-4.99	9	2.8%	64.2%	2	1.2%	45.1%	7	4.4%	83.7%
5.00-5.99	70	21.6%	85.8%	61	37.2%	82.3%	9	5.6%	89.4%
6.00-6.99	4	1.2%	87.0%	1	0.6%	82.9%	3	1.9%	91.2%
7.00-7.99	25	7.7%	94.8%	23	14.0%	97.0%	2	1.2%	92.5%
8.00-8.99	0	0.0%	94.8%	0	0.0%	97.0%	0	0.0%	92.5%
9.00-9.99	17	5.2%	100.0%	5	3.0%	100.0%	12	7.5%	100.0%
Mean		$3.42			$4.09			$2.73	
Median		$2.51			$5.00			$2.00	
Mode		$5.00			$5.00			$2.50	
min/max		$0.15/$9.99			$ .40/$9.99			$0.15/$9.99	

Question 7d. For foreign order with bill required

COPYRIGHTED JOURNALS

Journals by Subject

	Pure Sciences (N=109)		Applied Sciences (N=109)		Social Sciences (N=80)		Humanities (N=26)	
	Absolute Frequency	Adjusted Frequency	Abs. Fr.	Adj. Fr.	Abs. Fr.	Adj. Fr.	Abs. Fr.	Adj. Fr.
0.01-0.25	5	4.6%	0	0	1	1.2%	1	3.8%
0.26-0.50	0	0	2	1.8%	4	5.0%	2	7.7%
0.51-0.99	26	23.9%	12	11.0%	5	6.3%	3	11.5%
1.00-1.99	6	5.5%	20	18.3%	22	27.5%	9	34.6%
2.00-2.99	22	20.2%	10	9.2%	9	11.2%	4	15.4%
3.00-3.99	2	1.8%	23	21.1%	9	11.2%	2	7.7%
4.00-4.99	0	0	3	2.8%	6	7.5%	0	0
5.00-5.99	31	28.4%	23	21.1%	14	17.5%	2	7.7%
6.00-6.99	1	.9%	0	0	0	0	3	11.5%
7.00-7.99	13	11.9%	7	6.4%	5	6.3%	0	0
8.00-8.99	0	0	0	0	0	0	0	0
9.00-9.99	3	2.8%	9	8.3%	5	6.3%	0	0
mean		$3.50		$3.70		$3.33		$2.20
median		$2.50		$3.00		$2.50		$1.50
mode		$5.00		$3.00		$5.00		$1.00
min/max		$0.15/ $9.99		$0.32/ $9.99		$0.15/ $9.99		$0.20/ $6.00

Question 7d: For foreign order with bill required

Copyrighted Journals by Size of Circulation

	For Profit			Non-profit		
	(N=129) 0-2999	(N=17) 3000-9999	(N=18) 10000-max	(N=61) 0-2999	(N=59) 3000-9999	(N=39) 10000-max
0.01-0.25	0	0	0	8.2%	1.7%	2.6%
0.26-0.50	0	5.9%	5.6%	3.3%	3.4%	5.1%
0.51-0.99	24.0%	5.9%	0	13.1%	6.8%	5.1%
1.00-1.99	2.3%	5.9%	11.1%	36.1%	27.1%	33.3%
2.00-2.99	4.7%	5.9%	11.1%	14.8%	35.6%	15.4%
3.00-3.99	3.9%	41.2%	61.1%	8.2%	10.2%	5.1%
4.00-4.99	1.6%	0	0	3.3%	3.4%	7.7%
5.00-5.99	45.0%	11.8%	5.6%	4.9%	1.7%	10.3%
6.00-6.99	.2%	0	0	3.3%	1.7%	0
7.00-7.99	17.1%	5.9%	0	1.6%	1.7%	0
8.00-8.99	0	0	0	0	0	0
9.00-9.99	.7%	17.6%	5.6%	3.3%	6.8%	15.4%
mean	$4.20	$4.36	$3.12	$2.19	$2.75	$3.48
median	$5.00	$3.08	$2.99	$1.26	$2.49	$2.50
mode	$5.00	$3.00	$3.00	$1.00	$2.50	$9.99
min/max	$0.52/ $9.99	$0.40/ $9.99	$0.50/ $9.99	$0.15/ $9.99	$0.20/ $9.99	$0.15/ $9.99

Question 8. How many reprints or authorized photocopies of articles did you sell from this journal in your last calendar or fiscal year?
______________copies of articles.

Sale of Reprints or Authorized Photocopies During Last Calendar or Fiscal Year

Thirty-eight percent of the 579 responding journals report no reprint or photocopy sales whatsoever, and, when added to the group which reported sales of less than 300 copies, represents a majority of all respondents at 66.2%. Commercial journals reported a greater incidence of reprint or copy sales for those who sold at least some, but an even greater percentage, 43.0%, of commercial journals reported selling no copies whatsoever. At the other end of the spectrum, 13.1% of responding journals reported the sale of more than 8000 copies, with a considerably higher (22.0%) level of response among commercial than among non-profit (8.4%) journals.

Applied science and technology journals showed a far greater pattern of sale of reprints or photocopies than any other subject discipline. The 26.8% of journals who sold more than 8000 copies represents almost three times the response level of social science, and more than six times the level reported in the pure sciences and humanities.

Journals with larger circulations were more apt to sell reprints and photocopies, and since these journals reach more readers, this is not surprising. In particular, large commercial journals reported the sale of over 8000 copies for 65.7% of the journals reporting. The percentage even for large non-profit journals is considerably smaller, at 17.4%.

Question 8: How many reprints or authorized photocopies of articles did you sell from this journal in your last calendar or fiscal year? ____________copies of articles

	Total Journal Response (N=579)	Type of Publisher For Profit (N=200)	Non-profit (N=379)	Journals by Subject Pure Science (N=126)	Applied Science (N=183)	Social Science (N=197)	Humanities (N=73)
0	38.0%	43.0%	35.4%	42.9%	25.1%	44.7%	43.8%
1-299	28.2%	9.0%	38.3%	27.8%	21.3%	31.0%	38.4%
300-599	2.4%	2.0%	2.6%	1.6%	3.8%	1.5%	2.7%
600-999	2.9%	4.0%	2.4%	4.0%	2.2%	3.0%	2.7%
1000-2999	8.3%	9.5%	7.7%	12.7%	9.8%	4.6%	6.8%
3000-7999	7.1%	10.5%	5.3%	7.1%	10.9%	5.6%	1.4%
8000-max	13.1%	22.0%	8.4%	4.0%	26.8%	9.6%	4.1%
mean	6617.017	13484.305	2993.119	1846.873	15328.08	3201.756	2229.616
median	12.375	100.000	10.176	3.250	550.000	4.250	3.000

Question 8: How many reprints or authorized photocopies of articles did you sell from this journal in your last calendar or fiscal year?

____________copies of articles

Journals by Size of Circulation

	For Profit 0-2999 (N=133)	3000-9999 (N=32)	10000-max (N=35)	Non-profit 0-2999 (N=167)	3000-9999 (N=126)	10000-max (N=86)
0	60.2%	15.6%	2.9%	42.5%	34.1%	23.3%
1-299	6.8%	18.8%	8.6%	38.3%	42.1%	32.6%
300-599	3.0%	0	0	4.2%	1.6%	1.2%
600-999	4.5%	0	5.7%	1.8%	2.4%	3.5%
1000-2999	9.0%	12.5%	8.6%	7.8%	6.3%	9.3%
3000-7999	9.8%	15.6%	8.6%	1.8%	4.8%	12.8%
8000-max	6.8%	37.5%	65.7%	3.6%	8.7%	17.4%
mean	2018.955	21419.938	49797.200	1088.012	1949.532	8221.547
median	3.313	4000.500	40600.000	4.250	9.50	50.500

Question 9. What speed of service do you (or your agent) give in dispatching reprints or authorized photocopies from receipt of order to dispatch of copies? Average number of days ______________.

Speed of Service in Dispatching Reprints or Copies—Direct or Through Agent

Over half of the 703 journal respondents indicated that copies were dispatched, either directly or by an agent, within 5 days of the receipt of the order. Non-profit journals reported a greater rapidity of response than commercial journals, with 60.2% of responses in this time range, compared to 43.3% for commercial journals. The mean for all journals reporting was 12 days, for non-profit journals 10 days, and for commercial journals 15 days. It would appear that commercial organizations give a relatively lower level of priority to this endeavor, which can be identified as producing a fair amount of work for little if any return. Response time was most rapid for pure science and, perhaps surprisingly, humanities journals. It can be assumed that in the latter case it results from a desire to satisfy a request, and not from an attempt to gain a financial advantage. The mean response time for the humanities, 7 days, was the lowest reported for any subject discipline.

Circulation size of journal has no clear impact on response time. In general, the larger circulation journals, particularly in the profit sector, are slower to respond to requests.

Responses to this question can be compared to those made to question 5 of the publisher questionnaire, which asked for anticipated speed of service by those publishers who do not now sell reprints or authorized photocopies. The anticipated mean of 12 days in that questionnaire matches closely the responses in this journal questionnaire, and only the median publisher figure of 7 days appears somewhat optimistic in comparison.

Question 9: What speed of service do you (or your agent) give in dispatching reprints or authorized photocopies from receipt of order to dispatch of copies?

Average number of days_____________.

	Total Journal Response (N=703)	Type of Publisher: For Profit (N=263)	Non-profit (N=440)	Journals by Subject: Pure Science (N=176)	Applied Science (N=205)	Social Science (N=250)	Humanities (N=72)
0-5 Days	53.9%	43.3%	60.2%	65.3%	40.0%	54.4%	63.9%
6-10 Days	14.4%	11.8%	15.9%	5.1%	18.0%	16.0%	20.8%
11-25 Days	14.4%	17.9%	12.3%	12.5%	11.7%	18.8%	11.1%
26-60 Days	16.1%	26.6%	9.8%	15.3%	28.8%	10.0%	2.8%
61-99 Days	1.3%	.4%	1.8%	1.7%	1.5%	.8%	1.4%
Mean	12	15	10	11	15	11	7

Journals by Size of Circulation

	For Profit 0-2999 (N=159)	3000-9999 (N=34)	10000-max (N=42)	Non-profit 0-2999 (N=184)	3000-9999 (N=151)	10000-max (N=104)
0-5 Days	60.4%	26.5%	21.4%	60.3%	65.6%	52.9%
6-10 Days	11.9%	5.9%	23.8%	16.3%	13.2%	19.2%
11-25 Days	1.3%	17.6%	26.2%	13.0%	8.6%	15.4%
26-60 Days	25.8%	50.0%	28.6%	7.6%	11.9%	10.6%
61-99 Days	.6%	0	0	2.7%	.7%	1.9%
Mean	13	20	16	10	8	10

Question 10. If you authorized photocopying on the basis of individual permission requests, please attach a copy of your fee schedule.

a. Fee schedule attached ___________

b. Fee schedule not attached (no fixed or standard schedule) ________

Provision of Fee Schedule

Only about 12% of the journals in the survey supplied fee schedules. Failure to provide fee schedules could be due either to the absence of a practice of authorizing photocopying based on individual permissions, or of the absence of a policy and the coverage of such requests on a case-by-case basis. A number of the comments received indicated that no fee was charged, that the journal was too small to have a fee schedule, or that it was too cumbersome to develop and implement a policy. Where fee schedules were supplied, the fact that some related to individual copies, some to bulk shipment, and some specifically to copies for authors, made correlation impossible. Perhaps surprisingly, commercial journals are only marginally more likely to have fee schedules than non-profit journals. The practice is most common (perhaps 1 journal in 6 or 7) for applied science and social science journals; it is quite uncommon (about 1 in 20) for pure science and humanities journals.

As might be expected, large circulation journals are more apt to have published fee schedules than small circulation journals. However, even the largest of these categories, large commercial journals, only report fee schedules in 24.5% of the cases.

Question 10: If you authorized photocopying on the basis of individual permission requests, please attach a copy of your fee schedule.

a. Fee schedule attached____________
b. Fee schedule not attached (no fixed or standard schedule)________

	Total Journal Response (N=974)	Type of Publisher		Journals by Subject			
		For Profit (N=308)	Non-profit (N=666)	Pure Science (N=216)	Applied Science (N=264)	Social Science (N=371)	Humanities (N=123)
a. fee schedule attached	11.8%	12.0%	11.7%	5.1%	15.2%	15.6%	4.9%
b. fee schedule not attached	88.2%	88.0%	88.3%	94.9%	84.8%	84.4%	95.1%

Journals by Size of Circulation

	For Profit			Non-profit		
	0-2999 (N=177)	3000-9999 (N=47)	10000-max (N=49)	0-2999 (N=297)	3000-9999 (N=234)	10000-max (N=134)
a. fee schedule attached	10.7%	12.8%	24.5%	10.4%	11.6%	14.9%
b. fee schedule not attached	89.3%	87.2%	75.5%	89.6%	88.4%	85.1%

Question 11. **If you do not supply authorized reprints or photocopies from this journal what would you consider a fair price, for an authorized copy or reprint of an article of up to ten pages which you would supply from this journal, including postage?**

a. For United States order with accompanying payment $____________

Determination of Fair Price for Reprints or Photocopies, Copyrighted Journals Not presently Supplied

Accompanying Payment for Domestic Order

Journals were asked to repond to either question 7 or question11, the former if authorized reprints or photocopies were presently being supplied, question 11 if they were not. The fact that 432 copyrighted journals responded to question 11 indicates at least the possibility of some overlap in responses between this question and question 7, the extent of which cannot be determined. However, it can be assumed that question 11 tabulates responses from journals at least the strong majority of which do not presently furnish authorized reprints or photocopies.

In their responses, 135 journals, or 31.3%, indicated that they wished to receive no payment whatsoever for supplying copies. Since they do not presently supply copies, their lack of interest in receiving payment can be interpreted as something of an absolute unwillingness to supply copies in the future, rather than as a willingness to supply such copies for nothing. Of the 297 copyrighted journals which did indicate a price, the greatest response range was between $1 and $3 for an article of up to 10 pages, including postage, with method of postal transmission not specified. More than half, or 55.2% of the responding journals who indicated a willingness to supply reprints or photocopies for a price were willing to do so for $3 or less. However, a very large group of responses, 37.4%, is clustered at the $5 to $6 range. Virtually all respondents are willing to supply these articles for under $6.

Among commercial publishers, the response of those wishing to receive no payment was up to 34.6%, giving at least some credence to the belief that the unwillingness to state a price resulted from a residual unwillingness to supply copies. For commercial journals, better than half, or 62.7% of those willing to supply reprints for a price indicated that a price between $5 and $6 was considered fair. By contrast, non-profit journals, only 29.3% of which stated no price at which they would be willing to supply copies, tended to cluster into lower price ranges, with 69.2% satisfied with $3 or less, although a substantial minority of 24.1% still holds out for the $5-$6 range.

The most significant trend indicated in an analysis by subject disciplines is the far greater willingness of pure science journals which do not presently supply copies to do so for a price. Only 11.6% failed to name what they con sidered a fair price. By the same token, pure science journals also project the highest prices, with 47.4% in the $5-$6 range. Size of journal indicates significant trends in the growing unwillingness, as journals have larger cir culations, to name a fair price. Almost three fourths of the largest (over 10,000) commercial and one third of the largest non-profit journals indicated that they desired no payment for supplying copies which, as stated above, is interpreted not as altruism but as an unwillingness to participate, particu larly for journals which do not presently supply copies. For journals which do express a willingness, commercial journals cluster most heavily in the $5-$6 range, regardless of circulation size. Non-profit journals are, as reported previously, generally satisfied with payments of up to $3, although a sizeable minority, particularly for medium circulation journals, is in the $5 range.

Question 11. If you do not supply authorized reprints or photocopies from this journal what would you consider a fair price, for an authorized copy or reprint of an article of up to ten pages which you would supply from this journal, including postage?

a. For United States order with accompanying payment $______________

COPYRIGHTED JOURNALS

	Total Journal Response (N=297) Absolute Frequency	Adjusted Frequency	Cumulative Frequency	For Profit Journals (N=102) Abs. Fr.	Adj. Fr.	Cum. Fr.	Non-profit Journals (N=195) Abs. Fr.	Adj. Fr.	Cum. Fr.
0.01-0.25	1	.3%	.3%	0	0	0	1	.5%	.5%
0.26-0.50	5	1.7%	2.0%	0	0	0	5	2.6%	3.1%
0.51-0.99	12	4.0%	6.1%	6	5.9%	5.9%	6	3.1%	6.2%
1.00-1.99	75	25.3%	31.3%	2	2.0%	7.8%	73	37.4%	43.6%
2.00-2.99	71	23.9%	55.2%	21	20.6%	28.4%	50	25.6%	69.2%
3.00-3.99	12	4.0%	59.3%	5	4.9%	33.3%	7	3.6%	72.8%
4.00-4.99	4	1.3%	60.6%	3	2.9%	36.3%	1	.5%	73.3%
5.00-5.99	111	37.4%	98.0%	64	62.7%	99.0%	47	24.1%	97.4%
6.00-6.99	0	0	98.0%	0	0	99.0%	0	0	97.4%
7.00-7.99	4	1.3%	99.3%	0	0	99.0%	4	2.1%	99.5%
8.00-8.99	0	0	99.3%	0	0	99.0%	0	0	99.5%
9.00-9.99	2	.7%	100.00%	1	1.0%	100.00%	1	.5%	100.%
mean		$3.09			$4.03			$2.60	
median		$2.50			$4.99			$2.00	
mode		$5.00			$5.00			$5.00	
min/max		$ .25/$9.99			$ .75/$9.99			$ .25/$9.99	
0*	135	31.3%		54	34.6%		81	29.3%	

*These responses not included in the above tabulations

Question 11a. For United States order with accompanying payment

COPYRIGHTED JOURNALS

Journals by Subject

	Pure Sciences (N=76) Absolute Frequency	Adjusted Frequency	Applied Sciences (N=68) Abs Fr	Adj Fr	Social Sciences (N=114) Abs Fr	Adj Fr	Humanities (N=39) Abs Fr	Adj Fr
0.01-0.25	0	0	0	0	1	.9%	0	0
0.26-0.50	4	5.3%	0	0	1	.9%	0	0
0.51-0.99	1	1.3%	5	7.4%	5	4.4%	1	2.6%
1.00-1.99	15	19.7%	12	17.6%	33	28.9%	15	38.5%
2.00-2.99	14	18.4%	19	27.9%	23	20.2%	15	38.5%
3.00-3.99	1	1.3%	7	10.3%	4	3.5%	0	0
4.00-4.99	0	0	0	0	4	3.5%	0	0
5.00-5.99	36	47.4%	24	35.3%	43	37.7%	8	20.5%
6.00-6.99	0	0	0	0	0	0	0	0
7.00-7.99	4	5.3%	0	0	0	0	0	0
8.00-8.99	0	0	0	0	0	0	0	0
9.00-9.99	1	1.3%	1	1.5%	0	0	0	0
mean		$3.61		$3.16		$2.98		$2.31
median		$4.96		$2.52		$2.50		$1.99
mode		$5.00		$5.00		$5.00		$1.00
min/max		$ .37/$9.99		$ .75/$9.99		$ .25/$5.00		$ .75/$5.00
0*	10	11.6%	48	41.4%	60	34.5%	17	30.4%

*These responses not included in the above tabulations

Question 11a. For United States order with accompanying payment

Copyrighted Journals by Size of Circulation

	For Profit			Non-profit		
	(N=82) 0-2999	(N=13) 3000-9999	(N=7) 10000-max	(N=88) 0-2999	(N=73) 3000-9999	(N=34) 10000-max
0.01-0.25	0%	0%	0%	0%	1.4%	0%
0.26-0.50	0%	0%	0%	2.3%	2.7%	2.9%
0.51-0.99	4.9%	7.7%	14.3%	2.3%	1.4%	8.8%
1.00-1.99	1.2%	0%	14.3%	38.6%	30.1%	50.0%
2.00-2.99	15.9%	53.8%	14.3%	34.1%	19.2%	17.6%
3.00-3.99	3.7%	7.7%	14.3%	3.4%	4.1%	2.9%
4.00-4.99	3.7%	0%	0%	1.1%	0%	0%
5.00-5.99	70.7%	30.8%	28.6%	17.0%	38.4%	11.9%
6.00-6.99	0%	0%	0%	0%	0%	0%
7.00-7.99	0%	0%	0%	1.1%	2.7%	2.9%
8.00-8.99	0%	0%	0%	0%	0%	0%
9-00-9.99	0%	0%	14.3%	0%	0%	2.9%
mean	$4.22	$2.95	$3.84	$2.38	$3.05	$2.23
median	$4.99	$2.34	$3.00	$2.00	$2.49	$1.25
mode	$5.00	$2.00	$5.00	$2.50	$5.00	$1.00
min/max	$1.75/$5.00	$.80/$5.00	$.92/$9.99	$.50/$7.50	$.25/$7.50	$.50/$9.99
	no. fr.	no. fr.	no. fr.	no. fr.	no. fr.	no. fr.
0*	24 22.6%	11 45.8%	19 73.1%	33 27.3%	31 29.8%	17 33.3%

* These responses not included in the above tabulations.

Question 11b. For foreign order with accompanying payment

Accompanying Payment for Foreign Orders

Response patterns do not differ substantially from those reported for domestic orders with accompanying payment. Patterns of unwillingness to receive payment (interpreted as unwillingness to participate) are only fractionally higher, since payment with order assures safety even in a foreign transaction. Generally commercial journals are willing to charge approximately the same, or only slightly more, for filling a foreign order. Non-profit journals, by contrast, tend to slide their pricing scale upward by about 50 cents. Since these prices are designed to include postage, the method of transmittal assumed by the journal is important, although not divulged. Air mail shipment overseas is reasonably rapid, but expensive, and probably not covered in a 50 cent charge increase. Surface mail is probably too slow to be practical, and less than first class mail service becomes extremely chancy. However, it is possible that some responding journals assumed a slow low-cost method of shipment, with a higher priced alternative made available to the customer at his option, since it is known that a number of publications do in fact offer this option at present.

Question 11b. For foreign order with accompanying payment

COPYRIGHTED JOURNALS

	Total Publisher Response (N=283)			For Profit Publishers (N=101)			Non-profit Publishers (N=182)		
	Abs Freq	Adj Freq	Cum Freq	Abs. Freq.	Adj. Freq.	Cum. Freq.	Abs. Freq.	Adj. Freq.	Cum. Freq.
0.01-0.25	0	0	0	0	0	0	0	0	0
0.26-0.50	1	.4%	.4%	0	0	0	1	.5%	.5%
0.51-0.99	6	2.1%	2.5%	3	3.0%	3.0%	3	1.6%	2.2%
1.00-1.99	61	21.6%	24.0%	3	3.0%	5.9%	58	31.9%	34.1%
2.00-2.99	61	21.6%	45.6%	21	20.6%	26.7%	40	22.0%	56.0%
3.00-3.99	29	10.2%	55.8%	5	5.0%	31.7%	24	13.2%	69.2%
4.00-4.99	7	2.5%	58.3%	4	4.0%	35.6%	3	1.6%	70.9%
5.00-5.99	94	33.2%	91.5%	64	63.4%	99.0%	30	16.5%	87.4%
6.00-6.99	18	6.4%	97.9%	0	0	99.0%	18	9.9%	97.3%
7.00-7.99	4	1.4%	99.3%	0	0	99.0%	4	2.2%	99.5%
8.00-8.99	0	0	99.3%	0	0	99.0%	0	0	99.5%
9.00-9.99	2	.7%	100.0%	1	1.0%	100.0%	1	.5%	100.0%
mean		$3.52			$4.19			$3.15	
median		$3.01			$4.99			$2.51	
mode		$5.00			$5.00			$5.62	
min/max		$ .50/$9.99			$ .80/$9.99			$ .50/$9.99	
0*	140	33.1%		55	35.3%		85	31.8%	

*These responses not included in the above tabulations.

Question 11b. For foreign order with accompanying payment

COPYRIGHTED JOURNALS
Journals by Subject

	Pure Sciences (N=73)		Applied Sciences (N=63)		Social Sciences (N=110)		Humanities (N=37)	
	Absolute Frequency	Adjusted Frequency	Abs Freq	Adj Freq	Abs Freq	Adj Freq	Abs Freq	Adj Freq
0.01-0.25	0	0	0	0	0	0	0	0
0.26-0.50	0	0	0	0	1	.9%	0	0
0.51-0.99	3	4.1%	0	0	3	2.7%	0	0
1.00-1.99	12	16.4%	9	14.3%	30	27.3%	10	27.0%
2.00-2.99	13	17.8%	18	28.6%	18	16.4%	12	32.4%
3.00-3.99	4	5.5%	8	12.7%	11	10.0%	6	16.2%
4.00-4.99	0	0	2	3.2%	4	3.6%	1	2.7%
5.00-5.99	36	49.3%	25	39.7%	26	23.6%	7	18.9%
6.00-6.99	0	0	0	0	17	15.5%	1	2.7%
7.00-7.99	4	5.5%	0	0	0	0	0	0
8.00-8.99	0	0	0	0	0	0	0	0
9.00-9.99	1	1.4%	1	1.6%	0	0	0	0
mean		$3.91		$3.60		$3.43		$2.88
median		$4.97		$3.48		$3.00		$2.49
mode		$5.00		$5.00		$6.00		$2.00
min/max		$ .65/$9.99		$1.00/$9.99		$ .50/$6.00		$1.00/$6.0
0*	10	12.0%	51	44.7%	61	35.7%	18	32.7%

*These responses not included in the above tabulations.

Question 11b. For foreign order with accompanying payment

Copyrighted Journals by Size of Circulation

	For Profit (N=82) 0-2999	(N=13) 3000-9999	(N=6) 10000-max	Non-profit (N=83) 0-2999	(N=67) 3000-9999	(N=32) 10000-max
0.01-0.25	0%	0%	0%	0%	0%	0%
0.26-0.50	0%	0%	0%	0%	0%	3.1%
0.51-0.99	2.4%	7.7%	0%	2.4%	1.5%	0%
1.00-1.99	3.7%	0%	0%	28.9%	26.9%	50.0%
2.00-2.99	14.6%	53.8%	33.3%	25.3%	19.4%	18.8%
3.00-3.99	3.7%	7.7%	16.7%	19.3%	9.0%	6.3%
4.00-4.99	4.9%	0%	0%	3.6%	0%	0%
5.00-5.99	70.7%	30.8%	33.3%	13.3%	23.9%	9.4%
6.00-6.99	0%	0%	0%	6.0%	16.4%	6.3%
7.00-7.99	0%	0%	0%	1.2%	3.0%	3.1%
8.00-8.99	0%	0%	0%	0%	0%	0%
9.00-9.99	0%	0%	16.7%	0%	0%	3.1%
mean	$4.30	$3.25	$4.67	$2.92	$3.64	$2.74
median	$4.98	$2.81	$3.75	$2.50	$2.99	$1.52
mode	$5.00	$2.50	$5.00	$3.00	$5.62	$1.00
min/max	$.80/$5.00	$.84/$5.00	$2.00/$9.99	$.65/$9.50	$.75/$7.50	$.50/$9.99
0*	no. fr. 24 22.6%	no. fr. 11 45.8%	no. fr. 20 76.9%	no. fr. 35 29.7%	no. fr. 33 33.0%	no. fr. 17 34.7%

*These responses not included in the above tabulations.

Question 11c. For United States order with bill required

Domestic Order With Bill Required

The percentage of responses who indicated that they wished to receive no payment rose to 36.4% (from the 31.3% who had indicated a desire for zero payment for orders with accompanying payment) giving credence to the assumption, expressed earlier, that this is a body ofjournals which in fact does not wish to supply copies at all. For the 260 journals which did indicate a price, the price range appears to run about $1 higher than with prepayment, reflecting both the inconvenience of billing and the risk of not being able to collect. The half-way point in journal responses was not reached until a price of $4 (compared to the $2-$3 range for domestic prepayment), and almost half of the responses indicate a desire for payment of more than $5, with about 19% in fact desiring more than $6. Commercial journals were solidly above $5, with two thirds specifying payment of between that amount and $6. Non-profit journals, which for accompanying payment were largely (69.2%) content with $3 or less, are satisfied with this amount in only 46.6% of the cases where billing is required, and better than 35% indicate a need for more than $5 in payment.

As with domestic orders with payment, pure science journals are most willing to name a price, with only 15.4% of the responding journals in this discipline unwilling to do so. By the same token, and as with pre-paid orders, pure science journals are also prepared to charge the highest prices, with half in the $5-$6 range, and only about 40% below that figure. Almost half of the applied science journals refused to indicate a desire for payment, and thereby indicated an unwillingness to furnish copies. For those which did, the heaviest concentration was again in the $5-$6 range. Social science and humanities journals, particularly the latter, were somewhat lower in their price estimates for the more than 60% willing to supply copies for a price, with 56% of humanities journals willing to supply copies for under $3, despite the requirement for billing.

As with pre-paid orders, unwillingness to name a price grows as the circulation of the journal increases, particularly in the for-profit sector, with 80% of the largest circulation commercial journals reporting zero as a figure. By contrast, the largest circulation non-profit journals, approximately as unwilling (37.5%) as smaller non-profit journals to indicate a price, tend to be willing to accept a lower price for bills with shipment, with 43.3% content with under $2, and 60% satisfied with a $3 ceiling.

Question 11c. For United States order with bill required.

COPYRIGHTED JOURNALS

	Total Publisher Response (N=260)			For Profit Publishers (N=99)			Non-profit Publishers (N=161)		
	Abs. Freq.	Adj. Freq.	Cum. Freq.	Abs. Freq.	Adj. Freq.	Cum. Freq.	Abs. Freq.	Adj. Freq.	Cum. Freq.
0.01-0.25	1	.4%	.4%	0	0	0	1	.6%	.6%
0.26-0.50	0	0	0	0	0	0	0	0	0
0.51-0.99	8	3.1%	3.5%	6	6.1%	6.1%	2	1.2%	1.9%
1.00-1.99	38	14.6%	18.1%	1	1.0%	7.1%	37	23.0%	24.8%
2.00-2.99	42	16.2%	34.2%	7	7.1%	14.1%	35	21.7%	46.6%
3.00-3.99	40	15.4%	49.6%	14	14.1%	28.3%	26	16.1%	62.7%
4.00-4.99	4	1.5%	51.2%	1	1.0%	29.3%	3	1.9%	64.6%
5.00-5.99	78	30.0%	81.2%	66	66.7%	96.0%	12	7.5%	72.0%
6.00-6.99	33	12.7%	93.8%	3	3.0%	99.0%	30	18.6%	90.7%
7.00-7.99	13	5.0%	98.8%	0	0	99.0%	13	8.1%	98.8%
8.00-8.99	1	.4%	99.2%	0	0	99.0%	1	.6%	99.4%
9.00-9.99	2	.8%	100.0%	1	1.0%	100.0%	1	.6%	100.0%
mean		$3.91			$4.32			$3.66	
median		$3.99			$4.99			$2.99	
mode		$5.00			$5.00			$6.50	
min/max		$ .25/$9.99			$ .75/$9.99			$ .25/$9.99	
0 *	149	36.4%		56	36.1%		93	36.6%	

*These responses not included in the above tabulations.

Question 11c. For United States order with bill required

COPYRIGHTED JOURNALS

Journals by Subject

	Pure Science (N=66)		Applied Science (N=57)		Social Science (N=103)		Humanities (N=34)	
	Absolute Frequency	Adjusted Frequency	Abs. Freq.	Adj. Freq.	Abs. Freq.	Adj. Freq.	Abs. Freq.	Adj. Freq.
0.01-0.25	0	0	0	0	1	1.0%	0	0
0.26-0.50	0	0	0	0	0	0	0	0
0.51-0.99	2	3.0%	1	1.8%	5	4.9%	0	0
1.00-1.99	4	6.1%	5	8.8%	22	21.4%	7	20.6%
2.00-2.99	8	12.1%	8	14.0%	14	13.6%	12	35.3%
3.00-3.99	13	19.7%	15	26.3%	8	7.8%	4	11.8%
4.00-4.99	0	0	2	3.5%	2	1.9%	0	0
5.00-5.99	33	50.0%	23	40.4%	18	17.5%	4	11.8%
6.00-6.99	6	9.1%	2	3.5%	19	18.4%	6	17.6%
7.00-7.99	0	0	0	0	13	12.6%	0	0
8.00-8.99	0	0	0	0	0	0	1	2.9%
9.00-9.99	0	0	1	1.8%	1	1.0%	0	0
mean		$4.11		$3.87		$3.98		$3.37
median	$	$4.98		$3.75		$4.01		$2.54
mode		$5.00		$5.00		$5.00		$6.50
min/max		$ .60/$6.50		$ .92/$9.99		$ .25/$9.99		$1.00/$8.00
0*	12	15.4%	53	48.2%	65	38.7%	19	35.8%

*These responses not included in the above tabulations.

Question 11c. For United States order with bill required.

Copyrighted Journals by Size of Circulation

	For Profit (N=81) (0-2999)	(N=13) (3000-9999)	(N=5) (10000-max)	Non-Profit (N=71) (0-2999)	(N=60) (3000-0000)	(N=30) (10000-max)
0.01-0.25	0	0	0	0	1.7%	0
0.26-0.50	0	0	0	0	0	0
0.51-0.99	4.9%	7.7%	20.0%	2.8%	0	0
1.00-1.99	0	0	20.0%	21.1%	15.0%	43.3%
2.00-2.99	8.6%	0	0	29.6%	15.0%	16.7%
3.00-3.99	7.4%	53.8%	20.0%	14.1%	16.5%	20.0%
4.00-4.99	1.2%	0	0	2.8%	1.7%	0
5.00-5.99	74.1%	38.5%	20.0%	9.9%	5.0%	6.7%
6.00-6.99	3.7%	0	0	16.9%	26.7%	6.7%
7.00-7.99	0	0	0	1.4%	16.7%	6.7%
8.00-8.99	0	0	0	0	1.7%	0
9.00-9.99	0	0	20.0%	1.4%	0	0
mean	$4.45	$3.60	$4.08	$3.36	$4.41	$2.86
median	$4.99	$3.57	$3.00	$2.56	$4.03	$2.49
mode	$5.00	$3.00	$ .92	$6.50	$6.50	$1.50
min/max	$ .75/6.00	$ .80/5.00	$ .92/9.99	$ .60/9.99	$ .25/8.00	$1.00/7.00
	no. fr.	no. fr.	no. fr.	no. fr.	no. fr.	no. fr.
0*	25 23.6%	11 45.8%	20 80.0%	40 36.0%	35 36.8%	18 16.5%

*These responses not included in the above tabulations.

Question 11d. For foreign order with bill required.

Foreign Orders With Bill Required

While the percentage of respondents unwilling to state a price is up to 37.5%, this is still considered surprisingly low considering the difficulties in collecting from or dunning overseas customers. There is virtually no difference in reluctance between commercial and non-profit journals. For the 253 journals willing to indicate a price to supply copies with billing to foreign customers, the mid-point is not reached until the $5-$6 range, and the $4.38 mean and $4.98 are $1 and $2 greater, respectively, than for foreign orders with accompanying payment. Again, since the assumed method of shipment is not specified in either the question or the response it is not possible to determine whether these journals intend, at that price, any but the lowest level method of communication.

Commercial journals are solidly in the $5-$6 range, with non-profit journals reaching a cumulative 55% at a top of $4. As with previous responses, pure science journals are the most willing to specify a price for filling orders on this basis, and these and applied science journals also concentrate in the $5-$6 range. Humanities journals are again the lowest priced, with over 60% included in a $4 maximum.

Willingness to state a desired price hovers consistently around 37% for non-profit journals, regardless of the circulation of the journal, but decreases sharply as the circulation of commercial journals increases, with 84% of the largest circulation for profit journals unwilling to even indicate a price at which billing with shipment would be handled for foreign customers.

Question 11d. For foreign order with bill required.

COPYRIGHTED JOURNALS

	Total Publisher Response (N=253)			For Profit Publishers (N=96)			Non-profit Publishers (N=157)		
	Abs. Freq.	Adj. Freq.	Cum. Freq.	Abs. Freq.	Adj. Freq.	Cum. Freq.	Abs. Freq.	Adj. Freq.	Cum. Freq.
0.01-0.25	0	0	0	0	0	0	0	0	0
0.26-0.50	0	0	0	0	0	0	0	0	0
0.51-0.99	5	2.0%	2.0%	4	4.2%	4.2%	1	.6%	.6%
1.00-1.99	29	11.5%	13.4%	1	1.0%	5.2%	28	17.8%	18.5%
2.00-2.99	33	13.0%	26.5%	7	7.3%	12.5%	26	16.6%	35.0%
3.00-3.99	47	18.6%	45.1%	15	15.6%	28.1%	32	20.4%	55.4%
4.00-4.99	6	2.4%	47.4%	1	1.0%	29.2%	5	3.2%	58.6%
5.00-5.99	73	28.9%	76.3%	63	65.6%	94.8%	10	6.4%	65.0%
6.00-6.99	12	4.7%	81.0%	4	4.2%	99.0%	8	5.1%	70.1%
7.00-7.99	30	11.9%	92.9%	0	0	99.0%	30	19.1%	89.2%
8.00-8.99	14	5.5%	98.4%	0	0	99.0%	14	8.9%	98.1%
9.00-9.99	4	1.6%	100.0%	1	1.0%	100.0%	3	1.9%	100.0%
mean		$4.38			$4.46			$4.33	
median		$4.98			$4.99			$3.48	
mode		$5.00			$5.00			$7.12	
min/max		$ .75/$9.99			$ .75/$9.99			$ .75/$9.99	
0*	152	37.5%		57	37.3%		95	37.7%	

*These responses not included in the above tabulations.

Question 11d. For foreign order with bill required

	Copyrighted Journals by Subject							
	Pure Sciences (N=64)		Applied Sciences (N=55)		Social Sciences (N=101)		Humanities (N=33)	
	Absolute Freq.	Adjusted Freq.	Abs. Freq.	Adj. Freq.	Abs. Freq.	Adj. Freq.	Abs. Freq.	Adj. Freq.
0.01-0.25	0	0.0%	0	0.0%	0	0.0%	0	0.0%
0.26-0.50	0	0.0%	0	0.0%	0	0.0%	0	0.0%
0.51-0.99	1	1.6%	0	0.0%	4	4.0%	0	0.0%
1.00-1.99	1	1.6%	3	5.5%	21	20.8%	4	12.1%
2.00-2.99	8	12.5%	7	12.7%	9	8.9%	9	27.3%
3.00-3.99	13	20.3%	14	25.5%	12	11.9%	8	24.2%
4.00-4.99	2	3.1%	1	1.8%	3	3.0%	0	0.0%
5.00-5.99	32	50.0%	25	45.5%	14	13.9%	2	6.1%
6.00-6.99	1	1.6%	1	1.8%	7	6.9%	3	9.1%
7.00-7.99	6	9.4%	2	3.6%	16	15.8%	6	18.2%
8.00-8.99	0	0.0%	1	1.8%	13	12.9%	0	0.0%
9.00-9.99	0	0.0%	1	1.8%	2	2.0%	1	3.0%
mean		$4.39		$4.32		$4.52		$4.04
median		$4.97		$4.96		$4.98		$3.01
mode		$5.00		$5.00		$5.00		$3.00
min/max		$0.75/$7.12		$1.06/$9.99		$0.75/$9.99		$1.00/$9.0
	no.	fr.	no.	fr.	no.	fr.	no.	fr.
*0	1.	15.8%	54	49.5%	66	39.5%	20	37.7%

*These responses not included in the above tabulations.

Question 11d. For foreign order with bill required.

	Copyrighted Journals by Size of Circulation											
	For Profit						Non-Profit					
	(N=80) 0-2999		(N=12) 3000-9999		(N=4) 10000-max		(N=69) 0-2999		(N=58) 3000-9999		(N=30) 10000-max	
0.01-0.25	0%		0%		0%		0%		0%		0%	
0.26-0.50	0%		0%		0%		0%		0%		0%	
0.51-0.99	3.7%		8.3%		0%		1.4%		0%		0%	
1.00-1.99	1.2%		0%		0%		15.9%		12.1%		33.3%	
2.00-2.99	7.5%		0%		25.0%		23.2%		10.3%		13.3%	
3.00-3.99	8.8%		58.3%		25.0%		17.4%		20.7%		26.7%	
4.00-4.99	1.2%		0%		0%		2.9%		5.2%		0%	
5.00-5.99	72.5%		33.3%		25.0%		8.7%		1.7%		10.0%	
6.00-6.99	5.0%		0%		0%		8.7%		3.4%		0%	
7.00-7.99	0%		0%		0%		17.4%		27.6%		6.7%	
8.00-8.99	0%		0%		0%		1.4%		17.2%		10.0%	
9.00-9.99	0%		0%		25.0%		2.9%		1.7%		0%	
mean	$4.52		$3.78		$5.25		$4.10		$5.08		$3.42	
median	$4.99		$3.82		$4.00		$3.02		$5.05		$2.98	
mode	$5.00		$3.50		$2.50		$7.12		$7.12		$3.00	
min/max	$.75/$6.50		$.90/$5.00		$2.50/$9.99		$.75/$9.99		$1.00/$9.00		$1.00/$8.75	
	no.	fr.	no.	fr.	no.	fr.	no.	fr.	no.	fr.	no.	fr.
0*	25	23.8%	11	47.8%	21	84.0%	41	37.3%	36	38.3%	18	37.5%

*These responses not included in the above tabulations.

Question 12. If authorized copies were supplied by an agent or a clearinghouse, what would you consider an appropriate payment to you for each copy of an article of up to ten pages from this journal?

Payment to be Recovered from Clearinghouse or Authorized Agent

More than 50% of the 412 copyrighted journals which responded to this question answered that they expected no payment to be made to them from the supply of copies by a clearinghouse or agent. These journals are presumably satisfied to use such a clearinghouse (if indeed they like the concept at all--responses in the publisher questionnaire indicate a strong preference for direct mailing over the clearinghouse concept) as a convenience mechanism, or perhaps as a copying deterrent, and do not expect to obtain any funds in this manner. Clearinghouse charges for these journals would presumably be those necessary to meet operating costs (the question of whether or not there was a willingness to subsidize the operation of a clearinghouse was not raised). Perhaps, surprisingly, journals in the for profit sector were even more strongly committed to zero recovery from the clearinghouse than non-profit journals, in 58.4% of the cases.

Where compensation through an agent or clearinghouse mechanism was desired, there was a willingness to receive 50 cents or less in about half the cases, with commercial journals perhaps surprisingly more willing to settle for this ceiling than non-profit journals. However there were substantial numbers of journals who wanted much larger payments, with the 75th percentile not reached until $2, and with 10% desiring to recover more than $4.

Applied science and humanities journals were more desirous of receiving payment than either pure or social science journals. However, pure science journals which did wish to make a payment recovery did, in 15% of the cases, demand $7 or more, a figure not approached by any other subject discipline. By contrast, however, more than half of the pure and applied science journals expecting remuneration are willing to settle for 50 cents or less, while social science and humanities journals tend to have greater expectations in more than half of the instances, and therefore report medians of $ .99 and $ .78, respectively.

Willingness to forego recompense from an agent or clearinghouse decreases in the for profit sector as the journal distribution increases, with 70.6% of the smallest commercial journals willing to forego a return, compared to only 27.6% of those with the largest circulations. However, the majority of these journals indicate a desire for a payment of 50 cents or less, but a significant fraction insists on substantially higher returns, with 38% expecting $3 or more, and 19% desiring $5 or more. Non-profit journals are willing to forego payment in a fairly consistent approximately 45% of the cases. Where payment is expected, smaller journals appear less satisfied with the emerging "target" of 50 cents, with only 35.9% content with this figure, compared to 45.5% of large circulation non-profit journals. Smaller circulation non-profit journals fall heavily into the $1 to $2 range, a ceiling which will satisfy over 80% of all but the smallest non-profit journals, 18.8% of which expect payment of between $2 and $3.

Question 12. If authorized copies were supplied by an agent or a clearinghouse, would you consider an appropriate payment to you for each copy of article of up to ten pages from this journal?

COPYRIGHTED JOURNALS

	Total Publisher Response (N=203)			For Profit Publishers (N=67)			Non-profit Publishers (N=136)		
	Abs. Freq.	Adj. Freq.	Cum. Freq.	Abs. Freq.	Adj. Freq.	Cum. Freq.	Abs. Freq.	Adj. Freq.	Cum. Freq.
0.01-0.25	37	18.2%	18.2%	1	1.5%	1.5%	36	26.5%	26.5%
0.26-0.50	59	29.1%	47.3%	38	56.7%	58.2%	21	15.4%	41.9%
0.51-0.99	13	6.4%	53.7%	3	4.5%	62.7%	10	7.4%	49.3%
1.00-1.99	45	22.2%	75.9%	7	10.4%	73.1%	38	27.9%	77.2%
2.00-2.99	24	11.8%	87.7%	6	9.0%	82.1%	18	13.2%	90.4%
3.00-3.99	5	2.5%	90.1%	4	6.0%	88.1%	1	.7%	91.2%
4.00-4.99	4	2.0%	92.1%	2	3.0%	91.0%	2	1.5%	92.6%
5.00-5.99	9	4.4%	96.6%	5	7.5%	98.5%	4	2.9%	95.6%
6.00-6.99	0	0	96.6%	0	0	98.5%	0	0	95.6%
7.00-7.99	4	2.0%	98.5%	0	0	98.5%	4	2.9%	98.5%
8.00-8.99	0	0	98.5%	0	0	98.5%	0	0	98.5%
9.00-9.99	3	1.5%	100.0%	1	1.5%	100.0%	2	1.5%	100.0%
mean		$1.44			$1.50			$1.41	
median		$ .74			$ .52			$ .98	
mode		$ .50			$ .50			$1.00	
min/max		$ .05/$9.99			$ .25/$9.99			$ .05/$9.99	
0*	209	50.7%		94	58.4%		115	45.8%	

*These responses not included in the above tabulations.

Question 12. If authorized copies were supplied by an agent or a clearing house, what would you consider an appropriate payment to you for each copy of an article of up to ten pages from this journal?

Copyrighted Journals by Subject

	Pure Sciences (N=39)		Applied Sciences (N=73)		Social Sciences (N=61)		Humanities (N=30)	
	Abs. Freq.	Adj. Freq.	Abs. Freq.	Adj. Freq.	Abs. Freq.	Adj. Freq.	Abs. Freq.	Adj. Freq.
0.01-0.25	11	28.2%	7	9.6%	14	23.0%	5	16.7%
0.26-0.50	11	28.2%	32	43.8%	8	13.1%	8	26.7%
0.51-0.99	1	2.6%	4	5.5%	5	8.2%	3	10.0%
1.00-1.99	5	12.8%	9	12.3%	23	37.7%	8	26.7%
2.00-2.99	3	7.7%	8	11.0%	8	13.1%	5	16.7%
3.00-3.99	0	0	4	5.5%	0	0	1	3.3%
4.00-4.99	1	2.6%	2	2.7%	1	1.6%	0	0
5.00-5.99	1	2.6%	7	9.6%	1	1.6%	0	0
6.00-6.99	0	0	0	0	0	0	0	0
7.00-7.99	4	10.3%	0	0	0	0	0	0
8.00-8.99	0	0	0	0	0	0	0	0
9.00-9.99	2	5.1%	0	0	1	1.6%	0	0
mean		$2.06		$1.45		$1.24		$1.03
median		$ .51		$ .52		$ .99		$ .78
mode		$ .50		$ .50		$1.00		$1.00
min/max		$ .05/$9.99		$ .10/$5.50		$ .10/$9.99		$ .10/$3.00
0*	48	55.2%	50	40.7%	90	59.6%	21	41.2%

*These responses not included in the above tabulations.

Question 12. Payment for each copy supplied by an agent or a clearinghouse.

Copyrighted Journals by Size of Circulation

	For Profit (N=32) 0-2999	(N=14) 3000-9999	(N=21) 10000-max	Non-profit (N=64) 0-2999	(N=50) 3000-9999	(N=22) 10000-max
0.01-0.25	3.1%	0	0	28.1%	26.0%	22.7%
0.26-0.50	43.8%	92.9%	52.4%	7.7%	22.0%	22.7%
0.51-0.99	6.3%	0	4.8%	4.7%	6.0%	18.2%
1.00-1.99	18.7%	0	4.8%	31.2%	28.0%	18.2%
2.00-2.99	18.7%	0	0	18.8%	8.0%	9.1%
3.00-3.99	6.3%	0	9.5%	0	2.0%	0
4.00-4.99	0	0	9.5%	1.6%	2.0%	0
5.00-5.99	3.1%	7.1%	14.3%	4.7%	2.0%	0
6.00-6.99	0	0	0	0	0	0
7.00-7.99	0	0	0	1.6%	4.0%	4.5%
8.00-8.99	0	0	0	0	0	0
9.00-9.99	0	0	4.8%	1.6%	0	4.5%
mean	$1.32	$ .81	$2.23	$1.50	$1.24	$1.55
median	$ .75	$ .50	$1.61	$1.00	$ .68	$ .73
mode	$ .50	$ .50	$ .50	$1.00	$1.00	$ .50
min/max	$ .25/$5.00	$ .30/$5.00	$ .50/$9.99	$ .05/$9.99	$ .10/$7.50	$ .15/$9.99
0*	no. fr.	no. fr.	no. fr.	no. fr.	no. fr.	no. fr.
	77 70.6%	9 39.1%	8 27.6%	49 43.4%	49 49.5%	17 43.6%

*These responses not included in the above tabulations.

Question 13. If you would wish to license directly (or through an agent or clearinghouse) individual user organizations to make photocopies of articles from your journals rather than selling reprints or authorized copies directly or through an agent, what would you consider to be a fair license payment to you for each copy of an article of up to ten pages from this journal?

Willingness to License Directly or Through an Agent or Clearinghouse

This question asked journals willing to license photocopying to indicate what they considered a fair license payment for a copy of an article. Better than half of the copyrighted journals in the survey declined to respond to this question, which may indicate either an unwillingness to license or uncertainty about the implications of the question, with a particularly large (54.2%) percentage of non-profit publishers unwilling to respond. Of those which did respond, more than half indicated that they expected no payment at all from licensing arrangements. This response, which was particularly prevalent from commercial journals (63.4%) may be taken at face value, or it may also be interpreted as some residual reluctance to license at all, since the only opportunity provided to opponents of licensing was an avoidance of the entire question.

Of the 203 journals which specifically indicated both a willingness to license and named an expected payment, slightly more than half expressed a willingness to accept 50 cents or less. However, a sizeable minority held out for considerably larger payments, with only 3/4 of the respondents satisfied with $2, and almost 10% still dissatisfied with $5. Among for profit journals the clustering within the 50 cent limit was much greater (66.1%) than in the non-profit journals (44.2%).

There was relatively little variance between subject disciplines based on willingness to respond and willingness to set a price figure. Among those journals which did specify, pure and applied science journals were in the majority, content with a recovery of 50 cents or less, although a number of pure and social science journals hung to the upper reaches of $7 or more. Humanities journals tended to cluster more heavily in the $1 and $2 range, with only 39.3% satisified with a 50 cent payment. However, humanities journals also did not display the extremes at the higher end of the spectrum.

Circulation size contributed no significant variations, except for the fact that the great majority of small circulation commercial journals (73.3%)

indicated a willingness to license without recompense. In general, larger for-profit journals are most willing to accept a 50 cent payment than either smaller commercial or any non-profit journals, but even non-profit journals increase their tendency to accept such a payment as they increase in circulation. This may be because larger circulation journals have greater familiarity with licensing arrangements and what can reasonably be expected, or simply because, with larger expected volume, they can accept a lower unit transaction price.

It is significant to note that both with respect to question 12 and 13 publishers of more than one journal reported the same price or license fee per article for all of their journals. In other words, the price or license fee per article for multiple journal publishers was not greater for journals with higher subscription prices than for journals with lower subscription prices.

Question 13. If you would wish to license directly (or through an agent or clearinghouse) individual user organizations to make photocopies of articles from your journals rather than selling reprints of authorized copies directly or through an agent, what would you consider to be a fair license payment to you for each copy of an article of up to ten pages from this journal?

COPYRIGHTED JOURNALS

	Total Publisher Response (N=203)			For Profit Publishers (N=56)			Non-profit Publishers (N=147)		
	Abs. Freq.	Adj. Freq.	Cum. Freq.	Abs. Freq.	Adj. Freq.	Cum. Freq.	Abs. Freq.	Adj. Freq.	Cum. Freq.
0.01-0.25	31	15.3%	15.3%	2	3.6%	3.6%	29	19.7%	19.7%
0.26-0.50	71	35.0%	50.2%	35	62.5%	66.1%	36	24.5%	44.2%
0.51-0.99	8	3.9%	54.2%	2	3.6%	69.6%	6	4.1%	48.3%
1.00-1.99	44	21.7%	75.9%	10	17.9%	87.5%	34	23.1%	71.4%
2.00-2.99	24	11.8%	87.7%	2	3.6%	91.1%	22	15.0%	86.4%
3.00-3.99	4	2.0%	89.7%	2	3.6%	94.6%	2	1.4%	87.8%
4.00-4.99	2	1.0%	90.6%	1	1.8%	96.4%	1	.7%	88.4%
5.00-5.99	9	4.4%	95.1%	1	1.8%	98.2%	8	5.4%	93.9%
6.00-6.99	0	0	95.1%	0	0	98.2%	0	0	93.9%
7.00-7.99	4	2.0%	97.0%	0	0	98.2%	4	2.7%	96.6%
8.00-8.99	0	0	97.0%	0	0	98.2%	0	0	96.6%
9.00-9.99	6	3.0%	100.0%	1	1.8%	100.0%	5	3.4%	100.0%
mean		$1.53			$1.06			$1.71	
median		$ .53			$ .51			$ .98	
mode		$ .50			$ .50			$ .50	
min/max		$ .10/$9.99			$ .10/$9.99			$ .10/$9.99	
0*	214	51.3%		97	63.4%		117	44.3%	

*These responses not included in the above tabulations.

Question 13. If you would wish to license directly (or through an agent or clearinghouse) individual user organizations to make photocopies of articles from your journals rather than selling reprints of authorized copies directly or through an agent, what would you consider to be a fair license payment to you for each copy of an article of up to ten pages from this journal?

Copyrighted Journals by Subject

	Pure Sciences (N=34)		Applied Sciences (N=70)		Social Sciences (N=71)		Humanities (N=28)	
	Abs. Freq.	Adj. Freq.	Abs. Freq.	Adj. Freq.	Abs. Freq.	Adj. Freq.	Abs. Freq.	Adj. Freq.
0.01-0.25	9	26.5%	6	8.6%	8	11.3%	8	28.6%
0.26-0.50	10	29.4%	33	47.1%	25	35.2%	3	10.7%
0.51-0.99	1	2.9%	3	4.3%	3	4.2%	1	3.6%
1.00-1.99	6	17.6%	8	11.4%	20	28.2%	10	35.7%
2.00-2.99	1	2.9%	11	15.7%	7	9.9%	5	17.9%
3.00-3.99	1	2.9%	2	2.9%	1	1.4%	0	0
4.00-4.99	0	0	2	2.9%	0	0	0	0
5.00-5.99	1	2.9%	4	5.7%	3	4.2%	1	3.6%
6.00-6.99	0	0	0	0	0	0	0	0
7.00-7.99	4	11.8%	0	0	0	0	0	0
8.00-8.99	0	0	0	0	0	0	0	0
9.00-9.99	1	2.9%	1	1.4%	4	5.6%	0	0
mean		$1.87		$1.45		$1.59		$1.17
median		$ .51		$ .52		$ .85		$ .99
mode		$ .50		$ .50		$ .50		$1.00
min/max		$ .10/$9.99		$ .10/$9.99		$ .20/$9.99		$ .10/$5.00
0 *	50	56.8%	54	43.5%	90	55.9%	20	41.7%

*These responses not included in the above tabulations.

Question 13. Fair license payment for each copy

Copyrighted Journals by Size of Circulation

	For Profit (N=28) 0-2999	(N=14) 3000-9999	(N=14) 10000-max	Non-profit (N=70) 0-2999	(N=54) 3000-9999	(N=23) 10000-max
0.01-0.25	7.1%	0	0	17.1%	16.7%	38.8%
0.26-0.50	39.3%	92.9%	78.6%	18.6%	33.3%	21.7%
0.51-0.99	3.6%	0	7.1%	4.3%	3.7%	4.3%
1.00-1.99	35.7%	0	0	28.6%	22.2%	8.7
2.00-2.99	7.1%	0	0	12.9%	14.8%	21.7%
3.00-3.99	7.1%	0	0	2.9%	0	0
4.00-4.99	0	0	7.1%	1.4%	0	0
5.00-5.99	0	7.1%	0	8.6%	3.7%	0
6.00-6.99	0	0	0	0	0	0
7.00-7.99	0	0	0	1.4%	3.7%	4.3%
8.00-8.99	0	0	0	0	0	0
9.00-9.99	0	0	7.1%	4.3%	1.9%	4.3%
mean	$1.00	$ .81	$1.45	$1.91	$1.49	$1.61
median	$ .78	$ .50	$ .53	$1.00	$ .53	$ .51
mode	$ .50	$ .50	$ .50	$1.00	$ .50	$ .50
min/max	$ .10/$3.50	$ .30/$5.00	$ .50/$9.99	$ .10/$9.99	$ .10/$9.99	$ .10/$9.99
0 *	no. fr. 77 73.3%	no. fr. 9 39.1%	no. fr. 11 44.0%	no. fr. 44 38.6%	no. fr. 53 49.5%	no. fr. 20 46.5%

*These responses not included in the above tabulations.

Question 14. Do you sell directly or through an agent(s) microform versions of this journal?

a. Directly ___________ Through an agent(s) _____________
b. Current issues Yes _____________ No _____________
c. Yearly volumes of back issues Yes _________ No _________

Sale of Microform Versions of the Journal

A total of 28.2% of all survey journals did not respond to a question which inquired into sale of microforms either directly or through an agent, and it can therefore be assumed that these journals do not produce microform copies, although it is of course possible that some journals which do produce microforms simply did not answer the question. Of respondents, sale through an agent was preferred to direct sale by a ratio of more than 4 to 1. In particular, non-profit journals rely almost entirely on microform sale through agents, by almost 8 to 1. By contrast, commercial journals make direct distribution in microforms more than one third of the cases in which microform is available. Pure science journals are most apt to handle their own microform distribution, while humanities journals hardly do so at all. For-profit journals with small circulations appear more likely to distribute their own microforms; larger commercial journals and the non-profit sector prefer working through an agent.

Less than half of responding journals sell current year issues on micro form, whether through an agent or directly. Commercial journals are less likely to do so than non-profit journals, perhaps because of fear that current distribution of microforms could cut into full sized subscriptions. Social science and humanities journals are more willing to distribute current issues in microform.

All journal groups indicated a practice of furnishing back issues on microform, by a margin of almost 5 to 1 for responding journals. There is little difference between profit and non-profit journals, or within subject disciplines. Large journals, both commercial and non-profit, indicate the greater trend toward back year availability on microform. This could be expected, since these journals also provide the most attractive potential market.

Question 14. Do you sell directly or through an agent(s) microform versions of this journal?

a. Directly ______________ Through an agent(s) __________
b. Current issues Yes ______________ No ______________
c. Yearly volumes of back issues Yes ______________ No ______

	Total Journal Response (N=974)	Type of Publisher: For Profit (N=308)	Non-profit (N=666)	Journals by Subject Breakdown: Pure Science (N=216)	Applied Science (N=264)	Social Science (N=371)	Humanities (N=123)
a. Directly	13.9%	25.3%	8.6%	35.2%	12.5%	6.5%	1.6%
through an agent	57.9%	40.6%	65.9%	41.2%	57.6%	63.3%	71.5%
No answer	28.2%	34.1%	25.5%	23.6%	29.9%	30.2%	28.4%
b. Current issues							
YES	37.5%	22.1%	44.6%	25.9%	36.7%	43.1%	42.3%
NO	43.0%	58.1%	36.0%	49.5%	42.4%	41.0%	39.0%
No answer	19.5%	19.8%	19.4%	24.5%	20.8%	15.9%	18.7%
c. Yearly back issues							
YES	68.1%	64.6%	69.7%	73.6%	65.9%	66.8%	66.7%
NO	13.9%	13.6%	14.0%	9.7%	11.4%	17.8%	14.6%
No answer	18.1%	21.8%	16.3%	16.7%	22.7%	15.4%	18.7%

Question 14. Do you sell directly or through an agent(s) microform versions of this journal?

a. Directly ______________ Through an agent (s) __________
b. Current issues Yes ______________ No ______________
c. Yearly volumes of back issues Yes ______________ No ______

Journals by Size of Circulation

	For Profit 0-2999 (N=177)	3000-9999 (N=47)	10000-max (N=49)	Non-profit 0-2999 (N=297)	3000-9999 (N=234)	10000-max (N=134)
a. Directly	36.2%	23.4%	6.1%	4.7%	14.1%	7.5%
Through Agent	30.5%	42.6%	79.6%	63.0%	66.2%	71.6%
No and No answer	33.3%	34.0%	14.3%	32.3%	19.7%	20.9%
b. Current Issues						
YES	11.9%	23.4%	49.0%	39.7%	44.4%	56.0%
NO	66.7%	55.3%	38.8%	37.1%	36.3%	33.6%
No answer	21.4%	21.3%	12.2%	23.2%	19.3%	10.4%
c. Yearly volumes of back issues						
YES	68.9%	63.8%	71.4%	58.9%	78.7%	77.7%
NO	9.0%	14.9%	6.2%	19.5%	8.1%	11.9%
No answer	22.1%	21.3%	22.4%	21.6%	13.2%	10.4%

Question 15. If you sell microform editions of this journal, do you authorize copying without further payment, of articles from these microform editions?

a. Current year issues Yes ____________ No ______

b. Back year issues Yes ____________ No ______

Authorization of Copying Without Further Payment from Microform Editions

With regard to current year issues, only 8.6% of journals responded positively to this question, a number which drops to 1.6% for commercial journals, compared to 11.9% for non-profit journals. No clear patterns concerning the impact of size of circulation emerge. Large commercial journals appear most willing to permit copying from current microform issues among the for-profit sector, but that may be partially true because larger journals are more likely to have microform of current year issues. The willingness to permit copying without charge from back year issues is somewhat greater, but not substantially so. The overall positive response is 10.2%, with commercial journals indicating a willingness in only 3.2% of the answers, compared to 13.4% for non-profit journals. No clear patterns emerge among disciplines. Humanities journals appear the least willing, but since they also show the highest percentage of non-responses, they may simply be less likely to be available in microform. As with the question concerning current issue microform copying, larger circulation journals appear more willing to permit the practice than smaller circulation journals, but, as pointed out earlier, that may be in part because larger circulation journals are more likely to be available in microform.

The 32.3% of the journals which did not respond to this question can be assumed not to sell microform editions, and can therefore be added to the impact of those who refuses permission. However, since the non-responses grew to 35.1% for the question concerning current year, it leaves open to conjecture whether in fact 2.8% of the journals supply back but not current years (a response which can not really be elicited from the previous question) or whether a varying number simply chose not to answer the question. In any case, the truly significant measure is of those willing to permit copying from microforms without further payment.

Question 15: If you sell microform editions of this journal, do you authorize copying without further payment, of articles from these microform editions?

Current year issues Yes__________ No__________
Back year issues Yes__________ No__________

	Total Journal Response (N=974)	Type of Publisher: For Profit (N=308)	Type of Publisher: Non-profit (N=666)	Journals by Subject: Pure Science (N=216)	Journals by Subject: Applied Science (N=264)	Journals by Subject: Social Science (N=371)	Journals by Subject: Humanities (N=123)
a. Current back issues							
Yes	8.6%	1.6%	11.9%	10.2%	9.5%	8.4%	4.9%
No	56.3%	65.6%	52.0%	49.5%	58.0%	58.0%	59.3%
No answer	35.1%	32.8%	36.1%	40.3%	32.5%	33.6%	35.8%
b. Back year issues							
Yes	10.2%	3.2%	13.4%	11.6%	10.6%	9.7%	8.1%
No	57.5%	68.5%	52.5%	53.7%	60.2%	58.2%	56.1%
No answer	32.3%	28.3%	34.1%	34.7%	29.2%	32.1%	35.8%

Question 15: If you sell microform editions of this journal, do you authorize copying without further payment, of articles from these microform editions?

Current year issues Yes __________ No __________
Back year issues Yes __________ No __________

Journals by Size of Circulation

	For Profit: 0-2999 (N=177)	For Profit: 3000-9999 (N=47)	For Profit: 10000-max (N=49)	Non-profit: 0-2999 (N=297)	Non-profit: 3000-9999 (N=234)	Non-profit: 10000-max (N=134)
a. Current year issues						
Yes	.6%	0	8.2%	8.8%	15.4%	12.7%
No	63.2%	53.2%	75.5%	47.1%	56.4%	55.2%
No answer	36.2%	46.8%	16.3%	44.1%	28.2%	32.1%
b. Back year issues						
Yes	2.8%	0	10.2%	9.4%	18.4%	13.4%
No	63.9%	68.1%	77.6%	48.8%	54.7%	56.7%
No answer	33.3%	31.9%	12.2%	41.8%	26.9%	29.9%

Copying by Non-Profit Libraries After December 31, 1977

Question 16. Would you be willing to authorize (and to include a printed statement to this effect in each issue) non-profit libraries open to the public and specialized researchers to copy articles or to secure copies through interlibrary loan from this journal, without limitation or payment, current year"s issues as well as back issues?

YES ________ NO ________

Willingness to Authorize Non-Profit Libraries to Copy Without Limitation or Payment

Response to this question was calculated only for those journals which had indicated earlier that they were copyrighted. For the 872 journals in the response sample, an overwhelming majority, 71.9%, responded negatively, with only 22.5% agreeing to such blanket permission, and 5.6% failing to answer the question. Reaction was particularly negative from commercial journals, only 5.1% of which agreed to such unrestricted free copying from non-profit libraries. Among subject disciplines, humanities journals were most willing to permit such copying in 31.4% of the cases, but even here refusals outnumbered permissions by almost two to one. Pure science journals were very unwilling to permit free unrestricted copying, with only 10.0% of the journals agreeing to such a practice, and 86.5% refusing.

Perhaps surprisingly, smaller circulation commercial journals were more reluctant to agree to such copying than large circulation journals. In the for-profit sector, only 4.0% of small circulation journals were willing to agree to unrestricted free copying, compared to 15.9% in the largest stratum. No clear pattern by distribution size emerges among non-profit journals, with refusals generally outnumbering permissions by 2 to 1.

Question 16. Would you be willing to authorize (and to include a printed statement to this effect in each issue) non-profit libraries open to the public and specialized researchers to copy articles or to secure copies through interlibrary loan from this journal, without limitation or payment, current year's issues as well as back issues?

YES ____________ NO ____________

COPYRIGHTED JOURNALS

	Total Journal Response (N=872)	Type of Publisher: For Profit (N=296)	Non-profit (N=576)	Journals by Subject Breakdown: Pure Science (N=200)	Applied Science (N=238)	Social Science (N=329)	Humanities (N=105)
YES	22.5%	5.1%	31.4%	10.0%	22.7%	27.1%	31.4%
NO	71.9%	92.9%	61.1%	86.5%	74.4%	64.4%	61.9%
No answer	5.6%	2.0%	7.5%	3.5%	2.9%	8.5%	6.7%

Journals by Size of Circulation

	For Profit: 0-2999 (N=173)	3000-9999 (N=44)	10000-max (N=44)	Non-profit: 0-2999 (N=237)	3000-9999 (N=213)	10000-max (N=125)
YES	4.0%	2.3%	15.9%	35.9%	25.8%	32.0%
NO	93.6%	97.7%	79.5%	60.8%	62.4%	60.0%
No answer	2.4%	0	4.6%	3.3%	11.8%	8.0%

Question 17. If your answer to 20 is NO, would you be willing to authorize (and to include a printed statement to the effect in each issue) non-profit libraries open to the public and specialized researchers to copy articles from this journal or to secure copies through interlibrary loan without limitation or payment from earlier years?

YES ____________ NO ____________

Willingness to Authorize Non-profit Libraries to Copy or Secure on Interlibrary Loan Without Limitation or Payment from Earlier Years

Responses to this question, which differed from the previous question in that it specified only earlier years and excluded current issues, were nevertheless heavily negative. Negative reaction outweighed positive response by more than 4 to 1 for all journals responding. For commercial journals the ratio was more than 17 to 1, for non-profit journals close to 2 1/2 to 1. There was relatively little difference among subject disciplines, although applied science and technology journals were most unwilling to permit such copying. Size of journal distribution also had relatively little impact. Larger commercial journals were highly unwilling to permit such copying or borrowing without limitation, while larger non-profit journals were willing in 25.2% of the journal sample.

A high rate of non-response (22.5%) may have been caused in part by a typographical error, in which response to this question was incorrectly tied to question 20 rather than question 16, as intended. However, the meaning was sufficiently clear so that most journals were able to figure out the intention of the question and respond accordingly.

Question 17. **If your answer to 20 is NO, would you be willing to authorize (and to include a printed statement to the effect in each issue) non-profit libraries open to the public and specialized re searchers to copy articles from this journal or to secure copies through interlibrary loan without limitation or payment from earlier years?**

YES __________ **NO** __________

COPYRIGHTED JOURNALS

	Total Journal Response (N=872)	Type of Publisher: For Profit (N=296)	Non-profit (N=576)	Journals by Subject Breakdown: Pure Science (N=200)	Applied Science (N=283)	Social Science (N=329)	Humanities (N=105)
YES	14.4%	5.1%	19.3%	17.0%	10.1%	16.1%	14.3%
No	63.1%	89.2%	49.7%	72.5%	66.8%	57.8%	53.3%
No answer	22.5%	5.7%	31.0%	10.5%	23.1%	26.1%	32.4%

Journals by Size of Circulation

	For Profit: 0-2999 (N=173)	3000-9999 (N=44)	10000-max (N=44)	Non-profit: 0-2999 (N=237)	3000-9999 (N=213)	10000-max (N=125)
YES	6.4%	4.5%	4.5%	11.4%	24.4%	25.6%
No	88.4%	95.5%	77.3%	55.7%	47.4%	42.4%
No answer	5.2%	0	18.2%	32.9%	28.2%	32.0%

Question 18. If your answer to 17 is YES, what would you consider to be the lapse of time from publication date of the journal appropriate for permitting copying by non-profit libraries of articles without limitation or payment?

______________ Years

Lapse of Time Before Permission for Unlimited Copying by Non-Profit Libraries

Response to this question was requested only from those journals which had expressed a willingness to permit copying from earlier years. The question sought the journal's definition of "earlier years", and 401 journals responded to the question. Of these, better than two thirds set one year as the cut-off factor. Response after that dropped off rapidly, so that 19.7% of responding journals still insisted on a waiting period of five years or more. Commercial journals were considerably more willing to set the limit at only one year, and did so in 84.1% of responses, with only 13.3% insisting on a waiting period of 5 years or more. By contrast, non-profit journals willing to permit copying after one year totaled only 61.2%, and those insisting on a five year or longer waiting period represented 23.6% of the response. Pure science journals were most unwilling to grant rapid permission, with 61.1% willing to do so after one year, and 28.9% insisting on a minimum 5 year period. By contrast, applied science journals, with perhaps a shorter half life, were willing to grant reproduction permission after one year in 76.4% of the responses. Size of journal distribution appears to be a significant factor for non-profit journals (more unwilling to grant permission to start with). Larger non-profit journals were more unwilling to release their journals for distribution than smaller ones, with only 55.8% of such journals with circulation above 10,000 copies willing to do so after one year, and 23.1% demanding a delay of five years or more.

Question 18. If your answer to 17 is YES, what would you consider to be the lapse of time from publication date of the journal appropriate for permitting copying by non-profit libraries of articles without limitation or payment? ________Years.

COPYRIGHTED JOURNALS

	Total Publisher Response (N-401)	Type of Publishers		Journals by Subject Breakdown			
		For Profit (N-151)	Non-Profit (N-250)	Pure Science (N-90)	Applied Science (N-110)	Social Science (N-157)	Hum. (N-44)
1 year	69.8%	84.1%	61.2%	61.1%	76.4%	69.4%	72.7%
2 years	7.7%	1.3%	11.6%	7.8%	2.7%	10.8%	9.1%
3 years	2.5%	1.3%	3.2%	1.1%	1.8%	4.5%	0
4 years	.2%	0	.4%	1.1%	0	0	0
5 years	13.0%	6.0%	17.2%	25.6%	8.2%	9.6%	11.4%
6-10 years	4.5%	7.3%	2.8%	2.2%	9.1%	3.2%	2.3%
11- years	2.2%	0	3.6%	1.1%	1.8%	2.5%	4.5%
mean	2.76	1.099	3.764	2.856	1.827	3.076	3.773
median	.257	.099	.399	.349	.188	.255	.286

Question 18. If your answer to 17 is YES, what would you consider to be the lapse of time from publication date of the journal appropriate for permitting copying by non-profit libraries of articles without limitation of payment?

_____________ Years.

COPYRIGHTED JOURNALS

Journals by Size of Circulation

	For Profit			Non-profit		
	0-2999 (N=103)	3000-9999 (N=24)	10000-max (N=24)	0-2999 (N=92)	3000-9999 (N=105)	10000-max (N=52)
1 year	86.4%	66.7%	91.7%	69.6%	56.2%	55.8%
2 years	1.0%	0	4.2%	6.5%	14.3%	15.4%
3 years	1.9%	0	0	3.3%	2.9%	3.8%
4 years	0	0	0	0	0	1.9%
5 years	6.8%	4.2%	4.2%	13.0%	22.9%	13.5%
6-10 years	3.9%	29.2%	0	2.2%	1.9%	5.8%
11- years	0	0	0	5.4%	1.9%	3.8%
mean	.806	3.125	.333	3.696	3.638	4.212
median	.079	1.250	.071	.280	.472	.750

Copying by For-Profit Organizations After December 31, 1977

Question 19. Would you be willing to authorize (and to include a printed statement to this effect in each issue) for-profit organizations (other than organizations in the business of making and selling photocopies), open to the public or specialized researchers without limitation or payment to copy articles or to secure copies through interlibrary loan from this journal current year's issues as well as back issues? YES ________ NO ________

Willingness to Permit Unlimited Current and Back Year Copying in For-Profit Organizations

The vast majority of responding copyrighted journals were unwilling to grant such permission. Only 10.4% were willing to permit such carte blanche copying in for-profit organizations while 81.7% objected. The negative reaction was particularly strong among commercial journals, 93.9% of which opposed such authorization, and only 3.0% of which approved. Non-profit journals were somewhat more lenient, but refusals still outnumbered permissions by more than 5 to 1. While no subject discipline countenanced such unlimited copying by for-profit organizations in even 1 out of 6 cases, pure science journals objected particularly, refusing authorization by a margin of more than 16 to 1. Size of journal distribution mattered in responses only for commercial journals, where the larger journals were more willing than the almost unanimous negation by smaller for-profit journals. Even large journals were unwilling, however, by more than 7 to 1.

Question 19. Would you be willing to authorize (and to include a printed statement to this effect in each issue) for-profit organizations (other than organizations in the business of making and selling photocopies), open to the public or specialized researchers without limitation or payment to copy articles or to secure copies through interlibrary loan from this journal current year's issues as well as back issues?

YES ________ NO ________

COPYRIGHTED JOURNALS

	Total Journal Response (N=872)	Type of Publisher: For Profit (N=296)	Non-profit (N=576)	Journals by Subject Breakdown: Pure Science (N=200)	Applied Science (N=238)	Social Science (N=329)	Humanities (N=105)
YES	10.4%	3.0%	14.2%	5.5%	10.5%	12.5%	13.3%
NO	81.7%	93.9%	75.3%	91.0%	81.1%	78.4%	75.2%
No Answer	7.9%	3.1%	10.5%	3.5%	8.4%	9.1%	11.4%

Journals by Size of Circulation

	For Profit 0-2999 (N=173)	3000-9999 (N=44)	10000-max (N=44)	Non-profit 0-2999 (N=237)	3000-9999 (N=213)	10000-max (N=125)
YES	1.7%	2.3%	11.4%	15.2%	12.2%	15.2%
NO	96.0%	93.2%	84.1%	76.8%	76.1%	72.0%
No Answer	2.3%	4.5%	4.5%	8.0%	11.8%	12.8%

Question 20. If your answer to 19 is NO, would you be willing to authorize (and to include a printed statement to this effect in each issue) for-profit organizations(other than organizations in the business of making and selling photocopies), open to the public and specialized researchers to copy articles or to secure copies through interlibrary loan without limitation or payment, from back issues of this journal from earlier years?

YES ________ NO ________

Willingness to Permit Copying of Back Issues by For-Profit Organizations

Journals which had expressed opposition to permitting for-profit organizati to copy current issues without restriction were asked whether they would be willing to allow copying from earlier years. The negative reaction abated somew but only slightly. Only 11.9% of 872 responding journals indicated such a willingness, contrasted to 70.5% which expressed the intention of denying such permission even for earlier years, and 17.5% which did not respond , presumably in part because they had already indicated their willingness in response to question 19, although this category may also include non-respondents for other reasons. In any case, the 70.5% who specifically and categorically refuse back issue unlimited copying permission to for-profit organizations represent a resoundingly negative vote. As with the earlier question, this unwillingness is particularly strong among commercial journals, 86.5% of which were unwilling to grant such permission, while the negative response from the non-profit sector was 62.3%. There was little apparent differentiation by subject discipline, or by size of circulation.

Question 20. If your answer to 19 is NO, would you be willing to authorize (and to include a printed statement to this effect in each issue) for-profit organizations (other than organizations in the business of making and selling photocopies), open to the public and specialized researchers to copy articles or to secure copies through interlibrary loan without limitation or payment, from back issues of this journal from earlier years?

YES ________ NO ________

COPYRIGHTED JOURNALS

	Total Journal Response (N=872)	Type of Publisher		Journals by Subject Breakdown			
		For Profit (N=296)	Non-profit (N=576)	Pure Science (N=200)	Applied Science (N=238)	Social Science (N=329)	Humanities (N=105)
YES	11.9%	9.1%	13.4%	18.0%	10.1%	11.2%	6.7%
NO	70.5%	86.5%	62.3%	75.5%	71.4%	66.9%	70.5%
No Answer	17.5%	4.4%	24.3%	6.5%	18.5%	21.9%	22.8%

Journals by Size of Circulation

	For Profit			Non-profit		
	0-2999 (N=173)	3000-9999 (N=44)	10000-max (N=44)	0-2999 (N=237)	3000-9999 (N=213)	10000-max (N=125)
YES	8.1%	20.5%	9.1%	9.3%	17.4%	14.4%
NO	88.4%	77.3%	79.5%	67.9%	59.2%	57.6%
No Answer	3.5%	2.2%	11.4%	22.8%	23.5%	28.0%

Question 21. If your answer to 20 is YES, what would you consider to be the lapse of time from the publication date of this journal appropriate for permitting the copying by for-profit organizations (other than organizations in the business of making and selling photocopies) of articles without limitation or payment?

________ YEARS.

Appropriate Lapse of Time Before Copying Permission for For-Profit Organizations

Since question 21 was only supposed to be answered by those journals which answered affirmatively to question 20, and only 104 journals fell into this category, the fact that 373 journals answered question 21 indicates that a considerable number of journals wanted to have their wishes recorded in any case. It is therefore surprising, based on the heavy negative response to question 20, that 73.5% of the 373 respondents to question 21 were willing to permit copying by for-profit organizations after a lapse of one year, with only 17.7% of a group which, to a considerable extent had earlier said "never", now insisting on a waiting period of 5 years or more. Even more surprising is the response of commercial journals, most negative with regard to question 20, 83.0% of which are willing to permit copying after one year in response to question 21. However, this willingness is consistent with their attitude toward non-profit organizations. The number insisting on a wait of 5 years or more, by for-profit organizations, is only 13.6%. Pure science journals are least willing to permit copying by commercial organizations, as they are for non-profit organizations, with 62.2% willing to permit such activity after one year, and 33.4% insisting on a delay of five years or more. Analysis by size of journal circulation yields deviations, but no identifiable trends.

Question 21. If your answer to 20 is YES, what would you consider to be the lapse of time from the publication date of this journal appro priate for permitting the copying by for-profit organizations (other than organizations in the business of making and selling photocopies) of articles without limitation or payment?

____________YEARS.

COPYRIGHTED JOURNALS

	Total Publisher Response (N=373)	Type of Publisher		Journals by Subject Breakdown			
		For Profit (N=147)	Non-profit (N=226)	Pure Sciences (N=90)	Applied Sciences (N=104)	Social Sciences (N=144)	Humanities (N=35)
1 year	73.5%	83.0%	67.3%	62.2%	76.0%	75.0%	88.6%
2 years	7.2%	2.0%	10.6%	3.3%	2.9%	12.5%	8.6%
3 years	1.3%	1.4%	1.3%	0	0	3.5%	0
4 years	.3%	0	.4%	1.1%	0	0	0
5 years	11.3%	6.1%	14.6%	27.8%	8.7%	4.9%	2.9%
6-10 years	5.6%	7.5%	4.4%	5.6%	10.6%	3.5%	0
11 and above	.8%	0	1.3%	0	1.9%	.7%	0
mean	1.767	1.143	2.173	1.989	2.202	1.660	.343
median	.199	.107	.274	.318	.167	.192	.083

Question 21. If your answer to 20 is YES, what would you consider to be the lapse of time from the publication date of this journal appropriate for permitting the copying by for-profit organizations (other than organizations in the business of making and selling photocopies) of articles without limitation or payment?

_______________ YEARS

COPYRIGHTED JOURNALS

Journals by Size of Circulation

	For Profit 0-2999 (N=100)	3000-9999 (N=23)	10000-max (N=24)	Non-profit 0-2999 (N=84)	3000-9999 (N=95)	10000-max (N=46)
1 year	86.0%	65.2%	87.5%	75.0%	61.1%	65.2%
2 years	2.0%	0	4.2%	10.7%	11.6%	8.7%
3 years	2.0%	0	0	1.2%	2.1%	0
4 years	0	0	0	0	0	2.2%
5 years	6.0%	4.3%	8.3%	7.1%	21.1%	15.2%
6-10 years	4.0%	30.4%	0	3.6%	3.2%	8.7%
11 and above	0	0	0	2.4%	1.1%	0
mean	.800	3.261	.542	2.405	2.179	1.783
median	.081	1.333	.100	.189	.364	.293

Publisher Questionnaire

Definition of Survey Population
(Also described in Journal Questionnaire)

The population for this survey was drawn from the list of U.S. scholarly and research journals identified by the Indiana University Graduate Library School Research Center in its study on "Economics and Interaction of the Publisher-Library Relationship in the Production and Use of Scholarly and Research Journals", prepared for the National Science Foundation under Grant GN-41398*.

This study, which identified 2459 journals, published by 1634 publishers, defined scholarly and research journals through the exclusion of certain categories of periodicals believed to be inappropriate because the category would not ordinarily contain communications useful for scholarly purposes or would have little economic impact. Journals were therefore excluded if they fell into any of the following categories: 1) newsletters; 2) house organs; 3) general mass audience magazines; 4) popular culture magazines; 5) periodicals intended for a juvenile audience; 6) "little" magazines; 7) reprints;

*A book describing the methodology and conclusions of this study is available as "Publishers and Libraries: A Study of Scholarly and Research Journals", by Bernard M. Fry and Herbert S. White. D.C. Heath & Co., Lexington, Mass. 1976.

8) patents; 9) secondary periodicals or services; 10) periodicals intended for a local audience; 11) trade journals; 12) periodicals not indexed by an indexing or abstracting service except in subject areas in which such services are inadequate, or where the journal began publication after 1970 and might therefore not reasonably be expected to be indexed; 13) processed periodicals; 14) tabloids; 15) free periodicals; 16) government publications; and 17) controlled circulation periodicals. On the advice of statistical consultants, any journal with a circulation above 100,000 was excluded under category 3), because it was felt that data from these journals would hopelessly skew reported information and conclusions.

The initial list, compiled in 1974 through reviews of Current Contents and Ulrich's International Periodicals Directory, was then updated through a review of Ulrich's 16th Edition 1975-76, since Ulrich's lists both cessations and new journal starts. Finally, the list was impacted by the responses of publishers themselves, some of which indicated that journals still listed had actually ceased publication, and some of which called our attention to journals not in our survey for a variety of reasons, including the fact that they were new. These publisher-induced changes to the list of scholarly and research journals were relatively minor. Our survey is ultimately based on potential responses from 1672 publishers, who distribute 2552 scholarly and research journals.

Rate of Response

The overall rate of response as of May 10, 1977, the cut-off date, was 31.8% of the publishers contacted. Moreover, an analysis performed at the Library of Congress and reported elsewhere in this report indicates that the percentage of publishers of copyrighted journals responding was considerably greater than the average. This suggests that at least a portion of the non-response came from publishers of journals who did not feel affected by the implications of the questionnaire, and further indicates that the impact of the trends reported from publisher and journal responses is in fact greater than the percentage response might project, since copyrighted journals, far more directly impacted by changes in the Copyright Law, responded in greater percentages. Some publishers, in fact, replied only to state that, since their material was not copyrighted, they saw no point in responding to other questions, and these responses were not counted. Other publishers who do not copyright did answer the questions and were included. Of the responding publisher groups, for-profit publishers had the lowest rate of response, as expected, and despite the assurance of anonymity. This reluctance was also evidenced in the NSF survey, in which only 13.66% of commercial publishers contacted responded, but which included a wide range of information considered by many to be proprietary. In this survey, which did not request organizational financial data, the rate of response, at 26.6%, is almost twice that of the original NSF survey, and yields what in our judgment are significant patterns. Response rates in the not-for-profit sector were higher, at 32.9%. Since the not-for-profit sector represents 82.2% of the survey population, it represents 85.1% of the responding publisher population. As in the NSF study, not-for-profit publishers were divided into three groups: a) society (if membership is professionally involved in subject areas defined as scholarly or research); b) university press (presses owned and operated by universities); and c) other not-for-profit (university departments, research institutes, and other generally small and scattered scholarly organizations). Among not-for-profit publishers, university presses, at 48.8%, offered the greatest rate of response, again consistent with the NSF study. University presses, a small and cohesive group which maintains close contacts, also demonstrates a high level of awareness of sensitivity to issues which affect the entire community. Societal publishers responded at a rate of 34.1%, and the small scattered "other" sector responded at the lowest rate, 30.0%, probably because small staffs and inadequate records make response to any questionnaire difficult.

Correlation of Survey Population and Response Population

To the extent to which publisher groups replied in percentages above or below the average response rate of all publishers, this affected their impact on questionnaire responses as a whole. For example, university presses, which represented only 2.6% of the survey population, are 4.0% of the response population, because almost half of the surveyed university presses responded. Societal publishers, which were 45.9% of the survey, are almost half, 49.3%, of the responses. By contrast, both commercial publishers and the small other-not-for-profit grouping represent a smaller percentage in the response population than in the initial survey population. Commercial publishers fell from 17.8% of the survey to 14.9% of the response, while the "other" small miscellaneous group dropped from 33.7% to 31.8%.

Although some of these deviations are significant, they do not change the ranking of frequency of response from publisher groups. Societal publishers are also the largest non-responding group, and make up 44.3% of the queried publishers who did not respond. As with responses, other not-for-profit publishers also rank second in non-responses, with commercial publishers third and university presses lowest in both instances.

Publisher Response to Survey

Total Queries N=1672

	Number	Percentage
Responding Publishers	531	31.8%
Non-Responding Publishers	1141	68.2%

	Total in Survey Pop	%of Survey Population	No. Responding	% Response	% of Response Population
For Profit Publishers	297	17.8%	79	26.6%	14.9%
Not-for-profit Publishers	1375	82.2%	452	32.9%	85.1%
a) Societies	768	45.9%	262	34.1%	49.1%
b) University Press	43	2.6%	21	48.8%	4.0%
c) Other NFP Publishers	564	33.7%	169	30.0%	31.8%

	No. not Responding	% of Non-response Population
For Profit Publishers	218	19.1%
Not-for-profit Publishers	923	80.9%
a) Societies	506	44.3%
b) University Press	22	1.9%
c) Other NFP Publisher	395	34.7%

Number of Journals Per Publisher

The overwhelming majority of publishers who responded, 84.6%, distributed only one journal. The five publishers who responded although they do not presently publish a journal considered scholarly or research under the definitions used were included because they now publish similar material, or plan to publish other journals, and because their views are therefore significant to an overall impression of publisher responses. Obviously, these publishers are not reflected in journal questionnaire tabulations. Over 95% of the responding publishers distribute 5 or fewer journals. While this scattering of small and isolated publishers is most prevalent among the "other not-for-profit" sector, it is also surprisingly evident even among commercial publishers.

Of the 966 journals identified in publisher questionnaire response (an additional 8 were submitted in response to only the journal questionnaire), almost half, or 46.5%, are distributed by publishers who publish only that one scholarly journal. Publishers who distribute 5 or fewer journals account for 61.8% of the journals in the survey. If publishers of 20 or more journals are considered as large, this group accounts for 23.8% of the total. If the number for this definition is lowered to 10, large publishers represent 31.7%. It would appear, therefore, that scholarly publishing is generally scattered among individual publishers, with a group of large publishers who would represent perhaps 25% of the total.

The 452 responding not-for-profit publishers distribute 658 journals, for an average of 1.47. Over 87% of the publishers responding publish only one journal, and over 96% publish five or less. Of the 658 journals, 59% are published by organizations which distribute only that one journal, pointing to the heavy concentration of small university departments and research institutes in this group. Publishers who distribute 5 or less journals account for an overwhelming percentage of the total, 75.8%. By contrast publishers of 20 or more journals account for only 10.2% of the total, and this percentage rises only to 15.3% when publishers of 10 or more journals are included.

The 79 for-profit publishers exhibit somewhat differing characteristics. Although even in this group 69.3% of the publishers distribute only one journal, the average number of journals published is 3.90. These single journal pub lishers account for only 18.1% of the commercial journals distributed and less than one third of the not-for-profit group. Similarly, commercial publishers who distribute 5 or less journals account for only 32.2% of the journals pub lished in this field. By contrast with the not-for-profit sector, commercial publishers of 20 or more journals account for 53.6% of the total. Clearly, in the for-profit sector, unlike the not-for-profit sector, publication appears, from our responses, to be more concentrated in a few large publishers.

No. of Journals Per Publisher

Total Response N=531 Publishers

Category Label: No. of journals	No. of Publishers Absolute Frequency	Relative Frequency (Percent)	Cumulative Adj. Freq. (Percent)
* 0	5	.9	.9
1	449	84.6	85.5
2	27	5.1	90.6
3	15	2.8	93.4
4	6	1.1	94.5
5	5	.9	95.5
6	7	1.3	96.8
7	1	.2	97.0
9	1	.2	97.2
10	5	.9	98.1
12	1	.2	98.3
14	1	.2	98.5
20	2	.4	98.9
21	1	.2	99.1
25	1	.2	99.2
27	2	.4	99.6
28	1	.2	99.8
62	1	.2	100.0

*Responses were received from publishers who were sent the questionnaires but who no longer publish a journal considered scholarly or research. These responses were included because of their intention to again publish such journals.

No. of Journals per Publisher
Subfile: Not for Profit N=452 Publishers

Category Label: No. of journals	No. of Publishers Absolute Frequency	Relative Frequency (Percent)	Cumulative Adj. Freq. (Percent)
* 0	4	.9	.9
1	394	87.2	88.1
2	21	4.6	92.7
3	11	2.4	95.1
4	5	1.1	96.2
5	2	.4	96.7
6	7	1.5	98.2
7	1	.2	98.5
9	1	.2	98.7
10	2	.4	99.1
14	1	.2	99.3
20	2	.4	99.8
27	1	.2	100.0

*Responses were received from publishers who were sent the questionnaires but who no longer publish a journal considered scholarly or research. These responses were included because of their intention to again publish such journals.

No. of Journals Per Publisher
Subfile: For Profit N=79 Publishers

Category Label No. of Journals	No. of Publishers Absolute Frequency	Relative Frequency (Percent)	Cumulative Adj. Freq. (Percent)
*0	1	1.3	1.3
1	55	69.3	70.9
2	6	7.6	78.5
3	4	5.1	83.5
4	1	1.3	84.8
5	3	3.8	88.6
10	3	3.8	92.4
12	1	1.3	93.7
21	1	1.3	94.9
25	1	1.3	96.2
27	1	1.3	97.5
28	1	1.3	98.7
62	1	1.3	100.0

*Responses were received from publishers who were sent the questionnaires but who no longer publish a journal considered scholarly or research. These responses were included because of their intention to again publish such journals.

Universal Numbering System for Journal Articles

Question 2. If a universal system of sub-numbers to be added to the International Serial Number (ISSN), which would identify the issue and the individual article (and be printed on the first page of the individual articles) were adopted, to what extent would this in your opinion enable publishers to supply authorized reprints or photocopies at less cost to buyers?

a. Greatly? __________ b. Substantially? __________

c. Minimally? __________ d. Not at all? __________

Only a small percentage of the publishers who responded to the question felt that the use of a universal system of sub-numbers would enable publishers to supply reprints or photocopies at a reduced cost, and this negative re action was consistent with only slight variation among various publisher groups. Only 13.2% of publishers as a whole felt that such a system would help greatly or at least substantially. Not-for-profit publishers were more favorably inclined, to the extent of 13.7%, while commercial publishers were favorably recorded in only 10.2% of the cases. Larger (2 or more journals) not-for-profit publishers were the most favorably inclined, at 22.3%, but larger for-profit publishers were the most negative, with only 8.6% favoring the concept either greatly or substantially.

Question 2. Universal Numbering System for Journal Articles

If a universal system of sub-numbers to be added to the International Serial number (ISSN), which would identify the issue and the individual article (and be printed on the first page of the individual articles) were adopted, to what extent would this in your opinion enable publishers to supply authorized reprints or photocopies at less cost to buyers?

	Total Publisher Response (N=531)	Type of Publisher: For Profit (N=79)	Type of Publisher: Non-profit (N=452)	Publishers by no. of journals published: For profit Less than 2 (N=56)	For profit 2 and more (N=23)	Non-profit Less than 2 (N=398)	Non-profit 2 and more (N=54)
a. Greatly	1.3%	1.3%	1.3%	0.0%	4.3%	1.3%	1.9%
b. Substantially	11.9%	8.9%	12.4%	10.7%	4.3%	11.3%	20.4%
c. Minimally	36.3%	29.1%	37.6%	26.8%	34.8%	36.4%	46.3%
d. Not at al	42.9%	57.0%	40.5%	57.1%	56.5%	42.0%	29.6%
e. No answer	7.6%	3.7%	8.2%	5.4%	0.1%	9.0%	1.8%

Note: See responses to Question 1d in the journal questionnaire.

Question 3. Please rank in order of preference the possible ways of authorizing (licensing) users to copy materials from journals you publish: (Show first choice as '1', second as '2', etc).

a. Directly ________ b. Through an agent __________ c. By delegation to a Clearinghouse or other general agent __________

d. Other (explain) ______________________________________

Preference for Licensing Arrangements

All but 6.6% of the 531 publishers responding to the survey were able to select a first choice from among the three options posed in the questionnaire, with 4.0% electing to write in a different response, and only 2.6% failing to indicate a preference. There was a drop-off after the statement of a first choice, with 26.7% of responding publishers indicating no second choice among the three alternatives stated, and 36.9% having no third choice.

All publishers, regardless of for-profit status or number of journals published, showed an overwhelming preference for direct licensing to the alternatives of using an agent or a clearinghouse or general agent. This preference was particularly strong in the for-profit sector, where 73.4% of the respondents made direct licensing their first choice, and most particularly for small (less than two journals) commercial publishers, who favored this approach in 3 out of 4 responses. However, even the least favorably inclined group, non-profit publishers of two or more journals, preferred this approach in 55.6% of the cases. In all publisher groups the use of a clearinghouse or general agent was preferred as a first choice by remaining responders, by a margin exceeding 2 to 1 for small publishers and more than 3 to 1 and more than 4 to 1 for large non-profit and commercial publishers, respectively. However, the selection of a second choice of those preferring to license directly was not as clear, with non-profit publishers in this group preferring an agent to a clearinghouse, and commercial publishers equally divided. Larger publishers, in both the commercial and non-profit sectors, preferred agents to clearinghouses as their second choice to a greater extent than small publishers. Clearly, however, all publishers show a consistent preference for direct licensing over any of the other alternatives presented.

It should be noted that responses to this questionnaire were received before the Association of American Publishers developed and publicized its program for the implementation of a copyright clearinghouse. Publishers who reacted to the concept of a clearinghouse were therefore reacting to what was still only an undefined concept, and it is probable that the development of a specific proposal will have sharpened reactions, and perhaps substantially increased approval.

Responses to this question were subject to some ambiguity, since there was no opportunity for respondents to indicate that they did not desire to enter into any licensing agreement at all, either because they did not copy right their journals or because they considered any formal licensing arrange ment as too cumbersome. This difficulty is reflected in the theme of a large number of comments, although even these publishers decided, in most cases, to respond to the question.

Question 3. Licensing.

Please rank in order of preference the possible ways of authorizing (licensing) users to copy materials from journals you publish: (Show first choice as '1', second as '2', etc.).

	Total Publisher Response N=531				
	First	Second	Third	Fourth	Unranked
a. Directly	68.7%	8.1%	14.9%	.6%	7.7%
b. Through an agent	7.0%	37.5%	25.6%	.4%	29.6%
c. Clearinghouse or other general agent	17.7%	27.7%	22.6%	1.1%	30.9%
d. Other	4.0%	1.1%	.2%	58.8%	36.0%
e. No choice	2.6%	25.6%	36.7%	39.1%	

	For Profit Publishers N=79				
	First	Second	Third	Fourth	Unranked
a. Directly	73.4%	6.3%	10.1%	1.3%	8.9%
b. Through an agent	6.3%	30.4%	20.3%	0	43.0%
c. Clearinghouse or other general agent	15.2%	30.4%	17.7%	1.3%	35.4%
d. Other	2.5%	2.5%	0	43.0%	51.9%
e. No choice	2.6%	30.4%	51.9%	54.4%	

	Non-profit Publishers N=452				
	First	Second	Third	Fourth	Unranked
a. Directly	67.9%	8.4%	15.7%	.4%	7.5%
b. Through an agent	7.1%	38.7%	26.5%	.4%	27.2%
c. Clearinghouse or other general agent	18.1%	27.2%	23.5%	1.1%	30.1%
d. Other	4.2%	.9%	.2%	61.5%	33.2%
e. No choice	2.7%	24.8%	34.1%	36.6%	

Question 3.
Please rank in order of preference the possible ways of authorizing (licensing) users to copy materials from journals you publish: (Show first choice as '1', second as '2', etc.).

	For Profit, Less than 2 journals N=56				
	First	Second	Third	Fourth	Unranked
a. Directly	75.0%	5.4%	7.1%	0	12.5%
b. Through an agent	7.1%	28.6%	16.1%	0	48.2%
c. Clearinghouse or other general agent	14.3%	30.4%	16.1%	0	39.3%
d. Other	0	1.8%	0	37.5%	60.7%
e. No choice	3.6%	33.8%	60.7%	62.5%	

	For Profit, 2 or more journals N=23				
	First	Second	Third	Fourth	Unranked
a. Directly	69.6%	8.7%	17.4%	4.3%	0
b. Through an agent	4.3%	34.8%	30.4%	0	26.1%
c. Clearinghouse or other general agent	17.4%	30.4%	21.7%	4.3%	26.1%
d. Other	8.7%	4.3%	0	56.5%	30.4%
e. No choice	0	21.8%	30.5%	34.9%	

	Non-profit, Less than 2 journals N=398				
	First	Second	Third	Fourth	Unranked
a. Directly	69.6%	8.0%	14.1%	.3%	8.0%
b. Through an agent	6.8%	38.2%	26.4%	.3%	28.4%
c. Clearinghouse or other general agent	16.1%	27.1%	23.9%	1.3%	31.7%
d. Other	4.5%	.8%	0	60.1%	0
e. No choice	3.0%	25.9%	35.6%	38.0%	

Question 3.

Please rank in order of preference the possible ways of authorizing (licensing) users to copy materials from journals you publish: (Show first choice as '1', second as '2', etc.).

	Non-profit, 2 or more journals N=54				
	First	Second	Third	Fourth	Unranked
a. Directly	55.6%	11.1%	27.8%	1.9%	3.7%
b. Through an agent	9.3%	42.6%	27.8%	1.9%	18.5%
c. Clearinghouse or other general agent	33.3%	27.8%	20.4%	0	18.5%
d. Other	1.8%	1.9%	1.9%	72.2%	22.2%
e. No choice	0	16.6%	22.1%	24.0%	

Question 4. Please rank in order of your preference the following possible ways of selling copies of articles from your journals, adding in the space provided any other means you wish to suggest (Show first choice as '1', second '2', etc.)

a. Supply directly by publisher ___________ b. Supply through an agent _________ c. Supply through a clearinghouse or periodical bank or other general agent ____________________ d. Other (explain) ______________________________

Supplying Authorized Copies

All but 8.5% of the 531 responding publishers were able to select a first choice from among the three alternatives suggested. As with licensing preferences, direct supply of authorized copies was by far the most popular choice, although some of the comments raised the concern that some of these publishers intend to distribute copies only in bulk orders (such as to authors) and not in response to individual single copy requests most freq uently favored by libraries.

While favored by all publishers, direct supply of authorized copies is particularly preferred by commercial publishers, 70.9% of which expressed this as their first choice, and even more particularly small commercial pub lishers, who selected direct supply in 3 out of 4 cases. Larger not-for-profit publishers are the only group for which direct supply, at 42.6%, does not represent a majority choice, although it is the choice most frequently named. For these publishers the use of a clearinghouse ranked a close second, at 38.9%. However, while the use of a clearinghouse or general agent is the second most frequently named preference for both profit and non-profit publishers, it is less popular in the commercial sector, where this alternative was the first choice in only 15.2% of the cases, than in the non-profit sector, where it is the first choice in 19.9% of the cases. Moreover, when it comes to listing second choices, publishers who largely preferred to deal directly were quite negative to the use of a clearinghouse, and preferred the use of agents as a second alternative.

It must be pointed out, as with the response to the question concerning licensing, that this questionnaire pre-dated the development of a specific copyright clearinghouse proposal by the Association of American Publishers. Respondents were still reacting to an abstract concept, and it is probable that, confronted by a specific proposal, responding publishers would react more definitively, and perhaps more positively.

This question posed similar difficulties to the problems raised in the licensing question, in that it provided no opportunity for publishers to indicate either that they had no interest in selling copies from their articles at all, or that they had no interest in even supplying any, with or without charge. This concern was addressed in a number of the comments, although even these publishers tended to respond to the questionnaire. A number of publishers, for example, leave all secondary distribution to the author. Others, particularly those which do not presently copyright, don't care where copies are obtained, as long as they are not involved. Still another group differentiated between current and back copies, a distinction which the wording of the question did not permit the respondents to make. Finally, some publishers distribute, and intend to distribute, only in bulk quantities (such as to authors) and not in response to the individual single copy requests typical of library requirements.

Question 4. Supplying Authorized Copies

Please rank in order of your preference the following possible ways of selling copies of articles from your journals, adding in the space provided any other means you wish to suggest (Show first choice as '1', second '2', etc.).

	Total Publisher Response N=531				
	First	Second	Third	Fourth	Unranked
a. Directly	60.6%	8.5%	19.4%	.8%	10.7%
b. Through an agent	11.7%	38.0%	24.3%	.4%	25.6%
c. Clearinghouse or other general agent	19.2%	29.4%	21.5%	.9%	29.0%
d. Other	4.9%	1.3%	.2%	60.1%	33.5%
e. No choice	3.6%	21.8%	34.6%	37.8%	

	For Profit Publishers N=79				
	First	Second	Third	Fourth	Unranked
a. Directly	70.9%	6.3%	17.7%	0	5.1%
b. Through an agent	10.1%	36.7%	16.5%	0	36.7%
c. Clearinghouse or other general agent	15.2%	26.6%	20.3%	1.3%	36.7%
d. Other	2.5%	1.3%	0	49.4%	46.8%
e. No choice	11.3%	29.1%	45.5%	49.3%	

	Non-profit Publishers N=452				
	First	Second	Third	Fourth	Unranked
a. Directly	58.8%	8.8%	19.7%	.9%	11.7%
b. Through an agent	11.9%	38.3%	25.7%	.4%	23.7%
c. Clearinghouse or other general agent	19.9%	29.9%	21.7%	.9%	27.7%
d. Other	5.3%	1.3%	.2%	61.9%	31.2%
e. No choice	4.1%	21.7%	32.7%	35.9%	

Question 4.

Please rank in order of your preference the following possible ways of selling copies of articles from your journals, adding in the space provided any other means you wish to suggest (Show first choice as '1', second '2', etc.).

For profit, Less than 2 journals N=56					
	First	Second	Third	Fourth	Unranked
a. Directly	75.0%	5.4%	12.5%	0	7.1%
b. Through an agent	7.1%	35.7%	16.1%	0	41.1%
c. Clearinghouse or other general agent	16.1%	23.2%	17.9%	0	42.9%
d. Other	0	0	0	42.9%	57.1%
e. No choice	1.8%	35.7%	53.5%	57.1%	

For profit, 2 or more journals N=23					
	First	Second	Third	Fourth	Unranked
a. Directly	60.9%	8.7%	30.4%	0	0
b. Through an agent	17.4%	39.1%	17.4%	0	26.1%
c. Clearinghouse or other general agent	13.0%	34.8%	26.1%	4.3%	21.7%
d. Other	8.7%	4.3%	0	65.2%	21.7%
e. No choice	0	13.1%	26.1%	30.5%	

Non-profit, Less than 2 journals N=398					
	First	Second	Third	Fourth	Unranked
a. Directly	61.1%	8.3%	17.3%	.1%	12.6%
b. Through an agent	11.8%	37.4%	25.1%	.5%	25.1%
c. Clearinghouse or other general agent	17.3%	29.6%	22.9%	1.0%	29.1%
d. Other	5.5%	1.5%	0	60.3%	32.7%
e. No choice	4.3%	23.2%	34.7%	37.4%	

Question 4.

Please rank in order of your preference the following possible ways of selling copies of articles from your journals, adding in the space provided any other means you wish to suggest (Show first choice as '1', second '2', etc.).

	Non-profit, 2 or more journals N=54				
	First	Second	Third	Fourth	Unranked
a. Directly	42.6%	13.0%	37.0%	1.9%	5.6%
b. Through an agent	13.0%	44.4%	29.6%	0	13.0%
c. Clearinghouse or other general agent	38.9%	31.5%	13.0%	0	16.7%
d. Other	3.7%	0	1.9%	74.1%	20.4%
e. No choice	1.8%	11.1%	18.5%	24.0%	

Question 5. If you do not now sell reprints or authorized photocopies on a regular basis, what speed of service do you anticipate you (not your agent) would be able to give in supplying reprints or authorized photocopies from receipt of an order to dispatch of copies? Number of days ____________.

Speed of Service in the Sale of Reprints or Photocopies

The 322 publishers who responded indicated that they would be able to supply copies in a mean of 12.07 days, and a median 7.13 days. The mean is substantially larger because 13.4% of responding publishers indicated that such service would take in excess of 26 days, and 1.9% in excess of two months. For these reasons, the median is considered the more significant statistic, although it does cause a concern that publishers taking 4 weeks and longer could effectively negate the usefulness of such a system. In general, mean responses varied little between commercial and non-profit publishers, and between large and small publishers. With the use of medians, large commercial publishers are the most receptive, with a promised median response of 5.5 days. Larger non-profit publishers were the second most rapid group, with a median response of 7 days. Small publishers were slower, and small commercial publishers slowest of all.

The wording of the question did not allow a distinction between those of the 209 non-responding publishers who did not respond to the question (as instructed) because they presently do sell reprints, and those who simply chose not to answer the question although they were asked to respond, as non-sellers of reprints. Moreover, it is not possible to determine if any publishers who do sell reprints, and were asked to skip this question, answered it anyway.

A further caution must also be introduced. Some publishers indicated in their comments that, in their willingness to supply reprints and photocopies, they were not talking about individual single orders which libraries can be assumed to generate. They were discussing only orders for minimum quantities, which were not defined, but which could be assumed to be at least 5 or 10 copies, and therefore impractical for libraries. In some cases they even specified a minimum of 100 copies, or indicated that they supply exclusively to authors. The wording of the questionnaire did not permit this distinction to be made.

Question 5.

If you do not now sell reprints or authorized photocopies on a regular basis, what speed of service do you anticipate you (not your agent) would be able to give in supplying reprints or authorized photocopies from receipt of an order to dispatch of copies? Number of days________________.

	Total Publisher Responses (N=322)	Type of Publisher		Publishers by no. of journals published			
		For Profit (N=43)	Non-profit (N=279)	For Profit Less than 2 (N=31)	For Profit 2 and more (N=12)	Non-profit Less than 2 (N=241)	Non-profit 2 and more (N=38)
0-5 days	42.5%	34.9%	43.7%	29.1%	50.0%	44.4%	39.5%
6-10 days	27.3%	34.9%	26.1%	42.0%	16.7%	25.7%	29.0%
11-25 days	16.8%	23.3%	15.9%	22.5%	25.0%	15.8%	15.8%
26-60 days	11.5%	4.7%	12.5%	3.2%	8.3%	12.4%	13.1%
61-99 days	1.9%	2.2%	1.8%	3.2%	--	1.7%	2.6%
mean	12.068	12.023	12.075	11.935	12.250	11.929	13.000
mode	5.000	10.000	5.000	10.000	1.000	5.000	5.000
median	7.125	9.727	6.982	9.850	5.500	6.979	7.000

Note: Percentages adjusted for missing cases.

Question 6. Do you have a teletype installation so that orders for reprints or copies might be received by teletype? YES ________ NO ______

Question 7. If you do not have a teletype for receipt of orders, would you be willing to install a teletype for this purpose? YES _____ NO ______

Use of Teletype Equipment

Only 5.8% of the overall publisher responses indicate the availability of teletype equipment, undoubtedly because of the prevalence of small single-journal publishers, particularly in the non-profit sector. Only large commercial publishers report the existence of such equipment to any appreciable extent, with 43.5% indicating that such equipment is available for copy ordering in their organizations. No other publisher group remotely approaches this percentage, with large non-profit publishers second at a distant 13%.

Publishers were asked to indicate, if they do not have teletype equipment at present, whether they would be willing to install it for this purpose. Since the 9.2% non-response to this question exceeds the 5.8% who answered the previous question affirmatively (and were therefore asked not to respond) and the 1.3% which did not answer the previous question at all, the non-response to this question includes at least some publishers who did indicate in the earlier question that they did not have teletype equipment, but who simply did not choose to speculate as to whether or not they would obtain it. Moreover, it is not possible to determine without considerable analysis whether any publishers who had responded affirmatively to the previous question answered this one improperly.

In any case, response was resoundingly negative. Only 3.6% of responding publishers indicated a willingness to install teletype equipment specifically or primarily for the purpose of receiving orders. What positive response there was came from large non-profit publishers, 14.8% of whom expressed the willingness to install such equipment. By contrast, no large commercial publishers who do not already have teletype equipment indicated that they were prepared to install it to receive orders.

Question 6.

Do you have a teletype installation so that orders for reprints or copies might be received by teletype? YES_____ NO_____

	Total Publisher Response (N=531)	Type of Publisher: For Profit (N=79)	Non-profit (N=452)	Publisher by no. of journals published: For profit Less than 2 (N=56)	For profit 2 or more (N=23)	Non-profit Less than 2 (N=398)	Non-profit 2 or more (N=54)
Yes	5.8%	17.7%	3.8%	7.1%	43.5%	2.5%	13.0%
No	92.9%	81.0%	94.9%	91.1%	56.5%	96.2%	85.1%
No answer	1.3%	1.3%	1.3%	1.8%	0	1.3%	1.9%

Question 7.

If you do not have a teletype for receipt of orders, would you be willing to install a teletype for this purpose? YES_____ NO_____

	Total Publisher Response (N=531)	Type of Publisher: For Profit (N=79)	Non-profit (N=452)	Publisher by no. of journals published: For profit Less than 2 (N=56)	For profit 2 or more (N=23)	Non-profit Less than 2 (N=398)	Non-profit 2 or more (N=54)
Yes	3.6%	2.5%	3.8%	3.6%	0	2.3%	14.8%
No	87.2%	75.9%	89.2%	82.1%	60.9%	92.0%	68.5%
No answer	9.2%	21.6%	7.0%	14.3%	39.1%	5.7%	16.7%

Question 8. Do you now or would you be willing to take telephone orders for reprints or authorized photocopies

a. For the standard charge? ____________

b. For an extra charge? __________

Acceptance of Telephone Orders

Of the 68% of publishers in the entire response population who expressed a willingness to accept telephone orders, more than 3/4 expressed their read iness to accept orders via telephone for a standard charge, with commercial publishers particularly willing, by more than 10 to 1. Non-profit publishers were far more conservative, accepting such an arrangement by a margin of 3 to 1, and large non-profit publishers were almost equally divided between those who would accept telephone orders at the standard charge, and those who would impose an extra charge.

This question shares the problem of a number of previous questions, in that it does not permit differentiation between those who chose not to answer the question because of an unwillingness to accept telephone orders under any circumstances, and those who simply chose not to answer the question. Moreover, appended comments indicate that a number of publishers who do not accept telephone orders answered the question, and these comments state some of the conditions under which orders might be accepted, including both pre-payment and established deposit accounts. Other publishers will accept telephone orders, but only for bulk quantities, and still others will only respond to requests from the author. Since these differentiations could not be statistically recorded, care in the use of the numerical conclusions must be taken.

Question 8.

Do you now or would you be willing to take telephone orders for reprints or unauthorized photocopies

a. For the standard charge? ___________

b. For an extra charge? ___________

	Total	Type of Publisher		Publisher by no. of journals published			
	Publisher Response (N=531)	For profit (N=79)	Non-profit (N=452)	For profit Less than 2 (N=56)	For profit 2 or more (N=23)	Non-profit Less than 2 (N=398)	Non-profit 2 or more (N=54)
a. Standard Charge	52.9%	58.2%	52.0%	58.9%	56.5%	53.5%	40.7%
b. Extra Charge	15.1%	5.1%	16.8%	3.6%	8.7%	14.3%	35.2%
No and No answer	32.0%	36.7%	31.2%	37.5%	34.8%	32.2%	24.1%

Question 9. Do you anticipate that some form of electronic communication other than teletype might be more effective for the electronic receipt of orders?

YES ___________ NO ___________

Anticipation of Electronic Equipment Other than Teletype

Relatively few publishers (about 1/5 of those responding) anticipated that such equipment would be useful. For profit publishers were the most positive in their responses, with 39.1% of large commercial publishers foreseeing such a development. By contrast, small publishers were strikingly more negative. This may have been because they did not envisage the usefulness of such equipment to small operations such as their own, or because they simply were not sufficiently familiar with the characteristics of such equipment. Since no time frame was specified in the question, it is probable that most respondents considered the question in terms of presently developed and commercially available electronic communication equipment.

Question 9.

Do you anticipate that some form of electronic communication other than teletype might be more effective for the electronic receipt of orders?

	Total Publisher Response (N=531)	Type of Publisher		Publisher by no. of journals published			
		For profit (N=79)	Non-profit (N=452)	For profit Less than 2 (N=56)	For profit 2 or more (N=23)	Non-profit Less than 2 (N=398)	Non-profit 2 or more (N=54)
Yes	15.8%	20.3%	15.0%	12.5%	39.1%	13.1%	29.6%
No	61.6%	62.0%	61.5%	62.5%	60.9%	63.3%	48.1%
No answer	22.6%	17.7%	23.5%	25.0%	0	23.6%	22.3%

Question 10. What do you believe to be the most practical method of payment to you by your customers for reprints or authorized copies for journal articles; that is, the methods you think you would accept if you begin providing copies directly? (Please check each method acceptable to you).

a. Check with orders ________

b. Deposit account ________

c. Billing each individual order ________

d. Open account with larger customers ________

e. Stamps or coupons sold in advance ________

f. Other, specify ________________________

Evaluation of Payment Methods

Since multiple choices were possible (and did not require ranking) the responses exceeded 100%. Check with order was far and away the preferred method of payment. It is not surprising that over 86% of all publishers and over 92% of commercial publishers found such a method acceptable, since payment is received before fulfillment of the order. Billing individual orders was the second choice with all publisher groups, with 45.4% of responding publishers finding this method acceptable, and only large non-profit publishers indicating any degree of resistance. It should be noted that the question did not require indication of any minimum billing, and it is possible that at least some publishers anticipate a minimum charge, regardless of size of orders, which might negate the practicality of individual library requests.

Open accounts with large customers and the use of deposit accounts, which are similar practices which tend to differ only in the timing of pay ment, were acceptable to about 20% of the publishers, with for-profit pub lishers, particularly large for-profit publishers, finding this approach ac ceptable. Small non-profit publishers favor this approach in only 18.9% and 13.6% of responses, respectively, presumably because they don't really en visage having large volume customers. The use of stamps and coupons did not draw strong support, particularly not from small publishers. Only large pub lishers show any acceptance of this approach, with 26.1% of commercial and 20.4% of non-profit publishers finding it acceptable.

Question 10.

What do you believe to be the most practical method of payment to you by your customers for reprints or authorized copies for journal articles; that is the methods you think you would accept if you begin providing copies directly? (Please check each method acceptable to you).

a. Check with orders ______ b. Deposit account ______ c. Billing each individual order ______ d. Open account with larger customers ______

e. Stamps or coupons sold in advance ______ f. Other, specify ______

	Total Publisher Response (N=531)	Type of Publisher: For profit (N=79)	Type of Publisher: Non-profit (N=452)	Publisher by no. of journals published: For profit Less than 2 (N=56)	For profit 2 or more (N=23)	Non-profit Less than 2 (N=398)	Non-profit 2 or more (N=54)
a. Check with orders	86.3%	92.4%	85.2%	91.1%	95.7%	84.9%	87.9%
b. Deposit account	18.1%	25.3%	16.8%	17.9%	43.5%	13.6%	40.7%
c. Billing each individual order	45.4%	40.5%	46.2%	37.5%	47.8%	48.5%	29.6%
d. Open account with larger customers	21.7%	29.1%	20.4%	28.5%	30.4%	18.9%	31.5%
e. Stamps or coupons sold in advance	7.0%	10.1%	6.4%	3.6%	26.1%	4.5%	20.4%
f. Other	4.0%	1.3%	4.2%	1.8%	4.3%	3.8%	7.4%

Question 11. If you do not sell reprints or authorized photocopies of articles from your journals directly or through an agent, are you seriously considering doing so? YES ________ NO ________

Willingness to Consider Sale of Reprints or Photocopies Through an Agent

Of the 231 publishers who responded, about three fourths stated an unwillingness to consider sale, either direct or through an agent. Commercial publishers, particularly large commercial publishers, were more willing to consider the practice, but even in this group a majority of responders were negatively inclined. For small non-profit publishers, the negative reactions outnumbered the positive ones by more than 5 to 1.

Difficulties similar to those encountered with other questions were caused by the wording. Publishers were asked to respond only if they did not presently sell reprints or photocopies, and the failure of 56.5% to respond may indicate that they already sell directly or through an agent, or simply a failure to answer the question for other reasons.

Question 11.

If you do not sell reprints or authorized photocopies of articles from your journals directly or through an agent, are you seriously considering doing so?

	Total Publisher Response (N=531)	Type of Publisher		Publisher by no. of journals published			
		For profit (N=79)	Non-profit (N=452)	For profit Less than 2 (N=56)	For profit 2 or more (N=23)	Non-profit Less than 2 (N=398)	Non-profit 2 or more (N=54)
Yes	8.7%	15.2%	7.5%	14.3%	17.4%	7.0%	11.1%
No	34.8%	20.3%	37.4%	19.6%	21.7%	37.2%	38.9%
No answer	56.5%	64.5%	55.1%	66.1%	60.9%	55.8%	50.0%

APPENDIX

Publisher Questionnaire:

NATIONAL COMMISSION ON NEW TECHNOLOGICAL USES OF COPYRIGHTED WORKS (CONTU)

Tel: (202) 557-0996 Washington, D.C. 20558

SURVEY ON JOURNAL COPYING
BASIC (PUBLISHER) QUESTIONNAIRE

Name of Publisher ______________________

Address of Publisher ______________________

____

____

For Profit Publisher ____

Non-Profit Publisher ____

Person Supplying Information ______________________
NAME
____
TITLE
____
TELEPHONE NUMBER

Instructions.

Please return this questionnaire when completed and the individual journal questionnaires using the enclosed government franked mailing label addressed to the Graduate Library School Research Center, Indiana University, Bloomington, Indiana 47401. If corrections in the name and address of the publisher are required, please insert them.

Explanatory comments are welcome.

The questions in this basic questionnaire relate to the publisher. Questions on the supplementary form pertain to individual journals. Fill out one supplementary form for each journal you publish which has been selected for inclusion in this survey and listed in List A.

1. Attach a copy of List A, your journal(s) selected for this survey, and check those for which you are supplying information in the supplementary questionaire.

Universal Numbering System for Journal Articles

2. If a universal system of sub-numbers to be added to the International Serial Number (ISSN), which would identify the issue and the individual article (and be printed on the first page of the individual articles) were adopted, to what extent would this in your opinion enable publishers

to supply authorized reprints or photocopies at less cost to buyers?

a. Greatly? ______ b. Substantially? ______ c. Minimally? ______

d. Not at all? ______

Licensing

3. Please rank in order of preference the possible ways of authorizing (licensing) users to copy materials from journals you publish: (Show first choice as '1', second as '2', etc).

	Rank	Comment (Optional)
a. Directly	____	____________
b. Through an agent	____	____________
c. By delegation to a Clearinghouse or other general agent	____	____________
d. Other (explain) ____________	____	

Supplying Authorized Copies

4. Please rank in order of your preference the following possible ways of selling copies of articles from your journals, adding in the space provided any other means you wish to suggest (Show first choice as '1', second '2', etc.)

	Rank	Comment (Optional)
a. Supply directly by publisher	____	____________
b. Supply through an agent	____	____________
c. Supply through a clearinghouse or periodical bank or other general agent	____	____________
d. Other (explain) ____________	____	____________

5. If you do not now sell reprints or authorized photocopies on a regular basis, what speed of service do you anticipate you (not your agent) would be able to give in supplying reprints or authorized photocopies from receipt of an order to dispatch of copies? Number of days ______.

6. Do you have a teletype installation so that orders for reprints or copies might be received by teletype? YES ______ NO ______

7. If you do not have a teletype for receipt of orders, would you be willing to install a teletype for this purpose? YES ______ NO ______

8. Do you now or would you be willing to take telephone orders for reprints or authorized photocopies

   a. For the standard charge? ______

   b. For an extra charge? ______

9. Do you anticipate that some form of electronic communication other than teletype might be more effective for the electronic receipt of orders?

   YES ________ NO________

10. What do you believe to be the most practical method of payment to you by your customers for reprints or authorized copies for journal articles; that is the methods you think you would accept if you began providing copies directly? (Please check each method acceptable to you).

    a. Check with orders ________

    b. Deposit account ________

    c. Billing each individual order ________

    d. Open account with larger customers ________

    e. Stamps or coupons sold in advance ________

    f. Other, specify ____________________________

11. If you do not sell reprints or authorized photocopies of articles from your journals directly or through an agent, are you seriously considering doing so? YES ________ NO________

Journal Questionnaire:

NATIONAL COMMISSION ON NEW TECHNOLOGICAL USES OF COPYRIGHTED WORKS
(CONTU)

Tel: (202) 557-0996 Washington, D.C. 20558

____
(Title of Journal)

____
(Name of Publisher)

SUPPLEMENTARY FORM FOR EACH INDIVIDUAL JOURNAL
LISTED FOR THIS PUBLISHER IN LIST A

(please return this questionnaire using the enclosed government franked mailing label addressed to the Graduate Library School Research Center, Indiana University, Bloomington, Indiana 47401).

Instructions

The following information is sought in reference to each individual journal you publish which is included in List A of this survey. Please fill out one form for each such journal. Your answer to certain questions after question 1 may be the same for all of your journals. If this is the case you may, if you wish answer these questions for one journal and mark this questionnaire as "Journal A" and then enter after these questions for your other journals "Same as Journal A".

Journal Description

1 a. What is the publication frequency? ________ times per year

b. Circulation as of January, 1977

(1) Total ________ copies per issue

(2) Outside U.S. _________ copies per issue

(3) 'Special' subscription(s) ________ copies per issue
(Please report here only subscriptions, either in hard copy or microform, which include some authorization to copy greater than that for regular subscriptions).

c. Total circulation as of January, 1972: _________ copies per issue

d. International Standard Serial Number (ISSN) ______________________
(Enter the ISSN only if the ISSN is printed in each issue of the journal itself).

2 a. Do you copyright each issue of this journal? YES ________ NO _____

b. Are individual articles in this journal copyrighted by the authors or others?

None_____; Few _____; Some _____; Many _____

3. Page charges

a. Not employed ________

b. Required __________

c. Employed but not mandatory ________

Present Sales of Reprints or Authorized Photocopies

4. Do you now sell directly or through an authorized agent reprints or authorized photocopies of articles from this journal? If you do not sell copies directly or through an agent skip to question 10 after answering this question.

a. Directly YES ________ NO ________

b. Through an authorized agent YES ________ NO ________

c. Name of authorized agent(s) ________________________________

5. If so, for how many years back do you or your agent sell reprints or authorized copies for this journal? Back to ________
year

6. What was the starting date of publication of this journal? ________
year

7. If reprints or authorized photocopies are regularly sold, what is the price you charge or your authorized agent charges, including postage, for an article of up to ten pages from this journal?
a. For United States order with accompanying payment $________

b. For foreign order with accompanying payment $________

c. For United States order with bill required $________

d. For foreign order with bill required $________

8. How many reprints or authorized photocopies of articles did you sell from this journal in your last calendar or fiscal year?
________ copies of articles.

9. What speed of service do you (or your agent) give in dispatching reprints or authorized photocopies from receipt of order to dispatch of copies?
Average number of days ________.

10. If you authorized photocopying on the basis of individual permission requests, please attach a copy of your fee schedule.

a. Fee schedule attached ________

b. Fee schedule not attached (no fixed or standard schedule) ________

If Reprints or Authorized Photocopies Not Now Supplied

11. If you do not supply authorized reprints or photocopies from this journal what would you consider a fair price, for an authorized copy or reprint of an article of up to ten pages which you would supply from this journal, including postage?

a. For United States order with accompanying payment $ ________

b. For foreign order with accompanying payment $ ________

c. For United States order with bill required $ ________

d. For foreign order with bill required $ ________

12. If authorized copies were supplied by an agent or a clearinghouse, what would you consider an appropriate payment to you for each copy of an article of up to ten pages from this journal? $ ________

13. If you would wish to license directly (or through an agent or clearinghouse) individual user organizations to make photocopies of articles from your journals rather than selling reprints or authorized copies directly or through an agent, what would you consider to be a fair license payment to you for each copy of an article of up to ten pages from this journal?

$ ________

MICROFORMS

14. Do you sell directly or through an agent(s) microform versions of this journal?

a. Directly ________ Through an agent(s) ________

b. Current issues Yes ________ No ________

c. Yearly volumes of back issues Yes ________ No ________

15. If you sell microform editions of this journal, do you authorize copying without further payment, of articles from these microform editions?

a. Current year issues Yes ________ No ________

b. Back year issues Yes ________ No ________

Copying by Non-Profit Libraries After December 31, 1977

(The questions in this and the following section are asked in order to find out from the publishers side, whether there are any significant number of journals the publishers of which do not, for one reason or another, expect at this time to bother with the collection of copying fees or selling reprints or authorized photocopies, after the new copyright act comes into effect on January 1, 1978. An announced policy of permitting certain copying could, of course, be changed at any time with respect to future issues. Your present indication is, of course, in no way binding and will not be publicized in identifying form.)

16 Would you be willing to authorize (and to include a printed statement to this effect in each issue) nonprofit libraries[1] open to the public and specialized researchers to copy articles or to secure copies through interlibrary loan from this journal, without limitation or payment, current year's issues as well as back issues?

YES ________ NO ________

17. If your answer to 20 is NO, would you be willing to authorize (and to include a printed statement to the effect in each issue) nonprofit libraries[1] open to the public and specialized researchers to copy articles from this journal or to secure copies through interlibrary loan without limitation or payment from earlier years?

YES ________ NO ________

18. If your answer to 17 is YES, what would you consider to be the lapse of time from publication date of the journal appropriate for permitting copying by nonprofit libraries of articles without limitation or payment?

________ YEARS.

Copying by For-Profit Organizations After December 31, 1977

19. Would you be willing to authorize (and to include a printed statement to this effect in each issue) for-profit organizations (other than organizations in the business of making and selling photocopies), open to the public or specialized researchers without limitation or payment to copy articles or to secure copies through interlibrary loan from this journal current year's issues as well as back issues?

YES ________ NO________

20. If your answer to 19 is NO, would you be willing to authorize (and to include a printed statement to this effect in each issue) for-profit organizations (other than organizations in the business of making and selling photocopies), open to the public and specialized researchers to copy articles or to secure copies through interlibrary loan without limitation or payment, from back issues of this journal from earlier years?

YES ________ NO________

21. If your answer to 20 is YES, what would you consider to be the lapse of time from the publication date of this journal appropriate for permitting the copying by for-profit organizations (other than organizations in the business of making and selling photocopies) of articles without limitation or payment? ____________________YEARS.

---

[1] Including public libraries, school libraries, academic libraries and special libraries of foundations, government agencies and other not-for-profit organizations.

CONTU Memo:

NATIONAL COMMISSION ON NEW TECHNOLOGICAL USES OF COPYRIGHTED WORKS (CONTU)

Tel: (202) 557-0996 Washington, D.C. 20558

February 15, 1977

TO: Publishers of some 2600 U. S. Scientific, Technical, Professional and Scholarly Journals.

SUBJECT: Survey of Publishers' Practices and Present Attitudes on Authorized Journal Article Copying and Licensing

The National Commission on New Technological Uses of Copyrighted Works (CONTU) has asked the Graduate Library School, Indiana University, Bloomington, Indiana, to develop information not heretofore available on publishers' practices in providing copies of journal articles, and on publishers' present attitudes toward alternative ways of supplying or licensing copies. Participation in the Indiana University survey by publishers of journals will contribute to developing an equitable means for providing access to copyrighted journal works with appropriate recognition and/or compensation to the copyright owners.

Background Information

As you may know, this Commission was established by Public Law 93-473 to study and collect data on the problems of (1) computer use of copyrighted works, and (2) photocopying of copyrighted works, and to make recommendations on these two subjects not later than December 31, 1977. These recommendations are to deal with "such changes in copyright law or procedures that may be necessary to assure.... access to copyrighted works, and to provide recognition of the rights of copyright owners".

The Congress has recently passed and the President has signed a new copyright act - Public Law 94-553 - which comes into effect on January 1, 1978. The new law imposes copyright liability for certain copying of periodical articles. Part of the assignment to the Commission is to make recommendations to the President and the Congress as to copyright procedures to facilitate the effective operation of the photocopying provisions of the new statute for those desiring to copy or to secure authorized copies when the permission of the copyright proprietor is required. The Commission is also authorized to recommend further changes in the copyright law.

Possibilities for Supplying Copying

In the discussions between copyright proprietors and copyright users over the last several years, various methods of providing authorization to copy or for securing authorized copies have emerged. Some of the principal alternatives which have been discussed are as follows:

A. A voluntary clearinghouse or clearinghouses organized by copyright proprietors, by users of copyrighted material, or by commercial firms acting as agents for copyright proprietors. Fees for copying could be collected in a variety of ways:

1. The collection of fees for photocopying on the basis of a certain price per page or per article, which might be a uniform price or vary with the publication. The level of these fees could be left to economic forces, or set by statute, or left to be determined and/or adjusted by the Copyright Royalty Tribunal established by Chapter 8 of Public Law 94-553. (This last alternative would required additional legislation.)

2. The authorization of certain amounts of photocopying for a fixed payment, or a sliding scale of payment.

3. The clearinghouse(s) might issue licenses to institutions to photocopy for individual publications, or groups of publications, or the whole repertoire.

4. Voluntary, or statutory, arrangements could be established with respect to placing machine (and eye) readable code numbers on copyrighted materials to facilitate the clearinghouse operations. A subcommittee of Committee Z-39 of the American National Standards Institute is studying a system of numbers identifying individual journals and articles to be added as a supplement to the International Standard Serial Number (ISSN).

B. A government operated clearinghouse or clearinghouses rather than a voluntary clearinghouse organized by proprietors (possible fee structures as in A).

C. One or more national or regional "periodical banks" established by users, or by the government, which would pay royalties on photocopies made, with fees set in one or more of the various ways listed in A.

D. A compulsory licensing scheme which would supplement either clearinghouse(s) or periodical bank(s), (possible fee structures as in A).

E. The supply of reprints or authorized photocopies by the publisher or his authorized agent(s).

F. Increased hard copy periodical subscription prices with a photocopying privilege.

G. The supply by publishers of microform editions with reproduction privileges.

H. Increased book prices with photocopying privileges.

Information Needed from Publishers

At the present time there is no comprehensive collection of data on the attitudes of publishers of journals on these various alternatives or on their present practices with respect to authorizing photocopying. The attached questionnaires are designed to develop a body of factual information on these points for the consideration of the Commission and also for the use of proprietors and users of copyrighted materials. The periodicals being surveyed are of a scholarly and research nature, because this seems to be the type of periodical most frequently copied.

The results of this survey when tabulated in anonymous form will also be made available to King Research of Bethesda, Maryland which is under contract to the National Commission for Libraries and Information Science an behalf of the Conference an Resolution of Copyright Issues (the "Upstairs-Downstairs" group): (1) to make a further factual study of library photocopying in both not-for-profit and for-profit organizations, including photocopying for interlibrary loans and, (2) to develop various possible systems for dealing with authorized photocopying with costs estimates (a royalty payment mechanism). An advisory committee on this study consists of three publishers and three representatives of library organizations. The contract to King Research is scheduled to be completed in the early summer of 1977, and therefore the results of this CONTU journal survey are needed by April, 1977 in order to be used by King Research in the second aspect of the NCLIS contract. There are two other efforts underway which have a bearing on a system or systems for authorized photocopying:

> (1) A task force of the National Commission on Libraries and Information Science, studying a periodical bank or banks for the supplying of photocopies analogus to the British Lending library Division at Boston Spa, Yorkshire, England. This task force is expected to report to NCLIS in February, 1977.
>
> (2) Studies by publishers and information firms of copyright proprietor's clearinghouses. A presentation to CONTU by the Association of American Publishers and the Information Industry Association on these proposed clearinghouses are expected by late March or early April, 1977.

The journals being surveyed constitute an update of the list of 2,459 U.S. journals of a research and scholarly nature screened out by the Graduate Library School at the University of Indiana for the November 1975 study prepared by Bernard M. Fry and Herbert S. White for the National Science Foundation on "Econmics and Interaction of the Publisher-Library Relationship in the Production and Use of Scholarly and Research Journals". The distribution of this earlier list of 2,459 journals by type of publisher and broad disciplines is shown in Appendix I. Appendix II shows the distribution of these journals in terms of the number of journals published by individual publishers.

The publishers' questionnaire and the journal questionnaire address a considerable number of items, in order to illuminate preferences among the multiple possibilities. However, the questions have been designed so as to require only the entry of easily available information and the expressions of opinions on topics of direct current interest and importance and publishers. The questionnaire forms have been tested by a few journal publishers, and the time required is modest considering the value of the information supplied.

The choices expressed by respondents will be interpreted as tentative preferences, in light of what is now known, and not as commitments. The opportunity for publishers of research and scholarly journals to express preferences and to volunteer further suggestions is especially important to CONTU, in order to take into account the varied interests and circumstances of the diverse journals of the country.

Return of Questionnaire to Respondents

You will note in the attached contractors letter that the contractor will return the completed questionnaires have been tabulated without identification of individual publishers or journals and that such identification will appear in the contractor's report to the Commission.

Attachments: Appendix I
Appendix II

APPENDIX I

DISTRIBUTION BY TYPE OF PUBLISHER AND BROAD DISCIPLINES

N - 2,459 Journals

Publisher Population

Type of Publisher	Number of Publishers	Number of Journals Published
Commercial	256	645
Society	768	1073
University Press	40	127
Other Not-for-Profit	570	614
Total	1634	2459

Distribution by Type of Publisher and Discipline

Discipline	Commercial		Society		University Press		Not-for-Profit		Total
	Number	%	Number	%	Number	%	Number	%	
Pure Science	147	31.1	209	44.2	40	8.5	77	16.2	473
Applied Science and Technology	276	38.5	356	49.6	9	1.3	76	10.6	717
Humanities	40	13.4	84	28.1	28	9.4	147	49.1	299
Social Sciences	182	18.8	424	43.6	50	5.2	314	32.4	970
Total	645	26.2	1073	43.6	127	5.2	614	25.0	2459

APPENDIX II

NUMBER OF JOURNALS DISTRIBUTED BY EACH PUBLISHER

(Raw Data From NSF Study Does Not Match Study Totals Exactly Because of Later Changes and Corrections)

Number of Publishers

No. of Journals	Societies Pub.	Societies Jnls.	Univ. Presses Pub.	Univ. Presses Jnls.	Other N.F.P. Pub.	Other N.F.P. Jnls.	Commercial Pub.	Commercial Jnls.	Total Pub.	Total Jnls.
1	666	666	20	20	565	565	212	212	1463	1463
2	66	132	4	8	26	52	27	54	123	246
3	16	48	3	9	8	24	13	39	40	120
4	7	28	4	16	2	8	7	28	20	80
5	6	30	4	20	1	5	2	10	13	65
6	6	36	1	6	—	—	2	12	9	54
7	1	7	2	14	—	—	3	21	6	42
8	—	—	—	—	—	—	1	8	1	8
9	2	18	1	9	—	—	—	—	3	27
10	—	—	—	—	—	—	2	20	2	20
11	1	11	—	—	—	—	3	33	4	44
12	1	12	—	—	—	—	1	12	2	24
13	1	13	—	—	—	—	—	—	1	13
14	—	—	—	—	—	—	2	28	2	28
15	—	—	—	—	—	—	2	30	2	30
17	1	17	—	—	—	—	—	—	1	17
22	1	22	—	—	—	—	—	—	1	22
24	—	—	—	—	—	—	2	28	2	48
25	1	25	—	—	—	—	1	25	2	50
26	—	—	—	—	—	—	1	26	1	26
27	—	—	1	27	—	—	—	—	1	27
36	1	36	—	—	—	—	—	—	1	36
64	—	—	—	—	—	—	1	64	1	64
	777	1101	40	129	602	654	282	670	1701	2554

Press Release:

NATIONAL COMMISSION ON NEW TECHNOLOGICAL USES OF COPYRIGHTED WORKS
(CONTU)

Tel: (202) 557-0986 Washington, D.C. 20558

Press Release No. 1
for IMMEDIATE Release
February 23, 1976

COMMISSION HOLDS FOURTH MEETING FEBRUARY 11, 12 and 13
AND SCHEDULES APRIL, MAY AND JUNE MEETINGS

The National Commission on New Technological Uses of Copyrighted Works (CONTU) held its fourth meeting on February 11, 12 and 13, 1976 in Bethesda, Maryland.

The emphasis in the fourth meeting was on one of the two problems assigned to the Commission by the Congress in the enabling statute (P. L. 93-573) - the "computer issue". The statute charges the Commission to study, compile data on, and make recommendations on changes in the copyright law and procedures with respect to the reproduction and use of copyrighted works of authorship "in conjunction with automatic systems capable of storing, processing, retrieving and transferring information", and "the creation of new works by the application or intervention of such automatic systems."

Nine invited experts were heard on computerized storage and retrieval systems of a general nature and in the specialized fields of medicine, law, chemistry and economic statistics.

The Commission is required to make a preliminary report to the President and the Congress not later than October 8, 1976. A final report and recommendations are required by December 31, 1977.

The next three meetings of the Commission are scheduled for April 1 and 2 (probably in the New York City area), May 6 and 7, and June 3 and 4 (probably in the Washington, D.C. area). All four of the Commission meetings to date have been open to the public. Inquiries concerning the work and schedule of the Commission may be addressed to Arthur J. Levine,

Executive Director, National Commission on New Technological Uses of Copyrighted Works (CONTU), Washington, D.C. 20558, Telephone (202) 557-0996.

Attachments: Text of Title II of Public Law 93-573

Members and professional staff of the Commission

NATIONAL COMMISSION ON NEW TECHNOLOGICAL USES OF COPYRIGHTED WORKS (CONTU)

Tel: (202) 557-0996 Washington, D.C. 20558

MEMBERS OF THE COMMISSION

Selected from the public:

Stanley H. Fuld — Chairman
Retired Chief Judge, New York Court of Appeals
Special Counsel, Kaye, Scholer, Fierman, Hays and Handler

Melville B. Nimmer — Vice Chairman
Professor of Law
UCLA Law School

George D. Cary
Retired Register of Copyrights

Rhoda H. Karpatkin
Executive Director
Consumers Union

Selected from authors and other copyright users:

John Hersey
President
Authors League of America

Dan Lacy
Senior Vice President
McGraw-Hill, Inc.

E. Gabriel Perle
Vice President-Law
Time, Inc.

Hershel B. Sarbin
President
Ziff-Davis Publishing Company

Selected from copyright users:

William S. Dix
Librarian Emeritus of Princeton University
Princeton, New Jersey

Arthur R. Miller
Professor of Law
Harvard Law School

Robert Wedgeworth
Executive Director
American Library Association

Alice E. Wilcox
Director
MINITEX

EX OFFICIO MEMBERS OF THE COMMISSION

Daniel Boorstin (voting)
Librarian of Congress

Barbara Ringer (nonvoting)
Register of Copyrights

PROFESSIONAL STAFF OF THE COMMISSION

Arthur J. Levine
Executive Director

Robert W. Frass
Assistant Executive Director/Economist

Michael S. Keplinger
Senior Attorney

Jeffrey L Squires
Staff Attorney

NATIONAL COMMISSION ON NEW TECHNOLOGICAL USES OF COPYRIGHTED WORKS
(CONTU)

Tel: (202) [illegible] Washington, D.C. [illegible]

ARTHUR J. LEVINE

Arthur J. Levine, Executive Director of the National Commission on New Technological Uses of Copyrighted Works, has had extensive experience as a lawyer and lecturer of copyright law. A native of Connecticut, Mr. Levine was educated at Wesleyan University (1958) and at Columbia Law School (1962). He joined the Examining Division of the Copyright Office in 1963 and served as Assistant Chief of the Division from 1966 to 1971, when he left to enter private practice. In March 1975 he was appointed by the Librarian of Congress as special consultant on planning for the new Commission and in October was named its executive director.

Since 1967 Mr. Levine has lectured on copyright law and book and magazine publishing at the Practicing Law Institute, and last year he was named an adjunct professor of law at Georgetown Law Center. He presently serves on the board of trustees of the Copyright Society of the U.S.A. and as chairman of the copyright committee of the District of Columbia Bar Association. He has been chairman of the American Bar Association's committees on Copyright Office affairs and on copyright law revision and a member of the Association's committee on government relations to copyright. Mr. Levine is a member of the District of Columbia, the Maryland, and the Supreme Court bars. He was a contributing editor for the American Society for Information Science's Omnibus Copyright Revision in 1973.

Mr. Levine resides in Bethesda, Maryland.

NATIONAL COMMISSION ON NEW TECHNOLOGICAL USES OF COPYRIGHTED WORKS (CONTU)

Tel: (202) [illegible] Washington, D.C. [illegible]

ROBERT W. FRASE

Robert W. Frase, Assistant Executive Director and Economist of the National Commission on New Technological Uses of Copyrighted Works, has written widely on economic and public policy issues relating to publishing, libraries, and copyright. Most recently, he was a consulting economist is private practice.

A native of Chicago, he was educated at the University of Wisconsin and at Harvard University. From 1938 to 1950, he served in economic and administrative positions in several Federal and international agencies, including the Department of Labor, Agriculture, and Commerce. From 1950 to 1972 he was vice president and economist of the Association of American Publishers and its predecessor organizations. In 1973 he was appointed director of the Library Statistics Project of the American Library Association and in November 1975 he was named to his present post with the Commission

Mr. Frase resides in Falls Church, Virginia.

Public Law 93-573
93rd Congress, S. 3976
December 31, 1974

An Act

88 STAT. 1873

To amend title 17 of the United States Code to remove the expiration date for a limited copyright in sound recordings, to increase the criminal penalties for piracy and counterfeiting of sound recordings, to extend the duration of copyright protection in certain cases, to establish a National Commission on New Technological Uses of Copyrighted Works, and for other purposes.

Be it enacted by the Senate and House of Representatives of the United States of America in Congress assembled,

TITLE II—NATIONAL COMMISSION ON NEW TECHNOLOGICAL USES OF COPYRIGHTED WORKS

ESTABLISHMENT AND PURPOSE OF COMMISSION

SEC. 201. (a) There is hereby created in the Library of Congress a National Commission on New Technological Uses of Copyrighted Works (hereafter called the Commission).

(b) The purpose of the Commission is to study and compile data on:

(1) the reproduction and use of copyrighted works of authorship—

(A) in conjunction with automatic systems capable of storing, processing, retrieving, and transferring information, and

(B) by various forms of machine reproduction, not including reproduction by or at the request of instructors for use in face-to-face teaching activities; and

(2) the creation of new works by the application or intervention of such automatic systems or machine reproduction.

(c) The Commission shall make recommendations as to such changes in copyright law or procedures that may be necessary to assure for such purposes access to copyrighted works, and to provide recognition of the rights of copyright owners.

MEMBERSHIP OF THE COMMISSION

SEC. 202. (a) The Commission shall be composed of thirteen voting members, appointed as follows:

(1) Four members, to be appointed by the President, selected from authors and other copyright owners;

(2) Four members, to be appointed by the President, selected from users of copyright works;

(3) Four nongovernmental members to be appointed by the President, selected from the public generally, with at least one member selected from among experts in consumer protection affairs;

(4) The Librarian of Congress.

(b) The President shall appoint a Chairman, and a Vice Chairman who shall act as Chairman in the absence or disability of the Chairman or in the event of a vacancy in that office, from among the four members selected from the public generally, as provided by clause (3) of subsection (a). The Register of Copyrights shall serve ex officio as a nonvoting member of the Commission.

(c) Seven voting members of the Commission shall constitute a quorum.

(d) Any vacancy in the Commission shall not affect its powers and shall be filled in the same manner as the original appointment was made.

COMPENSATION OF MEMBERS OF COMMISSION

SEC. 203. (a) Members of the Commission, other than officers or employees of the Federal Government, shall receive compensation at the rate of $100 per day while engaged in the actual performance of Commission duties, plus reimbursement for travel, subsistence, and other necessary expenses in connection with such duties.

(b) Any members of the Commission who are officers or employees of the Federal Government shall serve on the Commission without compensation, but such members shall be reimbursed for travel, subsistence, and other necessary expenses in connection with the performance of their duties.

STAFF

SEC. 204. (a) To assist in its studies, the Commission may appoint a staff which shall be an administrative part of the Library of Congress. The staff shall be headed by an Executive Director, who shall be responsible to the Commission for the Administration of the duties entrusted to the staff.

(b) The Commission may procure temporary and intermittent services to the same extent as is authorized by section 3109 of title 5, United States Code, but at rates not to exceed $100 per day.

EXPENSES OF THE COMMISSION

SEC. 205. There are hereby authorized to be appropriated such sums as may be necessary to carry out the provisions of this title until June 30, 1976.

REPORTS

SEC. 206. (a) Within one year after the first meeting of the Commission it shall submit to the President and the Congress a preliminary report on its activities.

(b) Within three years after the enactment of this Act the Commission shall submit to the President and the Congress a final report on its study and investigation which shall include its recommendations and such proposals for legislation and administrative action as may be necessary to carry out its recommendations.

(c) In addition to the preliminary report and final report required by this section, the Commission may publish such interim reports as it may determine, including but not limited to consultant's reports, transcripts of testimony, seminar reports, and other Commission findings.

POWERS OF THE COMMISSION

SEC. 207. (a) The Commission or, with the authorization of the Commission, any three or more of its members, may, for the purpose of carrying out the provisions of this title, hold hearings, administer oaths, and require, by subpena or otherwise, the attendance and testimony of witnesses and the production of documentary material.

(b) With the consent of the Commission, any of its members may hold any meetings, seminars, or conferences considered appropriate to provide a forum for discussion of the problems with which it is dealing.

TERMINATION

SEC. 208. On the sixtieth day after the date of the submission of its final report, the Commission shall terminate and all offices and employment under it shall expire.

Approved December 31, 1974.

Letter Mailed with Questionnaires:

INDIANA UNIVERSITY

Graduate Library School

UNIVERSITY LIBRARY

BLOOMINGTON, INDIANA 47401

RESEARCH CENTER FOR LIBRARY AND INFORMATION SCIENCE

TEL. NO. 812—337-5388

February 15, 1977

Dear Journal Publisher:

The National Commission on New Technological Uses of Copyright Works (CONTU) has awarded the Graduate Library School a contract to survey U.S. publishers of scientific, technical, professional and scholarly journals with respect to their attitudes on permitting photocopying and various methods of dealing with licensing photocopying or the supply of authorized photocopies. The background and purposes of this survey are covered in the attached memorandum of the Commission.

The Graduate Library School of Indiana University was awarded this contract because of experience gained in the conduct of the study completed in November, 1975 for the National Science Foundation on "Economics and Interaction of the Publisher-Library Relationship in the Production and Use of Scholarly and Research Journals". Lexington Books, D.C. Heath and Company, 1976, (also available from the National Technical Information Service - NTIS - Document #PB 249108)

In this earlier survey 2,459 U.S. journals (excluding government publications) of this nature were identified. This earlier universe has now been brought up to date, taking into account new journals and journals discontinued and the present universe includes about 2600 journals. The procedure for the current survey is as follows:

1. Each of the publishers having one or more journals in the universe of some 2600 journals and listed in the attached List A is requested to fill out and return to the Indiana University Graduate Library School the enclosed franked, self-addressed postcard concerning participation in the survey.
2. List A attached contains the titles of your journal(s) which are included in the survey.
3. The basic questionnaire is to be filled out for each publisher.
4. The supplementary questionnaire is to be filled out for each journal in List A.

By participating in this survey, you will provide information which will help the National Commission to develop recommendations to the Congress to implement the provisions relating to photocopying in the new copyright law (Public Law 94-553) or to suggest further legislation. Tabulations from this survey will deal only with various aggregates. No data for individual publishers or individual journals will be made public by the contractor or the Commission, and the completed survey forms will be returned to the respondents after the data supplied on the forms have been recorded in anonymous form. Each journal publisher participating in the survey will be furnished with a copy of our report to CONTU including the tabulated results of the survey.

Sincerely,

Bernard M. Fry

Bernard M. Fry
Dean
Graduate Library School

Attachments:

1. List A - the list of your journals to be reported on the supplemental questionnaire.
2. Background memorandum of the National Commission on New Technological Uses of Copyrighted Works relating to the survey.
3. Return franked postcard addressed to the Indiana University Graduate Library School.
4. Basic (publisher) questionnaire for the survey.
5. Supplementary questionnaire(s) to be filled out for each journal in List A.
6. A government franked mailing label addressed to the Indiana University Graduate Library School to be affixed to a plain envelope for the return of the completed questionnaires.
7. CONTU Press Release No. 2.

Follow-up Letter:

INDIANA UNIVERSITY
Graduate Library School
UNIVERSITY LIBRARY
BLOOMINGTON, INDIANA 47401

RESEARCH CENTER FOR
LIBRARY AND INFORMATION SCIENCE

TEL. NO. 812—337-5388

April 15, 1977

Dear Journal Publisher:

On February 15, 1977, we mailed a questionnaire to you on behalf of the National Commission on New Technological Uses of Copyright Works (CONTU). This questionnaire, which addressed the publishers of U.S. scholarly and research journals, asked for information concerning attitudes toward photocopying and various methods for dealing with licensing of the supply of authorized photocopies. Responses, which were originally requested by March 25, 1977, will help the National Commission to develop recommendations to the Congress to implement the provisions of the new copyright law (Public Law 94-553), and to suggest further legislation.

It was stressed in the earlier communication, which requested responses for each journal in the survey population as well as an overall response from each publisher, that tabulations would deal only with aggregates. No data for individual publishers or individual journals will be made public, and the completed survey forms will be returned after the data has been recorded in anonymous form.

As of this date, we have not received your response. If you have delayed or hesitated in responding to this important request for information which is intended to assist the publishing industry, we urge you to reconsider. YOUR COOPERATION IS IMPORTANT TO THE SUCCESS OF THIS SURVEY OF PUBLISHER VIEWS.

If the questionnaires have been mislaid or never received, or if you have any questions, please do not hesitate to call the Research Center of the Graduate Library School collect at (812) 337-5388. Thank you for your cooperation.

Sincerely yours,

Bernard M. Fry
Principal Investigator
Dean, Graduate Library School

Herbert S. White
Co-Principal Investigator
Professor and Director of the
Research Center

Statement by the National Serials Data Program (NSDP), Library of Congress on the Status of the Assignment of International Standard Serial Numbers (ISSN) to Journals to which the Survey Questionnaires were sent.

Although only 36.0% of the 974 journals responding to this survey reported that the ISSN was printed on the journal issues, this percent may be expected to increase rapidly. The Library of Congress will be developing facilities to enable NSDP routinely to notify publishers of the validated ISSN assigned to their journals. Specific requests from publishers on the Serial Data Sheet (copy attached) for the assignment of ISSN are continuing to be handled expeditiously, with particular attention given to pre-publication requests.

A mailing by the R.R. Bowker Company in the spring of 1977 reporting to publishers the ISSN assigned to their publications, which was made in connection with the preparation of a new edition of Ulrich's Directory, also contained a letter from NSDP. The letter urged publishers either to use the ISSN reported to them by Bowker, or to request an assignment from NSDP. This appeal has resulted in a fourfold increase in the weekly volume of publisher requests submitted to NSDP for the assignment of ISSN. Several other developments are likely still further to increase the number of requests from publishers for the assignment of ISSN. The new copyright registration forms, being developed by the Copyright Office for copyright registration under the new copyright act after December 31, 1977, will contain a place for the insertion of the ISSN. Similar arrangements are being discussed with the U.S. Postal Service in connection with filings for second class mailing privileges. It is also expected that ISSN will be used in various mechanisms for payment of royalties for copying or for the supplying of authorized copies of serial articles.

The NSDP records show the following as of June 23, 1977 with respect to the assignment of ISSN to the journals which were sent the questionnaire in this survey (respondents and non-respondents alike). It should be noted that publishers requesting assignment of ISSN on the serial data sheet form are notified only of fully validated ISSN.

ISSN Assignments

Validated ISSN	1,405	58%
Unvalidated LC record	62	2%
CONSER record with ISSN	326	13%
CONSER record	17	1%
OCLC record with ISSN	349	14%
OCLC record	74	3%
No on-line record	146	6%
Not searchable on OCLS	38	1%
Insufficient information in title list to perform creditable search or to distinguish among multiple records	(155)	1%
	2,418	98% (because of rounding the total is not 100%)

Exhibit A

NSDP Library of Congress National Serials Data Program Washington, D.C. 20540

SERIAL DATA SHEET FOR PUBLISHERS

Your assistance is requested in order for the National Serials Data Program to assign your serial an ISSN (International Standard Serial Number) and an accompanying Key title. There is no charge for making this assignment. When you have completed the application form, send both parts back to NSDP at the above address.

This form MUST be accompanied by a sample issue of the publication, or if this is inconvenient, a photo copy of the cover, title page, and masthead. If the serial has not yet been published, a mock-up of the items above will suffice, provided that a sample issue (or photocopies) is sent as soon as it is available.

If you have any questions, feel free to contact NSDP for assistance. Your cooperation is greatly appreciated.

☐ This is a request for prepublication assignment of an ISSN. The first issue of the serial will appear (date): with the following numbering:

☐ This is a request for assignment of an ISSN for a serial which began publication (date): with the following numbering:

1. TITLE (from the title page, or the cover if there is no title page)

2. VARIANT FORMS OF THE TITLE on the cover, masthead, or other parts of current issues. Please specify source of each title on the issue.

3. EARLIER TITLES which this serial continues

4. PUBLISHER

5. CITY AND STATE OF PUBLISHER

6. SUBSCRIPTION ADDRESS

7. SUBSCRIPTION PRICE (indicate differential rates)

8. FREQUENCY

9. LANGUAGE(S) OF TEXT

10. ADDITIONAL INFORMATION, COMMENTS, QUESTIONS

TO BE PROCESSED, THIS DATA SHEET MUST BE ACCOMPANIED BY AN ISSUE OF THE SERIAL OR PHOTOCOPIES AS SPECIFIED ABOVE. APPLICATION FOR A NEW ISSN MUST BE MADE IF THE TITLE OF THE PUBLICATION CHANGES.

11. CONTACT PERSON

(name) (telephone)

(address if different from subscription address)

(date this form completed)

For NSDP Use ONLY

Comments and Instructions

Date received by NSDP ________

Date publisher notified of assignment ________

Request postpub. issue ☐

ISSN:

Key title:

67-60 (rev 11/76) GPO 929 352

Legal Protections of Computer Software: An Industrial Survey

SUMMARY OF FINDINGS

A written survey of the computer software industry, as represented by membership in the major trade association and readers of the principal trade periodical, characterized the typical company as follows:

It is independently owned and is less than 10 years old. It has fewer than 100 employees, annual sales of under $5 million and spends slightly under $100,000 per year on research and development. It could be located almost anywhere in the U.S. but is more likely to be in the Northeast or California than elsewhere. Its principal markets are apt to be consulting, contract programming, the development of proprietary software packages and data center operations and management. Although its revenues are fairly distributed over each of its markets, it tends to specialize in specific products or service lines. It develops from one to two dozen computer programs per year at its own expense and an equal number are purchased and/or developed at its customer's expense.

This company relies largely upon its technological resourcefulness in a burgeoning industry. It is not particularly concerned with the protection of the software that it develops or purchases and, to the extent that it is, would prefer to rely upon physical, technological, and contractual modes of protection rather than legal monopolies. It is not at all convinced that legal protection is necessary and feels that it is generally ineffective even when invoked. The company may – just "may" – take advantage of legal protection if it is offered, provided that it is simple, accessible and inexpensive. The absence of legal protection, however, will not in any way deter it from developing or marketing new programs.

These perceptions are likely to change as the company gets larger, particularly if it is involved in general business and systems software programs. Indeed, a large company which develops business programs on a proprietary basis, or for the management of a facility, is likely to support legal protection with some degree of enthusiasm. Relative to the number of firms in the indifferent majority, however, it is a lonely, albeit loud, voice in its industry.

The typical company would not change its development or marketing plans if the copyright law were to substantially strengthen available legal protection. It is not especially interested in the recent development of "trapdoor functions" which promise unbreakable ciphers and would probably be even less interested in the creation of utility models or other imaginative new legal devices. The more engineering and technically oriented the company's programming, the more prepared it is to rely upon the uniqueness of its product and its skills for protection – to the extent that it is conscious of protection at all. Conversely, the more generalized its applications or systems programming, the more sensitive it is to the need for protection. But these are shadings at the extremities: the singular outstanding conclusion of the survey is that for the most part the issue of legal protection through a grant of limited monopoly is a matter of monumental insignificance to the industry.

I. BACKGROUND TO THE SURVEY

A. The Software Subcommittee Report

This report presents results of a survey conducted by Harbridge House under the auspices of CONTU (National Commission on New Technological Uses of Copyrighted Works) to assess the attitudes of the computer software industry on legal protection for services and their products under existing patent, copyright and other laws.

The CONTU "Software Subcommittee" report of April 1977 reviewed the literature, the law and testimony concerning the conflicting social interests in the protection of computer software and concluded that " . . . these interests can best be balanced with respect to computer programs, as with all other works of authorship, by affording such works copyright protection."[1] However, the Subcommittee also noted expressions of reservations among the commissioners, the witnesses, and scholarly commentators. Indeed, tabulating merely the oral and written testimony from 20 Commission witnesses representing 18 organizations it was observed that "11 favored copyright, three favored patent, three favored trade secrecy, eight had no preference, and two perceived no need for protection."[2]

Harbridge House was retained against this background to secure additional empirical data on the nature and effects of software protection to assist the Commmission in its deliberations.

B. Highlights of Legal Issues

Thirteen years have passed since the Copyright Office's 1964 decision to accept computer programs as registerable for copyright protection. Yet the adequacy of laws that protect the proprietary interest in computer software, as well as their substance and application, are still in controversy. Section 117 of P.L. 94-553 clearly preserves the legal status quo on computer related works – and leaves all of the outstanding questions open.[3] Nevertheless, this youthful industry has burgeoned: The EDP Industrial Reporter estimated that $900 million would be spent on software development in 1976.[4] Rough estimates suggest that as many as 10,000 separate computer programs are created daily in the U.S.[5]

Given the limited availability of the legal mechanisms available for protecting computer software, it is not surprising that many software developers feel the legal system is unresponsive to their needs. Two recent Supreme Court decisions Gottschalk v. Benson, 409 U.S. 63 (1972), which characterized the computer program in question as an unpatentable mathematical algorithm or formula, and Dann v. Johnston, 96 S. Ct. 1393 (1976), which for the most part sidestepped the software patentability issue – have generally barred patent protection for computer software.[6] Ironically, though, if the same set of logical steps contained in a computer program were permanently embodied in the circuitry of an item of computer hardware, the resulting "firmware" might presumably be patentable. The peculiar character of computer software complicates the task of devising appropriate legal mechanisms to protect the proprietary interests of computer program producers. Not until the hearings surrounding the passage of the Copyright Act of 1976 did the Congress explicitly proclaim the copyrightability of computer programs.

---

[1] Report, p. 2.

[2] Id., p. 25.

[3] See H.R. Rep. No. 1476, 94 Cong. 2d Sess.; Sen. Rep. No. 473, 94th Cong. 2d Sess. (1976).

[4] EDP Industry Report, published by International Data Corp., March 26, 1976.

[5] Goldberg, Morton D., Legal Protection for EDP Software, 18 Datamation 66 (S/1971).

[6] A complete list of all computer software cases is set forth in Appendix A below.

Computer programs are classified as books by the Copyright Office. As with books, the holder of a software copyright has exclusive right to copy the form of expression of the author's ideas. It is reasonably easy to envision the type of protection offered by statutory copyright to literary works. For computer software, however, what is protected is not as readily discerned. For example, while an unauthorized photo or magnetic copy of a registered computer program would constitute an infringement, the real value of a computer program is not captured until the program is actually put to use in a computer. Yet the unauthorized use of a computer program by entering it into a computer without copying it may not constitute an infringement, nor may storage of that program in an electronic memory or on tape. Moreover, many question the value of copyright protection when a plagiarist can derive the value of a program by substantially duplicating the ideas and techniques embodied in it without technically infringing. The copyright law for literary works is designed to provide the copyright holder a means to control or benefit from the wide distribution of his work. Copyright laws do not intend to limit use of literary works but instead to encourage widespread usage. However, a computer program does not necessarily derive its monetary value from the breadth of its distribution, but rather from the type of application for which it is used.

Bolstering protection for computer software is not without hazards. Arthur Miller characterizes computer programs as processes and warns that a copyright system that grants a monopoly on the utilization of a process, approaches the monopoly power granted by the patent system without the safeguards attached to the patent examination process.[7] Furthermore, an abundance of software copyrights might seriously hamper future software development. Developers would have to extensively research existing copyrights to avoid infringing other programs. Complex disagreements would occur regarding priority, originality, and private rights versus public domain.

Other observers question the need for further software protection. Keefe and Mahn[8] note that the marketing of most software packages includes significant supporting services by the seller without which successful marketing or use of the software by a copier would be prohibitively difficult. It is argued that the importance of these support services which accompany software products decrease the need for further software protection. On the other hand, software is early in the product life cycle and many buyers of computer software may be at a stage of relative unsophistication with the product. Perhaps as users become more knowledgeable about the use and maintenance of computer software, protection of proprietary software products may become increasingly important to the survival of the industry.

Many feel that proprietary software products that are distributed on a limited basis and which can be classified as "unpublished" can obtain generous protection through a combination of common law copyright and trade secret law. Common law copyright may offer broader protection than statutory copyright since use as well as copying of a program is often prohibited. But the laws are complicated and vary between states. Common law copyright applies only to products of fairly limited distribution. To preserve trade secret protection, software developers must employ extensive techniques to closely limit disclosure of information about the protected secret. Furthermore, questions have been raised about the future of common law copyright and trade secret laws. The Copyright Act of 1976 specifically preempts state copyright laws pertaining to unpublished works fixed in a tangible medium of expression. Trade secret laws that confer

---

[7] Miller, Arthur, "Computers and Copyright Law," Michigan State Bar Journal 4/67 p. 11-18. See also "Additional Views on Computer Software" by John Hersey, an addendum to the CONTU Software Subcommittee Report of April 1977.

[8] Keefe, Arthur J. and Mahn, Terry G., "Protecting Software: Is It Worth All the Trouble" 62 A.B.A.J. 906 (1976).

rights equivalent to those within the scope of the Copyright Act are also preempted.[9] How this will affect "unpublished" software products which previously may have benefited from the generally broader state copyright laws cannot be precisely predicted.

C. The 1973 National Science Foundation Study

To a degree, this work is an expanded update of a modest survey conducted in 1973 for the National Science Foundation as part of a larger project on legal incentives and barriers to utilizing technological innovation. The 1973 study included a brief survey of modes of legal protection utilized by the computer services industry and the perceived adequacy of the laws.[10] At that time, while considering the application of laws to developing technologies which did not fit neatly into established legal categories, we became concerned with computer software, which we defined as the series of instructions and documentary material which makes possible the functioning of computer hardware.

With the assistance of the Association of Data Processing Service Organizations (ADAPSO) we conducted the first survey on modes of legal protection utilized by the software industry. This study indicated that copyright protection ranked third in preferred modes of protection, behind trade secret licenses and leases with confidential disclosure clauses. There was a moderate interest in software protection but little evidence that its presence or absence affected business decisions. Protection was regarded as most significant for general business and financial programs. Eight-seven percent of the respondents could not recall a single instance in which computer programs representing a significant level of innnovation were not developed or marketed because of inadequate protection.

However, this survey reported only the views of 31 respondents of a professional organization of 46 members in a young industry. In an industry which reckons generations as fractions of decades it was appropriate to question the current validity of such a primitive census.

D. The Software Industry

The computer services industry is composed of 2,584 companies who produced $5.3 billion in sales, and $573 million in profits, in 1976.[11] The industry forecasts a compounded growth rate of 18 percent over the next five years as contrasted to a 13 percent growth rate for the computer manufacturing industry.

The industry can be said to be divided into four basic markets which are displayed below in terms of their earned and projected revenues:

---

[9] H.R. Report #1476, Ibid., and §301 of P.L. 94-533. See also, p. 20 of CONTU report cited supra.

[10] See Miller, R.I., Legal Aspects of Technology Utilization (D.C. Heath & Co., published 1974), Chap. 8. This survey covered 46 companies; there were 31 respondents.

[11] See 1977 Annual Report on "The Computer Services Industry," published by International Data Corporation, Waltham, Massachusetts, and the Association of Data Processing Service Organizations, Inc., of Montvale, New Jersey.

EXHIBIT 1

Product Categories	1976 Revenues ($ millions)	Projected 1981 Revenues
Processing Services	3,065	8,038
Software Packages	550	1,856
Staff Support Services	675	1,087
Facilities Management	495	1,020

All of these markets generate computer programs. That is, they design – and to some extent market – writings which set forth instructions which can direct the operation of an automatic system capable of storing, processing, retrieving or transfering information. Each of them may be presumed to have an interest in the protection of software. The products of these markets are displayed in Exhibit 2 in terms of the fundamental utility or value added by the vendor.

For the purposes of the CONTU software industry survey, these markets were presumed to be represented principally by the 305 member company Association of Data Processing Service Organizations (ADAPSO) and, to a lesser degree, the membership of the Computer and Business Equipment Manufacturer's Association (CBEMA) and the readership of the trade newspaper, Computerworld.

E. Software Protection Publications

An impressive body of scholarly and speculative legal literature has been published on software protection during the past decade. This literature is listed in the Appendix B bibliography. It is noteworthy, however, that in addition to the NSF study cited above, only two other empirical studies have previously been published – one in the United Kingdom and one in Sweden.[12] The British survey concluded that 53 percent of the respondents in the United Kingdom computer industry want stronger legal methods of protecting computer programs. The desirable features of such protection would be informality, immediacy, low cost, and protection against foreign infringers – all of which is quite compatible with copyright. The Swedish study disclosed that although 60 percent of the organizations polled are interested in a system of legal protection that makes it easier than at present to regain investments in software, a clarification of existing legal alternatives might well be sufficient. A degree of copyright and trade secret protection is available in both countries. In neither country did the surveys uncover any industry reluctance to develop programs because of insufficient legal protection.

[12] Anderson, M. and Niblett, B., "Software Protection: A Survey of the U.K. Industry"; Siepel, P., "Software Protection and the Law", Data, June 1975, pp. 43-46.

EXHIBIT 2

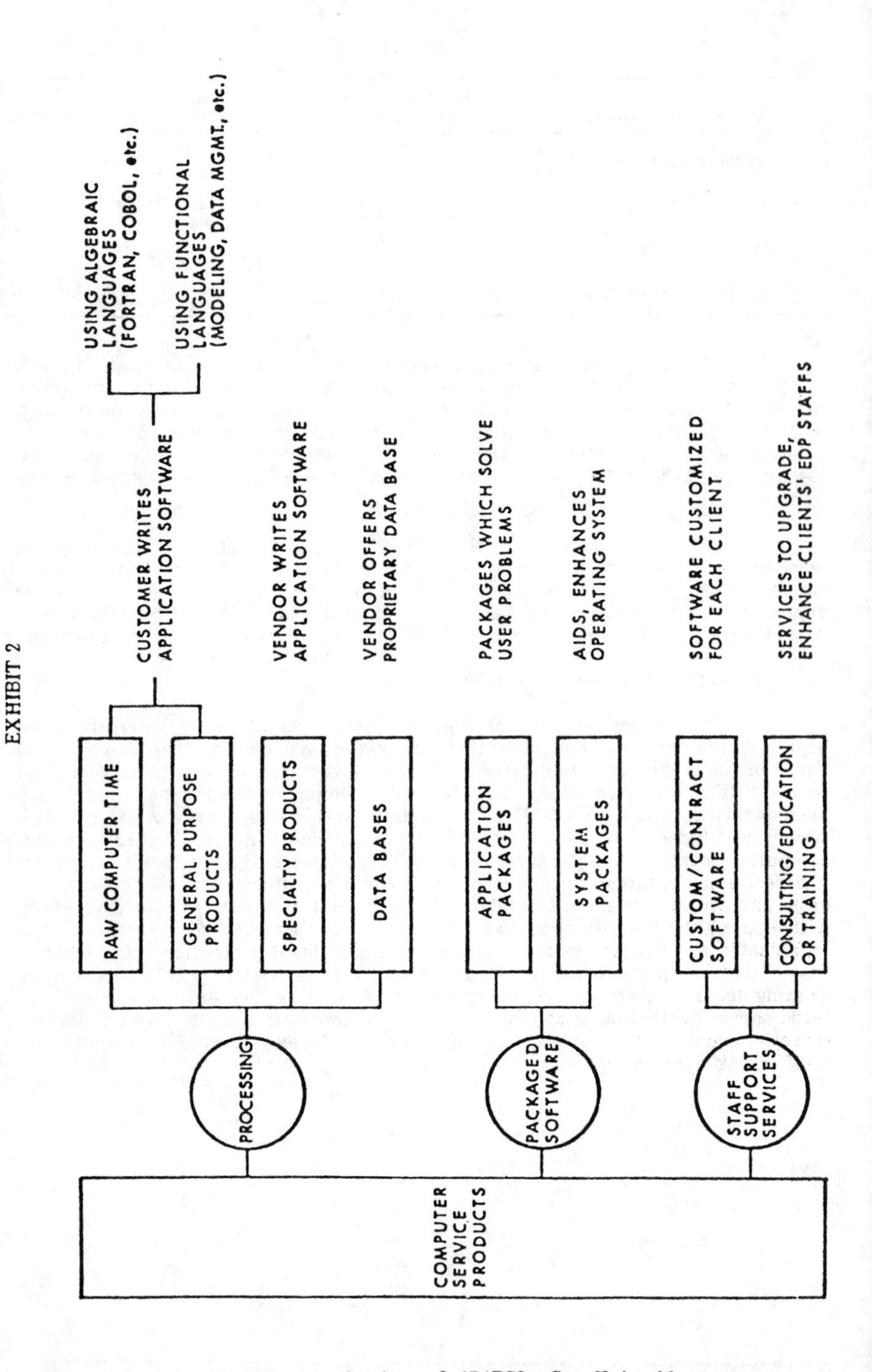

***Chart reproduced with permission of ADAPSO. See Note 11 above.**

II. THE SURVEY

A. Objective of the Survey

The basic purpose of this study was to secure data relating investment, development, and marketing of computer software to legal protection. In elaboration of this basic information, however, we wanted to examine the following questions:

(i) If more effective legal protection for software were available, would companies make greater investment in computer software?

(ii) Are companies discouraged from marketing particular products because software elements are not adequately protected by legal structure?

(iii) Have there been any inhibiting effects on technological development because of a lack of confidence in computer software protective procedures?

B. Method of Approach

The first step was the design of a questionnaire to examine the questions discussed above. Drafts of the questionnaire were reviewed by members of CONTU and various persons in the software industry, to obtain their inputs and reactions. The questionnaire was revised and distributed in the form shown in Appendix C.

In order to sample the attitudes that are generally held by industry, we needed a universe for our study which was accessible and representative. With the cooperation of ADAPSO, we developed a mailing list of computer software industrial executives to whom the questionnaire was mailed. Since the membership of ADAPSO is persons rather than firms, there were instances where many persons from one firm were ADAPSO members. We limited the mailing so that only one response from each firm was solicited.

After receiving the initial response, the replies were analyzed by Harbridge House consultants. In many cases nonresponding recipients were called to determine whether or not they would be participating. In other situatuions, respondents were called to explain entires on their replies which were not clear to the analysts.

Finally, cross tabulation of mailed questionnaires was programmed for the Hewlitt-Packard 3000 computer. The smaller number of replies to the published Computerworld questionnaire were manually tabulated and used as a cross check to the larger ADAPSO population.

C. Characteristics of the Sample

Questionnaires were distributed to 308 member companies of ADAPSO. Replies were received from 116 companies, which constitutes a 38 percent response rate. There were 10 responses to the published Computerworld questionnaire. Since this was presumbly an infinitisimal fraction of an indeterminate sample, the Computerworld responses were treated as a control and the responses were not included in the statistical base; they were, however, included in the base of anecdotal information. In this section we shall report on the kinds of companies that participated in terms of their size, product interest, kinds of ownership, and so forth. Some of the information supplied is expressed as a function of some of other information about the applicants.

1. Services and Products

The following is a tabulation of the kinds of services provided by the respondents followed by the percentage of firms that indicated they were active in this area. Since most respondents were active in several markets, the total exceeds 100 percent. The four principal services are underscored.

EXHIBIT 3

Service	Percent
<u>Consulting</u> (feasibility studies, systems analysis and design)	39%
<u>Contract Programming</u> (including custom software packages)	51%
<u>Proprietary Software Packages</u>	44%
<u>Data Center Operations and Management</u>	47%
Time-Sharing	16%
Telecommunications	9%
Facility Management	9%
Education	9%
Hardware Products	16%
Batch Processing	5%
Service Bureau	5%
Data Entry	4%
Data Processing	3%
Computer Services	2%
Miscellaneous	8%

Although most of the respondents said that they were involved in four major services/products markets, many reported that no single market dominated revenues. Exhibit 4 expresses services and products as a function of company sales. For example, reading horizontally along the top line, for 27 percent of the respondents "consulting" represents 1 to 10 percent of sales; for 4 percent of the respondents 11 to 20 percent of sales is in consulting, for 2.5 percent, consulting represents 31 to 40 percent of sales and so on. The large percentage of "nones" in the chart may mean that respondents taken individually tend to specialize in the products and services sold. (It may also mean that the categories were strictly construed.) The grouping on the low side of the sales classifications suggests that although four service/products are most frequently marketed, revenues are more broadly distributed among all of the markets than might be expected from their dominance.

2. Company Ownership

Seventy-one percent of the responding companies were independently owned. Fifteen percent identified themselves as a "subsidiary" while 8 percent called themselves a "division." Another 7 percent provided no answer to this question.

3. Number of Employees

Over two thirds of the ADAPSO responding companies had fewer than 100 employees. Nine of the 10 firms which replied to the published Computerworld questionnaire also had fewer than 100 employees. (The tenth had 13,000.) As the graph in Exhibit 5 displays, this seems to be characteristic of the industry.

4. Annual Investment in Research

Exhibit 6 is a summary of the volume of research activity sponsored by the respondents, as measured by the amount spent annual on internally-funded software development, including research.

5. Annual Sales

Exhibit 7 is a breakdown of respondents by their total volume of sales.

Systems programs are the detailed and voluminous programs stored on the machine that allow the computer to function efficiently and take on other programs. Applications programs use the computer to solve problems in the outside world. Exhibit 8 is a breakdown of total annual sales of respondents as between systems software programs and application software programs.

6. Indices of Software Activity

a. Financing of Program Development

Respondents were asked how many programs they had developed over the last three years, which they considered proprietary to their firm. They were

EXHIBIT 4
SERVICES AND PRODUCTS EXPRESSED AS A FUNCTION OF RESPONDENT SALES

SERVICES/ PRODUCTS	PERCENTAGE OF RESPONDENTS SALES											
	1-10%	11-20	21-30	31-40	41-50	51-60	61-70	71-80	81-90	91-100	No. Ans.	None
CONSULTING	.27	.04		.025	.01		.01		.01		.07	.55
CONTRACT PROGRAMMING	.32	.09	.035	.035		.01	.01	.01		.01	.07	.41
PROPRIETARY SOFTWARE	.155	.07		.025	.01	.02	.01	.01	.035	.07	.11	.48
TIME SHARING	.04	.02	.01	.01	.01			.01	.01	.04	.08	.775
TELECOMMUNI-CATIONS	.05	.02	.01								.09	.835
DATA CENTER OPERATIONS	.02	.02	.025	.025	.01	.01	.035	.06	.12	.14	.07	.465
FACILITY MANAGEMENT	.025	.02	.02		.01						.075	.85
EDUCATION	.085										.08	.79
HARDWARE PRODUCTS	.06	.01	.02	.01			.01			.02	.08	.79
OTHER	.08	.025	.03	.01			.02		.03	.05	.08	.68

EXHIBIT 5
NUMBER OF EMPLOYEES IN RESPONDENT FIRMS

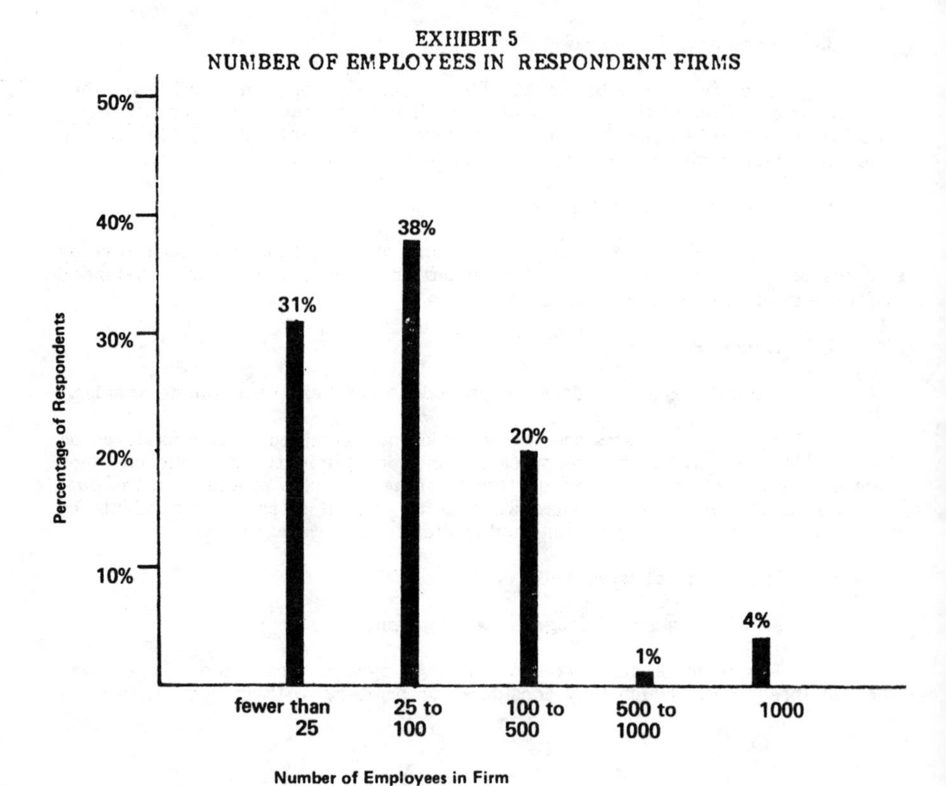

EXHIBIT 6
ANNUAL INVESTMENT IN RESEARCH

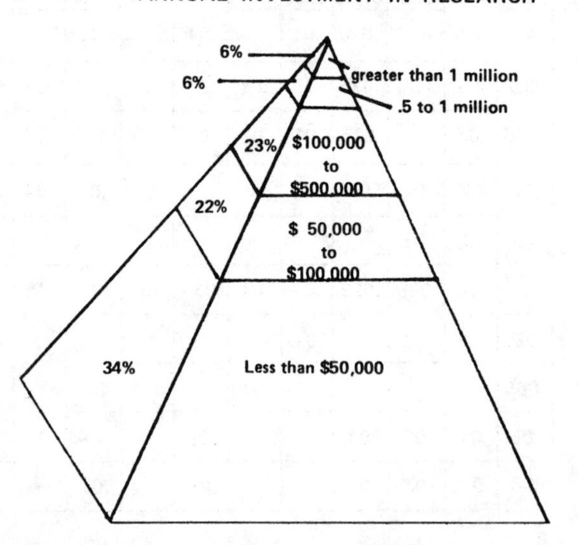

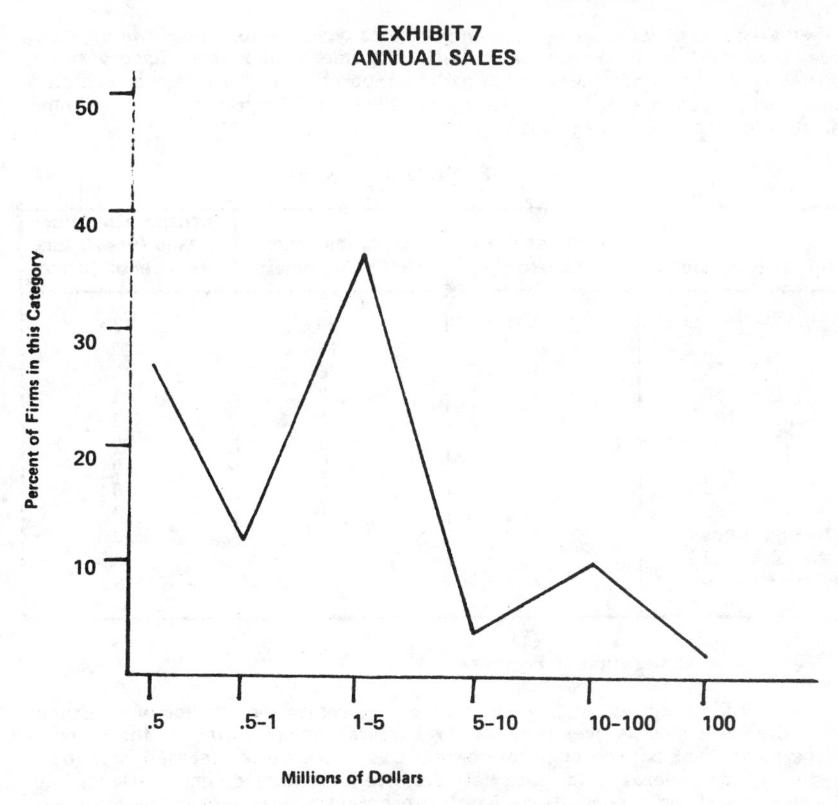

EXHIBIT 7
ANNUAL SALES

EXHIBIT 8
SALES IN SYSTEMS AND APPLICATION SOFTWARE PROGRAMS

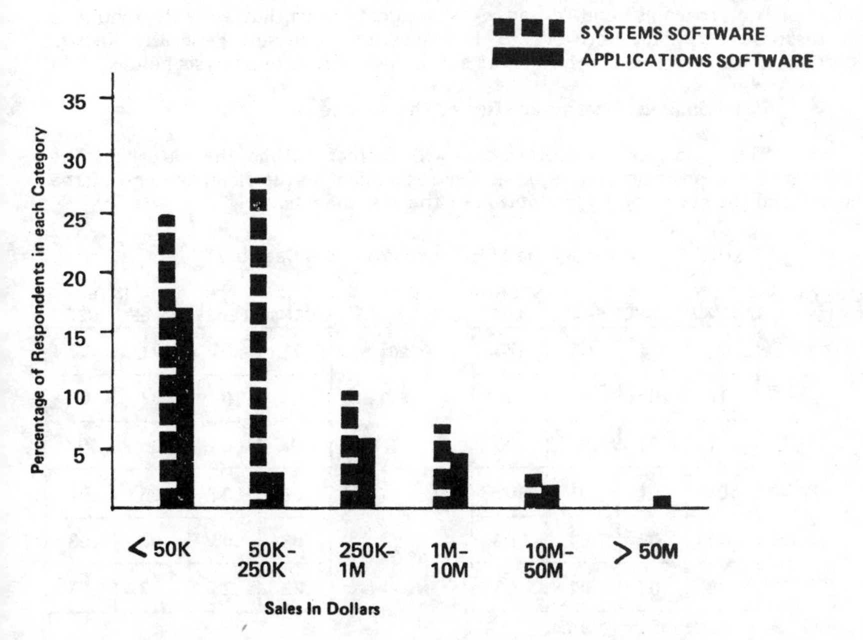

further asked to differentiate between programs developed at their own expense, those developed in a shared basis with customers, and those incorporating proprietary products of others which had been purchased. The listing in Exhibit 9 shows the percentage of respondents who developed programs in the volumes indicated for the three categories stated:

EXHIBIT 9

No. of Programs	Solely at Own Expense	Expenses Shared with Customers	Incorporating Purchased Proprietary Products of Others
No Programs	9%	39%	57%
1 - 10	28	16	12
11 - 25	9	6	3
26 - 50	9	3	1
51 - 100	5	3	2
101 - 200	6	3	0
201 - 500	3	2	0
501 - 999	1	0	0
- 999	3	1	0
Don't Know	6	7	3
Not Applicable	4	4	3
No Answer	16	16	19

b. Generation of Programs

The tabulation in Exhibit 10 below expresses the number of programs produced by respondents over the last three years, differentiated by the purpose of generation, that is, whether the program was to be leased, licensed, sold (permanent use) or generated for internal use. Each verticial column reflects 100 percent of the sample population. The "no programs" entry means that, for example, "44 percent of the sample does not generate programs for licensing"; ". . . 53 percent does not generate programs for lease", and so on. The large number of "no programs" and "no answers" suggests to us that, notwithstanding a high response rate, the answers to the question were not generally known. Accordingly, we used this characteristic sparingly in our data analysis below.

7. Miscellaneous Characteristics of the Sample

The following characteristics will further outline the nature of the sample as to the position of the particular respondent in the firm, the age of the company and the geographic distribution of the respondents.

EXHIBIT 10 Percentage of Respondents in this Category

VOLUME OF ACTIVITY*	LICENSE	LEASE	SALE	INTERNAL USE
No Programs	.44	.53	.51	.24
1-10	.17	.09	.1	.1
11-25	.01	.01	.02	.05
26-50	.01	.01	.01	.05
51-100	.01	.02	.01	.04
101-200	.03	.01	.01	.09

VOLUME OF ACTIVITY*	LICENSE	LEASE	SALE	INTERNAL USE
201-500	.01	.01	.01	.05
501-999	0	0	.02	0
7999	.01	0	0	.07
Don't Know	.06	.04	.05	.07
Not Applicable	.03	.03	.03	.03
No Answer	.22	.25	.23	.21

*Expressed as number of programs.

a. Respondent's Position in Firm

EXHIBIT 11

Position	Percent of Those Replying
President	56%
Vice President	19
General Manager	3.5
Controller	1
Managing Partner	1
Systems Analyst	1
Division Manager	1
Treasurer	2
Financial Analyst	2.5
Marketing Representative	1
Director, Market Research	2
Director, DP	1
Director, Corporate Development	1
Administrative Director	1
Director, Computer Services	1
Manager, Creative Services	1
General Counsel	1
No Answer	6

b. Age of Company

EXHIBIT 12

Firm's Age	Percent of Those Responding
< 1 year	0%
1 - 2 years	3
3 - 5 years	9
6 - 10 years	42
11 - 15 years	13
16 - 20 years	12
21 - 20 years	2
26 - 100 years	4
No Answer	14

c. Geographic Distribution of Respondents

The distribution of the sample is shown in Exhibit 13.

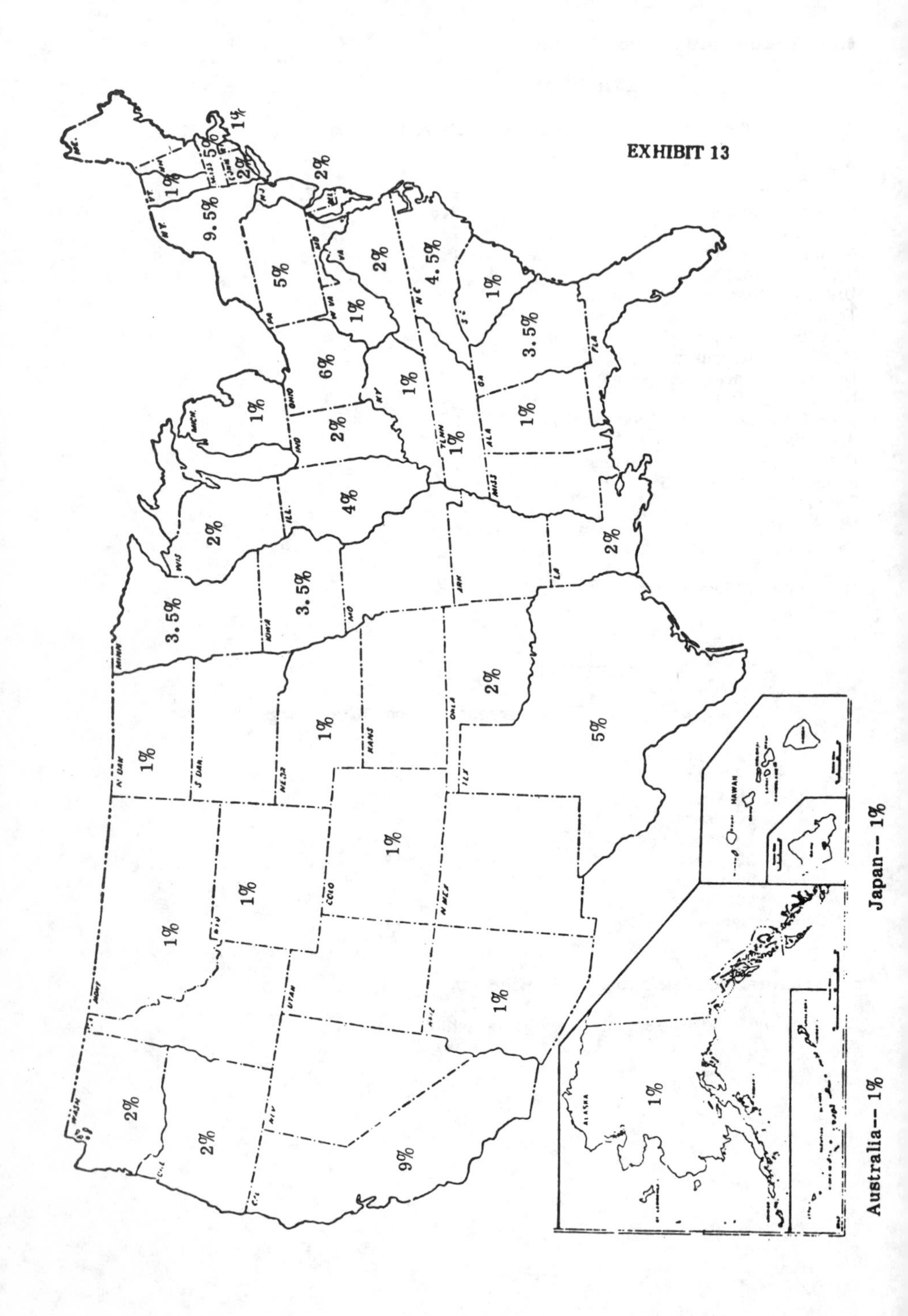
EXHIBIT 13
Japan-- 1%
Australia-- 1%

8. The Sample Summarized

The typical respondent to this survey is the President of his company, which is independently owned and is less than 10 years old. The company has fewer than 100 employees, annual sales of under $5 million, and spends less than $100,000 annually on research. The firm could be located almost any place in the United States, but is most likely to be located in the Northeast or in California. The firm is most likely to be involved in consulting, contract programming and the development of proprietary software. To the extent that it is able to discriminate among markets, its revenues are fairly evenly divided among them unless it engages in data center operations, in which case it will derive most of its revenues from that single activity.

D. Attitudes of the Respondents

1. Use and Evaluation of Various Protection Techniques

The respondents were asked to indicate their utilization of various techniques to protect software and to state their assessment of its effectiveness on a ranking scale of 0-5 with "0" designated as "not at all effective" and 5 as "completely effective."

EXHIBIT 14
PREFERRED MODE OF PROTECTION
(Figures Indicate Percentage of Respondents Answering in Each Category)

	Degree of Effectiveness						
Mode of Protection	Not at all Effective	Rarely Effective	Somewhat Effective	Fairly Effective	Very Effective	Completely Effective	Frequency of Use*
Patent	.82	0	0	.18	0	0	.04
Copyright	.55	0	.05	.1	.15	.15	.2
Trade Secret	.29	.05	.14	.24	.14	.14	.21
Release of Object Program Only	.17	0	.04	.08	.33	.38	.3
Know-How Requirement	.28	.17	0	.17	.17	.22	.13
Cryptographic Coding	.5	0	.17	.25	.08	0	.4
Other Means of Limiting Access	.27	0	0	.13	.06	.53	.17

*The figures in this column relate to the entire sample.

Only 30 percent of the sample responded to this question with 20 percent indicating that the question was "not applicable" and 50 percent replying that they did not know or simply leaving the question blank. Although it might be presumed from this low response that 70 percent of the sample simply do not believe that protection of programs is particularly important, this may be stretching the implications of silence. Exhibit 14 should be read by observing, for example, that 20 percent of the sample used copyright protection. Of that total population, 55 percent of them believe that it is not at all effective; only 15 percent stated that it was completely effective.

Those firms which had rated the various protection techniques as being completely effective ("5") or not at all effective ("0") were asked to indicate in terms of their experience whether a form of protection has differential effects: Does it tend to be effective against contracting parties? Against those who have obtained unauthorized possession? Against plagiarizers? Against pirates who sell stolen programs to others?

The most common response was that nonlegal modes of protection were sufficient for most purposes. In this connection it should be noted that 17 percent of the respondents said that they used other (undesignated) means of limiting access, and that well over half regarded these means as completely effective. The next most common observation was that legal protection was inadequate. A somewhat smaller number volunteered that protection itself was unnecessary in any event. If this view is shared by any sizable number of those who did not respond to this question – and we believe that to be a reasonable presumption – then the ranks of the disinterested may be substantial. The Computerworld sample suggests that this view is not shared by those who develop and/or market proprietary business programs.

There were also a handful of enthusiastic responses from some of the larger firms indicating a heavy reliance upon legal protection and satisfaction with the protection afforded for particular proprietary programs. One firm, for example, noted that copyright was extensively used and highly regarded for a series of graphic packages composed in Fortran III, while another graphic series in BASIC was less efficiently protected by copyright and less frequently used.

Six companies (5 percent of the total sample) indicated that their use of a particular form of protection resulted in a legal action of some sort (which could include a threat of lawsuit as well as actual litigation). Four of these used copyright while two used trade secrets.

In the 1973 NSF survey, the smaller sample of respondents rated effectiveness on a scale of 0-3. Moreover, the modes of protection were largely restricted to legal alternatives. In the CONTU survey not only was the ranking scale (0-5) larger, but the alternatives included a greater technological range, such as the release of an object program only, as well as cryptographic coding. Therefore, the two studies cannot be directly compared on a numerical basis. But with appropriate allowances for differences in scale and choice of alternatives it is possible to compare the two surveys in some respects:

The NSF survey included the legal alternative of "leases with confidential disclosure clauses." In the fact-oriented CONTU survey this category was subsumed by releasing of the object program only and other means of limiting access. The restricted release, by whatever legal or commercial arrangement the restriction was secured, ranked first in the preferred modes of protection.

There was virtually no shift in opinion between the NSF and CONTU surveys among those who used trade secret. That is, if you could use them at all, they were fairly effective. However, the more sophisticated CONTU survey also asked for an evaluation of a know-how requirement on the part of a user. To the extent that this may be considered a kind of trade secret, it was less frequently used and less effective than a program which could be withheld by its authors.

Copyright, as in 1973, ranked third in the preferred modes of protection. However, the ratio of respondents in the NSF survey who reported using copyright protection compared to the ratio in the CONTU survey was almost two to one. We are uncertain as to why this is so. It might have been a function of the product lines represented by the respective surveys (that is, more business programming represented in the survey); or it may have been a consequence of the ambiguity of silence rather than a quality of the sample. On the other hand, with respect to those who said they did use copyright, three times as many respondents (on a percentage basis) in 1977 said it was not at all effective as compared to 1973. A slightly increased number also said that it was completely effective. We explain these developments by observing that as copyright usage has increased, more respondents have used this relatively inexpensive, accessible mechanism to try to protect more programs that are easily designed around.

Patent protection kept its place on the bottom of the list for utility and efficacy. Moreover, the overwhelming opinion of the small number that used it was that it was not at all effective. However, a few firms found it fairly effective; they were generally among that small proportion of the CONTU sample which observed that the hardware protects the software.

2. Importance of Protection for Various Product Lines

Respondents were asked to assess the importance of legal protection for various proprietary software product lines. The table below expresses the respondents' answers as a percentage of all affirmative responses for a particular category. Thus, 50 percent of all firms which market general business and financial programs state that protection has great significance whereas 53 percent of the firms which market engineering and scientific programs believe that protection is of no significance at all. (The data has been expressed in this form since the response rate for each category differed depending upon the respondents markets.)

EXHIBIT 15
SIGNIFICANCE OF SOFTWARE PROTECTION BY FUNCTION*

	No Significance	Some Significance	Great Significance
(a) General business and financial applications (e.g., accounting, inventory control, payroll)	.17	.33	.5
(b) Business planning operations (e.g., planning models, simulations, operations research)	.5	.24	.26
(c) Complex production/distribution control operations (e.g., linear programming)	.55	.19	.26
(d) Engineering and scientific applications	.53	.19	.28
(e) Data and statistical analysis	.51	.17	.31
(f) Project management and control	.54	.23	.23
(g) Systems software (e.g., compilers, monitors, new techniques for more efficient machine utilization)	.4	.17	.43

*Figures indicate percentage of respondents answering in each category.

With allowances for a difference in the way in which the data is expressed,[13] the CONTU results are strikingly similar to those of the 1973 NSF survey. What they show is that the more universal and widely marketed the program the more important is protection. This is a characteristic of general business programs, which can be addressed to such functions as payroll and receivables anywhere, and also of systems software in which a program can be used for a particular computer in a variety of installations. On the other hand, the more technical and unique the program the less significant protection appears to be. This finding is consistent with information which was supplied to us about the programs which were being marketed.

Respondents were requested to provide information about their best selling programs. Thirty-five percent of the sample reported about 113 computer programs. Fifty-four percent of the programs pertained to systems software. All of the rest of the respondents reported programs in categories "b" through "f" in Exhibit 15 above. We regard it as highly significant that the overwhelming majority of those respondents who chose to provide information about programs

---

[13] In the NSF survey "not applicable" answers were included as a part of the population. In the CONTU survey, for the purposes of this question, the population was defined to include only those answered affirmatively.

were those for whom software protection is regarded as of great significance. Accordingly, we cross tabulated some of the data about the sample (presented in Section C above) with the attitudes of the firms which were predominantly in general business and systems software programming. For each of the characteristics below, we sought to determine what percentage of the sample in that group believed that software protection had ("some" or "great") significance.

Significance of protection as a function of:

a. **Internal Cost of Development**

EXHIBIT 16

	<$50K	$50–$100K	$100–$500K	$500K–$1M	$1–$10M
General Business	.49	.58	.63	.29	.43
Systems Software	.18	.32	.37	.57	.57

b. **Annual Sales**

EXHIBIT 17

	<$500K	$500K–$1M	$1M–$5M	$5M–$10M	$10–$100M	>$100M
General Business	.39	.57	.68	.40	.33	.50
Systems Software	.19	.29	.39	.40	.33	.50

c. **Services and Products**

EXHIBIT 18

	Consulting	Contract Programming	Proprietary Software	Time-Sharing	Telecommunications	Data Center Operations	Facility Management	Education	Hardware
General Business	.53	.56	.63	.61	.40	.60	.70	.30	.61
Systems Software	.33	.30	.43	.39	.10	.25	.50	.40	.33

The displays above should be read as follows: Looking, for example, at the first entry under "Internal Cost of Development for General Business – "Forty-nine percent of all respondents who said that they had sales of less than $50,000 felt that software protection was significant."

A ranking order immediately becomes apparent: of the two markets in the software industry interested in legal protection, it is more important to the general business market than to the systems software market, as measured by any selected function. Since most of the respondents are small firms it is important to note that measured in terms of either the cost of development or sales, less than half of that majority thought that protection was important. The degree of importance appears to increase to a peak of investment cost between $100,000 and $500,000 and sales at $1 to $5 million. On the basis of some of the comments on questionnaires, we might be tempted to generalize "the larger the company, the more important is protection." However, this conclusion cannot be statistically supported because our sample had too few large companies. The most positive statement we can make is that this is demonstrable to a point. The product lines most impacted are facilities management and proprietary software. Thus, protection is most important to larger general business firms which might be generating programs for security systems or accounting functions.

3. Effectiveness of Contractual Restraints

It will be recalled from Exhibit 14 above that 53 percent of the sample indicated that "other means" of limiting access were completely effective. The NSF survey and the comments of respondents suggested that contractual arrangements with customers were the most commonly used devices to minimize unauthorized dissemination. Respondents were asked whether contractual arrangements normally restrain customers from duplicating programs: Fifty-five percent replied in the affirmative, 16 percent in the negative and the balance either felt that the question was inapplicable or had no opinion. This response should be considered in the light of the normal means by which programs are ordinarily transferred from the developers to their customers. A somewhat larger proportion of programs which are generated for the use of customers (rather than for internal use) appear to be transferred by lease or by license than by outright sale.[14] It is not surprising, then, that contractual restraint is regarded as effective. The developer exercises a maximum degree of contractual control when title to a program (and, presumably, update services) remain with the firm.

4. Effect of Legal Protection on Marketing Plan

The critical test of the effectiveness of laws is the degree to which their presence or absence influences behavior. Accordingly, our sample was asked whether it had ever rejected or abandoned a marketing program for a proprietary software product because of the inadequacy of legal protection. Conversely, they were asked whether they would change a marketing program because legal protection was improved. Note that in each instance the stress was on legal protection, a narrower category than the full scope of protection probed earlier. The response was unequivocal: Seventy-four percent of the sample had never rejected or abandoned a program because of the presence or absence of protection and 65 percent would not change their marketing even if protection were provided.

The minority opinion was represented by the 4 percent of the entire sample which had rejected or abandoned programs for lack of protection and 15 percent which would change its marketing program if legal protection were improved. The affirmative responses, broken down into the categories set forth above were:

a. Internal Cost of Development **EXHIBIT 19**

	<$50K	$50-$100K	$100-$500K	$500K-$1M	$1-$10M
General Business	.03	0	.04	.2	.2
Systems Software	.1	.2	.15	.14	.33

[14]See Exhibit 10 above.

b. **Annual Sales**

EXHIBIT 20

	<$500K	$500K-$1M	$1M-$5M	$5M-$10M	$10-$100M	>$100M
General Business	0	.13	.3	.33	.10	0
Systems Software	.1	.21	.17	.2	.17	0

c. **Services and Products**

EXHIBIT 21

	Consulting	Contract Programming	Proprietary Software	Time-Sharing	Telecommunications	Data Center Operations	Facility Management	Education	Hardware
General Business	.3	.2	.1	.6	0	0	.13	0	0
Systems Software	.13	.14	.24	.11	0	.13	.1	.3	.18

In this instance an affirmative response appears to be linear with the quantitative factors, that is, the larger a company is, the more likely it is to change its marketing plan because of the presence or absence of legal protection. Indeed, the marketing plans of the small companies which make up a majority of the sample would be almost completely unaffected by any change in the law. By product line, the only services that would be even nominally affected seem to be the marketing or proprietary systems software and general business consulting. (We have reservations about the latter; the reader should note that the minority opinion was so small that 30 percent refers to only four companies.)

5. **Effects on Research and Development Plans**

The lack of significance of legal protection on marketing plans was reaffirmed by the responses to an open question with a substantially larger scope. The question was expanded in three respects:

- The respondent was not restricted to his own business experience. He was asked whether he was "aware of <u>any</u> situation" of rejection or abandonment for lack of protection.

- The "legal" modification was omitted.

- The question was expanded to include <u>development</u> as well as marketing.

Since a particular concern of the survey is the effect of legal protection on technological development of software, the response to the open question was highly significant. The response was almost precisely identical to the answers to the marketing inquiry: Seventy-seven percent of the sample knew of no instance of aborted marketing or development. Only 3 percent responded in the affirmative. We regarded the 3 percent as too small a fraction of the sample to cross tabulate against research and development investment.

There is no question that development programs have been occasionally abandoned because of inadequate protection. One company with annual sales of $140,000 stated that it had abandoned development of a "system implementation language" and would resume development if it could be protected. A second company with annual sales of $400 million stated that it refrains from developing applications packages that can be used with the hardware of other companies because of the lack of protection. But these situations appear to be so few and far between that they are statistically insignificant. Whether they have sufficient technological significance to have policy implications beyond their numbers was beyond the scope of the survey.

6. Effect of the Copyright Act of 1976

We asked the respondents whether the Copyright Act of 1976 will cause changes in the company marketing program in 1978. Seventy-six percent replied in the negative, 3 percent in the affirmative. (We were rather surprised that of the 21 percent which failed to give a "yes" or "no" answer, only 3 percent said they did not know, since only 1 percent of the respondents were identified as lawyers.) We believe that the response to this question should be considered with the opinion disclosed earlier, that 15 percent said that an improvement in legal protection would cause a change in their marketing program. If so, it would appear that the Copyright Act of 1976 is (correctly) perceived by most as not affecting their markets.

7. Other Comments

Thirty-eight percent of the respondents were kind enough to offer miscellaneous responses to an open solicitation for advice that might be helpful to CONTU. The comment most often repeated was that an apparent lack of interest in legal protection was related to the fact that they did not market proprietary software. Some felt that legal protection is inherently complex and expensive. A few observed that the rapid development of new technology helps to deter pirating. Some suggested that a new mode of intellectual property protection might be appropriate. Only 1 percent of the sample underscored a positive need for further legal protection.

APPENDIX A
TABLE OF CASES

An Overview

In re Calma Co., 5 C.L.S.R. 216 (Comp. Gen. 1969)

Computer Science Corp. v. Commissioner, 57 T.C. 600, 5 C.L.S.R. 786 (1974)

Com-Share, Inc. v. Computer Complex, Inc., 3 C.L.S.R. (E.D. Mich. 1971)

Data General Corp. v. Digital Computer Controls, Inc., 5 C.L.S.R. 1073 (Del. Ch. New Castle County Ct. 1975)

Futuronics Corp., 4 C.L.S.R. 900 (Comp. Gen. 1973)

Goldstein v. California, 4 C.L.S.R. 180, 41 L. Week 4829 (Sup. Ct. L.A. 1973)

Hancock v. Decker, 379 F.2d 552, 1 C.L.S.R. 858 (5th Cir. 1967)

Hancock v. State, 402 S.W. 2d 906, 1 C.L.S.R. 562 (Crim. App. Tex. 1966)

J. Dirats and Co. v. Nat'l. Cash Register Co., 5 C.L.S.R. 1295 (Mass. App. Div. of Dist. Cts. W. Dist. Ct. Springfield 1975)

In re McDonnell Automation Co., 49 Comp. Gen. 124, 2 C.L.S.R. 291 (1969)

Perma Research and Development Co. v. Singer Co., 542 F.2d 111, 6 C.L.S.R. 98 (2nd Cir. 1976)

Shepard v. Commissioner, 57 T.C. 600, 4 C.L.S.R. 1021 (1972)

Smithsonian Institute v. Datatron Processing, Inc., 3 C.L.S.R. 393 (E.D.N.Y. 1971)

Patent Protection

In re Abrams, 788 F.2d 165, 4 C.L.S.R. 607 (C.C.P.A. 1951)

In re Benson and Tabbot, 441 F.2d 216, 169 U.S.P.Q. (BNA) 548, 2 C.L.S.R. 1030 (C.C.P.A. 1971)

In re Benson and Tabbot, 4 C.L.S.R. 574 (Ger. Fed. Patent Ct. 1973)

In re Bernhart and Fetter, 417 F.2d 1395, 2 C.L.S.R. 359 (C.C.P.A. 1969)

In re Booz-Allen Applied Research, Inc., 4 C.L.S.R. 617 (N.A.S.A. 1965)

In re Brandstadter, 484 F.2d 1395, 4 C.L.S.R. 976 (C.C.P.A. 1973)

In re Brown, 4 C.L.S.R. 56 (C.C.P.A. 1973)

Bullard v. General Electric Co., 348 F.2d 985, 4 C.L.S.R. 1016 (4th Cir. 1965)

In re Chatfield, 545 F.2d 152, 6 C.L.S.R. 52 (C.C.P.A. 1976)

In re Christensen, 4 C.L.S.R. 66 (C.C.P.A. 1973)

Com-Share, Inc. v. Tymshare, Inc., 3 C.L.S.R. 480 (E.D. Mich. 1972)

In re Comstock, 481 F.2d 905, 4 C.L.S.R. 818 (C.C.P.A. 1973)

Dann v. Johnston, 96 S. Ct. 1393, 5 C.L.S.R. 1133 (1976)

Data General Corp. v. Digital Computer Control, Inc., 5 C.L.S.R. 1073 (Del. Ch. New Castle Co. 1975)

In re Doyle, 4 C.L.S.R. 933 (C.C.P.A. 1973)

Electronic Assistance Corp. v. N.Y., 17 F.R. Serv. 2d 1048, 4 C.L.S.R. 945 (S.D.N.Y. 1973)

In re Fielder, 471 F.2d 640, 4 C.L.S.R. 738 (C.C.P.A. 1973)

In re Foster, 438 F.2d 1011, 2 C.L.S.R. 994 (C.C.P.A. 1971)

Frederick v. Irasek, 397 F.2d 342, 4 C. L. S. R. 1017 (C. C. P. A. 1968)

In re Freeman, 5 C. L. S. R. 518 (C. C. P. A. 1974)

Ghiram v. Ulrieh, 442 F.2d 985, 3 C. L. S. R. 70

Gottschalk v. Benson, 93 S. Ct. 253, 3 C. L. S. R. 256 (1972)

Hamilton Humidity, Inc. v. I. B. M., 168 U. S. P. Q. 626, 3 C. L. S. R. (N. D. Ill. 1971)

Hemstreet v. General Electric Co., 168 U. S. P. Q. 683, 3 C. L. S. R. 664 (D. C. 1971)

Honeywell, Inc. v. Sperry Rand Corp., 180 U. S. P. Q. 673, 5 C. L. S. R. 78 (D. Minn. 1967)

I. B. M. v. Sperry Rand Corp., 44 F. R. D. 10, 1 C. L. S. R. 882 (D. Del. 1968)

I. B. M. v. Sperry Rand Corp., 44 F. R. D. 7, 1 C. L. S. R. 879 (D. Del. 1967)

Iowa State University Research Foundation, Inc. v. Honeywell, Inc., 15 F. R. Serv. 2d 1595, 3 C. L. S. R. 614 (8th Cir. 1972)

Iowa State University Research Foundation, Inc. v. Sperry Rand Corp., 447 F.2d 406, 2 C. L. S. R. 1041 (4th Cir. 1971)

In Re Johnston, 502 F.2d 765, 4 C. L. S. R. 1491 (C. C. P. A. 1974)

Kewanee Oil Co. v. Bicron Corp., 4 C. L. S. R. 37 (6th Cir. 1973)

In re King, 46 U. S. P. Q. 590, 1 C. L. S. R. 302 (B. P. Q. 1964)

In re Knowlton, 4 C. L. S. R. 1480 (C. C. P. A. 1974)

In re Knowlton, 481 F.2d 1357, 4 C. L. S. R. 799 (C. C. P. A. 1973)

Lundy Electronics and Systems, Inc. v. Optical Recognition Systems, Inc., 493 F.2d 1222, 5 C. L. S. R. 676 (4th Cir. 1974)

Lundy Electronics and Systems, Inc. v. Optical Recognition Systems, Inc., 3662 F. Supp. 230, 178 U. S. P. Q. (BNA) 525, 4 C. L. S. R. 1327 (E. D. Va. 1973)

In re McIlroy, 442 F.2d 1397, 3 C. L. S. R. 81 (C. C. P. A. 1971)

In re Mahoney, 421 F.2d 742, 2 C. L. S. R. 587 (C. C. P. A. 1976)

In re Noll, 545 F.2d 141, 6 C. L. S. R. 69 (C. C. P. A. 1976)

Mici-Shield Co. v. First National Bank of Miami, 404 F.2d 157, 2 C. L. S. R. 1 (5th Cir. 1968)

In re Musgrave, 431 F.2d 882, 2 C. L. S. R. 920 (C. C. P. A. 1970)

In re Naquin, 398 F.2d 863, 4 C. L. S. R. 441 (C. C. P. A, 1968)

Porter Instrument Co. v. ODEC Computer Systems, Inc., 37 F. Supp. 198, 5 C. L. S. R. 1146 (D. R. I. 1944)

Potter Instrument Co. v. Control Data Corp., 2 C. L. S. R. 988, 169 U. S. P. Q. (BNA)

In re Peater, 415 F. 2d 1378, 160 U. S. P. Q. (BNA) 230, 2 C. L. S. R. 8 (C. C. P. A. 1968)

Reeves Instrument Corp. v. Beckman Instruments, Inc., 444 F. 2d 263, 3 C. L. S. R. 693 (9th Cir. 1971)

Schmierer v. Newton, 397 F. 2d 1010, 4 C. L. S. R. 1016 (C. C. P. A. 1968)

Shepard v. Commissioner, 57 T. C. 600, 4 C. L. S. R. 1021 (1972)

Sperry Rand Corp. v. Bell Telephone Laboratories, Inc., 208 F. Supp. 598, 5 C. L. S. R. 68 (S. D. N. Y. 1962)

Sperry Rand Corp. v. Control Data Corp., 319 F. Supp. 629, 2 C. L. S. R. 907 (D. Md. 1970)

Technitrol, Inc. v. Control Data Corp., 394 F. Supp. 511, 5 C. L. S. R. 1144 (D. Md. 1975)

Technitrol, Inc. v. Control Data Corp., 164 U. S. P. Q. (BNA) 552, 2 C. L. S. R. 493 (D. Md. 1970)

Technitrol, Inc. v. Memorex, 5 C. L. S. R. 403 (N. D. Ill. 1974)

Technitrol, Inc. v. United States, 169 U. S. P. Q. (BNA) 732, 2 C. L. S. R. 384 (Ct. Cl. 1971)

Technitrol, Inc. v. United States, 164 U. S. P. Q. (BNA) 51, 2 C. L. S. R. 371 (Ct. Cl. 1969)

In re Waldbaum, 3 C. L. S. R. 173 (C. C. P. A. 1972)

In re Wheeling, 413 F. 2d 1187, 2 C. L. S. R. 297 (C. C. P. A. 1969)

Copyright

Data General Corp. v. Digital Computer Controls, Inc., 5 C. L. S. R. 1073 (Del. Ch. New Castle Co. 1975)

Goldstein v. California, 4 C. L. S. R. 180, 41 L. Week 4829 (Sup. Ct. L. A. 1973)

Telex v. I. B. M., 5 C. L. S. R. 3 (10th Cir. 1975)

Trade Secrets

Automated Systems Inc. v. Service Bureau Corp., 401 F. 2d 619, 1 C. L. S. R. 581 (10th Cir. 1968)

Automated Systems Inc. v. Service Bureau Corp., 1 C. L. S. R. 570 (D. Kansas 1966)

Adams v. Dan River Mills, Inc., 15 F.R. Serv. 2d 1275, 4 C. L. S. R. 33 (W.D. Va. 1972)

Com-Share, Inc. v. Computer Complex, Inc., 3 C. L. S. R. 479 (E. D. Mich. 1972)

Com-Share, Inc. v. Computer Complex, Inc., 3 C. L. S. R. 462 (E. D. Mich. 1971)

Com-Share, Inc. v. Tymshare, Inc., 3 C. L. S. R. 480 (E. D. Mich. 1972)

Data General Corp. v. Digital Computer Controls, Inc., 6 C. L. S. R. 88 (Del. Ch. New Castle Co. 1976)

Data General Corp. v. Digital Computer Controls, Inc., 5 C. L. S. R. 1073 (Del. Ch. Ct. New Castle Co. 1975)

Data General Corp. v. Digital Computer Controls, Inc., 3 C. L. S. R. 499 (Del. Ch. Ct. 1971)

Electronic Assistance Corp. v. N.Y., 17 F. R. Serv. 2d 1048, 4 C. L. S. R. 945 (S. D. N. Y. 1973)

Electronic Data Systems v. Kinder, 360 F. Supp. 1044, 5 C. L. S. R. 502 (1973)

Goldstein v. California, 4 C. L. S. R. 180, 41 L. Week 4829 (Sup. Ct. L.A. 1973)

International Data Corp. v. Infomart, Inc., 3 C. L. S. R. 1163 (C.D. Cal. 1971)

Kewanee Oil Co. v. Bicron Corp., 94 S. Ct. 1879, 4 C. L. S. R. 1203 (1974)

Kewanee Oil Co. v. Bicron Corp., 4 C. L. S. R. 37 (6th Cir. 1973)

Lear, Inc. v. Adkins, 395 U. S. 653, 89 S. Ct. 1902, 23 L. Ed. 2d 610, 2 C. L. S. R. 235 (1969)

Lundy Electronics and Systems, Inc. v. Optical Recognition Systems, Inc., 3662 F. Supp. 230, 178 U. S. P. Q. (BNA) 525, 4 C. L. S. R. 1327 (E. D. Va. 1973)

Painton and Co., Ltd. v. Bourns, Inc., 442 F.2d 216, 2 C. L. S. R. 558 (2d Cir. 1971)

Painton and Co., Ltd. v. Bourns, Inc., 309 F. Supp. 271, 2 C. L. S. R. 550 (S. D. N. Y. 1970)

Republic Systems and Programming, Inc. v. Computer Assistance, Inc., 440 F. 2d 996, 3 C. L. S. R. 49 (2d Cir. 1971)

Republic Systems and Programming, Inc. v. Computer Assistance, Inc., 322 F. Supp. 619, 3 C. L. S. R. 35 (D. Conn. 1970)

Sigma Systems Corp. v. Electronic Data Systems Corp., 467 S. W. 2d 675, 3 C. L. S. R. 66 (Tex. Civ. App. 1971)

Shepard v. Commissioner, 57 T. C. 600, 4 C. L. S. R. 1021 (1972)

Sperry Rand Corp. v. Pentronix, Inc., 353 F. Supp. 1291, 4 C. L. S. R. 731 (E. D. Pa. 1973)

Sperry Rand Corp. v. Pentronix, Inc., 311 F. Supp. 910, 2 C. L. S. R. 600 (E. D. Pa. 1970)

Telex v. I. B. M., 5 C. L. S. R. 3 (10th Cir. 1975)

Telex v. I. B. M., 5 C. L. S. R. 1 (10th Cir. 1975)

Telex v. I. B. M., 4 C. L. S. R. 1071 (N. D. Okla. 1973)

Telex v. I. B. M., 4 C. L. S. R. 275 (N. D. Okla. 1973)

Texas Instruments v. United States, 407 F. Supp. 1326, 5 C. L. S. R. 1529 (N. D. Tex. 1976)

Trilog Associates, Inc. v. Famularo, 455 Pa. 243, 314 A. 2d 287, 5 C. L. S. R. 625 (Penn. Sup. Ct. 1974)

United States v. Antosz, 4 C. L. S. R. 551 (N. D. Ill. 1971)

United States v. I. B. M., 5 C. L. S. R. 1022 (S. D. N. Y. 1974)

United States v. I. B. M., 5 C. L. S. R. 1019 (S. D. N. Y. 1974)

United States v. I. B. M., 4 C. L. S. R. 486 (S. D. N. Y. 1973)

United States v. I. B. M., 4 C. L. S. R. 499 (S. D. N. Y. 1973)

University Computing Co. v. Lykes-Youngstown Corp., 504 F. 2d 518, 183 U. S. P. Q. (BNA) 705, 5 C. L. S. R. 1248 (5th Cir. 1974)

Waul v. Superior Court of California, 3 C. L. S. R. 206 (Cal. Super. Ct. Almeida 1971)

Other Means

Aerojet General Corp. v. Computer Learning and Systems Corp., 358 U. S. P. Q. (BNA) 170, 4 C. L. S. R. 111 (Pat. Off. Treadmark Trial and App. Bd. 1971)

Computer-In-Look, Inc., 5 C. L. S. R. 891 (Pat. Off. Trademark Trial and App. Bd. 1972)

In re Delta Packaging Corp., 161 U. S. P. Q. (BNA) 52, 4 C. L. S. R. 98 (Pat. Off. Trademark Trial and App. Bd. 1969)

Harris Intertype Corp., 518 F. 2d 629, 5 C. L. S. R. 1243 (C. C. P. A. 1975)

Minnesota Mining and Manufacturing Co. v. Electronic Memoirs, Inc., 455 F. 2d 1391, 3 C. L. S. R. 611 (C. C. P. A. 1972)

APPENDIX B
BIBLIOGRAPHY

I. The Protection of Proprietary Rights

Generally

Kayton, Irving (Ed.), The Law of Software--1968 Proceedings, Computers-In-Law Inst., Geo. Wash. U. (1968).

Id., The Law of Software--1969 Proceedings, Computers-In-Law Inst., Geo. Wash. U. (1969).

Milde, K. F., Jr, Can a Computer be an "Author" or an "Inventor"?, 51 J. P. O. S. 378 (June 1969); reprinted in 2 Patent L. Rev. 568 (1970).

Miller, Richard I., Legal Aspects of Technology Utilization, (Lexington: D.C. Heath & Co., 1974) Ch. 8, Copyright and Data.

Tanaka, Richard I., Fee or Free Software, 13 Datamation 205 (Oct. 1967).

Program to Police Proprietary Packages, 2 Comp. Decisions 99 (April 1970).

An Overview

Association of Independent Software Companies, Legal Protection for Computer Programs, Computers and Automation 12 (Feb. 1969).

Association of Patent Law Attorneys Quarterly Journal, Vol. V(1) (1977).

Bender, David, Last Battle in the War (Letter to the Ed.), 19 Datamation 32 (Oct. 1968).

Bigelow, Robert P. (Ed.), Computer Law Service, 4 Callaghan and Co. (1976).

Id., Legal Aspects of Proprietary Software, 14 Datamation 32 (Oct. 1968).

Bigelow, Robert P., and Nycum, Susan, Your Computer and the Law, (Prentice-Hall, 1975) pp. 64-95, 193-195.

Blaustein, Albert P., Rothman, S. Hackensack, Intellectual Property; Cases and Materials 1960-1970, (1971).

Boonin, L. I., Patents and Copyrights--What Should Be Protected?, 8 Comm. A. C. M. 474 (July 1965).

Bricker, Seymour M., Thirty Months After Sears and Compco, Bull. Cr. Soc. 293 (April 1967).

Brown, Ralph S., Kaplin, Benjamin, Lacy, Dan, Haskins, Caryl P.,

5-0 G. R. E. 1 at pg. 189; reviewed in 13 C. R. 22,544 by R. N. Freed (Feb. 1972).

Buckman, T., Protection of Proprietary Interest in Computer Programs, 51 J. P. O. S. 135 (March 1969).

Dixon, Sharon P., Parker, Kellis E., West, Togo, D., Software, Statutes and Stare Deisis, 13 Howard L.J. 420 (Spring 1967).

Duggan, Michael A., Patents and Programs: the A.M.C.'s Position, Comm. A.C.M. 278 (April 1971).

Felsman, Robert A., Crisman, Thomas L., Hope, Henry W., Holder, John E., Medlock, V. Bryan Jr., Computer Program Protection, 34 Tex. B.J. 127 (Jan. 22, 1971).

Fisher, Thomas E., Lear v. Adkins--Enforcement of Contractual Provisions Restricting Disclosure of Confidential Information, 6 Law Notes 115 (July 1970).

Freed, Roy N., "Protection of Proprietary Software Programs in the U.S." in Winkler, Stanley (Ed.), Computer Communication Impacts and Implication--First Int'l. Conf. on Computer Communication (Northridge: I.E.E.E. Computer Society, 1972); reprinted in 13 J.J. 139 (Spring 1973).

Id., Some Program Patents OK, But Trade Secrets Better, 6 Computerworld 20 (Dec. 1972-Jan. 1973).

Id., Trade Secrets, Tax Issues Confuse Software Sector, 7 Computerworld 24 (Jan. 1973).

Galbi, Elmer W., Software and Patents: A Status Report, 14 Comm. A.C.M. 274 (April 1971).

Galler, B.A., Pinkerton, T.D., Arden, B.W., Proprietary Packages: A Point of View, 11 Comm. A.C.M. 802 (Dec. 1968).

Gambrell, James B., "Problems of Software" in Leninger and Gilchrist, Computers, Society and Law: The Role of Legal Education (Montvale, N.J.: A.F.I.P.S. Press, 1973) pg. 59.

Goldberg, Morton David, Legal Protection of EDP Software, 18 Datamation 66 (May 1972); reprinted in 4 Law & Comp. Tech. 97 (July-Aug. 1972); reviewed in 13 C.R. 23,812 (Sept. 1972).

Id., Patent and Copyright Implications of Electronic Data Processing, 8 Idea 183 (1964).

Goldstein, Bernard, Program Protection, Data Systems News 20 (Feb. 26, 1968).

Haanstra, John W., "Software: An Independent Existence?" in Kayton (Ed.), The Law of Software--1968 Proceedings, Computers-In-Law Inst., Geo. Wash. U. (1968) A-1.

Jacobs, Morton C., Legal Approaches for Protecting Computer Programs, 8 Data Processing 450 (1965).

Id., "Patent, Copyright and Trade Secret Aspects of Computers" in Bigelow (Ed.), Computers and the Law: An Introductory Handbook (2d ed.), A.B.A. Comm. on Elec. Data Retrieval (1966) pg. 90.

Id., Commission's Report (Re: Computer Programs), 49 J. P. O. S. 372 (May 1967).

Id., "Proprietary Protection of Hardware and Software" in Bigelow (Ed.), Computers and the Law: An Introductory Handbook (2d ed.), A. B. A. Standing Committee on Law and Technology (1969) pg. 148.

Katona, G. P., Legal Protection of Computer Programs, 47 J. P. O. S. 995 (Dec. 1965).

Kaul, Donald A., And Now State Protection of Intellectual Property?, 60 A. B. A. J. 198 (Feb. 1974).

Kayton, Irving, Protection and Licensing of Computer Software: Before and After Lear (Lear v. Adkins), 2 Licensing Law & Practices Inst., Proc 432 (1970).

Keefe, Arthur J., with Mahn, Terry G., Protecting Software: Is It Worth All The Trouble?, 62 A. B. A. J. 906 (1976).

Koller, Herbert R., Computer Software Protection: Report of an Institute Clinic, 13 Idea 351 (Fall 1969-1970).

Lawlor, Reed C., Software Protection--The American View, Conf. Rpt. British Comp. Soc. 22 (Nov. 1969).

Martin, Julian Clark, Spinggate, Jack R., Protection of a Businessman's Proprietary Information, 32 La. L. Rev. 497 (June 1972).

McFarlane, G., Legal Protection of Computer Programs, 1970 J. Bus. L. 204 (July 1970).

Morris, Grant E., Protecting Proprietary Rights of Computer Programs: The Need for New Legislative Protection, 2 Catholic U. L. Rev. 181 (Fall 1971).

Patent Resources Group, Software Protection by Trade Secret Contract Patent, (Washington, D. C., 1969) pg. 358.

Puckett, Allen W., Protecting Computer Programs, 13 Datamation 55 (Nov. 1967); letter regarding article in 14 Datamation 12 (Feb. 1968).

Rackman, M. I., Legal Protection of Computer Programs, 48 J. P. O. S. 275 (April 1966).

Silber, Howard A., A Hypothetical Interview Between the President of a Computer Software Company and a Patent Attorney Specializing in Protection of Computer Programs, 19 Comp. & Auto. 16 (Feb. 1970); reprinted in 2 Comp. Services 21 (March-April 1970); C. R. 19, 703.

Smith, L. W., What is Proprietary in Mathematical Programming?, 4 Comm. A. C. M. 542 (Dec. 1961).

Titus, James P., The Government Increases Its Regulations of Computers, 2 Comm A. C. M. 645 (Sept. 1968).

Weiss, Eric A., Response to Galler, Pinkerton, Arden Letter, 12 Comm A. C. M. 302 (June 1969).

Wessel, Milton R., Legal Protection of Computer Programs, 43 Harv. Bus. Rev. 97 (March-April 1965).

Id., Software Protection--A Need to Work Together for Survival, 2 Comp. Services 70 (March-April 1970).

Young, Melvin L., Precarious Path to Adequate Legal Protection of Software, 10 Data Mgt. 10 (Aug. 1972).

A. C. M. Will Register Software Names--Registry Will Indicate Whether the Name Is Legally Protected, e.g. a Trademark, Computerworld (Nov. 15, 1967).

Adequate Legal Protection for Computer Programs, 1968 Utah L. Rev. 369 (Sept. 1968).

Computer Programs and Proposed Revisions of the Patent and Copyright Laws, 81 Harv. L. Rev. 1541 (May 1968); C.R. 17,611.

Computer Program Protection: The Need to Legislate a Solution, 54 Cornell L. Rev. 586 (April 1969).

Software Protection: Patents, Copyrights, and Trade Secrets, 35 Albany L. Rev. 695 (1971).

Protection of Proprietary Rights, 7 Honeywell Comp. J. 61 (1973).

Computer Software: Beyond the Limits of Existing Proprietary Protection Policy, 40 Brooklyn L. Rev. 116 (Summer 1973); noted in 20 Bus. Law 1062 (April 1974).

Patent Protection

Barnaby, Howard B. Jr., Patent Law--Computer Programs Unpatentable Mental Process: Gottschalk v. Benson, 14 B.C. Ind. & Com. L. Rev. 1050 (May 1973).

Bender, David, Computer Programs: Should They Be Patentable?, 68 Colum. I. Rev. 241 (Feb. 1968).

Berteau, C. Donald, Don't Give Up Hope on Software Patents, 5 Comp. Decisions 45 (Feb. 1973).

Bigelow, R.P., The Patentability of Software, 5 Mod. Data 34 (June 1972).

Id., Infosystems, The Law and Patents, 20 Infosystems 34 (Feb. 1973); reprinted in 13 Jurimetrics J. 129 (Spring 1973).

Brenner, Edward J., "The Future of Computer Programs in the United States Patent Office" in Kayton (Ed.), The Law of Software--1969 Proceedings, Computers-In-Law Inst., Geo. Wash. U. (1969).

Brothers, Robert F., Grimaldi, Alan M., In re Prater and Patent Reform Proposals: "Debugging" the Patent Office's Administration of Computer Program Applications, 18 Catholic U. L. Rev. 389 (Spring 1969); reprinted in 51 J. P. O. S. 581 (Sept. 1969).

Bureau of National Affairs, Analysis, Are Computer Programs Ever Patentable? Did the Patent Office Win?, 24 P. T. C. J. C-1 (1973).

Coe, Roger Norman, A Second Sword of Damocles for Licenses, 54 J. P. O. S. 175 (March 1972).

Cohen, Eric, Patentability of Computer Programs, 27 U. Miami L. Rev. 494 (1973).

"Supreme Court Again Ducks Software Patentability Issue", Computer Law Tax Reporter (May 1976) pg. 1.

Davidson, Leon, Practical Considerations in Program Patentability, 17 Comp. & Auto 12 (May 1968).

Duggan, Michael A., Patents on Computer Programs? Round Six and No Decision in View!, 12 Comm. A. C. M. 589 (Oct. 1969).

Id., Patents and Programs: The A. C. M.'s Position, 14 Comm. A. C. M. 278 (April 1971); C.R. 21,639.

Id., Patents on Programs? The Supreme Court Says No, 16 Comm. A. C. M. 60 (Jan. 1973); reprinted in 13 Jurismetrics J. 135 (Spring 1973).

Dunner, Donald R., Gambrell, James B., White, Stuart A., Kayton, Irving, Nonstatutory Subject Matter, 14 Jurismetrics J. 113 (Winter 1973); reprinted from Dunner, Gambrell, White & Kayton, Patent Law Perspectives--Current Service.

Goetz, Martin, Letter to the Editor, Comm. A. C. M. (May 1973).

Etienne, A. J., Patent and Copyright Implications of Electronic Data Processing, 8 Idea 153 (1964).

Falk, James W., Mental Steps and the Patent Law--A Rumination, 8 Patent L. Ann. 203 (1970).

Id., The Use of Apparatus and Operational Method Claims by Patentees, 54 J. P. O. S. 723 (Nov. 1972).

Id., Knowledge, Patents, and the Market Place, Loyola U. L. J. 279 (Summer 1972).

Galbi, Elmer W., Software and Patents: A Status Report, 17 Bull. Cr. Soc. 280 (April 1970); C.R. 21,638.

Id., The Prospect of Future Legislation and Court Action Concerning the Protection of Programming, 13 Jurimetrics J. 235 (Summer 1973).

Goetz, Martin A., Revise Don't Sacrifice the Software Patent System, Computerworld (April 18, 1977).

Graham, M. W. J. Jr., Process Patents for Computer Program Patents, 56 Calif. L. Rev. 466 (April 1968).

Hamlin, Kenneth B., Computer Programs Are Patentable, 7 Comm. A.C.M. 581 (Oct. 1964).

Hauptman, Gunter A., Joint Inventorship of Computers, 7 Comm. A.C.M. 579 (Oct. 1964).

Heitezman, George A., Computer Programs "Are" Patentable, 1 Seton Hall L. Rev. 113 (1970).

Hirsch, Phil, The Patent Office Examines Software, Datamation 79 (Nov. 1966).

Iandiorio, Joseph S., Which Wei Did They Go?, 53 J.P.O.S. 712 (Nov. 1971).

Id., Protecting Computer Programs--The Conventional Forms of Protection Are Still Available, Boston B.J. 25 (Nov. 1972).

Jacobs, Morton C., Patent Protection of Computer Programs, 7 Comm. A.C.M. 583 (Oct. 1964); reprinted in 47 J.P.O.S. 6 (Jan. 1965).

Id., "Patentable Machines--Systems Embodiable in Hardware or Software (The Myth of the Non-Machine)" in Kayton (Ed.), The Law of Software--1968 Proceedings, Computers-In-Law Inst., Geo. Wash. U. (1968) A-1.

Id., Commission Report Regarding Computer Programs, 49 J.P.O.S. 5 (1967).

Id., Patents for Software Inventions--The Supreme Court's Decision, 55 J.P.O.S. 59 (Jan. 1973); reprinted in 13 Jurismetrics J 132 (Spring 1973).

Id., Patents for Software Inventions--The Supreme Court's Computer Programming Decision, 16 Comm A.C.M. 586 (Oct. 1973).

Kayton, Irving, Patent Protectability of Software: Background and Current Law, reprint in Jurimetrics J. 153 (Dec. 1968); C.R. 18, 383.

Koller, Herbert R., Moshman, J., "Patent Protection for Computer Software: Implications for the Industry" in Kayton (Ed.), The Law of Software--1968 Proceedings, Computers-In-Law Inst., Geo. Wash. U. (1968) A-45; reprinted in 12 Idea 1109 (Winter 1968).

Kurtz, Richard E., Patents and Data Processing, 6 Data Proc. Mag. 9 (Nov. 1964); letter regarding article in Data Proc. Mag. 13 (Jan. 1965) by John F. Banzhaf III.

Leavitt, Don, C.C.P.A. Again O.K.'s Program Patent, Computerworld 1, 4 (Dec. 13, 1976).

Mandelbaum, Howard F., Gottschalk v. Benson--The Supreme Court Takes a Hard Line on Software, 471 St. John's L. Rev. 635 (May 1973).

Milgrim, Roger M., Software, Carfare and "Benson", 19 Datamation 75 (April 1973); reprinted in 13 Jurimetrics J 240 (Summer 1973).

Milbank, Robert, Finders Keepers, Licensors Weepers, 52 J.P.O.S. 343 (June 1970).

Nimtz, Robert O., The Patentability of Computer Programs, 1970 Rutgers J. Comp. & Law 38 (Spring 1970).

Painter, M.A., Recent Developments in the Protection of Computer Programs Under the Patent System, 5 J. Beverly Hills 32 (Nov.-Dec. 1972).

Popper, Howard R., "Method Claims for Programmable Processes" in Kayton (Ed.), The Law of Software--1968 Proceedings, Computers-In-Law Inst., Geo. Wash. U. (1968) B-55.

Id., Prater II (Prater, In re, 415 F2d 1393), 19 Am. U.L. Rev. 25 (Dec. 1969).

Rackman, Michael I., Patentability of Computer Programs, 38 N.Y.U.L. Rev. 981 (1963).

Reese, William, Patent Law Computer Programs for Processing Data with a Digital Computer Cannot be Patented Under Present U.S. Laws, 4 Loyola U.L.J. 560 (Summer 1973).

Schuyler, William E. Jr., "Protecting Property in Computer Software" in Kayton (Ed.), The Law of Software--1969 Proceedings, Computers-In-Law Inst., Geo. Wash. U. (1969) H.

Sheers, and Encke, Ernest L., Copyrights of Patents for Computer Programs?, 49 J.P.O.S. 323 (May 1967).

Sher, Melvin, Comment: Commissioner of Patents v. Benson et al, 56 J.P.O.S. 179 (March 1974).

Soltysinski, Stanislaw J., Computer Programs and Patent Law, 3 Rutgers J. Comp. Law (1973).

Spaeth, Harold J., High Court Seen Likely To Reject Patents, 5 Law & Comp. Tech. 50 (March-April 1972).

Titus, James P., Supreme Court Ruling Fails To Settle Issue of Patenting Computer Programs, 16 Comm. A.C.M. 63 (Jan. 1973).

Stanford Research Institute, Legal Protection of Proprietary Rights in Software, prepared by Susan Nycum for the Nat'l. Science Fdn. (1976).

Wessel, Milton R., Some Implications of the Software Decision, 14 Jurimetrics J. 110 (Winter 1973); reprinted in 19 Datamation 165 (Feb. 1973), 20 Data Proc. Dig. 9 (May 1974).

Woodcock, Virgil E., "The Implications of the Software Decision" in Kayton (Ed.), The Law of Software--1969 Proceedings, Computers-In-Law Inst., Geo. Wash. U. (1969) D-1.

Id., Mental Steps and Computer Programs, 52 J.P.O.S. 275 (May 1970); C.R. 20,412.

Analysis of Gottschalk v. Benson, B.N.A.'s Patent, Trademark & Copyright J. (April 1973).

Are Computer Programs Ever Patentable? Did the Patent Office Win?, B. N. A. 's Patent, Trademark & Copyright J. C1 (April 19, 1973); reprinted in 13 Jurimetrics J. 248 (Summer 1973).

Comment, Computer Programs for Processing Data with a Digital Computer Cannot Be Patented Under Present U.S. Laws--Gottschalk v. Benson, 4 Loyola U. L. J. 560 (1973).

Computer Programmers Are Not Inventors, New Scientist 30 (Nov. 1972).

Gottschalk v. Benson: Case Comments, 4 Loyola U. L. J. 560 (Summer 1973).

Limits of Copyright and Patent Protection for Computer Programs, 16 Copyright L. Sym. (ASCAP) 81 (1968).

Mathematics, Computers, and In re Prater: The Medium and the Message, 58 Georgetown L. J. 391 (1969); reprinted in 2 Patent L. Rev. 615 (1970).

"Mental Steps" Doctrine: A Critical Analysis in Light of Prater and Wei (Prater & Wei, In re, 159 U.S.P.Q. 583), 52 J. P. O. S. 479 (Aug. 1970).

Nonstatutory Subject Matter (Re: Gottschalk v. Benson), 2 Pat. L. Perspectives (1973).

Patentability of Computer Programs: Gottachalk v. Benson, 93 S. Ct. 253 (1972), 27 U. Miami L. Rev. 494 (Spring/Summer 1973).

Patent Law--Another Step Past Prater--"Patentable Process" Expanded--In re Musgrave, 2 Seton Hall L. Rev. 551 (1971).

Patently Untrue, 1 Group/3 J. 12 (Dec. 1972).

Patents--Patentability--A Process Performable on an Analog Computer Which Also Reads Upon a General Purpose Digital Computer Does Not Necessarily Fall Within the "Mental Step" Exclusion and May Be Patentable If the Specificity Requirements of Section 112 Are Fulfilled, 49 Tex. L. Rev. 971 (May 1970).

Process Patents for Computer Programs, 56 Calif. L. Rev. 466 (April 1968).

Programs Must Be Disclosed for Computer Which Is Not Used in "Conventional" Manner, B.N.A.'s Patent, Trademark & Copyright J. (Sept. 13, 1973).

Copyright

Banzhaf III, John F., Copyright Protection for Computer Programs, 64 Columbia L. Rev. 1274 (Nov. 1964); C.R. 8093.

Id., On Computers and Programs--Copyrights and Patents, 8 Comm. A.C.M. 220 (April 1965); C.R. 8094.

Id., Copyrighted Computer Programs: Some Questions and Answers, Comp. & Auto. 22 (July 1965).

Id., Statement Before House Judiciary Committee-Subcommittee, 3 Comp. & Auto 9 (Sept. 1965); Comp. & Auto. (Oct. 1965).

Id., "Copyright Protection for Computer Programs" in Kayton (Ed.), The Law of Software--1968 Proceedings, Computers-In-Law Inst., Geo. Wash. U. (1968) C-33.

Breyer, Stephen, The Uneasy Ease for Copyright: a Study of Copyright in Books, Photocopies and Computer Programs, 84 Harv. L. Rev. 281 (1970).

Cary, G.D., Copyright Registration and Computer Programs, 11 Bull. Cr. Soc. 362 (Aug. 1964).

Id., "The Registrability of Computer Programs" in Kayton (Ed.), The Law of Software--1968 Proceedings, Computers-In-Law Inst., Geo. Wash. U. (1968) C-15.

Computerworld, editorial, A Realistic Method, (March 21, 1977).

Committee to Consider the Law on Copyright and Designs, report of, Copyright and Designs Law, Her Majesty's Stationery Office (1977).

Computer Law Association, Transcript of Proceedings March 9, 1977 (Washington, D.C.).

Cunningham, Joseph, Information Retrieval and the Copyright Law, 14 Bull. Cr. Soc. 223 (Oct. 1966).

Detner, J.M., Savage, B.I., Copyrighted Computer Programs: Some Comments, 14 Comp. & Auto. 13, 56 (Dec. 1965).

Doud, Wallace C., "The Business of Software and Its Protection" in Kayton (Ed.), The Law of Software--1969 Proceedings, Computers-In-Law Inst., Geo. Wash. U. (1969) P.

Freed, Roy N., Copyright Act Protects Programs Form, Not Contents, Computerworld (April 25, 1975).

Hill, James, Scope of Protection for Computer Programs Under the Copyright Act, 14 De Paul L. Rev. 360 (Spring-Summer 1965).

Holf, J.F., Software Copyrights, 11 Datamation 13 (April 1965).

Iskrant, John, The Impact of the Multiple Forms of Computer Programs on Their Adequate Protection by Copyright, 18 Copyright L. Sym. (ASCAP) 92 (1970).

Mahn, Terry, Copyrighting Software--Is It Worth All the Trouble?, 4 On Line 3 (May 1976).

McTiernen, C.E., Copyright Protection for Computer Programs, 4 Data Proc. 28 (Jan. 1966).

Miller, Arthur R., Computers and Copyright Law, Mich. St. B. J. 11 (April 1967).

Id., "Computers and Copyrights" in Holmes and Norville (Ed.s), The Law of Computers (Ann Arbor: Inst. of Contin. Legal Ed., 1971) pg. 107.

Mooers, Calvin N., Copyright Seen as Best Program Protection, Covers Unauthorized Use, Translations, Computerworld (Oct. 13, 1971).

National Commission on New Technological Uses of Copyrighted Works, Software, Subcommittee Report and Additional Views (1977).

Nelson, G. J., Copyrightability of Computer Programs, 7 Ariz. L. Rev. 204 (Spring 1966).

Oberman, Michael S., Copyright Protection for Computer Produced Directories, 41 Fordham L. Rev. 767 (May 1973).

Prasinos, Nicholas, Worldwide Protection of Computer Programs by Copyright, 4 Rutgers J. Comp. L. 42 (1974).

Savelson, R.S., Electronic Music and the Copyright Law, 13 Copyright L. Sym. (ASCAP) 133 (1964).

Scafetta, Joseph Jr., Computer Software Protection; the Copyright Revision Bills and Alternatives, 8 J. Mar. J. Prac. Proc. 381.

Smoot, Oliver R., Development of an International System for Legal Protection of Computer Programs, 19 Comm. A.C.M. 171 (1976).

Titus, James P., Copyrighting Computer Programs, 9 Comm. A.C.M. 879 (Dec. 1966).

Computer Programs To Be Registered for Copyright, 23 Lib. Cong. Info. Bull. 226 (May 18, 1964).

Copyright Protection for Computer Programs, 14 Copyright L. Sym. 118 (ASCAP) (1966).

Copyright Laws in the Computer Age, 19 Datamation 138 (May 1973).

Impact of the Mutliple Forms of Computer Programs on Their Adequate Protection by Copyright, 18 Copyright L. Sym. 92 (ASCAP) (1970).

Trade Secrets

Adelman, Martin J., Trade Secrets and Federal Pre-Emption--The Aftermath of Sears and Compco, 49 J.P.O.S. 713 (Oct. 1967).

Secrecy and Patenting: Some Proposals for Resolving the Conflicts, 1 A.P.L.A. J. 293 (1973).

Arnold, Tom, Durkee, Bill, Shadows Do Not Fight, 1 A.P.L.A. J. 244 (1973).

Arnold, Tom, Protecting Trade Secrets Today--In House, in Commerce, in Court, N.Y.P.L.I. 424 (1973).

Bender, David, "Trade Secret Protection of Software After Lear vs. Adkins" in Kayton (Ed.), The Law of Software--1969 Proceedings, Computers-In-Law Inst., Geo. Wash. U. (1969) F.

Id., Post-Adkins Trade Secret Protection of Software, 1970 Rutgers J. of Comp. & Law 5 (Spring 1970).

Id., Trade Secret Protection of Software, 38 Geo. Wash. L. Rev. 909 (July 1970).

Bigelow, Robert P., Opportunity Makes a Thief, 20 Infosystems 29 (Dec. 1973).

Doerfer, Gordon L., The Limits on Trade Secret Law Imposed by Federal Patent and Antitrust Supremacy, 80 Harv. L. Rev. 1432 (1967).

Foster, Stanley H., Comments on Painton and Company v. Bourns, Inc., 53 J.P.O.S. 732 (Nov. 1971).

Foy, Nancy, How Telex Got at Vital Secrets, Computing 14 (Nov. 15, 1973).

Fromholz, Haley J., Legal Protection of Computer Programs and Confidential Information, Comp. Conf. '73, San Francisco (Silver Springs: I.E.E.E., 1973).

Id., Legal Protection of Proprietary Software, 6 Computer 27 (Dec. 1973).

Fromson, David, The Safeguarding of Trade Secrets--Your Elusive Asset, N.Y.S.B.J. 53 (Jan. 1968).

Gamboni, Ciro A., Unfair Competition Protection After Sears and Compco, 15 Copyright L. Sym. (ASCAP) 1 (1965).

Goldstein, Paul, The Competitive Mandate: From Sears to Lear, 59 Calif. L. Rev. (June 1971); reprinted in 53 J.P.O.S. 627 (Oct. 1971).

Harding, Victor M., Trade Secrets and the Mobile Employee, 22 Bus. Law. 395 (Jan. 1967).

Kane Jr., Daniel H., Limitations on the Law of Trade Secrets, 53 J.P.O.S. 162 (March 1971).

Mahon Jr., John J., Trade Secrets and Patents Compared, 50 J.P.O.S. 536 (Aug. 1968).

Milgrim, Roger M., Trade Secret Protection and Licensing--A True Alternative, A.P.L.A. Bull. 396 (July 1972).

Pretty, Lawrence H., Industrial Processes and Formulas: Special Consideration for the Lawyer in Protecting Them, 8 Law Notes 91 (Spring 1972).

Schneider, Joseph, Protecting Trade Secrets, 8 Trial 55 (Jan.-Feb. 1972).

Schneider, Joseph; Halstrom, Frederic, A Program for Protecting Proprietary Information, 18 Prac. Law '71 (Oct. 1972).

Vandevoort, John R., Trade Secrets: Protecting a Very Special "Property", 26 Bus. Law 681 (Jan. 1971).

Wydick, Richard, Trade Secrets: Federal Preemption in the Light of Goldstein and Kewanee (Part I), 55 J.P.O.S. 736 (Dec. 1973); Part II, 56 J.P.O.S. 4 (Jan. 1974).

Theft of Trade Secrets: The Need for a Statutory Solution, 120 U. Pa. L. Rev. 378 (Dec. 1971).

Patent Law--Federal Patent Application Not a Prerequisite To Licensing a Trade Secret for Royalties--Painton v. Bourns, 50 J. Urban L. 159 (1972).

Unfair Compeitition--Patent Law--State Trade Secret Laws Protecting a Patentable Discovery Are Preempted by Federal Patent Laws--Kewanee Oil Co. v. Bicron Corp., 478 F.2d 1074 (6th Cir. 1973), cert granted, 42 USLW 3194 (U.S. Oct. 9, 1973) (No. 73-187), 53 B.U.L. Rev. 1142 (Nov. 1973).

Patent Preemption of Trade Secret Protection of Inventions Meeting Judicial Standards of Patentability, 87 Harv. L. Rev. 807 (Feb. 1974).

Other Means

Constantine, Larry L., The Processright: Protection for Programs, 2 Mod. Data 24 (June 1969).

Galbi, Elmer W., Proposal for New Legislation To Protect Computer Programming, 17 Bull. Cr. Soc. 280 (April 1970).

Galler, B.A., Mooers, C.N., Correspondence Relative to Usefulness of Trademark in Software Protection, 11 Comm. A.C.M. 148 (March 1968).

Gardner, Martin, Mathematical Games, Scientific American (Aug. 1977).

Lawlor, Reed C., Patent Attorney Sees Need To Revise IBM Proposal, 16 Datamation 154 (March 1970).

Mooers, Calvin N., Accommodating Standards and Identification of Programming Languages, 11 Comm. A.C.M. 574 (Aug. 1968); C.R. 15,506.

Senhenn, D.A., Wanted: A New Law To Protect Computer Program Material, 12 Comp. Bull. 112 (July 1968); C.R. 16,112.

Steel Jr., T.B., Commentary on Mr. Mooers' Paper, 11 Comm. A.C.M. 576 (Aug. 1968); C.R. 15,507.

Trademarks and Languages, Computerworld 4 (Sept. 11, 1968).

APPENDIX C
COMPUTERWORLD QUESTIONNAIRE

Page 10 COMPUTERWORLD July 11, 1977

Contu Researcher Asks Help

How Effective Is Your Software Protection?

The National Commission on New Technological Uses of Copyrighted Works (Contu) was established to consider problems related to the reproduction and use of copyrighted works on DP systems, among other things. To do this, it has contracted with various research firms to gather data in specific areas of interest.

One of these firms has turned to Computerworld, and particularly the software developers or vendors among our readers, for help.

Harbridge House developed the following questionnaire to accumulate statistics, rather than folklore, on what forms of protection are being used for software and how effective that protection is.

CW has been assured (by Harbridge House) that information provided by readers will be treated as confidential, not going forward in the company's report to Contu nor in a summary report of the results with which the researchers will provide CW.

The completed questionnaire should be sent to Richard I. Miller, Harbridge House, Inc., 11 Arlington St., Boston, Mass. 02116.

Contu Questionnaire

(Please Use 1976 for All "Annually" Based Questions)

1. Name of Company ______

 Address ______

 Respondent's Name, Phone No. and Company Position

 ______

2. Please list the three major services/products provided by your company, indicating also the percent of annual sales each represents.

 1. ______ % annual sales ______
 2. ______ % annual sales ______
 3. ______ % annual sales ______

3. How many employees does your company have? ______

4. What are the total annual sales of your company? $______

5. How much does your company invest annually in software development and research? $______

6. Please indicate below how often during the past year you utilized the following forms of software protection, and indicate how effective you consider them to be. (If you do not know, please indicate with "DK".)

PROTECTION TECHNIQUES	USE Number of Times in the Last Calendar or Fiscal Year: In Business Operations and/or Negotiations	In Legal Action	EFFECTIVENESS Rank order on scale of 0-5*
1. Contract or license backed up by: a. Patent			
b. Copyright			
c. State trade secret law			
d. Release of object program only			
e. None of the above			
2. Requirement for "know-how"			
3. Use of cryptographic protection			
4. Use of other means to limit access to the software program			

*0 = not effective at all; 5 = completely effective

7. Please list the proprietary software products you market below and indicate next to each whether there is no significance, some or great significance regarding the importance of legal protection for each of the products.

 1. ______
 2. ______
 3. ______
 4. ______
 5. ______
 6. ______

8. Have you ever rejected or abandoned a marketing program for a proprietary software product because of the inadequacy of legal protection

 Yes ______ No ______

9. Do you know of any situation where software products representing a significant level of innovation are not developed or marketed because of inadequate protection?

 Yes ______ No ______ Please Identify ______

10. Do you contemplate any change in your marketing program because of the Copyright Act of 1976, effective January 1, 1978?
 Yes ______ No ______

11. How would you change your marketing program if legal protection were otherwise improved for computer software? ______

Thank you for your participation.

APPENDIX D
ADAPSO QUESTIONNAIRE

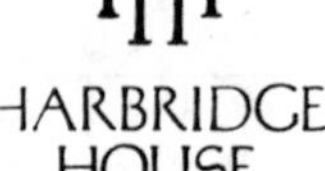

HARBRIDGE HOUSE INC

Eleven Arlington Street, Boston, Massachusetts 02116, Telephone (617) 267-6410, Cable: HARBRIDGE BOSTON

RICHARD I. MILLER
Vice President

June 1, 1977

Dear ADAPSO Member:

Public Law 93-573, enacted on December 31, 1974, established a National Commission on New Technological Uses of Copyrighted Works (CONTU). Among other things it requires the Commission to study and compile data on the reproduction and use of copyrighted works "in conjunction with automatic systems capable of storing, processing, retrieving, and transferring information . . . " and the creation of new works by application or intervention of such systems. The Commission must recommend such changes in copyright law or procedures as may be necessary to assure access to copyrighted works and provide recognition of the rights of copyright owners.

The ADAPSO Software Protection Committee has been monitoring CONTU hearings (as well as other developments pertaining to computer software). Accordingly, Marty Goetz and Jerry Dreyer--speaking for the organization as a whole--were quick to declare their interest in a fact-finding survey which this firm is performing for CONTU on software protection. They join me in requesting that you fill out and return the attached questionnaire by June 15 (a self addressed return envelope is enclosed). We feel that this is a unique and most valuable opportunity for you to play a significant part in the formulation of recommendations for new legislation which will affect your work for years to come, and your help is both needed and deeply appreciated.

The information you submit will be treated as confidential and disclosed only to regular employees of Harbridge House for their use in preparing the Harbridge House report to CONTU. The report will be presented in a form that will preclude attribution of statistics or comments to the company providing them, either directly or by inference.

The final question asks for general comments that may be helpful to the CONTU staff. Please describe here any problems encountered in software protection that were not identified in earlier answers, as well as any thoughts you have on the best overall approach to the protection of proprietary software (whether by changes in the copyright law or otherwise).

Do not hesitate to contact me or my associates, Francis J. Kelley and Deborah C. Notman, if you have any questions about the survey or any part of the questionnaire.

Very truly yours,

Richard Miller

Richard I. Miller
Vice President

Boston New York Washington Chicago Los Angeles London Paris Frankfurt am Main

ADAPSO QUESTIONNAIRE
by
Harbridge House, Inc.

Please fill in:
Name of Company ______

Address ______

Date Company Founded ______ State ______

Respondent's Position in Company ______

Respondent's Name and Phone Number ______

PLEASE RELATE ALL "ANNUAL" OR "BASE YEAR" QUESTIONS TO 1976 OR THE MOST RECENT YEAR FOR WHICH FIGURES ARE AVAILABLE. IF OTHER THAN 1976, PLEASE INDICATE THE YEAR ENDING ______.

1. What are the services and products provided by your company?

		% of Annual Sales
a. Consulting (feasibility studies, systems analysis and design).	______	______
b. Contract Programming (including custom software packages).	______	______
c. Proprietary Software Packages	______	______
d. Time-sharing	______	______
e. Telecommunications	______	______
f. Data Center Operations and Management	______	______
g. Facility Management	______	______
h. Education	______	______
i. Hardware Products	______	______
j. Others? Please list: ______		______
______		______
______		______

2a. Is your company a division or subsidiary of another company?

Division ______ Subsidiary ______ Neither ______

2b. Name of parent company (if applicable), or affiliates:

______

3. How many employees does your company have?

______ Fewer than 25
______ 25 to 100
______ 100 to 500
______ 500 to 1,000
______ More than 1,000

4. How much does your company spend annually on internally funded software development, including research?

______ Less than $50,000
______ $50,000 to $100,000
______ $100,000 to $500.000
______ $500,000 to $1 million
______ $1 to $10 million
______ More than $10 million

5. What are the **total annual sales** of your company?

____ Less than $500,000	____ $5 to $10 million
____ $500,000 to $1 million	____ $10 to $100 million
____ $1 to $5 million	____ More than $100 million

6. With respect to software products (including both contract programming and proprietary packages), please indicate the breakdown of total annual sales as between:

	Less than $50,000	$50,000 to $250,000	$250,000 to $1 million	$1 million to $10 million	$10 million to $50 million	More than $50 million
a. Systems software programs:						
b. Application software programs:						

7. How many programs have you developed over the last three years which are regarded as proprietary to your firm?
   a. Solely at your own expense ________.
   b. Incorporating in your own material proprietary products of others which you have purchased ________.
   c. Involving arrangements for sharing of expense with customer ________.

8. What is the number of new programs produced over the last three years for:
   a. License* ________.
   b. Lease* ________.
   c. Sale (permanent use) ________.
   d. Internal use ________.
   e. Other ________.

   *It would be helpful to the Commission if you could provide a sample of your standard form.

9. Please indicate below how often during the past year you utilized the following forms of software protection, and indicate how effective you consider them to be. (If you do not know, please indicate with "DK".)

PROTECTION TECHNIQUES	USE Number of Times in the Last Calendar or Fiscal Year: In Business Operations and/or Negotiations	In Legal Action	EFFECTIVENESS Rank order on scale of 0-5*
1. Contract or license backed up by: a. Patent			
b. Copyright			
c. State trade secret law			
d. Release of object program only			
e. None of the above			
2. Requirement for "know-how"			
3. Use of cryptographic protection			
4. Use of other means to limit access to the software program.			

*0 = not effective at all; 5= completely effective.

10. If in the preceding question you marked any protection as **completely effective** or **not effective at all**, please explain in terms of your actual business experience. Indicate if a protection technique is effective against some parties but not others; i.e. (i) the party with whom you have a contract, (ii) other parties who have obtained unauthorized possession of your proprietary products, (iii) someone who copies your ideas or programs for his own use, and (iv) someone who copies your ideas or programs and attempts to market them to others.

____

____

____

____

____

____

____

____

____

11. How important from a business standpoint is legal protection for each of the proprietary software products you market in the categories below?

	No Significance	Some Significance	Great Significance
a. General business and financial applications (e.g., accounting, inventory control, payroll)			
b. Business planning operations (e.g., planning models, simulations, operations research)			
c. Complex production/distribution control operations (e.g., linear programming)			
d. Engineering and scientific applications			
e. Data and statistical analysis			
f. Project management and control			
g. Systems software (e.g., compilers, monitors, new techniques for more efficient machine utilization)			

12. Please provide the following information for your **five** "best selling" programs (in terms of number of copies, not dollar value).

	Type of Program	Sold or Licensed /Leased	Date First Marketed	No. of Copies Distributed		Optional Information**	
				Since Inception	In latest calendar/ fiscal year	Development Cost	Price to Customer
Program 1							
Program 2							
Program 3							
Program 4							
Program 5							

*Designate "a" or "b", etc., according to type of program categories in question 11 above.

**This information would be helpful to the Commission if you are free to provide it.

13. Do your contractual arrangements with customers normally restrain them from duplicating programs supplied by you, beyond normal use and backup?

    Yes ____ No ____

14. Have you ever rejected or abandoned a marketing program for a proprietary software product because of the inadequacy of legal protection?

    Yes ____ No ____

    If yes, please describe:

    ____

    ____

    ____

15. Are you aware of any situation (other than one described in #14 above) where software products representing a significant level of innovation are not developed or marketed because of inadequate protection?

    Yes ____ No ____

    Please identify each situation by industry/function and comment on the loss of economic/social value in each case.

    ____

    ____

    ____

    ____

16. Do you contemplate any change in your marketing program because of the Copyright Act of 1976, effective January 1, 1978?

    Yes ____ No ____

17. Would your marketing program be changed if legal protection were otherwise improved for computer software?

    Yes ____ No ____

    If yes, how?

    ____

    ____

    ____

    ____

18. Please provide below any additional information or comments that you think would be helpful to CONTU in its study. [Include here any problems encountered in software protection that were not identified in earlier answers, as well as any thoughts you have on the best overall approach to the protection of proprietary software (whether by changes in the copyright law or otherwise).]

    ____

    ____

    ____

    ____

    ____

    ____

Thank you very much for your cooperation in this project.

Library Photocopying in the United States

SUMMARY OF LIBRARY PHOTOCOPYING
IN THE UNITED STATES

This report presents the results of a study of the amount of photocopying of library materials by library staff in United States libraries. A national survey was conducted from a sample of Public, Academic, Special and Federal libraries to determine the annual volume of photocopying undertaken for interlibrary loans, local users, and intrasystem loans. Since interpretations of the Law concerning eligibility for royalty payment appear to vary, data are also given for the amount of photocopying that occurs under various hypothetical conditions of eligibility as they might be interpreted in the new Copyright Law and in guidelines set forth by the National Commission on New Technological Uses of Copyrighted Works (CONTU) for photocopying for interlibrary loans. The report documents the effects of these hypothetical conditions from the perspective of both libraries and publishers. In addition, the report describes alternative royalty payment mechanisms and discusses some advantages and disadvantages of each from the standpoints of small and large libraries and small and large publishers. This summary presents estimates of total volume of photocopying, analyzes implications of the new Law from the perspectives of libraries and publishers, and describes alternative payment mechanisms.

Sampling and Data Collection

The sample of libraries for collection of data on the volume and characteristics of photocopies of library materials made on library staff-controlled equipment was a stratified random selection representing the five categories of libraries: Academic, Public, Federal, Special associated with profit-seeking organizations, and Special libraries associated with not-for-profit organizations. The target minimum number of participating libraries by type were: 100 Academic, 100 Public, 62 Federal, 108 Special (74 Profit associated, 34 Non-Profit associated). These target numbers were based in part on the estimated volumes of interlibrary lending for 1972, the most recent year for which comprehensive data could be assembled at the time.

Some large libraries were included in the sample with certainty, to represent themselves. The remaining libraries of each type were stratified by significant variables to facilitate selection of a representative sample from which to estimate totals for the non-certainty libraries. Academic libraries were stratified by size (measured by volumes in collection) and type of institution (University, four year, two year). Public libraries were stratified by population served and by region. Federal libraries were stratified by agency and by volume of interlibrary loans. Special libraries were stratified by size. Participation was invited from a sample larger than the minimum target number, so that ineligible libraries, refusals, and nonresponse would not disrupt the very tight time table.

In order to avoid excessive burden on any library, short sample periods were specified for collecting each major category of information. Each library was asked to record and report information on photocopying volumes for a sample period, to describe characteristics of library materials photocopied for selected days, and to report on requests made during a specified period for interlibrary loans, and on the disposition of those requests. These sample periods ranged from one day to three weeks, and were specified in light of volume reported on a preliminary screener form.

Subsequently, participating libraries were also asked to respond to a questionnaire which addressed questions of costs of photocopying operations, preferences among possible royalty payment mechanisms, judgments concerning relative costs of hypothetical recordkeeping procedures, and a few volume items. Thus, the data collection from libraries involved an initial screener inquiry and four separate, but closely related, requests for information.

In addition, the time limitation on the project did not permit data collection to be spread throughout the year. Therefore, it was important to find adjustment factors to correct for the difference between periods (days of the week and months of the year) when data were collected and the average activity over the year. Such adjustment weights were derived in the course of an analysis of interlibrary loan data for the MINITEX system for the year 1976. The MINITEX data were also used to verify a mathematical model used to project estimates of the distribution of photocopying to the entire year.

A total of 37,032 individual photocopy transactions were reported by the sampled libraries and analyzed. These reports of photocopying included information about each individual photocopy transaction such as type of material (serials, books, other materials), whether copyrighted, type of transaction (interlibrary loan, local user, intrasystem loan) as well as other relevant information.

Total Volume of Photocopying

In 1976, one full year prior to implementation of the new Copyright Law, a substantial amount of photocopying took place in libraries in the United States. It is estimated that there were 36.8 thousand paper-to-paper photocopying machines in the 21,280 libraries from which the sample was chosen. Of 35.3 thousand machines used regularly for photocopying of library materials, 15.4 thousand were used exclusively by patrons for photocopying library and other materials and 19.9 thousand were used by library staff. Thus, the average number of machines per library is less than one. This study addressed only the volume of photocopying performed by library staff of library materials. Even with this limitation, an estimated 114 million photocopy items were made by library staff in that year.

Less than one-half of this volume, however, was from copyrighted materials. This means that the per library average is about 2,500 copyrighted items from 54 million photocopies made from copyrighted materials.

Public libraries accounted for the largest share of photocopying of all library materials, with 64 million photocopy items. Special libraries were next, with 26 million photocopy items, followed by Academic libraries, with 17 million, and Federal libraries, with 7 million. (See Figure 1.) The 8,310 Public libraries in the population averaged 7,700 photocopy items per library. The 3,030 Academic libraries averaged 5,500 photocopy items per library, with Special libraries (8,510) averaging 3,100 and Federal libraries (1,430) averaging 4,900 items. The proportion of photocopying from copyrighted materials varied somewhat among the types of libraries. Public libraries had the lowest proportion of photocopying from copyrighted materials (37%) and Special libraries had the highest proportion (69%). Academic libraries did 48 percent and Federal libraries did 58 percent of their photocopying from copyrighted materials. This variation among types of libraries reflects differences in the types of materials photocopied by different types of libraries.

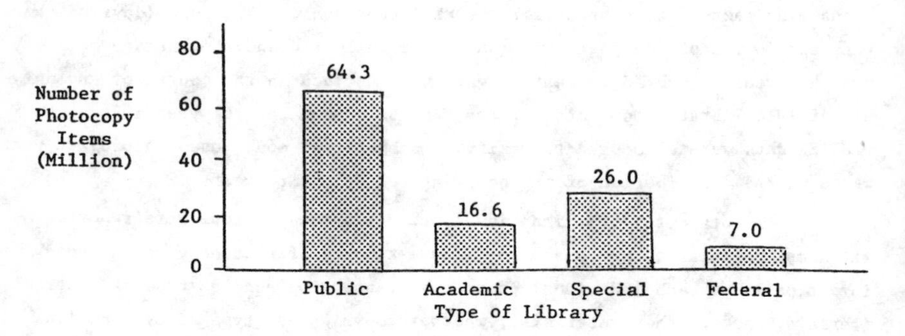

Figure 1. Number of Photocopy Items by Type of Library (1976)

Over all the libraries, serials accounted for 48 million photocopy items; books 14.9 million; and other materials 50.8 million. (See Figure 2.) Only 7 percent of the other materials, however, were identified as being copyrighted, whereas, 79 percent of the photocopy items of serials and 84 percent of the photocopy items made from books were from copyrighted materials. Public libraries accounted for nearly three-fourths of all the photocopying of other materials, which is why they had a low proportion of photocopying from copyrighted materials.

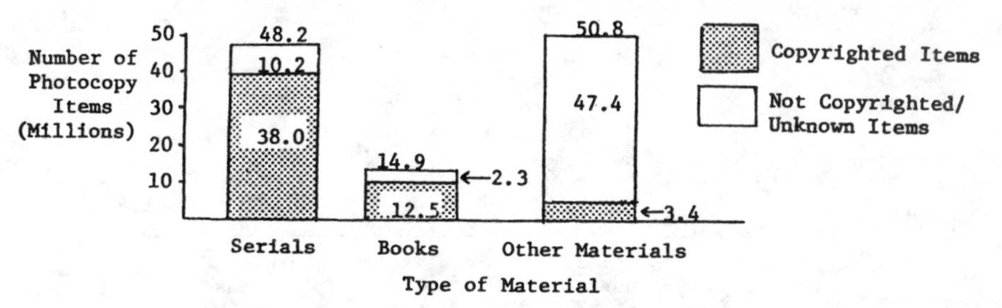

Figure 2. Number of Photocopy Items by Type of Material (1976)

Volume of Serial Photocopying

This report pays particular attention to volume of photocopying of serials. Serials accounted for the largest number of items photocopied from copyrighted materials, at about 38 million photocopy items. Also, libraries and publishers appear to be more concerned about serials than about books or other materials.

Special and Public libraries have the largest number of photocopy items from copyrighted serials, about 16 million and 14 million respectively. Academic and Federal libraries made, respectively, about 5 million and 4 million photocopy items from copyrighted serials. The disparity among the types of libraries is largely accounted for by the number of libraries within each type. When one considers the average number of photocopy items per library, the disparity is much less. Although Federal libraries averaged 2,500 photocopy items per library, the other three types ranged from 1,600 to 1,800 items per library.

It is especially important to observe the categories in which serial photocopying breaks down according to use (interlibrary loan, local use by patrons or library staff, and intrasystem loan to a branch library) since both the Copyright Law and CONTU Guidelines may have different implications for each. Most photocopy items of copyrighted serials (about 22 million) are made for local users. Twelve million items of copyrighted serials are made for intrasystem loans and about 4 million are made for interlibrary loan. (See Figure 3.) For each of the three types of transactions mentioned above, the amount of photocopying performed under different conditions of eligibility is summarized below.

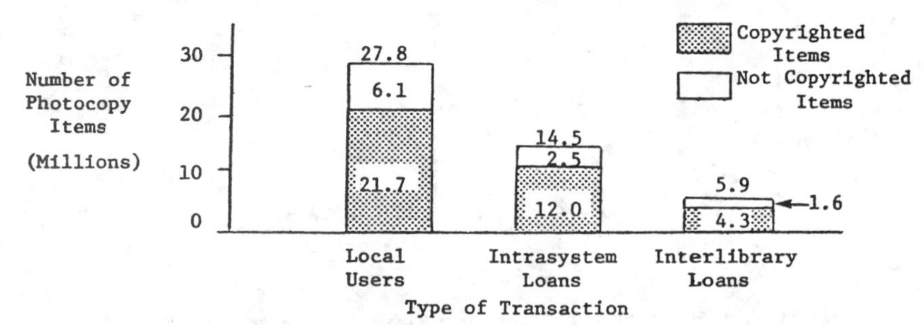

Figure 3. Number of Photocopy Items of Serials That Are Copyrighted by Type of Transaction (1976)

Filled serial interlibrary loan requests for domestic serials account for 3.8 million photocopy items, of which 3.1 million are estimated to be copyrighted. When CONTU guidelines are applied to the 3.1 million, it is estimated that 2.4 million are under six years old and 2.0 million are both under six years old and not used for replacement or classroom use. If the rule of six copies or more is applied, about 500 thousand photocopy items are subject to royalty payment. (See Figure 4.) This total increases to 1.9 million items if all photocopy items from serials over five years old are also considered eligible.

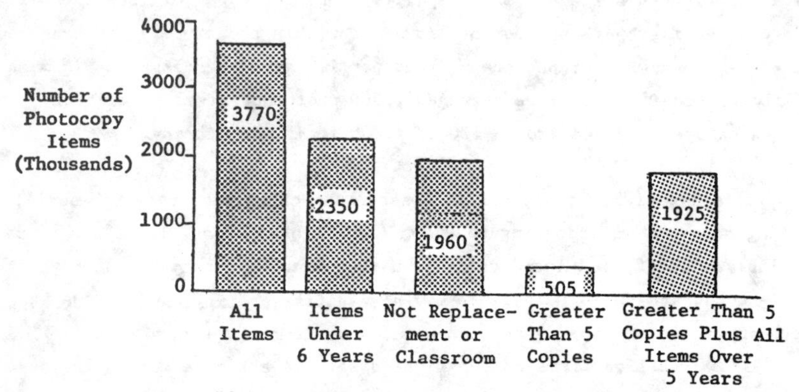

Figure 4. Number of Photocopy Items of Domestic Serials Requested for Interlibrary Loans-All Items, Items Under 6 Years, Items Not for Replacement or Classroom, Items With Greater Than Five Copies (1976)

Considering all interlibrary loan photocopy items, it is estimated that 81 percent of all U.S. libraries will have less than 250 items per year. These libraries, however, account for only 41 percent of the total interlibrary loan photocopy items, for there is a high degree of centralization of photocopying for interlibrary loans. Twenty percent of the libraries request 73 percent of the photocopied interlibrary loans. (See Figure 5.)

Local use accounts for the largest amount of photocopying at 28 million serial photocopy items. Of these, about 22 million are copyrighted and 19 million are from copyrighted domestic serials. If one hypothetically applies CONTU's eligibility conditions for local use as well as for interlibrary loan, one finds that 15 million photocopy items are from serials under six years old, 17 million are from serials having five or more copies made in a library, and 13 million are from serials under six years old with five or more copies made in a library. One also finds that 800 thousand photocopy items for local users were made for replacement or for classroom use by faculty. Another hypothetical condition of

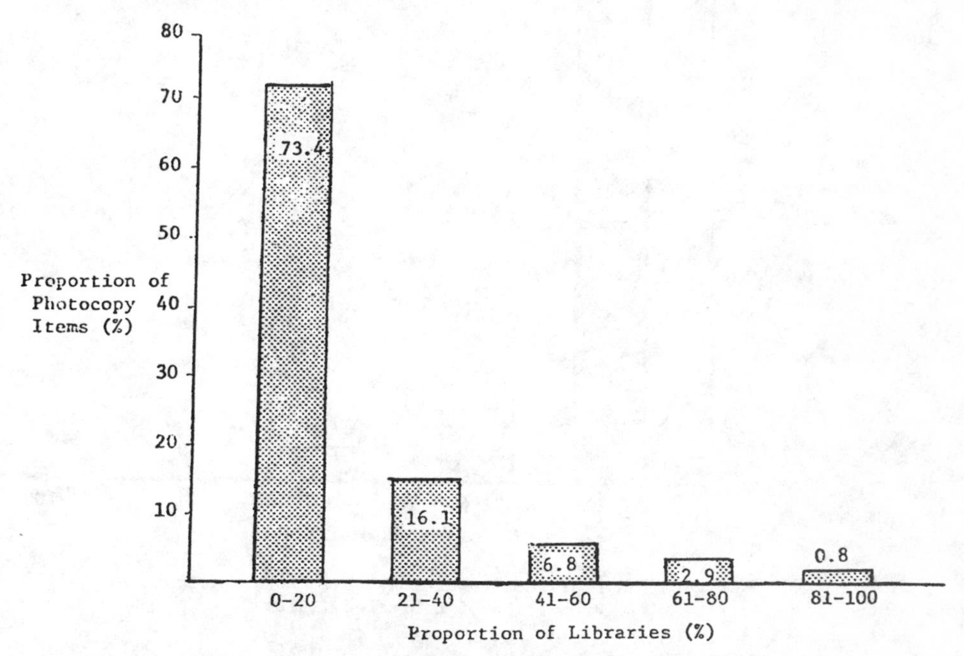

Figure 5. Distribution of Interlibrary Loan Photocopy Items by Proportion of Libraries (1976)

eligibility from Section 108(d) of the Law, involves single copies made for individuals. It is estimated that 82 percent of the photocopy items made for local users involve single copies made for individuals or institutions. Considering all photocopy items made for local use, it is estimated that 62 percent of all U.S. libraries will have less than 250 photocopy items. These libraries account for only seven percent of the total photocopy items made for local use, with the remaining 93 percent made by 40 percent of the libraries. A total of 78 percent of the photocopies made for local use are made by 20 percent of the libraries. (See Figure 6.)

Photocopying for intrasystem loan of serials comes to a total of 14 million photocopy items, of which 10 million are from copyrighted domestic serials. One-half million of these items involve replacement or classroom use. Approximately 7 million of the intrasystem loan photocopy items are from serials under six years old. Finally, it is estimated that about 76 percent of the items photocopied for intrasystem loan are single copies made for individuals

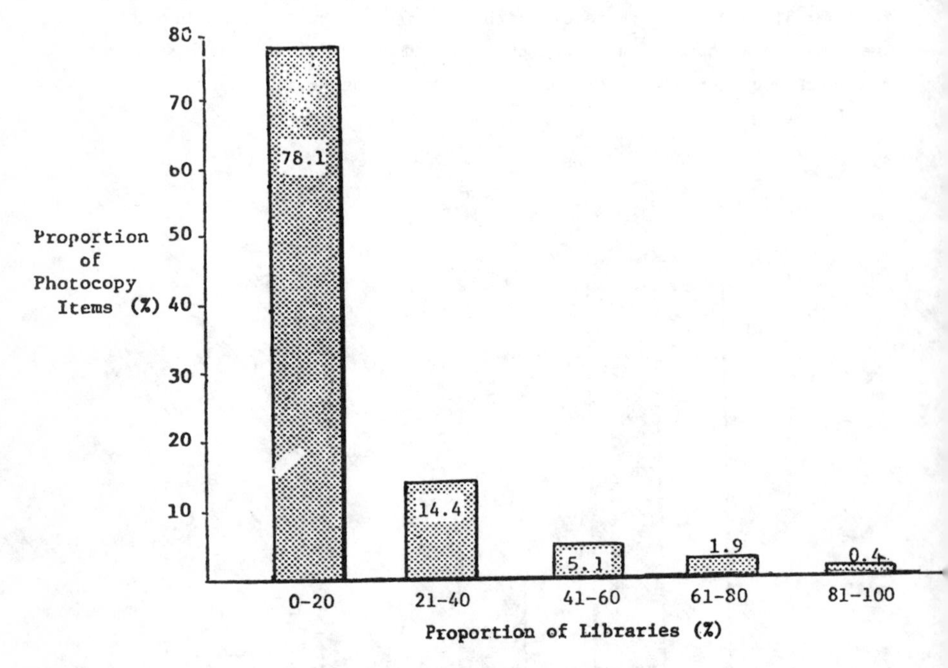

Figure 6. Distribution of Local Use Photocopy Items by Proportion of Libraries (1976)

or other institutions. Over one-third of the transactions for intrasystem loan involve multiple copies of one or two pages, which may be photocopies of tables of contents or title pages made for current awareness.

Libraries and Photocopying Operations

Depending upon final legal interpretation of the conditions of eligibility for royalty payment, libraries may be required to screen outgoing interlibrary loan requests to check for possible exemptions. A majority of libraries report that they would not incur extra costs which could not be absorbed if they were required to perform various screening operations for outgoing serial interlibrary loan requests. Depending upon the specific screening operation, this answer varies among libraries from 84 percent of all libraries to 62 percent of all libraries.

In similar proportions, libraries indicated that they would not incur higher costs if required to screen requests from local patrons. There is an exception, however. About 60 percent of responding libraries reported that extra non-absorbable costs would be incurred in the event that they were required to check for previously made photocopies from a requested title.

No single royalty payment mechanism stood out as being preferred over the others. Libraries in the survey rated as "most preferred" four mechanisms: higher subscription prices for all serials, purchase of royalty stamps or coupons, photocopying machine fees, and purchase of multiple copies or reprints from a single agency. No more than one-third of the libraries, however, rated any of these mechanisms as "most preferred."

In some instances, libraries charge their users for photocopying services. The average annual gross income per library for operation of photocopying machines is $3,085. The largest average annual gross income is $11,544 for Academic libraries, followed by $3,648 for Federal libraries, $2,964 for Public libraries, and $96 for Special libraries. The largest average annual income per machine is $3,607 for Academic libraries, followed by $2,432 for Federal libraries, $1,744 for Public libraries, and $87 for Special libraries. On the average, however, photocopying operations cost Public libraries $4,080 per year and Academic libraries $16,260 per year. This suggests that some libraries, on the average, may currently be incurring net losses for their photocopying operations when their gross income is compared to their operational costs. Sufficient data were not available to estimate annual costs for Federal and Special libraries.

Publishers and Photocopied Serials

Publishers have information needs unlike those of libraries. For example, they need to know how much photocopying of individual serials occurs across all libraries. The estimate is that, over all libraries, the total number of interlibrary loan photocopy items per serial title is 50 or less for 40 percent of serial titles, with these titles accounting for three percent of the total photocopy items. About seven percent of the serials have more than 500 photocopy items made from them. Considering only those photocopy items that are not for replacement or classroom use, that are less than six years old, and that have more than five copies, 91 percent of serial titles have 50 or fewer photocopy items and very few, if any, have more than 100 photocopy items made of them. There is, in fact, a high concentration of photocopying serials: 86 percent of the photocopying of serials occurs on only 20 percent of the serials. (See Figure 7.)

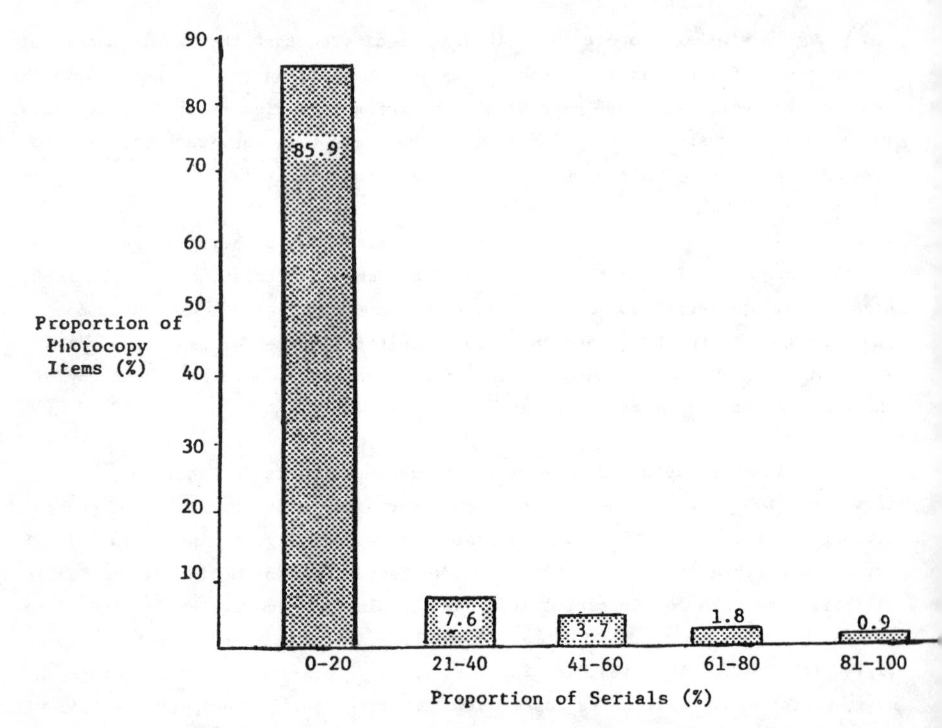

Figure 7. Distribution of Interlibrary Loan Photocopy Items by Proportion of Serials (1976)

For local user photocopying, the estimate is that 67 percent of the copied serials have less than 1,000 photocopy items and a small, but significant, five percent of the titles have more than 5,000 items made of them. Considering only those photocopy items of serials less than six years old and with more than five copies, nearly all of the serials have less than 500 photocopy items. Here, also, a significant proportion of the serials accounts for a major proportion of the photocopy items. About 68 percent of the photocopy items come from 20 percent of the serials. (See Figure 8.)

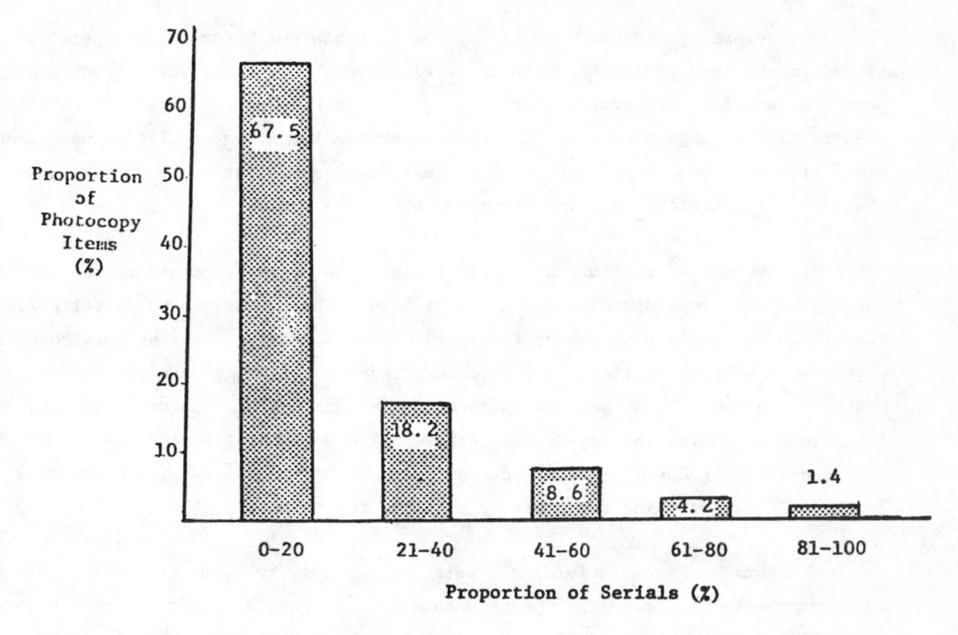

Figure 8. Distribution of Local Use Photocopy Items by Proportion of Serials

According to the recent Indiana University survey of publishers, nearly 50 percent of responding journals expected to receive no royalty payments from a clearinghouse arrangement supplying authorized copies. The average expected payment was about $1.50 per item for those publishers who expected payment. Many publishers appeared to prefer direct licensing of photocopying to clearinghouse arrangements. This survey, however, was made before the Association of American Publishers, Inc. had announced its intention to set up a Copyright Clearance Center. After that announcement, the response may have been different.

Implications for the Development of Royalty Payment Mechanisms

Although the implications of royalty payment mechanisms for libraries and publishers are different, it appears that only a minority of either group would be appreciably affected by the actual payment of royalties, since a large proportion of photocopying takes place in 20 percent of the libraries and with 20 percent of the serials.

No single mechanism appears suitable for all photocopying which might be eligible for royalty payment. Depending upon the final resolution of the eligibility question and the volume of photocopying involved, it is likely that a combination of mechanisms will be required.

Generally speaking, royalty payment mechanisms become more expensive to design and operate as the matching of eligible photocopying volume and royalty payments requires more accuracy and precision. As evidenced by their relatively high ranking of higher subscription prices as an alternative royalty payment mechanism, libraries appear willing to exchange some accuracy for a simplification of their mode of participation in a royalty payment mechanism.

Because of the low number of eligible photocopy items per serial for the majority of copyrighted domestic serials, and because of the potentially low proportion of eligible photocopy items at any one library, it may be more cost-effective, at least initially, for a central agency, clearinghouse, or payment center to concentrate on serving high-volume serials and high-volume libraries. Low-volume libraries and low-volume serials may also find it inexpensive when compared to their own monitoring, depending upon the proportion of photocopying in their libraries which was actually eligible for payment.

Monitoring and enforcing royalty payment may be among the most expensive components of a royalty payment mechanism. If publishers desire monitoring, these functions may be handled most effectively by a central agency if legal questions such as anti-trust can be resolved.

The impact of royalty payments in terms of subscription cancellations is uncertain. We hypothesize that, if this occurred, it would have the most negative impact on small, specialized journals.

Caveats and Statistical Precision of Results

One should keep in mind that behavior of libraries and publishers may be different after the Copyright Law goes into effect in 1978. A change in behavior could substantially alter the number of photocopy items eligible for royalty payment from the estimates made in the sample. Also, attitudes of libraries and publishers toward alternative royalty payment mechanisms may change (from those observed in recent surveys) after they become familiar with operating under the Law.

Since the data were obtained from a sample of libraries, there is some chance of estimates being higher or lower than those given in this report. In order to give some indication of the statistical precision of the results, standard errors of typical estimates are stated here. Statistical precision estimates made for all libraries are higher than those made by type of library because of the difference in sample sizes. The standard error for interlibrary loan for all photocopies made in all four types of libraries is 3.8 ± .58 million. The interpretation is that the number of photocopies made in all four types of libraries for interlibrary loan requests is between 4.4 million and 3.2 million at 66 percent level of confidence, or, 3.8 ± 1.16 million at 95 percent level of confidence. The number of photocopies made for interlibrary loans by Public libraries would be 1.0 ± .16 million, and for Academic libraries 1.1 ± .13 million. The standard errors for Special and Federal libraries are 1.3 ± .54 million and 0.4 ± .012 million respectively. The estimate for local users is 19.0 ± 3.4 million. The estimates for Public, Academic, Special and Federal libraries are 7.4 ± 3.7; 1.8 ± 1.4; 7.9 ± 2.2; and 2.0 ± 0.6 respectively. It is noted that estimates that involve the proportion of transactions such as the proportion of serials that are copyrighted, the proportion that are from domestic publishers, age of the publications and so on have a substantially higher statistical precision since the sample sizes are over 10,000.

Finally, the estimates derived from the MINITEX data base serve as an excellent verification of estimates of photocopying for interlibrary loans made from the national library survey. It appears that the national library survey data closely resemble those obtained from MINITEX. Also, data from another National Science Foundation study of scientific and technical publishing yield very similar overall results to estimates of total photocopying of scientific and technical serials observed in this study.

2.1 Background

During the past several years, significant progress has been made in the area of copyright that affects both libraries and holders of copyright. This area is the photocopying of copyrighted materials by United States libraries. Examples of the progress that has been made are the following:

- The establishment by the NCLIS and the Register of Copyrights of the Conference on Resolution of Copyright Issues (CORCI), also known as the "Upstairs-Downstairs Group" which included both publishers and librarians who agreed to lend their support to a study that would objectively analyze data relevant to the issues of library photocopying and the design of a royalty payment mechanism.
- The establishment of the National Commission on New Technological Uses of Copyrighted Works (CONTU).
- The signing by the President of the new Copyright Law on October 19, 1976, to go into effect January 1, 1978.
- CONTU's issuing of the Guidelines dealing with interlibrary loan (ILL) transactions.
- The concrete proposals put forth during 1977 by the Copyright Clearance Center Task Force of the Association of American Publishers (AAP).

This study is an outgrowth of the deliberations of the "Upstairs-Downstairs Group," a body of voluntary representatives of the various interested parties who met during 1974 and 1975 to see if they could reach an agreement on questions raised by library photocopying of copyrighted serials. On the one hand, publishers as copyright holders felt that they deserved monetary compensation for library photocopying since such copying--especially its transmission between libraries via existing channels of interlibrary loan--constituted, in their view, a breach of traditional concepts of "fair use" which was potentially damaging. On the other hand, librarians felt that most of the library photocopying was, indeed, "fair use" and any restrictions on photocopying would harm public access to information. They were also concerned that the record-keeping involved in some payment mechanism clearinghouse proposals might be an expensive administrative headache. Authors felt that their concerns were not being addressed. Finally, the Federal Government was interested in the controversy for many reasons:

- It subsidizes much of the scientific and technical information generated and disseminated in the United States by published material.
- The NCLIS advocates in its National Program Document, "Toward a National Program for Library and Information Services: Goals for Action," the establishment of a national library and information network based, in large part, on resource sharing.
- The Congress was anxious to have the librarians and publishers resolve their differences.
- The Copyright Office was equally anxious for a resolution on the difference for the above reasons.

Objective, quantitative data to evaluate the various arguments did not exist on a nationwide basis. The seminal study in this field, the one carried out in the mid-60s by Sophar and Heilprin of the Committee to Investigate Copyright Problems Affecting Communication in Science and Education (CICP), had put forth the concept of a clearinghouse (9), but the data collected in that study came from a restricted sample and could no longer be considered indicative of the national situation in the late 1970s. The Canadian study of Basil Stuart-Stubbs (10) provided significant insight into the problem, but its quantitative applicability to the American situation was questionable. CORCI found that it could make no further progress without up-to-date national data on library photocopying.

Accordingly, the NCLIS and the National Science Foundation (NSF) agreed to fund a research study to: (a) analyze the volume and distribution of library photocopying via a national survey of United States Public, Academic, Special, and Federal libraries,* and (b) test the feasibility of a royalty payment mechanism. A Request for Proposal (RFP) was issued by NCLIS, and King Research, Inc., a survey research firm located in Rockville, Maryland, was selected to perform the study. Following award of this contract, which began in May 1976, the National Commission on New Technological Uses of Copyrighted Works (CONTU) funded an amendment which provided for the study of one year's interlibrary loan requests received by the Minnesota Interlibrary Telecommunications Exchange (MINNITEX). This latter study, performed in conjunction with the NCLIS/NSF study, provided invaluable data on seasonal fluctuations in demand for individual libraries and on individual libraries' demand for individual serial titles, data which were to become of crucial importance in light of the subsequently-issued CONTU interlibrary loan guidelines.

---

* School libraries/media center were not included in the sampling universe.

2.2 The Studies

In this section we give an overview of the study approach.

The sample of libraries for the NCLIS/NSF photocopying study was a stratified random selection representing the four categories of libraries: Academic, Public, Federal, and Special libraries. The target number of participating libraries by type were: 108 Academic, 100 Public, 62 Federal, and 100 Special. These target numbers were based in part on the estimated volumes of interlibrary lending for 1972, the most recent year for which comprehensive data could be assembled at the time.

Very large libraries and some with unique characteristics were included in the sample with certainty. That is, the probability with which they were selected equalled one, and they were chosen to represent only themselves. The remaining libraries of each type were stratified by significant variables to facilitate selection of a representative sample from which to estimate totals for the non-certainty libraries. Participation was invited from a sample larger than the minimum target number, so that ineligible libraries, refusals, and nonresponses would not disrupt the very tight time table.

Academic libraries were stratified and sub-stratified according to bookstock (number of volumes) and type of academic institution (university/research, other four year, and two year), based on a data tape supplied by the National Center for Education Statistics.

Public libraries in the certainty stratum were selected on the basis of bookstock. For non-certainty Public libraries, stratification was based on the size of population served and geographic region.

Special library sampling was accomplished in stages. Initial samples were drawn from the American Library Directory, the Directory of the Special Libraries and Information Centers, and the Special Library Association Membership Directory. These were sorted into Legal, Medical, Religious, and Special. Overlap with Federal and Academic libraries was then determined.

Federal libraries were stratified according to aggregate interlibrary loans, based upon the 1972 survey of Federal libraries. The Federal library certainty stratum includes both large borrowers and large lenders.

The first solicitation to libraries designated for inclusion in the sample and for alternates was a "screener" form. Follow-up letters were mailed to all addressees that did not respond. Days for data collection for volume, for characteristics, and for purpose of requests were assigned to each library which provided a screener, based on the information reported therein. Volume logs, forms to record characteristics of library materials photocopied, and interlibrary loan forms for serials borrowed were then transmitted to each library which had answered the screener. At this stage, additional refusals and nonresponses occurred. Almost exactly 300 libraries reported on volume of photocopying and on the characteristics of materials copied, plus 44 reports of "no copying," as compared with the combined target of 370. Academic libraries reported very conscientiously on borrowings, but in each of the other library types, a significant number did not report on borrowings.

Subsequently, participating libraries were also asked to respond to a Copyright Royalty Library Survey questionnaire which addressed questions of costs of photocopying operations, preferences among possible royalty payment mechanisms, judgments concerning relative costs of hypothetical recordkeeping procedures, and a few volume items. (Data collection forms are displayed in Appendix A.)

A total of 2,350 volume logs were analyzed, representing a sample of approximately 13,095 transactions. 4,660 interlibrary loan forms were collected and analyzed. A total of 19,277 characteristics forms were analyzed, and 201 copyright royalty library survey questionnaires were returned and analyzed.

The time limitation on the project did not permit data collection to be spread throughout the year. Therefore, it was important to find adjustment factors to correct for the difference between periods (days of the week and months of the year) when data were collected and the average activity over the year. Such adjustments weights were derived in the course of an analysis of interlibrary loan data for the MINITEX system for the year 1976.

The statewide interlibrary loan system of Minnesota, MINITEX, handles approximately 130,000 requests per year from all types of libraries. These libraries are located mainly in Minnesota but also in Montana, North Dakota, and small portions of Wisconsin and Canada.

Analysis of MINITEX interlibrary loan transactions for a full year provided seasonal variations in ILL borrowing by type of library and thereby helped in determining annual volumes of library copying for those libraries participating in the Photocopying Study. It also provided other information including such items as whether or not the requesting library subscribed to the periodical requested, distribution of serial requests over the life of a journal, distribution of requests for specific journal titles, purpose of request, and requests for photocopying in lieu of loan. Detailed MINITEX tabulated data and national survey results will be given in another volume.

2.3 Categories of Photocopying

The categories of photocopying of particular interest to this study are presented in the following table:

TABLE 2.1

CATEGORIES OF LIBRARY PHOTOCOPYING

General Category	Specific Category	Hypothetical Eligibility for Royalty Payment	
		Eligible	Not Eligible
(1) Photocopying of Copyrighted serials by or for library staff	(1.1) for local users	x	
	(1.2) in response to intra-system loan (ISL) requests	x	
	(1.3) in response to inter-library loan requests from other libraries		x
(2) Interlibrary loan (ILL) requests for Copyrighted serials	(2.1) Unfilled requests		x
	(2.2) Requests filled by photocopying by other libraries	x	
	(2.3) Requests filled by other libraries with originals		x

In this table, categories of photocopying are classified as being either eligible or not eligible for royalty payments. We emphasize that this refers to <u>hypothetical</u> eligibility, since definitive legal interpretations of what proportion of photocopying in the "eligible" category would actually require royalty payments do not exist at this time.

There are two general categories of interest: (1) Photocopying of copyrighted serials by or for library staff, and (2) interlibrary loan requests for copyrighted serials. The qualifier "by or for library staff" is added to category (1) to show that photocopying by library users on unsupervised machines (e.g., coin-operated machines) is not considered here. Interlibrary loan "requests" are considered because of the impact of the CONTU ILL guidelines which make interlibrary loan photocopying normally the responsibility of the requesting rather than the photocopying library.

Category (1) may be subdivided into photocopying (1.1) for local users, (1.2) in response to intrasystem loan requests, and (1.3) in response to interlibrary loan requests from other libraries. "Local users" are library patrons and staff who are presumably able to initiate photocopying transactions on a walk-in or local phone call basis. Local users include employees of the library's parent institution. "Intrasystem loan requests" are requests transmitted from other branches or libraries within the same system. Photocopying in both of these categories may hypothetically be eligible for royalty payments. Category (1.3), however, photocopying in response to interlibrary loan requests from other libraries, is normally not considered to be the responsibility of the photocopying library, due to interpretation of the CONTU ILL guidelines.

Category (2) may also be subdivided into three categories: (2.1) unfilled requests, (2.2) requests filled by photocopying by other libraries, and (2.3) requests filled with originals. Normally, only category (2.2) is assumed in this report to be eligible for royalty payment. Loan requests for library materials are processed by an interlibrary loan department or office in the larger libraries, and in smaller libraries one or more staff members have the responsibility for handling interlibrary loans. Loan requests are transmitted from the requesting libraries on a variety of request forms. The most common form is the "standard" interlibrary loan form approved by the American Library Association. A special form is available for photocopy requests but few libraries use it. Teletype requests arrive in different formats. While the formats of the various forms differ, the content is reasonably similar. The vast majority of filled serial article requests are filled with photocopies, not with original issues of the requested serial title.

Two categories of photocopying are specifically not covered here: photocopying of non-library materials by library staff, and photocopying by library patrons of library materials on equipment provided by the library for unsupervised patron use.

A great deal of photocopying by library staff on library-controlled machines is composed of the copying of correspondence, letters, memos, catalog cards, and other types of office copying. While this is not directly relevant to the development of a royalty payment mechanism, the ability to distinguish between it and copying eligible for payment is. The existence of this category of photocopying requires estimates to be made from a sample of actual photocopying transactions, rather than from post-hoc estimates. This had implications for this study and for transaction-based royalty payment mechanisms.

Photocopying on unsupervised machines is particularly difficult to monitor, and was not included in this study under terms of the study contract. This category is significant in two respects. First, in some libraries the amount of photocopying in this category may be significant, as suggested in a later section of this report. Second, in some libraries, particularly the smaller ones, staff and patrons use the same machine(s). This complicates the monitoring of specific copying categories.

2.4 Special Considerations

After this study had started, the new Copyright Law was signed and CONTU issued its interlibrary loan (ILL) guidelines. These guidelines for the first time specified a maximum volume of allowable photocopying for serial articles requested by means of interlibrary loan. This quantitative limit, a product of considerable negotiation among interested parties, was included in a formal Congressional report, although not in the actual language of the final bill. Significantly, however, these guidelines made compliance the responsibility of individual libraries with respect to individual serial titles. The practical impact of the above was that for each library a potentially different mathematical distribution existed for the number of times each serial title was requested. This entailed considerably more complex statistical analysis than had been originally anticipated.

The MINITEX analysis allowed the demand for individual titles by individual libraries to be observed over an entire year, and this was useful in projecting to an annual level the findings from the photocopying study's shorter observation periods.

These developments necessitated a categorization of King Research data in line with the Copyright Law and the CONTU ILL guidelines. As will be noted later, however, there is still considerable uncertainty with regard to interpretation and application of the Law and guidelines. Reasons for some of this uncertainty are discussed below.

It is not always easy to determine if items are copyrighted, as will be shown in discussion of the large volume of "copyright unknown" photocopy items. Many alternative payment mechanisms rely upon the identification of photocopy items eligible for payment by library staff; a plain and visible statement of copyright status is a necessity for such mechanisms.

It is necessary to distinguish between two types of photocopying for replacement purposes. Items may be photocopied to replace out-of-print or otherwise unobtainable originals or source items, assuming that an effort has been made to obtain an original. Or, items may be photocopied for replacement use due to mutilation of an original.

It is assumed that serial articles photocopied by or for a teacher in a not-for-profit educational institution and which satisfy the Guidelines for Classroom Copying in Not-for-Profit Educational Institutions with Respect to Books and Periodicals (2) would not be eligible for royalty payment.

A continuing uncertainty is the definition of a library system for royalty payment purposes. We have assumed that libraries within the same system (e.g., branches in a public library system) are part of a single entity. The cohesiveness of systems differs, depending upon the basis of the system. Some are determined by locality or governmental sponsorship, such as public library systems and federal agency library systems. Others may be more loose-knit, such as multi-library cooperatives designed to share audiovisual resources. A definition of "library" and "library system" must still be developed for determining future payment responsibilities. This will also aid in defining what constitutes "intrasystem" photocopying.

The CONTU ILL guidelines would not apply if present interlibrary loan practices were "...supplemented or even largely replaced by a system in which one or more agencies or institutions, public or private, exist for the specific purpose of providing a central source for photocopies." The most practical implication for royalty payment mechanism operation related to ILL transactions of one or more such agencies would be, presumably, to make accounting and payment the responsibility of the photocopying library, as opposed to the requesting library. It may be useful to determine when existing or developing libraries and other agencies should be considered to "exist for the specific purpose of providing a central source for photocopies."

There is still some uncertainty regarding the interpretation of the concept of fair use and the prohibition against systematic copying with regard to non-ILL photocopying. The practical impact of this uncertainty is the following. It appears impossible to estimate for non-interlibrary loan photocopying, with the same degree of certainty as for interlibrary loan photocopying, the proportion of domestic copyrighted serial photocopy items which would be in excess of fair use and therefore potentially eligible for royalty payment. This uncertainty remains even if photocopying for classroom use by faculty and photocopying for library replacement use (still the subject of some uncertainty) and other possibly exempt categories, are excluded. The source of this uncertainty is the concept of "multiple copies" as opposed to "single copies." The essence of this uncertainty is the following: Several photocopy items of an individual source item might be made during the course of a single transaction. Or, several photocopy items of an individual source item might be made over the course of several transactions, for the same or different requesters. The CONTU ILL guidelines resolved this potential conflict mathematically for interlibrary loans by specifying limits on the number of photocopy items which could be received by a single requesting library from a single copyrighted serial title during a specific period of time, regardless of the number of photocopy items made during the course of a single transaction.

If it were assumed that single photocopy items made for local user or intrasystem loan requests were exempt from payment, without regard to the number of times single serial titles were photocopied during the course of single or multiple transactions, then only a small proportion of the total domestic copyrighted serial photocopy items would be eligible for payment. The data described in this report demonstrate that a very large number of single photocopy items are made in response to local user and intrasystem loan requests. Excluding these from the total number of potentially eligible photocopy items would significantly reduce the volume eligible for payment.

This does not take into account heavy use of individual titles, where the number of photocopy items over time, or the existence of numerous multiple photocopy items during the course of a single transaction, might conceivably cumulate within a single library or library system to the point where photocopying could be perceived as substituting for individual serial subscriptions. The CONTU ILL guidelines addressed these issues for interlibrary loan but the case may be somewhat different for non-ILL photocopying, since there is significantly more local user and intrasystem photocopying of copyrighted domestic serials, and since ILL transactions involve a somewhat higher proportion of single photocopy items per transaction.

A possible analytical solution to this problem would be the application of guidelines similar to those issued by CONTU regarding ILL to non-ILL photocopying. Some of the impacts of this on eligible photocopying volume are discussed in this report.

TOTAL VOLUME OF PHOTOCOPYING OF LIBRARY MATERIALS BY LIBRARY STAFF IN THE UNITED STATES

One of the most important issues of the past decade concerning library photocopying has been the amount of photocopying that actually takes place in libraries. This report provides estimates of the amount or volume of photocopying of library materials by or for the library staff in Public, Academic, Special, and Federal libraries in the United States.

This section is devoted to estimates of the total volume of photocopying in the United States presented by type of libraries (Public, Academic, Special and Federal), type of library materials (serials, books and other material), and whether the materials are currently copyrighted or not. The photocopying activities for which data were collected are also separated into three main categories -- photocopying of materials by library staff for local library users (patrons or staff) and copying of materials for other libraries, subdivided by intrasystem loans and interlibrary loans. These three types of transactions are referred to in the remainder of the report as local users, intrasystem loan and interlibrary loan.

One could choose among many units of measure to describe the volume of photocopying. However, the following units of measure were chosen to be presented in this report. Three types of library materials include serials, books and other materials (e.g., sheet music, reports, pamphlets, etc.). A transaction involves any request for a library's material that may come from an institution, individual or another library. A transaction could be filled or unfilled and it could be filled by presenting an original copy to the requestor or by presenting the requestor with a photocopy of the material. In this report, we include only those transactions that are filled by a photocopy made by library staff members. A source item is the unit of material being photocopied. This category includes such items as an article, a single page, or specified multiple pages from a serial or a chapter from a book. The number of requested photocopy items refers to the number of times the source item is copied in fulfillment of a transaction. This differs from the number of filled transactions that are processed at a machine. A single filled transaction may be for multiple copies of the same source item. The total number of photocopy items is the sum of the filled requested photocopy items. This will be the most common unit of measurement in the results presented in this report. Other units of measurement that will be mentioned are number of filled transactions, number of source item pages copied and the number of photocopy pages. Further definitions have been given in the Glossary at the beginning of this report.

* HIGHLIGHTS *

Total Volume of Photocopying

- There were an estimated 114 million photocopy items made of library materials by library staff in 1976. There was an estimated average of 5,400 photocopy items per library in the population of 21,280 libraries from which the sample was chosen.
- The largest share of photocopying of library materials was performed in Public libraries (64 million photocopy items) followed by Special libraries (26 million), Academic libraries (17 million) and Federal libraries (7 million).

- Public libraries also averaged the greatest amount of photocopying (7,700 photocopy items per library). Academic libraries also had a large average amount of photocopying at 5,500 photocopy items per library. Federal libraries averaged 4,900 photocopy items and Special libraries averaged 3,100 photocopy items.

- Most of the materials photocopied were serials (48 million photocopy items) and other materials (51 million). Books were photocopied to the extent of about 15 million photocopy items.

- Of 114 million photocopy items, approximately 76 million were made for local users (patrons and library staff), 27 million for intrasystem loan and 11 million for interlibrary loan.

Total Volume of Photocopying of Copyrighted Materials

- Less than one-half of the volume of photocopying was performed on copyrighted materials. There were about 54 million photocopy items of copyrighted materials made in 1976. This volume amounts to about 2,500 photocopy items per library throughout the United States. A total of 17 million photocopy items was made from materials in which copyright was unknown or unreported.

- The largest amount of photocopying of copyrighted materials was performed in Public libraries (24.0 million photocopy items). A total of 17.9 million photocopy items were made in Special libraries, 7.9 million in Academic libraries and 4.0 in Federal libraries.

- The average amount of photocopying was 2,900 copyrighted photocopy items per Public library, 2,600 copyrighted photocopy items per Academic library, 2,800 copyrighted photocopy items per Federal library, and 2,100 copyrighted photocopy items per Special library.

- A majority of the volume of photocopying of copyrighted materials was from serials (38.0 million photocopy items). There were 12.5 million photocopy items made from copyrighted books and 3.4 photocopy items made from other library materials.

- A total of 21.7 photocopy items of copyrighted serials was made for local users; 12.0 million for intrasystem loan; and 4.3 million for interlibrary loan.

3.1 Estimated Volume of Photocopy Items and Photocopy Pages

There is a very large amount of photocopying of library materials by or for library staff in the United States. It is estimated that in 1976 about 114 million photocopy items were made by staff in the 21,280 libraries from which the national sample was chosen. This means that about 5,400 photocopy items were made per library. Considered in another way, an average of about 20 photocopy items are made in libraries each regular working day of the year. The total volume of photocopying varies substantially among the four major types of libraries. The extent of this variation is displayed in Figure 3.1 below.

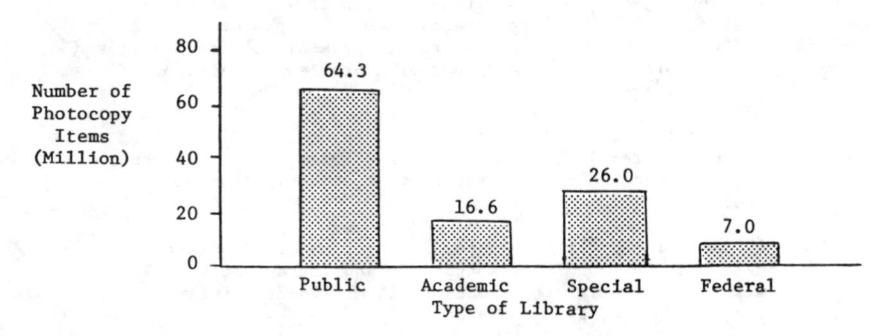

Figure 3.1. Number of Photocopy Items by Type of Library

Public library staff photocopied over one-half of the total volume of photocopy items. They made a total of 64.3 million photocopy items compared to 26 million made in Special libraries, 16.6 made in Academic libraries and 7.0 million made in Federal libraries.

A somewhat different picture emerges when one considers the average number of photocopy items per library as shown in Table 3.1 below.

Table 3.1 NUMBER OF PHOTOCOPY ITEMS AND PHOTOCOPY ITEMS PER LIBRARY, BY TYPE OF LIBRARY (1976)

Type of Library	Number of Photocopy Items (million)	Number of Libraries	Number of Photocopy Items Per Library
Public	64.3	8,310	7,700
Academic	16.6	3,030	5,500
Special	26.0	8,510	3,100
Federal	7.0	1,430	4,900
All Libraries	113.9	21,280	5,400

SOURCE: King Research, Inc.: Library Photocopying in the United States (hereafter referred to as National Library Survey).

Public libraries had the largest average volume of photocopy items among the types of libraries (7,700 photocopy items per library), but the average volume in Academic libraries is also quite large (5,500 photocopy items per library). As one might expect, the average photocopying volume in Special libraries and Federal libraries is lower, being 3,100 photocopy items per Special library and 4,900 photocopy items per Federal library.

Another measure of the volume of photocopying is the total number of photocopy pages made by library staff. In this instance, it is estimated that about 906 million photocopy pages were made in 1976. This represents an average of about 42,600 photocopy pages per library and eight photocopy pages per photocopy item. The latter average gives some indication that the number of item pages photocopied is not extensive. That is, there is little evidence that many books or journal issues are photocopied in their entirety, although there were some isolated reported instances where this appeared to be true for books. The breakdown of volume of photocopy pages by type of library is given in Table 3.2

Table 3.2 NUMBER OF PHOTOCOPY PAGES, PHOTOCOPY PAGES PER LIBRARY AND PHOTOCOPY PAGES PER PHOTOCOPY ITEM, BY TYPE OF LIBRARY (1976)

Type of Library	No. of Photocopy Pages (million)	No. of Photocopy Pages Per Library (000)	No. of Photocopy Pages Per Photocopy Item
Public	377	45.4	5.9
Academic	219	72.3	13.2
Special	238	28.0	9.2
Federal	72	50.3	10.3
All Libraries	906	42.6	8.0

SOURCE: King Research, Inc.: National Library Survey.

The number of photocopy pages per library ranges from 28,000 in Special libraries up to 72,000 in Academic libraries. The number of photocopy pages per photocopy item is also given in Table 3.2. In this instance, Academic libraries appear to have greater number of photocopy pages per photocopy item (13 pages). The other types of libraries range from about six pages in Public libraries to a little over nine pages in Special and ten in Federal libraries. It will be shown later that the type of materials photocopied varies among the different types of libraries which accounts for the differences in average number of pages photocopied observed above in Table 3.2.

3.2 Estimated Volume of Photocopying by Type of Material and Type of Transaction

Two important characteristics of photocopying are the type of library material involved and the type of transaction that led to photocopying of these materials. The type of material is sub-divided into serials, books and other materials because these types are often published by different organizations. For example, many serials are published by professional societies that are not concerned at all with extent of photocopying of books or other materials.

The breakdown of library photocopying by type of transaction (local user, intra-system loan, and interlibrary loan) is important because photocopy items from these three types of transactions might be treated differently concerning their potential eligibility for royalty payment. For example, guidelines have been set forth by CONTU for interlibrary loans and they have been made part of the Conference Report (2). These two characteristics of photocopying are discussed in detail below.

The total volume of photocopying of serials, books and other materials is shown in Figure 3.2 below.

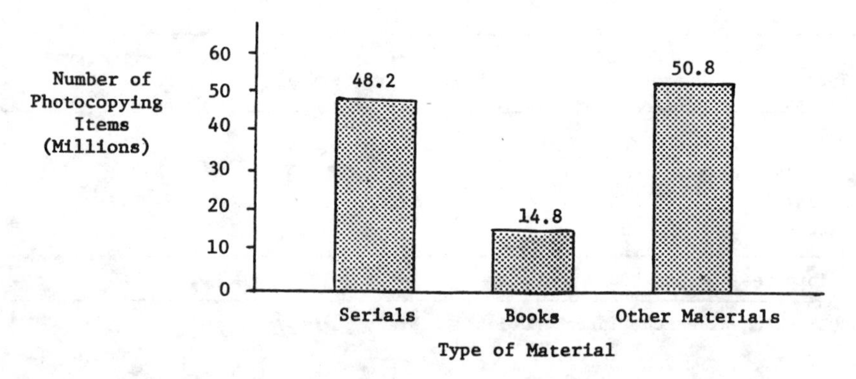

Figure 3.2 Number of Photocopy Items by Type of Material

The amount of photocopying in terms of photocopy items is about the same for serials (48 million) and other materials (51 million), while the total number of photocopy items for books is only 15 million. Although nearly one-half of the number of photocopy items are from other materials, most of these other materials are not copyrighted, as will be shown in Section 3.3.

The relative amount of photocopying from the three types of materials varies among the four types of libraries. These results are given in Table 3.3 on the following page.

Table 3.3 NUMBER OF PHOTOCOPY ITEMS, BY TYPE OF MATERIAL, BY TYPE OF LIBRARY (1976)

(Millions of Photocopy Items)

Type of Library	All Materials	Type of Material		
		Serials	Books	Other Materials
Public	64.3	16.6	8.8	38.9
Academic	16.6	6.3	3.8	6.5
Special	26.0	19.2	1.7	5.1
Federal	7.0	6.1	0.6	0.3
All Libraries	113.9	48.2	14.9	50.8

SOURCE: King Research, Inc.: National Library Survey

Well over one-half of the photocopy items made in Public libraries are from other materials and nearly twice as many photocopy items are made from serials as are made from books. Even within serials, it was observed that Public libraries had a substantial proportion of photocopied items from non-scientific materials such as newspapers and popular magazines or other non-science serials. The proportion of transactions that involved newspapers and popular magazines was 22 percent, the proportion of transactions for other non-scientific serials was 32 percent, and the proportion of transactions involving scientific serials was 46 percent.

About an equal number of photocopy items were made from serials and other materials in Academic libraries. There were about one-half as many photocopy items made from books as from serials in Academic libraries. As might be expected, the proportion of transactions in Academic libraries involving scientific serials was high (65 percent) compared to newspapers and popular magazines (14 percent) and other non-scientific serials (21 percent).

In Special libraries, nearly three-fourths of the photocopy items were from serials and nearly all of the remaining photocopy items were from other materials. As with Academic libraries, most of the transactions of serials involves scientific serials (87 percent) with four percent from newspapers and magazines and nine percent from other non-scientific serials.

Nearly ninety percent of the photocopy items made in Federal libraries were from serials with the remainder split between books and other materials. Of the transactions involving serials, 89 percent were from scientific serials, nine percent were from newspapers and magazines and two percent were from other non-scientific serials.

Public and Special libraries dominate the total volume of photocopy items of serials and Public libraries are dominant in the total volume of photocopy items made from books and other materials. However, the average amount of photocopy items made by libraries presents a different picture as shown in Table 3.4.

Table 3.4 NUMBER OF PHOTOCOPY ITEMS PER LIBRARY, BY TYPE OF MATERIAL, BY TYPE OF LIBRARY (1976)

(Average Number of Photocopy Items Per Library)

	Type of Material			
Type of Library	All Materials	Serials	Books	Other Materials
Public	7,700	2,000	1,100	4,700
Academic	5,500	2,100	1,300	2,100
Special	3,100	2,300	200	600
Federal	4,900	4,300	300	200
All Libraries	5,400	2,300	700	2,400

SOURCE: King Research, Inc.: National Library Survey

The number of photocopy items per library made from serials does not vary much among the four types of libraries. The range is 4,300 photocopy items per Federal library to about 2,000 photocopy items in the remaining types of libraries. However, the average number of photocopy items of books is much larger in Public (1,100 photocopy items) and Academic libraries (1,300 photocopy items) than in Special (200 photocopy items) and Federal (300 photocopy items) libraries. The same holds true for other materials where the average number of photocopy items is greatest in Public libraries (4,700 photocopy items) followed by Academic (2,100 photocopy items), Special (600 photocopy items) and Federal (200 photocopy items) libraries.

The relative amount of photocopying of library materials is different when measured by photocopy pages. The total number of photocopy pages is estimated to be nearly 1 billion of which 365 million come from other materials, 319 million come from serials and 220 million come from books. Data by type of library are given in Table 3.5 below.

Table 3.5 NUMBER OF PHOTOCOPY PAGES BY TYPE OF MATERIAL, BY TYPE OF LIBRARY (1976)

(Millions of Photocopy Pages)

Type of Library	Type of Material			
	All Materials	Serials	Books	Other
Public	377	54.8	100.0	221.7
Academic	219	64.3	100.8	53.4
Special	238	140.2	10.8	87.0
Federal	72	59.8	8.8	2.9
All Libraries	906	319.1	220.4	365.0

SOURCE: King Research, Inc.: National Library Survey

In terms of total volume of photocopy pages, Special libraries have the greatest amount for serials, Public and Academic libraries for books and Public libraries for other materials.

Considering the average number of pages per photocopy item, one finds that books have the largest amount at about 15 pages. Both serials and other materials are about one-half that amount. These data are displayed below in Table 3.6.

Table 3.6 NUMBER OF PHOTOCOPY PAGES PER PHOTOCOPY ITEM, BY TYPE OF MATERIAL, BY TYPE OF LIBRARY (1976)

(Average Number of Photocopy Pages Per Photocopy Item)

Type of Library	Type of Material			
	All Materials	Serials	Books	Other
Public	5.9	3.3	11.3	5.7
Academic	13.2	10.2	26.5	8.3
Special	9.2	7.3	6.5	16.8
Federal	10.3	9.8	17.3	8.5
All Libraries	8.0	6.1	14.9	7.2

Public libraries average fewer pages per serial than other libraries. However, as indicated above, they photocopy less scientific materials and more newspapers and magazines. The size of photocopy items is particularly large in Academic libraries, but, there was a small number of libraries in the sample where entire books were photocopied which accounts for this difference. The size of photocopy items involving other materials undoubtedly reflects the type of materials involved in the various types of libraries. However, we did not record this information.

As mentioned previously, the type of transaction is also an important factor in assessing photocopying in the United States with regard to the new Copyright Law and its implications. The types of transactions studied were those from local users, intrasystem loan and interlibrary loans. The total amount of photocopying from these transactions is given in Figure 3.3 below.

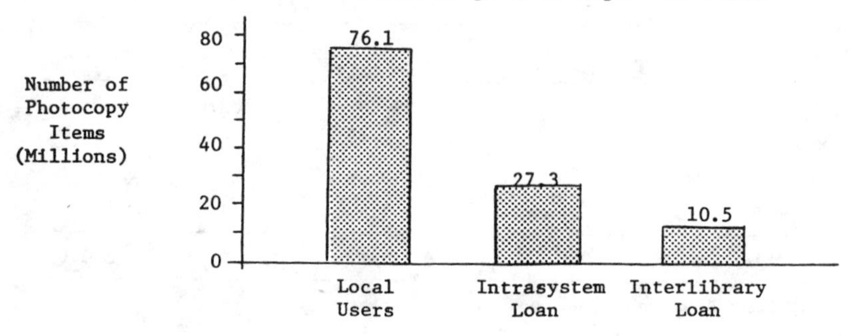

Figure 3.3. Number of Photocopy Items by Type of Transaction

Nearly two-thirds of the photocopy items are made for local users, a category that includes both patrons and library staff. However, as shown in Section 4, most of the photocopying for patrons is from serials. Only about 10 million photocopy items are prepared for interlibrary loan and 27 million are made for intrasystem loan. The breakdown of these by type of material will be shown subsequently. In Table 3.7, the volume by type of transaction is given by type of library

Table 3.7 NUMBER OF PHOTOCOPY ITEMS BY TYPE OF TRANSACTION, BY TYPE OF LIBRARY (1976)

(Millions of Photocopy Items)

Type of Library	All Transactions	Type of Transaction: Local Users	Intrasystem Loan	Interlibrary Loan
Public	64.3	45.3	13.7	5.3
Academic	16.6	9.9	3.8	2.9
Special	26.0	16.5	7.9	1.6
Federal	7.0	4.4	1.9	0.7
All Libraries	113.9	76.1	27.3	10.5

SOURCE: King Research, Inc.: National Library Survey

More than one-half of the photocopy items in all types of libraries are made for local users. The proportion of photocopying for type of transaction seems to be relatively consistent among the four types of libraries. Obviously, that relationship also holds for average number of photocopy items per library, as shown in Table 3.8 below.

Table 3.8 NUMBER OF PHOTOCOPY ITEMS PER LIBRARY BY TYPE OF TRANSACTION, BY TYPE OF LIBRARY (1976)

(Average Number of Photocopy Items Per Library)

Type of Library	Type of Transaction			
	All Transactions	Local Users	Intrasystem Loan	Interlibrary Loan
Public	7,700	5,500	1,600	600
Academic	5,500	3,300	1,200	1,000
Special	3,100	1,900	900	200
Federal	4,900	3,100	1,300	500
All Libraries	5,400	3,600	1,300	500

SOURCE: King Research, Inc.: National Library Survey

There appear to be some slight differences among types of library, however. Based on average photocopying per library, intrasystem lending seems to be relatively highest for Public and Federal libraries. Interlibrary lending is particularly high in Academic libraries. The relative proportion of photocopying for local users is highest with Public libraries and lowest with Special libraries.

The number of photocopy pages appears to be fairly consistent across sources of transactions. These data are given in Table 3.9.

Table 3.9 NUMBER OF PHOTOCOPY PAGES BY TYPE OF TRANSACTION, BY TYPE OF LIBRARY (1976)

(Millions of Photocopy Pages)

Type of Library	Type of Transaction			
	All Transactions	Local Users	Intrasystem Loan	Interlibrary Loan
Public	377	290.3	51.6	34.7
Academic	219	121.3	46.0	51.7
Special	238	161.1	68.5	8.3
Federal	70	44.2	18.2	7.7
All Libraries	906	615.2	184.8	106.0

SOURCE: King Research, Inc.: National Library Survey

Photocopying for local users accounts for the largest proportion of total volume of photocopy pages in all types of libraries. Photocopying for intrasystem loan is greater than interlibrary loan in all types of libraries except with Academic libraries. In the latter instance, much of the photocopying involves books where the number of pages per transaction item is large.

The average number of photocopy pages per photocopy item is presented in Table 3.10 which follows.

Table 3.10 NUMBER OF PHOTOCOPY PAGES PER PHOTOCOPY ITEM BY TYPE OF TRANSACTION, BY TYPE OF LIBRARY (1976)

(Average Number of Photocopy Pages Per Photocopy Item)

Type of Library	Type of Transaction			
	All Transactions	Local Users	Intrasystem Loan	Interlibrary Loan
Public	5.9	6.3	3.7	6.4
Academic	13.2	12.0	12.0	17.3
Special	9.2	10.6	9.4	5.6
Federal	10.3	10.6	10.1	11.5
All Libraries	8.0	7.9	6.6	9.9

SOURCE: King Research, Inc.: National Library Survey

When average number of photocopy pages per photocopy item is considered, there is not an appreciable difference among types of libraries or type of transaction. The principal difference is with Public libraries where the average number of pages is low across all types of transaction.

A much clearer picture of the amount of photocopying is presented with the number of photocopy items broken down by type of transaction, type of material and type of library as displayed on the following page. In all types of libraries and with all types of material, the number of photocopy items is greatest for local users, then intrasystem loan, and finally, interlibrary loan. The difference is less pronounced with serials when comparing photocopying for local users (27.8 million) and intrasystem loans (14.5 million) than with interlibrary loans (5.9 million). There is a large drop in the number of books by Public libraries from local users (5.7 million) to intrasystem loans (2.2 million). Perhaps Public libraries are more likely to lend original book copies than are the other types of libraries.

A somewhat different picture occurs when the average number of photocopy items per library is considered. These data are given in Table 3.12 which follows.

Table 3.11 NUMBER OF PHOTOCOPY ITEMS BY TYPE OF TRANSACTION, BY TYPE OF MATERIAL, BY TYPE OF LIBRARY (1976)

(Millions of Photocopy Items)

	Type of Transaction															
	All Transactions				Local Users				Intrasystem Loans				Interlibrary Loans			
Type of Library	All Mat.	Serials	Books	Other Mat.	All Mat.	Serials	Books	Other Mat.	All Mat.	Serials	Books	Other Mat.	All Mat.	Serials	Books	Other Mat.
Public	64.3	16.6	8.8	38.9	45.3	9.0	5.7	30.6	13.7	5.4	2.2	6.1	5.3	2.2	0.9	2.2
Academic	16.6	6.3	3.8	6.5	9.9	2.5	1.7	5.7	3.8	2.0	1.6	0.2	2.9	1.8	0.5	0.6
Special	26.0	19.2	1.7	5.1	16.5	12.3	0.8	3.4	7.9	5.6	0.7	1.6	1.6	1.3	0.2	0.1
Federal	7.0	6.1	0.6	0.3	4.4	4.0	0.3	0.1	1.9	1.5	0.2	0.2	0.7	0.6	0.1	<.1
All Libraries	113.9	48.2	14.9	50.8	76.1	27.8	8.5	39.8	27.3	14.5	4.7	8.1	10.5	5.9	1.7	2.9

SOURCE: King Research, Inc.: National Library Survey

Table 3.12 NUMBER OF PHOTOCOPY ITEMS PER LIBRARY BY TYPE OF TRANSACTION, BY TYPE OF MATERIAL, BY TYPE OF LIBRARY (1976)

(Average Number of Photocopy Items Per Library)

	Type of Transaction															
	All Transactions				Local Users				Intrasystem Loans				Interlibrary Loans			
Type of Library	All Mat.	Serials	Books	Other Mat.	All Mat.	Serials	Books	Other Mat.	All Mat.	Serials	Books	Other Mat.	All Mat.	Serials	Books	Other Mat.
Public	7,700	2,000	1,000	4,700	5,500	1,100	700	3,700	1,600	600	300	700	600	300	100	300
Academic	5,500	2,100	1,300	2,100	3,300	800	600	1,900	1,200	700	500	100	1,000	600	200	200
Special	3,100	2,300	200	600	1,900	1,400	100	400	900	700	100	200	200	200	-	-
Federal	4,900	4,300	400	200	3,100	2,800	200	100	1,300	1,000	100	100	500	400	10C	-
All Libraries	5,400	2,300	700	2,400	3,600	1,300	400	1,900	1,300	700	200	400	500	300	100	100

SOURCE: King Research, Inc.: National Library Survey

The average number of photocopy items per library reflects the fact that individual Federal libraries have the greatest serial photocopying for local users and intrasystem loans. The average number of photocopy items is least with serial and book interlibrary loans, but by far the heaviest by individual Academic libraries. Book photocopying for local users is greatest in Public and Academic libraries. Individual Academic libraries seem to have greater intrasystem loans of photocopy items of books than do the other types of libraries, and this appears to hold for interlibrary loans, but to a less pronounced degree.

3.3 Estimated Volume of Photocopying of Library Materials that Are Copyrighted and Not Copyrighted

One of the most important questions addressed by this study is what proportion of photocopied library materials is currently copyrighted. It is noted that determination of the copyright was established by the librarians who reported on the volume logs and photocopy characteristics sheets. Some copyright data were not found by them or were not reported. However, the proportion of reported data is very high. The number of photocopies of library materials that are copyrighted is given in Figure 3.4.

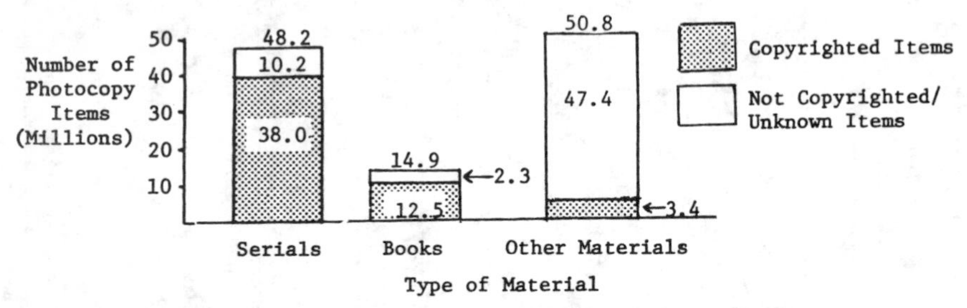

Figure 3.4. Number of Photocopy Items by Type of Material

It is clear that a very high proportion of serials and books are copyrighted and that only a small proportion of other materials are copyrighted. If the proportion of materials in which it is unknown whether they are copyrighted is the same as those known, the proportion of copyright is estimated to be 85 percent for serials, 87 percent for books and only nine percent for other materials. This proportion of copyrighted serials that were photocopied (85%) is much higher than the proportion of serial titles reported to be copyrighted by publishers in a survey conducted by Indiana University (3). In that study, about 70 percent of the serials were reported to be copyrighted.

A more complete breakdown of the amount of photocopied items that were made from copyrighted materials is given on the following page in Table 3.13 by type of material and by type of library. From the standpoint of potential royalty payments, the picture is very different from that presented with non-copyrighted materials included. The annual volume of photocopy items of copyrighted materials is substantially greater in serials (38 million) than in books (12.5 million), or other materials (3.4 million). The relationship of volume of photocopy items of copyrighted material is highest for serials in all types of libraries. The volume is highest for copyrighted serials in Public and Special libraries, but highest for copyrighted books in Public and Academic libraries. With other materials most of the photocopy items made from copyrighted materials were made in Public libraries, which made about 2.2 million photocopy items of copyrighted other materials. Special libraries made about 1 million photocopy items of other materials, while 150 thousand were made in Academic libraries and only about 40 thousand were made in Federal libraries.

As shown in Table 3.14, individual libraries of each of the four types average about the same amount of photocopying of copyrighted serials, ranging from 1,600 photocopies per library in Academic libraries to 2,500 photocopies per library in Federal libraries. Both Public and Academic libraries average many more photocopy items of copyrighted books than Special and Federal libraries.

The annual volume and average number of photocopies per library are given by serials, books and other materials by source of transaction and by type of library in Tables 3.15 through 3.20. Number of photocopy items and average number per library of copyrighted serials are displayed in Tables 3.15 and 3.16. We find that most of the photocopying of copyrighted serials is done for local users (21.7 million) and intrasystem loans (12.0 million) with about 4 million done for interlibrary loan. This pattern holds among the four types of libraries. In all instances, the total number of photocopy items for local users is greater than photocopying for the other two sources of transactions combined.

With books (Tables 3.17 and 3.18), it is also found that more photocopying of copyrighted books is performed for local users than intrasystem or interlibrary loans. Public and Academic libraries photocopy more copyrighted books for requests from all three sources of transaction from the standpoint of total volume and average photocopies per library.

Nearly twice as much photocopying of copyrighted other materials is done for local users as intrasystem and interlibrary loans together. This pattern holds true for all four types of libraries, although most of the total annual volume is accounted for in Public libraries. Similar patterns hold for average photocopy per library.

Table 3.13 NUMBER OF PHOTOCOPY ITEMS BY TYPE OF MATERIAL, BY COPYRIGHTED AND NOT COPYRIGHTED, BY TYPE OF LIBRARY (1976)

(Millions of Photocopy Items)

	Type of Material															
	All Materials				Serials				Books				Other Materials			
Type of Library	All Items	Copyrighted	Not Copyrighted	Unknown	All Serials	Copyrighted	Not Copyrighted	Unknown	All Books	Copyrighted	Not Copyrighted	Unknown	All Other Mat.	Copyrighted	Not Copyrighted	Unknown
Public	64.3	24.0	29.2	11.0	16.6	14.2	1.6	0.8	8.8	7.6	0.9	0.3	38.9	2.2	26.7	9.9
Academic	16.6	7.9	5.2	3.4	6.3	4.7	1.0	0.6	3.8	3.1	0.6	0.1	6.5	0.1	3.6	2.7
Special	26.0	17.9	5.6	2.6	19.2	15.5	2.2	1.5	1.7	1.4	0.2	0.1	5.1	1.0	3.2	1.0
Federal	7.0	4.0	2.6	0.3	6.1	3.6	2.3	0.2	0.6	0.4	0.1	<.1	0.3	<.1	0.2	0.1
All Libraries	113.9	53.8	42.6	17.3	48.2	38.0	7.1	3.1	14.9	12.5	1.8	0.5	50.8	3.4	33.6	13.8

SOURCE: King Research, Inc.: National Library Survey

Table 3.14 NUMBER OF PHOTOCOPY ITEMS PER LIBRARY THAT ARE COPYRIGHTED AND NOT COPYRIGHTED BY THE TYPE OF MATERIAL, BY TYPE OF LIBRARY (1976)

(Average Number of Photocopy Items Per Library)

	Type of Material															
	All Materials				Serials				Books				Other Materials			
Type of Library	All Items	Copyrighted	Not Copyrighted	Unknown	All Serials	Copyrighted	Not Copyrighted	Unknown	All Books	Copyrighted	Not Copyrighted	Unknown	All Other Mat.	Copyrighted	Not Copyrighted	Unknown
Public	7,700	2,900	3,500	1,300	2,000	1,700	200	100	1,000	900	100	40	4,700	300	3,200	1,200
Academic	5,500	2,600	1,700	1,100	2,100	1,600	300	200	1,300	1,000	200	30	2,100	50	1,200	900
Special	3,100	2,100	700	300	2,300	1,800	300	200	200	200	20	10	600	100	40	1,200
Federal	4,900	2,800	1,800	200	4,300	2,500	1,600	100	400	300	50	30	200	30	100	100
All Libraries	5,400	2,500	2,000	800	2,300	1,800	300	100	700	600	90	30	2,400	200	1,600	600

SOURCE: King Research, Inc.: National Library Survey

Table 3.15 NUMBER OF PHOTOCOPY ITEMS OF SERIALS THAT ARE COPYRIGHTED AND NOT COPYRIGHTED BY SOURCE OF TRANSACTION, BY TYPE OF LIBRARY (1976)

(Millions of Photocopy Items)

	Source of Transaction															
	All Transactions				Local Users				Intrasystem Loan				Interlibrary Loan			
Type of Library	All Items	Copyrighted	Not Copyrighted	Unknown	All Local Users	Copyrighted	Not Copyrighted	Unknown	All Intrasystem Loans	Copyrighted	Not Copyrighted	Unknown	All Interlibrary Loans	Copyrighted	Not Copyrighted	Unknown
Public	16.6	14.2	1.6	0.8	9.0	7.6	0.9	0.6	5.4	4.7	0.5	0.2	2.2	1.9	0.2	0.1
Academic	6.3	4.7	1.0	0.6	2.5	2.0	0.3	0.2	2.0	1.6	0.3	0.1	1.8	1.1	0.5	0.3
Special	19.2	15.5	2.2	1.5	12.3	9.7	1.8	0.8	5.6	4.8	0.3	0.6	1.3	1.0	0.1	0.2
Federal	6.1	3.6	2.3	0.2	4.0	2.5	2.0	0.1	1.5	0.9	0.6	0.1	0.6	0.4	0.2	0.1
All Libraries	48.2	38.0	7.1	3.1	27.8	21.7	4.5	1.6	14.5	12.0	1.7	0.8	5.9	4.3	0.9	0.7

SOURCE: King Research, Inc.: National Library Survey

Table 3.16 NUMBER OF PHOTOCOPY ITEMS OF SERIALS PER LIBRARY THAT ARE COPYRIGHTED AND NOT COPYRIGHTED BY SOURCE OF TRANSACTION (1976)

(Average Number of Photocopy Items Per Library)

	Source of Transaction															
	All Transactions				Local Users				Intrasystem Loan				Interlibrary Loan			
Type of Library	All Items	Copyrighted	Not Copyrighted	Unknown	All Local Users	Copyrighted	Not Copyrighted	Unknown	All Intrasystem Loans	Copyrighted	Not Copyrighted	Unknown	All Interlibrary Loans	Copyrighted	Not Copyrighted	Unknown
Public	2,000	1,700	200	100	1,100	900	100	100	600	600	100	-	300	200	-	-
Academic	2,100	1,600	300	200	800	700	100	100	700	500	100	-	600	400	100	100
Special	2,300	1,800	300	200	1,400	1,100	200	100	700	600	-	100	150	100	-	-
Federal	4,300	2,500	1,600	100	2,800	1,700	1,000	100	1,000	600	400	-	400	200	100	-
All Libraries	2,300	1,800	300	100	1,300	1,000	200	100	700	600	100	-	300	200	-	-

SOURCE: King Research, Inc.: National Library Survey

Table 3.17 NUMBER OF PHOTOCOPY ITEMS OF BOOKS THAT ARE COPYRIGHTED AND NOT COPYRIGHTED BY SOURCE OF TRANSACTION, BY TYPE OF LIBRARY (1976)

(Millions of Photocopy Items)

	Source of Transaction											
	Local Users				Intrasystem Loan				Interlibrary Loan			
Type of Library	All Local Users	Copy-righted	Not Copy-righted	Un-known	All Intra-System Loans	Copy-righted	Not Copy-righted	Un-known	All Inter-Library Loans	Copy-righted	Not Copy-righted	Un-known
Public	5.7	4.9	0.6	0.2	2.2	2.0	0.2	0.0	0.9	0.8	0.1	0.1
Academic	1.7	1.4	0.2	0.1	1.6	1.5	0.1	0.0	0.5	0.2	0.3	0.0
Special	0.8	0.6	0.1	0.0	0.7	0.6	0.0	0.0	0.2	0.2	0.0	0.0
Federal	0.3	0.2	0.0	0.0	0.2	0.1	0.1	0.0	0.1	0.0	0.0	0.0
All Li-braries	8.5	7.1	1.0	0.3	4.7	4.8	0.4	0.1	1.7	0.4	0.4	0.1

SOURCE: King Research, Inc.: National Library Survey

Table 3.18 NUMBER OF PHOTOCOPY ITEMS PER LIBRARY OF BOOKS THAT ARE COPYRIGHTED AND NOT COPYRIGHTED, BY SOURCE OF TRANSACTION, BY TYPE OF LIBRARY (1976)

(Average Number of Photocopy Items Per Library)

	Source of Transaction											
	Local Users				Intrasystem Loan				Interlibrary Loan			
Type of Library	All Local Users	Copy-righted	Not Copy-righted	Un-known	All Intra-System Loans	Copy-righted	Not Copy-righted	Un-known	All Inter-Library Loans	Copy-righted	Not Copy-righted	Un-known
Public	700	590	80	20	300	240	20	6	100	90	10	7
Academic	600	450	80	30	500	500	30	1	200	50	100	4
Special	100	80	10	5	100	70	5	3	-	20	6	2
Federal	200	4	1	8	100	100	40	-	100	6	10	20
All Li-braries	400	340	40	20	200	230	20	4	100	50	20	6

SOURCE: King Research, Inc.: National Library Survey

Table 3.19 TOTAL NUMBER OF PHOTOCOPY ITEMS OF OTHER MATERIALS THAT ARE COPYRIGHTED AND NOT COPYRIGHTED, BY SOURCE OF TRANSACTION, BY TYPE OF LIBRARY (1976)

(Millions of Photocopy Items)

	Source of Transaction											
	Local Users				Intrasystem Loan				Interlibrary Loan			
Type of Library	All Local Patrons	Copy-righted	Not Copy-righted	Un-known	All Intra-System Loans	Copy-righted	Not Copy-righted	Un-known	All Inter-Library Loans	Copy-righted	Not Copy-righted	Un-known
Public	30.6	1.2	20.5	8.9	6.1	0.5	4.9	0.6	2.2	0.5	1.2	0.4
Academic	5.7	0.1	3.4	2.1	0.2	0.0	0.2	0.0	0.6	0.0	0.0	0.5
Federal	3.4	0.7	1.7	0.5	1.6	0.2	1.4	0.0	0.1	0.0	0.1	0.0
Special	0.1	0.0	0.1	0.0	0.2	0.0	0.1	0.1	<1	-	0.0	0.0
All Libraries	39.8	2.1	25.7	12.0	8.1	0.7	6.6	0.8	2.9	0.6	1.3	1.0

SOURCE: King Research, Inc.: National Library Survey

Table 3.20 NUMBER OF PHOTOCOPY ITEMS PER LIBRARY OF OTHER MATERIALS THAT ARE COPYRIGHTED AND NOT COPYRIGHTED BY SOURCE OF TRANSACTION, BY TYPE OF LIBRARY (1976)

(Average Number of Photocopy Items Per Library)

	Source of Transaction											
	Local Users				Intrasystem Loan				Interlibrary Loan			
Type of Library	All Local Patrons	Copy-righted	Not Copy-righted	Un-known	All Intra-System Loans	Copy-righted	Not Copy-righted	Un-known	All Inter-Library Loans	Copy-righted	Not Copy-righted	Un-known
Public	3,700	145	2,470	1,070	700	55	595	75	300	65	145	45
Academic	1,900	45	1,115	7,010	100	3	55	4	200	21	7	185
Special	400	90	200	115	200	25	165	4	-	1	10	2
Federal	100	20	45	20	100	4	80	50	-	-	2	14
All Libraries	1,900	100	1,210	565	400	30	3,120	35	100	25	60	45

SOURCE: King Research, Inc.: National Library Survey

IMPLICATIONS OF THE COPYRIGHT LAW AND CONTU GUIDELINES CONCERNING SERIALS FROM THE LIBRARIANS' PERSPECTIVE

The results of the national library survey can be presented from two quite distinct perspectives depending on whether they are directed to an organization that is subject to royalty payments (libraries) or one that is eligible to receive the payments (publishers and authors). In the first instance, librarians may wish to know how many libraries appear to have materials subject to royalty payment, how much photocopying of library materials is involved, and what proportion of the materials is subject to royalty payment. Publishers, on the other hand, are interested in knowing how many published materials in a library are eligible for payment, but even more so how much photocopying of a single publication is performed across all libraries and what proportion of the titles achieve certain levels of photocopying. This section is addressed to the extent of photocopying of serials that takes place in an individual library. Section 5 presents data for individual serial titles summed across libraries which is more important to publishers. In these two sections, we concentrate on photocopying of serials since they represent the largest amount of photocopying of library materials that are copyrighted and they seem to be of most concern to all participants.

The first part of this section deals with the overall estimates of serial photocopying that involves copyrighted material. Since the Copyright Law involves different interpretations concerning photocopying for the three principal types of transactions, the following three parts are directed to each type (interlibrary loan, local users, and intrasystem loan). The total amount of photocopying subject to royalty payment is discussed for photocopying from each type of transaction. The impact of CONTU guidelines on this number is discussed in detail for interlibrary loans. Some hypothetical eligibility conditions are also applied to photocopying for local users and intrasystem loans in order to simulate the impact of possible future guidelines involving these photocopy items. The final section discusses librarians' attitutdes toward possible royalty payment mechanisms, their ability to implement these mechanisms, and other library data related to photocopying.

* HIGHLIGHTS *

Volume of Serial Photocopying

- 48.2 million photocopy items are made of serials, of which 38.0 million are copyrighted. This comes to an average of 2,300 and 1,800 photocopy items per library, respectively.
- Public libraries make 14.2 million photocopy items per year, which comes to 1,700 per library. Academic libraries make

4.7 million photocopy items or 1,600 per library. Special libraries make 15.5 photocopy items or 1,800 per library. Federal libraries make 3.6 million photocopy items or 2,500 per library.

- Most photocopy items of copyrighted serials are made for local users (21.7 million), followed by intrasystem loan (12.0 million) and interlibrary loan (4.3 million).

Volume of Interlibrary Loan Photocopying

- Of 6.0 million serial requests for interlibray loan, 4.3 million are from domestic publications. The ones filled by photocopies yielded 3.8 million photocopy items of which 3.1 million are copyrighted.

- When CONTU guidelines are applied to the number of photocopy items made for interlibrary loans, it is estimated that 2.4 million are under six years old and 2.0 million are under six years old and are not used for replacement or classroom use. When the rule of six copies or more is also applied, there are about 500 thousand photocopy items remaining that are subject to royalty payment.

- If photocopy items for serials over five years old are all eligible for royalty payment, the total increases to 1.9 million photocopy items.

- Of 132 libraries served by MINITEX, only 58 are found to be required to pay any royalty payments when CONTU guidelines are applied (not considering serials over five years old). These libraries averaged 53 photocopy items subject to royalty payments.

- Considering only serials under six years old and excluding photocopy items made for replacement or classroom use, 93 percent of all U.S. libraries should have less than 250 photocopy items eligible for royalty payment and 2 percent should have more than 1,000 copies eligible for payment. The latter percent will decrease substantially if the rule of six copies or more is applied.

Volume of Local User Photocopying

- Of 27.8 million photocopy items made for local users (patrons and library staff), 21.7 million are estimated to be copyrighted. Of these, 19.0 million are estimated to be made from domestic serials.

- There are about 800 thousand photocopy items made for replacement by library or classroom use by faculty.

- Approximately 14.9 million photocopy items are made for local users from serials under six years old.

- About 17.4 million photocopy items are made for local users for serials that have more than five copies made within a library.

- Approximately 12.9 million photocopy items are made from serials under six years old and that have more than five copies made within a library.

- About 82 percent of the transactions for local use involve single copies made for local patrons (individuals and institutions).

- Considering only serials under six years old and excluding photocopy items made for replacement or classroom use, 67 percent of the libraries should have less than 250 photocopy items eligible for royalty payment. About 20 percent of the libraries will have over 1,000 such photocopy items, five percent over 5,000 photocopy items and one percent of the libraries over 10,000 photocopy items.

Volume of Intrasystem Loan Photocopying

- Of the 14.5 million photocopy items prepared for intrasystem loan, 12.0 million are copyrighted. Of these 9.8 are estimated to be made from domestic serials.
- There are about 500 thousand photocopy items of intrasystem loans made for replacement by the library or classroom use by faculty.
- Approximately 7.2 million photocopy items made for intrasystem loan are from serials under six years old.
- About 76 percent of the transactions involve single copies made for local patrons (individuals and institutions).

4.1 Estimated Volume of Photocopying of Serials

The estimated total amount of photocopying for serials is shown in Figure 4.1 below for number of photocopy items made for local users, intrasystem loan and interlibrary loan.

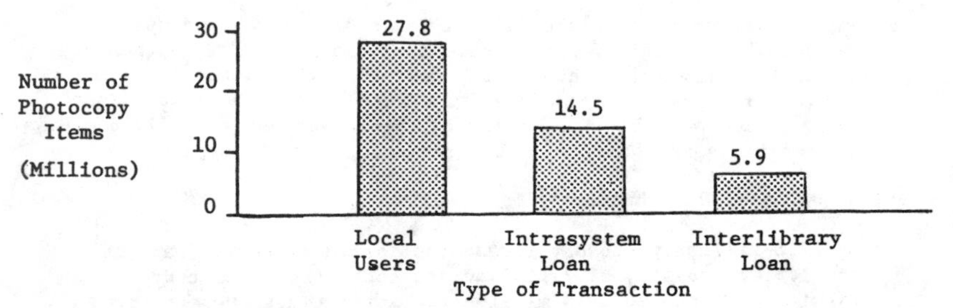

Figure 4.1 Number of Photocopy Items for Serials by Type of Transaction (1976

The total volume of photocopying for local patrons (27.8 million) is greater than either interlibrary loan (5.9 million) or intrasystem loan (14.5 million).

Estimates of the total annual volume of photocopy items made from serials is given in Table 4.1 by source of transaction and by type of library.

TABLE 4.1 NUMBER OF PHOTOCOPY ITEMS OF SERIALS BY TYPE OF TRANSACTION, BY TYPE OF LIBRARY (1976)

(Millions of Photocopy Items)

Type of Library	All Transactions	Type of Transaction		
		Local Users	Intrasystem Loan	Interlibrary Loan
Public	16.6	9.0	5.4	2.2
Academic	6.3	2.5	2.0	1.8
Special	19.2	12.3	5.6	1.3
Federal	6.1	4.0	1.5	0.6
All Libraries	48.2	27.8	14.5	5.9

SOURCE: King Research, Inc.: National Library Survey

The relationship over type of transaction exists for Public, Special and Federal libraries. However, Academic libraries have nearly as many interlibrary loans as intrasystem loans.

Even though Public libraries account for the largest proportion of serial photocopying from all sources of transaction, they are not at all dominant when considering average photocopying per library, as shown in Table 4.2.

TABLE 4.2 NUMBER OF PHOTOCOPY ITEMS PER LIBRARY OF SERIALS BY TYPE OF TRANSACTION, BY TYPE OF LIBRARY (1976)

(Average Number of Photocopy Items Per Library)

Type of Library	All Transactions	Type of Transaction		
		Local Users	Intrasystem Loan	Interlibrary Loan
Public	2,000	1,100	600	300
Academic	2,100	800	700	600
Special	2,300	1,400	700	200
Federal	4,300	2,800	1,000	400
All Libraries	2,300	1,300	700	300

SOURCE: King Research, Inc.: National Library Survey

The Federal libraries have the largest average amount of photocopying at 4,300 photocopy items per library. The other types of libraries are remarkably close in average amount of photocopying at just about 2,000 photocopy items per library. However, the average amount of photocopying for local users varies more among the four types of libraries. Federal libraries have by far the most photocopying for local users with 2,800 photocopy items per library. The other libraries range from 800 to 1,400 photocopy items per library. The pattern of photocopying for intrasystem loans follows that of the total with Federal libraries making the most on the average (1,000 photocopy items per library) and with the other three types of libraries very close to one another. The average photocopying per librar of interlibrary loan is highest for Academic libraries (600) and somewhat less for Federal (400), Public (300) and Special (200) libraries. It is emphasized that these estimates are for lending and not borrowing. Estimates for the latter will be given in the next section. There is some difference since some types of libraries appear to lend more than they borrow and vice versa.

The proportion of photocopying of serials that are copyrighted is shown in Figure 4.2 for local users, intrasystem loans and interlibrary loans.

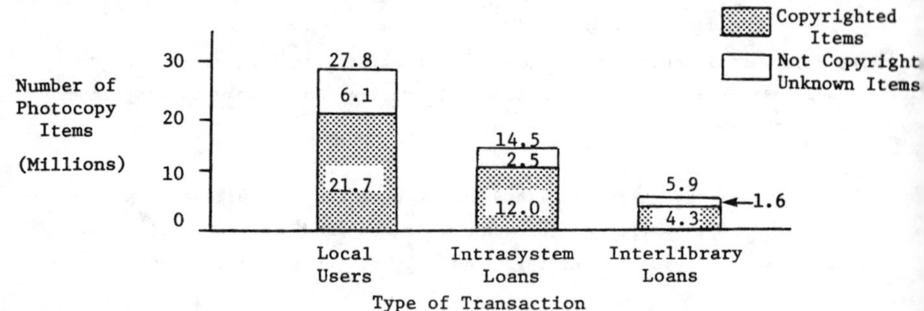

Figure 4.2 Number of Photocopy Items of Serials that are Copyrighted by Type of Transaction (1976)

Special libraries have the greatest volume of photocopying of copyrighted serials at about 15.5 million photocopy items. Public libraries also have a large amount with 14.2 million photocopy items. Academic and Federal libraries account for 4.7 and 3.6 million photocopy items, respectively.

The amount of photocopying of serials that is copyrighted is given by type of transaction and type of library in Table 4.3.

TABLE 4.3 NUMBER OF PHOTOCOPY ITEMS OF SERIALS THAT ARE COPYRIGHTED BY TYPE OF TRANSACTION, BY TYPE OF LIBRARY (1976)

(Millions of Photocopy Items)

Type of Library	All Transactions	Type of Transaction		
		Local Users	Intrasystem Loan	Interlibrary Loan
Public	14.2	7.6	4.7	1.9
Academic	4.7	2.0	1.6	1.1
Special	15.5	9.7	4.8	1.0
Federal	3.6	2.5	0.9	0.4
All Libraries	38.0	21.7	12.0	4.3

SOURCE: King Research, Inc.: National Library Survey

Most of the analysis in this report is based on the amount of copyrighted serials that is photocopied. We find a total of at least 38 million photocopy items made of copyrighted serials in the United States. However, over the remainder of section 4, we will show that a large portion of these photocopy items may not be eligible for royalty payment depending on one's interpretations of the Copyright Law. These alternative royalty payment conditions vary by type of transaction, which is why this breakdown is emphasized in the remainder of this section. As mentioned above, photocopying for local users forms the greatest proportion of photocopying of serials that are copyrighted. Of this amount, Special and Public libraries account for 80 percent of the total. The same proportion also holds for intrasystem lending of photocopied serials. The largest amount of interlibrary lending of serials is performed by Public libraries. They account for about 45 percent of the total. Again, however, when average photocopy items per library is studied a some what different picture is revealed. These data are given in Table 4.4 below.

TABLE 4.4 NUMBER OF PHOTOCOPY ITEMS PER LIBRARY OF SERIALS THAT ARE COPYRIGHTED BY TYPE OF TRANSACTION, BY TYPE OF LIBRARY (1976)

(Average Photocopy Items Per Library)

Type of Library	All Transactions	Type of Transaction		
		Local Users	Intrasystem Loan	Interlibrary Loan
Public	1,700	900	600	200
Academic	1,600	700	500	400
Special	1,800	1,100	600	100
Federal	2,500	1,700	600	200
All Libraries	1,800	1,000	600	200

SOURCE: King Research, Inc.: National Library Survey

By eliminating non-copyrighted serials and those that were listed as unknown or not reported, we find a similar array of data as that observed with all materials included. However, the average number of intrasystem loans of serials that are photocopied is about the same for all types of libraries.

It is emphasized that, while analysis of the average number of photocopy items per library is interesting, a far more significant statistical result is the distribution of libraries that have various levels of photocopying. In the next sub-sections, we will present an estimate of the proportion of libraries that make less than 250 photocopy items per year; 250 to 1,000; 1,000 to 5,000; 5,000 to 10,000; and over 10,000 photocopy items per year. These data will be presented under different conditions of eligibility for royalty payment.

The next three sub-sections discuss details of photocopying performed for interlibrary loans, local users and intrasystem loans respectively. The interlibrary loans are discussed first since a great deal of effort has been devoted by CONTU in providing guidelines for interpreting allowable levels of photocopying for interlibrary loan. Some of these guidelines might also be applied in the future to photocopying involving other types of transaction as well. Also, MINITEX provided us with an enormously valuable data base for analysis of interlibrary loans which they processed from December, 1975 through November, 1976. (We refer to these as 1976 data). These data were used to correct national data for seasonal and day-of-the-week effects. They were also used to develop mathematical models for estimation of distributions of photocopying by serial titles. Finally, they provided an excellent means of verifying results of photocopying of interlibrary loans observed in the national library survey.

4.2 Estimated Volume of Photocopying of Serials for Interlibrary Loan

One portion of library photocopying that has received particular attention is the photocopying done by one library for another library outside its organization (interlibrary loan). The substitution of photocopies for the lending of the original publication is common practice in the case of serials. For the year 1976, it is estimated from the national library survey that a total of 5.9 million photocopy items of serials were made by United States libraries for interlibrary loans to other libraries. The libraries in the national survey also reported receiving about 6 million borrowed requests. Approximately three-fourths of the photocopies were of identified copyrighted materials. Serials accounted for about 60 percent of all photocopies made for interlibrary loan. Palmour et al, found, in 1971, that photocopies accounted for about 42 percent of all interlibrary loans made by Academic libraries (7). The same study estimated that 95 percent of the photocopying for interlibrary loans involved serials materials. This evidence suggests that other libraries may be lending a higher proportion of books and other materials.

The proportion of photocopying for interlibrary loans of copyrighted serials is displayed by type of library in Figure 4.3.

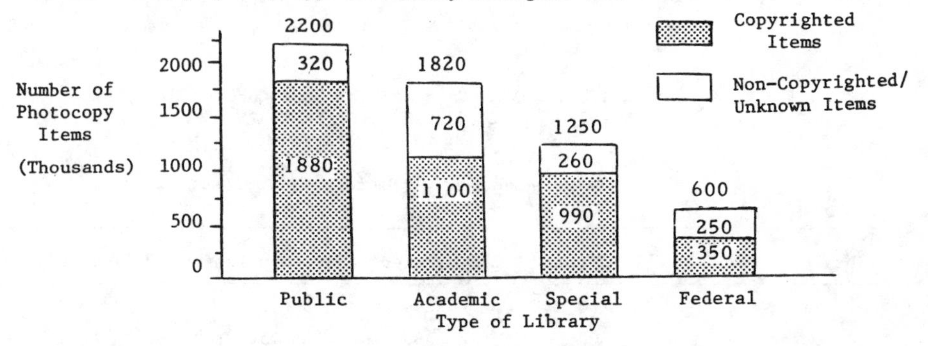

Figure 4.3 Number of Photocopy Items of Serials for Interlibrary Loans by Type of Library (1976)

The largest amount of photocopying for interlibrary loans is in Public and Academic libraries at 2.2 and 1.8 million photocopy items respectively. Special libraries had about 1.3 million and Federal libraries 600 thousand photocopy items respectively. The Association of Research Libraries (ARL) reported that the libraries of their member institutions provided about 1.7 million photocopies to other libraries through interlibrary loan in the year 1975-76 (1). This suggests that a large portion of the photocopying for interlibrary loans comes from large Academic libraries. Many of the ARL libraries were included in the national library survey.

The number of photocopy items of copyrighted serials is given by the type of libraries in Table 4.5.

TABLE 4.5 NUMBER OF PHOTOCOPY ITEMS OF SERIALS FOR INTERLIBRARY LOANS, COPYRIGHTED AND NOT COPYRIGHTED, BY TYPE OF LIBRARY (1976)

(Thousands of Photocopy Items)

Type of Library	All Serials	Copyrighted	Not Copyrighted	Unknown
Public	2,200	1,880	180	140
Academic	1,820	1,100	460	260
Special	1,250	990	50	210
Federal	600	350	190	60
All Libraries	5,870	4,320	880	670

SOURCE: King Research, Inc.: National Library Survey

The total numbers of photocopy items of copyrighted serials that are given in Table 4.5 are not those used in most of the analysis in the remainder of this section. These data are compared with the number of photocopy items borrowed since the CONTU guidelines indicate that responsibility for royalty payment is with the borrowing library. As a matter of interest, the average numbers of photocopy items lent are given in Table 4.6.

TABLE 4.6 ESTIMATED AVERAGE NUMBER OF PHOTOCOPIED INTERLIBRARY LOANS OF SERIALS BY WHETHER THEY ARE COPYRIGHTED, BY TYPE OF LIBRARY (1976)

(Average Number of Photocopy Items Per Library)

Type of Library	All Serials	Copyrighted	Not Copyrighted	Unknown
Public	260	230	20	4
Academic	600	360	150	90
Special	150	120	10	20
Federal	420	240	130	40
All Libraries	280	200	40	30

SOURCE: King Research, Inc.: National Library Survey

Academic and Special libraries lend similar amounts of copyrighted photocopy items (360 and 116 respectively). Also, the average amount lent by Public and Federal libraries is similar (230 and 240 respectively). Even though the estimated and average total numbers of photocopy items for interlibrary loans are high, the rules under the CONTU guidelines reduce the total number of photocopies subject to royalty payment to a small fraction of the total. The CONTU guidelines are discussed first in section 4.2.1, the distinction is made between photocopies loaned and borrowed in section 4.2.2, and the estimated total number of photocopy items made for interlibrary loans and the impact of CONTU guidelines are provided in section 4.2.3.

4.2.1 CONTU Guidelines Concerning Interlibrary Borrowing of Serials

Section 108 of the new Copyright Law, effective January 1, 1978, prohibits systematic photocopying of copyrighted materials but permits interlibrary arrangements "that do not have, as their purpose or effect, that the library or archives receiving such copies or phonorecords for distribution does so in such aggregate quantities as to substitute for a subscription to or purchase of such work." The National Commission on New Technological Uses of Copyrighted Works (CONTU) consulted with the principal library, publisher, and author organizations to reach a workable and fair interpretation of the term "such aggregate quantities." Agreement was reached and resulted in what are now referred to as the CONTU Guidelines.

The CONTU Guidelines place the burden of responsibility upon the borrowing library. Because of their importance, the Guidelines are repeated in full text.

Guidelines for the Proviso of Subsection 108(g)(2)

1. As used in the proviso of subsection 108(g)(2), the words "...such aggregate quantities as to substitute for a subscription to or purchase of such work" shall mean:

(a) with respect to any given periodical (as opposed to any given issue of a periodical), filled requests of a library or archives (a "requesting entity") within any calendar year for a total of six or more copies of an article or articles published in such periodical within 5 years prior to the date of the request. These guidelines specifically shall not apply, directly or indirectly, to any request of a requesting entity for a copy or copies of an article or articles published in any issue of a periodical, the publication date of which is more than 5 years prior to the date when the request is made. These guidelines do not define the meaning, with respect to such a request, of "...such aggregate quantities as to substitute for a subscription to (such periodical)".

(b) with respect to any other material described in subsection 108(d), (including fiction and poetry), filled requests of a requesting entity within any calendar year for a total of six or more copies or phonorecords of or from any given work (including a collective work) during the entire period when such material shall be protected by copyright.

2. In the event that a requesting entity --

(a) shall have in force or shall have entered an order for a subscription to a periodical, or

(b) has within its collection, or shall have entered an order for, a copy of phonorecord of any other copyrighted work, material from either category of which it desires to obtain by copy from another library or archives (the "supplying entity"), because the material to be copied is not reasonably available for use by the requesting entity itself, then the fulfillment of such request shall be treated as though the requesting entity made such copy from its own collection. A library or archives may request a copy or phonorecord from a supplying entity only under those circumstances where the requesting entity would have been able, under the other provisions of Section 108, to supply such copy from materials in its own collection.

3. No request for a copy or phonorecord of any material to which these guidelines apply may be fulfilled by the supplying entity unless such request is accompanied by a representation by the requesting entity that the request was made in conformity with these guidelines.

4. The requesting entity shall maintain records of all requests made by it for copies or phonorecords of any materials to which these guidelines apply and shall maintain records of the fulfillment of such requests, which records shall be retained until the end of the third complete calendar year after the end of the calendar year in which the respective request shall have been made.

5. As part of the review provided for in subsection 108(i), these guidelines shall be reviewed not later than 5 years from the effective date of this bill.

Part of the national library survey on photocopying was devoted to the collection of data on interlibrary loan borrowing requests for serials made by the sample libraries. All estimates in this section were derived from the borrowing data, in contrast to estimates in previous sections on interlibrary loans made to other libraries.

4.2.2 Estimated Volume of Photocopying of Interlibrary Loans Versus Interlibrary Requests.

It is important to make a distinction between interlibrary loans (lending library photocopying) and interlibrary requests (borrowing library use) since the CONTU guidelines indicate that the borrowing libraries might be responsible for royalty payments for photocopies of interlibrary loans of serials that are photocopied. The previous section gave an estimate of interlibrary loans by whether they were copyrighted. Unfortunately, borrowing data from the interlibrary loan form is not broken down by copyrighted or not copyrighted because borrowing forms do not contain this information.

The relationship between interlibrary loans and interlibrary requesting is given by type of library in Table 4.7

TABLE 4.7 NUMBER OF PHOTOCOPY ITEMS OF SERIALS LENT AND BORROWED BY TYPE OF LIBRARY (1976)

(Thousands of Photocopy Items)

Type of Library	Photocopy Items Lent	Photocopy Items Borrowed	Net Photocopies Lent*
Public	2,200	1,340	+ 860
Academic	1,820	2,060	- 240
Special	1,250	1,800	- 550
Federal	600	830	- 230
All Libraries	5,870	6,030	- 160

SOURCE: King Research, Inc.: National Library Survey

* These data present some evidence of the balance of lending and borrowing. However, much of the difference observed can be accounted for by statistical variation.

It appears that Public libraries lend more than they borrow by a total of about 860 thousand photocopy items. On the other hand, the Academic, Special and Federal libraries together borrowed about 1 million more copies than they lent. The net effect is that there are about 160,000 more borrowing requests than loans from the 21,280 libraries included in the sampling universe.

The average number of photocopy items of serials lent and borrowed from other libraries is given in Table 4.8 below.

TABLE 4.8 NUMBER OF PHOTOCOPY ITEMS OF SERIALS PER LIBRARY LENT AND BORROWED BY TYPE OF LIBRARY (1976)

(Average Number of Photocopy Items Per Library)

Type of Library	Photocopy Items Lent	Photocopy Items Borrowed	Net Photocopy Items Lent
Public	260	160	+ 100
Academic	600	680	- 80
Special	150	210	- 60
Federal	420	580	- 160
All Libraries	280	280	- 7

SOURCE: King Research Inc.: National Library Survey

There is an average net excess of loans for Public libraries. Academic, Special and Federal libraries all tend to borrow more than they lend. The next table shows, however, that most of the Academic borrowing is from other Academic libraries.

The number of photocopy items requested that were indicated to be from various types of libraries are given in Table 4.9.

TABLE 4.9 NUMBER OF PHOTOCOPY ITEMS OF SERIALS MADE FOR INTERLIBRARY LOAN BY TYPE OF LENDING LIBRARY AND BY TYPE OF BORROWING LIBRARY (1976)

(Thousands of Photocopy Items)

Type of Borrowing Library	All Libraries	Type of Lending Library					
		Academic	Federal	Public	School	Special	Unkn
Public	1,340	470	0	450	10	60	35
Academic	2,060	1,360	60	60	0	190	39
Special	1,800	430	450	50		620	25
Federal	830	300	140	30	--	230	13
All Libraries	6,030	2,560	650	590	10	1,100	1,12

SOURCE: King Research, Inc.: National Library Survey

Unfortunately, a large proportion of the responses indicated that the lending sou was unknown or was not recorded on the form. For the most part, results show that Public libraries borrow mostly from Public and Academic libraries (450 and 470 thousand photocopy items respectively); most Academic libraries borrow from Academic libraries; Special libraries borrow heavily from Special libraries, Federal and Academic libraries; and Federal libraries borrow mostly from Academic and Special libraries. The data seem to corroborate data from Table 4.7 and 4.8.

The remainder of this section is devoted to interlibrary borrowing requests. Data came from the national library survey interlibrary loan form and the MINITEX data base. From the national library survey data, it is estimated tha there are about 6 million borrowing requests, of which about 4.3 million are requests for domestic publications. Of these, a total of 3.8 million had photocop made. The remaining were reported to be filled by original serial copies or to be unfilled. These data are given by type of borrowing library in Table 4.10.

TABLE 4.10 NUMBER OF PHOTOCOPY ITEMS OF SERIALS REQUESTED FOR INTERLIBRARY LOAN BY TYPE OF BORROWING LIBRARY (1976) (MILLIONS OF PHOTOCOPY ITEMS)

Type of Borrowing Library	Number of Borrowing Requests	Number of Domestic Requests	Number of Domestic Photocopy Items	Number of Copyrighted Domestic Photocopy Items
Public	1.34	1.18	1.01	0.91
Academic	2.06	1.28	1.13	0.83
Special	1.80	1.35	1.25	1.14
Federal	0.83	0.52	0.38	0.23
All Libraries	6.03	4.33	3.77	3.11

SOURCE: King Research, Inc.: National Library Survey

The number of copyrighted photocopy items was found from the proportion of copyrighted loaned photocopy items to the total of copyrighted and not copyrighted found in Table 3.15. The values were 0.905 for Public, 0.733 for Academic, 0.909 for Special and 0.600 for Federal libraries. The Academic libraries seemed to have a higher proportion of borrowed photocopies from foreign serials than did other types of libraries. The total number of requests for photocopies of domestic serials is given in Table 4.10 and the average number of interlibrary loan photocopied requests per library is given in Table 4.11.

TABLE 4.11 NUMBER OF PHOTOCOPY ITEMS PER LIBRARY OF SERIALS MADE FOR INTERLIBRARY LOANS BY TYPE OF BORROWING LIBRARY (1976) (AVERAGE NUMBER OF PHOTOCOPY ITEMS PER LIBRARY)

Type of Borrowing Library	Number of Borrowing Requests Per Library	Number of Domestic Requests Per Library	Number of Domestic Photocopy Items Per Library	Average Number of Domestic Copyrighted Photocopy Items Per Library
Public	160	140	120	110
Academic	680	420	370	270
Special	210	160	150	140
Federal	580	360	270	160
All Libraries	280	200	180	150

SOURCE: King Research, Inc.: National Library Survey

The average number of photocopy items made from copyrighted domestic serials per library is highest in Academic libraries (270) and lowest in Public libraries (110). It is cautioned that the results involve only copyrighted domestic serials. Libraries should recognize that they may have a liability for copyrighted foreign serials as well.

The total and average number of photocopy items for interlibrary loan requests are given in Tables 4.12 and 4.13.

TABLE 4.12 NUMBER OF PHOTOCOPY ITEMS OF SERIALS REQUESTED FOR INTERLIBRARY LOAN BY TYPE OF REQUESTOR, BY TYPE OF BORROWING LIBRARY (1976)

(Thousands of Photocopy Items)

Type of Borrowing Library	All Requestors*	Type of Requestor: Teacher	Student	Individual	Library	Other Institution	Not Specified
Public	1,340	10	440	460	210	200	20
Academic	2,080	780	1,040	30	170	50	10
Special	1,810	170	100	1,270	140	80	50
Federal	814	100	20	690	3	1	0
All Libraries	6,044	1,070	1,600	2,450	530	320	80

SOURCE: King Research, Inc.: National Library Survey

TABLE 4.13 NUMBER OF PHOTOCOPY ITEMS PER LIBRARY OF SERIALS REQUESTED FOR INTERLIBRARY LOAN BY TYPE OF REQUESTOR, BY TYPE OF BORROWING LIBRARY (1976) (AVERAGE NUMBER OF PHOTOCOPY ITEMS PER LIBRARY)

Type of Borrowing Library	All Requestors**	Type of Requestor: Teacher	Student	Individual	Library	Other Institution	Not Specified
Public	162	2	53	55	26	24	2
Academic	686	256	343	10	57	15	5
Special	211	20	12	149	16	9	5
Federal	576	76	15	483	2	-	-
All Libraries	285	50	76	115	25	15	4

SOURCE: King Research, Inc.: National Library Survey

* Totals do not agree with Table 4.10 due to rounding.

** Averages do not agree with Table 4.11 due to rounding.

It is found, as expected, that Academic libraries are serving teachers and students much more frequently than other types of libraries. Teachers also rely on Special libraries and Federal libraries to a fair degree. About one-fourth of the students' requests are processed through Public libraries and nearly all the rest come from Academic libraries.

4.2.3 CONTU Guidelines and Interlibrary Loan

Of the 3.77 million interlibrary loan photocopy items of domestic serials, a substantial proportion are not subject to royalty payment based on

CONTU guidelines for interlibrary loans. One way to display this fact is by sequentially screening out photocopy items by those publications over five years old, those used for replacement or classroom use and the number of photocopy items less than six copies per serial title made in the past year within an individual borrowing library. These data are given in Figure 4.4.

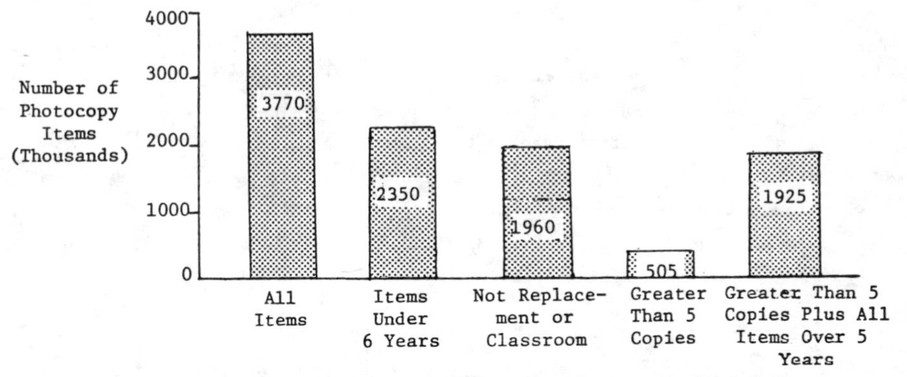

Figure 4.4 Number of Photocopy Items of Domestic Serials Requested for Interlibrary Loans-All Items, Items Under 6 Years, Items Not for Replacement or Classroom, Items With Greater Than Five Copies (1976)

The total annual number of photocopy items drops from 3.77 million to 2.4 million when publications over five years old are dropped from consideration. Of these, about 2.0 million photocopy items remain after replacement copies and copies made for classroom use are dropped from consideration. Thus, roughly one-half of the original photocopies are exempt after these aspects of the CONTU guidelines and fair use doctrine are applied. When the five and under rule applies, it is estimated that the number of eligible photocopy items decrease to about 505 thousand.

The most difficult observation involves the number of photocopy items which are not eligible for royalty payment because fewer than six copies of them are made in a library within a one-year period of time. A rather complex mathematical model was used to make this estimate. The difficulty in making this estimate comes from the fact that observations of photocopy items were made not only from a sample of libraries but also from a sample of time in the year. One can project quite well the estimate of total volume of photocopying but the estimate of the proportion (distribution) of serials that has 1, 2, 3, 4, 5 or greater photocopy items is quite difficult. If one observes that 95 percent of the serials had less than six photocopies in one week, there are found to be fewer serials that will have less than six photocopies over the entire year. The data from the MINITEX files were extremely useful in formulating an estimate for this figure. This was done by observing the mathematical distribution of photocopies for one week and one year for all libraries and serial titles in MINITEX. From these data an extrapolation factor was derived for each type of library. A detailed discussion of this approach is given in Appendix C. This approach yields a very small proportion of photocopies that are subject to royalty payments under the conditions mentioned above when the serials with five or less photocopies are made and, when the first five copies of the remaining titles are excluded.

Table 4.14 gives the eligible photocopy items by type of library. It is noted that the number of exemptions for classroom use is much higher in Academic and Public libraries than in the others. We find also that only 13 percent of the total domestic photocopy items are subject to royalty payments after the exemptions are applied. This proportion ranges from 9 percent in Public libraries up to 18 percent in Special libraries. This proportion of serial titles involved is discussed in Section 5.

TABLE 4.14 NUMBER OF PHOTOCOPY ITEMS OF DOMESTIC SERIALS REQUESTED FOR INTERLIBRARY LOAN THAT ARE UNDER SIX YEARS OLD, NOT FOR REPLACEMENT OR CLASSROOM USE, AND GREATER THAN FIVE COPIES BY TYPE OF BORROWING LIBRARY (1976)

(Thousands of Photocopy Items)

Type of Borrowing Library	All Domestic Photocopy Items	and*	Serial Characteristic: Publication Under Six Years	and*	Not for Replacement or Classroom use	and*	Greater Than Five Copies	Proportion of Total
Public	1,010		620		440		90	0.09
Academic	1,130		610		430		140	0.12
Special	1,250		850		830		220	0.18
Federal	380		270		260		55	0.14
Total	3,770		2,350		1,960		505	0.13

*Includes only serials observed in previous column. Thus, each column total is a sub-set of the previous column total.

SOURCE: King Research, Inc.: National Library Survey

A similar analysis was performed on MINITEX data for an entire year from 132 of their Public, Academic and Special libraries. Age is given first, is followed by the other exemptions. These data are presented in Table 4.15.

TABLE 4.15 COMPARISON OF RESULTS OF PHOTOCOPY ITEMS OF DOMESTIC SERIALS REQUESTED FOR INTERLIBRARY LOAN FROM NATIONAL LIBRARY SURVEY AND MINITEX DATA BASE (1976)

Type of Borrowing Library	No. of Domestic Photocopy Items Borrowed Per Library		Prop. of Serials Under Six Years		No. of Eligible Photocopy Items Per Library		Prop. of Photocopy Items Eligible	
	Survey	MINITEX	Survey	MINITEX	Survey	MINITEX	Survey	MINITEX
Public	120	138	.50	.51	10.8	4.8	0.09	.04
Academic	370	629	.60	.53	46.2	34.7	0.12	.06
Special	150	150	.62	.69	25.6	15.0	0.18	.10

SOURCE: King Research, Inc.: National Library Survey
MINITEX Data Base

The comparisons can be made with national library survey data as follows. In Public libraries, the average number of domestic photocopy items borrowed is quite similar for the national library survey data (120) and the MINITEX data base (138), the proportion of serials under six years old is almost identical, and the average number of eligible photocopy items per library was estimated to be 11 in the national library survey and about 5 in the MINITEX data base. The proportion of photocopy items subject to royalty payment was estimated to be 9 percent in the national library survey and 4 percent from the MINITEX data base. The average number of domestic photocopy items is different only for Academic libraries, where the average number of photocopy items is estimated to be higher in the national library survey. The proportion of photocopy items from publications less than six years old is within ten percent for all types of libraries. The national library survey estimate of eligible photocopies per library seems to be somewhat higher than the MINITEX data base average, but not too far off. This is reflected in the proportion of eligible photocopy items given in the last column where the proportion for the national library survey data is larger than for the MINITEX data base. The data from MINITEX seem to provide good evidence to support the national library survey data for estimates of the number of photocopy items made in request of interlibrary loans.

One hypothetical condition of eligibility subject to question has to dc with the disposition of photocopy items made from publications over five years old. One view is that all these photocopy items are eligible except those exempt under fair use. Thus the five copy rule would not apply. One argument is that, if this were not true, there would be an implication that the copyright has a five year duration. If this eligibility condition exists, the total number of photocopy items subject to royalty payment would be as follows:

Type of Library	No. of Eligible Photocopy Items
Public	480,000
Academic	660,000
Special	620,000
Federal	165,000
All Libraries	1,925,000

Thus, if this condition of eligibility is valid, the number of photocopy items subject to royalty payment would increase from 505 thousand to 1.9 million, or nearly a four-fold increase. (This assumes, of course, that none of these older extra photocopy items fall into the fair use category.)

TABLE 4.16 NUMBER OF PHOTOCOPY ITEMS OF DOMESTIC SERIALS REQUESTED FOR INTERLIBRARY LOAN THAT ARE OVER FIVE YEARS OLD, LESS THAN SIX COPIES, CURRENT SUBSCRIBER REPLACEMENT COPY AND FACULTY/CLASSROOM BY TYPE OF LIBRARY--MINITEX, 1976

Type of Borrowing Library	Total Photocopies	Over Five Years Old		Less Than Six Copies		Current Subscriber		Replace-ment Copy		Faculty/ Classroom	
		Tot.	Prop.	Tot.	Prop.	Tot.	Prop.	Tot.	Prop.	Tot.	Prop.
Public	3,582	1,755	.49	640	.18	316	.09	11	.003	153	.04
Academic	42,122	19,758	.47	12,917	.31	5,675	.13	140	.003	2,157	.05
Special	5,715	1,792	.31	1,644	.29	279	.05	0	0	41	.01
All Libraries	51,419	23,305	.45	15,201	.30	6,270	.12	151	.002	2,351	.05

SOURCE: King Research, Inc.: MINITEX Data Base

The largest number of exemptions came from the age rule, then, in order, five copies or less per serial, current subscriber, classroom use and replacement copy. It is noted that the total number of exemptions is less than the sum of those given in Table 4.16 since many exemptions are common to a given photocopy item.

4.2.4 Distribution of Photocopy Items Made By Libraries for Interlibrary Loan

From the perspective of libraries, one important question concerns the proportion of libraries that will not have any photocopy items that are subject to royalty payments. One source of evidence to answer this question is from the MINITEX data base. These data are given in Table 4.17 with serials over five years excluded. Of the 132 libraries, only 58 have photocopy items that are subject to royalty payments. These 58 libraries have a total of 3,057 photocopy items of domestic serials that are subject to royalty payments for an average of about 53 photocopy items each. The average number of serials involved per library is ten which yields about five photocopy items each that are subject to royalty payments. Results for the number of eligible photocopy items summed across libraries are given in Section 5. It appears that only a moderate number of journals are eligible for royalty payment for photocopying interlibrary requests. Furthermore, less than one-half of the libraries that MINITEX serves have any interlibrary photocopy items that are subject to royalty payments, and these libraries average only 53 eligible photocopy items per library.

TABLE 4.17 NUMBER OF LIBRARIES WITH ALL ROYALTY EXEMPTIONS NOT INCLUDED-MINITEX (1976)

Type of Borrowing Library	Public	Academic	Special	All Libraries
No. of Libraries	26	68	38	132
No. of Libraries (All Ex.)	12	34	12	58
Prop. of Libraries (All Ex.)	.46	.50	.32	.44
No. of Photocopy Items (All Ex.)	126	2,360	571	3,057
Photocopy Items Per Library*	10.5	69.4	47.6	52.7
No. of Serials (All Ex.)	27	464	87	578
Serials Per Library*	2.3	13.6	7.3	10.0
Photocopy Items Per Library Per Serial*	4.6	5.1	6.6	5.3

SOURCE: King Research, Inc.: MINITEX Data Base

*Average based on libraries that are eligible for any royalty payment.

The proportion of libraries that photocopy at various levels are given below for different conditions of eligibility. These data are for national estimates.

TABLE 4.18 PROPORTION OF LIBRARIES THAT HAVE VARIOUS LEVELS OF PHOTOCOPY ITEMS BY THREE CONDITIONS OF ELIGIBILITY (1976)

(Proportion of Libraries)

Serial Characteristics	0 - 250	Number of Eligible Photocopy Items		
		251 - 500	501 - 1,000	>1,000
All Domestic Photocopy Items	0.81	0.10	0.05	0.04
Publication <Six Years	0.93	0.04	0.02	0.02
Not for Replacement/ Classroom Use	0.93	0.03	0.01	0.02

SOURCE: King Research, Inc.: National Library Survey

Thus, when all domestic photocopy items are considered, about 81 percent of the libraries will have less than 250 photocopy items and 4 percent of the libraries will have more than 1,000. When the five and under rule is applied, the proportions will shift substantially to the left. If the eligibility condition concerning photocopy items is valid, the picture would be closer to the one with all domestic photocopy items since the fair use eligibility criteria are not too very restrictive.

Table 4.18 does not show the dramatic picture portrayed by the large proportion of photocopy items made for interlibrary loan for a small proportion of libraries. This picture is presented in Figure 4.5 on the next page.

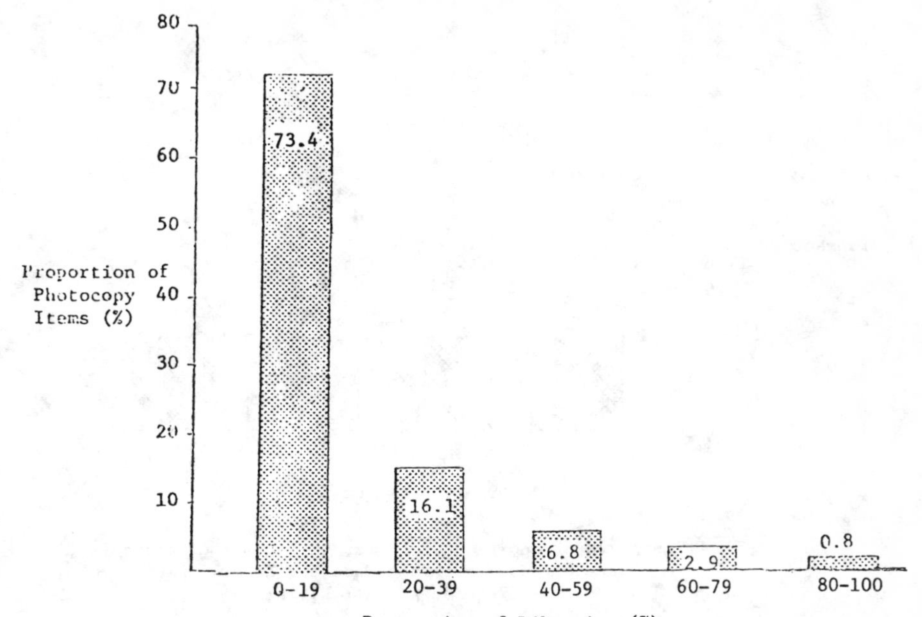

Figure 4.5 Distribution of Interlibrary Loan Photocopy Items by Proportion of Libraries (1976)

Figure 4.5 shows that 73.4 percent of the photocopy items for interlibrary loan are prepared for 20 percent of the libraries, when all libraries are included. One-half of the libraries request only about seven percent of the interlibrary loans and the other half requests 93 percent of the loans.

Also of interest is the distribution of the number of pages in each photocopy transaction. These data are displayed in Figure 4.6, and show that 16 percent of the transactions are 1 page, 13 percent 2 pages, 52 percent 3-10 pages, and 20 percent over 10 pages.

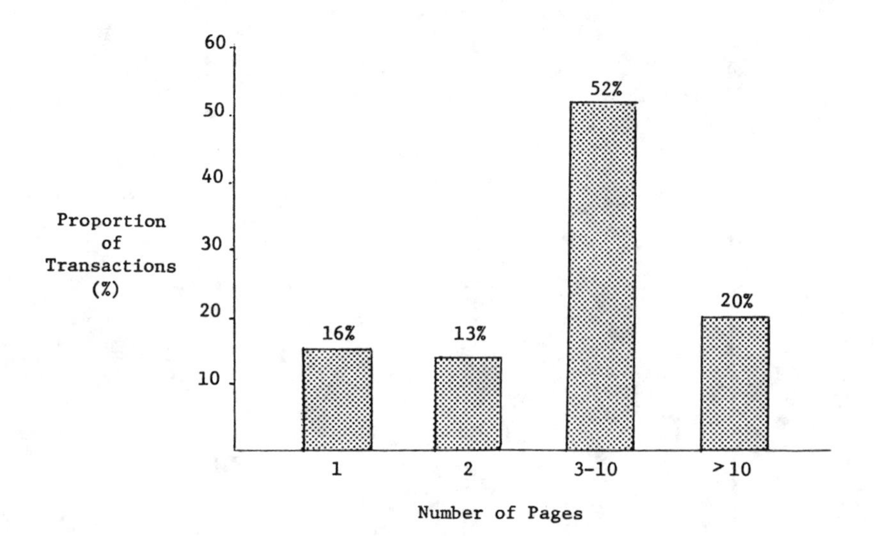

Figure 4.6 Proportion of Number of Pages of Photocopy Transactions of Serials Made for Interlibrary Loan Request for All Libraries

4.3 Estimated Volume of Photocopying of Serials for Local Users

The photocopying of serials by library staff for local users comprises the largest volume among the three types of transactions. In fact, it is estimated that about 27.8 million such photocopy items are made in a year. Of these, about 78 percent are copyrighted, 16 percent are not copyrighted and copyright status is unknown or not reported for six percent of the transaction responses. These data are given in Table 4.19, and the average number per library is given in Table 4.20.

Table 4.19 NUMBER OF PHOTOCOPY ITEMS OF SERIALS FOR LOCAL USERS COPYRIGHTED AND NOT COPYRIGHTED, BY TYPE OF LIBRARY (1976)

(Thousands of Photocopy Items)

Type of Library	All Serials	Copyrighted	Not Copyrighted	Unknown
Public	9,010	7,560	900	550
Academic	2,530	2,020	340	170
Special	12,280	9,670	1,790	820
Federal	4,020	2,470	1,960	90
All Libraries	27,840	21,720	4,490	1,630

SOURCE: King Research, Inc.: National Library Survey

Table 4.20 NUMBER OF PHOTOCOPY ITEMS PER LIBRARY OF SERIALS FOR LOCAL USERS COPYRIGHTED AND NOT COPYRIGHTED, BY TYPE OF LIBRARY (1976)

(Average Number of Photocopy Items Per Library)

Type of Library	All Serials	Copyrighted	Not Copyrighted	Unknown
Public	1,100	900	100	100
Academic	800	700	100	100
Special	1,400	1,100	200	100
Federal	2,800	1,700	1,000	100
All Libraries	1,300	1,000	200	100

SOURCE: King Research, Inc.: National Library Survey

The pattern of copyrighted serials over all sources seems to hold for photocopying for local users.

The largest volume of serial photocopy items for local users occurs for Special libraries, with approximately 12.3 million local user photocopy items. Next are Public libraries with 9 million, trailed by Federal and Academic libraries. Public libraries photocopy the largest proportion of copyrighted serials for users (84%) while Federal libraries have the lowest proportion (61%).

The estimated number of photocopy items of domestic and foreign serials for local users is given in Table 4.21.

Table 4.21 NUMBER OF PHOTOCOPY ITEMS OF COPYRIGHTED SERIALS FOR LOCAL USERS BY DOMESTIC AND FOREIGN PUBLISHERS, BY TYPE OF LIBRARY (1976)

(Thousands of Photocopy Items)

		Type of Publisher		
Type of Library	All Publishers	Domestic	Foreign	Unknown
Public	7,560	7,383	125	52
Academic	2,020	1,758	258	4
Special	9,670	7,933	1,698	39
Federal	2,470	1,958	511	0.7
All Libraries	21,720	19,032	2,592	96

SOURCE: King Research, Inc.: National Library Survey

The proportion of photocopying of foreign published materials is slightly more than ten percent. This proportion is highest in Federal libraries (21%) and lowest in Public libraries (2%). The average number of foreign serials photocopied in libraries for local users is given in Table 4.22.

Table 4.22 NUMBER OF PHOTOCOPY ITEMS OF COPYRIGHTED SERIALS FOR LOCAL USERS BY DOMESTIC AND FOREIGN PUBLISHERS, BY TYPE OF LIBRARY (1976)

(Average Number of Photocopy Items Per Library)

		Type of Publisher		
Type of Library	All Publishers	Domestic	Foreign	Unknown
Public	900	890	15	6
Academic	700	580	86	1
Special	1,100	930	201	5
Federal	1,700	1,370	357	.5
All Libraries	1,000	890	122	5

SOURCE: King Research, Inc.: National Library Survey

The number is appreciably high in any type of library, ranging from 15 photocopy items per library in Public libraries to 357 in Federal libraries.

Several conditions of eligibility for royalty payment are discussed in the remainder of this section. These conditions include characteristics of photocopying that are described by fair use, as well as classroom use by faculty, and application of guidelines similar to those suggested by CONTU for interlibrary loans. The following section discusses the effect of these conditions and presents results for domestic and copyrighted serials. One problem is to determine how many of the items photocopied for local users are for either replacement use by libraries or classroom use for faculty. Of the 21.7 million domestic, copyrighted serial photocopy items, replacement or classroom status of about twenty percent was not known or was unreported. Of the remaining photocopy items, however, less than one percent was for replacement by libraries and about five percent was for classroom use by faculty. The rest were classified as "other" responses. The breakdown of this result by type of library is given in Table 4.23 for total photocopy items.

Table 4.23 TOTAL NUMBER OF PHOTOCOPY ITEMS OF COPYRIGHTED SERIALS FOR LOCAL USERS BY PURPOSE OF REQUEST, BY TYPE OF LIBRARY (1976)

(Thousands of Photocopy Items)

		Purpose of Request				
Type of Library	All Purposes	Replacement by Library	Classroom Use by Faculty	Other	Unknown	Unreported
Public	7,560	73	325	4,747	1,540	875
Academic	2,020	8	220	1,139	458	195
Special	9,670	10	88	8,993	150	429
Federal	2,470	<1	40	1,521	237	672
All Libraries	21,720	91	673	16,400	2,385	2,171

SOURCE: King Research, Inc.: National Library Survey

The greatest amount of replacement is found in Public libraries (73,000) and Special libraries (10,000). The Public and Academic libraries account for most of the volume of photocopying performed for classroom use by faculty as local users (325 and 220 thousand, respectively). Not surprisingly, Academic libraries report the largest proportion of local user photocopy items with "classroom use by faculty" as purpose of request (11%). If such classes of local user photocopying were exempt from payment, the effects would appear to be minimal.

Average local user photocopy items per library are shown in Table 4.23. This table expecially points out the large proportion of "other" local user photocopying (75.5%) which, on the average, occurs in U.S. libraries.

The average amount of photocopying per library (shown in Table 4.24) follows the pattern in total volume, except that Academic libraries average 73 photocopy items for faculty classroom use and Public libraries average 39 photocopy items in this same category. Not surprisingly, Special libraries average the smallest number (10) of photocopy items for local user classroom use by faculty.

Table 4.24 NUMBER OF PHOTOCOPY ITEMS OF COPYRIGHTED SERIALS FOR LOCAL USERS BY PURPOSE OF REQUEST, BY TYPE OF LIBRARY (1976)

Type of Library	All Purposes*	Purpose of Request: Replacement of Library	Classroom Use by Faculty	Other	Unknown	Unreported
Public	909	9	39	571	185	105
Academic	667	3	73	376	151	64
Special	1,136	1	10	1,057	18	50
Federal	1,729	1	28	1,064	166	470
All Libraries	1,021	4	32	771	112	102

SOURCE: King Research, Inc.: National Library Survey

*Averages, All Purposes, do not agree with Table 4.22 due to rounding.

It is possible that single photocopy items made for individuals are eligible for royalty payment for photocopy items made for local use. One way to distinguish these photocopy items is to display the distribution of photocopy items by use: for local patrons (individuals and institutions) or for internal library staff use. These data are given in Table 4.25 on the next page, which may be read as follows. In Public libraries, 4.36 million transactions for patrons involved a single photocopy item, 200 thousand transactions involved two photocopy items, 160 thousand transactions involved between three and ten photocopy, and 20 thousand transactions involved over ten photocopy items. If one does not include any unknown (or unreported) exposures and assumes

Table 4.26 NUMBER OF SINGLE COPY TRANSACTIONS OF SERIALS FOR LOCAL USERS, BY TYPE OF LIBRARY (1976)

Type of Library	Total Number of Transactions (000)	Reported Single Copy Transactions for Local Users (000)	Estimated Total Single Copy Transactions For Local Users (000)
Public Libraries	4,850	3,310	3,800
Academic Libraries	1,650	1,320	1,460
Special Libraries - Profit	5,510	4,070	4,260
Special Libraries - Non-Profit	3,770	3,430	3,570
Federal Libraries	1,190	400	760
All Libraries	16,980	12,530	13,850

SOURCE: King Research, Inc.: National Library Survey

In this instance the number of transactions equal the number of photocopy items, so that the values in Table 4.26 can be used as an estimate of the number of photocopy items involved in this condition of royalty payment eligibility.

Another hypothetical condition of eligibility in this category concerns photocopy items from publications over five years old. Here it is found that a smaller proportion of publications are photocopied than with interlibrary loan where about 40 percent of the photocopies are found to be exempt due to the CONTU interlibrary loan rule. The proportion of photocopy items made for serials over five years old is found to be about 20 percent. The proportion of older publications is highest for Academic libraries (40 percent) and lowest for Federal libraries (18 percent). This results in a relative change in average volume per library between the Academic and Federal libraries. One might speculate that the major reason for interlibrary loans being older is that libraries did not subscribe to older issues of serials and therefore, need to get copies of articles from other libraries. The distribution of the age of photocopy items is given in Section 5.

they are the same as those reported, we have the number of photocopy items that have single copies made for local patrons given in Table 4.26.

Table 4.25 DISTRIBUTION OF NUMBER OF TRANSACTIONS OF SERIALS MADE FOR LOCAL USERS BY TYPE OF USER, BY TYPE OF LIBRARY (1976)

(Thousands of Transactions)

		Number of Photocopy Items					
Type of Library	Type of User	1	2	3-10	>10	Unknown	All Photocopy Items*
Public	Patron	3,310	60	80	0	50	3,500
	Staff	660	60	60	10	70	850
	Unknown	390	80	20	10	0	500
	All Users	4,360	200	160	20	120	4,850
Academic	Patron	1,320	30	10	0	10	1,370
	Staff	100	10	20	0	0	130
	Unknown	110	10	10	0	20	150
	All Users	1,530	50	40	0	30	1,650
Special (Profit)	Patron	4,070	480	20	30	40	4,640
	Staff	640	0	20	0	0	660
	Unknown	210	0	0	0	0	210
	All Users	4,920	480	40	30	40	5,510
Special (Non-Profit)	Patron	3,430	50	50	0	20	3,550
	Staff	80	0	0	10	0	90
	Unknown	100	10	0	10	10	130
	All Users	3,610	60	50	20	30	3,770
Federal	Patron	400	110	20	10	90	630
	Staff	60	20	10	0	0	90
	Unknown	420	50	0	0	0	470
	All Users	880	180	30	10	90	1,190
All Libraries	Patron	12,530	730	180	40	210	13,690
	Staff	1,540	90	110	20	70	1,830
	Unknown	1,230	150	30	20	30	1,460
	All Users	15,300	970	320	80	30	16,980

*Total transactions do not necessarily reflect number of photocopy items since transactions are estimated only from characteristic forms. Photocopy items are estimated from volume logs and characteristic forms.

SOURCE: King Research, Inc.: National Library Survey

Tables 4.27 and 4.28 are given below to present another perspective of the total and average numbers of photocopy items within libraries. Here we give these figures for serials under six years, for serials with less than six copies, and for serials meeting both conditions.

We made an attempt to estimate the proportion of photocopying that would involve serial titles having more than five photocopies made for local users in the past year. We applied the same estimation procedure that was used in the interlibrary loan estimates of the distributions of photocopy items. Results were tabulated for each library to determine the number of serial titles having one, two, three, and so on, photocopy items made during the sampling peirod. Obviously, substantially more photocopy items were observed for local use than were observed for interlibrary loan.

It was found that a much lower proportion of photocopy items are under six copies. In fact, over all libraries, total photocopy items drop only 32 percent after serials over five years and under six copies are excluded. The distribution of photocopy items by serial title is highly skewed. For example, in Public libraries, 54 percent of the serials have fewer than five copies, which accounts for seven percent of the photocopy items. Similar shaped distributions are found for the other types of libraries as well.

Table 4.27 NUMBER OF PHOTOCOPY ITEMS OF DOMESTIC, COPYRIGHT SERIALS MADE FOR LOCAL USERS BY PUBLICATIONS UNDER SIX YEARS OLD, AND MORE THAN FIVE COPIES, BY TYPE OF LIBRARY (1976)
(Thousands of Photocopy Items)

Type of Library	All Serials	Serial Characteristics			
		>5 Years	<6 Years	>5 Copies	<6 Years and >5 Copies
Public	7,390	1,460	5,930	6,850	5,520
Academic	1,760	700	1,060	1,740	1,040
Special	7,940	1,580	6,360	5,830	4,960
Federal	1,950	360	1,590	1,880	1,570
All Libraries	19,040	4,090	14,940	17,390	12,880

SOURCE: King Research, Inc.: National Library Survey

Table 4.28 NUMBER OF PHOTOCOPY ITEMS PER LIBRARY OF DOMESTIC, COPYRIGHT SERIALS MADE FOR LOCAL USERS BY PUBLICATIONS UNDER SIX YEARS OLD, MORE THAN FIVE COPIES, BY TYPE OF LIBRARY (1976)

(Average Number of Photocopy Items Per Library)

Type of Library	All Serials	Serial Characteristics			
		> 5 Years	< 6 Years	> 5 Copies	< 6 Years and > 5 Copies
Public	890	170	710	820	660
Academic	580	230	350	570	340
Special	930	190	750	680	580
Federal	1,370	260	320	1,320	1,100
All Libraries	890	190	700	810	480

SOURCE: King Research, Inc.: National Library Survey

Since the number of photocopy items is higher for local users than for interlibrary loans, the distribution spreads out somewhat more. Data for all domestic photocopy items and for those for publications over five years old and those that are not used for replacement or classroom use by faculty are given in Table 4.29 below.

Table 4.29 PROPORTION OF LIBRARIES THAT HAVE VARIOUS LEVELS OF PHOTOCOPY ITEMS BY THREE CONDITIONS OF ELIGIBILITY (1976) (Proportion of Libraries)

Serial Characteristics	Number of Eligible Photocopy Items				
	0-250	251-1000	1001-5000	5001-10000	> 10000
All Domestic P/C Items	0.62	0.14	0.20	0.02	0.02
Publication < 6 Years	0.66	0.15	0.15	0.04	0.01
Not for Replacement/ Classroom Use	0.67	0.14	0.15	0.04	0.01

SOURCE: King Research, Inc.: National Library Survey

Only two percent of the libraries have over 10,000 photocopy items made for local users and that number decreases to about one-half when publications over five years old and photocopying for replacement and classroom use are not included. By excluding single photocopy items made for individuals, or by applying the five and under rule, the distribution would shift substantially to the left. It would probably closely resemble that observed for interlibrary loan.

As with photocopy items made for interlibrary loan, we find that a large proportion of photocopy items made for local users are prepared by a small proportion of libraries. These data are displayed in Figure 4.7.

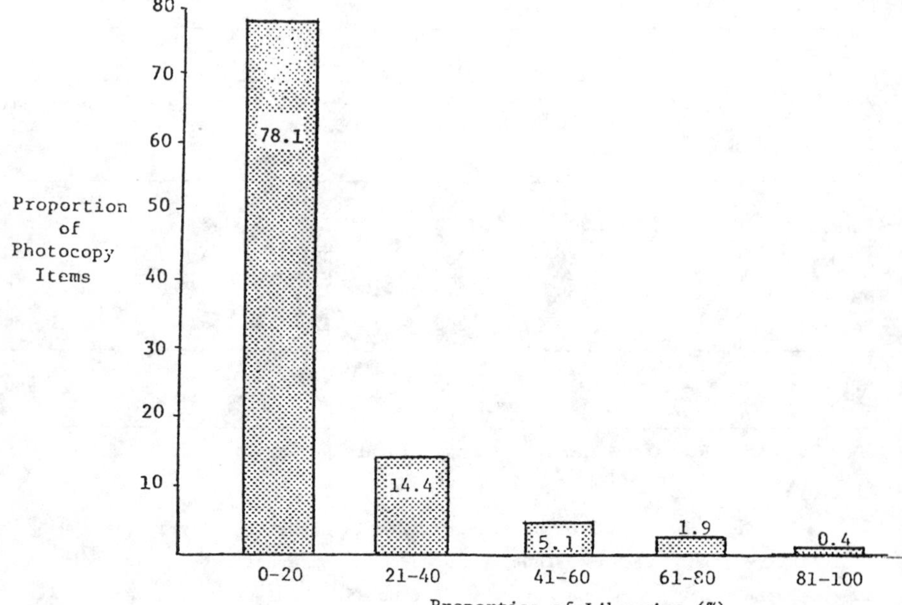

Figure 4.7 Distribution of Local Use Photocopy Items by Proportion of Libraries (1976)

Approximately 20 percent of the libraries are found to make 78 percent of the photocopy items prepared by library staff for local users. About four percent of the photocopy items are made for local users by 50 percent of the libraries and the remaining 50 percent of the libraries made 96 percent of photocopy items for local users.

Considering the distribution of number of pages per photocopy transaction (Figure 4.8), we find that 17 percent of the transactions are 1 or 2 pages, 29 percent are 3-10 pages, and 55 percent are more than 10 pages. This distribution is quite different from that for interlibrary loan photocopy items (see p. 76).

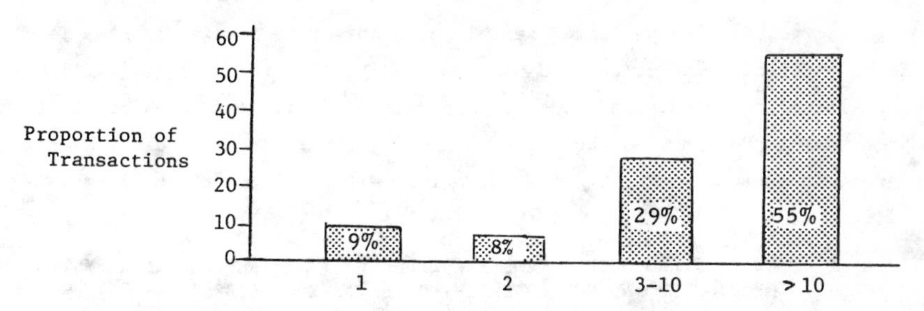

Figure 4.8 Proportion of Number of Pages of Photocopy Transactions of Serials Made for Local User Request

4.4 Estimated Volume of Photocopying of Serials for Intrasystem Loan

As noted earlier, photocopying for intrasystem loan requests (i.e., in response to requests from branch libraries or other libraries within a system) has an uncertain status regarding the proportion eligible for royalty payment. In this section we provide some breakdowns of ISL photocopying of serials which might be useful in this regard.

The amount of photocopying by library staff for intrasystem loan (ISL) is quite high. In fact, it appears that the total volume of photocopying for this source of request is higher than for interlibrary loan. However, in reviewing individual responses, it was noticed that a fair amount of photocopying involved a large number of photocopy items (say, 20) of a single page. Perhaps some of this is a regular photocopying of title pages or tables of contents that may be used for display in branch libraries or for current awareness distribution for organizational offices.

The total photocopying for intrasystem loan comes to nearly 14.5 million photocopy items. Of those about 82 percent were indicated to be copyrighted, and the copyright status of approximately 5.5 percent was recorded as unknown or was not reported. These results are reported in Table 4.30 by type of library.

Table 4.30 NUMBER OF PHOTOCOPY ITEMS OF SERIALS FOR INTRASYSTEM LOAN BY COPYRIGHTED AND NOT COPYRIGHTED, BY TYPE OF LIBRARY (1976)

(Thousands of Photocopy Items)

Type of Library	All Serials	Copyrighted	Not Copyrighted	Unknown
Public	5,370	4,680	540	150
Academic	2,010	1,630	300	80
Special	5,630	4,780	290	560
Federal	1,460	860	600	< 10
All Libraries	14,470	11,950	1,730	790

SOURCE: King Research, Inc.: National Library Survey

The largest volume of copyrighted serial photocopy items for intrasystem loan is found in Special libraries (4.8 million) and Public Libraries (4.7 million) and the least in Academic and Federal libraries (1.6 million and .9 million, respectively). However, as shown in Table 4.31, the Federal libraries average the greatest photocopying for intrasystem loan with 1,000 photocopy items per library.

Table 4.31 NUMBER OF PHOTOCOPY ITEMS PER LIBRARY OF SERIALS FOR INTRASYSTEM LOAN F COPYRIGHTED AND NOT COPYRIGHTED, BY TYPE OF LIBRARY (1976)

(Average Number of Photocopy Items Per Library)

Type of Library	All Serials	Copyrighted	Not Copyrighted	Unknown
Public	600	600	100	-
Academic	700	500	100	-
Special	700	600	-	100
Federal	1,000	600	400	-
All Libraries	700	600	100	-

SOURCE: King Research, Inc.: National Library Survey

Of the total copyrighted photocopy items prepared in response to intrasystem loan requests, 9.8 million are from serials published domestically (Tables 4.32 and 4.33). The estimated number of photocopy items of foreign published serials is highest for Special libraries (714 thousand) and this number is very low for Public libraries (less than 1,000 photocopy items). Thus, the average photocopying of domestic serials remains high in Public libraries (550 photocopy items per library) and decreases for the other three types of libraries (ranging from 230 to 440 photocopy items per library). We note that the largest proportion of unknown or unreported domestic or foreign publisher status is for Federal libraries.

Table 4.32 NUMBER OF PHOTOCOPY ITEMS OF COPYRIGHTED SERIALS FOR INTRASYSTEM LOAN, BY DOMESTIC AND FOREIGN SERIALS, BY TYPE OF LIBRARY (1976)

(Thousands of Photocopy Items)

		Type of Publisher		
Type of Library	All Publishers	Domestic	Foreign	Unknown
Public	4,680	4,590	<1	88
Academic	1,630	1,150	461	22
Special	4,780	3,750	714	318
Federal	860	330	189	337
All Libraries	11,950	9,820	1,365	765

SOURCE: King Research, Inc.: National Library Survey

Table 4.33 NUMBER OF PHOTOCOPY ITEMS PER LIBRARY OF COPYRIGHTED SERIALS FOR LOAN, BY DOMESTIC AND FOREIGN SERIALS, BY TYPE OF LIBRARY (1976)

(Average Number of Photocopy Items Per Library)

Type of Library	All Publishers	Type of Publisher		
		Domestic	Foreign	Unknown
Public	600	550	0	10
Academic	500	380	152	7
Special	600	440	84	37
Federal	600	230	132	236
All Libraries	600	460	64	36

SOURCE: King Research, Inc.: National Library Survey

The volume of photocopying for intrasystem loans for replacement by libraries or for classroom use by faculty is low, as was found in photocopying of serials requests from the other two sources of transactions. In fact, it is estimated that only about 215 thousand replacements by libraries and 237 thousand photocopy items for classroom use by faculty are for intrasystem photocopying. Again, as depicted in Tables 4.34 and 4.35, the total number of photocopy items reported in the national survey as unknown or not reported is fairly high. Public libraries have the highest volume of replacement but they and Federal libraries have the highest average. Academic libraries have the highest volume and average of photocopying for classroom use by faculty from intrasystem loans.

Table 4.34 NUMBER OF PHOTOCOPY ITEMS OF COPYRIGHTED SERIALS FOR INTRASYSTEM LOANS BY PURPOSE OF REQUEST, BY TYPE OF LIBRARY (1976)

(Thousands of Photocopy Items)

Type of Library	All Purposes	Purpose of Request				
		Replacement by Library	Classroom Use by Faculty	Other	Unknown	Unreported
Public	4,680	163	14	3,013	1,057	433
Academic	1,630	25	205	1,308	49	43
Special	4,78C	--	--	3,582	239	959
Federal	860	27	18	464	209	142
All Libraries	11,950	215	237	8,367	1,554	1,577

SOURCE: King Research, Inc.: National Library Survey

Table 4.35 NUMBER OF PHOTOCOPY ITEMS PER LIBRARY OF COPYRIGHTED SERIALS FOR INTRASYSTEM LOANS BY PURPOSE OF REQUEST, BY TYPE OF LIBRARY (1976)

(Average Number of Photocopy Items Per Library)

Type of Library	All Purposes*	Purpose of Request: Replacement by Library	Classroom Use by Faculty	Other	Unknown	Unreported
Public	564	20	2	363	127	52
Academic	538	8	68	432	16	14
Special	562	--	--	421	28	113
Federal	601	19	13	324	146	99
All Libraries	561	10	11	393	73	74

SOURCE: King Research, Inc.: National Library Survey

*Averages, All Purposes, do not agree with Table 4.33 due to rounding.

Fewer hypothetical conditions of eligibility for royalty payment have been studied for intrasystems loans than for interlibrary loans and local users. We have, however, looked at the number of photocopy items made for serials over five years old (see Tables 4.37 and 4.38). Data for photocopy items that are single copies made for local patrons (individuals and institutions) are presented in Table 4.36 on the following page.

Table 4.36 DISTRIBUTION OF NUMBER OF TRANSACTIONS OF SERIALS MADE FOR INTRA-SYSTEM LOANS BY TYPE OF USER, BY TYPE OF LIBRARY (1976)

(Thousands of Transactions)

Type of Library	Type of User	Number of Photocopy Items: 1	2	3-10	>10	Unknown	All Photocopy Items*
Public	Patron	600	10	10	–	40	660
	Staff	230	40	80	0	40	390
	Unknown	360	0	0	–	10	370
	All Users	1,190	50	90	0	90	1,420
Academic	Patron	1,260	30	60	0	0	1,350
	Staff	150	20	0	0	-	170
	Unknown	50	–	0	–	0	50
	All Users	1,460	50	60	0	0	1,570
Special (Profit)	Patron	680	10	60	–	10	710
	Staff	140	50	60	–	–	250
	Unknown	70	10	40	–	–	120
	All Users	840	70	160	0	10	1,080
Special (Non-profit)	Patron	40	–	10	–	–	50
	Staff	–	–	–	–	–	0
	Unknown	–	–	–	–	–	0
	All Users	40	0	10	0	0	50
Federal	Patron	330	0	10	0	0	340
	Staff	10	–	–	0	–	10
	Unknown	30	0	0	0	–	30
	All Users	370	0	10	0	0	380
All Libraries	Patron	2,860	50	150	0	50	3,110
	Staff	530	110	140	0	40	820
	Unknown	510	10	40	0	10	570
	All Users	3,900	170	330	0	100	4,500

*Total transactions do not necessarily reflect number of photocopy items since

The numbers of photocopy items over 5 years old are displayed in Table 4.37 by type of library.

Table 4.37 NUMBER OF PHOTOCOPY ITEMS OF DOMESTIC, COPYRIGHT SERIALS MADE FOR INTRASYSTEM LOAN FROM PUBLICATIONS OVER FIVE YEARS OLD BY TYPE OF LIBRARY (1976)

(Thousands of Photocopy Items)

Type of Library	All Serials	Age of Serials > 5 Years	Age of Serials < 6 Years
Public	4,590	1,330	3,260
Academic	1,150	320	830
Special	3,750	790	2,960
Federal	330	170	150
All Libraries	9,820	2,650	7,170

SOURCE: King Research, Inc.: National Library Survey

The average numbers of photocopy items per library for serials over five years old are given in Table 4.38.

Table 4.38 NUMBER OF PHOTOCOPY ITEMS PER LIBRARY OF DOMESTIC, COPYRIGHT SERIALS MADE FOR INTRASYSTEM LOAN FOR PUBLICATIONS OVER FIVE YEARS OLD BY TYPE OF LIBRARY (1976)

(Average Number of Photocopy Items Per Library)

Type of Library	All Serials	Age of Serials >5 Years	Age of Serials <6 Years
Public	550	160	390
Academic	380	106	274
Special	440	92	348
Federal	230	115	115
All Libraries	460	124	336

SOURCE: King Research, Inc.: National Library Survey

One feature of intrasystem loans that has been noted is the number of loans that involve transactions with one or two pages of a number of copies. These transactions may be for photocopies of the title pages and/or tables of content that are sent to branch libraries for current awareness. The extent of this phenomenon is displayed in Table 4.39.

The distribution of number of pages for intrasystem loan photocopying items is shown in Figure 4.9 below. It indicates that 25 percent of photocopy items are one page, 11 percent are two pages, 48 percent are 3-10 pages, and 17 percent are more than 10 pages.

transactions are estimated only from characteristic forms. Photocopy items are estimated from volume longs and characteristics forms.

SOURCE: King Research,- Inc.: National Library Survey

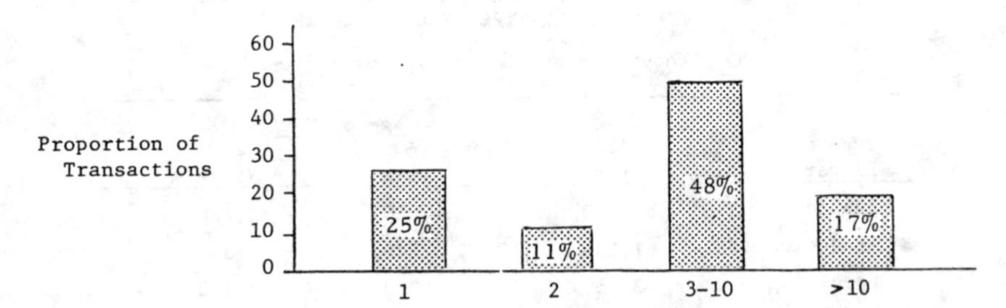

Figure 4.9 Proportion of Number of Pages of Photocopy Transactions of Serials Made for Intrasystem Loan Request For All Libraries

Table 4.39 NUMBER OF PHOTOCOPY TRANSACTIONS OF SERIALS MADE FOR INTRASYSTEM LOAN THAT HAVE SINGLE PAGE AND MULTIPLE COPIES BY TYPE OF LIBRARY (1976)

(Thousands of Transactions)

Pages	Type of Library	Public	Academic	All Special	Federal	All Libraries
	All Transactions*	1,045	1,500	990	340	3,870
1	1 Copy	380	150	100	10	640
	2 Copies	30	20	10	2	60
	>2 Copies	70	20	30	<1	120
2	1 Copy	120	150	90	30	390
	2 Copies	10	<1	30	<1	40
	>2 Copies	-	<1	30	<1	30
3-10	1 Copy	390	770	480	190	1,830
	2 Copies	10	10	20	<1	40
	>2 Copies	20	10	60	5	90
10	1 Copy	20	340	140	110	610
	2 Copies	<1	20	10	<1	30
	>2 Copies	8	10	6	-	20

*Transactions do not include those where number of pages or copies are not reported.

SOURCE: King Research, Inc.: National Library Survey

4.5 Copyright Royalty Library Survey

As part of our study, a questionnaire was sent to the sample of libraries from the national survey after data on photocopying had been collected. This "Copyright Royalty Library Survey" requested data on the following:

- Number of photocopying machines and number of exposures
- Photocopying and ILL costs
- Librarians' preferences for alternative royalty payment mechanisms
- Librarians' assessment of the impact of a royalty payment mechanism.

This section describes responses to this survey.

4.5.1 Estimated Number of Photocopying Machines

Librarians were asked to report the number of paper-to-paper photocopying machines in their libraries in each of the following categories:

1. Total number of paper-to-paper photocopying machines operated by or in the library.
2. Number of machines reported in (1) which are regularly (at least once per week) used by or for library staff or patrons for copying library materials.
3. Number of machines reported in (2) used exclusively by library patrons for the unsupervised copying of library materials.

These questions were asked so that we could distinguish machines used exclusively for office copying from those used totally or partially for the copying of library materials. We discovered in several pretests of this questionnaire that it is difficult for librarians, especially in smaller libraries with fewer machines, to distinguish between machines used only by staff and machines used only by patrons, hence the wording of Question 2. Question 3 was included to differentiate machines used exclusively by patrons from other machines. This was done so that we could identify copies or machines which would not be included in the category, "by or for library staff."

Results are displayed in the Table 4.40. The average number of photocopying machines in Academic libraries is 3.7 machines per library. The highest value reported is 64 machines, while the low value is 1, evidence of a very skewed distribution. The low average is due to the large proportion of U.S. Academic libraries that are small colleges such as community colleges and other small academic institutions.

The average number of Academic library machines used by staff or patrons for the photocopying of library materials is slightly less, 3.2. The average number of machines used exclusively by library patrons for their own copying of library materials is 2.0. If 2.0 is subtracted from 3.2, the number 1.2 is generated, which represents an estimate of the average number of machines in U.S. Academic libraries responsible for the volume of Academic library photocopying estimated in the national library survey.

The average number of paper-to-paper photocopying machines in Public libraries is 1.7 machines. This low number is accounted for by the large number of small Public libraries in the United States serving populations of less than 25,000. When these smaller libraries are not included, (they comprise approximately 82 percent of the population of U.S. Public libraries), the average number of machines in the remaining population rises to 4.5 machines. This is evidence of a distribution skewed towards the high end of the scale.

Both Special and Federal libraries have fewer machines per library than Public and Academic libraries, with 1.1 and 1.5 machines. It is noted that both Special and Federal strata included significantly more libraries reporting zero machines of their own than the other two categories. The smaller size of most Special and Federal libraries presumably results from their reliance upon their parent institution's machines for their photocopying of library materials.

Table 4.40 NUMBER OF PAPER-TO-PAPER PHOTOCOPYING MACHINES PER LIBRARY OR LIBRARY SYSTEM BY CATEGORY OF MACHINE, BY TYPE OF LIBRARY (1976)

(Average Number of Machines Per Library)

Type of Library	Category of Machine	Average Number of Machines
Public	Total Number[1]	1.7
	Staff or Patrons[2]	1.7
	Patrons Only[3]	.7
Academic	Total Number	3.7
	Staff or Patrons	3.2
	Patrons Only	2.0
Special	Total Number	1.1
	Staff or Patrons	1.1
	Patrons Only	.3
Federal	Total Number	1.5
	Staff or Patrons	1.5
	Patrons Only	.6
All Libraries	Total Number	1.7
	Staff or Patrons	1.7
	Patrons Only	.7

SOURCE: King Research, Inc.: National Library Survey

[1] "What is the TOTAL number of paper-to-paper photocopying machines operated by or in your library?"

[2] "How many of the machines reported in (1) above are regularly (at least once per week) used by or for library staff *or patrons* for copying library materials? (Exclude machines used exclusively for office-type copying such as correspondence, catalog cards, etc.)"

[3] "How many of the machines reported in (2) above are used exclusively by library patrons for the unsupervised copying of library materials? (By "unsupervised" is meant that patrons may operate the machines without the direct permission or assistance of library staff, as in the case of patron-operated coin machines.)"

It may appear that the number of machines which might need to be monitored for photocopying is quite low. This impression, however, may be somewhat misleading, since there is evidence of very skewed distributions. Those libraries most likely to photocopy the largest volumes of copyrighted materials have more photocopying machine and make heavier use of them. Yet, the majority of libraries have few relevant machines, expecially when machines for office copying and exclusive patron use are excluded.

A more general picture is given by estimating the total number of paper-to-paper photocopying machines in U.S. libraries, by type of library, as shown in Table 4.41. Public, Academic, Special, and Federal libraries in the United States operate a total of approximately 37 thousand paper-to-paper photocopying machines. Of these, about 35 thousand machines are used by library staff or patrons for copying library materials.

Table 4.41 NUMBER OF PAPER-TO-PAPER PHOTOCOPYING MACHINES IN U.S. LIBRARIES BY CATEGORY OF MACHINE, BY TYPE OF LIBRARY (1976)

(Thousands of Photocopying Machines)

Type of Library	Category of Machine			
	Total Number	Staff or Patrons	Patrons Only	Relevant Machines
Public	14.1	14.1	5.8	8.3
Academic	11.2	9.7	6.1	3.6
Special	9.4	9.4	2.6	6.8
Federal	2.1	2.1	.9	1.2
Total	36.8	35.3	15.4	19.9

SOURCE: King Research, Inc.: National Library Survey

Approximately 15 thousand of these machines are used exclusively by library patrons.

If we subtract these last two figures, we obtain approximately 20 thousand "relevant machines." This is an estimate of the total number of machines in the United States upon which library materials are photocopied by library staff, excluding machines operated exclusively by patrons. Public libraries accounted for nearly 42 percent of these machines, Special libraries for 34 percent, Academic libraries for 18 percent, and Federal libraries for 6 percent.

4.5.2 Estimated Volume of Number of Photocopy Exposures

Librarians were also asked to record the total number of exposures* made on the three categories of paper-to-paper photocopying machines described in the previous section. These results are described in Table 4.42. Some librarians do not know the total annual exposures because maintenance of these machines is performed by a contractor or another department within the parent institution.

This lack of knowledge among librarians may have implications for some alternative royalty payment mechanisms. For example, if an exise tax or fee on machines (8) were to be levied only on machines operated in libraries, one would need to take into account libraries which do not have financial or accounting responsibility for their machines.

Again, these data show a substantial difference between total photocopies per library and the number of photocopies which are potentially eligible for royalty payment (i.e., those photocopies made by or for library staff). For example, the average annual number of total exposures for Academic libraries was 347 thousand. On machines used by Academic library staff or patrons for copying library materials, an average of 317 thousand exposures was made. Of these, an average of 202 thousand exposures per library was made on machines used exclusively for patron copies. Subtracting the last two figures, we find that, on the average, 115 thousand exposures per Academic library are potentially eligible for royalty payments. This number would be futher reduced through exclusion of non-library materials, fair use photocopying, non-copyrighted materials, etc.

*The reader is cautioned that the term "exposures" is not equal to the term "pages," since a single page of a source item may require more than one exposure to make a complete photocopy, and vice versa.

Table 4.42 NUMBER OF EXPOSURES ON PAPER-TO-PAPER PHOTOCOPYING MACHINES PER LIBRARY BY CATEGORY OF MACHINE, BY TYPE OF LIBRARY (1976)

(Average Number of Exposures Per Library in Thousands)

Type of Library	Category of Machine	Exposures per Library (Thousands)
Public	(1) Total	75
	(2) Staff or Patrons	57
	(3) Patrons Only	16
Academic	(1) Total	347
	(2) Staff or Patrons	317
	(3) Patrons Only	202
Special	(1) Total	162
	(2) Staff or Patrons	146
	(3) Patrons Only	Not Available
Federal	(1) Total	246
	(2) Staff or Patrons	234
	(3) Patrons Only	Not Available
All Libraries	(1) Total	160
	(2) Staff or Patrons	141
	(3) Patrons Only	Not Available

SOURCE: King Research, Inc.: National Library Survey

This figure would be reduced even futher if we excluded non-copyrighted materials. books, occasional unsupervised patron copying and non-library materials that are also copied on machines operated by or for library staff.

When exposures per library are considered, Academic libraries have the largest number, with 347 thousand exposures per library, followed by Federal (246 thousand), Special (162 thousand), and Public (75 thousand). A slightly different picture is created by looking at exposures per machine, which takes into account the different number of total machines per library.

In Table 4.43 we see that, in terms of use made of individual machines, Federal libraries are the largest, followed by Special libraries, then Academic libraries and Public libraries. The Federal libraries ratio is affected by the large national libraries, while presumably the Special library ratio is also affected by the heavy use of individual machines relative to Academic and Public libraries.

Table 4.43 RATIO OF AVERAGE ANNUAL PHOTOCOPY EXPOSURES TO MACHINES PER LIBRARY, BY TYPE OF LIBRARY (1976)

Type of Library	Total Exposures per Library (Thousands)	Average Total Machines per Library	Exposures per Machine[1] (Thousands)
Public	75	1.7	44
Academic	347	3.7	94
Special	162	1.1	147
Federal	246	1.5	164

SOURCE: King Research, Inc.: National Library Survey

[1](Total exposures per library) ÷ (Average machines per library)

4.5.3 Other Photocopying Machines

Librarians were asked if there were other paper-to-paper photocopying machines operated within other local offices or departments of their parent institution or company. Table 4.44 shows the responses by percentage to this question. Respondents who replied "yes" to this question were then asked, "To the best of your knowledge, is the volume of exposures made of *copyrighted books and serials* on these other machines greater than, less than or about the same as the volume of exposures of copyrighted books and serials made on all library staff- and user-operated machines?" Responses to this question are displayed in Table 4.45.

Table 4.44 PROPORTION OF LIBRARIES REPORTING THE EXISTENCE OF OTHER PHOTOCOPYING MACHINES WITHIN THEIR PARENT INSTITUTION OR COMPANY, BY TYPE OF LIBRARY (1976)

(Proportion of Responses in %)

Type of Library	Response				
	Yes	No	Not Applicable	No Response	Total
Public	23.9	34.1	40.9	1.2	100.1
Academic	93.7	6.2	0.0	0.1	100.0
Special	74.7	17.6	7.6	0.1	100.0
Federal	62.3	9.5	28.2	0.0	100.0
All Libraries	56.7	21.9	21.0	0.5	100.1

SOURCE: King Research, Inc.: National Library Survey

Table 4.45 PROPORTION OF LIBRARIES ESTIMATING THE VOLUME OF EXPOSURES MADE OF COPYRIGHTED BOOKS AND SERIALS ON NON-LIBRARY MACHINES, BY TYPE OF LIBRARY (1976)

(Proportion of Responses in %)

Type of Library	Response					
	Greater Than	Less Than	About the Same	Don't Know	No Response	Total
Public	3.6	78.8	0.0	12.8	4.8	100.0
Academic	1.7	64.8	1.4	32.0	0.1	100.0
Special	12.9	45.4	3.3	32.1	6.3	100.0
Federal	4.6	21.9	0.0	73.5	0.0	100.0
All Libraries	7.1	59.5	1.5	27.5	4.4	100.0

SOURCE: King Research, Inc.: National Library Survey

Table 4.44 shows that, except for Public libraries (which tend to be "stand-alone" institutions), most libraries report that their parent institution has photocopying machines. This question was asked so that we could determine if there were other machines, not included in this study, upon which photocopy items of copyrighted materials (not necessarily library materilas) could be made. Academic libraries' high affirmative response (93.7%) is presumably accounted for by other machines in administrative and departmental offices.

Table 4.45 is based upon the replies of those respondents who replied neither "no" nor "not applicable" to the previous question. It is cautioned that this question should only be considered suggestive of the volume of copyright-photocopying on non-library machines. The high rate of "don't knows" among Federal libraries could be due to either a lack of knowledge or legal advice within the organization. Still, all types of libraries estimated this photocopying to be less than the library's photocopying of coprighted material.

4.5.4 Impact of Copyright Guidelines on Serial Photocopying Requested or Received by Interlibrary Loan

According to guidelines issued by CONTU, responsibility for interlibrary loan photocopying of copyrighted serial articles belongs to the requesting library as of January 1, 1978. Since this responsibility might include payment of royalties to copyright owners for serial article photocopying which is not exempt from payment, librarians were asked several questions about the effect that implementation of these guidelines might have upon their libraries' interlibrary loan operations where implementation of such guidelines require the checking of outgoing serial article requests.

This question was asked for each of four categories representing four possible screening checks which a library might make in determining compliance with photocopying guidelines. (We note here that the CONTU interlibrary loan guidelines and the Guidelines for Classroom Copying have been considerably condensed in this question in an attempt to simplify respondent effort.)

The question was asked as follows:

> "Were your library to determine the following royalty exemption category for each serial article photocopy requested or received via ILL on a regular basis, would your library incur any extra costs which your budget would be unable to absorb without obtaining additional staff or funding?"

Results are displayed in Table 4.46 on the following page.

The minimum "yes" response occurs for screening type (a), since checking a title is a common practice prior to making an interlibrary loan request.

Screening type (b) implies that a file of some sort has been set up upon which outgoing photocopy requests are tallied by serial title, date of serial, and date of request. Here, significantly more libraries report some difficulty in absorbing the added cost, especially Federal libraries (56.8%). Special libraries would appear to have the least trouble with this category (only 32.1% respondents replied "yes"). Perhaps this is because of their smaller size and less frequent use of interlibrary loan channels. Sixty-one percent of Academic libraries report they would not incur extra operational costs, perhaps due to their pre-existing files which could be used or adapted.

Screening types (c) and (d) both refer to CONTU guidelines and Classroom use criteria which may require a "purpose of request" distinction be made at the time an interlibrary loan is negotiated. Special libraries, not surprisingly, have the least trouble with these categories, since their clientele are not generally drawn from the educational community. Federal libraries would have the most problems. In summary, a majority of Public, Academic, and Special libraries estimate that they would be able to absorb the costs of making the extra purpose of request and use by classroom teacher determinations.

Table 4.46 PROPORTION OF LIBRARIES INDICATING THAT COST WOULD BE INCURRED FOR CHECKING OUTGOING SERIAL ILL REQUESTS BY TYPE OF SCREENING, BY TYPE OF LIBRARY (1976)

(Proportion of Responses in %)

Type of Screening	Type of Library	Would Library Incur Extra Cost Which Could Not Be Absorbed? Yes	No	No Response	Total
(a) To determine if your library has a current subscription (or one on order) for a title which is still being published at the time you make the request.	Public	17.6	78.6	3.9	100.1
	Academic	8.7	89.8	1.5	100.0
	Special	7.2	85.5	7.3	100.0
	Federal	4.6	92.4	3.0	100.0
	All Libraries	11.3	83.9	4.9	100.0
(b) To determine if your library has already requested a photocopy from this same title via ILL at any time during the current calendar year.	Public	40.7	55.5	3.9	100.1
	Academic	37.5	61.1	1.5	100.1
	Special	32.1	58.1	9.8	100.0
	Federal	56.8	42.2	1.0	100.0
	All Libraries	37.9	56.4	5.7	100.1
(c) To determine if the requested article will be used for scholarly research by a teacher in a not-for-profit educational institution.	Public	38.5	57.6	3.9	100.0
	Academic	22.8	75.7	1.5	100.0
	Special	17.9	65.3	16.8	100.0
	Federal	42.1	39.6	18.3	100.0
	All Libraries	28.3	62.0	9.7	100.0
(d) To determine if the requested article will be used for classroom purposes by a teacher in a not-for-profit educational institution.	Public	41.7	54.5	3.9	100.1
	Academic	24.4	74.1	1.5	100.0
	Special	15.1	68.0	16.9	100.0
	Federal	42.0	39.5	18.5	100.0
	All Libraries	28.7	62.0	9.8	100.0

SOURCE: King Research, Inc.: National Library Survey

4.5.5 Impact of Copyright Guidelines on Serial Photocopying for Local Patrons

In the previous section we described librarians' assessments of their ability to absorb increased costs if they were required to screen outgoing serial interlibrary loan requests to determine if they were complying with various photocopying guidelines set up to aid in defining "fair use." At this time guidelines comparable to the CONTU/interlibrary loan guidelines, which limit the number of photocopy items that can be made from a given copyrighted serial title, have not been developed or added to the Copyright Law to deal with non-classroom photocopying by library staff. Therefore, we ask librarians in the national library survey to respond to an analagous set of guidelines that might be applied to photocopying in response to local user requests. The question was phrased as follows:

"For the photocopying of copyrighted serial articles made by or for your library staff for your local patrons, would regular determination of the following categories result in your library incurring any extra costs which your budget would be unable to absorb without obtaining additional staff or funding? (Please exclude from consideration photocopies of copyrighted serial articles which your library makes for or receives via interlibrary loan (ILL)."

Responses are displayed in Table 4.47.

The lowest "yes" response occurs for screening type (a). The majority of libraries estimate that they would not have cost problems associated with checking for a current title.

There are, except for Federal libraries, significantly more "yes" responses to type (b) screening for local patron copying than for interlibrary loan requests, presumably because of the savings associated with pre-existing interlibrary loan files. Nearly 64 percent of Public libraries would incur extra costs for screening previous photocopying of a serial title requested by a local patron, versus 41 percent for screening outgoing interlibrary loan requests. (It is noted here that it is presently difficult to know without examination of an item whether or not it is subject to copyright protection. This problem might be remedied for pre-1978 items by a list of titles such as the one proposed for the AAP's Copyright Clearance Center.)

Table 4.47 PROPORTION OF LIBRARIES INDICATING THAT COST WOULD BE INCURRED FOR CHECKING PHOTOCOPYING OF SERIALS FOR LOCAL PATRONS BY TYPE OF SCREENING, BY TYPE OF LIBRARY (1976)
(Proportion of Responses in %)

Type of Screening	Type of Library	Would Library Incur Extra Costs Which Could Not Be Absorbed?			
		Yes	No	No Response	Total
(a) To determine if your library has a current subscription (or one on order) for a title which is still being published at the time you process the request.	Public	26.7	69.5	3.9	100.1
	Academic	18.2	76.2	5.6	100.0
	Special	9.8	87.6	2.6	100.0
	Federal	14.3	76.4	9.3	100.0
	All Libraries	17.9	78.1	4.0	100.0
(b) To determine if your library has already made a photocopy from this same serial title for a local patron at any time during the current calendar year.	Public	63.8	32.3	3.9	100.0
	Academic	61.1	33.2	5.6	99.9
	Special	52.5	45.0	2.5	100.0
	Federal	55.4	35.5	9.1	100.0
	All Libraries	58.3	37.7	4.0	100.0
(c) To determine if the requested article will be used for scholarly research by a teacher in a not-for-profit educational institution.	Public	45.7	50.4	3.9	100.0
	Academic	28.4	64.7	6.9	100.0
	Special	19.9	68.0	12.1	100.0
	Federal	28.9	52.6	18.5	100.0
	All Libraries	31.8	59.6	8.6	100.0
(d) To determine if the requested article will be used for classroom purposes by a teacher in a not-for-profit educational institution.	Public	45.7	50.4	3.9	100.0
	Academic	30.0	63.0	6.9	99.9
	Special	17.7	70.3	12.0	100.0
	Federal	28.9	52.6	18.5	100.0
	All Libraries	31.1	60.3	8.6	100.0

SOURCE: King Research, Inc.: National Library Survey

Reactions to type (c) and (d) screening are comparable. Special libraries do not generally perceive screening for purpose of request or for use to be much of a cost problem. Both Public and Academic libraries find that checking of local patrons' photocopying requests is more expensive than interlibrary loan checking, but the difference is not large. However, significantly more Public, Academic, and Federal libraries would incur extra costs which could not be absorbed than would Special libraries.

To summarize:

- A majority of libraries would not incur unabsorbable extra costs if they were required to determine if their library had a current or on-order subscription.
- Except for Federal libraries, significantly more libraries would incur extra costs if regularly required to determine if they had made a photocopy from a serial title previously for a local patron than would incur such costs if required to make this determination for interlibrary loan.
- Determination of requestor status for copying for local patrons would be somewhat more costly than for interlibrary loan requests, except Federal libraries.

4.5.6 Preferences for Alternative Royalty Payment Mechanisms

Based upon a review of the literature and upon discussions with this study's Advisory Committee, a list of hypothetical royalty payment mechanisms was developed. In this list an attempt was made to address as many design aspects of the RPM as possible. The payment mechnaisms included in the list do not reflect a prior assessment of feasibility or preference. Rather, our objective was to provide librarians responsible for setting or stating library policy an opportunity to rank a broad range of alternatives according to their preferences.

The question was asked as follows:

"What are your library's relative preferences for the following mechanisms for making royalty payments for photocopying of copyrighted serial articles? Assume that each alternative would result in the same amount being paid by your library for royalties, and rank the alternatives from 1 to 8, with 1 = MOST PREFERRED and 8 = LEAST PREFERRED."

"Multiple Copies" were defined as follows:

"MULTIPLE COPIES - more than 5 copies from the same serial title either made for local patrons by or for your library staff or received by your library in response to an ILL request."

Since it was impossible to agree upon a definition of systematic photocopying, we were not able to specify a time period over which multiple photocopying would take place. That is, it was impossible to tell the respondent to distinguish between five photocopy items made during a single transaction and five photocopy items made over several transactions or days.

Respondents were also asked to assume that each alternative would result in their libraries paying the same amount for royalties. This was added to suggest that the respondent evaluate the alternatives according to criteria other than gross royalty payments, since it was not feasible to give any indication of what the amount for royalty payments might be. In effect, then, the respondent was asked to evaluate the responses by criteria such as practicality, fairness or complexity.

Table 4.48 displays the proportion of respondents ranking each alternative as "most preferred."

Alternative G, the royalty stamp or coupon option, was ranked most often as "most preferred" by Public libraries (19 percent). The alternative ranked least often by Public librarians as "most preferred" is alternative A, the agreement to buy multiple copies or reprints of serial articles directly from the serial publishers or their agents.

Table 4.48 PROPORTION OF LIBRARIES RANKING ONE OF EIGHT ALTERNATIVE ROYALTY PAYMENT MECHANISMS AS "MOST PREFERRED" BY TYPE OF LIBRARY (1976)

(Proportion of Responses Ranked as "Most Preferred" in %)

	Type of Library				
Alternative Royalty Payment Mechanisms	Public	Academic	Special	Federal	All Libraries
(a) Libraries would agree to purchase multiple copies or reprints of serial articles directly from the serial publisher or their agents.	5	0	5	0	4%
(b) Libraries would pay an optional extra subscription price for those serials from which multiple copies would be made.	8	4	7	3	7%
(c) Libraries would pay a fee for each photocopying machine to a central agency, which would then distribute these payments as royalties to copyright owners.	13	14	11	14	12%
(d) Payment for copyright royalties would be made by libraries to individual publishers, requiring a tally to be kept by libraries for multiple copies of affected serial titles.	9	2	0	3	4%
(e) Payment for copyright royalties would be made by libraries to a centralized agency which would have the responsibility for making a count of individual libraries' photocopies and for transmitting payments to publishers.	11	6	3	2	6%
(f) Libraries would agree to purchase multiple copies or reprints of serial articles from a centralized agency authorized or designated by publishers which would then distribute copyright royalties.	10	14	5	16	9%
(g) Libraries would purchase "royalty stamps" or coupons from a centralized agency which would then be affixed to multiple copies of a copyrighted serial article.	19	23	16	5	17%
(h) All subscription prices would be higher, automatically giving libraries permission to make multiple copies.	16	34	25	30	23%
Average non-response	15	15	15	15	15%

SOURCE: King Research, Inc.: National Library Survey

*Non-response percents were computed for each library type and for each alternative. Individual non-response percents were then averaged over all alternatives for each library type. Since response percents were calculated independently for each alternative, columns do not total to 100%.

Academic libraries most often ranked alternatives H, higher subscription prices, as "most preferred" (34 percent). Here also the alternative ranked least often as "most preferred" is the agreement to purchase multiple copies from serial publishers or their agents.

The alternative ranked most often as "most preferred" by Special libraries is alternative H, higher subscription prices (25 percent).

The alternative ranked most often as "most preferred" by Federal libraries is again higher subscription prices (30 percent). Direct purchase of multiple copies is ranked by Federal libraries least often as the "most preferred" alternative.

It is obvious that no single alternative is ranked as "most preferred" by an overwhelmming majority of any library types. This could be due to a broad distribution of preferences across the alternatives or to librarians' lack of understanding of the intricacies of the briefly described alternatives. Four of the higher ranked alternatives -- higher subscription prices, royalty stamps or coupons, purchase of copies from a central agency, and photocopyingmachine fees -- incorporate a very wide variety of characteristics. The alternative that is most like the Copyright Clearance Center -- alternative (E), a centralized agency responsible for counting individual photocopying and transmission of payments to publishers -- is not included in this group. However, some additional analysis of this question shows that this alternative increases in importance if those alternatives ranked as 1 _or_ 2 are aggregated.

Not surprisingly, this particular question generated the most comments. Some librarians pointed out that they found all of the alternatives repugnant, since their budgets were already strained. Some threatened that their recourse to increased costs would be subscription cancellations. A few -- particularly Special librarians -- said they would agree to payments if the mechanism were easy and efficient. On the whole, the written objections to royalty payment mechanisms fell into three categories:

1. The cost to the participating library of administration of the mechanism.
2. The added "red tape" and complexity of the mechanism, which could delay the library's service to the user.
3. Moral opposition and the principle of free access to information.

Keeping in mind the hypothetical nature of this question, the following hypotheses about libraries' preferences concerning royalty payment mechanisms are suggested:

1. Libraries react relatively positively to stamp or coupon mechanisms which would not require that individual counts of photocopying transactions be made by library staff.
2. Libraries react negatively to alternatives involving significantly greater responsibility on their part for the "bookkeeping" functions of the payment mechanism.

3. Libraries react positively to mechanisms which involve utilization of existing payment channels (cf. photocopying machine fee, higher subscription prices).

4. Libraries react more positively to dealing with a centralized agency than to dealing with individual publishers.

5. The probability of delay or degradation of service to users is a major concern to libraries when they consider participation in a royalty payment mechanism.

While the final list of mechanisms considered in the last section of this report is different from that described here, readers should keep these general preferences in mind as additional criteria for their own evaluation of the alternatives.

4.5.7 Estimated Current Gross Income from Photocopying and Interlibrary Loan

Libraries were asked to report their average monthly inoss income for photocopying and interlibrary loan operations. These estimates were then projected to an annual basis by multiplying by 12. Results are reported in the following table.

Table 4.49 ANNUAL GROSS INCOME FOR PHOTOCOPYING AND INTERLIBRARY LOAN OPERATIONS PER LIBRARY, BY TYPE OF LIBRARY (1976)

(Average Income in $)

Type of Library	Average Annual Gross Income	
	Photocopying Income/Fees	Interlibrary Loan Income/Fees
Public	2,964	72
Academic	11,544	504
Special	96	0
Federal	3,648	1,668
All Libraries	3,085	212

SOURCE: King Research, Inc.: National Library Survey

For all types of libraries, gross income or fees from ILL (operational costs are not excluded here) is substantially less than income or fees from photocopying. On the average, Academic libraries derive the largest annual income from photocopying operations ($11,544), perhaps because of the relatively large number of coin-operated machines in Academic libraries. Next are Federal libraries with $3,648 per year, Public libraries with $2,964 per year, and Special libraries with $96 per year.

The figures for Special and Federal libraries deserve some comment. The average for Special libraries is extremely low, chiefly because most Special libraries are smaller and do not have their own photocopying machines. We hypothesize also that, even in Special libraries which have their own machines, charges and income are not incurred or earned by the library. Instead, they accrue to the parent organization.

The majority of Federal and Special libraries report zero average annual income for photocopying income and fees. The relatively high average of $3,648 for Federal libraries is chiefly due to the few large "national" libraries. If these were removed from the calculations, the average annual photocopying income for Federal libraries would drop to a figure at or below the figure for Special libraries. Federal libraries average $1,668 per year for interlibrary loan income and fees. Again, this average is primarily a result of the large national libraries. If they were excluded, annual ILL income would be nearer zero.

Academic libraries report $504 average annual income from ILL, or slightly more than 4 percent of photocopying income. Public libraries report $72, or slightly more than 2 percent of the annual photocopying income. Special libraries report $0 for ILL income.

Libraries were not asked directly how much they charged per exposure or per photocopy, because of the wide variety of pricing schedules. Indirect evidence of these pricing practices can be obtained by dividing the average annual photocopying income by the average number of exposures on staff or patron machines per library. This generates the following rough estimates of the price per exposure received by libraries:

- Public 5.2¢ per exposure
- Academic 3.6¢ per exposure
- Special 0.7¢ per exposure
- Federal 1.6¢ per exposure

According to these estimates, Public libraries probably charge the most per exposure, followed by Academic libraries and then by Federal libraries. The low cent-per-exposure figure for Special libraries may be evidence of a high degree of subsidization by Special libraries' parent institutions, since Special libraries have a higher exposure-per-machine ratio than either Public or Academic libraries.

It is possible to calculate rough estimates of "income per machine" for machines which may be used by library staff or patrons for the copying of library materials. These figures are given in the following table.

Table 4.50 ANNUAL INCOME PER PAPER-TO-PAPER PHOTOCOPYING MACHINES, PER LIBRARY BY TYPE OF LIBRARY (1976)

(Income in $)

Type of Library	Annual Photocopying Income Per Library	Average Machines per Library[1]	Annual Income Per Machine[2]
Public	2,964	1.7	1,744
Academic	11,544	3.2	3,607
Special	96	1.1	87
Federal	3,648	1.5	2,432

SOURCE: King Research, Inc.: National Library Survey

[1]Excludes machines used exclusively for copying other than library materials

[2](Annual photocopying income per machine) ÷ (Average machines per library)

Here we see that, on the average, Academic libraries have the largest income per machine, followed by Federal libraries, then Public libraries and Special libraries.

4.5.8 Costs for Photocopying

Many libraries already perceive photocopying operations to be a burden according to Whitestone (13). The following summarizes some of the data reported by librarians on the costs of their photocopying operations.

Libraries were asked to report average monthly costs for their photocopying operations. Responses projected to an annual level are reported in the following table. Because of the large nonresponse rate to this series of questions by Special and Federal libraries (perhaps evidence that many of their librarians do not have budget-making responsibilities within the many small organizations and agencies represented by our survey) data for Public and Academic libraries only will be presented.

The question was asked as follows:

"On an average monthly basis, what is your library's cost for operating and maintaining all the paper-to-paper photocopying machines for which it is responsible? Include only the costs which the library pays."

Summaries of responses by cost category are displayed in the following table.

Table 4.51 AVERAGE ANNUAL COST FOR PHOTOCOPYING OPERATIONS PER LIBRARY FOR PUBLIC AND ACADEMIC LIBRARIES (1976)

(Cost in $)

Type of Library	Cost Category					
	Annual Rental or Lease	Supplies (Paper, toner, etc.)	Annual Maintenance Contract	Annual Staff Costs	Other Costs*	Total Costs
Public	2,640	672	240	528	-	4,080
Academic	6,000	4,368	300	4,932	660	16,260

SOURCE: King Research, Inc.: National Library Survey
*e.g., special accounting arrangements, insurance, etc.

The reported average total cost for Public libraries is $4,080 per year, and for Academic libraries, $16,260 per year. This figure is an estimate of the cost for all paper-to-paper machines in the library rather than only those machines used for photocopying library materials.

Using these data, we can make some estimates of the operational costs per machine. By dividing average annual operational cost by average number of machines per library, we find that Public library machines cost $2,400 per year per machine, and that Academic library machines cost $4,395 per year. By dividing these costs by total exposures per year, we can obtain rough estimates of cost per exposure. For Public libraries this estimated cost is 3.2¢ per exposure and for Academic libraries, it is 1.3¢ per exposure. (We caution against comparing these costs per exposure with the price per exposure figures given previously. Price per exposure was calculated by using exposures made on machines used by staff or patrons for copying library materials. Costs per exposure as shown above includes all machines and all exposures, a significant portion of which involve photocopying by library staff of office work correspondence, catalog cards, etc.).

Average annual rental or lease costs per machine are very similar for Public and Academic libraries. Average annual rental or lease cost for Public libraries is $1,553 per library per machine. For Academic libraries this cost is $1,620 per library per machine. Because of this similarity, the disparity between Public library and Academic library operational costs must be due to other cost categories. These are supplies (paper, toner, etc.) and staff costs (operation and maintenance costs which are paid by the library). Average annual supply costs for Public libraries are $672 per library ($395 per Public library machine), and for Academic libraries, $4,368 per library ($1,180 per Academic library machine). Average annual staff costs for Public libraries are $528 per library ($311 per Public library machine), and for Academic libraries $4,932 per library ($1,333 per Academic library machine).

A possible explanation for this disparity is that both supplies and staff costs vary for individual machines while rental or lease costs per machine are fixed for individual machines. This makes sense when we recall that the ratio of exposures per machine is different for Public and Academic libraries: 44 thousand per machine for Public and 94 thousand per machine for Academic libraries. Since Academic library machines are more heavily used than Public library machines, their variable costs are higher.

While the categories of machines for which gross income and cost figures are reported may not be comparable, the data for Public and Academic libraries suggest that, on the average, these libraries may be incurring net losses for their photocopying operation when their gross income is compared to their operational costs on a per-library basis.

Some caveats are in order here. First, most costs reported in this section probably do not include general overhead inflation factors. If such factors were introduced, unit and total costs would be increased. Second, a very few libraries reported that they purchased machines during the past year, and these data are not included here as operational costs. However, if purchase costs were included, in their entirety or on a depreciated basis, they would increase these costs only slightly.

IMPLICATIONS OF THE COPYRIGHT LAW AND CONTU GUIDELINES CONCERNING SERIALS FROM THE PUBLISHERS' PERSPECTIVE

Estimates in Section 4 give the total amount of photocopying of serials and the proportion of the photocopying that is eligible for royalty payments based on the Copyright Law and CONTU guidelines for interlibrary requests. Some analysis was presented for hypothetical conditions of eligibility for royalty payment for photocopy items made for interlibrary loan, local users and intrasystem loan. Estimates of the total number of photocopy items are derived by summing the amount of photocopying over libraries. These total data are useful from the perspective of the library and publishing communities, for they provide an estimate of the total photocopying subject to royalty payments under several conditions. However, these estimates do not show individual publishers the extent of photocopying for individual serial titles. In order to provide such an estimate, it is useful to sum the number of photocopy items eligible for royalty payment over all libraries for each title for publishers. This gives a basis for estimating total photocopy items for individual titles. The clearest picture of the extent of photocopying of individual titles comes from the MINITEX data base. The national library survey data are difficult to make estimates because of problems of differential weights applied to sampled libraries. Nevertheless, a technique to provide rough estimates of the distribution of number of photocopy items by serial titles was developed. The approach is discussed in detail in Appendix C.

This section is sub-divided into four parts. The first part gives the proportion of serial titles that are photocopied within libraries at various levels of copies per titles. These estimates are given for both interlibrary borrowing (MINITEX data base and national library survey) and photocopying performed by library staff for local users. The second part deals with the extent of photocopying of individual serial titles subject to royalty payment observed in 132 MINITEX libraries over an entire year. Estimates are also provided for distribution of photocopy items by serial title under hypothetical conditions of eligibility for royalty payment. The total number of interlibrary requests are correlated with total number of subscribers given in Ulrich's International Periodicals Directory 1975-76 (11). Also, the distribution of transactions by year of publication is given since this result may have some bearing on when royalty payments may be made. The third part deals with a summary of publishers attitudes concerning the Copyright Law and potential royalty payment mechanisms. The final part presents some data for scientific and technical serials only.

* HIGHLIGHTS *

- Considering the number of photocopy items per serial title obtained by an individual MINITEX library, it is found that 2-3 percent of serial titles are borrowed more than five times and about 1 percent are borrowed more than ten times. On the national level, the proportion of serial titles with more than five photocopy items within a library is 2 percent for Public and Federal libraries, 3 percent for Special libraries, and 8 percent for Academic libraries. The proportion of serial titles having more than 10 photocopy items is .2 percent for Public libraries, .7 percent for Federal libraries, 9 percent for Special libraries, and 3 percent for Academic libraries.

- Over all libraries, it is estimated that the total number of interlibrary loan photocopy items made per serial title is distributed in the following manner: 40 percent of serial titles have 50 or fewer photocopy items each, 21 percent have 51-100 photocopy items, 32 percent have 101-500 photocopy items, and 7 percent have more than 500 photocopy items. Considering only those photocopy items not for replacement or classroom use, less than six years old, and with greater than five copies, the distribution over several titles changes to 91 percent of the titles having 50 or less photocopy items.

- For local use photocopy items over all libraries, only 10 percent of the serial titles photocopied have 100 or less photocopy items; 37 percent have 101-500 items; 20 percent have 501-1000 items, 28 percent 1001-5,000 items, and 5 percent of the serial titles will have more than 5,000 photocopy items. Considering only those photocopy items of serials less than six years old and with more than five copies, 24 percent of the serial titles will have 100 or less photocopy items. 50 percent of the serial titles will have 101-500 photocopy items, and 26 percent will have 501 items or more.

- In response to a survey conducted by Indiana University for CONTU, many publishers expressed concern about the potential complexities or bureaucracy of a royalty payment mechanism similar to concerns voiced by librarians. Publishers also appeared to prefer direct licensing of photocopying over clearinghouse arrangements for authorizing photocopying. The direct sale of reprints was more preferable to large circulation journals than to small circulation journals. Small circulation journals showed greater preference for sale of reprints through agent or clearinghouse arrangements. Publishers and libraries do not appear to share similar preferences for direct licensing; publishers rated it more highly than libraries, which prefer to minimize contracts with individual publishers.

- Based upon data from our National Library Survey, it appears that a minority of serial publishers would benefit significantly if many classes of photocopying were exempt from payment. According to the recent Indiana University survey of serials and publishers conducted during the first five months of 1977, over 50 percent of responding journals expect to receive zero royalty payments from a clearinghouse arrangement which would supply authorized copies.

5.1 Estimates of the Distribution of Photocopying and Interlibrary Loan Requests of Individual Serial Titles Within Libraries

5.1.1 Distribution of Photocopying of Interlibrary Loan Requests of Individual Serial Titles Within MINITEX Libraries

Detailed data were collected for 132 Public, Academic and Special libraries that used the MINITEX system during 1976. There was a total of 51,419 domestic serial interlibrary loan requests from these 132 libraries for an average of 390 interlibrary loan requests per library. These requests involve an average of 194 serial titles per library. Obviously, some serial titles are requested by more than one library. Over the 132 libraries, 25,624 titles were identified. However, there were only 6,345 unique serial titles when data from all 132 libraries were combined. Section 5.2 is partially devoted to an analysis of the requests summed over the 132 libraries for these 6,345 unique serial titles.

The average number of serial titles per library having at least one photocopy item for interlibrary loan is given in Table 5.1 below by type of library. The average number of photocopy items per title is also given.

Table 5.1 NUMBER OF SERIAL TITLES PER LIBRARY, NUMBER OF PHOTOCOPY ITEMS AND NUMBER OF PHOTOCOPY ITEMS PER TITLE BY TYPE OF LIBRARY-MINITEX (1976)

Type of Borrowing Library	No. of Libraries	No. of Titles	No. of Titles Per Library	No. of Photocopy Items	No. of Photocopy Items Per Title
Public	26	2,160	33	3,582	1.7
Academic	68	20,638	304	42,122	2.0
Special	38	2,826	74	5,715	2.0
All Libraries	132	25,624	194	51,419	2.0

SOURCE: King Research, Inc.: MINITEX Data Base

Academic libraries are by far more active in interlibrary loan requests and they request the most serial titles at 304 titles per library. Special libraries are next, with 74 titles and are followed by Public libraries at only 33 titles. It is significant that the average number of photocopy items per title within libraries was only 2 photocopy items per title per library.

A better portrayal of interlibrary requests by serial title is presented by the number of serial titles that have one, two, three or more interlibrary requests in a given library. Data on number of serial titles having 1, 2,..., 10 (and greater) requests are given in Table 5.2 for Public, Academic and Special libraries. The data in Table 5.2 may be read as follows. There were 1,571 serial titles in the 26 Public libraries that had a single photocopy item (for a total of 1,571 photocopy items); there were 326 serial titles in 26 Public libraries that had two photocopy items (for a total of 652 photocopy items) and so on. Two columns were added to the table. They indicate the number of titles and photocopy items that involved more than five photocopy items per title and more than 10 photocopy items per title. In Public libraries, only 62 serial titles out of 2,160 titles had more than five photocopy items (3 percent) and only 16 titles (.7 percent) had more than ten photocopy items over the 26 Public libraries. These titles had 640 (18 percent) and 305 (9 percent) total photocopy items respectively.

The proportion of serial titles that have greater than five photocopy items is between three and five percent for the three types of borrowing libraries. Similarly, the proportion of titles that have more than ten photocopy items is .007, .016 and .024 for Public, Academic and Special libraries respectively. The number of photocopy items for these titles is 305, 7,371, and 1,017 photocopy items for Public, Academic and Special libraries respectively. The average number of photocopy items for these titles is 19.1 photocopy items per title in Public libraries, 21.2 photocopy items per title in Academic libraries and 15.2

photocopy items per title in Special libraries. Clearly, the proportion of serial titles that have over ten photocopy items for given libraries is small, but the number of photocopy items is high for these serials.

Table 5.2 DISTRIBUTION OF NUMBER OF SERIAL TITLES AND NUMBER OF PHOTOCOPY ITEMS FOR INTERLIBRARY LOAN REQUESTS BY TYPE OF LIBRARY-MINITEX (1976)

Type of Borrowing Library	Public	Academic	Special	All Libraries
No. of Libraries	26	68	38	132
Number of Photocopy Items Per Serial Title	Serials Items	Serials Items	Serials Items	Serials Items
1	1,571 1,571	13,394 13,394	1,901 1,901	16,866 16,866
2	326 652	3527 7054	429 858	4282 8564
3	113 339	1439 4317	185 555	1737 5211
4	60 240	755 3020	118 472	933 3732
5	28 140	414 2070	57 285	499 2495
Total >5	62 640	1,109 12,917	136 1,644	1,307 15,201
6	19 114	291 1746	33 198	343 2058
7	11 77	183 1281	7 175	219 1533
8	5 40	138 1104	11 88	154 1232
9	6 54	85 765	14 126	105 945
10	5 50	65 650	4 40	74 740
Total >10	16 305	347 7371	67 1017	412 8693
Total	2,160 3,582	20,638 42,122	2,826 5,715	51,419

SOURCE: King Research, Inc.: MINITEX Data Base

This phenomenon becomes even more pronounced when serial publications that are over five years old are excluded. These results are given in Table 5.3. The number of serial titles that have greater than ten photocopy items in a given library is as follows: Public libraries have 7 titles that had more than 10 photocopy items, or an average of 18.7 photocopy items per title. Academic libraries have 126 titles with more than ten photocopy items for an average of 20.2 photocopy items per title, and Special libraries have 35 titles, or an average of 19.5 photocopy items per title. Many more serial titles have greater than ten photocopy items when all the photocopy items for a given title are summed over the 132 libraries. Similarly, there are substantially more photocopy items per title on the average. These results are given in Section 5.2. First, however, estimates are given in Section 5.1.2 for the estimated average number of photocopy items per serial per library. These data are based on data from libraries chosen in the national library survey.

5.1.2 Distribution of Photocopying of Interlibrary Loan Requests of Individual Serial Titles Within the National Survey Libraries

It is substantially more difficult to compute the estimates of the proportion of journals having specified levels of copies made. The difficulty is that one must use the MINITEX data to establish an extrapolation factor for the mathematical distribution of requests per title. The technique used to do this extrapolation is given in Appendix C. The estimated proportions of serials with greater than five photocopy items and greater than ten photocopy items are given in Table 5.4 below.

Table 5.4 PROPORTION OF SERIAL TITLES WITH GREATER THAN FIVE AND TEN PHOTOCOPY ITEMS WITHIN A LIBRARY FOR NATIONAL LIBRARY SURVEY AND MINITEX LIBRARIES (1976)

(Proportion of Titles)

Type of Borrowing Library	Proportion of Titles With >5 Photocopy Items		Proportion of Titles With >10 Photocopy Items	
	Nat. Library Survey	MINITEX	Nat. Library Survey	MINITEX
Public	0.02	0.02	0.002	0.004
Academic	0.08	0.03	0.030	0.009
Special	0.03	0.03	0.009	0.012
Federal	0.02	-	0.007	-

SOURCE: King Research, Inc.: National Library Survey

Table 5.3 DISTRIBUTION OF NUMBER OF SERIAL TITLES AND NUMBER OF PHOTOCOPY ITEMS FOR INTERLIBRARY LOAN REQUESTS FROM SERIALS PUBLISHED IN THE PAST FIVE YEARS BY TYPE OF LIBRARY-MINITEX (1976)

Type of Borrowing Library	Public	Academic	Special	All Libraries
No. of Libraries	26	68	38	132
Number of Photocopy Items Per Serial Title	Serials Items	Serials Items	Serials Items	Serials Items
1	919 919	7,926 7,926	1,346 1,346	10,191 10,191
2	173 346	2014 4028	320 640	2507 5014
3	50 150	747 2241	127 381	924 2772
4	25 100	407 1628	74 296	506 2024
5	11 52	203 1015	39 195	253 1265
Total >5	24 262	529 5526	89 1065	642 6853
6	6 36	156 936	22 132	184 1104
7	3 21	77 539	15 105	95 665
8	1 8	68 544	9 72	78 624
9	4 36	52 468	5 45	61 549
10	3 30	50 500	3 30	56 560
Total >10	7 131	126 2539	35 681	168 3351
Total	1,202 1,827	11,826 22,364	1,995 3,923	15,023 28,114

SOURCE: King Research, Inc.: MINITEX Data Base

It appears that Academic libraries at the national level tend to have a somewhat higher proportion of titles that have greater than five and ten photocopy items within individual libraries. Otherwise, the data are comparable.

5.2 Distribution of Photocopying of Interlibrary Loan Requests of Individual Serial Titles Over All Libraries

Publishers probably have greater interest in data that indicate the amount of photocopying of individual serial titles over all libraries, since this provides some evidence of what publishers can expect concerning total royalty payments for their serials. Unfortunately, national totals are not available in this study, but strong evidence of this result is available from MINITEX data and one can extrapolate these results to national totals with some broad assumptions. The MINITEX data are presented for the 6345 unique domestic serial titles that have at least one request from one or more of the 132 libraries used for analysis. The results are presented for a sample of 317 serials by total requests, requests of titles published less than six years ago, and requests that are eligible for royalty payment under the CONTU guidelines. Some results given in this section correlate the number of requests with number of subscribers (when data are available).

The distribution of the number of serial titles having one request, two, three and so on, is given in Table 5.5. The results displayed in Table 5.5 clearly demonstrate that the CONTU guidelines have a substantial screening effect on the number of titles with photocopy items eligible for royalty payments. To a lesser degree, they affect the total number of photocopy items for these titles that are eligible for royalty payment. Even when the photocopy items are added over 132 libraries, we find that only 140 out of 6,345 titles have more than 40 photocopy items made of them. When the number of photocopy items from publications over five years old and with fewer than six copies are not included, it is found that only 40 serial titles have more than 20 photocopy items. However, these 40 serials account for 2,620 photocopy items. Thus, they average about 65 photocopy items each. The results clearly show that only a small proportion of the serial titles have a large number of photocopy items. In fact, the number is not appreciable except with a small proportion of the serial titles.

Table 5.5 DISTRIBUTION OF NUMBER OF SERIAL TITLES AND NUMBER OF PHOTOCOPY ITEMS REQUESTS, BY CONDITION OF ELIGIBILITY, MINITEX (1976) FOR INTERLIBRARY LOAN

(Sample Size 317 Serial Titles)

Condition of Eligibility	Total Number of Photocopy Items Per Serial Title										
	0	1	2	3	4	5	6-10	11-20	21-30	31-40	>40
All Photo copying Items											
Serials	0	1,920	960	520	420	260	1,200	600	180	140	140
Items	0	1,920	1,920	1,560	1,680	1,300	9,600	8,400	4,320	4,760	10,660
Photocopy Items <6 Years	0	1	2	3	4	5	6-10	11-20	>20	-	-
Serials	1,665	1,580	740	500	360	220	720	340	220	-	-
Items	0	1,580	1,480	1,500	1,440	1,100	5,760	4,760	9,470	-	-
Photocopy Items <6 Years and >5 Photocopy Items	0	1	2	3	4	5	6-10	11-20	>20	-	-
Serials	5,925	0	0	0	0	0	260	120	40	-	-
Items	0	0	0	0	0	0	1,860	1,900	2,620	-	-

SOURCE: King Research, Inc.: MINITEX Data Base

Table 5.6 NUMBER OF REQUESTS BY INDIVIDUAL SERIALS ACROSS 132 LIBRARIES - MINITEX 1976

	No. of Serials	All Photocopy Items	Photocopy Items <6 Years	Photocopy Items < 6 Years and > 5 Photocopy Items
	65	> 60	> 39	> 4.5
	125	> 43	> 27	> 3.5
	315	> 27	> 15	-
	635	> 16	> 9	-
	1270	> 8	> 6	-
Total	6345	51,419	28,114	
Average	-	8.1	4.4	

SOURCE: King Research, Inc.: MINITEX Data Base

The table above may be interpreted as follows. All of the top 65 serial titles have more than 60 photocopy items. Those serials published less than six years ago have at least 39 photocopy items each. Those serials that were published less than six years ago <u>and</u> that have more than five photocopy items have at least 4.5 photocopy items each.

The average number of photocopy items per title with over ten photocopy items is 28.3 photocopy items per title. If one assumes that the 132 MINITEX libraries are typical of the 21,280 libraries found nationally, these 160 serial titles might yield as many as 4,500 photocopy items per title that are eligible for royalty payments. Similarly, 420 titles could yield an average of 2,400 photocopy items per title that are eligible for such payment.

There is some evidence concerning the representativeness of the serials in the MINITEX system that were requested. A publisher survey was conducted for CONTU by Indiana University (3) in which the proportion of journals was estimated for those having fewer than 3,000 subscribers, between 3,000 and 10,000 subscribers and over 10,000 subscribers. A similar distribution was compiled by King Research (4) from data from a study conducted at New York University (6) and <u>Ulrich's International Periodicals Directory 1975-76</u> (11). The latter data were gathered from a random sample of scientific and technical journals (4175). The sample of 317 MINITEX serial titles was noted and the number of subscribers looked up in Ulrich's. The number of subscribers was found for 160 serial titles. The distributions of subscribers for these three sources are compared below in Table 5.7.

Table 5.7 NUMBER OF SERIAL TITLES WITH LESS THAN 3,000 SUBSCRIBERS: 3,000 to 10,000 SUBSCRIBERS: AND OVER 10,000 SUBSCRIBERS, FROM THREE SOURCES

Source of Data		Number of Subscribers <3,000	3,000-10,000	>10,000	Total
MINITEX	No. of Serials	76	39	45	160
	Prop. of Serials	.48	.24	.28	1.00
Indiana University	No. of Serials	441	244	253 *	938
	Prop. of Serials	.50	.30	.20	1.00
King Research, Inc.	No. of Serials	2288	1353	534	4175
	Prop. of Serials	.54	.32	.13	1.00

* The Indiana University study did not include serials with greater than 100,000 circulation.

SOURCE: Indiana University; King Research, Inc.: MINITEX Data Base

The distribution of subscribers of the serials found in MINITEX seems to be more like that of the Indiana University serials than that of the King Research serials, although both are reasonably close. One would expect the Indiana University results to be closer since their journals are from a broader range of fields which may more correctly reflect the MINITEX titles.

Contrary to other results (5), it is found that the number of requests per serial title does not appear to be directly correlated with number of subscribers. The number of requests are plotted against number of subscribers (on a square root scale). The number of titles is also given in Table 5.8.

Table 5.8 NUMBER OF TITLES THAT ARE REQUESTED MORE OR LESS THAN 20 TIMES AND HAVE MORE OR LESS THAN 10,000 SUBSCRIBERS-MINITEX 1976

(Sample Size 160 Titles)

No. of Subscribers	No. of Requests ≤20	>20	Total
≤ 10,000	106	11	117
> 10,000	42	1	43
Total	148	12	160

SOURCE: King Research, Inc.: MINITEX Data Base
Ulrich's International Periodicals Directory, 1975-76.

One could characterize this distribution by the following three statements:

(1) The serial titles that have a large number of subscribers (>10,000) tend to have a relatively few number of requests (≤20).

(2) The serial titles that have a large number of requests (>20) tend to have a relatively few number of subscribers (≤10,000).

(3) The serial titles that have a few number of requests (≤20) and few number of subscribers (≤10,000) are uncorrelated.

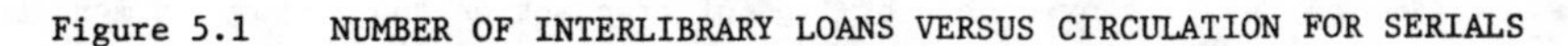

Figure 5.1 NUMBER OF INTERLIBRARY LOANS VERSUS CIRCULATION FOR SERIALS

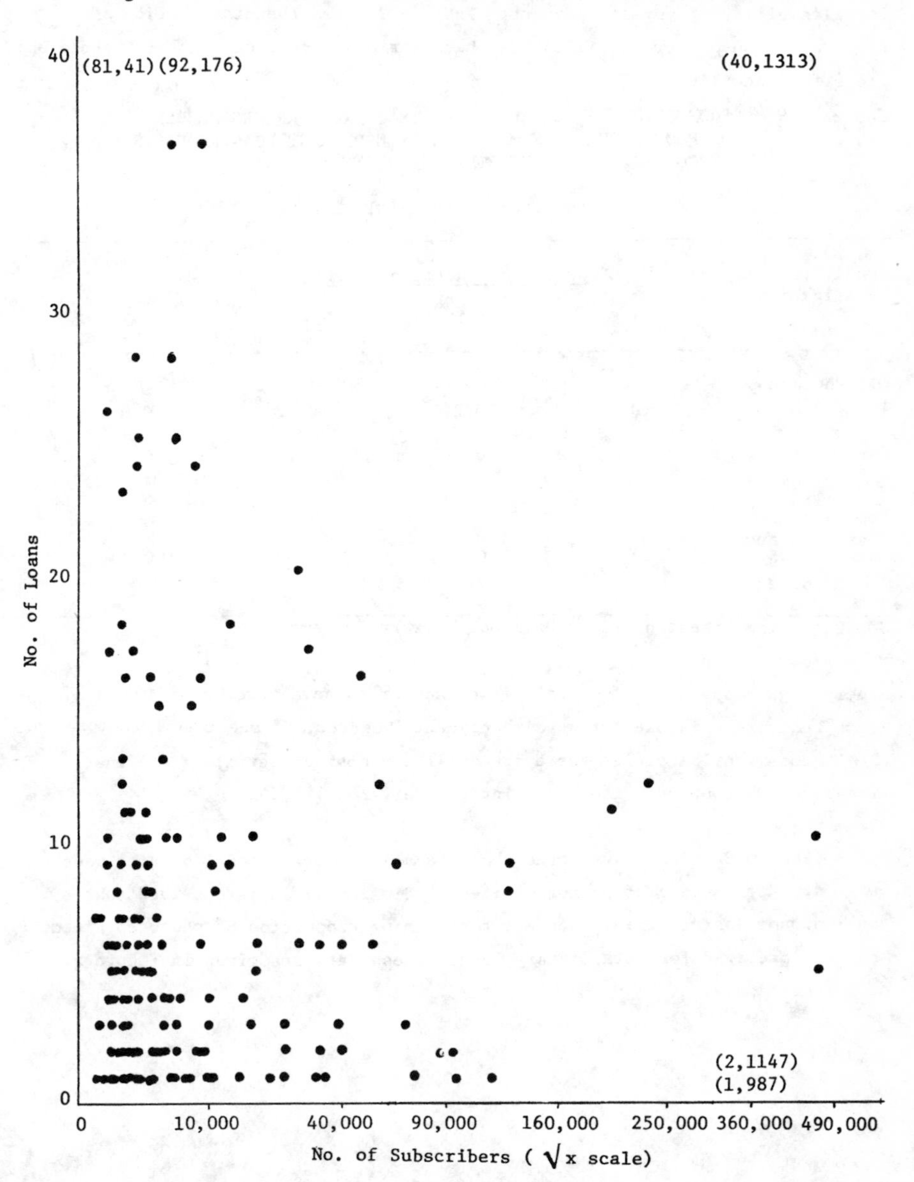

It is not known whether these results hold for libraries in the remaining parts of the country. However, it does give some evidence as to what publishers might expect.

Of particular interest is the number of serial titles that have various levels of photocopy items summed over libraries. A procedure for making gross estimates for these data has been derived (Appendix C). These estimates are presented here by type of transaction and by various conditions for eligibility of royalty payment. Table 5.9 gives the distribution of the proportion of serial titles that have various levels of number of photocopy items for interlibrary loans.

Table 5.9 PROPORTION OF SERIAL TITLES THAT HAVE VARIOUS NUMBERS OF PHOTOCOPY ITEMS MADE FOR INTERLIBRARY LOAN REQUESTS BY CONDITION OF ELIGIBILITY (1976)

(Proportion of Serial Titles)

Condition of Eligibility	Number of Photocopy Items			
	0-50	51-100	101-500	>500
All Photocopy Items	0.40	0.21	0.32	0.07
< 6 Years	0.51	0.28	0.21	0.00
Replacement/ Classroom and < 6 Years > 5 Copies	0.91	0.09	0.00	0.00

SOURCE: King Research, Inc.: National Library Survey

A very high proportion of serial titles appear to have fewer than 100 photocopy items that are eligible for royalty payment. However, if one assumes a total of 10,000 total serial titles, there are still a number of serials (700) that have over 500 photocopy items for interlibrary loan.

In Section 4, we found that a small proportion of libraries made a very large proportion of photocopy items. Similarly, it is observed that a small proportion of serials account for a major proportion of photocopy items that are prepared for interlibrary loan. These data are given in Figure 5.2 on the next page.

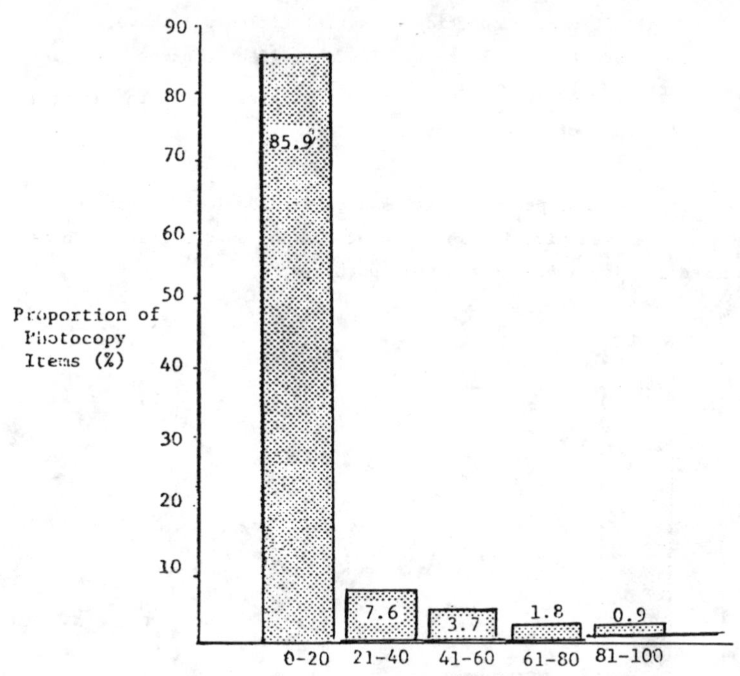

Figure 5.2 Distribution of Serial Photocopy Items for Interlibrary Loan by Proportion of Libraries (1976)

It is roughly estimated that approximately 86 percent of the photocopy items prepared for interlibrary loan are made from only 20 percent of the serials. About four percent of the photocopy items are made from 50 percent of the serials and the remaining 50 percent of the titles account for 96 percent of the photocopy items made for interlibrary loan.

This picture is somewhat different when considering photocopy items made for local users. Only ten percent of the serials will have fewer than 101 photocopy items; thirty-seven percent will have fewer than 501 photocopy items, and one-fifth of the serial titles will have less than 1001 photocopy items.

Table 5.10 PROPORTION OF SERIAL TITLES THAT HAVE VARIOUS NUMBERS OF PHOTOCOPY ITEMS MADE FOR LOCAL USER REQUESTS BY CONDITION OF ELIGIBILITY (1976)
(Proportion of Serial Titles)

Condition of Eligibility	Number of Photocopy Items				
	0-100	101-500	501-1000	1001 -5,000	>5,000
All Photocopy Items	0.10	0.37	0.20	0.28	0.05
< 6 Years	0.20	0.50	0.30	0.00	0.00
< 6 Years and >5 Copies	0.24	0.50	0.26	0.00	0.00

SOURCE: King Research, Inc.: National Library Survey

Here, we see that a significant proportion of serial titles will have over 1,000 photocopy items made for local users. In fact, if we assume 10,000 serial titles, there are 2,600 to 5,300 serial titles over 500 photocopy items, depending on the condition of eligibility.

Since there are more photocopy items made for local users, there appears to be a less skewed distribution of photocopying over serials. These data are displayed in Figure 5.3 on the next page.

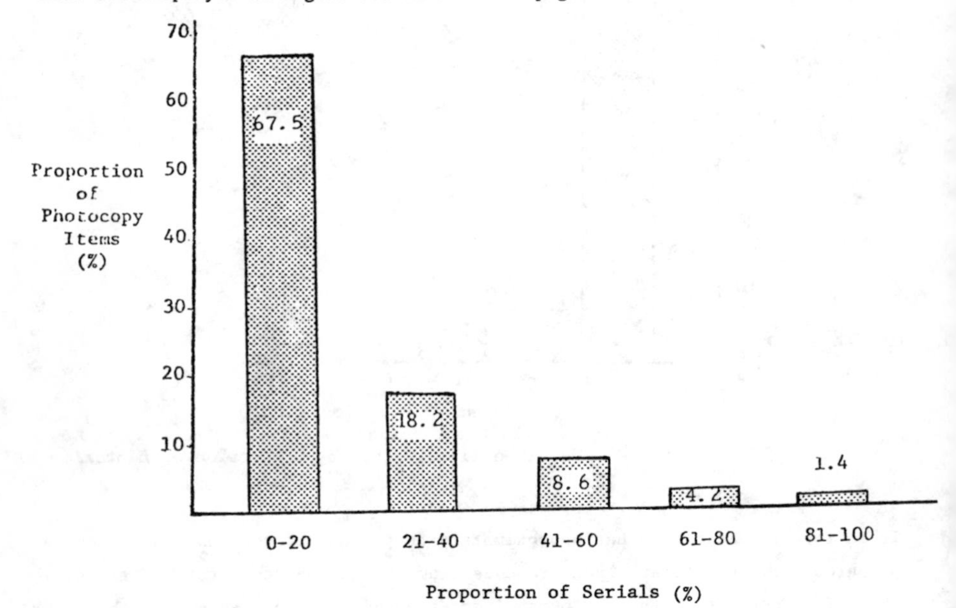

Figure 5.3 Distribution of Photocopy Items for Local Users by Proportion of Serials

It is grossly estimated that 68 percent of the photocopy items made for local users, are prepared from 20 percent of the serials. About ten percent of the photocopy items are made on 50 percent of the serial titles and the remaining 90 percent made on the rest of the serial titles.

Publishers may be particularly interested in data from the distribution of age of transactions. This has two implications. The first matter has to do with the number of royalty payments that might be received for previously published serials of various ages. The second, and perhaps, most important consideration concerns when royalty payments might be made in the future for currently published serials. The reason that this may be important is that the age of royalty payments has implications for cash flow of income. Serials have a preferred financial situation because much of their income is received ahead of expenses, so that the cash flow and return on investment is very favorable.

If the Copyright Law results in some cancellations of subscriptions in favor of payment of royalties on photocopies, the advantage of the cash flow of subscriptions will be diminished somewhat.

Table 5.11 DISTRIBUTION OF PROPORTION OF TRANSACTIONS OF SERIAL TITLES BY AGE OF PUBLICATION, BY TYPE OF LIBRARY, BY TYPE OF TRANSACTION (1976)

(Proportion of Transactions)

Type of Library/ Type of Transaction	Age of Serial in Years						
	1	2	3	4	5	6-10	>10
Public							
Interlibrary Loan	.277	.120	.135	.048	.030	.127	.262
Intrasystem Loan	.290	.147	.203	.049	.020	.052	.239
Local Users	.329	.278	.054	.038	.040	.088	.109
Academic							
Interlibrary Loan	.126	.162	.089	.083	.075	.177	.287
Intrasystem Loan	.312	.205	.083	.091	.037	.148	.125
Local Users	.334	.135	.118	.084	.054	.137	.261
Special							
Interlibrary Loan	.246	.165	.060	.113	.093	.197	.126
Intrasystem Loan	.481	.081	.128	.031	.072	.076	.131
Local Users	.453	.162	.080	.051	.057	.099	.099
Federal							
Interlibrary Loan	.289	.219	.082	.093	.022	.095	.200
Intrasystem Loan	.353	.036	.033	.015	.066	.200	.300
Local Users	.384	.170	.144	.080	.039	.117	.070
All Libraries							
Interlibrary Loan	.107	.167	.112	.090	.070	.183	.266
Intrasystem Loan	.352	.140	.131	.055	.043	.101	.178
Local Users	.409	.204	.076	.050	.048	.098	.114

SOURCE: King Research, Inc.: National Library Survey

Evidence of the age distribution for royalty payments is given in Table 5.11. (It is noted that data of use of past publications must be normalized because there were fewer serial titles as time goes back).

Table 5.11 DISTRIBUTION OF PROPORTION OF TRANSACTIONS OF SERIAL TITLES BY AGE OF PUBLICATION, BY TYPE OF LIBRARY, BY TYPE OF TRANSACTION 91976) (Cont'd)

(Proportion of Transactions)

Type of Library/ Type of Transaction	Age of Serial in Years				
	11-15	16-20	21-25	26-50	>50
Public					
Interlibrary Loan	.055	.054	.096	.050	.007
Intrasystem Loan	.081	.075	.031	.019	.033
Local Users	.031	.016	.009	.037	.015
Academic					
Interlibrary Loan	.083	.062	.056	.049	.036
Intrasystem Loan	.064	.032	.019	.007	.003
Local Users	.127	.056	.031	.032	.014
Special					
Interlibrary Loan	.056	.025	.026	.019	*
Intrasystem Loan	.036	.032	.016	.047	-
Local Users	.055	.019	.021	.004	-
Federal					
Interlibrary Loan	.065	.055	.008	.048	.024
Intrasystem Loan	.127	.034	.051	.070	.017
Local Users	.028	.026	.004	.002	.009
All Libraries					
Interlibrary Loan	.075	.057	.068	.048	.019
Intrasystem Loan	.067	.046	.025	.025	.015
Local Users	.049	.021	.017	.020	.008

SOURCE: King Research, Inc.: National Library Survey

As noted in Section 4, in all types of libraries, the interlibrary loans tend to be older than intrasystem loans or local uses when a distinction is made between current (first year) and older publications. Although, this distinction is less pronounced in Public libraries where the library materials tend to be more heavily popular magazines and newspapers rather than scholarly journals which are more frequently photocopied in other types of libraries. In nearly all instances, at least 10 percent of the transactions are over ten years old. Over all interlibrary transactions, 45 percent are over five years old and 27 percent are over ten years old for interlibrary loans; 28 percent are over five years old and 18 percent are over ten years old for intrasystem loans; and 21 percent are over five years old and 11 percent over ten years old for photocopy items made for local users. The age distribution for photocopy transactions is given in Figure 5.4.

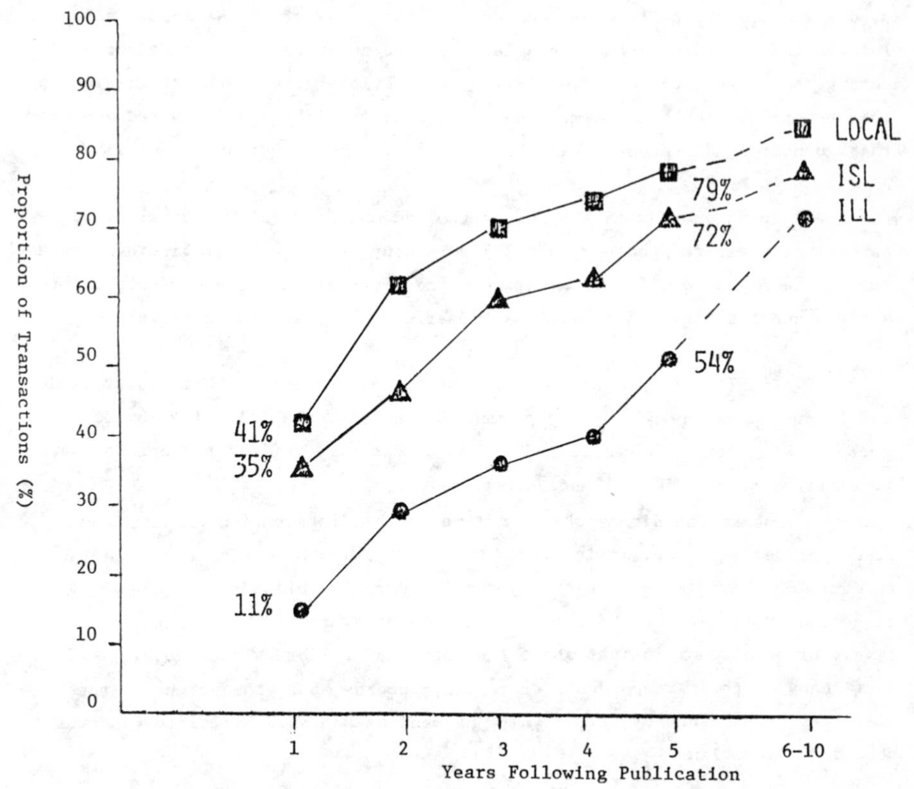

Figure 5.4 Age Distribution of Photocopy Transactions

5.3 Publishers' Preferences

We did not survey a sample of the publishers of the serials whose photocopying we measured in this study, therefore we cannot say with certainty how they might react to specific alternative royalty payment mechanisms. In the study recently completed for CONTU by Fry, White, and Johnson at Indiana University (3), publishers of journals were surveyed regarding their policies for page charges, reprint sales, and their feelings about the possible benefits to be derived from royalty payments for photocopying. Before we discuss the implications of this study, the following points should be noted:

First, the journals and journal publishers surveyed in the Indiana University study came from all fields of study but were primarily "scholarly" and "research" journals, perhaps a narrower category than the serial titles studied by King Research.

Second, as discussed by Fry, White and Johnson, the operational details of specific royalty payment mechanisms, including those considered in this study, the Copyright Clearance Center, and the plans of the National Technical Information Service, were not available to the publishers whom they surveyed during the first five months of 1977. Nor, obviously, were the statistics in this report available to them. Their respondents might have answered some of their questions differently had this information been available to them.

Third, approximately 70% of the Indiana University journals (and 59 percent of their responding journals) were copyrighted. Their findings suggest that there might be differences between the views of publishers of copyrighted serials and the views of publishers of serials which are not copyrighted.

Finally, regarding the implications of the Indiana University study and on our own study of royalty payment mechanisms, the following comments are those of King Research, Inc., and do not necessarily reflect the opinions or conclusions of Fry, White, and Johnson.

Due to the highly skewed nature of the distribution of photocopy items per serial title, it is likely that a minority of serial titles would account for the bulk of royalty payments. Journal publishers in general, as suggested by Fry, White and Johnson, seem to be aware of this, either intuitively or because of insight about the patterns of library photocopying. In fact, many of their respondents expressed concerns about the potential complexities or bureaucracy of a royalty payment mechanism, similar to concerns voiced by librarians.

Nearly 60% of the journals responding in the Indiana University survey sell reprints directly, and about one third sell reprints through an agent. Large circulation ($\geq$ 10,000) journals are more likely to sell reprints directly (87.8%) than small circulation ($\leq$ 2,999) journals (56.5%). It is not possible to tell from this how many journals are willing to sell single reprints as opposed to more than one reprint in response to a single order. One of the alternative royalty payment mechanisms considered in Section 6 of this report would require libraries to purchase photocopy items or reprints in excess of fair use and guidelines from individual publishers. These data suggest that this would be more feasible for large serials than for small serials. Another alternative royalty payment mechanism, the purchase of single photocopy items or reprints in excess of fair use or guidelines from a central agency, might be more appropriate for smaller journals which do not currently offer single reprint sales or which might not expect to receive significant royalty income. In fact, of those journals in the Indiana University survey which do offer reprint sales through an authorized agent, a larger proportion of small circulation journals ($\leq$ 2,999, 50.8%) and medium circulation journals (3,000-9,999, 27.7%) offer such a service than do large circulation journals ($\geq$10,000, 30.6%).

Fry, White, and Johnson report that the majority of journals do not display the International Standard Serial Number (ISSN) -only 36% of the responding journals reported displaying the ISSN in each issue, with small circulation journals being more likely than large circulation journals to display this identification number. Display of the ISSN is essential for a transaction-based royalty payment mechanism. The Copyright Clearance Center is mounting a special effort, with the cooperation of the National Serials Data Program (NSDP) at the Library of Congress, to convince serial publishers to display the ISSN along with specially-designed individual article coding. Wide-scale display of the ISSN would not only aid in development of a transaction-based royalty payment mechanism but would also aid in ongoing development and utilization of serials data bases, such as the Council of Library Resources-initiated Conversion of Serials (CONSER) project. We should note here that there is at the present time no way to "force" publishers to display the ISSN or individual article coding. Perhaps the possibility of obtaining royalty income through a payment mechanism or some type of government regulation would offer some inducement. With regard to the former, however, data presented elsewhere in this report suggest that the number of publishers which would benefit significantly would be in a minority if many classes of photocopying become exempt from payment.

As noted in the Indiana University study, publishers appear to prefer direct licensing of copying over clearinghouse arrangements for authorizing photocopying. An overwhelming majority of 68.7 percent of responding publishers preferred to license photocopying directly rather than through an agent, clearinghouse, or other method of licensing. This finding is subject to the caveat that the publishers were not presented an example of a specific mechanism to evaluate in the Indiana University survey. Fry, White and Johnson interpret this as an additional argument for a campaign to inform publishers about the existence and advantage of a royalty payment mechanism involving licensing agreements. In addition, we hypothesize that this feeling of publishers might have its roots in publishers' fears of the cost or complexity of such a licensing clearinghouse. On the other hand, publishers might feel that the number of potential licensees would be small enough so that direct licensing would be both feasible and cost effective. Perhaps significantly, publishers' relatively greater preferences for direct licensing are not necessarily shared by librarians, since we found that librarians generally oppose royalty payment mechanisms involving a direct contract between library and publisher.

Publishers of copyrighted journals were asked with respect to specific journal titles in the Indiana University survey what they felt would be "an appropriate payment" if authorized copies were supplied by an agent or clearinghouse.

Surprisingly, more than 50% of the 412 responding journals specified that they would expect a zero payment from such an arrangement. Fry, White, and Johnson speculate that this is due to publishers' preferences for direct mailing or their perceptions of such a clearinghouse as a "convenience mechanism, or ... copying deterrent." When all non-zero publisher responses are considered, a mean payment of $1.44 per copy was obtained, with a minimum of $.05 and a maximum of $9.99. Publishers of copyrighted journals who do not supply authorized reprints were also asked to supply the price they would charge for their supplying of an authorized copy or reprint of an article of up to ten pages for a United States order with accompanying payment. The mean response was $3.09 with a minimum of $.25 and a maximum of $9.99. For publishers who do currently supply reprints, a mean U.S. order price of $3.38 was reported, with a minimum of $.15 and a maximum of $9.99.

These responses do not directly address what portion of payment should be considered to be a "copyright royalty." In the case of publisher sale of reprints, labor and materials costs plus overhead must be covered before a royalty can be obtained. In the case of a sale by a clearinghouse or agent, a transaction or processing cost must be covered in addition to any royalties which would be transmitted to a publisher.

5.4 Photocopying of Scientific and Technical Serials

A large proportion of the serial publishing industry involves scientific and technical materials. This section provides estimates of the amount of photocopying that is performed on scientific and technical periodicals. These data were derived from the titles given on the characteristics forms so that they include only copyrighted serials. The publications are sub-divided by scientific and technical, non-science and newspapers and magazines. These subdivisions are given by type of library and type of transaction in Table 5.12.

Overall, about 64 percent of the photocopied serials are from scientific and technical publications. It is noted that Public libraries have a much smaller proportion of scientific publications photocopied (46%). Academic libraries do 65 percent of their photocopying from scientific and technical serials, Special libraries do 80 percent and Federal libraries do 89 percent. There is not quite the disparity among types of transactions. About 76 percent of photocopying of interlibrary loans are from scientific and technical serials, 59 percent of intrasystem loans from them and 63 percent of photocopying for local users from them.

We find that most of the scientific and technical serials are prepared by domestic publishers. Overall, about 70 percent of them are from domestic publishers. However, Special libraries photocopy the highest proportion of

Table 5.12 NUMBER OF TRANSACTIONS BY TYPE OF PUBLICATION, BY TYPE OF LIBRARY, BY TYPE OF TRANSACTION

(Thousands of Transactions)

Type of Library/	Type of Publication			Proportion
Type of Transaction	Science	Non-Science	Paper/Magazine	Science
Public				
Interlibrary Loan	802	319	151	.63
Intrasystem Loan	391	443	578	.28
Local Users	2,756	2,040	1,119	.47
Total	3,949	2,802	1,848	.46
Academic				
Interlibrary Loan	1,009	188	58	.80
Intrasystem Loan	930	370	272	.59
Local Users	982	390	306	.59
Total	2,921	948	636	.65
Special				
Interlibrary Loan	755	105	35	.84
Intrasystem Loan	976	174	61	.85
Local Users	4,103	645	476	.79
Total	5,834	924	512	.80
Federal				
Interlibrary Loan	167	6	7	.93
Intrasystem Loan	365	10	<1	.97
Local Users	924	16	146	.85
Total	1,456	32	154	.89
All Libraries				
Interlibrary Loan	2,733	618	251	.76
Intrasystem Loan	2,662	997	852	.59
Local Users	8,765	3,091	2,047	.63
Total	14,160	4,706	3,150	.64
Proportion of Total	.64	.21	.14	

SOURCE: King Research, Inc.: National Library Survey.

foreign serials (43%), and the Federal Libraries' proportion of foreign serials is about 29 percent. In Public libraries, only about one percent of photocopying is from foreign serials. The variation among types of transactions ranges from 19 percent of photocopies from foreign publications for intrasystem loan to 35 percent for local users. These results are displayed in Table 5.13.

Table 5.13 DISTRIBUTION OF PROPORTION OF TRANSACTIONS OF FOREIGN AND DOMESTIC COPYRIGHTED SCIENTIFIC SERIALS BY TYPE OF LIBRARY AND BY TYPE OF TRANSACTION

(Proportion of Transactions)

	Type of Copyrighted Scientific Serial	
	Foreign	Domestic
Type of Library		
Public	.011	.989
Academic	.117	.883
Special	.431	.569
Federal	.288	.712
All Libraries	.301	.699
Type of Transaction		
Interlibrary Loan	.225	.775
Intrasystem Loan	.193	.807
Local Users	.346	.654
All Transactions	.301	.699

SOURCE: King Research, Inc.: National Library Survey.

The age distribution of domestic, copyrighted scientific and technical serials is given in Table 5.14 by type of library and type of transaction. Overall, the age distribution of these serials seems to reflect that observed in Table 5.11 for all serials. However, when foreign, copyrighted serials are considered, it appears that the age distribution is somewhat different. For the most part, for all types of transactions, more of the photocopied serials are younger than domestic serials. These data are displayed in Table 5.15.

Age distribution was also established for the MINITEX data base. All of these responses were coded into the nine NSF fields of science. These data are displayed in Tables 5.16 through 5.18 for Public, Academic and Special libraries respectively. Because the characteristics of scientists and engineers in Minnesota are likely to be different from those in the rest of the U.S., comparison of total number of loans among the fields of science for the MINITEX database is not advised. However, use of the age distributions within a particular field of science by type of library seems reasonable. In Public libraries 26 percent of the loans are for publications over ten years old, Academic libraries 28 percent and Special libraries 15 percent. This is reasonably similar to the national library survey results where Academic libraries were 28 percent and Special libraries 11 percent. However, Public libraries were 40 percent compared to 26 percent in MINITEX.

Across all types of libraries, we find that Mathematics, Environmental Science, and Other Sciences appear to have loans from older publications. These three sciences have between 37 and 39 percent of their loans from publications over ten years old. In Computer Sciences only 19 percent of the loans were from serials over 10 years. All of the remaining sciences and engineering ranged from 22 to 28 percent over ten years old.

Table 5.14 DISTRIBUTION OF PROPORTION OF TRANSACTIONS OF DOMESTIC, COPYRIGHT, SCIENTIFIC SERIAL TITLES BY AGE OF PUBLICATION, BY TYPE OF LIBRARY, BY TYPE OF TRANSACTION

(Proportion of Transactions)

Type of Library/	Age of Serial in Years											
Type of Transaction	1	2	3	4	5	6-10	>10	11-15	16-20	21-25	26-50	>50
Public												
Interlibrary Loan	.203	.054	.171	.019	.017	.136	.399	.093	.073	.134	.043	.057
Intrasystem Loan	.555	.090	.086	.055	.014	.086	.115	.085	-	.015	.015	-
Local Users	.428	.188	.091	.051	.054	.116	.072	.019	.014	.005	.026	.009
Academic												
Interlibrary Loan	.118	.147	.097	.101	.068	.192	.276	.086	.076	.066	.024	.024
Intrasystem Loan	.323	.163	.101	.082	.037	.170	.123	.072	.020	.023	.003	.006
Local Users	.296	.109	.150	.057	.060	.154	.173	.082	.052	.024	.014	.002
Special												
Interlibrary Loan	.115	.440	.104	.040	.052	.139	.109	.102	.003	.002	.002	.001
Intrasystem Loan	.367	.236	.070	.052	.039	.082	.153	.029	.042	.010	.071	-
Local Users	.631	.060	.052	.043	.038	.087	.089	.041	.016	.027	.005	.001
Federal												
Interlibrary Loan	.295	.252	.087	.074	.061	.098	.133	.032	.017	.009	.032	.044
Intrasystem Loan	.354	.037	.033	.014	.043	.194	.326	.148	.035	.053	.071	.018
Local Users	.293	.205	.155	.079	.044	.135	.090	.045	.027	.013	.001	.003
All Libraries												
Interlibrary Loan	.152	.190	.119	.063	.050	.159	.266	.088	.056	.068	.025	.030
Intrasystem Loan	.370	.163	.079	.060	.036	.134	.160	.069	.027	.021	.036	.005
Local Users	.512	.108	.083	.050	.045	.106	.095	.041	.021	.020	.010	.002

SOURCE: King Research, Inc.: National Library Survey.

Table 5.15 DISTRIBUTION OF PROPORTION OF TRANSACTIONS OF FOREIGN, COPYRIGHTED, SCIENTIFIC SERIAL TITLES BY AGE OF PUBLICATION, BY TYPE OF LIBRARY, BY TYPE OF TRANSACTION (Proportion of Transactions)

Type of Library/ Type of Transaction	Age of Serial in Years 1	2	3	4	5	6-10	>10	11-15	16-20	21-25	26-50	>50
Public												
Interlibrary Loan	.010	-	.005	-	.469	-	.517	.005	-	-	-	.512
Intrasystem Loan	-	-	-	-	-	-	-	-	-	-	-	-
Local Users	.131	.013	.023	.013	.032	.520	.269	.082	.050	.054	.047	.036
Academic												
Interlibrary Loan	.243	.153	.099	.063	.078	.184	.181	.116	.012	.005	.026	.022
Intrasystem Loan	.213	.125	.099	.042	.146	.290	.085	.027	.057	.001	-	-
Local Users	.592	.091	.051	.041	.026	.102	.097	.056	.013	.012	.008	.007
Special												
Interlibrary Loan	.205	.245	.026	.187	.053	.172	.111	.066	.022	.021	.002	*
Intrasystem Loan	.318	.247	.172	.159	-	.034	.070	.036	.034	-	-	-
Local Users	.415	.206	.121	.041	.066	.092	.047	.024	.007	.014	.001	-
Federal												
Interlibrary Loan	.331	.126	.153	.120	.050	.113	.106	.018	.041	.004	.039	.004
Intrasystem Loan	.498	.054	.062	.028	.152	.150	.057	.027	.028	.001	.001	.001
Local Users	.367	.122	.167	.055	.092	.101	.096	.044	-	.009	.043	-
All Libraries												
Interlibrary Loan	.034	.224	.110	.148	.089	.206	.181	.097	.027	.013	.026	.025
Intrasystem Loan	.346	.133	.106	.070	.107	.167	.071	.030	.040	*	*	*
Local Users	.424	.200	.120	.042	.066	.096	.052	.027	.007	.014	.003	*

SOURCE: King Research, Inc.: National Library Survey

*Less than one-half of one-tenth of one percent.

Table 5.16 AGE OF INTERLIBRARY LOANS FOR PUBLIC LIBRARIES BY FIELD OF SCIENCE

(Number of Loans)

	Year Published											
Field of Science	1976	1975	1974	1973	1972	1971	1970	1969	1968	1967	≤1966	Total
Physical Science	2	4	3	3	7	3	4		1	1	27	55
Mathematics		30	19	3		1					5	58
Computer Science	2	4	1	3	1	1	2					14
Environmental Science	6	21	9	12	9	4	8	3	6		46	124
Engineering	12	41	24	15	6	3	7	6	1	2	56	173
Life Science	68	163	160	121	71	51	36	50	28	46	302	1,096
Psychology	7	53	42	39	30	26	17	23	17	11	65	330
Social Science	41	122	110	69	55	48	10	25	15	13	144	652
Comprehensive (All Other)	6	24	17	9	4	2	5	5	1	4	46	123
Total	144	462	385	274	183	139	89	112	69	77	691	2,625

SOURCE: King Research, Inc.: MINITEX database.

Table 5.17 AGE OF INTERLIBRARY LOANS FOR ACADEMIC LIBRARIES BY FIELD OF SCIENCE

(Number of Loans)

	Year Published											
Field of Science	1976	1975	1974	1973	1972	1971	1970	1969	1968	1967	≤1966	Total
Physical Science	204	170	93	78	44	45	31	34	34	25	305	1,063
Mathematics	15	25	14	15	11	9	7	6	3	5	97	207
Computer Science	2	36	22	18	20	12	5	13	9	5	41	183
Environmental Science	28	179	148	88	67	41	65	36	37	26	485	1,200
Engineering	68	223	184	137	73	57	47	32	21	26	375	1,243
Life Science	597	2,437	2,170	1,382	919	683	559	444	361	337	3,640	13,529
Psychology	97	530	561	299	211	169	128	79	88	79	668	2,909
Social Science	368	1,457	1,334	842	538	399	266	216	221	162	1,976	7,779
Comprehensive (All Other)	61	246	172	107	74	63	38	51	39	30	696	1,577
Total	1,440	5,303	4,698	2,966	1,957	1,478	1,146	911	814	695	8,285	29,693

SOURCE: King Research, Inc.: MINITEX database.

Table 5.18 AGE OF INTERLIBRARY LOANS FOR SPECIAL LIBRARIES BY FIELD OF SCIENCE
(Number of Loans)

	Year Published											
Field of Science	1976	1975	1974	1973	1972	1971	1970	1969	1968	1967	≤1966	Total
Physical Science	112	59	40	33	17	19	10	14	14	12	52	382
Mathematics	4	2	3	3	1	1	2	2	2		15	35
Computer Science	14	10	6	8	2	1		2	2	2	7	54
Environmental Science	49	22	18	13	6	9	2	4		4	15	142
Engineering	44	43	33	24	15	9	6	3	7	4	38	226
Life Science	559	365	232	160	100	68	56	28	31	31	230	1,860
Psychology	43	102	47	47	29	34	22	20	17	15	83	459
Social Science	176	228	148	111	88	69	45	38	47	20	224	1,194
Comprehensive (All Other)	46	58	42	31	18	15	11	5	2	3	32	263
Total	1,047	889	569	431	276	225	154	116	122	91	696	4.616

SOURCE: King Research, Inc.: MINITEX database.

This section is divided into four parts. In 6.1 we describe the factors relevant to the evaluation of alternative royalty payment mechanisms. Section 6.2 lists hypothetical mechanisms developed to serve as examples of several different design aspects.

The feasibility of these alternatives is examined in Section 6.3 in terms of speed, accuracy, transition cost, and operational cost. We summarize our conclusions in Section 6.4.

6.1 Factors to be Considered in Selecting from Among Alternative Royalty Payment Mechanisms

In this section, we describe some factors which should be taken into account in selecting among alternative mechanisms. These factors are presented from the perspective of individual libraries and publishers to aid them in selecting from among alternatives. The purpose of the evaluation is not to make specific recommendations, but rather to point out the advantages and disadvantages, as we see them, to individual libraries and publishers. It appears that certain advantages and disadvantages become important with libraries that have high or low volume eligible photocopying. Similarly, the relative advantages and disadvantages of alternative royalty payment mechanisms vary by the volume of photocopying that is eligible for payment to serial publishers. Therefore, the advantages and disadvantages are presented for libraries with high and low volumes of eligible photocopying and publishers that have serials with high and low volumes of eligible royalty payments. Clearly, it is unlikely that any one single royalty payment mechanism will be universally adapted by all libraries and all publishers. Thus, it would seem to be helpful to libraries and publishers to know their options and what the advantages and disadvantages are for each.

As shown in previous sections, one of the most important constraints, the volume of eligible photocopying, is still an uncertanty. Another important consideration is the need to balance public access to information with the need of copyright holders for a fair return. At the least, the existing segments of the copyright environment (libraries, users, authors, publishers, Federal government, etc.) should be able to absorb the added cost of a royalty payment mechanism. From a different perspective, a shift of resources should occur from one segment to another which would not result in a degradation of existing levels of performance or service for any of the segments. This shift hopefully would result in improvements in performance or service (or increased survivability) for at least one of the segments. Such optimality and social welfare considerations, however, need to be translated into more practical terms. The important question is whether it is feasible to develop a mechanism which will transmit royalty payments to copyright holders in proportion to the amount of library photocopying of individual copyright holders' materials which would be eligible for royalty payments.

The following assumptions should also be kept in mind when reading the following discussion:

- Copyright holders are assumed to be publishers.
- At least initially, royalty payment mechanisms will be concerned chiefly with photocopying of domestic (U.S.) published materials.
- The published material of chief concern to the mechanisms (at least initially) will be serial articles.

These assumptions may only hold over the next few years, but they do simplify the discussion of specific factors that might be used in selecting among alternative royalty payment mechanisms.

Additional factors which need to be taken into account are the following:

The amount of photocopying for individual serial titles.

This is particularly important since a large proportion of serial titles will have a small amount of photocopying and a small proportion of serials will have a substantial number of photocopying items eligible for payment.

The prevailing attitudes of libraries and publishers concerning alternative royalty payment mechanisms.

Clearly, alternative mechanisms must have some degree of acceptance by all parties or they will not be successful. This is especially important in a voluntary mechanism.

The market economic implications of alternative mechanisms.

The payment of royalties will have some economic impact on libraries. They could increase budgets to absorb the payments or require reallocation of their budgets to absorb the costs.

The capability of libraries and publishers to implement alternative mechanisms.

Each mechanism has practical and economic implications for the parties involved and whether they have the capability to implement mechanisms.

The proportion of photocopying at individual libraries which would be eligible for payment.

At some point, individual libraries' liability for payment must be determined. The proportion of photocopying eligible for payment will affect how efficient various measurement techniques will be. The proportion of photocopying that is eligible also has some bearing on the complexity of accounting for the number of eligible photocopy items.

Use of existing payment channels versus development of new payment channels.

The use of existing payment and distribution channels, such as interlibrary loan systems and information retrieval networks, would tend to make start-up and operation of a payment mechanism easier than if a totally new mechanism had to be designed and implemented. On the other hand, there is no guarantee that existing mechanisms could be easily adapted.

Differentiation Between Interlibrary Loan Photocopy and Photocopy for Local Users and Intrasystem Lending

As noted many times in this report, ILL payments would be, under the CONTU ILL guidelines, the responsibility of the requesting library. Thus, a library would not be responsible for the photocopying it does in response to other libraries' ILL requests. Volume estimates by the library or some other party would have to take this into account.

Method used for estimating or counting eligible photocopying.

To determine eligible photocopying volume, census or sampling approaches might be used. This study employed a sampling approach: a sample of libraries and a sample of photocopying within these libraries were observed, and national and annual estimates were projected from these samples. A census approach to determine eligible photocopy items might start with all potentially eligible libraries, and then some method would be applied to record all eligible photocopy items. From the standpoint of royalty payments, a census of all libraries and photocopying would provide the most accurate data. The uncertainty of sampling would be avoided. On the other hand, such a scheme would probably be expensive to operate, especially if the cost to participating libraries is also taken into account. In addition, careful sampling procedures would generate statistically valid data.

Degree to which non-standardization can be tolerated.

Interlibrary loan (ILL) forms have been standardized by the American Library Association (ALA). Photocopying operations and ILL operations within libraries are not standardized. Neither are serial publishers' formats for copyright notice display (although it is noted that standards have been proposed and partially implemented over the years). Any royalty payment mechanism must take into account the current variety of practices. Even though standardization might be initially expensive, it should aim for a reduction in long-run costs. For cost savings to be realized, however, standards for different purposes or operations should be compatible. Examples that might be cited are the standardization of bibliographic data used by abstracting and indexing services and the standardization of article coding such as that proposed for AAP's Copyright Clearance Center.

Relationship between data collection and distribution channels.

Data collection is defined here as the detection of photocopying that requires payment, and the estimation of its volume. A distribution channel is the way materials and payments are transmitted among copyright holders and libraries. If it were possible to combine data collection and distribution channels, or at least make them compatible, operational costs of the payment mechanism might be reduced. On the other hand, a lack of standardization in ordering and billing procedures might negate these savings.

Relationship between transaction level and payment level.

There are several variations of the relationship between transaction level and payment level. Royalty payments to copyright holders might be made on a one-to-one basis to the number of eligible photocopy items. Second, in an intermediate variation, royalty payments might be made on a "sliding scale" roughly related to the number of actual or potential eligible photocopy items. Third, royalty payments might be only indirectly related to the number of eligible photocopy items. The first two require potentially expensive data collection procedures to be developed and implemented. The last variation would be less expensive, but would be less accurate, and would still require the implementation of an accounting and billing operation.

From the above discussion of relevant factors, it should be possible to develop a list of criteria against which alternative royalty payment mechanisms might be compared. Before this is done, however, it is useful to describe the nature of the mechanisms which will be compared for their feasibility. This is best done by describing the functions to be performed by the mechanisms.

The primary function of the royalty payment mechanisms is to facilitate the following six separate "flows" of documents, information, or payments:

1. The flow of requests (orders) for photocopy items from individual to libraries and from libraries to suppliers of photocopy items.
2. The flow of data from libraries to or through a mechanism (and possibly to copyright owners) concerning the volume and characteristics of eligible photocopy items.
3. The flow of payments from libraries to copyright owners based upon the volume and characteristics of eligible photocopy items.
4. The flow of requests for authorizations to copy from libraries to copyright owners.
5. The flow of authorizations to copy from copyright owners to libraries.
6. The actual flow of photocopy items from and between libraries.

The feasibility of a royalty payment mechanism is defined as the degree to which it satisfactorily facilitates the flow of documents, information or payments. In order to evaluate these flows, the following general criteria are proposed:

- Speed
- Transition Cost
- Accuracy
- Operational Cost

Speed refers to the relative speed with which a request, document, payment, or information about a photocopy item is transmitted between interested parties. One of the most critical components in which speed is important is the speed of delivery, the time between a user's expression of a request and the time the request is satisfied with an original document or a photocopy item. A mechanism which imposes a delay between the time a request for a photocopy item is made and the time it is received by its user which is greater than the delay experienced in an alternative mechanism is, other things being equal, less desirable than the other mechanism. Another aspect of speed particularly relevant to publishers is the speed of payment, reflecting the time delay between a transaction involving an eligible copy and receipt of payment by the publisher.

Accuracy here refers to the positive correlation between a serial title's eligible photocopying and the payment received by its publisher. Other things being equal, the larger the number of eligible photocopy items, the greater would be the royalty payment to the publisher. Conversely, the smaller the number of eligible photocopy items for which a library is responsible, the smaller would be that library's royalty payments.

Transition Cost refers to the time, effort, and resources necessary to start up a mechanism and thereby make it operational. It is emphasized that transitional cost refers to more than the actual dollar cost of physical activities or facilities. It also refers to the difficult-to-measure time and energy lost to the design and setting up of a mechanism which is at least a step removed from providing the user "legal" photocopy and the publisher with a royalty payment. In a sense, this present study is an example of a transitional cost, since it does not contribute directly to either of these goals, but is more useful to the initial stages of planning and the evaluation of alternatives.

Operational Cost refers to the cost imposed upon the participants by administration of the mechanism. Generally speaking, an increase in accuracy may result in increased costs, due to the need for more accurate counting or estimation of eligible transactions. Since royalty payments are assumed to be for value received, they are not included in Transition Cost or Operational Cost.

6.2 Description of Alternative Royalty Payment Mechanisms

For the Copyright Royalty Library Survey, capsule descriptions of alternative royalty payment mechanisms were developed in order to obtain expressions of libraries' preferences. Based upon responses to this survey and upon further research, King Research developed a revised list of alternative royalty payment mechanisms (RPMs):

RPM-1 Libraries would purchase photocopy items in excess of fair use and guidelines from a central agency. The central agency would transmit payments to publishers.

RPM-2 Libraries would purchase photocopy items in excess of use and guidelines from individual publishers.

RPM-3 Libraries would pay an optional higher subscription price for those serials from which they anticipated making sufficient photocopy items to be eligible for payments.

RPM-4 Libraries would pay higher subscription prices for all serials, in effect paying for a "blanket" photocopying license.

RPM-5 Publishers of high-volume serials would establish direct licensing agreements with libraries which make a high volume of eligible photocopy items.

RPM-6 A central agency or clearinghouse would estimate or measure eligible photocopying volume and would perform accounting and billing operations as well as serving as an agent for publishers.

RPM-7 Libraries would purchase royalty stamps or coupons from a central agency which would then be affixed to photocopy items eligible for payment.

RPM-8 Libraries would pay royalties through existing and developing ILL and document delivery systems.

RPM-9 Libraries would pay a fee for each photocopying machine to a central agency which would then distribute these payments as royalties to copyright owners.

RPM-1 the purchase of excess photocopy items from a central agency, requires a library to determine the point at which fair use or guidelines would be exceeded. At this point, purchase of additional or excess photocopy items would be made from a central agency.

RPM-2, the purchase of excess photocopy items from individual publishers, also requires a library to determine the point at which fair use or guidelines would be exceeded. At this point, purchase of additional or excess photocopy items or reprints would be made from the individual publishers.

RPM-3, optional higher subscription price, would result in a library's identifying those serial titles from which it expected to photocopy in excess of fair use or guidelines. The library would then agree to pay an optionally higher subscription price (set by the publisher) for these serials, thereby obtaining in advance permission to make excess copies.

For RPM-4, blanket higher subscription price, libraries would pay higher subscription prices for all their serial titles, thereby obtaining in advance permission to do excess photocopying.

RPM-5, direct licensing between high-volume libraries and high-volume serials, would involve individual agreements between publishers and libraries concerning royalty payment for photocopy items in excess of fair use and guidelines, agreements which might vary among the various participants. (This alternative is not likely to be relevant to low-volume libraries.)

RPM-6, a central agency for counting, billing, and payment, would perform these functions as an agent for the publishers which were its sponsors. Through some method it would estimate or count the level of eligible photocopying of libraries, and bill or license them accordingly. The Copyright Clearance Center designed by the Association of American Publishers (AAP) is a specific example of some aspects of this alternative.

In mechanism alternative RPM-7, libraries would purchase royalty stamps or coupons from a central agency. Required royalty payments would be stated in the serial. These stamps would be affixed to eligible photocopy items to demonstrate that a required royalty payment had been made. Distribution of payments to publishers might be made in one of two ways. First, a central agency would monitor the volume of stamps affixed to copies from specific serials on a census or sampling basis, and distribute payments to individual publishers based on the data collected in such a monitoring operation. Second, the central agency would distribute the payments on some other basis, possibly not directly related to the volume of photocopying of specific titles.

RPM-8 involves the payment of royalties through existing systems. Examples of "existing systems" are the following: interlibrary loan networks, document delivery services, both for-profit and not-for-profit (e.g., Institute for Scientific Information, National Technical Information Service, University Microfilms International), and local information brokers and information-on-demand services. Some of these systems already have royalty or licensing agreements in operation, but many do not.

RPM-9, the payment of a photocopying machine fee to a central agency, would require the development of a mechanism to allocate royalty payments proportional to photocopying volume among the various publishers whose serials are photocopied.

In the next section, these hypothetical mechanisms are evaluated. We note that these mechanisms are not entirely independent. An operating mechanism might need to adopt operational details from more than one alternative.

6.3 Comparative Evaluation of Alternative Royalty Payment Mechanisms

As more exemptions and guidelines are established, the screening process to determine whether photocopying is eligible for payment also becomes more complex. If accuracy of payments is important, a transaction-based mechanism, where royalty payments are correlated with per-title copying, is appropriate, other things being equal. If transition cost and operational cost are to be minimized, a limited transaction-based system, possibly using existing payment and delivery channels, appears more appropriate. The trade-offs are somewhat complex, due to the potentially small proportion of libraries and serial titles likely to be involved operationally to a significant degree. In a transaction-based mechanism, the actual number of eligible photocopy items made or requested by a specific library or library system would need to be determined in order for accurate payments to be made. If libraries are completely responsible for this screening, a burden is placed upon them. A significant variable is the proportion of photocopy items within a given library which would be eligible for royalty payments, as well as the actual number. A large proportion of libraries have indicated that they would not be able to absorb the cost of having to perform such screening for photocopying for their local patrons. In addition, a large proportion of photocopy items made or requested by the majority of libraries would in all likelihood not be eligible for payments. A significant proportion of their added effort would be wasted due to the low proportion of eligible photocopy items.

A good argument can be made for the creation of a central agency which would perform this screening process, as well as the associated accounting, billing, and payment operations. Here again, however, the proportion of eligible photocopy items in a given library is an important factor to consider. If one assumes that the royalty fees paid through such an agency would be its primary support, these royalty fees would have to cover the input and processing costs of a significant number of non-eligible items, which might tend to dilute the royalty payments which would be transmitted to publishers. A better screening of records of photocopy items before they reach the central agency would improve this situation, but this would shift some of the burden back on the libraries.

The purpose of this section is to present a discussion of the relative feasibility of various alternative royalty payment mechanisms. The evaluation criteria related to feasibility are speed, accuracy, transition cost, and operational cost. Each of these complex criteria may contain both quantitative and qualitative elements; this makes it difficult to specify a single "best alternative," so our discussion will center around a comparative or relative analysis of the hypothetical alternatives.

We alluded earlier to the potential shifting of resources among the various segments of the copyright environment which might be brought about by a royalty payment mechanism. Someone must pay the costs associated with the mechanism. Because of this, the evaluation of various mechanisms must take into account the viewpoints of the various parties involved. We have chosen to do this by dividing this section into two parts. In the first part, the mechanisms will be discussed from the viewpoint of libraries; in the second, from the viewpoint of serial publishers.

It is useful to subdivide both libraries and serials publishers into two groups, high-volume and low-volume. High volume libraries and serials are those which account for a comparatively large number of eligible photocopy items. Low-volume libraries and serials are those which account for a comparatively low volume of eligible photocopy items.

Additional considerations in analysis are the distinction between ILL and local user and intrasystem copying, and the still-unresolved questions regarding limitations on local user and intrasystem loan copying. Finally, the treatment of ILL copies older than 5 years and non-U.S. copyrighted serials is not discussed here. We note that coverage of these categories would tend to increase the number of photocopy items eligible for royalty payments.

6.3.1 Low-Volume Libraries

The majority of libraries in the United States have a comparatively small number of photocopy items of copyrighted domestic serials which might be eligible for royalty payments. The following is a discussion of the relative feasibility of the hypothetical alternative royalty payment mechanism from the standpoint of the general criteria: (1) speed of delivery of eligible copies to a requester; (2) the accuracy of the royalty payment in relation to the actual volume of eligible photocopy items; (3) the transitional cost; and (4) the operational cost (excluding the actual cost of royalty payments).

6.3.1.1 RPM-1: Purchase of Excess Photocopy Items from a Central Agency

Speed of Delivery

RPM-1 would have a minimal impact on low-volume libraries, due to the low number of photocopy items which would be eligible for payment. ILL would not be materially affected. Other eligible photocopy items (e.g., local user and intrasystem loan requests) might be delayed due to the necessity for going to other libraries, but again, the small number would not be a significant detriment except for requesters who required their photocopy items quickly.

Accuracy

Assuming that excess photocopy items are purchased from a central agency, RPM-1 would be highly accurate in matching a library's royalty payments with the actual number of photocopy items it needs in excess of fair use and guidelines set forth by CONTU.

It is worthwhile to mention here that users would not necessarily have to go through the library to obtain photocopy items from the central agency; it is conceivable that direct orders from the user to the central agency could be made, as is possible with some document delivery services. Whether or not low-volume libraries would be inclined to shift this responsibility onto their users is unknown.

Transition Costs

The transition cost for RPM-1 for the low-volume library might be significant for that library depending upon the proportion of photocopy items made or requested which would be eligible for payment, and dependent upon the amount of screening to identify eligible photocopy items. If the proportion of eligibles is low, and the screening process is simple, the transition cost should not be significant. The major variable will be local user and intrasystem request photocopy items, since interlibrary loan files are more adaptable to screening for eligibles than the somewhat more informal non-ILL copying operations.

Operational Cost

The operational cost of RPM-1 for low-volume libraries might be significant, depending upon the proportion of photocopy items eligible for payment and the screening process required. This is because some means must be achieved in the library to screen for eligibility. However, we should note here that, if speed of delivery can be guaranteed, and if costs are competitive, the operation of a central agency for providing excess copies conceivably might benefit the low-volume library by providing quick access to a large central file for ILL and local user and intrasystem requests. In this sense, RPM-1 would be functioning as much more than a royalty payment mechanism for the low-volume library. In other words, it might be cheaper for the low-volume library to order a significant proportion of copies from RPM-1 rather than perform the screening operation. Overcoming the inherent delay in such a system might be a major obstacle, however.

6.3.1.2 RPM-2: Purchase of Excess Photocopy Items from Individual Publishers

Speed of Delivery

For low-volume libraries, RPM-2 might have a slightly more serious impact on the speed of delivery of requested items. Ordering requested photocopy items exceeding fair use or guidelines from individual publishers would be facilitated by standardized ordering and fulfillment procedures, standardization which does not currently exist with respect to reprint or subscription sales. (This is one case where development of a new centralized agency might outweigh the benefits of using existing channels.) Since low-volume libraries by definition would be infrequent sources of orders, setting up deposit accounts might not be feasible with individual publishers; such accounts might otherwise speed delivery.

Accuracy

Accuracy of RPM-2 for low-volume libraries would be high. Their payment to indivdiual publishers for orders would probably include royalty fees. Publishers could tie those directly to the volume of photocopy items ordered.

Transition Cost

Transition cost for RPM-2 for the low-volume library would be slightly more than RPM-1, since the library will have to develop procedures for dealing potentially with several publishers as well as develop the screening process to identify excess photocopy items. The transition cost attributable to dealing with several publishers would probably not be significant, however, due to the low number of eligible requests for copies.

Operational Cost

Operational cost for RPM-2 for low-volume libraries would be slightly more than RPM-1, due to dealing with several publishers. Again, however, the significant cost component would be the screening process, not the ordering process. However, ordering from multiple sources presents some added costs.

6.3.1.3 RPM-3: Optional Higher Subscription Price

Speed of Delivery

Assuming the accurate identification of serials from which excess photocopy items would be made, speed of delivery will not be affected by RPM-3 for the low-volume library. Mis-identification of titles for the low-volume library would not be too serious a problem, due to the library's overall low volume of eligible photocopy items.

Accuracy

RPM-3 would not be as accurate as a transaction-based system which involved library payment on an actual or estimated per-photocopy item basis. Accuracy might not be directly related to the library's actual volume, but possibly to some other statistic such as number of subscriptions, annual volume of exposures, or number of paper-to-paper photocopying machines. If a low-volume library paid for a subscription price option, then made fewer than expected photocopy items, it might feel it was over-paying.

Transition Cost

The low-volume library would have to identify the serial titles eligible for the RPM-3 subscription price option. The cost of this might be significant depending upon how accurate this determination would have to be. Because of the low-volume of eligible photocopy items, however, it is conceivable that a librarian with close familiarity with the use of serial titles would be readily able to identify the eligible titles, especially if (eventual) guidelines for local user and intrasystem request photocopy items are easy to implement.

Operational Cost

The RPM-3 operational cost for the low-volume library would be minimal, depending largely on the type of on-going monitoring necessary to guarantee compliance with the option agreement.

6.3.1.4 RPM-4: Blanket Higher Subscription Price

Speed of Delivery

RPM-4 would not decrease speed of delivery for the low-volume library.

Accuracy

Photocopying from individual titles may vary significantly among different libraries paying the same royalty surcharge for those titles, so a possible inequity (as compared with transaction-based mechanism) might develop. Also, the majority of the low-volume library's photocopying would probably not be eligible for royalty payment; this might result in overcharging for low-volume serial titles. The seriousness of this, of course, would depend upon the structure of the royalty surcharge payment schedule.

Transition Cost

For the low-volume library, transition cost for the RPM-4 would be minimal. Slightly more paperwork might be necessary at the beginning if subscription agreements need to be in the form of a legally-based licensing agreement. (This would also hold for RPM-3.)

Operational Cost

Other than the higher subscription charges, current photocopying and interlibrary loan operations could continue with no significant increase in operational cost due to RPM-4.

6.3.1.5 RPM-5: Direct Licensing Between High-Volume Libraries and High-Volume Serials

This alternative is not likely to be relevant to low-volume libraries. In this alternative, publishers and libraries would make individual agreements concerning royalty payment for photocopy items in excess of fair use and guidelines, agreements which might vary among the various participants. The cost may not justify the means.

6.3.1.6 RPM-6: Central Agency for Counting, Billing, and Payment

One example of this type of mechanism is the Copyright Clearance Center (12).

Speed of Delivery

The low-volume library's speed of delivery of payment-eligible photocopy items to requesters would not be affected, since the purpose of this mechanism is to relieve libraries of as much of the burden of accounting as possible. (This assumes that it would be cost-effective from the publishers' viewpoints for the central agency to monitor low-volume libraries' photocopying.)

Accuracy

Accuracy would be high to moderate, depending upon how the low-volume libraries' eligible photocopy items were screened. A transaction-based mechanism, in which all eligible photocopy items were recorded, would be the most accurate. A modified transaction-based system, based on a sampling of libraries stratified by various copying-related characteristics, would be less accurate, but possibly cost-effective from the central agency's point of view due to the large number of low-volume libraries necessary to deal with in a minor way.

Transition Cost

Transition costs for RPM-6 for low-volume libraries would be minimal, under the assumption that they would have little need for contact with the central agency.

Operational Cost

Again, minimal for low-volume libraries. As mentioned earlier in this section, actual costs depend greatly upon how much of the screening burden is borne by libraries. It might be even less expensive to perform the screening and counting at the Agency except where the proportion of exempt photocopy items is high.

6.3.1.7 RPM-7: Royalty Stamps or Coupons

Speed of Delivery

RPM-7 would not significantly affect the speed of delivery of requested photocopy items.

Accuracy

Assuming the low-volume library did not over-buy or under-buy the stamps or coupons, affixing stamps to photocopy items would be a very accurate way to decrement the pre-paid "account" which consisted of the stamps. (Note that accuracy here refers only to the accuracy of the library's payments being related to the volume of photocopying, not to the accuracy with which serial publishers would receive royalties for photocopying of their serials.)

Transition Cost

Other than the initial purchase price of the stamps, transition would not be costly, except for the expense of developing a screening operation to identify the photocopy items to which the stamps would have to be affixed.

Operational Cost

Operational costs for the low-volume library would be minimal.

6.3.1.8 RPM-8: Payment of Royalties Through Existing Systems

Speed of Delivery

Speed of delivery for the low-volume library would not be affected for interlibrary loan requests. Some delay might be experienced with requests for local users and intrasystem requests, as in RPM-1 and RPM-2.

Accuracy

This would be dependent upon the financial arrangement with the system. For example, a small library might contract with a local information broker for the provision of photocopy items not in that library's local collection. The library's bill would presumably include a percentage covering royalty payments.

Transition Cost

For low-volume libraries, transition cost for interlibrary loan would be minimal. For local user and intrasystem loan photocopying, transition costs are dependent upon the type of system which would be developed or adopted. The existing ILL networks in the U.S. might not be appropriate for handling non-ILL copying. Therefore, some transition costs might be passed on to libraries.

Operational Cost

For low-volume libraries, the cost for RPM-8 would be minimal.

6.3.1.9 RPM-9: Payment of Photocopying Machine Fee to a Central Agency

Speed of Delivery

RPM-9 would have no impact on speed of delivery.

Accuracy

The accuracy of RPM-9 would depend upon the way in which the photocopying of individual serial titles is estimated. The collection of machine fees would probably have to be separate from the estimation of relative photocopying volume, since automatic recording of individual transaction data such as title, publisher, page, etc., is not economically feasible at this time. Assuming that the low-volume library would pay a low machine fee, however, accuracy may not be an issue if low-volume libraries are willing to trade off accuracy (on a per-title basis) for ease of mechanism administration. Also, this alternative would not directly address the distinction between interlibrary loan photocopying and photocopying for local users or in response to intrasystem requests.

Transition Cost

For the low-volume library, transition costs for RPM-9 would be minimal. An exception might be the small libraries which do not have control over their own photocopying machines; these might require somewhat more complex accounting or payment operations.

Operational Cost

Operational cost for RPM-9 would be minimal for the low-volume library.

6.3.2 High-Volume Libraries

A minority of libraries in the United States account for a large proportion of photocopying of copyrighted domestic serials which might be eligible for royalty payments.

6.3.2.1 RPM-1: Purchase of Excess Photocopy Items from a Central Agency

Speed of Delivery

For a high-volume library - say, a large academic library which does a large volume of copying for local users and in response to intrasystem loan requests - speed of delivery would suffer if exess photocopy items were purchased from a central agency. This would be especially true if the library had a traditionally fast turnaround time on requests. In addition, the requests experiencing delay might be shifted into a seasonal variation, due to high-volume titles running out of "free" photocopy items early in the calendar or academic year.

Accuracy

Accuracy for high-volume libraries of RPM-1 would be high.

Transition Cost

Transition costs for high-volume libraries would be significant, for two reasons: screening operations would have to be developed to identify excess photocopy items, and ordering operations (perhaps similar to outgoing ILL requests) would have to be developed for excess local user and intrasystem loan requests.

Operational Costs

High-volume libraries' operational costs for RPM-1 would be signficant, due to the two operations mentioned above. However, as noted for low-volume libraries, a balancing factor would be the transfer of photocopying operations out of the library to an agency specifically designed for that purpose. Record-keeping within the library for non-ILL photocopying would still have to be developed to keep track of "excess" requests awaiting fulfillment.

6.3.2.2 RPM-2: Purchase of Excess Photocopy Items from Individual Publishers

Speed of Delivery

RPM-2 would have a major negative impact on speed of delivery due to high-volume libraries' requests' possible clustering around high-volume serial titles; speed of delivery would be degraded for just those serial titles which generated most demand. In addition, individual publishers' reprint operations might not operate as quickly or efficiently as the centralized RPM-1.

Accuracy

RPM-2 accuracy for high-volume libraries would be high.

Transition Cost

Transition cost for this alternative mechanism for high-volume libraries would be more than RPM-1, since ordering operations to deal with single publishers would have to be developed.

Operational Cost

Operational costs would be somewhat greater than for RPM-1, due to the need to deal with individual publishers. Screening operations would need to be conducted, and files of requests maintained, updated, and purged.

6.3.2.3 RPM-3: Optional Higher Subscription Price

Speed of Delivery

There would be no impact on speed of delivery if serial titles were properly identified from which excess photocopy items would be made. There might be some delay if mis-identified titles resulted in special requests being made to publishers, but efficient methods could be developed to deal with this potential "mid-stream" problem.

Accuracy

RPM-3 would not be as accurate for high-volume libraries as a transaction-based mechanism. It would, however, be more accurate than RPM-4, Blanket Higher Subscription Price (q.v.).

Transition Cost

For a high-volume library concerned with accurate payments (and the avoidance of possible legal entanglements) the transition cost of identifying and marking special titles, plus the cost of possible internal monitoring operations, might be significant.

Operational Cost

Operational costs for RPM-3 would be minimal to moderate, depending upon the need to monitor the copying volume status of individual serial titles.

6.3.2.4 RPM-4: Blanket Higher Subscription Price

Speed of Delivery

RPM-4 would not result in an impact on speed of delivery.

Accuracy

RPM-4 would be less accurate than RPM-3 (which is tailored to concentrate on specific titles) and much less accurate than a transaction-based mechanism since some degree of overpayment and underpayment by subscription is inevitable.

Transition Cost

Transition costs for RPM-4 would be minimal for high-volume libraries, unless each serial with a higher subscription price required special paperwork to form a legally-based licensing agreement.

Operational Cost

Operational costs for RPM-4 would be minimal, when the increase in price is not considered.

6.3.2.5 RPM-5: Direct Licensing Between High-Volume Libraries and High-Volume Serials

Speed of Delivery

Since the terms of these licensing agreements would be presumably left up to the participants in RPM-5, there is an opportunity here for copying licenses which would not result in a reduction in delivery speed. Licensing agreements which require special permissions (say, for especially large copying runs) might produce some delay.

Accuracy

This is totally dependent upon the nature of the licensing agreements. Some publishers will prefer transaction-based mechanisms, and some libraries may be able to provide data on a per-title basis.

Transition Cost

For high-volume libraries, the transition cost for RPM-5 would be significant if licensing agreements needed to be negotiated within a limited amount of time with numerous publishers.

Operational Cost

The operational cost for high-volume libraries would depend upon the nature of the licensing agreements. Transaction-based mechanisms requiring screening and counting would be the most expensive.

6.3.2.6 RPM-6: Central Agency for Counting, Billing, and Payment

An example of a central agency is the Copyright Clearance Center designed by the AAP (12).

Speed of Delivery

RPM-6 would have no impact on speed of delivery for high-volume libraries.

Accuracy

The accuracy of RPM-6 for high-volume libraries would be high to moderate, depending upon how eligible photocopy items would be screened. A strict transaction-based mechanism, in which all eligible photocopy items were recorded, would be most accurate. A sampling approach would be somewhat less accurate, but possibly more cost-effective to libraries on the average.

Transition Cost

Transition costs would be high for the high-volume library if the library were responsible for significant portions of the screening operation. Transition costs would be low if such screening were the responsibility of the central agency. There are many variations possible depending upon the way data are transmitted to the central agency, which might significantly affect the way photocopying or interlibrary loan operations would be managed in the high-volume library.

Operational Cost

Operational costs for the high-volume library depend upon the counting or estimating methods adopted by the central agency. If the proportion of exempt photocopies is low, the Agency might be able to screen and count at a low cost, relieving the large libraries of this burden.

6.3.2.7 RPM-7: Royalty Stamps or Royalty Coupons

Speed of Delivery

The use of such stamps or coupons sold by a central agency for use by a high-volume library might result in a slight delay in delivery simply because of a slight increase in request processing time.

Accuracy

As with low-volume libraries, affixing stamps to eligible photocopy items would be an accurate way for decrementing the prepaid account.

Transition Cost

The development of a screening operation to identify eligible photocopy items would probably be more costly than the initial purchase of stamps, excluding the cost of royalty payments per se.

Operational Cost

For a high-volume library, a stamp approach may not be the most cost-effective way to pay royalties, simply because of the slight increase in operational paperwork and complexity which the stamp approach might bring about. Again, the screening operation for the identification of eligible photocopy items would probably be more expensive than the actual use of stamps, coupons, or meters.

6.3.2.8 RPM-8: Payment of Royalties Through Existing Systems

The use of existing or developing state, multi-state, or national ILL networks would greatly simplify royalty payments for eligible ILL photocopy items. However, such systems would not be useful for local user and intra-system loan copy payments without a great deal of modification and standardization. For document delivery services operated outside of or in conjunction with library operations, which already charge for their photocopying services, royalty payments could be included as a portion of the library's service charge.

Speed of Delivery

Use of existing ILL and document delivery systems would not decrease delivery speed unless in-house copying by high-volume libraries was curtailed.

Accuracy

The accuracy of such systems is potentially high, especially for those services which already charge on a per-document basis.

Transition Cost

For the high-volume library, the transition cost for RPM-8 for ILL would not be significant, assuming that the ILL system would do the screening. For local user and intrasystem loan copying, the transition cost would depend upon the proportion of photocopying which was done by the system or operation which would be responsible for the royalty payment. If all payment-eligible photocopying were done by an outside organization which was responsible for the photocopying, then the transition cost would be minimal.

Operational Cost

Assuming that screening and counting operations were performed for the high-volume library, the operational cost would be low.

6.3.2.9 RPM-9: Payment of Photocopying Machine Fee to a Central Agency

Speed of Delivery

RPM-9 would have no impact on the speed of delivery of photocopy items by high-volume libraries.

Accuracy

As noted for low-volume libraries, accuracy would be difficult to achieve for RPM-9. This might be of some consequence for the high-volume library, since over-payments of royalties (in comparison with other alternatives) would be a definite concern.

Transition Cost

Transition costs for high-volume libraries would be minimal, unless high-volume libraries were required at the beginning to estimate accurately the expected volume of eligible photocopy items they might produce in order to qualify for a specific fee level graduated by eligible photocopying volume.

Operational Cost

RPM-9 operational cost for the high-volume library would be minimal.

6.3.3 Low-Volume Serials

A majority of copyrighted domestic serials can be characterized as low-volume. That is, the majority of serials accounts for a relatively small proportion of photocopy items eligible for royalty payment. The following is a discussion of the relative feasibility of the hypothetical alternative royalty payment mechanisms from the standpoint of the general criteria: (1) speed of payment for eligible photocopy items which are made by U.S. libraries; (2) the accuracy of the royalty payment in relation to the actual volume of eligible photocopying; (3) the transition cost borne by the serial publisher; (4) the operational cost borne by the serial publisher. (Note that potential royalty incomes are not discussed in detail here; we deal primarily with the practical feasibility of the development and operation of the mechanism.)

6.3.3.1 RPM-1: Purchase of Excess Photocopy Items from Central Agency

Speed of Payment

In RPM-1, royalty payments would be collected by a central agency in the course of selling photocopy items. These payments would then be transferred to the serial publisher in the form of a check after some period of time. In other words, there would be some delay coupled with the central agency's normal accounting period. Low-volume serials, by definition, have on the average relatively low eligible photocopying. This also might affect the frequency with which royalty checks are transmitted to the publishers of low-volume serials.

Accuracy

RPM-1 accuracy would be high, since presumably the payments transmitted to the serial publisher would be directly related to the number of photocopy items purchased.

Transition Cost

For RPM-1, a central file of serial originals would be maintained which could be duplicated upon demand. The contribution to this central file would determine the low-volume serials' transition cost.

Operational Cost

Assuming that the central agency could be self-supporting through fees and/or royalty payments, the low-volume serials' operational cost for RPM-1 would be minimal.

6.3.3.2 RPM-2: Purchase of Excess Photocopy Items from Individual Publishers

Speed of Payment

The speed of payment would be high, since payment would arrive with an order or during the course of a normal billing cycle.

Accuracy

RPM-2 accuracy for the low-volume serial would be high, since each transaction would require payment.

Transition Cost

The transition cost for RPM-2 for a low volume serial should be low to moderate, since many publishers already sell reprints or authorize reprint sales through an agent or another publisher. Marketing the service directly to libraries, however, could be expensive, out of proportion to the low volume or orders which might be generated.

Operational Cost

Actual operational costs for low-volume serials should not be significant due to the relatively low number of photocopy items which would actually be eligible for royalty payment.

6.3.3.3 RPM-3: Optional Higher Subscription Price

Speed of Payment

There is a substantial long-range financial advantage to publishers for them to obtain a royalty return through increased subscription prices since the income will occur before expenses are incurred. The age of photocopied materials can be quite old so that income is delayed by that amount. This advantage is probably greater for low-volume serials than for high-volume serials.

Accuracy

RPM-3 for low-volume serial titles for which this option was selected would have low to moderate accuracy, depending on how closely "tuned" the royalty surcharge was to the library's expected volume of photocopy items in excess of fair use and guidelines.

Transition Cost

For low volume serials, the transition cost would be moderate, since an additional subscription price category would need to be provided. In addition, written subscription agreements or licenses might be required by the publisher. Finally, this option does not directly provide for a monitoring of photocopying to determine such facts as over-copying of a title for which a library has not paid the optional surcharge.

Operational Cost

Operational costs to the low-volume serial publisher would be minimal for RPM-3, unless a monitoring operation were selectively instituted.

6.3.3.4 RPM-4: Blanket Higher Subscription Price

Speed of Payment

Same considerations as RPM-3.

Accuracy

RPM-4 might be less accurate than RPM-3 since all the low-volume serial's institutional subscribers would pay the higher subscription price, thereby giving them permission to photocopy in excess of fair use and guidelines. If the publisher related prices to some measurement of library size, it is conceivable that some libraries would pay the same royalty payment while making significantly more or fewer photocopy items than another library within the same payment category.

Transition Cost

Transition cost for the low-volume serial would be minimal.

Operational Cost

Operational costs for this alternative would be minimal, unless blanket increases in subscription prices inclined libraries to respond by dropping low-volume serials.

6.3.3.5 RPM-5: Direct Licensing Between High-Volume Libraries and High-Volume Serials

This alternative is not practical for low-volume serials.

6.3.3.6 RPM-6: Central Agency for Counting, Billing, and Payment

An example of RPM-6 is the Copyright Clearance Center designed by the AAP (12).

Speed of Payment

For low-volume serials, speed of payment through RPM-6 would depend upon its accounting period. Due to the low-volume status of the serial, payments might be infrequent (in relation to high-volume serials), and therefore delayed until some time after the actual eligible copy was made.

Accuracy

Accuracy of RPM-6 would be high to moderate, depending upon the counting method used. A sampling approach to estimating the number of eligible photocopy items for low-volume serials were such an approach to be employed, would need to be very carefully designed in order to make accurate estimates for the majority of serials which are low-volume. A census of all libraries which photocopy would be much more accurate.

Transition Cost

For the low-volume serial, the transition cost for RPM-6 would be minimal, depending upon the initial investment required of participants for development of the central agency. It might be necessary for copyrighted serials to place special article coding on the first page of articles for which it would require royalty payments.

Operational Cost

The operational costs for RPM-6 for low-volume serials would be minimal.

6.3.3.7 RPM-7: Royalty Stamps or Royalty Coupons

Speed of Payment

The speed of payment would depend upon the agency selling the royalty stamps, and upon how it determines royalties are to be distributed to the publishers for which it is a licensing agent.

Accuracy

Accuracy would depend chiefly upon how the central stamp agency determined how royalties are distributed. With low-volume serials, accuracy would be relatively expensive to achieve, due to the low and infrequent volume of eligible photocopy items.

Transition Cost

For the low-volume serial, RPM-7 transition costs would be low, depending for the most part on the type of contribution (financial or otherwise) which would be made to the central agency.

Operational Cost

Operational costs would be minimal, assuming that operational costs for RPM-7 would be allocated to serial publishers in proportion to the volume of eligible copies for which their serials accounted.

6.3.3.8 RPM-8: Payment of Royalties Through Existing Systems

Speed of Payment

Since all existing systems (except many publishers' sale of reprints) interpose an extra step or agency between the responsible library and the serial publisher, RPM-8 would result in some delay in payment.

Accuracy

Existing systems which utilize payment systems based on units of service (or documents provided) would be able to provide highly accurate payments, but only for the eligible photocopies which they handled.

Transition Cost

For low-volume serials, transition costs would be moderate, chiefly composed of having to set up agreements and rate structures with existing systems such as ILL networks, document delivery services, and information brokers.

Operational Cost

RPM-8 operational costs for low-volume serials would be minimal.

6.3.3.9 RPM-9: Payment of Photocopying Machine Fee to a Central Agency

Speed of Payment

Since a central agency would be established to collect and distribute machine fees, some delay in payment would occur.

Accuracy

Accuracy in recording and transmitting payments for eligible photocopy items of low-volume serials would be difficult to achieve through RPM-9 without some method of obtaining fairly detailed data on photocopy items per title distributions.

Transition Cost

A central mechanism or agency would have to be developed for RPM-9. Because the low-volume serial would benefit little from this alternative, the serial would presumably have little need to make a significant contribution to such an agency.

Operational Cost

RPM-9 operational costs for the low-volume serial would be minimal.

6.3.4 High-Volume Serials

A minority of copyrighted domestic serials can be characterized as high-volume. That is, this minority of serials accounts for a comparatively large proportion of photocopy items potentially eligible for royalty payment. Their special considerations are addressed in this section.

6.3.4.1 RPM-1: Purchase of Excess Copies from Central Agency

Speed of Payment

As with low-volume serials, there would be some delay in payment imposed through interposition of a central agency between the libraries and high-volume serials. However, high-volume serials might make special arrangements to receive payments more frequently than low-volume serials, perhaps quarterly or monthly.

Accuracy

Royalty payments to high-volume serials through RPM-1 would have high accuracy.

Transition Cost

Transition costs for RPM-1 might be high if a central file of originals must be developed. Since high-volume serial publishers would be expected to be the chief beneficiaries of this mechanism, they might have to bear a large proportion of its cost.

Operational Cost

It may be desirable to minimize the potential labor-intensive costs for operation of such a central document sales agency. This could be accomplished through semi-automation (e.g., microfiche-to-paper) of its duplication operations, but such automation might only be cost-effective for high-volume serials due to infrequent request for low-volume serials. Comparatively speaking, the bulk of operational costs would fall upon high-volume serials.

6.3.4.2 RPM-2: Purchase of Excess Photocopy Items for Individual Publishers

Speed of Payment

RPM-2 would have a high payment speed since royalty payments would accompany an order for photocopy items or would be expected within a normal billing cycle.

Accuracy

RPM-2 would result in a very close correspondence between the volume of eligible photocopy items and actual royalty payments, assuming royalty payments were charged on a per-item basis.

Transition Cost

Transition costs for RPM-2 for the high-volume serial would be significant if the publisher did not already have a reprint sale mechanism in operation. Direct marketing of the service by individual publishers for individual serials would also be expensive.

Operational Cost

Operational costs for the high-volume serial for direct sale of photocopy items of individual articles would be moderate to high (in terms of clerical time) but this would at least partially be offset by service and royalty fees.

6.3.4.3 RPM-3: Optional Higher Subscription Price

Speed of Payment

For those high-volume serials for which libraries would choose to pay a higher subscription price in advance for a license to photocopy in excess of fair use and guidelines, speed of payment would be no problem. There also is a great financial advantage due to improved cash flow.

Accuracy

Accuracy for high-volume serials would be low to moderate, depending on the pricing mechanism used for the option. Possible over-charging and undercharging might arise due to use of flat-fee systems. RPM-3's accuracy would be higher than RPM-4's accuracy, the Blanket Higher Subscription Price.

Transition Cost

Transition cost for adding the subscription price option to existing payment channels would be low to moderate, depending partly upon the amount of additional contacts to be made with subscribers who choose the option, and partly on increased internal accounting costs for establishment of an additional price category. A possible extra cost would be a monitoring or enforcement mechanism to determine if a library should be paying an option price but is not.

Operational Cost

Operational costs for the high-volume serial for RPM-3 would be minimal, unless selective monitoring or enforcement operations were initiated.

6.3.4.4 RPM-4: Blanket Higher Subscription Price

This alternative mechanism is similar to RPM-3 except that subscribers would not have the option of choosing or not choosing to pay the higher subscription price, which would then give them a license to make photocopies in excess of fair use and guidelines.

Speed of Payment

As in RPM-3, payment would be "cash return" prior to libraries' actual making of excess photocopy items during any given subscription period.

Accuracy

Accuracy might be somewhat lower than the accuracy of RPM-3 since both high-volume and low-volume libraries would be covered. Accuracy would be improved by using a graduated scale for the blanket higher subscription price -- smaller or lower-volume libraries paying a smaller differential as a consequence of their lower expected volume of excess photocopy items.

Transition Cost

The transition cost for RPM-4 for high-volume libraries would be minimal. This might change, however, depending upon the different payment scales which might be introduced to increase the accuracy of the mechanism. Development of a monitoring or enforcement mechanism would also increase transition costs for high-volume serials.

Operational Cost

Operational costs for RPM-4 for high-volume serials would be minimal, unless operation of a monitoring or enforcement mechanism were necessary, or unless some serials classified as high-volume were actually peripheral to some libraries and therefore dropped.

6.3.4.5 RPM-5: Direct Licensing Between High-Volume Libraries and High-Volume Serials

Speed of Payment

Speed of payment would depend upon the nature of the licensing agreement. Flat-fee payment might be made in advance, in anticipation of copying. Libraries with the capability for regular tallying of copying might be licensed on the basis of a regular payment.

Accuracy

This also would depend on the nature of the licensing agreement.

Transition Cost

The chief transition cost would be the negotiation of a number of licensing agreements within a given length of time. A lack of standardization in the agreements, designed to take into account legitimate differences among high-volume libraries, would result in an increased transition cost. Therefore, an important determinant of the transition cost for RPM-5 for high-volume libraries will be the actual number of libraries which fall into the high-volume category.

Operational Cost

Operational costs for RPM-5 for the high-volume serial should not be high, once initial licensing agreements are made.

6.3.4.6 RPM-6: Central Agency for Counting, Billing, and Payment

An example of RPM-6 is the Copyright Clearance Center designed by the AAP to go into operation January 1, 1978 (12).

Speed of Payment

There would be some delay in payment to high-volume serials due to interposition of an agency between libraries and high-volume serial publishers.

Accuracy

The accuracy of RPM-6 for high-volume serials would depend upon the method used for counting or estimating photocopy items. As mentioned previously, the most accurate method would be a census of eligible photocopy items, followed by a sample approach, then by a graduated-scale licensing system operated by the central agency.

Transition Cost

The transition cost for RPM-6 for the high-volume serial would depend upon the need for input standardization (e.g., standardized coding on individual articles to facilitate data collection), but mainly upon the cost borne by the high-volume serial for development of such a mechanism. Since high-volume serials would benefit significantly from development of such a mechanism (in terms of gross payments), they might be expected to share in a greater proportion of the transition costs.

Operational Cost

The RPM-6 operational cost for high-volume serials would be significantly less than the direct licensing alternative. The cost of operation would be borne by the collected copyright royalties. One method of support would be for the central agency to collect fees from participating serials based on royalties collected or the number of eligible photocopy items counted. One determinant of the level of these "transaction fees" would be the proportion of non-eligible copy records screened and processed by the central agency.

6.3.4.7 RPM-7: Royalty Stamps or Royalty Coupons

Speed of Payment

Speed of payment to high-volume serials by RPM-7 would depend upon its accounting period. Payment to high-volume serials could be made more frequently than payment to low-volume serials.

Accuracy

Accuracy of RPM-7 would be high to moderate, depending upon the counting or estimation method used. A method would be needed for allocation of payments. If a sample survey method were used, it would be relatively more easy to obtain accurate (and statistically precise) data concerning high-volume serials than for low-volume serials, due to the highly skewed nature of the photocopy item per title distribution.

Transition Cost

The transition cost for RPM-7 for high-volume serials depends upon the same factors as other alternative mechanisms which are not involved in the actual sale of photocopy items or reprints.

Operational Cost

The operational cost for a royalty stamp mechanism to high-volume libraries would depend upon the number of eligible photocopy items estimated by the payment allocation mechanism and upon the processing fee required by the mechanism.

6.3.4.8 RPM-8: Payment of Royalties Through Existing Systems

Speed of Payment

Due to the interposition of an additional step between the responsible library and the high-volume serial, a payment delay would exist.

Accuracy

Payment accuracy to high-volume serials would potentially be high, due to the greater ease of identifying and counting high-volume serials, especially by existing document-delivery systems which already charge on a unit basis. Low-volume libraries and small for-profit document delivery services might find flat-rate licensing fees more feasible, so accuracy for these copying agents might be somewhat less than for high-volume libraries.

Transition Cost

Unless there is a central agency which could act on behalf of high-volume serials in setting up, say, licensing agreements with existing and developing document delivery systems, the cost for RPM-8 to high-volume serials would be high due to the necessity of dealing with so many potential sources for payment.

Operational Cost

Operational costs incurred by high-volume serials for use of developing and existing systems would be low since these systems would presumably absorb a significant proportion of the operational cost.

6.3.4.9 RPM-9: Payment of Photocopying Machine Fee to a Central Agency

Speed of Payment

Speed of payment for RPM-9 to high-volume serials would not be high, due to the need to interpose a central agency between library and publisher.

Accuracy

Accuracy would not be high unless potentially expensive monitoring capabilities were developed to insure that payments to individual serial publishers were actually proportional to photocopy items.

Transition Cost

Transition costs for the high-volume serial would be moderate since use of RPM-9 would probably require some compromise to be made on accuracy. The bulk of costs of designing and developing a central agency would be passed on to the high-volume serials.

Operational Cost

Operational costs for RPM-9 for the high-volume library would be minimal, chiefly due to a simplification of the data collection procedures which might be required of a central agency.

6.4 Comments and Conclusions

There are still uncertainties concerning the circumstances in which royalty payments would be legally required. Examples of these uncertainties are the following:

- The lack of a concrete definition of the universe of publications to be covered by a royalty payment mechanism
- The lack of an unambiguous, quantitative definition of "systematic" photocopying
- The lack of an unambiguous definition of the term "open to the public"
- The lack of guidelines concerning serials older than five years
- The lack of guidelines governing the photocopying of library materials in response to local user and intrasystem loan requests
- The lack of a definition of "library system"

Until these uncertainties are resolved it will continue to be difficult to assess the impacts of alternative royalty payment mechanisms.

Despite these uncertainties, it appears that no mechanism satisfies all feasibility criteria equally well. It appears that a mix of mechanisms would best accommodate the different volumes and types of photocopying. For example, interlibrary loan, with its special eligibility requirements and its potentially low volume, might be more efficiently handled separately from local user requests and/or intra-system loan requests.

The majority of libraries and serials account for a comparatively low volume of photocopying. A sampling approach to estimating eligible photocopying volume must be very carefully designed to generate accurate and precise statistics for these libraries and serial titles. For such statistics to be statistically valid and as acceptable to the parties involved as a census approach, the cost of a sampling approach, while lower than the cost of a census approach, should not be underestimated.

Also because the majority of libraries and serials account for a comparatively low volume of photocopying, it may be more cost-effective, at least initially, for a central agency, clearinghouse, or payment center to concentrate on serving high-volume serials and high-volume libraries. Over the long run such a facility might be advantageous to all libraries and publishers.

We have already stated that a mix of mechanisms is likely to be the most feasible approach. At the same time, the possibility of the development of competing or non-complementary mechanisms should not be ignored. It is conceivable that problems of access for library users might result if royalty payment procedures are not standardized or at least coordinated. If library compliance with royalty payment mechanisms is complex, more responsibility for access might be shifted to users by curtailment or modification of existing library services. This might initially result in decreased access for users. At the same time, it might help develop a market for other document delivery services which choose to comply with royalty payment requirements.

Monitoring or enforcing royalty payment is potentially one of the most expensive components of the development of a royalty payment mechanism. If monitoring and enforcement are desired by publishers, these functions would be most efficiently carried out by a central agency, assuming that legal questions such as antitrust are resolved.

Much depends upon the pricing mechanisms instituted by various publishers. Uniform royalty pricing would be easiest to adopt from the standpoint of libraries, and to a lesser extent by a centralized agency, but it may not be acceptable to publishers with different operational costs.

The potential impact of royalty payment mechanisms in terms of subscription cancellations is still uncertain. We hypothesize that, if cancellations occurred, they would have the most negative impact on small, specialized journals. It will be difficult, however, to isolate the effects of royalty payments and mechanism requirements due to the existence of intervening variables such as library network developments and library budget constraints.

The most potentially burdensome screening operation for libraries to perform is the maintenance and checking of a manual or machine-readable file for determining the number of past requests for photocopying of the same serial title. In an operating royalty payment mechanism this appears to be an operation which could most advantageously be centralized or which might be modified in order to simplify mechanism operations.

We conclude that many libraries are willing to trade some accuracy in royalty payments in return for a simplification of possible royalty accounting procedures, based upon their comparatively high ranking of the subscription price alternative in the national library survey. Unfortunately, we do not possess comparable data on preferences for publishers, subscription agents, government policy makers, and library users. Perhaps most important of all, data on authors' preferences for royalty payment mechanisms are also lacking.

BIBLIOGRAPHY

1. Association of Research Libraries. ARL Statistics, 1975-1976. Washington, D.C.: ARL, 1976.

2. Congressional Record-House. "Joint Explanatory Statement of the Committee of Conference," Sept. 29, 1976, pp. H11 728-H11 729.

3. Fry, Bernard M., Herbert S. White and Elizabeth L. Johnson. Survey of Publisher Practices and Present Attitudes on Journal Article Copying and Licensing. Bloomington, Indiana: Indiana University, Graduate Library School, June 30, 1977 (Draft).

4. King, Donald W., et al. Statistical Indicators of Scientific and Technical Communication (1960-1980); Volume I: A Summary Report (NSF C-878). Washington, D.C.: U.S. Government Printing Office, 1976.

5. Line, Maurice B. and D. N. Wood. "The Effect of a Large-Scale Photocopying Service on Journal Sales." Journal of Documentation 31:4:234-45 (December 1975).

6. Machlup, Fritz. "The Production and Distribution of Scientific and Technological Information." A study in process under NSF Contract SIS74-12756A01. New York: New York University.

7. Palmour, Vernon E., et al. A Study of the Characteristics, Costs and Magnitude of Interlibrary Loan in Academic Libraries. Westport, Connecticut: Greenwood Publishing Company, 1972.

8. Rudd, Benjamin. "Excise Tax Solution." Copyright and Photocopying; Papers on Problems and Solutions, Design for a Clearinghouse, and a Bibliography. Edited by Laurence B. Heilprin. College Park, Maryland: University of Maryland, College of Library and Information Services, 1977.

9. Sophar, Gerald J., and Laurence B. Heilprin. The Determination of Legal Facts and Economic Guideposts with Respect to the Dissemination of Scientific and Technical Information as It is Affected by Copyright - A Status Report. Final Report. Washington, D.C.: Committee to investigate Copyright Problems Affecting Communication in Science and Education, Inc., December 1967. (ERIC No. ED 014621)

10. Stuart-Stubbs, Basil. Purchasing and Copying Practices at Canadian University Libraries. Ottowa, Ontario, Canada: Canadian Library Association, 1971.

11. Ulrich's International Periodicals Directory. New York: R. R. Bowker and Company, 1975-1976.

12. Wagner, Susan. "AAP Spells Out Clearinghouse Plan for Photocopying at CONTU Meeting." Publishers Weekly 211:15:28 (April 11, 1977).

13. Whitestone, Patricia. Photocopying in Libraries, the Librarians Speak. White Plains, New York: Knowledge Industry Publications, 1977. (ISBN 0-914236-08-3).

14. The National Commission on Libraries and Information Science, Toward a National Program for Library and Information Services: Goals for Action. Washington, D. C.: The Commission, 1975.

APPENDIX A

1. Solicitation Letter

Dear Library Director:

I'm writing to ask your participation in an important study to clarify some of the issues in the area of copyright. The National Commission on Libraries and Information Science and the Division of Science Information of the National Science Foundation, have contracted with King Research, Inc. (KRI) of Rockville, Maryland for a survey of the volume and characteristics of library photocopying.

This is a national survey which includes academic, federal, public and special libraries. Your library is one of 370 selected to participate. Our present schedule calls for two 7-day collection periods, one in (month) and the other in (month). During each period, you will be asked to monitor the volume of photocopying using a simple log form furnished by King Research, Inc. For a short time during each data collection period, more detailed characteristics of photocopied, copyrighted serials will be recorded separately on a simple form especially designed for this purpose. You will also receive a short questionnaire on photocopying costs, charges to patrons for photocopying services and other data needed for analysis.

Please complete the enclosed screening form so that we may initiate your participation. Should you have any questions, telephone Pat Dowd, King Research, Inc. (301) 881-6766, collect.

NCLIS is aware that many libraries are overburdened with survey forms. I am sure you will agree, however, that this particular study is of the utmost importance to the library community. For the first time, we will have valid data describing library photocopying practices in the United States instead of conjecture and opinion. The validity of the study depends upon your cooperation. Please return the enclosed screening form to signify your willingness to participate in the research.

Sincerely,

Alphonse Trezza
Executive Director
NCLIS

AT/jh
Enclosures

American Library Association
Association of Research Libraries
Special Libraries Association

September 1976

Dear Colleague:

I am writing to urge your participation in the national study of library photocopying being sponsored by NCLIS, NSF and CONTU.

The quantity of library photocopying has been a controversial issue for many years. During the attempted negotiations in recent years between the library community and the publishing community (the Conference on the Resolution of Copyright Issues), published library statistics were not accepted by the publishers because they feared that such studies contained biases in favor of libraries. Therefore because no data on the volume and characteristics of this copying mutually acceptable to both sides could be considered, progress toward any kind of a solution was hindered. The proposed study will collect and analyze such photocopying data. The study is also to include a study of the feasibility of royalty payment mechanisms.

The validity of this study depends on the cooperation of the libraries that are selected to participate. Your library is one of 370 libraries selected by the contractor to represent all libraries in the United States. Your participation is essential.

This study is of utmost importance to the total library community and the importance of your participation cannot be overstated. The enclosed letter from Al Trezza, NCLIS Executive Director, presents additional information about the study.

Robert Wedgeworth
Executive Director
American Library Association

John G. Lorenz
Executive Director
Association of Research Libraries

F. E. McKenna
Executive Director
Special Libraries Association

enc.

NOTE: This report is authorized by Public Law 91-345. While you are not required to respond, your cooperation is needed to make the results of this survey comprehensive, accurate and timely.

King Research, Inc.
Rockville, Maryland
September 1976
OMB No. 186-5-76002

NCLIS PHOTOCOPYING CHARACTERISTICS STUDY
SCREENING FORM

Name/Title of Coordinator_______________

Mailing Address_______________

____

Please read the instructions on the reverse side carefully before completing this form.

1. Does this library have branches or other related facilities separate from the central library?

   1 - Yes (Include any branches or related facilities in answering the following questions.)   2 - No

2. Is the organization of which you are a part of considered to be non-profit?

   1 - Yes   2 - No

3. Does this library operate or have access to one or more photocopying machines?

   1 - Yes   2 - No (Thank you. Please return this form to KRI in the enclosed, stamped envelope.)

4. How many branch or department libraries operate, or have access to, photocopying machines? (Do not include the main or central library.)

   Number of Branches or Departments _______________

5. Please record the following information for the central library and any branches or departments. Try to be as accurate as possible. If actual counts are not available, please give your best estimate.

	CENTRAL LIBRARY	ALL OTHER BRANCHES/DEPTS.
A. INTERLIBRARY LOANS		
Number of Items Borrowed or Received per Year		
Number of Items Loaned or Sent per Year		
B. INTRA-SYSTEM LOANS		
Number Processed per Year		
C. COPYING MACHINES OPERATED BY OR FOR LIBRARY STAFF		
Number of Xerox-type Photocopying Machines		
Number of Microform Cameras or Duplicators		
Number of Microform Reader/Printers		
Number of Facsimile Transmission Sender/Printers		
D. COPYING MACHINES NOT LISTED IN ITEM C WHICH ARE LOCATED IN THE LIBRARY AND MAY BE USED BY PERSONS OTHER THAN LIBRARY STAFF TO COPY LIBRARY MATERIALS		
Number of Xerox-type Photocopying Machines		
Number of Microform Cameras or Duplicators		
Number of Microform Reader/Printers		
Number of Facsimile Transmission Sender/Printers		
E. AVERAGE NUMBER OF EXPOSURES PER WEEK		
Number of Exposures on All Photocopying Equipment Listed in Item C (staff-operated copiers)		
Number of Exposures on All Photocopying Equipment Listed in Item D (other copying machines)		

THANK YOU FOR YOUR HELP

2. ILL Borrowing Form

☐☐☐☐ Date__________

NCLIS PHOTOCOPYING CHARACTERISTICS STUDY

ILL BORROWING FORM

Complete this form <u>for serial ILL requests only</u>

King Research, Inc.
Rockville, Maryland
OMB No. 186-S-76003
Expires March 1977

THIS SECTION SHOULD BE COMPLETED BY THE REQUESTOR

Requestor:

Faculty	1
Student	2
Other individual	3
Library	4
Other institution	5

Purpose of Request:

Replacement	1
Class use	2
Personal use	3
Other	4

Year of Publication ☐

Publisher:

Domestic	1
Foreign	2

Number of Pages in Article ☐
Number of Copies Requested ☐

THIS SECTION SHOULD BE COMPLETED BY THE BORROWING LIBRARY

Disposition:

Filled/original	1
Filled/photocopy	2
Unfilled	3
Still in process	4

Lending Library:
(if request is filled)

Academic library	1
Federal library	2
Public library	3
School library	4
For-profit special library	5
Other special library	6
Type of library unknown	7

NAME OF SERIAL ______________________

ISSN ☐

3. ILL Borrowing Form Instuctions

INSTRUCTIONS FOR COMPLETING ILL BORROWING FORM

Please complete this form whenever serial material is to be borrowed from another library through the Interlibrary Loan System. One ILL Borrowing Form should be completed for each serial ILL request ______________________.

1. **When a patron makes a request for serial material, please ask him to complete the left side of the form by circling the appropriate numerical codes to indicate:**

   -- **his status, i.e., is he a teacher or student; does he represent a library or some other institution.**

   -- **the purpose for which he is requesting the material.**

   -- **the year of publication of the serial.**

   -- **whether the publisher is foreign or domestic. If both, indicate domestic.**

   -- **the number of pages in the requested material.**

   -- the number of copies of the material requested, e.g., if 5 copies are requested of a 10-page article (a total of 50 pages) the number of copies should be recorded here as <u>5</u>.

2. **After the left side of the form has been completed by the patron, attach the form to your file copy of the standard ILL request form.**

3. When the ILL request form is returned by the lending library, either with the material requested or with an indication as to why the material was not sent, pull the appropriate file copy with its attached ILL Borrowing Form. Detach the ILL Borrowing Form and complete the second column by circling:

   - the disposition of the request
   - the appropriate code for lending library type

   Academic - *College and university libraries*

   Federal - *Libraries of federal agencies (do not include libraries in universities or private research firms that are funded by federal contract)*

   School - *Libraries affiliated with schools other than colleges and universities*

   Special - *All other libraries (Circle "5" only if you know that the library is associated with a profit-making organization. Circle "6" for all other special libraries.)*

   The form is now ready for return to King Research, Inc.

4. On ____________________, pull from your file any remaining ILL Borrowing Forms and circle the Disposition code for "still in process". Add these forms to those already completed and return to KRI.

4. Characteristics Form and Instructions

King Research, Inc.
Rockville, Maryland
OMB No. 186-S-76003
Expires March 1977

☐☐☐☐ Date________________

NCLIS PHOTOCOPYING CHARACTERISTICS STUDY
CHARACTERISTICS FORM

PART I. FILL OUT FOR ALL COPYING OF LIBRARY MATERIALS

Type of Item

1 - Book 2 - Serial 3 - Other

Interlibrary Loan?

1 - Yes 2 - No

Copyrighted?

1 - Yes 2 - No 3 - Unknown

Intra-system Loan?

1 - Yes 2 - No

Year of Copyright ☐

Number of Pages ☐

Number of Copies ☐

PART II. FILL OUT THIS SECTION FOR COPYING OF COPYRIGHTED SERIALS ONLY

Serial Title________________________________

Name of Copyright Holder________________________________

Is Copyright Holder: Domestic - 1 Foreign - 2

ISSN ☐

Volume [ ] Issue [ ] Mo./Day/Year [| |] First Page [ ]

FILL OUT FOR INTERLIBRARY LOANS

Source of Request:

Academic library	1
Federal library	2
Public library	3
School library	4
For-profit special library	5
Other special library	6
Type of library unknown	7

FILL OUT FOR ALL OTHER COPYING

Source of Request:

Individual/institution	1
Internal/library staff	2
Unknown	3

Purpose of Request:

Replacement by library	1
Classroom use by faculty	2
Other	3
Unknown	4

OFFICE USE ONLY: Library Code [ ] Publisher Code [ ]

212

6. Volume Log

[| | |]

King Research, Inc.
Rockville, Md.
September 1976
OMB No. 186-S-76003
Expires March 1977

NCLIS PHOTOCOPYING CHARACTERISTICS STUDY

VOLUME LOG

Type of Photocopier ____________________

Manufacturer ____________________ Model Number_____

Date ____________________

Type of Library Material			Copyright			Library Loans		Number of Pages	Number of Copies
Book	Serial	Other	Year of Copr.	No Copr.	Don't Know	Inter-lib	Intra-system		

After the last transaction of the day is completed, please record the total number of exposures made on <u>this</u> photocopying machine. Include <u>all</u> copies made during the day.

TOTAL NUMBER OF EXPOSURES [ ]

7. Volume Log Instructions

INSTRUCTIONS FOR COMPLETING THE VOLUME LOG

For the period ________________, keep a copy of the Volume Log next to each photocopying machine used by or for library staff. Please record on the log each photocopying transaction involving library materials which takes place on that machine during the time specified.

Fill out one line of the form for each transaction, i.e., each photocopy request for a page or series of pages from one publication. If more than one series of pages from different articles is requested, record each series as a separate transaction. Record separate articles within the same publication as separate transactions. Remember to include only copying of library controlled materials done by or for library staff.

As was mentioned in the letter which accompanied these materials, you will be filling out the Characteristics Form for a short part of the data collection period. During the time you are scheduled to record transaction information on the Characteristics Form, do not use the Volume Log.

Identification Information -- Record the type of photocopier, e.g., Xerox-type machine, microfilm camera, etc.; the manufacturer; and the model number. Then, enter the date for which you are recording photocopying transactions. Please begin a new log sheet each morning even if there is space on the Volume Log of the preceding day.

Type of Material -- Under the heading "Type of Material", make a check mark (✓) in the appropriate column to show the type of library material being copied. Make a check mark in the first column to indicate a book or monograph; check the second column to show that the material requested is part of a serial publication; and check the third column to indicate any other type of library controlled material. The following definitions apply.

Book - Include monographs and any other items that are treated as books. This category also includes serial publications which appear annually or less frequently, e.g., annual reviews and other similar publications.

Serial - A publication issued in successive parts bearing numerical or chronological designations, which is intended to be continued indefinitely and which may be identified by an ISSN (International Standard Serial Number). Serials include periodicals, newspapers, and the journals, memoirs, proceedings, transactions, etc. of societies. Serials are subject to subscription prices paid in advance. (This eliminates publications that appear annually or less frequently.)

Other - Any other type of library controlled material, e.g., technical reports, photographs, etc.

Exceptions: Sheet music is a special exception. Information for any transactions involving sheet music should not be recorded on the Volume Log. Also excluded from this category are memos, forms, cataloging cards, etc. These are not considered library materials and should not be recorded on the Volume Log.

Copyright -- In books or monographs, the copyright usually appears on the reverse of the title page. In serials, check: (1) the owner of publisher's statement on the reverse of the title page; (2) the list of publishers or authors; or, (3) the first page of the article being copied. The copyright may be indicated in various ways (e.g., ©, copyr. or copyright) but it should always include the year and the name of the publisher or publishing society, or other copyright holder, e.g., © 1975 Name of Publisher; or Copr. 1948 Name of Publishing Society.

Under the heading, "Copyright", write the year of the copyright in the first column for any type of copyrighted material. If no copyright information is given, make a check mark (✓) in the second column to show that the material probably is not copyrighted. Make a check mark (✓) in the third column if it is impossible to tell whether or not the material is copyrighted because the cover, contents page, etc. is missing as when they have been removed in the binding process.

(Over)

Library Loans -- Under the heading "Library Loans", make a check mark (✓) in the first column under "ILL" (Interlibrary Loan) if the material has been requested as an Interlibrary Loan by a library outside your library system. Make a check mark (✓) in the second column under "ISL" (Intra-system Loan) if the material was requested by branch or department library within your library system.

Number of Pages -- Record the number of pages of original being copied.

Number of Copies -- Record the number of copies provided. For ex mple, if five copies of a 10-page article are provided (a total of 50 pages), enter "5" as the number of copies made.

Total Number of Exposures -- At the end of each day, please record the total number of exposures that were made on that machine on that day. Include all copies even if they did not involve the reproduction of library material. This information should be recorded on the last sheet of the Volume Log filled out for that particular machine on that date.

8. Copyright Royalty Library Survey Questionnaire

King Research, Inc.
6110 Executive Blvd.
Rockville, Md. 20852
(301) 881-6766

COPYRIGHT ROYALTY
LIBRARY SURVEY

OMb
186-
Expires:

ID# ☐☐☐☐

The purpose of this survey is to help in estimating what the impact might be on libraries of various arrangements for making royalty payments for the photocopying of copyrighted serial articles. Most of the questions concern background information related to interlibrary loan (ILL) or photocopying operations, or possible cost implications for these operations of participating in a royalty payment mechanism of some sort.

Some of the questions (4,5,6,7,8,9,10, & 11) would benefit from being answered by an individual responsible for setting or stating library policy. Remaining questions deal with important cost and volume data which will be used to help assess impacts of possible royalty payment mechanisms. Please insert below the names, titles, and telephone numbers of individuals whom we might contact if any questions arise about interpretation of responses:

Name	Title	Telephone
• ____________	____________	( ) ________
• ____________	____________	( ) ________
• ____________	____________	( ) ________

• Name of Library: ______________________

In answering questions, please try to adhere to the following definitions:

LIBRARY - this term includes both the central library/headquarters and the branch libraries/departments of your library, library system, or archives.

PAPER-TO-PAPER PHOTOCOPYING MACHINES - machines used to make duplicate copies of paper originals, such as Xerox, Olivetti, and IBM copiers.

PATRONS - refers to individuals who use or contact your library in person or by telephone. Patrons may or may not be employed by or associated with your library's parent institution.

EXPOSURES - refers to the number of sheets of paper produced by paper-to-paper photocopying machines when materials are being duplicated.

UNSUPERVISED - refers to photocopying machines within your library which may be used by patrons without copying assistance of library staff. Usually includes coin-operated machines.

SERIAL - A publication issued in successive parts bearing numerical or chronological designations, which is intended to be continued indefinitely and which may be identified by an ISSN (International Standard Serial Number). Serials include periodicals, newspapers, and the journals, memoirs, proceedings, transactions, etc. of societies. Serials are subject to subscription prices paid in advance. (This eliminates publications that appear annually or less frequently.)

BOOK - Include monographs and any other items that are treated as books. This category also includes serial publications which appear annually or less frequently, e.g., annual reviews and other similar publications.

CALENDAR YEAR - January through December

ROYALTY - a payment made to a copyright owner to help compensate for library photocopying of copyrighted serial articles.

MULTIPLE COPIES - more than 5 copies from the same serial title either made for local patrons by or for your library staff or received by your library in response to an ILL request.

ILL REQUEST FILE - any file or other collection of data, arranged in any filing order, for keeping track of incoming or outgoing ILL requests.

ONE-TIME COSTS - labor or non-labor costs incurred only once at the initiation of a project or activity.

RECURRING COSTS - labor or non-labor costs incurred on a regular basis, following initiation of a project or activity.

AVERAGE MONTHLY BASIS - average monthly cost based on (a) annual cost divided by 12 or (b) costs for an "average" month as determined by library management.

1. What is the TOTAL number of paper-to-paper photocopying machines operated by or in your library? (Insert zero (0) if none)

   (a) in central library or headquarters . . . . . _______ (17-19)

   (b) all other branches/departments of library . . _______ (20-22)

   (c) TOTAL (a + b) . . . . _______ (23-25)

   (d) What is the total annual volume of exposures made on all of these machines? . . . . _______ (26-32)

2. How many of the machines reported in (1) above are regularly (at least once per week) used by or for library staff *or patrons* for copying library materials? (Exclude machines used exclusively for office-type copying such as correspondence, catalog cards, etc. Insert zero (0) if none)

   (a) in central library or headquarters . . . . . _______ (33-35)

   (b) all other branches/departments of library . . _______ (36-38)

   (c) TOTAL (a + b) . . . . _______ (39-41)

   (d) What is the total annual volume of exposures made on these machines? . . . . _______ (42-48)

3. How many of the machines reported in (2) above are used exclusively by library patrons for the unsupervised copying of library materials? (By "unsupervised" is meant that patrons may operate the machines without the direct permission or assistance of library staff, as in the case of patron-operated coin machines).

(a) in central library or headquarters . . . . ______ (49-51)

(b) all other branches/departments of library . . . . . ______ (52-54)

(c) TOTAL (a + b) . . . . ______ (55-57)

(d) What is the total annual volume of exposures made on these machines used exclusively by library patrons? . . . ______ (58-64)

4. In addition to your library's photocopying machines, are there any paper-to-paper photocopying machines operated within *other* local offices or departments of your parent institution or company? (Circle 1, 2, or 3. Use 3 if you are an independent library without a parent institution or company)

Yes . . . . 1 (Go to Q. 5)

No . . . . 2 (Skip to Q. 6) (65-66)

Not Applicable . . . . . . 3 (Skip to Q. 6)

5. To the best of your knowledge, is the volume of exposures made of *copyrighted books and serials* on these other machines greater than, less than or about the same as the volume of exposures of copyrighted books and serials made on all library staff- and user-operated machines? (Circle appropriate response)

Greater than 1

Less than 2 (67-68)

About the same 3

Don't know 4

6. According to guidelines issued by the Commission on New Technological Uses of Copyright (CONTU), responsibility for interlibrary loan (ILL) photocopying of copyrighted serial articles will belong to the requesting library when the new Copyright Law goes into effect January 1, 1978. This responsibility might include payment of royalty fees to copyright owners for serial article photocopies which are not exempt from payment.

Were your library to determine the following royalty exemption category for each serial article photocopy requested or received via ILL on a regular basis, would your library incur any extra costs which your budget would be unable to absorb without obtaining additional staff or funding? (Please circle 1 (Yes) or 2 (No) for each item.)

Category	Extra Costs? Yes	No	
(a) To determine if your library has a current subscription (or one on order) for a title which is still being published at the time you make the ILL request	1	2	(69-70)
(b) To determine if your library has already requested a photocopy from this same serial title via ILL at any time during the current calendar year	1	2	(71-72)
(c) To determine if the requested article will be used for scholarly research by a teacher in a not-for-profit educational institution	1	2	(73-74)
(d) To determine if the requested article will be used for classroom purposes by a teacher in a not-for-profit educational institution	1	2	(75-76)

[ ] (77-79)

[1] (80)

[Dup.] (1-6)

7. For the photocopying of copyrighted serial articles made by or for your library staff for your local patrons, would regular determination of the following categories result in your library incurring any extra costs which your budget would be unable to absorb without obtaining additional staff or funding? (Please exclude from consideration photocopies of copyrighted serial articles which your library makes for or receives via interlibrary loan (ILL). (Please circle 1 (Yes) or 2 (No) for each item.)

Category	Extra Costs? Yes	No	
(a) To determine if your library has a current subscription (or one on order) for a title which is still being published at the time you process the request	1	2	(7-8)
(b) To determine if your library has already made a photocopy from this same serial title for a local patron at any time during the current calendar year	1	2	(9-10)
(c) To determine if the requested article will be used for scholarly research by a teacher in a not-for-profit educational institution	1	2	(11-12)
(d) To determine if the requested article will be used for classroom purposes by a teacher in a not-for-profit educational institution	1	2	(13-14)

8. What are your library's relative preferences for the following mechanisms for making royalty payments for photocopying of copyrighted serial articles? Assume that each alternative would result in the same amount being paid by your library for royalties, and rank the alternatives from 1 to 8, with 1 = MOST PREFERRED and 8 = LEAST PREFERRED. (PLEASE READ ALL ALTERNATIVES BEFORE RANKING THEM.)

ALTERNATIVE ROYALTY PAYMENT MECHANISMS	RANK	
(a) Libraries would agree to purchase multiple copies or reprints of serial articles directly from the serial publisher or their agents		(15-16)
(b) Libraries would pay an optional extra subscription price for those serials from which multiple copies would be made		(17-18)
(c) Libraries would pay a fee for each photocopying machine to a central agency, which would then distribute these payments as royalties to copyright owners		(19-20)
(d) Payment for copyright royalties would be made by libraries to individual publishers, requiring a tally to be kept by libraries for multiple copies of affected serial titles		(21-22)
(e) Payment for copyright royalties would be made by libraries to a centralized agency which would have the responsibility for making a count of individual libraries' photocopies and for transmitting payments to publishers		(23-24)
(f) Libraries would agree to purchase multiple copies or reprints of serial articles from a centralized agency authorized or designated by publishers which would then distribute copyright royalties. . .		(25-26)
(g) Libraries would purchase "royalty stamps" or coupons from a centralized agency which would then be affixed to multiple copies of a copyrighted serial article		(27-28)

(h) All subscription prices would be higher, automatically giving libraries permission to make multiple copies . . . . [ ] (29-30)

9. Assume that your library would be required to check each outgoing serial interlibrary loan (ILL) request to see if you had already requested, during the current calendar year, any articles from the last five years' issues of that same title. Do you think that this would require you to substantially restructure or rearrange your ILL request file (or begin a file of some sort) to facilitate this checking procedure? (Circle 1 or 2)

   Yes . . . . 1 (Go to Q. 10)
   No . . . . 2 (Skip to Q. 11) (31-32)
   Not Applicable . . . . 3 (Skip to Q. 11)

10. **What would be the one-time cost to your library of restructuring or starting this file? (Please round estimate to nearest dollar; insert zero (0) if none)**

   (a) One-time direct labor cost . . . . $_________ (33-38)
   (b) One-time materials cost . . . . $_________ (39-44)
   (c) Could your library absorb this cost without obtaining additional staff or funding?

   Yes 1
   No 2 (45-46)
   Don't Know 3

11. How much, on an average monthly basis, do you estimate it would cost your library to perform this checking procedure for outgoing interlibrary serial article requests? (Please round to nearest dollar; insert zero (0) if none)

   (a) Recurring direct labor costs . . . . $_________ (47-52)
   (b) Recurring materials costs . . . . $_________ (53-58)
   (c) Could your library absorb this cost without obtaining additional staff or funding?

   Yes 1
   No 2 (59-60)
   Don't Know 3

   [ ] (61-79)

   [2] (80)

   [Dup.] (1-6)

12. On an average monthly basis, how much do interlibrary loan operations cost your library? ("Interlibrary loan operations" includes: making and receiving requests; locating and verifying requests; and associated recordkeeping and billing operations. Exclude your photocopying labor and nonlabor costs. Please round to nearest dollar; insert zero (0) if none)

   (a) Labor (professional and other) . . . .$_________ (7-13)
   (b) Materials (wrapping, mailing bags, forms, etc.) . . _________ (14-17)
   (c) Postage . . . . _________ (18-21)
   (d) Other communication costs (e.g., telephone, teletype) _________ (22-25)
   (e) Photocopying and ILL fees paid to other libraries _________ (26-29)

(f) Other (Describe): ______________________ . . ________ (30-33)

(g) TOTAL . . . . $________ (34-39)

13. If your library receives a subsidy or grant for participation in an interlibrary loan network, please insert the portion of the subsidy or grant applied to cover ILL costs on an annual basis. (Please round to nearest dollar; insert zero (0) if none) . . . . $________ (40-45)
annually

14. On an average monthly basis, what is your library's cost for operating and maintaining all the paper-to-paper photocopying machines for which it is responsible? (Include only the costs which the library pays. Please round to nearest dollar; insert zero (0) for none)

(a) Monthly rental or lease cost . . . . $________ (46-51)

(b) Supplies (paper, toner, chemicals, parts, etc.) ________ (52-55)

(c) Monthly maintenance contract or fees . . . . . . ________ (56-59)

(d) Monthly staff costs for operation or maintenance of photocopying machines/photocopying dept. . . . . ________ (60-63)

(e) Other monthly costs for which library pays . . . ________ (64-67)

(f) TOTAL . . . . $________ (68-71)

15. Please insert the total purchase costs if you purchased any paper-to-paper photocopying machines during the last twelve months. (Please round to nearest dollar; insert zero (0) if none) . . . . . . $________ (72-77)

16. On an average monthly basis, how much gross income or fees does your library obtain from your photocopying and interlibrary loan operations? (Please round to nearest dollar; insert zero (0) if none)

[ ] (78-79)
[3] (80)
[Dup.] (1-6)

(a) Photocopying income/fees . . . . $________ (7-10)

(b) ILL income/fees . . . . $________ (11-14)

(c) TOTAL . . . . $________ (15-18)

17. Please describe your interlibrary loan request volume for calendar year 1976. (Please use zero (0) if none)

		Serials	Books	Other	Total	
(a) Requests <u>made</u> by your library	Total	(1)_____	(2)_____	(3)_____	(4)_____	(19-42)
	Filled	(5)_____	(6)_____	(7)_____	(8)_____	(43-66)

[ ] (67-79)
[4] (80)
[Dup.] (1-6)

		Serials	Books	Other	Total	
(b) Requests <u>received</u> by your library	Total	(1)_____	(2)_____	(3)_____	(4)_____	(7-30)
	Filled	(5)_____	(6)_____	(7)_____	(8)_____	(31-54)

18. To assist in our analysis, we also need the following information:

(a) Total number of serial *titles* which you currently receive (excluding government publications) ________ (55-60)

(b) Total number of serial *subscriptions* which you currently receive (excluding government publications) . . . . ________ (61-67)

(c) Current year's actual or projected acquisition budget for serials (exclude binding and round to nearest dollar) . . . . $________ (68-74)

(d) Total number of full-time equivalent (FTE) staff members (include both professional and other; please round to nearest unit) . . . . . ________ (75-78)

[ ] (79)

[5] (80)

19. Please use the space below to make additional comments:

Thank you. Please Return this Questionnaire to:

King Research, Inc.
6110 Executive Blvd.
Rockville, Md. 20852

APPENDIX B

SURVEY OF LIBRARY PHOTOCOPYING: METHOD

Population

In order to collect information on library photocopying, a sample of libraries was selected, representing the major types of libraries. The populations of Public and Academic Libraries as defined by the National Center for Education Statistics were used for those types. The population of Federal Libraries was based on the 1972 Federal Library Survey, a 1976 directory of Army Libraries, and update information provided by the 1975 edition of Library and Reference Facilities in the Area of the District of Columbia (ASIS) and by the members of the Advisory Committee to the project. For Special Libraries, the American Library Directory and Gale's Directory of Special Libraries and Information Centers were primary frames for sampling. The membership directory of the Special Libraries Association was used as a supplemental source list.

Sampling and Data Collection

The sample of libraries for collections of data on the volume and characteristics of photocopies of library materials made on library staff-controlled equipment was a stratified random selection representing the five categories of libraries: Academic, Public, Federal, Special associated with profit-seeking organizations, and special libraries associated with not-for-profit organizations. The target minimum number of participating libraries by type were: 100 Academic, 100 Public, 62 Federal, 74 Profit associated, 34 Non-profit associated. These target numbers were based in part on the estimated volumes of interlibrary lending for 1972, the most recent year for which comprehensive data could be assembled at the time. This was based on the expectation that most photocopying in libraries is for ILL purposes.

Large libraries and some with unique characteristics were included in the sample with certainty, to represent themselves. The remaining libraries of each type were stratified by significant variables to facilitate selection of a representative sample from which to estimate totals for the non-certainty libraries. Academic libraries were stratified by size (measured by volumes in collection) and type of institution (University, four year, two year). Public libraries were stratified by population served and by region. Federal libraries were stratified by agency and by volume of interlibrary loans. Special libraries were stratified by size. Participation was invited from a sample larger than the minimum target number, so that ineligible libraries, refusals, and nonresponse would not disrupt the very tight time table.

In order to avoid excessive burden on any library, short sample periods were specified for collecting each major category of information. Each library was asked to record and report information on photocopying volumes for a sample period, to describe characteristics of library materials photocopied for selected days, and to report on requests made during a specified period for interlibrary loans - and on the disposition of those requests. These sample periods ranged from one day to three weeks, and were specified in light of volume reported on a preliminary screener form.

Subsequently, participating libraries were also asked to respond to a questionnaire which addressed questions of costs of photocopying operations, preferences among possible royalty payment mechanisms, judgments concerning relative costs of hypothetical recordkeeping procedures, and a few volume items. Thus, the data collection from libraries involved an initial screener inquiry and four separate, but closely related, requests for information.

In addition, the time limitation on the project did not permit data collection to be spread throughout the year. Therefore, it was important to find adjustment factors to correct for the difference between periods (days of the week and months of the year) when data were collected and the average activity over the year. Such adjustment weights were derived in the course of an analysis of interlibrary loan data for the MINITEX system for the year 1976.

Data was collected on all photocopying of library materials on library staff-controlled equipment, including both copies made for interlibrary loan purposes and copies made for local patron or in-house use. A preliminary screener form collected information on annual volumes and types of equipment. A "Transaction Log" was used to record volume data for the sample period on all pertinent transactions, and a characteristics form was completed with additional information about a subset of the serial photocopies made. Purpose of request information for interlibrary loans was collected for a relatively small sample of ILL borrowing requests made by the sample libraries.

Among the data elements identified are the number of photocopying transactions; number of photocopies made; type of material copied; copyright status of the material; and, for journals, the title, copyright holder, date of publication, source of request, purpose of request, and (for requests to borrow) publisher (domestic or foreign), disposition of request and lending library if filled.

Response

The first solicitation to libraries designated for inclusion in the sample and for alternates was a "screener" form. Follow-up letters were mailed to all addressees that did not respond. The response was good for Public and Academic libraries (See Table B.1, Response Statistics). Roughly one-fourth of Federal libraries did not respond, and another one-fourth were found to be now ineligible or to do "no copying". Federal library activity is highly skewed, dominated by the national libraries. Hence KRI opted to emphasize special data collection arrangements with the largest libraries in order to ensure coverage of those certainty libraries. Among Special libraries the response to the original mailing was disappointing, leading to a decision to select and mail to a supplemental sample of 56 Special libraries. In the two mailings, 209 Special libraries were addressed, of which 49 refused or did not respond, 18 reported they did no copying, 39 responded and were found ineligible; and 100 quantitative responses to the screener were received.

Days for data collection for volume, for characteristics, and for purpose of requests were assigned to each library which provided a screener, based on the information reported therein. Volume logs, forms to record characteristics of library materials photocopied, and interlibrary loan forms for serials borrowed were then transmitted to each library which had answered the screener. At this stage, additional refusals and nonresponses occurred. Almost exactly 300 libraries reported on volume of photocopying and on the characteristics of materials copied, plus 44 reports of "no copying," as compared with the combined target of 370. Academic libraries reported very conscientiously on borrowings, but in each of the other library types, a significant number of libraries did not report on borrowings.

Table B 1 RESPONSE STATISTICS (NUMBERS OF LIBRARIES)

Survey Category	Type of Library				
	Public	Academic	Federal	Special	Combined
1. Target Sample Size	100	100	62	108[a/]	370
2. Original Mailing	145	164	77	153	539
3. Supplemental Mailing	0	0	0	56	56
4. Reported Ineligible (closed etc.)	1	0	9	39	46
5. Reports of "No Copying"	8	3	12	21	44
6. Substantive Responses to "Screener"	117	142	39	100	398
7. Panel Reporting Volume	96	115	29	61	301
8. Panel Reporting Characteristics	95	115	30	59	299
9. Panel Responding on ILL borrowings	78	118	25	50	271
a. Zero borrowings	35	16	5	17	73
b. Non-zero borrowings	43	102	20	33	198
10. Gross Non-Returns to Screener	19	19	17	49	104
11. Imputed Ineligible and "No Copying" among nonrespondents $\left[\text{Line 10 X } \frac{\text{(Line 4 \& Line 5)}}{\text{(Line 4 \& Line 5 \& Line 6)}}\right]$	1	0	6	18	25
12. Gross Non-Returns to Volume Q	21	27	10	39	97
13. Estimated Net Non-Response to Volume Q (Line 12 - Line 11)	20	27	4	21	72
14. Estimated Rate of Net Non-Response to Volume Q $100\left[\frac{\text{Line 13}}{\text{Line 7 \& Line 13}}\right]$	17	19	12	26	19
15. Estimated Rate of Net Non-Response on Borrowings (%) $100\left[\frac{\text{Line 9}}{\text{Line 7 \& Line 13}}\right]$	33	17	24	39	27

a/ This sample size is the sum of the allocations originally made with a view to the possible need for separate estimates for special libraries associated with profit- seeking organizations and non-profit special libraries. The smaller response actually attained supports estimates for special libraries as a whole, subject to qualifications described in the text.

Estimation

Estimates have been prepared by straightforward weighting up of sample observations corresponding to the probability of selection, the extent of nonresponse, and adjustments for the days of week and month of the year. The latter two adjustment factors were specific to the individual library. Nonresponse was computed by stratum within type of library, after taking out certain special cases for which tailored sampling and collection procedures were necessary for four very large libraries.

The estimates thus constructed are valid, with sampling variability, under certain "as if" conditions. Each estimate is valid if the reporting libraries' activities during the reporting intervals are in fact representative of all libraries in the population over the year. The sources of differences are in principle: (a) library population vs. library sample design; (b) library sample specified vs. panel of libraries which responded; (c) intervals in which data was collected vs. full year of activity; (d) data as interpreted from reports received and processed vs. activity which in fact occurred. Each possible "source of difference" calls for a corresponding qualification on the estimates.

The library sample was selected in such a way as to represent, on a stratified basis, the libraries in the sampling frame. As described earlier, the frames were updated to some extent, in particular those for Federal libraries and Special libraries. No LIBGIS-type collection has heretofore been done for Special libraries. The population is amorphous and ill-defined: both ALD and Gale's have inclusions of non-libraries and omissions of special libraries. To the extent there are Special Libraries omitted from all of the sources used, the estimates for Special libraries necessarily understate the activity. "Deaths", i.e., libraries no longer active, constitute a special problem. They have been estimated from the returns to the screener form mailed to the designated sample. Returns identified as inactive or merged into other libraries were used as a basis for estimating adjustments to the estimated population size by type of library. These were insignificant adjustments for Public and Academic libraries, and were substantial for Federal and Special. In summary, KRI's judgment is that the net effect on the estimates from source of difference (a) is probably small.

The second potential source of difference is that the average magnitude and characteristics of reporting libraries might be different from those not reporting. This has two aspects: the proportion of libraries having no photocopying, and amount and characteristics of photocopying by libraries which do so. Libraries which did not reply to the screener may in some cases have been libraries without photocopying who felt the survey simply didn't apply to them: "that they had nothing to tell us." If these are in the same proportion to all non-returns as the number reporting "no copying" to the total number of respondents, the estimates made are not thereby distorted. To the extent that a larger proportion of non-returns are in fact "no copying" libraries than we have estimated on the basis of the returns received, the aggregates estimated in the study are over-stated. Specifically, the effect of a probably extreme difference: that the rate of "no copying" libraries among nonrespondents to the screener was double the rate reported among respondents, on the estimated number of libraries with copying, (all four types combined) would be to reduce the number of libraries with photocopying by approximately 2%, and each of the other estimated aggregates by the same proportion.

The other aspect of potential bias from non-response is the possible differences in volumes and characteristics of photocopying of nonrespondents from those of respondents. Some libraries may have refused, feeling the size of their photocopying operations would entail a burden or some perceived legal risk which they chose to try to avoid. Libraries which returned screener data and then refused or failed to respond to the volume and/or characteristics surveys may have been motivated primarily by concerns about the work involved in completing the project. To assess the possible effects of this potential bias, if the 20% (net) of nonrespondents were to have on the average as much as 25% greater volume in any one category as the average responding library, then the estimates for that category presented herein would be understated by 5%; if they had 50% more, the corresponding understatement in their estimate would be 9%; if 100% more, the understatement would be 17%.

For the interlibrary borrowing project, one further consideration enters. The ILL form calls for information on disposition, so the library was required to retain the form for days or weeks, in order to complete it on an individual transaction. Distraction of attention over a period of time is inevitable, which may well explain the smaller number of reporting libraries for that survey. Incomplete reporting could easily occur on the part of other libraries, too, if "stragglers", held for request replies, finally are misplaced or not remembered. Speculatively, the libraries which reported on volume and characteristics, but not on borrowings, may tend to be smaller in average borrowings (therefore not having formal recordkeeping for them) than the libraries which reported on borrowings. If so, the estimates herein would be overstated. However, more than 80% of this panel reporting on volume reported on borrowings. If the nonrespondents had only one-half the number of borrowings on the average as those reporting on borrowing, the overstatement from this source would be 11%. Any incompleteness of reporting would tend to affect the estimate in the opposite direction.

The third source of difference is between the "seasonal" and "day of week" adjustments applied and the actual experience of the libraries nationally. The factors applied were derived from MINITEX libraries requests for interlibrary loans for a year, so the question becomes: How different may MINITEX libraries' ILL requests be from those of the rest of the libraries in the country, and how different may volume of photocopying patterns be from ILL request patterns? No other evidence is known to us on which to base a judgment. However, the straightforward inflation by the number of days in the year related to the number of days reported would be a defensible estimator. The correction factors provide a refinement, and alternative values of the factors would likely not have a consistent effect in the same direction, since collection occurred from October through April. KRI judgment is that this source of possible difference probably may have small effect for Public and Academic libraries, and possibly moderate effect for Federal and Special libraries (which are not numerous in MINITEX).

The fourth potential source of difference includes all the possible kinds of errors in interpretation of the information requests by libraries and all the mistakes in understanding and processing reported data. The conduct of the surveys included safeguards intended to minimize these problems. However, there is no evidence on which to judge what the residual error might be. An independent reliability and validity study would be necessary to provide such evidence. Time-interval sampling is probably the operational aspect of the study with the greatest potential for differences. It has been found that on verification calls to sample libraries a month or more after the sampling, the library staff involved typically are not able to reconstruct from memory and records the precise periods sampled. Thus, for future studies of this type, quality checks or R&V analysis should be conducted concurrent with basic data collection.

In summary, the main photocopying survey is believed to provide a good baseline representation of 1976-77 photocopying in libraries. Considerations of sampling variability as well as sources of possible systematic differences point to the borrowings data as subject to greater caution (as having potentially larger relative errors) than the volume and characteristics data. Similarly, estimates for Special libraries and to somewhat lesser extent for Federal libraries are subject to greater qualifications than those for Public and Academic libraries.

Standard Errors

Tables B.2 and B.3 present the standard errors of the estimates of the total number of photocopy items requested for local users and requested for interlibrary loan. These are presented separately for all domestic photocopy items, photocopy items under six years old and not for replacement or classroom use, and for greater than 5 copies.

Table B.2 STANDARD ERRORS OF TOTALS OF NUMBER OF PHOTOCOPY ITEMS REQUESTED FOR LOCAL USERS

(Thousands of Photocopy Items)

Type of Borrowing Library	All Domestic Photocopy Items		Under 6 Years		Under 6 Years and Greater Than 5 Copies	
	Size of Estimate	Estimated Standard Error	Size of Estimate	Estimated Standard Error	Size of Estimate	Estimated Standard Error
Public	7,383	3,739	5,930	2,789	5,520	2,773
Academic	1,758	1,402	1,060	973	1,040	822
Special	7,933	2,187	6,360	1,175	4,960	1,364
Federal	1,958	598	1,590	86	1,570	478
Total	19,032	3,424	14,940	3,054	12,880	1,849

Table B.3 STANDARD ERRORS OF TOTALS OF NUMBER OF PHOTOCOPY ITEMS REQUESTED FOR INTERLIBRARY LOAN

(Thousands of Photocopy Items)

Type of Borrowing Library	All Domestic Photocopy Items		Under Six Years and Not For Replacement Or Classroom Use		Under Six Years, Not Replacement or Classroom Use, & Greater Than 5 Copies	
	Size of Estimate	Estimated Standard Error	Size of Estimate	Estimated Standard Error	Size of Estimate	Estimated Standard Error
Public	1,010	155	440	116	90	10
Academic	1,130	128	430	98	140	12
Special	1,250	539	830	342	220	62
Federal	380	12	260	62	55	9
Total	3,770	580	1,960	379	505	49

APPENDIX C

AN ANALYSIS TO PROVIDE ESTIMATES OF THE DISTRIBUTION OF PHOTOCOPYING BY SERIAL TITLES

The CONTU guidelines, while making an important contribution to interpretation of the Copyright Law, created some statistical estimation problems unanticipated at the beginning of the project. The guidelines suggest that, for interlibrary loans, photocopy items be considered eligible for royalty payment only when six or more photocopy items are made for a given serial publication within a one year period. This rule applies after other fair use exemptions are excluded. This presents a difficult estimation problem since it is necessary to estimate the distribution of photocopying as well as totals and averages from a sample over time as well as libraries. Estimates of the volume of photocopying are based on observing the amount of photocopying that takes place over a designated period of time (say, one to three weeks) from a sample of libraries chosen from a population of 21,280 libraries in the United States. By observing the number of photocopy items that are made over one week, one can estimate the amount that the library makes in one year (considering seasonal variation and day of the week effects). By properly weighting the libraries in the sample, the total photocopying can be estimated for the 21,280 libraries in the population.

However, this relatively simple approach cannot be taken in estimating the distribution of photocopying. The problem is, for example, that if we observe in a library that twenty serial titles have fewer than six photocopy items made over a period of one week, it is not valid to project the twenty titles by 52 nor is it correct to project the number of photocopy items observed under six copies by a factor of 52. In order to make an estimate of the number of titles and photocopy items under six photocopy items over a year, it is necessary to estimate the entire distribution of photocopy items. That is, the proportion of titles having 1, 2, 3 -- and so on photocopy items over the sample period must be determined and this distribution then projected to the entire year. If this can be done, the estimate of the number of photocopy items under six observed in the sample of libraries can then be projected to the entire population of libraries.

A second major estimation problem is that it is useful to estimate the average number of eligible photocopy items that exist over all libraries for individual serial titles. The problem is that the principal sampling unit is not a serial title. As the number of sample libraries is increased, the number of serial titles observed in the sample also increases. The increase in the number of titles is not proportionate to the increase in sample size, however, since there is considerable overlap among the titles copied. Thus, as the number of sampled libraries increases, the estimated total number of photocopy items increases in proportion and the observed number of serial titles increases but at a decreasing rate. If one were to estimate the average number of photocopy items per title based on the titles observed in the sample, a small sample would yield a smaller estimate of photocopy items per title than a large sample would. Thus, a true estimate of the number of photocopy items per serial title requires a means of estimating the number of titles at various sample sizes as well as the number of photocopy items. Procedures for handling these two estimation problems are discussed below.

Both estimation problems (i.e., estimating the distribution of photocopy items per title and number of titles) are attacked by using data from MINITEX. MINITEX, an organization that serves libraries from Minnesota and surrounding states by processing interlibrary loan requests, graciously agreed to devote one year's accumulated interlibrary loan requests for use in this study. This amounted to approximately 130,000 transactions, of which about 55,000 were domestic serial titles. These data provided us with a means of weighting library observations for seasonal and day of the week effects. That is, we noted for each sample library the month and day of the week they counted their photocopy items. We then observed the average number of photocopy items observed in similar types of libraries in MINITEX (Public, Academic and Special) for the same months and days of the week. This provided an excellent means of adjusting all sample observations for these two time effects. The MINITEX data also provided evidence to cross-check the results from the national library survey that involved interlibrary loan estimates. Finally, and most importantly, the MINITEX data also provided a means of overcoming the two estimation problems mentioned above.

The procedure used to derive estimation methods, was to obtain a computer print-out of observations over one week and use this result to compare with results for the entire year. A "typical" week was chosen from an average month for each type of library. Included in the analysis are 26 Public libraries 68 Academic libraries and 38 Special libraries. There were no libraries classified as Federal in the MINITEX data base. The distribution of the number of photocopy items per serial title for the three types of libraries is given in Table C.1. It covers the sample week only.

Table C.1 SAMPLE WEEK DISTRIBUTION OF PHOTOCOPY ITEMS PER SERIAL TITLE - MINITEX (1976)

Type of Library		No. of Photocopy Items										
		1	2	3	4	5	6	7	8	9	10	>
Public	No. of Serials	54	7	2	2	0	0	0	0	0	0	
	Cum. Prop.	.831	.938	.969	1.00	1.00	1.00	1.00	1.00	1.00	1.00	1
Academic	No. of Serials	446	56	19	7	3	4	2	3	0	0	
	Cum. Prop.	.826	.930	.965	.978	.983	.991	.994	1.00	1.00	1.00	1
Special	No. of Serials	70	11	4	1	0	0	0	0	0	0	
	Cum. Prop.	.814	.942	.988	1.00	1.00	1.00	1.00	1.00	1.00	1.00	1

SOURCE: King Research, Inc.: MINITEX data base.

The entries in Table C.1 are totals over the types of libraries indicated. The table can be read as follows. In Public libraries, there were 54 serials that had one photocopy item, 7 serials that had two photocopy items, 2 serials that had three photocopy items and two serials that had four photocopy items. Thus, there were 65 serials that had a total of 82 photocopy items for an average (f)* of 1.26 photocopy items per serial title. Similarly, the cumulative proportion of serial titles is .831 for one photocopy item; .938 for two photocopy items and so on.

The data for the entire year is given in Table C.2.

Table C.2 ANNUAL DISTRIBUTION OF PHOTOCOPY ITEMS PER SERIAL TITLE - MINITEX (1976)

Type of Library		No. of Photocopy Items 1	2	3	4	5	6	7	8	9	10	>10
Public	No. of Serials	1,571	326	113	60	28	19	11	5	6	5	16
	Cum. Prop.	.728	.879	.931	.959	.972	.981	.986	.988	.991	.993	1.00
Academic	No. of Serials	13,394	3527	1439	755	414	291	183	138	85	65	347
	Cum. Prop.	.649	.820	.890	.926	.946	.960	.969	.976	.980	.983	1.00
Special	No. of Serials	1,901	429	185	118	57	33	25	11	14	4	70
	Cum. Prop.	.673	.824	.890	.932	.952	.964	.972	.976	.981	.983	1.00

SOURCE: King Research, Inc.: MINITEX data base.

These data may be interpreted in the same way as data in the Table C.1. The cumulative proportions from Tables C.1 and C.2 are plotted in Figure C.1 which is scaled as a lognormal probability distribution. The number of photocopy items are plotted (in logarithmic scale) against the corresponding cumulative proportion.

The distribution curves of the sample data are quite similar. The slopes are very close, except that the Special libraries drop off after two photocopy items. It is believed that this is an anomoly due to the small sample size. The averages for the three sample curves are 1.26 photocopy items per serial for Academic and Special libraries and 1.33 for Public libraries. The distribution curves for the entire year's data are also parallel but separated more.

It is highly significant that the curves of the sample distribution are parallel to the curves of the entire year's data. The f values (averages) and the distance between the sample curves and entire year's curves are given below:

	Sample f_1 Values	Year f_2 values	Relationship $(f_2 \div f_1)$	Relationship of Distance Between Curves	E
Public	1.26	1.66	1.32	1.55	1.17
Academic	1.33	2.07	1.56	1.95	1.25
Special	1.26	2.02	1.60	2.00	1.25

*Average here is designated as f because this measure, as shown later, will be used as an adjustment factor (f).

Since all of the curves appear to be parallel, the factor E will be used to extrapolate from short time period data from sample libraries in the national library survey to estimate the distribution over an entire year for these libraries.

Another very important characteristic of the relationship of the year's data is discussed at this point. As noted above, the averages for the three curves for the entire year's data are 2.07 photocopy items per serial for Academic, 1.66 for Public and 2.02 for Special libraries. It is noted that the distances between these three curves are very closely related to the three averages (f values). For example, the relationship of Academic to Public libraries is 2.07 ÷ 1.66=1.25. The distance between the two curves is found to be about 1.31 over the range of the curves. The relationship between the curves of Special and Public libraries is 1.22 and relationship of the distance between the two curves is about 1.23. Finally, the relationship between the curves of Academic and Special libraries is 1.03 and the relationship of the distance appears to be about 1.06. It is found that distribution curves from nearly all of the individual libraries are similarly shaped and that the relationship of the f factors and the distance between the curves are all very similar.

Another important issue is determination of a procedure for estimating the distribution of photocopy items summed over all libraries. Again, the MINITEX data provide a good basis for making this estimate. In this case only data from the entire year are analyzed. Data were tabulated by serial title for 6,345 titles found to have at least one photocopy item over the entire year. A sample of 317 of these titles were chosen to form a basis of the distribution of photocopy items per title (as well as to provide other analysis). The distribution observed for these 317 titles is given below:

	No. of Photocopy Items					
	1	2	3	4	5	6-10
No. of Serials	96	48	26	21	13	59
Cum. Prop.	.303	.454	.536	.603	.644	.830
	11-20	21-30	31-40	41-50	51-100	>100
No. of Serials	30	10	7	3	3	1
Cum. Prop.	.924	.956	.978	.987	.997	1.00

The cumulative distribution is plotted in Figure C.1 along with the three types of library data from Table C.2. The average (f) for the number of photocopy items per serial is 8.7 over all 132 MINITEX libraries. It is noted that all the curves are all nearly parallel. Also, the relationship between the three individual library curves and the curve of data summed over libraries is similar. These relationships are given as follows:

Type of Library	Year f_2 values	Total f_3 values	Relationship ($f_3 \div f_2$)	Relationship of Distance Between Curves
Public	1.66	8.7	5.2	5.5
Academic	2.07	8.7	4.2	4.0
Special	2.02	8.7	4.3	4.5

These data appear to show that one can project sample library data to the entire population if f_2 and f_3 factors are known. It is believed that this relationship holds because the number of observations are large enough that the effect of potential high clustering within individual libraries is balanced by the large number of photocopy items over the sample. The relationship holds very nicely for all libraries that have a large enough number of observations to plot more than three points on the curve. The fact that the curves are parallel and definable in terms of the averages (f) makes it possible to provide gross estimates from the national library sample for in dividual libraries (hence, the population totals) and for sums over libraries. However, to do this one must be able to estimate f at various values of number of photocopy items or corresponding number of serial titles.

The MINITEX data also provide a basis for estimating the relation ship between number of serial titles (x) and number of photocopy items (y). Values of x and y observed at MINITEX are plotted in Figure C.2. Here the one week sample data are plotted with circles around the points and the one year data are plotted without circles. The figure is given on three sheets with values of x ranging from 0 to 200 photocopy items, 201 to 2000 photocopy items and 2001 to 10,000 photocopy items. A line is drawn on each sheet to show the points at which x = y. The observations by definition must lie on or below that line since the total number of photocopy items must be greater than the number of serial titles (that have at least one photocopy item).

It is noted on the graph that there is no discernable difference between the week sample points and the total year points for values below 80 photocopy items. Perhaps they are a little bit higher. Similarly, there is no real distinction among Public, Academic and Special libraries. Clearly, as the number of photocopy items increase (x) the increase in number of serial titles (y) dampens and in fact approaches an asymptote which is the total number of serial titles in the population (6,345). This general form of curve is referred to as a modified exponential curve expressed as follows:

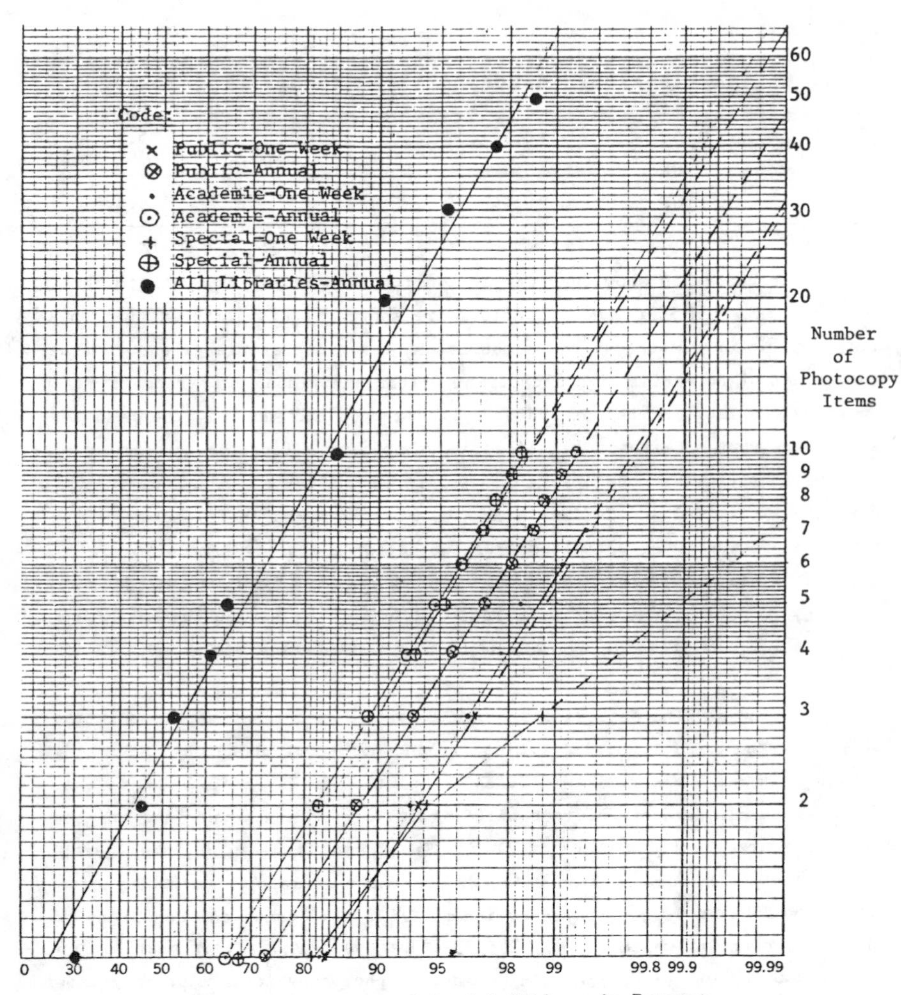

Figure C.1 Sample Week and Annual Distribution of Photocopy Items Per Serial Title-MINITEX (1976)

(1) $y = a + bc^x$

where: y is number of serial titles

x is number of photocopy items

a is an asymptote (total serial titles)

b is a model parameter

c is a model parameter

We would like this model to go through the origin since y = 0 when x = 0. Here we find that:

(2) $y = a\ (1-c^x)$

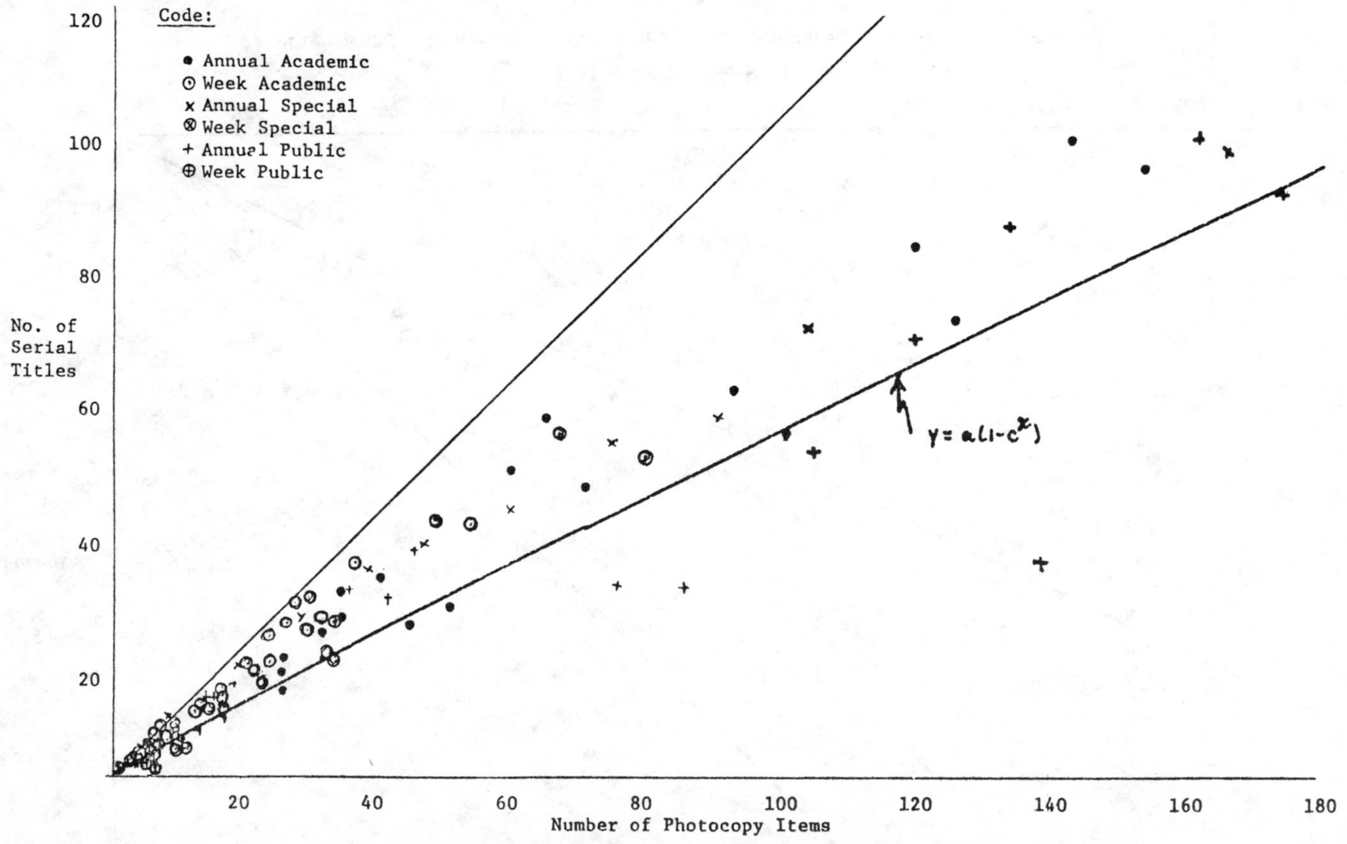

Figure C.2.a. Number of Photocopy Items (x) Versus Number of Serials (v)

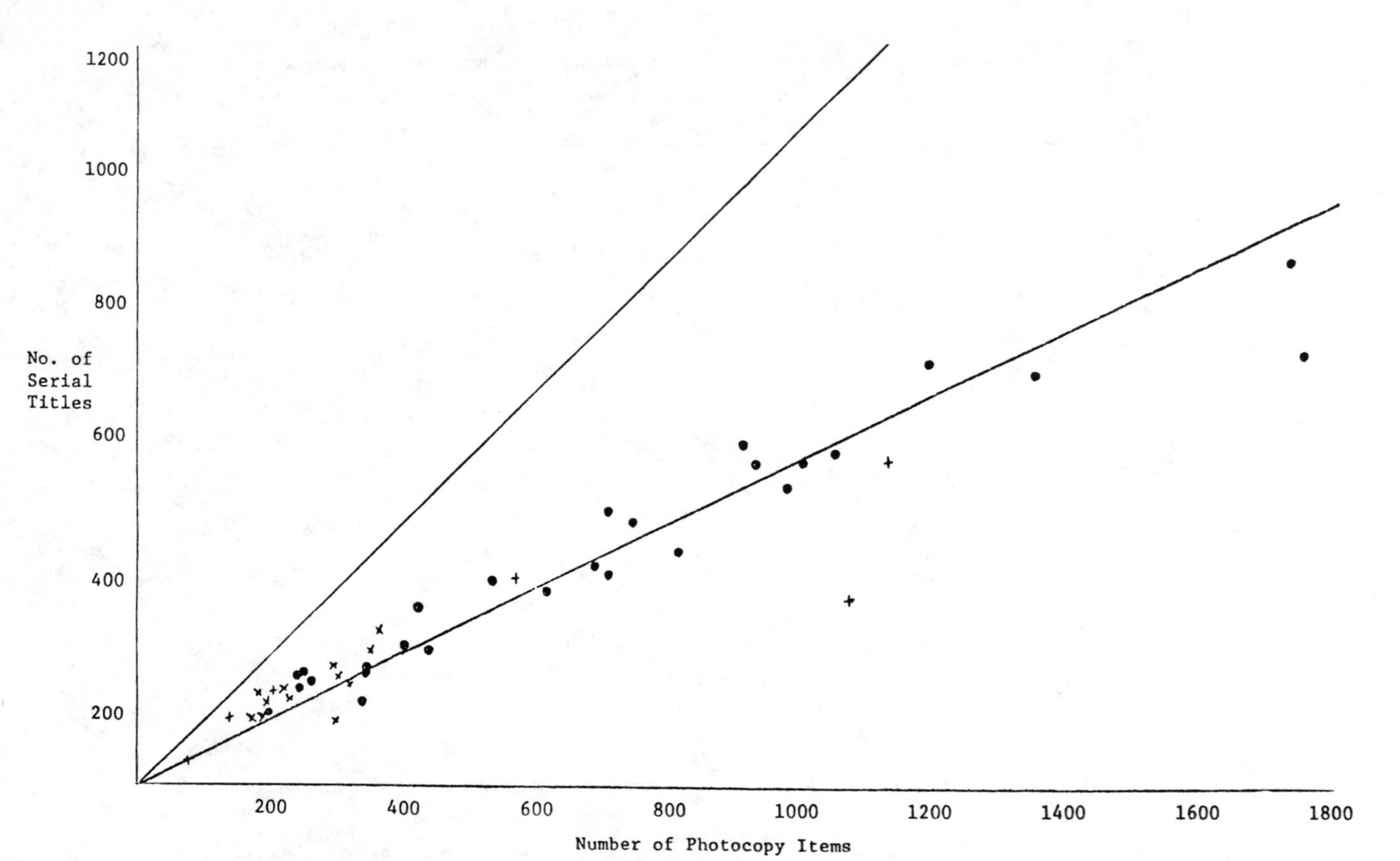

Figure C.2.b. Number of Photocopy Items (x) Versus Number of Serials (y)

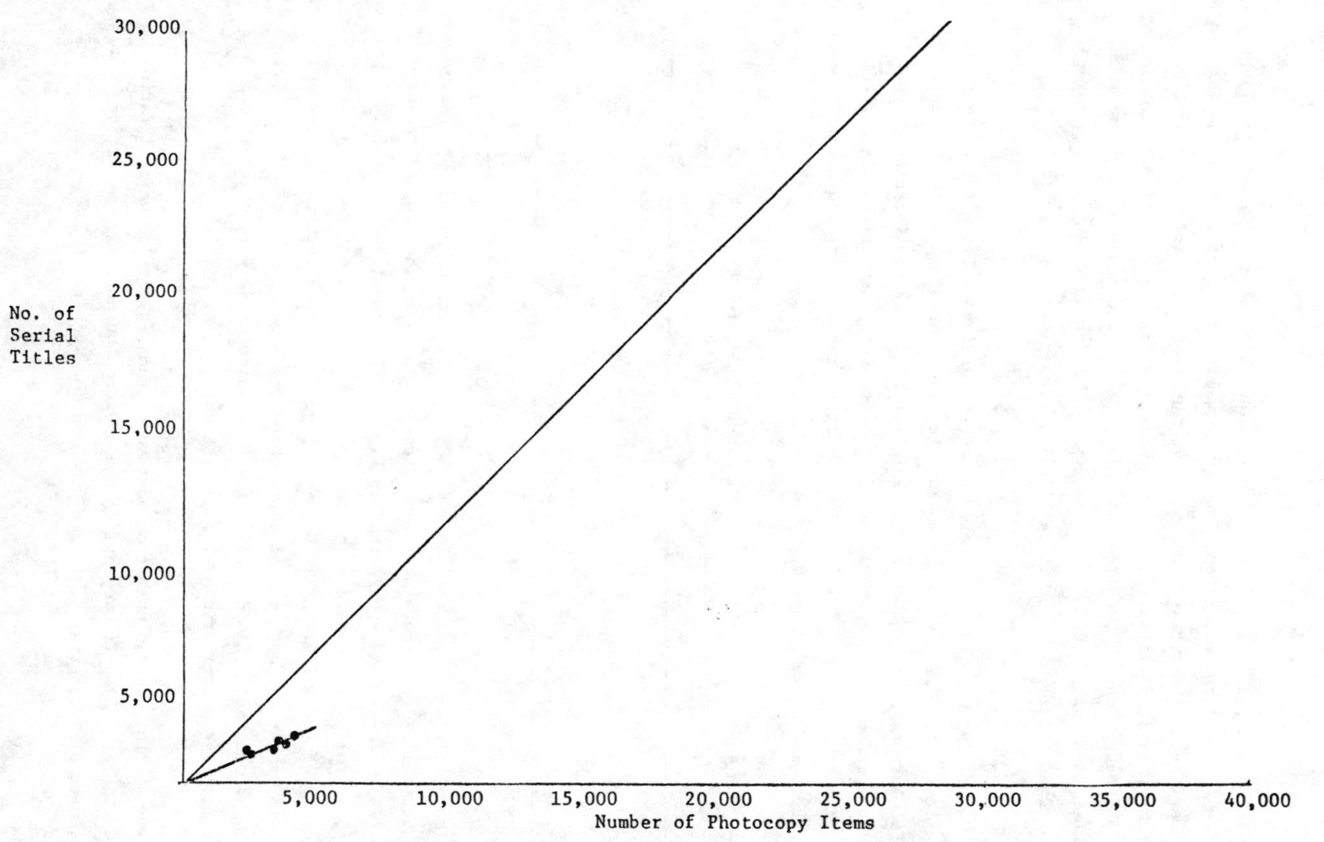

Figure C.2.c. Number of Photocopy Items (x) Versus Number of Serials (y)

Through trial and error we find that a reasonable fit of the data is

$$a = 6{,}345$$
$$c = .999918$$

This curve is given in Figure C.2. We find that the model predicts slightly low below 100 photocopy items but fits quite well above that value. The higher values are the ones that are most important from the standpoint of estimation from the national library survey. In other words, we can estimate the values of photocopy items (x) quite well. From these values of x we can estimate the number of serial titles (y) and, hence, the f-factor ($x \div y$). Some examples are given below for the national library survey data.

The example given below is for interlibrary loans for Academic libraries only. Figures are given for the other three types of libraries, the total across libraries and local users for all types of libraries without comment, since the results are self-evident after the explanation for one type of library is given. The distribution of photocopy items and number of serials is shown in Table C.3 below.

Table C.3 DISTRIBUTION OF NUMBER OF PHOTOCOPY ITEMS AND SERIALS FOR ACADEMIC LIBRARY

	Number of Photocopy Items									
	1	2	3	4	5	6	7	8	9	10
No. of Serials	838	77	34	12	5	1	1	1	1	2
Cum. Prop. of Serials	.862	.941	.976	.989	.994	.995	.9957	.9967	.9977	.9998

SOURCE: King Research, Inc.

This table can be read as follows: 838 serials had one photocopy item made, 77 serials had two photocopy items made and so on in the sampled Academic libraries. These data are plotted in Figure C.3. The line on the figure can be read as follows: 86 percent of the serial titles had one photocopy item; 94 percent of the serial titles had one or two photocopy items; 97.6 percent of the serial titles had one, two or three photocopy items made and so on. It is pointed out that individual libraries, in which there were observations, had very similar distributions slope of the curve.

The average number of photocopy items (x) in Academic libraries is 370 (Table 4.15). If one applies the equation on page 237 we arrive at an estimate of 190 serials (y) that produced the average of 370 photocopy items.

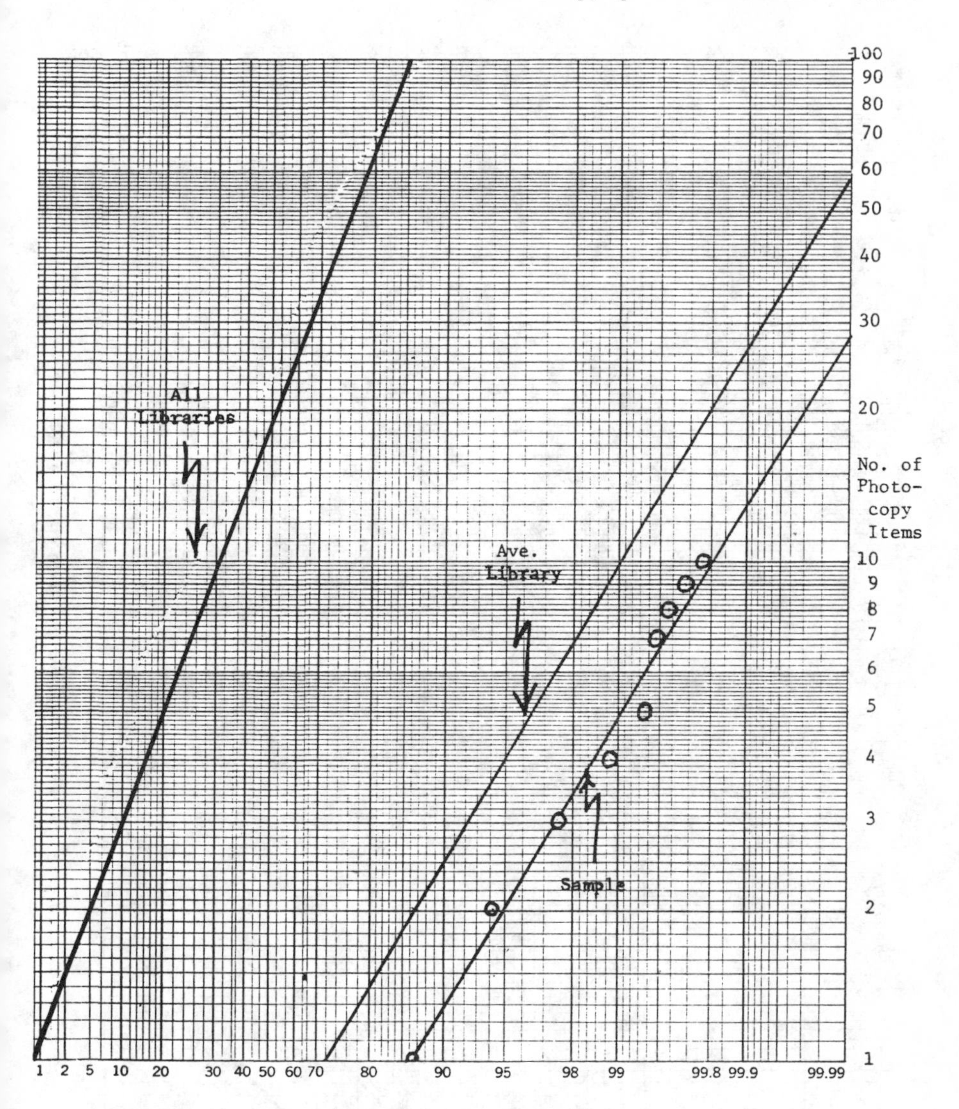

Figure C.3 Distribution of Photocopy Items by Serial Title for Academic Libraries

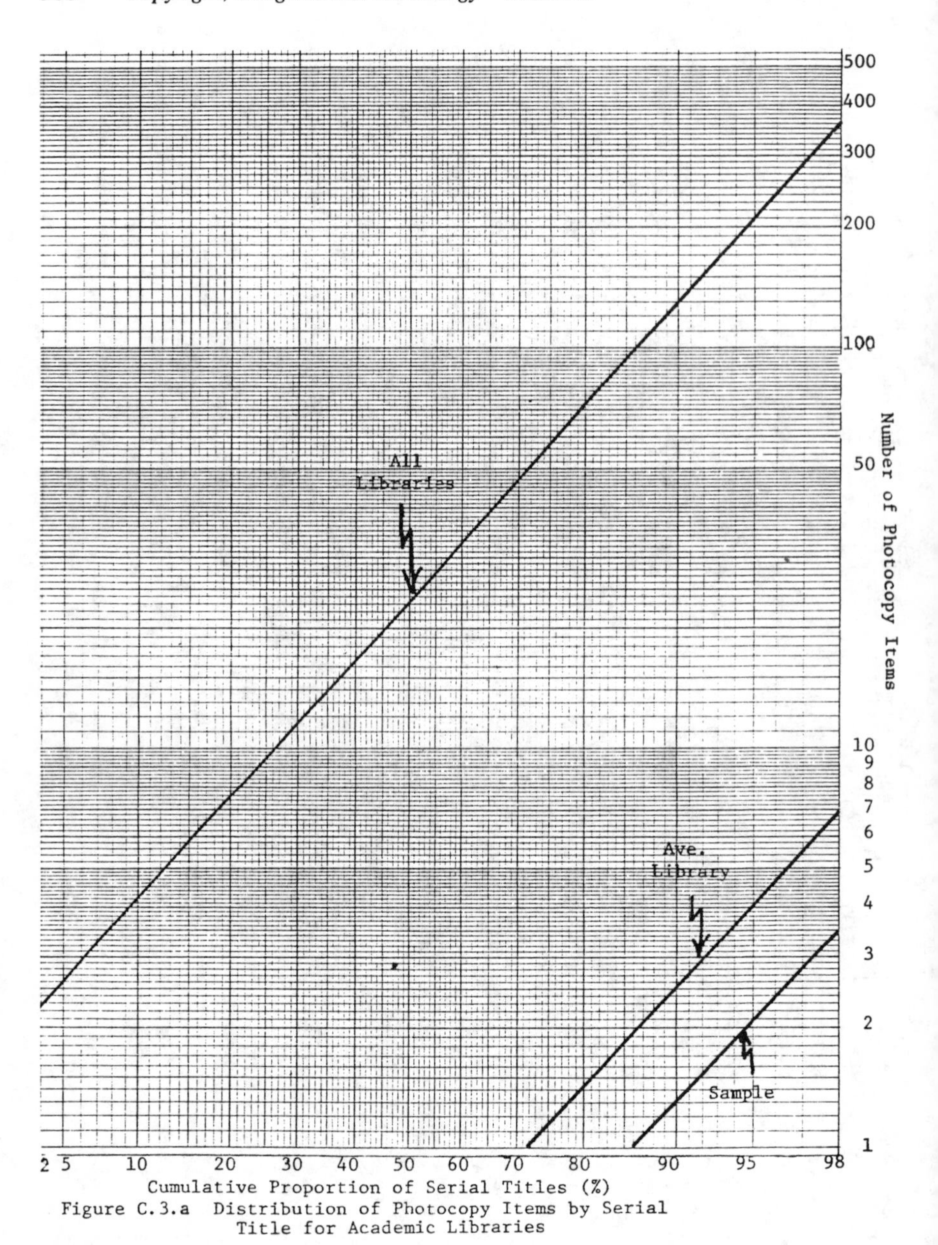

Figure C.3.a Distribution of Photocopy Items by Serial Title for Academic Libraries

Therefore, f is estimated to be 1.95 (370 ÷ 190). The extrapolation factor is computed as 2.00 (1.95 ÷ 1.25 x 1.28); where 1.28 is an adjustment factor observed in the MINITEX data. Therefore, the distribution of photocopying in an average Academic library is found by extrapolating each point on the line in Figure C.3 by 2.00. This distribution is also drawn on Figure C.3. As a check on the validity of this distribution, one can determine the total average number of photocopy items by summing the proportion of serials times number of photocopy items. This is done below.

Table C.4 DISTRIBUTION OF NUMBER OF PHOTOCOPY ITEMS BY SERIALS

	Number of Photocopy Items									
	1	2	3	4	5	6-10	11-20	21-30	31-40	41-50
Cum. Prop. of Serials	.72	.865	.921	.950	.965	.9815	.9910	.9985	.9995	.9998
Prop. of Serials (P)	.72	.145	.056	.029	.015	.0165	.0095	.0075	.0010	.0003
No. of Serials	.72	.29	.168	.116	.075	.124	.144	.188	.035	.014

SOURCE: King Research, Inc.

The average number of photocopy items is estimated to be 1.87 photocopy items per serial per library. This is found by multiplying the number of photocopy items times proportion of serials (last row). Summing the last row gives the average. Therefore, the total number of photocopy items for all Academic libraries is estimated to be 1.08 million photocopy items (1.87 x 190 serials x 3,030 libraries). This compares closely with 1.01 million photocopy items estimated for Academic libraries by straight projection (see Table 4.10). It is noted also that the proportion of photocopy items made from serials with fewer than six photocopy items is found by summing the last row (Serials times Proportion of Serials) from 6-10 through 41-50 photocopy items and dividing this by 1.87 photocopy items. This comes to 0.27 (0.501 ÷ 1.87). Thus, 27 percent of the photocopy items are estimated to be from serials that have more than five photocopy items made. Approximately 3.5 percent of the serials have more than five copies made. The approach above is that used to estimate distributions and proportion of photocopy items (under six copies) in Section 4 for the libraries' perspective.

The next step is to estimate the total number of photocopy items produced across all libraries. This information is of interest to publishers and is given in Section 5. These projections are not as analytically firm as with the previous results because we do not have a data base comparable to MINITEX to validate results. We have observed over the 132 MINITEX libraries that 6,345 serials produced the distribution shown in Figure C.1. This distribution is parallel to the observations from the three types of libraries. Also, the distance to the curve seems to be estimated by the ratio of f-values of the distributions. This relationship is used to extend the data even further to all libraries in the universe. Here, the equation given before can not be used to estimate number of serials (y) from number of photocopy items (x) because the values of y have approached an asymptote (a). Therefore, we have to make some judgement concerning the number of serials to estimate (f). We have chosen to use 10,000 titles because that is our best estimate of the current number of scientific and technical periodicals published in the U.S. (4). Also, we have estimated that a very large proportion of the photocopy items involve scientific and technical serials.

There are an estimated 1.01 million photocopy items made by Academic libraries for interlibrary loans. If there are 10,000 serials photocopied, the average number of photocopy items per serial title would be 100 (f). Therefore, an extrapolation factor (E) for the new distribution would be 51.3 (100 ÷ 1.95). This distribution is also plotted in Figure C.3. It is noted that the new distribution quickly goes over the scale provided in Figure C.3. Therefore, the three distribution curves are also displayed in Figure C.3(a). Here we find that 52 percent of the serials have less than 25 photocopy items, 20 percent have between 26 and 50 photocopy items; 14 percent have between 51 and 100 photocopy items and 14 percent have over 100 photocopy items. This distribution gives us the same proportion of serials that will have various levels of photocopying performed on them. With exemptions left out, one can then estimate the respective proportion of eligible serials that will achieve various levels of photocopying. If one believes that there are more or fewer serial titles, the curve can be moved up or down correspondingly.

APPENDIX D
STAFF ACKNOWLEDGEMENT

We would like to acknowledge here the support given by our staff during the many months of data collection, coding, editing, and analysis. The following individuals made the analysis given in this report possible:

D. Begosh
M. Bender
C. Brideau
J. Briggs

A. Caplan
R. Chaney
R. Clark
S. Clark
T. Connors
R. Cotton

T. Davis
E. Dowd
T. Dowd
M. Durham

S. Eckert
A. Esten

S. Fitzgerald
D. Fogel
C. Franklin
S. Fordham

M. Graziano

P. Jackson

M. Kane
T. Kellogg
C. Ketner
D. Ketner
L. King
M. King
S. King
K. Kott
J. Krintz
H. Kurtz

B. Long

M.J. Majowicz
M. Majowicz
J. Majowicz
R. Masonson
S. Molster
K. Motlagh

K. Oheim
M. Orsini

S. Price

C. Rohrbaugh
R. Rosenberg

H. Saba
R. Smith
G. Snyderman
C. Sullivan

T. Valeri

R. Woltman
S. Woltman

Costs of Owning, Borrowing, and Disposing of Periodical Publications

INTRODUCTION

Background

User needs for periodicals are satisfied in one of two ways by a library or information center: the library either maintains the publication in its own collection, or it borrows requested items from other libraries. Both cost money. To maintain a periodical in its own collection, the library must select, order, process, store and make the publication available. For a requested item in a publication not in its own collection, there is the staff cost to locate and borrow the item; and in many cases, a photocopy charge. The cost to satisfy a request by borrowing is roughly the same each time, whereas the average cost per use of a publication acquired for the library collection is a function of how frequently it is used. Consequently, for any given periodical title there is some frequency of use at which it becomes cheaper for a library to acquire the publication than to borrow it to satisfy patron demand.

Many libraries are now facing reduced budgets; the rapidly increasing costs of periodical subscriptions, the new copyright law and the proposed national periodicals system[1] have focused special attention upon periodical acquisitions and potentials for controlling or decreasing expenditures in this area.

To realize these potentials, it is highly desirable to be able to estimate the costs of options associated with acquiring periodicals. This report uses a mathematical model for estimating such costs to address the following question: Should a library own (i.e., subscribe to) or should it borrow, when needed, a specific periodical?

An earlier version of this model was developed by Westat, Inc. in 1968, under contract with The Center for Research Libraries; it computed the cost of owning versus borrowing to satisfy demand for serial publications.[2, 3, 4] Input to the 1968 model consisted of average cost data drawn from a survey of four university libraries, and use characteristics derived from interlibrary loan data collected at several large lending libraries. The model developed in this report uses cost figures drawn from a 1977 survey of two university libraries and one special library, and use characteristics derived from internal use data collected at two university libraries.

Overview of Model

Both the 1968 and the current models were designed to determine the frequency of use above which owning a periodical is cheaper than borrowing it. At this frequency, which is called the crossover point or breakeven point, the cost of borrowing equals the cost of owning. At frequencies of use below this point, borrowing is less costly than owning. At frequencies of use above the crossover point, owning is less costly than borrowing.

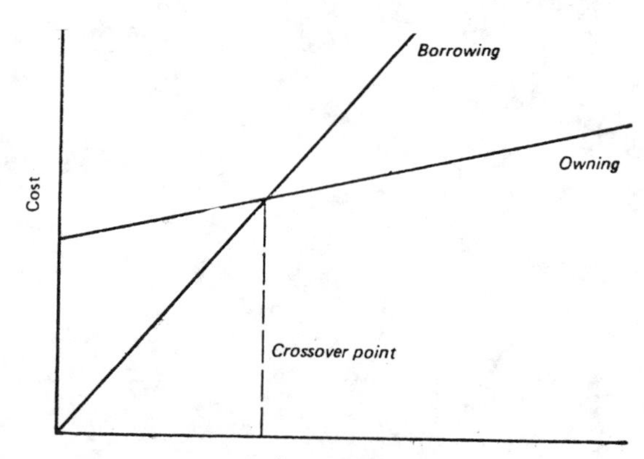

FIG. 1: COSTS AS A FUNCTION OF THE FREQUENCY OF USE FOR OWNING AND BORROWING

Figure 1 illustrates this phenomenon. It stems from the fact that there are two kinds of costs:

1. Costs that are independent of the frequency of use.

2. Costs that are proportional to the frequency of use.

As we shall see, owning a periodical involves both kinds of costs, while borrowing a periodical involves only the second kind of costs.

It should be noted that selecting the option that minimizes the cost for a single library does not necessarily coincide with minimizing the costs for society as a whole. Certain social costs are incurred when a library depends upon borrowing of a title for patrons, namely:

1. Loss of browsing capacity which may result in loss of use for marginal titles that a user will not request through interlibrary loan.

2. Delays to users when materials must be borrowed from another library.

3. Additional costs incurred by lending institutions that are not charged to the borrowing library.

From the social point of view, monies saved by libraries will have other effects. These might include increased subscription prices, loss of profits for commercial journal publishers, discontinuance of some periodicals, and pressure for some form of subsidy, to either libraries or journal publishers. Although the model was never intended for a cost benefit analysis of owning versus borrowing from a social point of view, a general observation can be made. The crossover points, in terms of level of use, would be lower for a social optimum than those calculated by the model from a single library's perspective.

The costs of owning and borrowing were computed for various frequencies of use as follows. The various costs incurred in each year of a specified planning period (25 years) were adjusted for inflation, discounted to the present value,[5] and then summed over all years of the period. The inflation rate and the discount rate were assumed to be 4 and 6 percent, respectively. Cost elements included in the model are:

1. Initial cost - The cost of ordering and cataloging a new title. This cost is applicable only if the periodical is ordered within the planning period.

2. Annual recurring cost - This includes annual review and selection, renewal of subscription, (exclusive of actual subscription cost), check-in, claiming, shelving, preparation of serials list, training, direct supervision of tasks, binding preparation, and bindery. The annual recurring cost does not include the actual subscription cost, and is independent of the number of years of back issues held or the average annual use of the periodical.

3. Internal use cost - Circulation cost, labor for reshelving of materials used, and for shelf maintenance, and in-library cost not recovered through fees for lending materials to other libraries through interlibrary loan, are included in this category. The total internal use cost is based on the average annual use of all issues of the title, and is dependent upon the number of volumes of back issues held.

4. Internal borrowing cost - The average unit cost within the library for borrowing an item through interlibrary loan. It includes staff time for verifying, locating, and forwarding a request for the desired item, and postage charges. Total cost reflects the number of items borrowed annually.

5. External borrowing cost - This is the charge made by the lending library for interlibrary loans or photocopies, and is again dependent upon the number of items borrowed annually.

2. Comparing the 1968 results to results based on current costs.
3. Applying the model to answer questions concerning the acquisition, maintenance, and discarding of back issues.
4. Updating and making the model available for use by librarians.

The remainder of this report consists of two chapters: Estimating Model Inputs and Crossover Points for Owning Versus Borrowing Decisions.

The appendices include:

- a detailed derivation of the cost model, and the associated computer program written in APL
- details concerning the cost surveys
- results generated by the model helpful in answering questions concerning the acquisition, maintenance, and discarding of back issues.

ESTIMATING MODEL INPUTS

Cost Inputs

In developing cost inputs for the model, an attempt was made to utilize, where possible, only those costs which would be altered by the addition or subtraction of a periodical title.[7] Costs of tasks related to periodicals which clearly are not affected by the number of subscriptions held in the library, such as overhead, general administration and supervision, and reference service have been excluded. Consequently, the summation of costs included in the model over a one year period does not result in the total annual cost for handling periodicals. While it would be desirable to have estimates of the marginal costs for handling one additional title, available data only allowed computation of average costs for the various tasks. For example, certain labor charges which make up the largest part of costs tend to increase in steps as a function of the number of titles owned; the addition or subtraction of a few titles does not affect the labor costs.

Data for the first four cost elements (initial cost, annual recurring cost, internal use cost, and internal borrowing cost) were collected from three main libraries and two branch libraries. See appendix B for details on the collection of cost data and appendix C for a step-by-step guide for the collection of these costs. For purposes of analysis, data were used from the three main libraries as follows:

A. The main library of a large university. The 1,000,000 volumes and almost 7,000 current journal subscriptions were primarily in the humanities, social sciences, and life sciences.

B. A smaller academic main library, with about 350,000 volumes, including 46,000 bound periodical volumes, and 2,615 current journal titles. The collection is similar to that of library A, with holdings in humanities, social sciences, and life sciences. A small percentage of basic physical science materials are also included.

C. A large special library (science and technology) with holdings in physics, chemistry, mathematics, and technology. About four-fifths of the 125,000 volume collection is bound journals; the library carries slightly over 2,200 current journal titles, including a substantial level of gifts and exchange.

The estimated unit costs of the four cost elements for the three libraries are shown in table 1. These estimated costs were used as inputs for model runs as discussed in the next chapter.

TABLE 1

UNIT COSTS FOR THREE LIBRARIES

Cost Element	Library A	Library B	Library C
Initial cost (per title added)			
New paid subscription	$70.65	$11.54	$53.53
New free subscription	44.61	—	37.91
Annual recurring cost (per current title)	24.45	9.31	25.94
Internal use cost (per use)	0.36	0.58	0.48
Internal borrowing cost (per item borrowed)	7.02	5.09	9.48

Other cost elements included in the model have been applied uniformly to each of the three libraries. (See appendix B for derivation of costs.) They are:

1. External borrowing costs - Borrowing costs have been calculated witn lending library charges of $0, $3, and $8.

2. Storage cost - Storage per annual volume (i.e., an annual volume is defined to include all issues for a calendar year, regardless of labeling or binding) is calculated at $0.50; for microfilm, storage costs are put at $0.05 per reel or $0.016 per annual volume. Storage costs are entered only is cases where weeding is being considered due to space constraints, since in other cases it is not considered a marginal cost.

3. Disposition (weeding cost) - Weeding costs are included at $0.65 per annual volume discarded.

4. Subscription cost - Five subscription costs are considered: $0, $20, $40, $80, and $120. An average 1977 subscription cost for academic libraries is estimated at about $40 across all subject areas, although actual subscription prices ranged from $0 to $3,000 in three libraries.[8] Subscription prices for scientific publications are much higher on the average.[9]

Total costs were computed for a planning period of 25 years, with an annual discount rate of 6 percent and an annual inflation rate of 4 percent.

Use Inputs

The model requires two kinds of inputs to specify use characteristics. First, the cumulative percentage of total use of a periodical volume as a function of its age is needed. This distribution specifies the annual decay in the frequency of use of an individual periodical issue as a function of its age. In other words, the cumulative distribution provides the "shape" of the decay in use over time, but does not specify the magnitude of use. Secondly, a normalized annual frequency of use is required to specify the magnitude or intensity of use.

Ideally the inputs on use would be derived from the same library as the cost inputs, but this is not essential. Libraries with similar collections should experience roughly the same percentage of total use for a title (as a function of its age) over comparable time periods.

Very few libraries have investigated the actual use of periodicals owned. Consequently, few data are available to estimate use levels for models such as the one used here. The use portion of the model developed in 1968 relied upon interlibrary loan data collected at several large lending libraries, i.e., National Library of Medicine, National Agricultural Library, John Crerar Library, and the National Lending Library for Science and Technology (now the British Library Lending Division). This data showed that, on the average, the use of each annual volume of a periodical title declined by about seven percent each year. Data were not available at that time on actual internal use of journals in libraries.

Internal use data recently became available from two university libraries. At the University of Pittsburgh, data have been published for three branch libraries: a physical science library, an engineering library, and a life sciences library.[10] Use of a general collection in the humanities, social, and life sciences, has been tabulated in a second university. This second library was one that provided cost data also, Library B mentioned in a previous section. As expected, the use of individual periodical issues in these libraries was more heavily concentrated in the years immediately following their publication than the use through interlibrary loan in 1968. This recent analysis showed that the prévious assumption of usage following a geometric distribution of decay as a function of age, while perhaps applicable to interlibrary loan, is not realistic for internal library use. Consequently, the model was reprogrammed to accept any empirical distribution of use as a function of age, as well as the geometric distribution.

The use data available from Library B seemed appropriate also for Library A since both collections are similar as far as subject coverage. An average distribution of use based on data from the physical science library and the engineering library of the University of Pittsburgh was used for Library C. The two cumulative distributions are given in table 2.

TABLE 2

CUMULATIVE PERCENTAGE OF TOTAL USE FOR AN INDIVIDUAL PERIODICAL ISSUE AS A FUNCTION OF AGE

Age, Years After Issue	Cumulative Percentage of Total Use: Science & Technology	Cumulative Percentage of Total Use: Social & Life Sciences
1	53	43
2	65	56
3	71	65.4
4	75	73
5	78	79
6	80	82
7	82	83.8
8	83.5	85.6
9	85	86.9
10	86.5	88.1
11	88	89.2
12	89.5	90.2
13	91	91.1
14	92.5	91.9
15	94	92.6
16	95	93.2
17	96	93.7
18	97	94.1
19	98	94.4
20	98.2	94.6
21	98.3	94.9
22	98.4	95.2
23	98.5	95.5
24	98.6	95.8
25	98.7	96.1

In addition to the cumulative distribution of use of a periodical volume as a function of its age, another input is required to specify the frequency of use of the title. The frequency of use in any particular time frame is related to the number of issues of the specific title which are available, either in the library or through interlibrary loan. Consequently, a use level of 10 items per year in the first year of publication of a new title represents a higher level of use than does an annual use of 10 items of an old title with, for example, 30 years of back issues.

To limit the number of cases required, annual use has been normalized in the model to reflect the use of a periodical title in its eleventh year of publication; in other words, a title with 10 years of back issues. Thus, in applying the model to a specific title it is necessary to adjust the estimated annual use upward or downward, depending upon the number of years the title has been published, to obtain the normalized annual use. This is done by multiplying the estimated annual use by an adjustment factor determined for the number of years of back issues for the title. Adjustment factors are calculated by dividing the cumulative use percentage for the tenth year (of the appropriate use curve) by the cumulative use percentage of the publication year being considered. Table 3 lists the adjustment factors for the science and technology and the general collection use distributions used here.

TABLE 3

ADJUSTMENT FACTORS FOR NORMALIZING ANNUAL USE
TO THE USE FOR A PERIODICAL WITH
TEN YEARS OF BACK ISSUES

	Adjustment Factor	
Years of back issues	Science and technology	Humanities, social and life sciences
1	1.63	2.06
2	1.33	1.57
3	1.22	1.35
4	1.15	1.21
5	1.11	1.11
6	1.08	1.08
7	1.05	1.05
8	1.04	1.03
9	1.02	1.01
10	1.00	1.00
12	.97	.98
15	.91	.95
17	.90	.94
20	.88	.93
25	.88	.92
30	.87	.91

Several values of annual use are input for each model run, as cost is calculated as a function of frequency of use. Typical values of the use ranged from 0 to 30.

Future annual use of a title may grow or decline depending on a number of factors such as:

1. Number of back issues available.
2. Size of user population.
3. Amount of available literature.

The model accounts only for the expected growth in annual use attributable to the availability of more back issues as the title ages. Estimating the effect of the user population size is more difficult due to the lack of necessary data. While the overall number of potential users may appear to be increasing in a specific field or discipline, the net effect of this growth on a particular title may be offset by the growth in the number of titles in the field. The rapid growth in highly specialized fields of science along with the corresponding increase in the number of new titles is a good example of this phenomenon. Although the 1968 model included a parameter to reflect the change in user population size, it was removed in the current model because adequate data were not available to estimate it.

CROSSOVER POINTS FOR OWNING VERSUS BORROWING DECISIONS

The model was used to investigate the basic question: should a library own (i.e., subscribe) or should it borrow, when needed, a specific periodical title? This question contains two cases:

Case 1. Library does not presently subscribe to the periodical title.
Case 2. Library does subscribe to the periodical title.

A decision with regard to Case 1 results in a library borrowing to meet patron demand for the title, or placing a subscription for the title. In Case 2 the decision outcomes are for the library to continue its subscription, or terminate the subscription and borrow to fulfill requests for items in future issues of the title. The decision to terminate a current subscription also raises the question of whether the library should continue to store the back files of the terminated title. The model was used also to examine a number of weeding options; these results are contained in appendix D.

An example of the model results for one library will be demonstrated first. Next, crossover points for the two cases will be examined for the three libraries. The chapter will conclude with some comments on how these results compare to the 1968 results and to the CONTU Guidelines.

Example Calculation

In order to acquaint the reader with the type of results available from the model and their application, consider the situation where a librarian wishes to decide on whether to continue a current subscription to a periodical title that has been published for 20 years. Available data indicated that the title (including all 20 years of back files assumed owned by the library) was used a total of 5 times during the last year. Further, assume that the current subscription price is $40 per year.

The cost inputs shown earlier in table 1 for Library A were used to calculate the crossover points shown in figure 2. Crossover points are shown for three interlibrary loan costs (external borrowing costs) -- $8, $3, and free. Most libraries charge for photocopies of periodicals supplied to other requesting libraries. The fees charged vary from library to library, but the $3 external borrowing cost is probably more typical of photocopy charges. The crossover point for a $3 external borrowing cost is seen as about 7-1/2 normalized uses per year. It is important to remember that the model operates in terms of normalized use per year. The actual number of uses in the previous year for the particular title being considered was assumed to be 5. On the expectation that the use over the next year will be the same, the actual use of 5 must be adjusted to correspond to a 10-year old title (which the model assumes) rather than its real age of 20 years. Going back to table 3 in chapter 2, the adjustment factor is .93 found under the heading of humanities, social and life sciences. Library A has that kind of collection. The adjustment factor is multiplied by the actual or observed demand (.93 x 5 = 4.65), which, in this case, does not really change that much. The adjusted expected use is less than the normalized use shown in figure 2 at the crossover point (7-1/2); therefore, the decision should be to terminate the subscription for the title. Up to 7-1/2 normalized uses per year, it is cheaper for the library to borrow, at $3 each time, in order to meet patron needs for the title. It becomes cheaper to subscribe and maintain the title if it is used greater than 7-1/2 times (in terms of normalized uses) per year, according to the model.

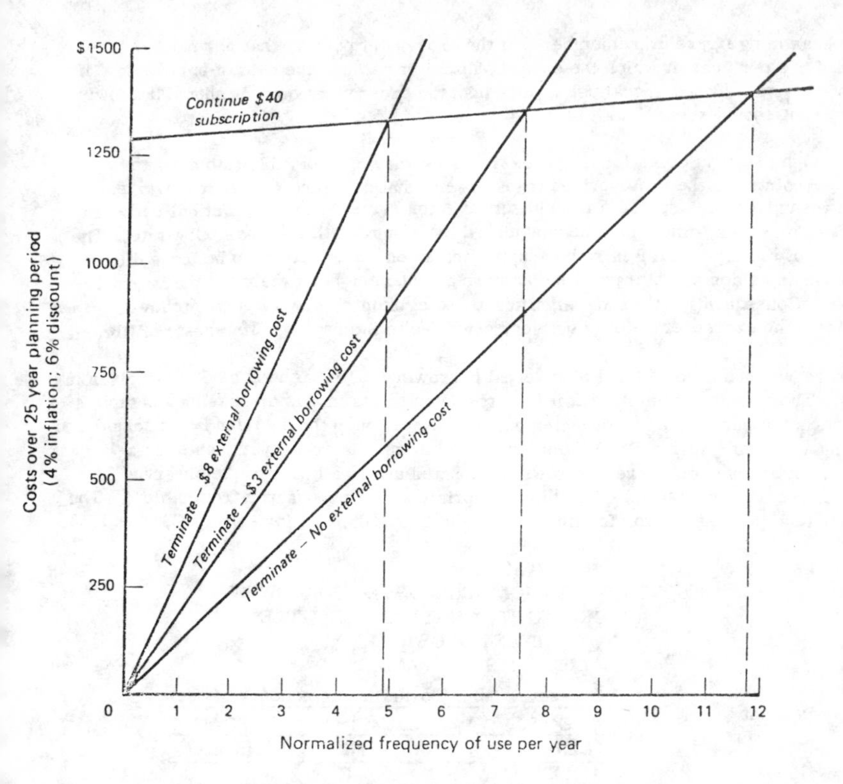

FIG. 2: COST CURVES FOR DECISION TO CONTINUE OR DISCONTINUE A SUBSCRIPTION FOR LIBRARY A

If library A had to pay $8 for each interlibrary loan, the crossover point would move down to just less than 5 normalized uses per year. The decision should be to retain the subscription in this case. Likewise, the library would be ahead to borrow in order to fill requests for a $40 title up to about 12 normalized uses per year if there are no external borrowing costs (free interlibrary loan). All of the calculations in this example assumed that back issues would be retained for titles terminated.

This example has shown the concept of the crossover point in decisions regarding the continuation or termination of a periodical subscription. The next section will expand upon the kind of investigation for the case in which a library does not presently subscribe to a title.

Decisions on Titles Not Presently Owned

Results were produced by the model for each of the three sets of costs inputs representing libraries A, B, and C. Libraries A and B are both university libraries with their journal collections primarily in the humanities, social sciences and life sciences. Library C is a large special library (science and technology) with collection strengths in physics, chemistry, mathematics, and technology. The purpose of using three libraries was to provide some comparisons based on differences in costs and collections.

Rather than showing a series of figures displaying the crossover points as in figure 2, we have chosen to first present in graphic form the crossover points as a function of annual subscription prices for each of three libraries. Figure 3 allows one to determine the crossover points for the decision on whether to borrow or subscribe to meet user needs for a newly-published title (no back files) with a single external borrowing cost of

$3. In examining figure 3, remember that the crosspoint point is that normalized frequency of use per year at which the cost of subscribing equals the cost of borrowing. If the library's normalized annual use is less than the crossover point, it should borrow; if greater, it should subscribe.

Although the input costs for the three libraries vary considerably (table 1), the crossover points for the lower priced titles are not that different. The crossover points are between about 5.7 and 7.4 for a $40 subscription price. For all practical purposes, the three crossover points could be considered the same for this subscription rate. The closeness of library A and B is rather surprising given what appears to be large difference in the input costs. Library A's costs are all much higher except for the internal use cost. Consequently, the most significant finding from figure 3 is that for lower priced periodicals the crossover point is not very sensitive to internal handling costs of libraries.

Crossover points for $0 and $8 external borrowing costs, as well as $3, are given in table 4. The reader is reminded that the crossover points in this discussion and table 4 are in terms of normalized frequencies of use. Even though the decision being considered concerns a new title with no back files, the model computes crossover points for a 10-year old title. In order to compare observed or expected use in a library, the observed frequency of use must be multiplied by the appropriate adjustment factor from table 3. The appropriate adjustment factor for libraries A and B is 2.06, and for library C, it is 1.63.

TABLE 4
CROSSOVER POINTS FOR DECISIONS ON BORROWING
OR SUBSCRIBING TO A 10-YEAR OLD TITLE
NOT PRESENTLY OWNED FOR
LIBRARIES A, B, AND C

Subscription cost	Crossover point (normalized frequency of use)								
	EBC[1]=$0			EBC=$3			EBC=$8		
	Library			Library			Library		
	A	B	C	A	B	C	A	B	C
Free	4	3	3	3	1	2	2	1	2
$20	8	7	6	5	4	4	4	3	3
$40	11	12	8	7	7	6	5	4	4
$80	17	21	12	12	12	9	8	8	7
$120	23	30	17	16	18	13	11	11	9

One other situation can exist under the case where the library does not presently subscribe to the periodical title under consideration. The above discussion centered on a newly-published title. The decision may concern an older title that the library has not subscribed to before.

A library considering a new subscription to a title which has been published for some time frequently utilizes user demand, as demonstrated by interlibrary loan requests, as the basis for such subscription decision. In determining the use level at which subscribing to an older title becomes less expensive than borrowing items from it, table 4 applies to titles of any age by the use of the appropriate adjustment factors from table 3. The crossover points in table 4 apply directly to the decision on whether to borrow or subscribe to a 10-year old title not presently owned by the libraries.

---

[1] EBC = External Borrowing Cost

The sensitivity of the crossover point to changes in the external borrowing cost can be seen in figure 4 for Library A. In the case of a $40 subscription price, the crossover point varies from about 11 for no external borrowing cost to about 5 for an $8 interlibrary loan charge. The crossover point for the $8 borrowing cost is observed to be approximately half of that for the $0 borrowing cost. This would be expected -- as the external borrowing cost goes up the library can afford to purchase a subscription at a lower frequency of use.

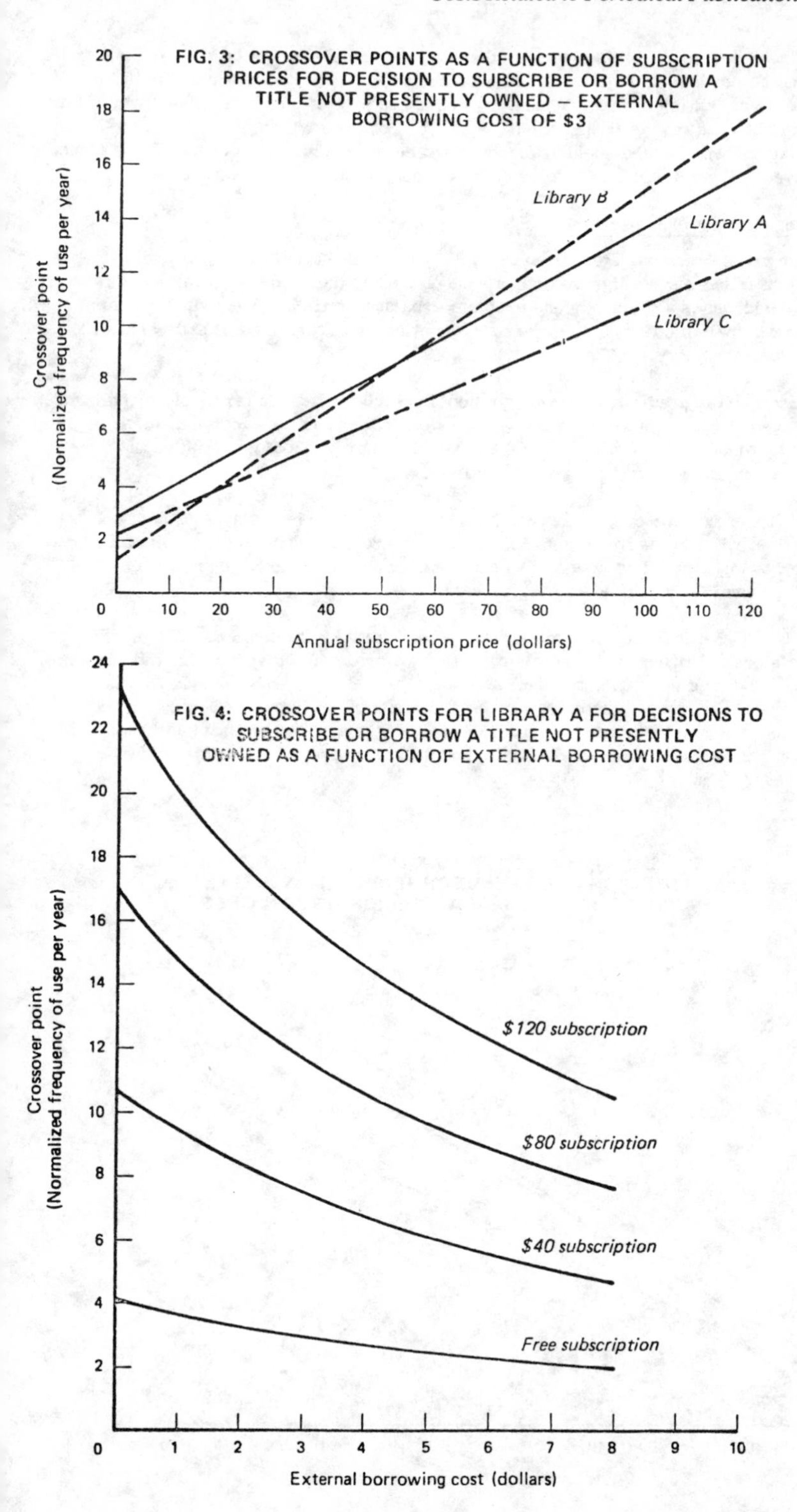
FIG. 3: CROSSOVER POINTS AS A FUNCTION OF SUBSCRIPTION PRICES FOR DECISION TO SUBSCRIBE OR BORROW A TITLE NOT PRESENTLY OWNED – EXTERNAL BORROWING COST OF $3
Crossover point (Normalized frequency of use per year)
Library B
Library A
Library C
Annual subscription price (dollars)
0
2
4
6
8
10
12
14
16
18
20
10
20
30
40
50
60
70
80
90
100
110
120
FIG. 4: CROSSOVER POINTS FOR LIBRARY A FOR DECISIONS TO SUBSCRIBE OR BORROW A TITLE NOT PRESENTLY OWNED AS A FUNCTION OF EXTERNAL BORROWING COST
Crossover point (Normalized frequency of use per year)
$120 subscription
$80 subscription
$40 subscription
Free subscription
External borrowing cost (dollars)
0
2
4
6
8
10
12
14
16
18
20
22
24
1
2
3
4
5
6
7
8
9
10

It has been assumed in this instance, that back issues are not to be acquired but will be borrowed as needed. Should back issues be acquired, initial costs should be increased by the cost of acquisition of these issues, including the cost of purchase. Borrowing costs will be eliminated as part of owning costs, since all requests will be filled from the collection. A comparison of added acquisition costs and deleted borrowing costs will show whether the breakeven use level will increase or decrease as a result of this option.

Decisions on Current Subscriptions

The second case investigated involves decisions on periodical titles that a library currently subscribes to. In light of present budget crises facing many libraries, this second case addresses a more serious problem area at this time. The primary decision is to decide whether to continue a current subscription or to terminate it and borrow to meet user requests for it.

As we saw in the previous section, the model calculates cost in terms of normalized use or the expected use in the 11th year, i.e., a 10-year old title. Decisions on titles of any age may be made from figures and tables based on normalized use by adjusting the observed use according to factors given in table 3.

Figure 5 presents the crossover points for all three libraries as a function of subscription price. The crossover points in the figure were computed on the basis of a $3 external borrowing cost. For free and $8 external borrowing costs, the crossover points can be seen in table 5.

There is little difference in the crossover points shown in table 5 and table 4. The case on decisions for titles not presently owned by a library (table 4) includes the one-time initial cost of adding a new title, but the influence of this cost is small over a 25-year planning period. Otherwise, the costs for the two kinds of decisions -- borrow or subscribe and continue to subscribe or borrow -- are the same. The sensitivity of the crossover points to changes in the external borrowing cost are also essentially the same (figure 4).

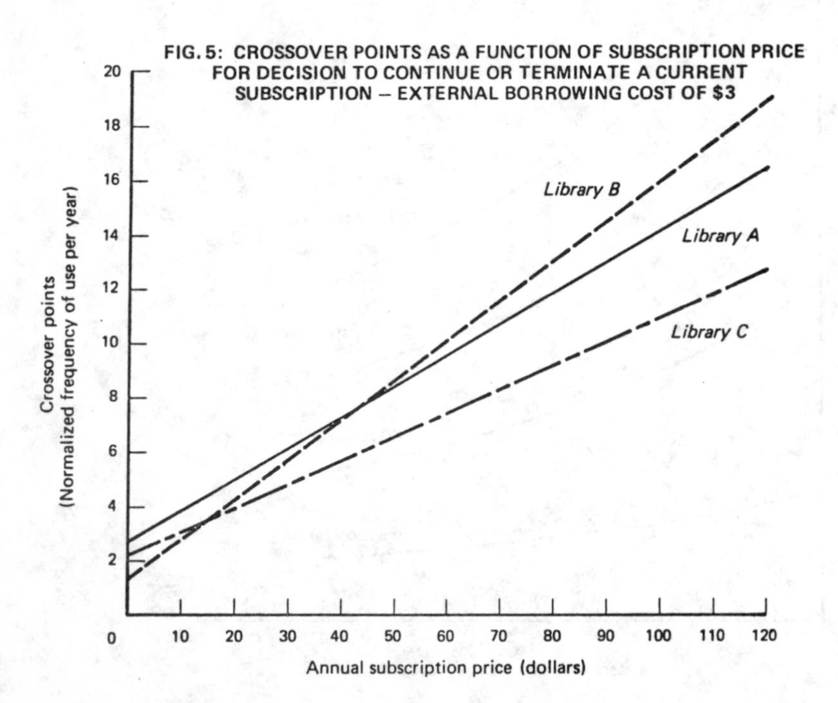

TABLE 5

CROSSOVER POINTS FOR DECISIONS ON BORROWING OR MAINTAINING A CURRENT SUBSCRIPTION FOR LIBRARIES A, B, AND C -- RETAIN 10 YEARS OF BACK ISSUES

Subscription cost	Crossover point (normalized frequency of use)								
	EBC[1]=$0			EBC=$3			EBC=$8		
	Library			Library			Library		
	A	B	C	A	B	C	A	B	C
Free	4	2	3	3	2	2	2	1	1
$20	7	7	6	5	5	4	3	3	3
$40	11	12	8	7	7	6	5	5	4
$80	18	22	13	12	13	9	8	8	7
$120	24	32	17	17	19	13	11	11	9

[1]EBC = External Borrowing Cost

Where use levels are below the crossover points and the decision is made to terminate the subscription, a second decision as to disposition of the ten years of back issues is required. Table 6 indicates the levels of use below which it remains cheaper to borrow, when termination includes discarding of back issues.

TABLE 6

CROSSOVER POINTS FOR DECISIONS ON BORROWING OR MAINTAINING A CURRENT SUBSCRIPTION FOR LIBRARIES A, B, AND C -- REMOVE AND DISCARD 10 YEARS OF BACK ISSUES

Subscription cost	Crossover point (normalized frequency of use)								
	EBC[1]=$0			EBC=$3			EBC=$8		
	Library			Library			Library		
	A	B	C	A	B	C	A	B	C
Free	3	2	3	2	1	2	1	1	1
$20	6	6	5	4	4	3	3	2	2
$40	9	10	7	6	6	5	4	4	3
$80	15	19	11	10	11	8	7	7	6
$120	20	27	15	14	16	11	9	10	8

[1]EBC = External Borrowing Cost

Storage of back issues has been assumed to be free. This is a valid assumption only for libraries with adequate space. Storage costs are not included in any of the calculations presented in this chapter. Appendix D contains results on weeding options under the assumption of space constraints and storage costs. With no storage costs taken into account, the cost differences between terminating a subscription and retaining back issues and terminating and discarding back issues are attributable to the lower internal use cost as compared to the external borrowing cost for back issues. Consequently, the retention of back issues offers the cheaper option as reflected in the higher crossover points in table 5 (as compared to those in table 6). The higher cost of borrowing to meet requests for items in the discarded back issues moves the crossover points down, making owning favorable at lower frequencies of use.

Comparison With 1968 Results

The validity of comparisons between current results and findings of the 1968 study is somewhat questionable in view of the differences in cost elements used in calculating the cost of the various alternatives. As noted earlier, such elements as general administration and reference service costs have been omitted from annual recurring costs, and selection and review of titles has been transferred from initial to annual costs. Overhead costs have been deleted throughout. In addition, discount and inflation rates were not generally applied in 1968. Labor costs, which comprise the major portion of all costs, have also increased substantially since 1968.

The crossover point for the decision to continue or discontinue a $20 subscription with the retention of back issues in 1968 was about six normalized annual uses; in 1977, it ranged from six to seven uses for a $40 subscription and a $3 external borrowing cost. One would conclude that the crossover points for similar cases have not changed much from 1968. Costs on both sides of the decision -- owning versus borrowing -- have apparently escalated about the same.

Impact of the "CONTU Guidelines"

The "CONTU guidelines" for photocopying periodical materials defines the securing of more than five copies per year from a title, of an article or articles published within the five previous years, as essentially substituting for subscribing to a periodical, and thus subject to authorization from the copyright proprietor, who may require royalty payment. Should a library apply cost-only considerations to their selection policies, and not subscribe to periodical titles which application of the model shows to be more economically borrowed, the necessary level of borrowing would place many of the more expensive titles in the area in which securing of over five copies is more economic than subscribing, even where the highest ($8) external borrowing costs apply. In these cases, to evaluate realistically the economy of borrowing, calculations of applicable external borrowing costs would necessarily include copyright royalty payments. In view of the substantial number of titles held in libraries that are not used at all (according to recent studies), however, it would appear unlikely that libraries would readily eliminate those with an average of more than five uses per year.

REFERENCES AND NOTES

[1] National Commission on Libraries and Information Science, Effective Access to the Periodical Literature: A National Program, Washington, D.C., April 1977.

[2] G. Williams, E.C. Bryant, R.R. V. Wiederkehr, V.E. Palmour, and C.J. Siehler, Library Cost Models: Owning Versus Borrowing Serial Publications, Chicago, Illinois: The Center for Research Libraries, 1968. (Study conducted by The Center for Research Libraries and Westat Research, Inc. for the National Science Foundation), PB 182 304.

[3] V.E. Palmour and R.R. V. Wiederkehr, "A Decision Model for Library Policies on Serial Publications." Paper presented at the XVII International Conference of the Institute of Management Sciences, London, England, July 1970.

[4] G. Williams, E.C. Bryant, R.R. V. Wiederkehr, V.E. Palmour, and C.J. Siehler, "Cost Models for Local Libraries," Reader in Library Cooperation, Edited by M.M. Reynolds, Washington, D.C.: NCR/Microcard Editions, 1972.

[5] For a discussion of the concept of present value, see Chapter 13, A.Alchian and W.Allen, University Economics, 2nd edition, Belmont, California: Wadsworth, 1969.

[6] The study reported here is one of several studies on various aspects of photocopy sponsored by CONTU, e.g., B.M. Fry, H.S. White and E.L. Johnson, Scholarly and Research Journals: Survey of Publisher Practices and Present Attitudes On Authorized Journal Article Copying and Licensing, Bloomington, Ind.: Indiana University, June 30, 1977. CONTU was one of three co-sponsors (National Commission on Libraries and Information Science,

National Science Foundation) of the study, Library Photocopying in the United States and Its Implications for the Development of a Copyright Royalty Payment Mechanism, Rockville, Md.: King Research, Inc., August 31, 1977 (Draft).

[7] For a discussion of relevant costs to be considered when comparing alternatives, see G.H. Fisher, Cost Considerations in Systems Analysis, New York: American Elsevier Pub. Co., 1971, Chapter 3, "Concepts of Economic Costs."

[8] F.F. Clasquin, "Periodicals Prices: 74-76 Update," Library Journal, Oct. 1, 1976, p. 2017.

[9] F.F. Clasquin and J.B. Cohen, "Prices of Physics and Chemistry Journals," Science, Vol. 197, No. 4302, 29 July 1977, pp. 432-438.

[10] A. Kent, K. L. Montgomery, J. Cohen, S. Bulick, W. Sabor, R. Flynn, D. Shirley, Progress Report on A Cost-Benefit Model of Some Critical Library Operations in Terms of Use of Materials, University of Pittsburg, April 1, 1977. (Current study funded by the National Science Foundation.)

APPENDIX A

A MODEL FOR THE PRESENT VALUE OF ALTERNATIVE LIBRARY POLICIES FOR PERIODICAL PUBLICATIONS

The cost over the planning period associated with a periodical title can be expressed as follows:

$$C = \sum_{y=1}^{P} \frac{C_y}{(1+r)^{y-1}} \qquad \text{(A-1)}$$

where C is the present value of costs, P denotes the planning period, y denotes a year in the planning period (i.e., $y = 1, 2, 3, \ldots, P$), C_y denotes the cost incurred in year y, and r denotes the nominal or monetary discount rate. This appendix develops an explicit expression for C.

The cost incurred in year y of the planning period, C_y, is given by:

$$C_y = I_y + P_y + M_y + S_y + W_y + U_y + B_y \qquad \text{(A-2)}$$

where the quantities on the right are defined in Table A-1.

TABLE A-1

COMPONENTS OF ANNUAL COST

Symbol in equation A-2	Cost Component
I_y	Initial cost of acquiring and cataloging a new title, zero except for y=1
P_y	Subscription cost in year y
M_y	Recurring annual costs such as check in, claiming, binding, marking, etc. in year y
S_y	Storage cost in year y
W_y	Disposal or weeding cost in year y
U_y	Cost of using in year y volumes of title held at library
B_y	Cost of borrowing from external sources in year y volumes not held by the library

The alternative policies for a periodical title affect the cost components in different ways, depending on which volumes of the title are held by the library. The first three cost components I_y, P_y and M_y are independent of the total number of volumes of a title held by the library. The storage cost, S_y, is porportional to the number of volumes of the periodical title held by the library in year y. The weeding cost is proportional to the number of volumes of the periodical discarded in year y.

The costs of using volumes held by the library in year y depends on which volumes are held by the library; and the cost of borrowing volumes not held by the library in year y depends on which volumes must be obtained from outside sources. These conditions are expressed by the following equations:

$$S_y = C_{vy} \alpha_y \qquad \text{(A-3)}$$

$$W_y = C_{wy} w_y \qquad \text{(A-4)}$$

$$U_y = C_{uy} D_y^+ \qquad \text{(A-5)}$$

$$B_y = C_{by} D_y^- \qquad \text{(A-6)}$$

where: C_{vy} = the cost of storing an annual volume* in year y

α_y = the number of annual volumes* held by the library in year y

C_{wy} = the cost of weeding an annual volumes in year y

w_y = the number of annual volumes weeded in year y

C_{uy} = the cost of satisfying a request for an annual volume held by the library in year y

D_y^+ = the number of satisfied requests (demand) fcr annual volumes held by the library in year y

C_{by} = the cost of satisfying a request for an annual volume not held by the library in year y

D_y^- = the number of satisfied requests (demand) for annual volumes not held by the library in year y.

Assuming that costs will increase at a steady rate of inflation i during the planning period gives the following equation:

$$\text{Cost in year } y = (1+i)^{y-1} \times \text{ cost in year } 1 . \qquad \text{(A-7)}$$

Substitution of Equations (A-2) to (A-7) in to Equation (A-1) gives:

$$C = I_1 + (M_1+P_1) \sum_{y=1}^{P} \theta^{y-1} + C_{v1} \sum_{y=1}^{P} \alpha_y \theta^{y-1} \qquad \text{(A-8)}$$

$$+ C_{w1} \sum_{y=1}^{P} w_y \theta^{y-1} + C_{u1} \sum_{y=1}^{P} D_y^+ \theta^{y-1} + C_{b1} \sum_{y=1}^{P} D_y^- \theta^{y-1}$$

where

$$\theta = \frac{1+i}{1+r} . \qquad \text{(A-9)}$$

*An annual volume is defined as all the articles contained in the periodical title in one year; it is not generally equal to a bound volume though it may be.

A computer program written in APL was used to calculate the cost C according to Equations (A-8) and (A-9). A listing of this program appears in Table A-2.

The quantities α_y and w_y, appearing in Equation (A-8), depend on the following parameters:

- the age of oldest volume of the periodical title held by the library in year y=1
- The age of the first volume of the periodical title in year y=1
- the cutoff age for the periodical title, the age at which annual volumes of a title are first weeded from the collection; i.e., annual volumes whose age equals or exceeds the cutoff age are weeded from the collection.

The quantities D_y^+ and D_y^- appearing in Equation (A-8) depend on the above quantities and the following as well:

- the normalized annual demand for the periodical title; i.e., the annual demand for a title with 10 years of back issues
- the decay of demand for a periodical title with age.

Equations relating α_y, W_y, D_y^+ and D_y^- to the above quantities are derived below and are embedded in the APL listing in Table A-2.

$\underline{\alpha_y}$

The number of annual volumes of the periodical title held by library in year y is:

$$\alpha_y = \alpha_y^+ - (\alpha_y^- - 1) \qquad \text{(A-10)}$$

where

α_y = the number of annual volumes held by the library in year y

α_y^+ = age of the oldest annual volume of the periodical title held by the library in year y

α_y^- = age of the youngest annual volume of the periodical title held by the library in year y.

We now derive expressions for α_y^+ and α_y^-.

First consider the case where the cutoff age is sufficiently large that no weeding takes place over the planning period. Then:

$$\alpha_y^+ = a_1 + y - 1 \qquad \text{(A-11)}$$

where

a_1 = the age of the oldest volume of the periodical title in year 1

$$\alpha_y^- = \begin{cases} 0 & \text{if the subscription is maintained} \\ y-1 & \text{if the subscription is terminated.} \end{cases} \qquad \text{(A-12)}$$

Now consider the effect of having a cutoff age which may require some weeding. No annual volumes with ages equal to or greater than the cutoff age will be held by the library. Hence, the more general experssion for α_y^+ is:

$$\alpha_y^+ = \min(a_1 + y - 1,\ a_c - 1) \qquad \text{(A-13)}$$

where

a_c = the cutoff age for the periodical title; when annual volumes reach the cutoff age, they are purged from the collection.

When the subscription to a periodical title is terminated, the age of the youngest title increases with a value of y-1 as we advance into the planning period. When this age equals $a_c - 1$, only one annual volume is held by the library. (This is in accord with Equation A-10.) We therefore define $\bar{\alpha}_y$ to be equal to a_c when all annual volumes of the periodical volume have been weeded from the library. This definition ensures that Equation A-10 remains valid when all annual volumes of a periodical title have been disposed of. Therefore, the more general expression for $\bar{\alpha}_y$ is:

$$\bar{\alpha}_y = \begin{cases} 0, & \text{subscription maintained} \\ \min(y-1,\ a_c), & \text{subscription terminated.} \end{cases} \quad \text{(A-14)}$$

$\underline{W_y}$

The number of volumes weeded in year y, W_y, will be 0 unless the age of the oldest volume as given by (A-11) equals or exceeds the cutoff age. For year 1 we have:

$$W_1 = \max\,[0, a_1 - (a_c - 1)] \quad \text{(A-15)}$$

For subsequent years, when the subscription is maintained, we have:

$$W_y = \begin{cases} 1, & \text{if } a_1 + y - 1 \geq a_c \\ 0, & \text{if } a_1 + y - 1 < a_c \end{cases} \quad \text{(A-16)}$$

When the subscription is terminated we have:

$$W_y = \begin{cases} 1, & \text{if } a_1 + y - 1 \geq a_c \text{ and } a_c \geq y-1 \\ 0, & \text{otherwise.} \end{cases} \quad \text{(A-17)}$$

$\underline{D^+_y \text{ and } D^-_y}$

These quantities can be derived from the cumulative demand curve for the periodical title, D(a), which is given by:

$$D(a) = \frac{F(a)}{F(10)} D(10) \quad \text{(A-18)}$$

where

D(a) = the demand for annual volumes of a periodical title whose ages are less than or equal to a.

D(10) = the normalized demand per year for a periodical title; i.e., the demand for a title with 10 years of back issues; or the demand for the most recent 10 years of a periodical title.

F(a) = the fraction of total demand for annual volumes of a periodical title whose ages are less than or equal to a, where a = 0, 1, 2, 3,...

The total demand for a periodical title in year y, D_y, is estimated to be:

$$D_y = D(\alpha^*_y) \quad \text{(A-19)}$$

where

D_y = total demand for a periodical title in year y.

α^*_y = age of the first annual volume of the periodical title in year y.

The quantity α^*_y is given by:

$$\alpha^*_y = b_1 + y - 1 \qquad \text{(A-20)}$$

where

b_1 = the age of the first volume of the periodical title in year 1.

The demand in year y for annual volumes of the title held by the library is:

$$D^+_y = D(\alpha^+_y) - D(\alpha^-_y - 1) \qquad \text{(A-21)}$$

The demand in year y for annual volumes not held by the library is:

$$D^-_y = D_y - D^+_y \qquad \text{(A-22)}$$

Because the current year (y=1) corresponds to an age of zero (a=0), it is convenient to define:

$$D(-1) = 0. \qquad \text{(A-23)}$$

This permits us to evaluate Equation (A-21) when $\alpha^-_y = 0$, a condition that occurs whenever the subscription is maintained.

Tables A-3 through A-7 show the input and output formats used in the APL program. Table A-3 shows the inputs for Library A for the use where the subscription is maintained, and table A-4 is the corresponding output. For the case where the subscription is terminated and back issues are retained, table A-5 gives the inputs, table A-6 gives the costs outputs, and table A-7 shows the values of the parameters used in this computer run.

A copy of the APL computer program is available at cost from the Public Research Institute. The current 1977 cost of the program is $50.

TABLE A-2

LISTING OF APL PROGRAM FOR COMPUTING COST

```
    ∇ INPUT
[1]     '                      LIBRARY COST MODEL  BE'
[2]     RID←QQ'RUN IDENTIFICATION='
[3]     INT←⍎QQ'INTEREST RATE='
[4]     INF←⍎QQ'INFLATION RATE='
[5]     PLN←⍎QQ'PLANNING PERIOD IN YEARS='
[6]     GD←(1 0 1 0 2)['YN10'⍳1↑QQ'DO DEMANDS DROP OF GEOMETRICALLY WITH AGE?']
[7]     →(B2,B1)[GD+1]
[8]    B1:DEC←⍎QQ'DEMAND DECAY FACTOR='
[9]     CUMS←(1-DEC*¯1+⍳(1+BEG+PLN))÷(1-DEC)
[10]    →B3
[11]   B3:CST←⍎QQ'STORAGE COST='
[12]    CWE←⍎QQ'WEEDING COST='
[13]    CUS←⍎QQ'INTERNAL USE COST='
[14]    CBINT←⍎QQ'INTERNAL COST OF BORROWING='
[15]    CBEXT←⍎QQ'EXTERNAL COST OF BORROWING='
[16]    CBR←CBINT+CBEXT
```

TABLE A-2 (Cont'd)

```
[17]   AGE←⍎QQ'AGE OF OLDEST VOLUME IN THE COLLECTION ='
[18]   BEG←⍎QQ'AGE OF FIRST VOLUME OF THE TITLE='
[19]   NSW←(1 0 1 0 2)['YN10'⍳1↑QQ'IS THIS A NEW SUBSCRIPTION?']
[20]   →(L8,L6)[NSW+1]
[21]  L1:SM←(1 0 1 0 2)['YN10'⍳1↑QQ'IS SUBSCRIPTION MAINTAINED?']
[22]   →(L5,L7)[SM+1]
[23]  L7:M←⍎QQ'RECURRING ANNUAL COST (EXCLUDING SUBSCR COST)='
[24]   NP←⍎QQ'HOW MANY SUBSCRIPTION COSTS DO YOU WISH TO ENTER?'
[25]   J←0
[26]   P←NP⍴0
[27]  L2:J←J+1
[28]   P[J]←⍎QQ'P(',(7⍕J),')='
[29]   →(J<NP)/L2
[30]  L4:NC←⍎QQ'HOW MANY VALUES OF CUTOFF AGE DO YOU WISH TO CONSIDER?'
[31]   COA←NC⍴0
[32]   J←0
[33]  L9:J←J+1
[34]   COA[J]←⍎QQ'COA(',(7⍕J),')='
[35]   →(J<NC)/L9
[36]   ND←⍎QQ'HOW MANY ANNUAL DEMANDS DO YOU WISH TO CONSIDER?'
[37]   DT←ND⍴0
[38]   J←0
[39]  L3:J←J+1
[40]   DT[J]←⍎QQ'D(',(7⍕J),')='
[41]   →(J<ND)/L3
[42]   'BBTHIS COMPLETES THE INPUT. TO COMPUTE COSTS TYPE COST AND PRESS RETURN
KEY.'
[43]   '                          TO CHECK INPUTS TYPE PARAMS AND PRESS RETURN K
EY.'
[44]   →0
[45]  B2:CUMS←⍎QQ'ENTER CUMULATIVE DEMAND SHAPE AS A VECTOR:LENGTH=PLN+BEG+1'
[46]   →B3×⍳(⍴CUMS=PLN+BEG+1)
[47]   'LENGTH OF VECTOR INCORRECT, TRY AGAIN.'
[48]   →B2
[49]  L5:M←0
[50]   NP←1
[51]   P←1⍴0
[52]   →L4
[53]  L6:SM←1
[54]   CIN←⍎QQ'INITIAL COST='
[55]   →L7
[56]  L8:CIN←0
[57]   →L1
     ∇


     ∇ R←QQ A
 [1]     ⍞←A,' '
 [2]     R←⍞
     ∇


     ∇ PARAMS
 [1]     'RUN IDENTIFICATION,RID= ';RID
 [2]     'INTEREST RATE,INT= ';INT
 [3]     'INFLATION RATE,INF= ';INF
 [4]     'STORAGE COST,CST= ';CST
 [5]     'WEEDING COST,CWE= ';CWE
 [6]     'INTERNAL USE COST,CUS= ';CUS
 [7]     'INTERNAL COST OF BORROWING,CBINT=';CBINT
 [8]     'EXTERNAL COST OF BORROWING,CBEXT=';CBEXT
 [9]     'BORROWING COST,CBR= ';CBR
 [10]    'INITIAL COST,CIN= ';CIN
 [11]    'AGE OF OLDEST VOLUME IN THE COLLECTION,AGE= ';AGE
 [12]    'AGE OF FIRST VOLUME OF THE TITLE,BEG= ';BEG
 [13]    'SUBSCRIPTION MAINTAINED SWITCH,SM= ';SM
 [14]    'NEW SUBSCRIPTION SWITCH,NSW=';NSW
 [15]    'PLANNING PERIOD,PLN= ';PLN
 [16]    'DEMAND DECAY FACTOR,DEC= ';DEC
 [17]    'RECURRING ANNUAL COST (EXCLUDING SUBSCR. COST),M= ';M
 [18]    'NUMBER OF CUTTOFF AGES,NC= ';NC
 [19]    'CUTTOFF AGES,COA= ';COA
 [20]    'NUMBER OF SUBSCRIPTION COSTS,NP= ';NP
 [21]    'SUBSCRIPTION COSTS,P=';P
 [22]    'NUMBER OF DEMANDS,ND= ';ND
 [23]    'DEMAND VALUES,DT= ';DT
 [24]    'CUMULATIVE DEMAND VS AGE SHAPE,CUMS:'
 [25]    CUMS
```

TABLE A-2 (Cont'd)

```
      ∇ COST
[1]     ⍝MASTER PROGRAM FOR COMPUTING COSTS OF OWNING AND BORROWING SERIAL TITLES
[2]     PRELIM
[3]     ANNUAL
[4]     STORE
[5]     WEED
[6]     DEMANDS
[7]     COSTIN
[8]     COSTOUT
[9]     CR←(NC,ND)⍴0
[10]    OUTPUT
      ∇

      ∇ PRELIM
[1]     CUT←COA+1
[2]     AGEV←NC⍴AGE
[3]     ⍝THETA
[4]     TH←(1+INF)÷(1+INT)
[5]     T←¯1+⍳PLN
[6]     X←⍳PLN+1
[7]     THT←0,TH*T
[8]     AGET←1,AGE+T+2
[9]     BEGT←1,BEG+T+2
[10]    TE←0,T
[11]    ALFP←CUT∘.⌊AGET
[12]    ALFM←2+(COA∘.⌊TE)×SM=0
[13]    ALFT←1+ALFP-ALFM
[14]    MV←NP⍴M
[15]    NCUM←CUMS×(÷CUMS[11])
[16]    CUMD←(,DT)∘.×NCUM
      ∇

      ∇ ANNUAL
[1]     ⍝PRESENT VALUE OF ANNUAL EXPENSES
[2]     TH←TH+0.000001×(TH=1)
[3]     DEC←DEC+0.000001×(GRO×TH×DEC=1)
[4]     A←(MV+P)×+/THT
      ∇

      ∇ STORE
[1]     ⍝PRESENT VALUE OF STORAGE COST
[2]     CV←CST×+/ALFT×(((⍴CUT)⍴1)∘.×THT)
      ∇

      ∇ WEED
[1]     ⍝WEEDING COST--
[2]     ALFW←(CUT+1)∘.⌊TE
[3]     WT1←CUT∘.<AGET
[4]     WT0←(CUT∘.<AGET)∧(CUT∘.≥TE)
[5]     WT←(WT0×(SM=0))+WT1×(SM=1)
[6]     W1←0⌈AGEV+1-COA
[7]     WT[;1 2]←⍉(2,NC)⍴W2←(NC⍴0),W1
[8]     CW←CWE×+/WT×(((⍴CUT)⍴1)∘.×THT)
      ∇

      ∇ DEMANDS
[1]     DIST←2 1 3⍉(ND,NC,PLN+1)⍴(CUMD[;,ALFP]-CUMD[;,ALFM-1])
[2]     DIST[;;1]←(NC,ND)⍴0
[3]     DTOT←(NC,ND,PLN+1)⍴CUMD[;,BEGT]
[4]     DTOT[;;1]←(NC,ND)⍴0
[5]     DOST←DTOT-DIST
[6]     DIS←+/DIST
[7]     DOS←+/DOST
      ∇

      ∇ COSTOUT
[1]     CB←CBR×+/DOST×((⍴DIST)⍴THT)
      ∇

      ∇ OUTPUT
[1]     '                              COST MODEL FOR SERIAL TITLES R'
[2]     DA←ND,1
[3]     →(L1,L2)[SM+1]
[4]    L1:'SUBSCRIPTION TERMINATED '
[5]     →L3
```

TABLE A-2 (Cont'd)

```
[6]    L2:'SUBSCRIPTION MAINTAINED'
[7]    L3:J←0
[8]    L4:J←J+1
[9]     K←0
[10]   L5:K←K+1
[11]    'EFOR CUTOFF AGE= ';COA[J]
[12]    'FOR SUBSCRIPTION COST= ';P[K]
[13]    'E  DEMAND     IN      AN       STO      RES    NEED  USE     BOR      TOT       DOS
   DIS     '
[14]    C←(DAρCIN),(DAρA[K]),(DAρCV[J]),(DAρ(-CR[J;])),(DAρCW[J]),(DAρCU[J;]),DAρ
CB[J;]
[15]    CT←+/C
[16]    B←C,CT
[17]    E←(DAρDOS[J;]),(DAρDIS[J;])
[18]    ((DAρDT+0.05)⍕7 4 2 0),' ',((B+0.5)⍕7 5 1 0),' ',((E+0.5)⍕6 4 1 0)
[19]    →(K<NP)/L5
[20]    →(J<NC)/L4
[21]    →L6×⍳CSW=0
[22]    'EE OPTIMUM CUTOFF AGE NOT COMPUTED IN THIS VERSION OF PROGRAM'
[23]  L6:'EEEND OF RUN  ',RID
    ∇
```

TABLE A-3

```
      INPUT
                    LIBRARY COST MODEL


RUN IDENTIFICATION= EXAMPLE OF INPUT AND OUTPUT
INTEREST RATE= .06
INFLATION RATE= .04
PLANNING PERIOD IN YEARS= 25
DO DEMANDS DROP OF GEOMETRICALLY WITH AGE? NO
ENTER CUMULATIVE DEMAND SHAPE AS A VECTOR:LENGTH=PLN+BEG+1 CSND
STORAGE COST= 0
WEEDING COST= 0
INTERNAL USE COST= .36
INTERNAL COST OF BORROWING= 7.02
EXTERNAL COST OF BORROWING= 3.00
AGE OF OLDEST VOLUME IN THE COLLECTION = 10
AGE OF FIRST VOLUME OF THE TITLE= 10
IS THIS A NEW SUBSCRIPTION? NO
IS SUBSCRIPTION MAINTAINED? YES
RECURRING ANNUAL COST (EXCLUDING SUBSCR COST)= 24.45
HOW MANY SUBSCRIPTION COSTS DO YOU WISH TO ENTER? 5
P(1)= 0
P(2)= 20
P(3)= 40
P(4)= 80
P(5)= 120
HOW MANY VALUES OF CUTOFF AGE DO YOU WISH TO CONSIDER? 1
COA(1)= 100
HOW MANY ANNUAL DEMANDS DO YOU WISH TO CONSIDER? 6
D(1)= .001
D(2)= 4
D(3)= 8
D(4)= 12
D(5)= 16
D(6)= 20


THIS COMPLETES THE INPUT. TO COMPUTE COSTS TYPE COST AND PRESS RETURN KEY.
                          TO CHECK INPUTS TYPE PARAMS AND PRESS RETURN KEY.
```

TABLE A-4

COST

COST MODEL FOR SERIAL TITLES

SUBSCRIPTION MAINTAINED

FOR CUTOFF AGE= 100
FOR SUBSCRIPTION COST= 0

DEMAND	IN	AN	STO	RES	WEED	USE	BOR	TOT	DOS	DIS
0.0	0.	491.	0.	0.	0.	0.	0.	491.	0.	0.
4.0	0.	491.	0.	0.	0.	31.	0.	522.	0.	108.
8.0	0.	491.	0.	0.	0.	62.	0.	553.	0.	216.
12.0	0.	491.	0.	0.	0.	93.	0.	584.	0.	323.
16.0	0.	491.	0.	0.	0.	124.	0.	615.	0.	431.
20.0	0.	491.	0.	0.	0.	155.	0.	646.	0.	539.

FOR CUTOFF AGE= 100
FOR SUBSCRIPTION COST= 20

DEMAND	IN	AN	STO	RES	WEED	USE	BOR	TOT	DOS	DIS
0.0	0.	893.	0.	0.	0.	0.	0.	893.	0.	0.
4.0	0.	893.	0.	0.	0.	31.	0.	924.	0.	108.
8.0	0.	893.	0.	0.	0.	62.	0.	955.	0.	216.
12.0	0.	893.	0.	0.	0.	93.	0.	986.	0.	323.
16.0	0.	893.	0.	0.	0.	124.	0.	1017.	0.	431.
20.0	0.	893.	0.	0.	0.	155.	0.	1048.	0.	539.

FOR CUTOFF AGE= 100
FOR SUBSCRIPTION COST= 40

DEMAND	IN	AN	STO	RES	WEED	USE	BOR	TOT	DOS	DIS
0.0	0.	1294.	0.	0.	0.	0.	0.	1294.	0.	0.
4.0	0.	1294.	0.	0.	0.	31.	0.	1325.	0.	108.
8.0	0.	1294.	0.	0.	0.	62.	0.	1356.	0.	216.
12.0	0.	1294.	0.	0.	0.	93.	0.	1387.	0.	323.
16.0	0.	1294.	0.	0.	0.	124.	0.	1418.	0.	431.
20.0	0.	1294.	0.	0.	0.	155.	0.	1449.	0.	539.

FOR CUTOFF AGE= 100
FOR SUBSCRIPTION COST= 80

DEMAND	IN	AN	STO	RES	WEED	USE	BOR	TOT	DOS	DIS
0.0	0.	2097.	0.	0.	0.	0.	0.	2097.	0.	0.
4.0	0.	2097.	0.	0.	0.	31.	0.	2128.	0.	108.
8.0	0.	2097.	0.	0.	0.	62.	0.	2159.	0.	216.
12.0	0.	2097.	0.	0.	0.	93.	0.	2191.	0.	323.
16.0	0.	2097.	0.	0.	0.	124.	0.	2222.	0.	431.
20.0	0.	2097.	0.	0.	0.	155.	0.	2253.	0.	539.

FOR CUTOFF AGE= 100
FOR SUBSCRIPTION COST= 120

DEMAND	IN	AN	STO	RES	WEED	USE	BOR	TOT	DOS	DIS
0.0	0.	2901.	0.	0.	0.	0.	0.	2901.	0.	0.
4.0	0.	2901.	0.	0.	0.	31.	0.	2932.	0.	108.
8.0	0.	2901.	0.	0.	0.	62.	0.	2963.	0.	216.
12.0	0.	2901.	0.	0.	0.	93.	0.	2994.	0.	323.
16.0	0.	2901.	0.	0.	0.	124.	0.	3025.	0.	431.
20.0	0.	2901.	0.	0.	0.	155.	0.	3056.	0.	539.

END OF RUN EXAMPLE OF INPUT AND OUTPUT

TABLE A-5

INPUT

LIBRARY COST MODEL

RUN IDENTIFICATION= EXAMPLE OF TERMINATING A SUBSCRIPTION
INTEREST RATE= .06
INFLATION RATE= .04
PLANNING PERIOD IN YEARS= 25
DO DEMANDS DROP OF GEOMETRICALLY WITH AGE? NO
ENTER CUMULATIVE DEMAND SHAPE AS A VECTOR:LENGTH=PLN+BEG+1 CSND
STORAGE COST= 0
WEEDING COST= 0
INTERNAL USE COST= .36
INTERNAL COST OF BORROWING= 7.02
EXTERNAL COST OF BORROWING= 3.00

```
AGE OF OLDEST VOLUME IN THE COLLECTION = 10
AGE OF FIRST VOLUME OF THE TITLE= 10
IS THIS A NEW SUBSCRIPTION? NO
IS SUBSCRIPTION MAINTAINED? NO
HOW MANY VALUES OF CUTOFF AGE DO YOU WISH TO CONSIDER? 1
COA(1)= 100
HOW MANY ANNUAL DEMANDS DO YOU WISH TO CONSIDER? 7
D(1)= .001
D(2)= 4
D(3)= 8
D(4)= 10
D(5)= 12
D(6)= 16
D(7)= 20

THIS COMPLETES THE INPUT. TO COMPUTE COSTS TYPE COST AND PRESS RETURN KEY.
                          TO CHECK INPUTS TYPE PARAMS AND PRESS RETURN KEY.
```

TABLE A-6

```
COST
                        COST MODEL FOR SERIAL TITLES

SUBSCRIPTION TERMINATED

FOR CUTOFF AGE=  100
FOR SUBSCRIPTION COST=  0
```

DEMAND	IN	AN	STO	RES	WEED	USE	BOR	TOT	DOS	DIS
0.0	0.	0.	0.	0.	0.	0.	0.	0.	0.	0.
4.0	0.	0.	0.	0.	0.	5.	728.	733.	93.	15.
8.0	0.	0.	0.	0.	0.	10.	1456.	1466.	186.	30.
10.0	0.	0.	0.	0.	0.	12.	1821.	1833.	233.	37.
12.0	0.	0.	0.	0.	0.	15.	2185.	2199.	279.	44.
16.0	0.	0.	0.	0.	0.	20.	2913.	2932.	372.	59.
20.0	0.	0.	0.	0.	0.	25.	3641.	3666.	465.	74.

```
END OF RUN  EXAMPLE OF TERMINATING A SUBSCRIPTION
```

TABLE A-7

```
     PARAMS
RUN IDENTIFICATION,RID= EXAMPLE OF TERMINATING A SUBSCRIPTION
INTEREST RATE,INT=  0.06
INFLATION RATE,INF=  0.04
STORAGE COST,CST=  0
WEEDING COST,CWE=  0
INTERNAL USE COST,CUS=  0.36
INTERNAL COST OF BORROWING,CBINT= 7.02
EXTERNAL COST OF BORROWING,CBEXT= 3
BORROWING COST,CBR=  10.02
INITIAL COST,CIN=  0
AGE OF OLDEST VOLUME IN THE COLLECTION,AGE=  10
AGE OF FIRST VOLUME OF THE TITLE,BEG=  10
SUBSCRIPTION MAINTAINED SWITCH,SM=  0
NEW SUBSCRIPTION SWITCH,NSW= 0
PLANNING PERIOD,PLN=  25
DEMAND DECAY FACTOR,DEC=  0.93
RECURRING ANNUAL COST (EXCLUDING SUBSCR. COST),M=  0
NUMBER OF CUTTOFF AGES,NC=  1
CUTTOFF AGES,COA=  100
NUMBER OF SUBSCRIPTION COSTS,NP=  1
SUBSCRIPTION COSTS,P= 0
NUMBER OF DEMANDS,ND=  7
DEMAND VALUES,DT=  0.001 4 8 10 12 16 20
CUMULATIVE DEMAND VS AGE SHAPE,CUMS:
 0 42.7 56 65.4 73.1 79.3 81.9 83.8 85.6 86.9 88.1 89.2 90.2 91.1 91.9 92.6 93.2
      93.7 94.1 94.4 94.6 94.9 95.2 95.5 95.8 96.1 96.3 96.5 96.7 96.9 97.1 97.3
      97.5 97.7 97.9 98.1 98.3 98.5 98.6
```

APPENDIX B

COST ELEMENTS FOR UTILIZING THE DECISION MODEL

LIBRARY COST FACTORS

Cost factors utilized in the decision model do not reflect total library costs for providing periodical (defined here as journal) services. General administration and supervision costs have been excluded, since such costs do not appear to have any direct relationship to the number of titles held. Reference service costs have similarly been excluded, since service is not limited to in-library journal collections alone, nor do reference costs necessarily vary with the number of titles held in-house.[1]

Use of data bases, which furnish bibliographic data and abstracts of journal articles, are an expanding phenomenon in research libraries and provide an increasingly common periodical service cost, although charges for them varies from full cost recovery from patron to full cost borne by the library. In some aspects, these data bases may be viewed as duplicate subscriptions (in another form) to reference journals also held in print. While in this study, data base costs have been considered reference rather than materials costs and excluded from the cost data, it may be pertinent at a future date to compare cost and use data for printed reference periodicals versus data base search, in reviewing continuance of increasingly costly reference journal subscriptions.

Library cost inputs comprised four of the cost categories used in the model. These are:

1. The average initial cost of acquiring and cataloging a new title.
2. The average annual per title cost for maintaining and servicing journal materials.
3. The average cost per use of journal materials, including circulation, interlibrary lending, and in-house use.
4. The average cost for borrowing a journal item through interlibrary loan.

In order to calculate the crossover or breakeven points in specific cost and use situations, these cost data were collected from five libraries. (The format for collection is shown in appendix C.) They are:

Library A: The main library of a large university. The 1,000,000 volumes and almost 7,000 current journal subscriptions are primarily in the humanities, social sciences, and life sciences. Almost one-quarter of total bookstock is bound journals.

Library A-1: The Engineering branch of Library A. Half of its approximately 130,000 volumes are bound periodicals, and the library has 1,425 current journal titles. The collection includes engineering fields and mathematics.

Library A-2: The Architecture branch of Library A. This small library holds 18,000 bound volumes (about one-fifth periodicals) and 145 current journal titles.

Library B: A smaller academic main library, with about 350,000 volumes, including 46,000 bound periodical volumes, and 2,615 current journal titles. The collection is similar to that of Library A, with holdings in humanities, social sciences, and life sciences. A small percentage of basic physical science materials are also included.

---

[1] For a discussion of relevant costs to be considered when comparing alternatives, see G.H. Fisher, Cost Considerations in Systems Analysis, New York: American Elsevier Pub. Co., 1971, Chapter 3, "Concepts of Economic Costs."

Library C: A large special library (science and technology) with holdings in physics, chemistry, mathematics, and technology. About four-fifths of the 125,000 volume collection is bound journals; the library carries slightly under 2,200 current journal titles, including a substantial level of gifts and exchanges.

Category I: Initial Costs for New Titles

Initial costs include labor for acquiring and cataloging new journal titles, as well as non-labor costs of providing catalog cards. Average acquisitions costs per new title have been calculated for both paid subscriptions and for subscriptions derived through gifts and exchanges. They do not include the actual subscription cost, nor, in the case of exchanges, the cost of the material exchanged.

For new paid subscriptions, acquisitions costs include:

1. Searching
2. Ordering
3. Preparation of invoices
4. Payment procedures.

Staff time spent in arranging gifts and exchanges accounts for acquisitions costs for materials received in that manner.

Selection of materials is not included among acquisition tasks in this one-time cost, since the total selection and title review process is considered to encompass review of all currently held titles in the collection. In addition, such staff time is a recurring cost which is not necessarily modified by the number of new titles added to the collection.

Cataloging costs apply to paid and free subscriptions alike, and include both cataloging and preparation of catalog cards. Where a shared cataloging system is used, costs for the bibliographic data base utilized as well as the cost of catalog cards would be included here.

Initial costs for the five sample libraries are shown in table B-1.

Category II: Annual Recurring Costs

Annual recurring costs are those labor and non-labor costs which result from routine maintenance and servicing of a periodical title. Labor tasks include:

1. Selection and review.
2. Renewal of subscriptions and preparation of invoices.
3. Ordering of missing, lost, or vandalized back issues.
4. Check-in and claiming of issues.
5. Shelving of new materials.
6. Catalog/shelf list/Kardex maintenance
7. Preparation of serials list.
8. Binding preparation, shipment and receipt, and marking.
9. Training.
10. Direct supervision (administration).

Non-labor costs include computer preparation and publication of serials list, and binding of journal volumes.

Table B-2 lists the annual recurring costs, by task, for the five libraries.

Category III: Internal Use Costs

Internal use of journals includes "circulation" of bound volumes and unbound issues, in-library use, or photocopying for use, and loaning of journal materials, or provision of photocopies of journal articles, in interlibrary loan. Unlike initial and maintenance costs which are based on the per title unit, internal use costs are based on total use of all journal items.

TABLE B-1
INITIAL COSTS FOR FIVE SAMPLE LIBRARIES

Library	Initial costs per title (dollars)[a]				
	A	A-1	A-2	B	C
New paid subscription					
Acquisitions (includes searching, orders, payments, and specific training and administration)	38.65[b]	38.65[b]	38.65[b]	7.17	29.42
Cataloging (includes cataloging and preparation of catalog cards)	32.00[c]	33.57[c]	33.57[c]	4.37	24.10
Total cost, paid subscription	70.65	72.22	72.22	11.54	53.52
New free subscription				None	
Acquisitions	12.61	12.61	12.61		13.81
Cataloging	32.00	33.57	33.57		24.10
Total cost, free subscription	44.61	46.18	46.18		37.91

[a] Labor costs include fringe benefits.

[b] All acquisitions are carried on in a single university serials department.

[c] Cataloging is done in the university serials department; branch libraries require an additional set of catalog cards.

TABLE B-2
ANNUAL RECURRING COSTS FOR FIVE SAMPLE LIBRARIES

Library	Cost per title (dollars)				
	A	A-1	A-2	B	C
Task					
Selection and review	1.95	0.15	1.76	0.66	0.85
Renewal and renewal payments (includes back issue orders)	2.74[a]	2.74[a]	2.74[a]	0.32	1.45
Check-in (includes catalog maintenance and shelving of new materials)	5.58	3.85	6.04	1.25	3.27
Claiming	0.16	0.76	0.86	0.08	0.89
Administration	0.94	3.77	1.71	Neg.	2.70
Serials list preparation	0.45[a]	0.45[a]	0.45[a]	0.56	2.43
Binding preparation	4.07	5.32	2.75	2.54	3.49
Other[b]	0.15	0.90	1.15	—	0.10
Total labor costs[c]					
Non-labor costs					
Serials list production	1.22[a]	1.22[a]	1.22[a]	d	0.63
Bindery (per annual volume)	7.17	9.14	7.42	3.90	10.13
Kardex cards	0.02	0.02	0.02	Neg.	Neg.
Total annual recurring cost per title	24.45	28.32	26.12	9.31	25.94

[a] Task performed by university serials department.

[b] Includes training, and transfer of materials.

[c] Includes fringe benefits

[d] Not charged to library.

Use patterns for journal materials in libraries vary substantially, ranging from the no circulation (outside the library) policy of many academic libraries, to the full circulation and free photocopying of the special library in our sample. Even where materials circulate, however, a substantial proportion of journal use takes place within the library. Where there is open access to materials, the measurement of internal use is difficult, and little data regarding the total volume of use of journal materials in libraries is available.

For the most part, use data in this category have been based on the reshelving of materials, both bound volumes and current issues. In libraries where observations have been made, approximately half of bound materials reshelved (including circulated monographs, etc) would appear to be journal volumes, and this has applied across most subject areas. The proportions of use of current issues to bound volumes (retrospective issues), however, varies widely by subject area.

Measuring use of journal materials by the counting of reshelved materials introduces the possibility of underestimating use because of materials reshelved by users. Among bound volumes, this may be insignificant, since user reshelving is considered to reflect a high proportion of rejection rather than use. Some underestimation of the use of current issues may result, however, since browsers of current materials frequently peruse them in adjacent seating and are more likely to return used materials to the open shelf.

Costs for internal use include:

1. Appropriate service desk "circulation" costs. This includes normal circulation costs where materials circulate, plus the labor costs of making materials available to users by locating them, directing users to them, etc. Reference costs are NOT included.
2. Photocopy costs if free photocopy service is provided to users.
3. Labor costs for reshelving of bound volumes and current issues.
4. The cost of lending periodical materials in interlibrary loan. This includes labor costs and photocopy and postage charges when these are not covered.

Unit costs per use of a periodical item is calculated by dividing total annual use costs of the four categories listed above, by the total number of items used (or reshelved, where use figures are not available). Total annual costs, annual units of use for the same period, and the resultant unit cost of internal use are shown in table B-3 for the five libraries.

TABLE B-3
INTERNAL USE COSTS FOR FIVE SAMPLE LIBRARIES

	Library				
A. Total annual costs	A	A-1	A-2	B	C
Circulation	$ 45,509	$ 3,223		$11,912	
Reshelving materials	10,608	2,288	$2,722	3,372	$21,285
In-library photocopying	a	a	a	a	11,137
Interlibrary lending	10,114	4,359	b	6,702	4,430
Total annual cost	$ 66,231	$ 9,870	$2,722	$21,986	$36,852
B. Total annual use					
Circulation	—	4,712[c]	—	—	5,109
Other items reshelved	183,165	28,559	4,185	37,488	71,469
Total items used	183,165	33,271	4,185	37,488	76,578
C. Unit cost of internal use	$ 0.36	$ 0.30	$ 0.65	$ 0.58	$ 0.48

[a] Patron pays for in-library photocopying.

[b] ILL is handled by main library.

[c] Materials are circulated only overnight.

Category IV. Cost of Borrowing Journal Materials Through Interlibrary Loan

Two components make up the total cost of borrowing journal materials through interlibrary loan. These are:

1. Internal borrowing costs.
2. External borrowing costs, or charges made by lending libraries.

Internal labor costs for verifying bibliographic data, locating materials, and preparing and forwarding requests have been calculated and unit costs developed on the basis of requests filled.

Many libraries are part of networks providing substantial levels of their interlibrary borrowing requirements with little or no lending library charge. Even where such arrangements do not exist, the number of libraries charging more than small amounts for processing and photocopying remains few, and average external borrowing charges reported by the sample libraries were minimal. External borrowing charges used as input for the model are not based on data collected in the libraries.

Table B-4 shows internal borrowing costs for the three sample libraries.

TABLE B-4

AVERAGE INTERNAL BORROWING COSTS FOR THREE SAMPLE LIBRARIES

Library	Average internal borrowing cost per item (dollars)
A	7.02
B	5.09
C	9.48

COST DATA FROM OTHER SOURCES

Other cost elements required for the model have been applied uniformly to all of the sample libraries. The remaining cost inputs used in the model are:

1. External borrowing costs
2. Storage costs
3. Disposition (weeding) costs
4. Subscription costs.

External Borrowing Costs

Although actual average external borrowing (or lending library) charges reported by the sample libraries are minimal, the increasing tendency to attempt to recover costs for such operations makes it necessary to illustrate the differences in crossover points if a library is required to fund the total costs of an interlibrary borrowing transaction. For this reason, external borrowing charges of $3 and $8, as well as the no charge situation, have been introduced in all decision situations.

Storage Costs

Few data are available concerning library storage costs, and most are not recent. Several problems arise in the use of this cost factor:

1. If space in existing buildings is not saturated, there is essentially no marginal storage cost; that is, there is no variation in overall cost which relates to the addition or subtraction of materials stored.

2. The costs of storage space vary greatly with the age of the buildings and equipment.

3. Replacement costs also vary with the availability of land already owned, local building costs, etc., and in addition, do not properly reflect costs of existing storage. Furthermore, replacement reflects an incremental rather than linear cost.

For use in the decision model, the assumption was made that when present storage areas are adequate sometime into the future, all materials are retained. In this case, the storage cost is "$0", since no additional costs accrue as the result of the addition. In cases where space is becoming critical, storage costs are calculated at $0.50 per annual volume.[1]

Disposal (Weeding) Costs

Published disposal or weeding costs have generally reflected the cost of moving materials from conventional to compact or off-site storage. Alternate kinds of storage were not addressed; here weeding represents complete loss of access to the materials removed. Several methods of weeding were analyzed and costed in Raffel and Shishko in 1969, including:

1. By publication date. Costs have been estimated at $0.20 and $0.40 per volume equivalent. This translates in 1977 dollars to $0.49 and $0.99 per annual volume, with a mean of $0.74.

2. By circulation criterion. The cost cited was $0.61, but a range of $0.80 to $1.00 per volume equivalent was considered more reasonable. In 1977 dollars this would be $1.50, or $1.97 to $2.46 per annual volume.

The primary cost difference between the two methods was the handling of individual materials to determine use, and the individual notation of catalog cards to indicate withdrawals. It is assumed that libraries would choose methods and means for minimizing weeding costs and that the average cost of the publication date method would be the more relevant. Inflated 1968 Westat weeding costs equaled $0.60. The mean of these two estimates was rounded to $0.65 per annual volume.

Subscription Costs

Clasquin, in Library Journal,[2] reported an average journal price for academic libraries in 1976 of about $40. For special libraries the average subscription price may be considerably higher. Subscription rates ranging from $0 to over $3,000 per year were reported by the sample libraries, with over 300 (almost 15 percent) of the subscriptions reported by the special library exceeding $120 in cost.

Five subscription rates, ranging from $0 to $120, were chosen to demonstrate the levels of average annual use below which borrowing is less costly than owning a title. Obviously, as subscription prices rise above $120 per year, the necessary level of use for cost economy also continues to increase.

---

[1] A 1969 study (J.A. Raffel and R. Shishko, Systematic Analysis of University Libraries: An Application of Cost-Benefit Analysis to the M.I.T. Libraries, Cambridge, Mass.: The M.I.T. Press, 1969) provides a storage cost for open access, conventional storage on campus, with moderate use, of $0.2825 per volume equivalent (2/3 annual volume). When inflated to 1977 dollars, this equals $0.46 per volume equivalent, or $0.70 per annual volume. The 1968 Westat study had shown a slightly lower storage rate, equal to $0.33 in 1977 dollars. The midrange of these two estimates, $0.52, has been rounded to $0.50 for use here.

[2] Clasquin, F.F., "Periodicals Prices: 74-76 Update," Library Journal, Oct. 1, 1976, p 2017.

APPENDIX C

METHODOLOGY FOR COLLECTION OF LIBRARY COST DATA

Library costs required for the owning vs. borrowing decision model are input in four cost categories as discussed in Appendix B. They are:

Category I. Initial Costs for New Titles

A. Acquisition of a new paid journal title
B. Acquisition of a new free journal title
C. Cataloging of a new title (free or paid)

Category II. Annual Recurring Costs

A. Costs involving maintenance and servicing of all current titles
   1. Selection and review of title
   2. Renewals of current subscriptions, including preparation of invoices and renewal payments
   3. Back issue orders
   4. Check-in of materials
   5. Check-in problems
   6. Claiming
   7. Catalog/Kardex additions, maintenance, and changes
   8. Shelving new materials
   9. Supervision (only of specific tasks)
   10. Training (for above tasks)

B. Binding Costs

C. Serials list costs

Category III. Internal Use Costs

A. Units of Use
B. Total Costs of Use
   1. "Circulation"
   2. Interlibrary lending
   3. Reshelving of materials

Category IV. Internal Borrowing Costs

INSTRUCTIONS

Most of the costs required are labor costs. Current salaries and fringe benefits should be used. The Personnel Office should be able to provide a schedule of total labor costs per employee (including fringe benefits) or a schedule of annual salaries plus the percentage to be applied for fringe benefits (Social Security and/or other retirement benefits, employer paid insurance benefits, etc.). Determine the hourly rate of pay for each employee involved in periodical service activities, by dividing annual salary plus fringe benefits by 52 (weeks of the year) and then by the number of hours in that person's normal work week. (Example: An employee works 35 hours per week for an annual salary of $9,825 plus 15 percent fringe benefits: $9,825 x 1.15 = $11,298.75/52 = $217.28/35 = $6.21 per hour. Time for hourly wage employees performing the same task at the same rate may be aggregated, with fringe benefits, if any, applied to an hourly rate.)

In general, data on the number of items processed in each task should be based on the latest data available for a full year. While the time spent on tasks will generally, of necessity, be based on current operations, if there is a substantial difference in operational procedures or quantities of materials processed between the time when numerical data are calculated and the current period when task times are collected, labor time should be adjusted to reflect an appropriate level of activity per item.

An example of the method for calculating costs of labor for the various tasks is shown. Hours and pay rates are entered for each employee engaged in the specific task.

Acquisition of new titles (228 new paid titles)

Tasks	Hours per week	Hourly pay	Cost per week	Cost per year	Unit Cost
Searching	3.7	$3.40	$12.58	$ 654.16	$ 2.86
Preparation of orders, invoices payments	14.5	6.72	97.44	5,066.88	
	3.8	3.90	14.82	770.64	
	0.6	4.75	2.85	148.20	
	1.3	4.10	5.33	277.16	
				$6,262.88	$27.46

Note: When an individual intermingles tasks which fall into two cost categories (examples: preparation of new title and renewal invoices, shelving of new materials and re-shelving of used materials, catalog filing and maintenance, supervision of acquisitions of new and renewal materials, etc.) time may be apportioned in proportion to the number of titles or items which fall into each of the cost categories. For example: An employee spends 26 hours per week on the preparation of invoices for new and renewal titles. The library has 1000 current paid subscriptions of which 50 are new titles in the survey year (5 percent). The amount of time apportioned to new titles (Initial Cost Category) is 5 percent of 26 hours or 1.3 hours, and the 24.7 hours are then allocated to costs of renewal (Category II. Annual Recurring Costs). Where the same employee or employees are engaged in all or most of the operations of a particular cost subdivision (multiple tasks) tasks may be merged (for example, total acquisitions labor costs for new paid titles may be treated as one aggregated task rather than separating time into the specific tasks of searching, ordering, etc.).

Unit costs can be calculated for each specific task or for aggregated tasks by adding total annual costs and dividing by the appropriate number of titles. Task unit costs are then combined to provide the unit (per title) cost for the category.

CATEGORY I. INITIAL COSTS (NEW TITLES ONLY)

A. Acquisition of New Paid Journal Subscriptions

Number of new paid titles acquired (last full year data)________________

Task	Hours per week	Hourly pay	Cost per week	Cost per year

(Complete for each employee involved)

Preparation of orders, invoices, payments

Other (list, if any)

$ _____ ÷ number of titles = $ _____ per title (A)

B. Acquisition of New Free (Gift and Exchange) Subscriptions

Show any time spent in arranging (procuring) new gifts or exchanges. DO NOT include the cost of the material exchanged.

Number of new free titles acquired (last full year data)________________

Task	Hours per week	Hourly pay	Cost per week	Cost per year

$ _____ ÷ number of titles = $ _____ per title (B)

C. Cataloging of New Journal Titles

Total number of new journal titles cataloged (last full year data)________________

Task	Hours per week	Hourly pay	Cost per week	Cost per year
Cataloging				
Supervision and review				
Training				
Preparation of Catalog cards				
Filing cards				

$ _____ ÷ number of titles = $ _____ per title (C1)

Non-Labor Costs	Unit costs
Total computer or network charges for on-line cataloging/number of titles cataloged (if applicable)	$________
Cost per set of catalog cards	________
Other, if any	________
Total Non-Labor Costs per Title	________(C2)
Total cataloging costs (labor and non-labor) per title (C1 + C2)	$________ (C)

Total Initial Costs (per title)

	New paid title	New free title
Acquisitions	(A) $________	(B) $________
Cataloging	(C) $________	(C) $________
Total Initial Cost of Adding a New Title	$________	$________

CATEGORY II. ANNUAL RECURRING COSTS

A. Annual Labor Costs for Maintenance and Servicing of a Journal Title

Total number of current journal titles (current data) ________________

Task	Hours per week	Hourly rate	Cost per week	Cost per year
Selection and review of titles				
Renewals, invoices, renewal payments				
Back issue orders				
Check-in				
Check-in problems				
Claiming				
Catalog/Kardex additions, maintenance, changes				
Shelving new materials				
Supervision	(only of specific tasks. EXCLUDE overall Administration)			
Training				

Total Labor Costs for Annual Maintenance $________ ÷ number of titles = $________ (A)

B. Binding

No. of journal titles bound (last full year data) ________________

Total no. of bound journal volumes (same period) ________________

Cost of binding, per bound volume ________________

1. Labor costs (preparation, shipment, receipt, marking, records)

Task	Hours per week	Hourly rate	Cost per week	Cost per year

Total labor cost (binding preparation and receipt) $________ ÷ number of titles bound = $________ (B1) per title

2. Binding costs

$$\frac{\text{Total number of bound journal volumes}}{\text{Number of journal titles bound}} = \text{average no. of volumes per title}$$

Average no. of volumes per title x cost of binding per volume = cost of binding an annual volume $_____ (B2)

C. Serials List

No. of journal titles in serials list ____________

1. Labor costs (in-library) for serials list entries, changes, corrections

Task	Hours per week	Hourly rate	Cost per week	Cost per year

Total labor costs, serials list preparation $_____ ÷ number of journal titles in list = $_____ per title (C1)

Number of Total Titles in Serials List ____________

2. Serials list production

Total cost for	Cost per year
Keypunch	
Programming	
Supervision	
Computer time	
Total cost for serials list production	$_____

Total cost for serials list production $_____ ÷ no. of total titles in serials list = $_____ per title (C2)

D. Cost of Record Keeping Materials

Kardex or other records used (per title) $_____ (D1)

Total Annual Recurring Costs (per title)

		Unit cost
Annual maintenance costs (labor)	(A)	_____
Labor costs, binding preparation	(B1)	_____
Cost of binding, per annual volume	(B2)	_____
Labor costs, serials list preparation	(C1)	_____
Serials list production costs	(C2)	_____
Record materials costs	(D1)	_____
Total annual recurring cost per title		$_____

CATEGORY III. INTERNAL USE COSTS

A. Units of Use

Unless the library uses another method of determining the use of journal materials, the reshelving of materials can be utilized as the measure of journal use. If use records have been maintained to include the age of materials used, record use data as follows:

Age of materials used (minimum breakdown)	Number of items used (or reshelved)	Cumulative percent of use as a function of age
< 1 (current issues)		
1-5		
6-10		
11-15		
16-25		
25+		
Total items used	_____	

To determine the use curve for library materials, the cumulative data above should be graphed with the curve extended to show projected use through the total age of the back issues held. Cumulations of use for each year through this period can then be entered into the model to provide a specific curve for the library or particular subject collections in the library, or for comparison with use data shown in the calculations in the text.

If no age records have been maintained, determine the total number of issues reshelved, including materials:

	Number of items reshelved
Circulated	
Used in interlibrary loan	
Collected from tables, reshelving areas, etc.	______
Total items used (reshelved)	______

B. Internal Use Costs

1. "Circulation" of journal materials.

a. Labor costs for "circulation"
(If journals do not circulate, include here the staff time spent in making the materials available to users - locating materials, directing users to materials, etc. DO NOT include reference time.)

Hours per week	Hourly pay	Cost per week	Cost per year

Total labor cost for "circulation" $______ (1a)

b. Non-labor costs of circulation
(Where journal materials are circulated and there is a mechanized or automated circulation systems used, enter the journal circulation proportion of total circulation system costs here.)

$______ (1b)

2. Interlibrary loan of journal items

a. Labor costs of lending

Task	Hrs per week	Hourly pay	Cost per week	Cost per year

Total labor cost for lending $______ (2a)

b. Non-labor costs of lending
(Where costs are not recovered by charges to the borrowing library, enter here the charges for postage and photocopying.)

	Cost per year
Postage	
Photocopying	
Other	
Total non-labor costs of lending	$______ (2b)

3. Reshelving of Materials (labor cost)

Hours per week	Hourly pay	Cost per week	Cost per year

Total cost (labor) of reshelving journal items (bound volumes and unbound issues) $______ (3)

Total Annual Internal Use Cost

		Total cost per year
Total labor cost for "circulation"	(1a)	$________
Total non-labor cost for circulation	(1b)	________
Total labor cost for lending	(2a)	________
Total non-labor cost for lending	(2b)	________
Total cost for reshelving journal items	(3)	________

Total annual use cost $________ ÷ total number of items used (or reshelved) = $______ per item used

CATEGORY IV. INTERLIBRARY BORROWING COSTS
(Internal Borrowing Cost)

Number of items borrowed (filled requests - last full year data) ____________

A. Labor Costs for Borrowing

Task	Hours per week	Hourly rate	Cost per week	Cost per year

Total labor costs for borrowing $______ ÷ total number of filled requests = $______ (A1)

B. Non-labor Costs of Borrowing

(If costs are not reimbursed by the patron requesting the item, enter here.)

	Cost per year
Postage	
Other	______

Total non-labor costs of borrowing (except lending library charges) $______ ÷ number of filled requests = $______ (A2)

Total Internal Borrowing Unit Costs

Labor costs for borrowing (A-1)	______
Non-labor costs for borrowing (A2)	______
Per item cost for borrowing in interlibrary loan	$______

Note: Average external borrowing costs for the library (lending library charges) may be calculated by dividing the total amount paid (last full year data) by the total number of requests filled (same period).

APPENDIX D

COLLECTION WEEDING OPTIONS

Few libraries are currently planning expansion of storage space, and the weeding of journal collections is a rapidly approaching prospect for many. Several studies in the late 1960s addressed weeding in the form of movement of lesser used materials to compact storage areas. Raffel and Shishko[1] determined that this was most economically done by a movement of gross classes of materials (for example, transferring a Dewey classification collection in a library which has primarily converted to the LC classification system, etc.).

Examination of individual use records and modification of individual bibliographic records are expensive procedures (see weeding costs in appendix B), although this method would undoubtedly insure optimal user access to materials. Moving to compact storage by date of publication is considerably less costly, although this decreases accessibility to some more heavily used materials and may necessitate more expensive location and retrieval methods.

Altogether, it is concluded that even in the less expensive cases, costs of transfer and access, coupled with decreased access to materials, tend to offset the slightly lower costs of compact storage as against conventional storage and there is relatively little cost benefit from the transfer. For this reason, cost factors associated with moving materials to compact storage for retention are not considered here and weeding decisions reflect the removal and discard of materials at optimal cutoff ages.

Utilizing the appropriate subject area use curve, the total cost per title for maintenance and use, or weeding and borrowing, of materials at various cutoff ages have been calculated. Optimal weeding ages are chosen on the use curve to reflect the point at which storage and use costs begin to exceed the cost of weeding and borrowing materials.

Subscription cost was not a factor in choosing the optimal cutoff age since the subscription was to be continued in force and only weeding of back issues was in question. Costs of five different options were compared. They are:

Option 1. Retain all issues
Option 2. Weed at 20 years
Option 3. Weed at 15 years
Option 4. Weed at 10 years
Option 5. Weed at 5 years

All options include binding of materials. Since storage was considered critical, storage costs were also included in all options.

Table D-1 shows the cheapest of these options (using numbers above) for the three libraries, with external borrowing costs of $0, $3, and $8, at levels of use from 0.1 to 30. Lines divide the levels of use at which borrowing is cheaper (above the line) from those at which maintaining the title is cheaper (below the line). Two figures (e.g., 4/3) indicate that costs are the same for both options.

[1] J.A. Raffel and R. Shishko, Systematic Analysis of University Libraries: An Application of Cost-Benefit Analysis to the M.I.T. Libraries, Cambridge, Mass.: The M.I.T. Press, 1969.

TABLE D-1

COST COMPARISONS FOR FIVE RETENTION OPTIONS
(Title with 10 years of back issues at
beginning of 25 year planning period)

Average annual use of periodicals in 11th year	Cheapest retention option[1]								
	EBC[2] = $0			EBC = $3			EBC = $8		
	Library			Library			Library		
	A	B	C	A	B	C	A	B	C
0.1	5	5	5	5	5	5	5	5	5
1	5	5	5	5	5	5	5	5	5
3	5	5	4	4	5	2	4	4	2
5	4	5	2	3	4	2	3	3	2
7	3	4	2	3	3	2	2	3	2
10	3	4/3	2	3	3	2	1	2	2
12	3	3	2	2	3	2	1	1	2
15	2	3	2	2/1	2	2	1	1	2
17	2	3	2	1	2	2	1	1	2
20	2	3	2	1	1	2	1	1	1
25	1	2	2	1	1	2	1	1	1
30	1	2	2	1	1	1	1	1	1

[1] Retention options for periodicals are defined in text.

[2] EBC = External Borrowing Cost.

Weeding at five or ten years is cheapest only for those levels of use at which borrowing is the less expensive alternative. The level of use at which cutoff ages of 15 and 20 years are cheapest decreases with the level of lending library charges. Where low cost borrowing is available, weeding at 20 years is feasible, in terms of cost, at the 20 annual use level in Library A, and through the level of 30 average annual uses in Libraries B and C. Only relatively low levels of use permit economical weeding with high external borrowing costs, except in Library C, where the high proportion of total use of a science or technology title during the earlier ages of issues makes weeding at 20 years effective through 20 average annual uses.

Two additional weeding options were also investigated. These options considered policies of brief retention without the costs of binding preparation and bindery. They are:

Option 6. Do not bind -- weed at five years

Option 7. Do not bind -- weed at three years.

Table D-2 shows the cheapest options for the three libraries at various use levels, when these two options are added to the first five. Again the lines separate the levels of use at which borrowing or maintaining materials is the cheaper alternative.

TABLE D-2

COST COMPARISONS FOR SEVEN RETENTION OPTIONS
(Title with 10 years of back issues at beginning of 25 year planning period)

Average annual use of periodicals in 11th year	Cheapest retention option								
	EBC = $0			EBC = $3			EBC = $8		
	Library			Library			Library		
	A	B	C	A	B	C	A	B	C
0.1	7	7	7	6	7	7	7	7	7
1	6	7	7	6	6	6	6	6	6
3	6	6	6	6	6	6	6	6	6
5	6	6	6	6	6	6	6	6	6
7	6	6	6	6	6	6	6	3	2
10	6	6	2	6	3	2	1	2	2
12	6	6	2	2	3	2	1	1	2
15	6	6	2	2/1	2	2	1	1	2
17	2	3	2	1	2	2	1	1	2
20	2	3	2	1	1	2	1	1	2
25	1	2	2	1	1	2	1	1	1
30	1	2	2	1	1	1	1	1	1

Brief retention of materials without binding is least expensive in all cases where materials are less expensively borrowed than held, as well as for some titles with use levels slightly above the breakeven level, even with the highest external borrowing cost. Beyond these use levels, however, options remain the same as in table D-1. Differences among libraries reflect the lower borrowing costs of Library B and the different use curve of Library C.

At least one additional option is available to libraries with space problems; that is, the retention of back issues on microform. The difficulty of estimating the average cost of microform subscriptions has been discussed in library literature and it has also been noted that the cost of dual subscriptions makes microform an expensive retention option. However, since one of the libraries providing cost data for this study has begun, in a limited way, the replacement of hard copy back issues with microfilm and could provide some cost data on their program, a cost comparison of this retention policy with other retention options was considered useful. Since no costs on microfiche were available, they are not included here.

Costs of microfilm averaged $24 per reel, and each reel contained an average of 3.2 annual volumes. Storage costs for microforms were estimated at slightly under five cents per reel per year. For purposes of the computations, average annual volumes were rounded to three per reel, and a figure of $0.016 per annual volume per year was used for microfilm storage. Costs were based on retention of hard copy for three years without binding, at which time it is replaced with microfilm. No borrowing costs accrue since all materials are available in-house. Table D-3 compares costs for all eight of the retention options discussed, showing the option which is cheapest at various levels of annual use.

Option 8. Weed hard copy at three years -- replace with microfilm.

The microfilm alternative is cheapest for almost all use levels at which maintaining a title is the preferred alternative. The combined savings in storage and binding costs more than compensates for the increased subscription costs, and since there are no borrowing costs, savings increase with the level of use. The relatively limited availability of micoform subscriptions, and the resistance to use of microfilm materials in some libraries, reduce the possibilities for implementing this option on a broad scale at the present time.

Better use data for titles and subject areas are needed to insure effective management of periodical collections. Use data collected at one of the universities mentioned earlier suggests that substantial portions of journal collections are used very little or not at all, and the library seeking to reduce journal expenditures may well begin with such titles. The model provides breakeven points for such decisions.

TABLE D-3

COST COMPARISONS FOR EIGHT RETENTION OPTIONS
(Title with 10 years of back issues at
beginning of 25 year planning period)

Average annual use of periodicals in 11th year	Cheapest retention option								
	EBC = $0 Library			EBC = $3 Library			EBC = $8 Library		
	A	B	C	A	B	C	A	B	C
0.1	7	7	7	7	7	7	7	7	7
1	6	7	7	6	6	6	6	6	6
3	6	6	6	6	6	6	6	6	6
5	6	6	6	6	6	8	8	6	8
7	6	6	8	8	6	8	8	8	8
10	8	6	8	8	8	8	8	8	8
12	8	6	8	8	8	8	8	8	8
15	8	8	8	8	8	8	8	8	8
17	8	8	8	8	8	8	8	8	8
20	8	8	8	8	8	8	8	8	8
25	8	8	8	8	8	8	8	8	8
30	8	8	8	8	8	8	8	8	8

As storage space becomes critical, the distribution of demand over the age of issues becomes the most important factor in determining the optimal cutoff age for holding back issues. Since much of the use of issues is in the early period after publication, analysis of the use of individual titles is necessary to determine the volume of demand beyond the suggested cutoff ages; even heavily used titles may have little use beyond a specific cutoff date. In broad terms, where the cost of storage exceeds the product of uses times borrowing cost, back issues should be discarded for greatest cost economy.

In general, it would appear that where acquired materials are little used, either subscriptions should be terminated or issues should remain unbound and retained only three to five years. Heavily used materials should be retained without cutoff; while for almost all economic levels of use, microfilm is the cheapest retention option, the greater convenience of use of hardcopy probably outweighs the considerations of lower cost. Decisions become more critical when focused on materials of moderate use, where close study of actual use beyond suggested cutoff ages should permit libraries to minimize both cost and space requirements.

Index

Compiled by Susan Ruth Stein